WHY THE SOUTH LOST THE CIVIL WAR

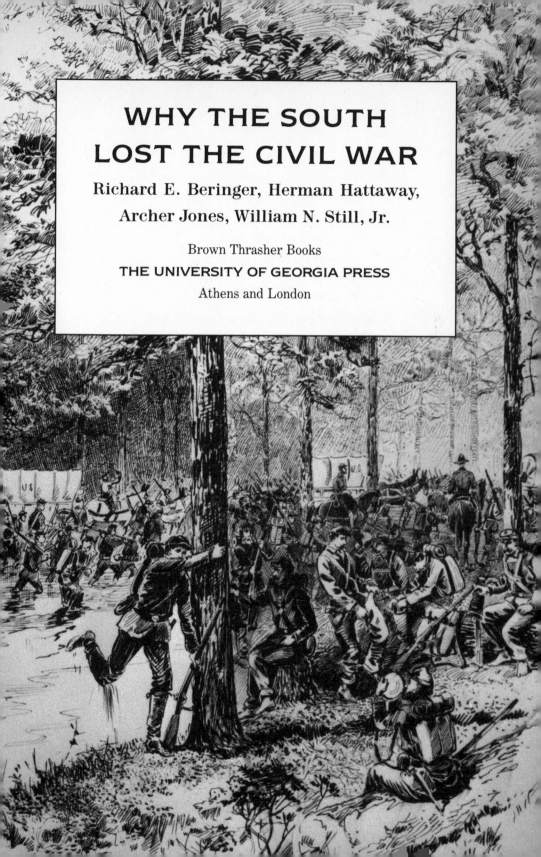

WHY THE SOUTH LOST THE CIVIL WAR

Richard E. Beringer, Herman Hattaway,
Archer Jones, William N. Still, Jr.

Brown Thrasher Books
THE UNIVERSITY OF GEORGIA PRESS
Athens and London

© 1986 by the University of Georgia Press
Athens, Georgia 30602
All rights reserved

Designed by Sandra Strother Hudson
Set in Linotron 202 ten on thirteen Century Expanded

The paper in this book meets the guidelines for
permanence and durability of the Committee on
Production Guidelines for Book Longevity of the
Council on Library Resources.

Printed in the United States of America

95 94 93 92 91   C   9 8 7 6
02 01 00   P   11 10 9 8

Library of Congress Cataloging in Publication Data

Main entry under title:
Why the South lost the Civil War.
Bibliography: p.
Includes index.
1. Confederate States of America—Historiography—
Addresses, essays, lectures.   2. United States—History
—Civil War, 1861–1865—Historiography—Addresses,
essays, lectures.   I. Beringer, Richard E., 1933–
E487.W48   1986   973.7′13   85–8638
ISBN 0–8203–0815–3
ISBN 0–8203–1396–3 (pbk.: alk. paper)

The illustrations on the title page and page one
are reproduced courtesy of the American Heritage
Picture Collection.

The map on pages 112–13 is from *How the North Won:
A Military History of the Civil War* by Herman
Hattaway and Archer Jones (University of Illinois
Press, 1983). Copyright 1983 by the Board of Trustees
of the University of Illinois.

British Library Cataloging
in Publication Data available

TO OUR PARENTS:

Martha Miriam Wupper Beringer, 1895–1970
William Beringer, 1887–1975

Mary Amelia Cook Hattaway
Samuel Morell Hattaway, 1913–1979

Helen Johnston Skinner
M. Osborne Jones, 1896–1979

Helen Morris Still
William N. Still, 1908–1963

Contents

Introduction

I N 1963, during the peak of the Civil War centennial, Henry Steele Commager wrote in the *New York Times Magazine,*

To most of us it is inconceivable that the Civil War should have had any outcome but that registered at Appomattox. It is inconceivable that the territory which now constitutes the United States should have been fragmented—like that of Latin America—into 20 states. It is inconceivable that the Confederacy should have made good its bid for independent nationhood.

But the doctrine of inevitability confronts us with two insuperable difficulties. If it was clear from the beginning that the South must lose, how can we explain the fact that men like Jefferson Davis, Judah P. Benjamin, R. B. Rhett, Howell Cobb and scores of others, men who were upright, virtuous, intelligent and humane, were prepared to lead their people to certain destruction? If defeat was inevitable, they must have discerned this, too, and their conduct takes on the character of criminal imbecility. And second, how can we explain the widespread assumption in Europe— and even in parts of the North—that the South would make good her bid for independence?[1]

How indeed! Commager tried to answer that question as have a host of others—historians, writers, and, of course, the participants themselves. As early as 1866 John Russell Bartlett published a book on the literature of the war containing several thousand items, including works by authors attempting to explain why the North won or the South lost. Since then the number of published items on the "Lost Cause" has run into tens of thousands.[2]

The authors of this study join that host in offering interpretations of their own about why the South lost the Civil War. We address the major interpretations advanced by contemporaries and subsequent scholars, including issues of the blockade, state rights, battlefield success, economic development, resources, and the like, and attempt to show that these are not sufficient to explain the outcome of the war. Indeed, some of these factors are better able to explain why the South lasted as long as it did than to reveal why it lost; other explanations seem, upon reflection, almost irrelevant. We hope that our analysis demonstrates the relationship between military success, morale, and will and the weakness of Confederate nationalism when undermined by battlefield defeat. We hope to suggest not only factors that led to the ultimate result, but also to explain how they interacted to produce an effect that was greater than the sum of the contributing parts.

The genesis of this book occurred several years ago when two of the authors had an animated discussion about the causes of Confederate defeat and concluded that much relevant research of the last decade and more was not receiving the consideration that it merited. A number of similar discussions were held at various meetings of the Southern Historical Association, in which the other two authors joined. With memories of recent conflict fresh in mind, we reminded ourselves that the victory does not inevitably go to the strong. Together we began to wonder whether superior availability of men and matériel to the Union really could explain southern disaster. We reminded ourselves that what seems logical to today's historians, or even to contemporary combatants, may not carry much explanatory weight. Ideas of appropriate behavior change, forcing twentieth-century historians to move beyond logic into the realm of a somewhat murky psychology. It did not take us long to realize that since the Civil War was more than a physical conflict, explanations had to be sought in the emotional, spiritual, and even mystical lives of its participants.

Originally we planned to present a series of papers in a session of the Southern Historical Association. The proposed session never took place, and we decided instead to put together a book on the subject, envisioning a collection of essays similar to those in David Donald's edited work *Why the North Won the Civil War*—the influence of which, incidentally, will be readily obvious to most of our readers.[3] In the end, however, we found that a series of short, discrete essays would not serve our purpose as well as an extended, integrated discussion.

We readily admit that much of this study is based on the work of others. Our effort, however, has been to synthesize the best and most appropriate conclusions of our predecessors in this field and to present the best and most provocative of that earlier work. Our goal is not to settle the controversy over Confederate defeat, once and for all, for we recognize that that is impossible. Rather, we hope to stimulate fresh thought and to move future discussion onto more complex ground. Of course, we accept full responsibility for our interpretations of the works of other historians.

We gratefully acknowledge the valuable assistance of Bruce Bubacz, David Danbom, Paul D. Escott, Edwin S. Gaustad, Margaret Hattaway, Cathy Heiraas, Gail Hokenson, Lloyd Hunter, Joanne L. Jones, Martin Marty, James McNeeley, James Moffat, Phillip S. Paludan, Robert Hill Porter, Thomas Regnary, Jerry A. Vanderlinde, James F. Vivian, and Charles Reagan Wilson. They are responsible for much of the quality of the manuscript but for none of its errors. In addition, Professor Beringer wishes to add special thanks to the graduate school of the University of North Dakota for the award of a Summer Research Professorship, which allowed him to spend the summer of 1984 working on this manuscript.

We are thankful for permission to quote from the following repositories and persons: the Samuel Latham Mitchill Barlow Papers, the Robert Alonzo Brock Papers, and the James William Eldridge Papers at the Huntington Library, San Marino, California; the Memoirs of W. S. Oldham at the Barker Texas History Center, University of Texas, Austin; the Thomas Bragg Diary, the John W. Brown Diaries, and the James G. Ramsay Papers, in the Southern Historical Collection, Library of the University of North Carolina at Chapel Hill; the Robert Charles Winthrop Papers in the Massachusetts Historical Society; the Reminiscences of J. A. Orr, Mississippi State Department of Archives and History; and Professors Dan T. Carter and William J. McNeill, for papers presented at annual meetings of the Southern Historical Association.

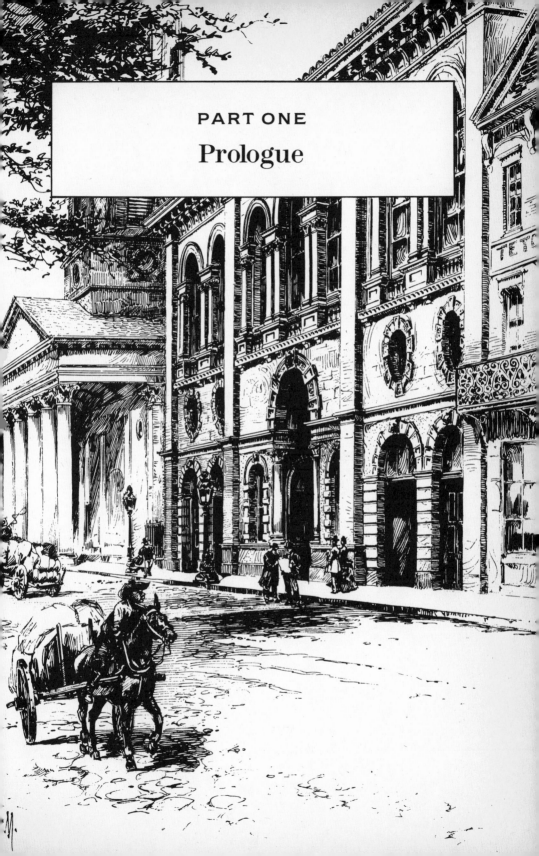

PART ONE
Prologue

Historians have assigned many causes for the South's defeat, some stressing a single cause, others many. But most have assigned first place to one, even as they acknowledge the importance of others. We do likewise in that we single out the weakness of southern nationalism as what lawyers would call the proximate cause of Confederate defeat. To show the primacy of this factor we not only explain Confederate nationalism's weak incidence and shallow roots but deal at length with other causes that may have a legitimate claim to supremacy. Included among these are military explanations, Confederate supply, and internal dissension and obstruction in the form of dedication to state rights. And, in dealing with Confederate morale, we find that religion played a vital role both in sustaining and diminishing Confederate confidence in victory.

This first brief section summarizes how historians have dealt with these questions and, in the process, indicates how we will treat them in our subsequent sections, which follow a topical as well as a chronological approach.

Chapter One

Historians
and the Civil War

F IVE EMINENT HISTORIANS gathered in November 1958 for a conference at Gettysburg College, at which each of them probed one of the familiar interpretations of why the North won the Civil War. David M. Potter chose the performance of Jefferson Davis and the impact of political factors; he believed that Jefferson Davis exhibited deficiencies in his relations with other people, his concept of the presidency, and his role as commander in chief. Potter even suggested that if Davis and Abraham Lincoln had been in each other's position, the Confederacy might have won the war. Norman A. Graebner assessed superior northern diplomacy and European neutrality, concluding that Secretary of State William H. Seward had made it clear that Europe would pay a high price if it chose to recognize the Confederacy. Richard N. Current reiterated that God had been on the side He usually chose, the one with the strongest battalions; he suggested that the real puzzle was how the Confederacy managed to stay afloat, for the economic supremacy of the Union made victory inevitable. T. Harry Williams examined the military question and cogently argued that northern victory resulted from superior northern and inferior southern military leadership because the South was undone by adherence to the place-oriented strategy of Antoine Henri Jomini. David Donald charged that the Confederacy lost the conflict because it refused to surrender its democratic ideals. Each of the five men admitted that he focused exclusively upon only one single theme for the sake of argument but that in many respects their total views overlapped. All of their essays had proved thought-provoking, but the ideas therein were hardly new or revolutionary.

The historiography of Civil War victory stretches as far back as the end of the war itself, when many northerners were convinced they had won the war because of the moral superiority of their cause, and many southerners thought they were defeated by their adversary's overwhelming resources. In the following generations interpretations became more subtle and less simplistic, as historians discussed military strategy, military superiority, leadership, political factors, diplomacy, and the tension between localism and centralism. Most historians still largely ascribe Confederate defeat to these issues, and Donald himself, in the introduction to the published version of the Gettysburg lectures, implies that all of the factors discussed on that occasion contributed to the result. Many historians have agreed with Donald's rejection of monocausation. Donald has written elsewhere that economic difficulties—including lack of resources, inflation, and the blockade; desertion; malnutrition; physical devastation; inferior manpower; and the lack of a system of political parties that would enable Jefferson Davis to mobilize political support—were all partly responsible for Confederate defeat.[1]

But there were other problems that the discussants at Gettysburg College in 1958 did not emphasize. In 1944, for example, Charles W. Ramsdell cited a wide range of economic difficulties that combined with military defeat to sap Confederate morale. Other historians agree on the vital role of the loss of morale, and E. Merton Coulter went so far as to say that the Confederacy lost because the people simply "did not will hard enough and long enough to win." One historian even contends that underlying the destructive loss of morale was a sense of guilt created by the dissonance between the South's knowledge of its own liberal tradition and its knowledge of the institution of slavery.[2]

Each of these hypotheses is interesting and, as David Donald suggests, doubtless all played some role in precipitating Confederate collapse. Causal effects do not operate with the same effect on every individual, however, and certainly the factors that caused Robert E. Lee and Joseph E. Johnston to lay aside their swords are not necessarily the same as those that may have caused a Mississippi plowboy or an Alabama herdsman to throw down his musket. Each generation of historians has selected what it felt to be the most likely causes of Confederate defeat, subjected them to scrutiny, and drawn its own conclusions. It may therefore be helpful to examine some of the more provocative previous suggestions, indicating as we do so the lines along which our argument will proceed.

ONE OF the most prominent themes of the first half of the twentieth century was that of internal dissension caused by the clash between the centralizing influence of the Confederate administration, led by Jefferson Davis, and the rights of the states, as interpreted by their governors, legislators, and citizens. In one way or another, most historians have equated internal dissent within the Confederacy with the philosophy of state rights. In this connection, David Donald's democratic liberties theme especially rings a familiar bell, for democratic liberties in many respects appears as only a positive-sounding label for state rights. As such, it reminds one of a vast array of Civil War scholarship since 1925, when Frank L. Owsley first explicitly championed the notion of state rights as a cause of Confederate defeat.

The Owsleian state-rights thesis crops up again and again and has had such a pervasive influence that any attempt to assess the ultimate cause for Confederate defeat must deal with Owsley's enormous impact on historiography for the last two generations. A legion of historians joined Owsley in deciphering the eroded letters on the tombstone of the Confederacy as reading "Died of State Rights."[3]

Yet considerable scholarship exists which reveals fundamental flaws in Owsley's thesis. To be sure, all of the elements pointed to by the persistent adherents of the thesis did exist, but the question remains whether these elements ruined the chances of the Confederacy. For example, even though various state governors of the Civil War era, especially Joseph E. Brown of Georgia and Zebulon Vance of North Carolina, complained about and even railed at what they perceived as losses in state rights, the Confederate government either responded adequately to their complaints or more likely ignored them with impunity. This study will demonstrate meticulously, as even some of Owsley's contemporaries perceived, that Owsley's work lacked good documentation and factual support.

Many subsequent historians, such as Thomas B. Alexander, Richard E. Beringer, Paul Escott, Raimondo Luraghi, and John B. Robbins, have examined the same questions as did Owsley, although from varying perspectives, and demonstrated in numerous ways that state rights probably had little effect on the war's outcome and certainly did not exert a decisive impact. So if Owsley's epitaph is not correct, what epitaph should the Confederacy have? A variety of observers have made other suggestions, beginning with one from newspaper editor Edward A. Pollard in 1865, just before the war ended. Referring to a famous episode in the Mexican War when Jefferson Davis deployed his regiment in an unorthodox wedge formation, which Pollard believed inspired Davis's conceit about his military competence, Pollard suggested that the Confederacy had "Died of a V." Davis himself later took a turn and chiseled the epitaph "Died of a Theory" into the southern headstone, reflecting his disgruntlement with those who had not supported his call for the use of blacks as soldiers.[4]

In our own time Bell I. Wiley suggested "Died of Big-man-me-ism" as the cause of Confederate demise, pointing to an exaggerated sense of self-importance that prevented many leading Confederates from subordinating their ideas and opinions to the general policy of the government. David Donald's variation on the tombstone metaphor reflects an argument slightly reminiscent of Wiley's and similar to that of Owsley. Contending that the South lacked the critical element of discipline because it had accepted wholeheartedly a series of democratic assumptions upon which white society had based its government, Donald concluded that the South "Died of Democracy."[5]

Much of what Donald had to say only amplified Owsley's recurrent state-rights thesis. But Donald was engaged in the proper quest. Like Owsley and other more recent "neo-Confederates," such as Ludwell H. Johnson, Donald felt, correctly, that historians too often see inevitability in the northern victory: "Nothing succeeds like success," Johnson recently wrote. "The historian," Donald scolded, "is a camp follower of the successful army." Lobbying further for his own thesis, Donald argued that the southern soldier showed too little discipline, sometimes having a Negro servant carry out the orders given him or hiring a substitute to perform his chores. This impertinent fighting man always "reserved his democratic rights to interpret his orders broadly" or simply to disobey them if they seemed unreasonable. Southern soldiers clung as long as possible to their right to determine the length of their tours of duty and to elect their own leaders. The South also outbungled the North, Donald asserted, in clinging to preservation of the basic freedoms of speech and press, freedom from arbitrary arrest, and due process of law: "The result, of course," says Donald, was that "disloyal elements throughout the South had almost unrestricted freedom."[6]

Finally, Donald addressed what he perceived as southern political weakness in rigorous adherence to law, as opposed to Lincoln and the North's cavalier and creative bending of the rules. Donald ultimately asserted, however, that "all of these were handicaps; but none was fatal. The real weakness of the Confederacy was that the Southern people insisted upon retaining their democratic liberties in wartime." This conclusion clearly revealed Donald as an Owsley disciple in modern dress; Donald's argument was much more sophisticated and convincing than Owsley's, but the two rested on the same foundation.[7]

Although the Donald-Owsley thesis is one that we must examine carefully if we are to understand Confederate failure, other theories have importance, too. What role did military superiority play? Did God, as Richard Current suggested, truly march with the strongest battalions, or did the Union display better generalship than the Confederacy, as T. Harry Williams maintained? And since armies needed supplies to fight, one must consider whether the army that stopped fighting did so because it no longer had the wherewithal to continue, or whether the troops or their leaders had lost the will to fight.

MOST HISTORIANS stipulate that the conflict between the North and South was an industrial war and that economic factors played an important role in determining its outcome. But did economics explain Confederate handicaps, or did they determine defeat? Current affirmatively concluded that "economic rather than strictly military superiority was the basic reason for the ultimate victory of the North." According to the 1860 census the North had approximately 1,300,000 industrial workers compared to the South's 110,000. The twenty-three states that remained in the Union manufactured more than nine-tenths of the industrial goods produced in the United States. At the outbreak of war the North produced annually, according to value, seventeen times as much cotton and woolen goods as did the South; thirty times as many boots and shoes; twenty times as much pig iron; thirteen times as much bar, sheet, and railroad iron; twenty-four times as many locomotive engines; more than five hundred times as much general hardware; seventeen times as much agricultural machinery; thirty-two times as many firearms; and five times as much tonnage in ships and boats. As Current states, "If wars are won by riches, there can be no question why the North eventually prevailed. The only question will be: How did the South manage to stave off defeat so long?"[8]

Much evidence indicates, however, that this disparity, present at the beginning of the conflict, diminished as the Confederacy proved able over the long pull to provide its military establishment with an adequate supply of arms and munitions. Although provisions rarely were plentiful, their scarcity resulted more from breakdowns in transportation than from production deficiencies. Nor is there evidence that Confederate armies suffered from starvation or even malnutrition. Throughout the war acquisition of sufficient clothing and shoes for the soldiers proved a serious but hardly a crippling problem in view of military operations that continued notwithstanding these deficiencies. The fact is, no Confederate army lost a major engagement because of the lack of arms, munitions, or other essential supplies.

As Raimondo Luraghi, Emory Thomas, and others have stressed, an economic revolution provided the basis for the effectiveness of Confederate logistics. The Confederacy, at least in terms of war matériel, transformed itself from an agrarian into an industrial economy. As Luraghi wrote, "The Confederate government acted immediately to nationalize the whole productive power of existing manufactures as far as war production was concerned." Thomas observed that "the Davis administration outdid its Northern counterpart in organizing for total war. Economically, the nation founded by planters to preserve commercial, plantation agrarianism became, within the limits of its ability, urbanized and industrialized."[9]

Confederate war industries achieved impressive results in expanding existing arsenals and armories and creating new ones. The army and the navy established ordnance works, foundries, laboratories, and iron manufacturing facilities. To create a fleet the Confederates built marine machinery works, shipyards, and even a rope walk. Private entrepreneurs launched clothing factories, leather works, rolling mills, and other industries. To provide raw materials such as lead, copper, iron, zinc, coal, and niter, the government created the Niter and Mining Bureau. Some of the manufacturing establishments such as Tredegar in Richmond and the Confederate Powder Works in Augusta, Georgia, grew into gigantic facilities, employing thousands of workers at their peak.

In view of the absence of an industrial base at the beginning of the conflict, these establishments produced at extraordinary rates. By the end of 1862 the output of eight government-owned armories reached 170,000 cartridges and 1,000 field-artillery rounds of ammunition daily and 155,000 pounds of lead monthly. Altogether the Augusta works turned out 2,750,000 pounds of powder during the conflict. By the end of 1864 the Niter and Mining Bureau had nearly a million cubic feet of niter beds in operation, fulfilling at least the bulk of all saltpeter needs. This successful manufacturing effort explains why the Confederates enjoyed an adequate supply of arms and munitions throughout the war.[10]

Even so, in an article published in 1983, Stanley Lebergott points out how much Confederate economic mobilization fell short of its potential. The Confederates failed, for example, to prohibit the raising of redundant cotton, thus tying up manpower that they could have used to raise corn, wheat, and hogs or that they could have applied to increasing mineral and manufacturing output. The Confederates also failed to allocate slaves both to the production of scarce supplies and to noncombatant tasks with the armies. With proper direction, this slave labor could have released thousands of soldiers who had been detailed to civilian pursuits and made them available for front-line service. Additional thousands of civilians could also have been sent to battle. These shortcomings reflected a policy of laissez-faire aimed at the planters that naturally undermined a war goal of establishing a world cotton monopoly. So planters used their labor to grow as much cotton as they wished, both to ensure short-term profits and to discourage Great Britain from developing alternate sources of supply that would hurt the South after the war. The commercial interests of the planters shaped war policy, says Lebergott, leading to ultimate defeat "because the South was not prepared to forego short-term monetary goals."[11]

But Lebergott expects an economic mobilization in the Confederacy without previous parallels and probably in excess of the power of most Confederate leaders—if not beyond their imagination—in view of the opposition of the large planters of cotton and owners of slaves. Precedents for the Confederacy's expansion in weapons and munitions production existed in the French Revolution, but not until World War I did nations exercise the economic controls that he envisions and that would have contributed so much to the Confederate war effort. Moreover, the Confederacy, a new government, could not benefit from long ties of loyalty and affection. As events proved, it could not even maintain public support when it made less extreme demands on its citizens. Yet the South maintained more than 3 percent of its population under arms, a figure higher than the North's and comparable to the average ratios attained by France and the United Kingdom during the wars of the French Revolution and Napoleon. The Confederacy attained this high level of armed manpower in spite of invasion and a large slave population, obstacles with which these European powers did not have to contend.

Lebergott also stresses the failure of Confederate finance. Avoidance of taxes together with totally inadequate taxation limited tax revenues to 1 percent of income, a significant contrast with the Union's 23 percent, and poor bond sales increased the reliance on printing money. Both resulted in an extreme inflation. Impressment of needed supplies at low fixed prices resulted in the enmity of producers and hardships to their families, as well as evasion of impressment and reduced production. But Confederate finance had its antecedents in both the American and French revolutions, and, in spite of this obvious handicap, the Confederacy did supply and equip its armies.[12]

The small navy also performed creditably. From 1861 to 1865, according to William N. Still, Jr., the South "converted, contracted for, or laid down within its borders at least 150 warships, including more than fifty ironclads. The twenty-two ironclads and dozens of wooden vessels completed and commissioned were armed primarily by ordnance from Tredegar and a naval foundry at Selma, Alabama." By the end of 1864 the navy, having more heavy guns than it needed, even began to provide the army with larger-caliber cannon for coastal fortifications.[13]

To be sure, some shortages and significant economic weaknesses did affect the Confederate war effort. Trying to fill the ranks of her constantly depleting armies, the South had to draw from the economic front a higher proportion of manpower than did the North. The Con-

federate government halfheartedly tried by exemption and detail to fill
the gaps left in the ranks of skilled labor, but its efforts proved unsuccessful. Toward the end of 1864 General Josiah Gorgas, chief of the
army's ordnance bureau, complained that, whereas two years earlier
there had been no machinery, he had now a surplus but no one to operate it.

Raw materials proved scarcer than machinery and as critical as
manpower. The supply of iron, especially, always seemed too scanty to
meet the need of the manufacturing establishments. Tredegar and
other foundries and rolling mills developed a productive capacity to
provide guns, machine parts, armor, and T-rails in excess of the meager raw materials available. Low pig iron production forced the Tredegar to operate at no more than one-third of plant capacity during the
four years of war. Even when the works had enough pig iron, production lagged because of a fuel shortage. In March 1863 the president of
Tredegar wrote to Stephen Mallory, Confederate secretary of the
navy: "We have iron to run six puddling furnaces instead of twenty and
these have been stopped much for want of coal."[14]

One of the ironies of the Civil War was that the South, with its overwhelming prewar emphasis on agriculture, sustained itself industrially
better than it did agriculturally. Several factors accounted for this
anomaly: the antebellum stress on the production of cash crops, the
federal occupation of extensive sections of southern cropland by the
end of 1862, and, finally, the breakdown in the Confederacy's transportation system. As Emory Thomas has observed: "People went hungry
in the midst of full cribs, barns, and smokehouses. A bountiful harvest
counted for little if local railroad tracks were destroyed by foes or can-
nibalized by friends, if the road to town were a quagmire, or if wagons
and mules were impressed to serve the army." Although the evidence
indicates that bountiful crops were produced during the war years,
soldiers and civilians alike, particularly the inhabitants of urban areas,
faced a constant shortage of food.[15]

The decline of the railway system seems likely the most important
economic factor in Confederate defeat. Catesby ap Roger Jones, while
commanding the naval ordnance facility at Selma, Alabama, wrote
that "the principal difficulty in coal now arises, not from its scarcity
. . . but from the limited means of transportation." Finished prod-

ucts—such as guns, armor plate, and shoes—often were delayed drastically long in reaching their destination.[16]

Although economic factors affected the outcome of the war, they did so primarily in an indirect manner. Despite all the problems of manpower, inadequate supplies of raw materials and food, and the deficient railway system, economic shortcomings did not play a major role in Confederate defeat. No Confederate army lost a crucial battle or campaign because of a lack of ammunition, guns, or even shoes and food, scarce though these latter items became. Economic liabilities played an important role in Confederate fortunes but primarily through the debilitating effect on the public will of the pervasive smell of defeat. A declining economy, added to other woes, caused southerners to recalculate the costs of war and to reconsider alternative decisions, with an effect on morale obvious to all.

When the war broke out no one foresaw that economic factors would affect the course of events by their influence upon public will. At first North and South stood at economic parity, in a military way, for each lacked more than rudimentary preparation for war. Southern industrial mobilization, although less productive than that of the North, nevertheless managed adequately to maintain that parity because the Civil War occurred at a time when equipping armies hardly could have been simpler or less expensive.

Since a man needed clothes whether soldier or civilian, the possession of a firearm defined the essential material difference between a combatant and a noncombatant. In earlier times soldiers often had required metal body armor, swords of good-quality steel, and bows or crossbows with suitable arrows. In contrast to the slow and expensive production of these handmade weapons, machines manufactured rifles relatively cheaply and quickly. The machine making of bullets and powder equally contrasted with the hand manufacture of arrows. The characteristic infrequency of battle meant that ammunition would constitute neither a problem nor a major cost. When the Confederates scavenged battlefields for lead, they were responding to inadequate transportation for resupply, not to the absence of lead. Further, since a smoothbore or rifle was far easier to learn to use than a sword or bow, both sides could quickly train effective forces. The main task was to learn how to march, drill, and deploy. Even drill had become much simplified by the new system adopted seventy years earlier during the French Revolution.

In addition to rifles, an army required artillery, one to four cannon per thousand men. Both the North and the South possessed plenty of coast-defense guns, and each had some serviceable muzzle-loading, smoothbore field guns—as well as facilities to make more. But the horses and mules that were required to move wagons and artillery and to equip the cavalry were costly. Even though the proportion of cavalry used by armies had declined steadily for a century and a half, an army still constituted a horse-intensive organization. Nevertheless civil life in both the North and South also depended heavily on horses, and the diversion of existing horses from civilian to military purposes soon provided an adequate supply.[17]

Thus the American Civil War occurred at a time when the task of preparing for war proved simpler than it had been for a long time and than it would become by the twentieth century. The Civil War also took place at a time when the power of the defense was approaching its apogee. Cavalry, the traditional offensive arm, already had lost much of its effectiveness when all infantry came to be armed with smooth-bores and bayonets. The combination of volleys and a bristling wall of bayonets presented by infantry in three lines rendered almost any frontal cavalry charge ineffective. The pre–Civil War introduction of the accurate, long-range rifle completed the devaluation: a cavalry charge became so nearly impossible that bayonets lost their most basic purpose. What little use bayonets received occurred less in hand-to-hand combat than in opening cans or preparing stray chickens for the stewpot. Indeed, bayonets inflicted less than 1 percent of the wounds suffered by the Union forces.[18]

During the Civil War a fluke in technological development made artillery almost exclusively a defensive weapon. The Napoleonic era saw development of new, more mobile artillery that could concentrate rapidly and fire upon infantry, which was vulnerable because the men had to stand to fire and reload as well as to resist cavalry charges. Artillery had the ability to come within three or four hundred yards, close enough to use grape or canister shot but still beyond the effective range of smoothbore muskets. Grape and canister shot, loads of small balls fired from a muzzle-loading smoothbore cannon, wreaked a devastating effect on infantry standing erect. But in the Civil War the infantryman's new rifle outranged the artilleryman's grape or canister. Since the infantrymen could shoot the gunners, the artillery had to stay out of the range of rifle as well as grape and canister fire and could no longer support the attack as in Napoleon's day. Because rifle-augmented firepower disposed of the danger of a cavalry charge, infantry on the defensive no longer needed to stand erect in serried ranks, vulnerable to grape, canister, and musket balls. Instead, infantrymen usually sought, or quickly devised, some cover against rifle bullets.

Smoothbore artillery, when firing cannon balls, had relatively little effect on infantry in defensive deployment. The available rifled artillery had little more effect, for extant designs did not yet result in sufficient strength to allow powerful charges to be used with reliable expectation that barrels would not burst—and ordnance designers had yet to develop a means of accurately exploding shrapnel shells in the air over the head of distant infantry. But the smoothbore, muzzle-loading cannon were just as deadly in the defense as ever, infantrymen fearing these more than rifled pieces. The grape and canister could inflict serious casualties upon attacking troops even though the attacking infantry no longer used lines three ranks deep. Infantry still had to advance erect, and the artillery, often as well protected from fire as the defending infantry, still provided a formidable asset to the defense just at the time it had lost most of its offensive value.[19]

The Civil War introduced to the North American continent the very large armies long characteristic of European warfare. Now armies in America routinely numbered forty or fifty thousand men, and often the Union had armies of one hundred thousand men, equal in size to major American cities. But European supply conditions did not prevail in the United States. Compared to Europe, where soldiers usually could find abundant food and fodder with ease, the American South was a sparsely populated area, which, in many cotton and tobacco regions, hardly grew any food crops at all, sometimes not even enough for local consumption. This difference in population density and agricultural productivity made it especially difficult to supply large forces if they remained long in one place. Civil War armies therefore had to depend far more on large-capacity lines of communications; horses and wagons over bad American roads would not suffice for very long.

Water communications fully met this criterion, as did the new railroads, though with less efficiency. Armies had to rely on a nationwide logistic network, and both belligerents had to use that of the invaded country, which placed a severe strain on the South's railroad and inland waterway system, which was less developed than that of the North. This exceptional logistic constraint also limited the mobility of American armies when compared with contemporary European armies because the Americans had to depend so much more on their communications. Thus, stationary or in motion, armies in the American theater of war, especially in the South, would face unusual logistic difficulties which further strengthened the defense.[20]

By remarkable and effective efforts the agrarian South did exploit and create an industrial base that proved adequate, with the aid of imports, to maintain suitably equipped forces in the field. Since the Confederate armies suffered no crippling deficiencies in weapons or supply, their principal handicap would be their numerical inferiority. But to offset this lack, Confederates, fighting the first major war in which both sides armed themselves with rifles, had the advantage of a temporary but very significant surge in the power of the tactical defensive. In addition, the difficulties of supply in a very large and relatively thinly settled region proved a powerful aid to strengthening the strategic defensive. Other things being equal, if Confederate military leadership were competent and the Union did not display Napoleonic genius, the tactical and strategic power of the defense could offset northern numerical superiority and presumably give the Confederacy a measure of military victory adequate to maintain its independence.

THIS CONCLUSION has led many students of the Civil War to a military explanation for the outcome of the war. Sometimes the military explanation goes no further than to claim that the results would have been different had a particular general, such as Albert Sidney Johnston or Thomas J. "Stonewall" Jackson, lived. But the thesis that superior manpower and industrial resources made Union victory inevitable must command respect. In dealing with the question of how much superiority would have made victory certain, we have appealed to the judgments found in the impartial writings of Karl von Clausewitz and Antoine Henri Jomini, the premier authorities on nineteenth-century war.

We have sought to use Clausewitz and Jomini in such a way as to deal with the most influential modern military interpretation of the course of the war. Presented by T. Harry Williams in his contribution to David Donald's *Why the North Won*, it relied on the thesis that Jomini strongly influenced Civil War generals and depicted him as an exponent of an obsolete, ineffective strategy that handicapped many Union generals and, at least hypothetically, could have given victory to the Confederates had not Lincoln and Ulysses S. Grant, ignorant of Jomini, displayed an intuitive grasp of the proper strategy and ultimately given a firm, modern direction to the Union war effort.

According to Williams, Jomini advocated warfare divorced from political considerations and aimed only at limited and essentially territorial military objectives. These ideas stultified Union commanders by making them see "cities and territory as their objectives rather than the armies of the enemy" and seek to conquer these "by maneuvering rather than by fighting." Like Jomini, Union generals wished to circumscribe the destructiveness of war. Jomini's prescription for the offensive, which involved, Williams said, "one big effort at a time in one theatre," inhibited Union offensives because generals never did "possess enough strength to undertake the movements recommended by Jomini."[21]

Lincoln always disagreed with these ideas, according to Williams, and, when he secured in Grant a commander not shackled by Jomini's precepts, the Union marched to victory in 1864 and 1865. Grant's strategy included the innovative and anti-Jominian elements of simultaneous advances on all fronts, aiming at the enemy's army, and the economic and psychological effect of William T. Sherman's marches.[22]

But Williams saw Jomini's ideas as having a different effect on Confederate generals. They stressed the important offensive element in Jomini's thought, particularly as interpreted by West Point professor Dennis Hart Mahan, as an emphasis on "celerity and the headlong attack." "More Jominian than the Federals," the Confederates, the "most brilliant practitioners of Jomini," successfully applied "the principles that Jomini emphasized—the objective, the offensive, mass, economy of force, interior lines, and unity of command."[23]

Confederates not only could not go beyond the restricted ideas of Jomini but, further, fought a strategically "conservative war" that was "designed to guard the whole circumference of the country." Because of this concern for territory, the "localistic South" could not "attempt on a grand strategic scale the movements its generals were so good at on specific battlefields—the concentrated mass offensive" prescribed by Jomini. Limited by their parochial outlook, Confederates could not concentrate in one theater and did not attempt such an offensive, which would have provided "probably the South's best chance to win its independence by a military decision."[24]

Although it is now clear that West Point taught very little of the strategy of Jomini or of anyone else and that Professor Dennis Hart Mahan had more influence as a teacher of the power of entrenchments than of the headlong attack, generals on both sides did read about the art of war, and many could have learned much more of Jomini than available through the brief exposure at West Point. For this reason, and because European authorities have had a different view of Jomini, it is still important to examine the Civil War in the light of his ideas, trying to show what they were, whether the commanders on both sides followed them, and whether his ideas facilitated or impeded military success.[25]

INEVITABLY WILLIAMS'S interpretation also brought in Clausewitz as a champion of Williams's view of the correct strategy in opposition to the behavior attributed to Jomini. Casting Clausewitz and Jomini as partisans in this controversy also necessarily placed these two expositors of the Napoleonic tradition in warfare in an opposition to each other that obscured the essential harmony between them. Using both of them as authorities enables us to deal with this interpretation, which has displayed amazing hardihood in spite of its fundamental misconception of what Jomini advocated.[26]

But we would also have appealed to Clausewitz in any case because his 1832 classic *On War* has far greater reputation and impact today than do Jomini's works, and very properly so. Not only does Clausewitz assume a knowledge of Jomini and go beyond him, but he treats much more exhaustively the lessons of Napoleonic warfare and many of the issues raised by the question whether the Confederacy could have won militarily. He also deals with the relationship between military and political factors more extensively and with more sophistication than Jomini.

This use of Clausewitz and Jomini also necessarily, though implicitly, involved us in a comparison of their military ideas. In showing how much they had in common and how rarely they disagreed significantly, we show—albeit indirectly—the inappropriateness of those understandings of Jomini that sharply differentiate him from Clausewitz and the Napoleonic tradition. In this way we deal adequately with the Williams interpretation without the fatiguing task of comparing Williams's ideas of Jomini with Jomini's writings. This approach also enables us to show that Union generals found difficulty in assuming the offensive, not because Jomini misled them but because they encountered obstacles to the offensive foreseen by Clausewitz.

Unfortunately, dealing with the Williams explanation of northern victory so thoroughly has involved us in a longer exposition of military operations than the importance of military factors in Confederate defeat seems to merit. But by analyzing military operations, and by relying so explicitly on two of the founders of modern military science, we link our treatment to contemporary operational ideas. In the nineteenth century the study of operations depended on Jomini and his disciples, and nineteenth-century thought, including that of Clausewitz, has continued to influence military thinking in our own time. For example, the United States Army's *Field Manual 100-5, Operations*, of August 20, 1982, employs the concepts of envelopment, the turning movement, and interior lines, ideas central to the thinking of Clausewitz and Jomini. In explaining military operations we make a few references to this manual to illustrate, in the Civil War context, some of the consonance between nineteenth-century and present-day thought.[27]

Using these ideas also enabled our treatment of the military question to harmonize well with Herman Hattaway and Archer Jones, *How the North Won: A Military History of the Civil War*. We have relied on this work, which, in turn, uses the classical approach to operations exemplified in Clausewitz, Jomini, and the United States Army's new operational doctrine. Because Hattaway and Jones answer most of the questions raised by Williams's interpretation of the conflict, we will rarely address it specifically and will let Clausewitz and Jomini speak for themselves about their views of the proper conduct of operations.

In spite of the relative comprehensiveness of invoking the enduring

concepts of Clausewitz and Jomini, this appeal does not directly deal
with the latest military interpretation of Confederate defeat. Grady
McWhiney and Perry D. Jamieson, in their *Attack and Die: Civil War
Military Tactics and the Southern Heritage*, have an ethnic interpretation for southern defeat that points to a peculiarly southern military
behavior. Rather than strategic, as Williams advocated, this behavior
is tactical, a southern addiction to the tactical offensive and to frontal
attacks. Clausewitz and Jomini do address the merits of the tactical
offensive and of frontal attacks, but their disagreement with Mc-
Whiney and Jamieson does not have to do with the effectiveness of
such tactics. Instead, the implicit argument over this interpretation
has to do with the degree to which southerners used the offensive,
whether it characterized Confederate operations significantly more
than northern, and, more fundamentally, whether heavy casualties
caused Confederate defeat. We address this interpretation and its
more basic thesis about the impact of casualties in an appendix.

IMPORTANT AS the discussion of state rights, economics, and military
operations will prove to be, however, we believe that the ultimate
causes of Confederate defeat were neither internal dissent, economic
inferiority, nor military inadequacy. No amount of argument along
those lines can obscure the fact that at the end the South still had large
combat-ready armies and that these armies surrendered and went
home. When Lee met Grant at Appomattox Court House, surrender
was not the only choice open to him. Therefore, the key question is,
why did not Confederates pursue another alternative? Why did they
lack the will to make different decisions?

Perhaps the answer may be found in a social-psychological interpretation of Confederate behavior. Charles W. Ramsdell closely examined the economic problems facing the South—shortages, inflation,
impressment, poor transportation, poverty among the soldiers' families, industrial weakness, and the like—and concluded "without much
hesitation" that the "greatest single weakness of the Confederacy . . .
was in this matter of finances." But Ramsdell touched on another vital
problem, for he pointed out that the disintegrating economy and the
deteriorating military situation created war weariness and destroyed
morale.[28]

Other historians have emphasized the problem of morale more forcefully, sometimes identifying it as will, determination, or even esprit de corps. Clement Eaton cites a variety of problems such as military defeats from 1863 onward, clashes over state rights, desertions from the army, the peace movement, impressment, and suspension of the writ of habeas corpus, discussing them all in a chapter titled "Loss of the Will to Fight." Charles P. Roland is in basic agreement. Contending that the South lacked the requisite resources, he claims that Confederates could still have won if they had displayed more skill, unity, and will than their adversary. In the event, however, "for want of necessary strength, or of its equivalent in superior unity and skill, the Southern will declined and the Confederacy fell."[29]

A generation earlier historians had raised the question of will, and a good deal more forcefully. In his multivolume *History of the United States*, Edward Channing declared that the Confederacy had not suffered military defeat by April 1865. Comparing the Civil War to "the history of other wars and other revolutions, the end had not yet come and was not even in sight had the Southern people, or the mass of the people of the seceded States, wished to continue the fight for Southern independence." Confederates, he maintained, had lost the "will to fight." Charles Wesley agreed. In a 1935 publication Wesley surveyed Confederate difficulties and asserted that all the causes so frequently mentioned were important and that "to attribute the collapse to a single cause is indefensible." He pointed, however, to "the absence of a wholehearted and sustained resistance, the complete renunciation of self, the popular support of its government's measures, the devoted and continued loyalty to its declared principles—without which no revolution has been successful." Of the causes that contributed to the final collapse, he concluded that "the psychological factor of morale was one of the most influential in the complex scene." E. Merton Coulter was more emphatic. The South lost because the people did not want to pay the price of victory. Inflation, internal dissension, conscription, defeat, uninspired leadership, and failure of the leadership to maintain morale by keeping the people informed had sapped the last ounce of willpower and morale. As a result, wrote Coulter, the Confederacy "never succeeded in developing an *esprit de corps* . . . and in that sense it did not deserve to win." Confederates evidently did not will their independence because in 1865 their sense of nationalism was too weak; return to the Union took less effort and seemed at least as attractive as separate nationhood, perhaps more.[30]

The logical answer to the question why the South chose the very distasteful option of surrender, these historians would say, was that most Confederates, both military and civilian, had no more stomach for war. In view of the loss of blood and treasure, and little of consequence to show for it, one can hardly blame them. This explanation has its foundation in the axiom that casualties, like defeats in battles and campaigns, eventually had nonmilitary consequences. Both casualties and consequences adversely affected the morale of the home front as well as of the soldiers, undermining Confederate will to achieve independence.

FOR MANY Confederates, doubts crippled morale and diminished will accordingly. Such southerners found little nobility in what they were doing. This feeling would have afflicted old hard-line Unionists, for example, but the South had relatively few of these. Whenever and wherever a southerner questioned the institution of slavery, he experienced a feeling of unease, and as the war continued and the casualty lists lengthened, more and more loyal Confederates fell into this category. Charles G. Sellers has noted this phenomenon and believes that a sense of guilt over the institution of slavery produced it. He suggests, further, that southerners found it difficult to make a conscious decision to betray their own traditional liberal values "and to wage war for the purpose of holding four million human beings in a bondage that violated their humanity." Thus early enthusiasm for the war "was rapidly supplanted by an apathy and a growing disaffection which historians have identified as major factors in the Confederacy's failure," and the South quickly and easily surrendered the cause when it became clear that it was lost. The unmistakable implication is that guilt over slavery provided one reason the Confederacy lost the Civil War.[31]

Some historians have displayed a distinctly negative reaction to Sellers's notion. Yet the guilt thesis has significant support. Bell I. Wiley discussed a wide range of contributing factors to the defeat, several of which one finds on the traditional list: military setbacks, loss of confidence in the leadership, internal dissension, failure of the leadership to communicate with the public, and others. He also suggested that "uneasiness about slavery gnawed at numerous Southern consciences. . . . When the tide of war turned against the South the guilt complex became more oppressive." Many saw justice in the looming defeat, while the turmoil created by the tension between morality and slavery contributed to the touchiness, the "Big-man-me-ism" that Confederates displayed toward each other. Carl N. Degler, thinking along the same lines, notes that the weight of guilt was so heavy that Confederates were relieved to see the destruction of slavery. More recently, Kenneth Stampp has also discussed the role of guilt, believing it caused many southerners to hope unconsciously for defeat, and distinguishing it from "the defeatism and demoralization that grew out of military reverses, shortages of civilian supplies, and financial collapse." He concludes that "weak morale was not simply the ultimate consequence of war weariness, for the problem was present at its birth" and was attributable partly to "widespread doubts and apprehensions about the validity of the Confederate cause." The South, says Stampp, suffered from a "weakness that matched in importance its physical handicaps. This was a weakness in morale."[32]

Guilt provides a useful aid to understanding Confederate behavior, especially when we consider it in the light of the fundamental Protestant Christianity that characterized southern religion. War, defeat, and religion caused many southerners to reevaluate their peculiar institution and their political system as well. The result of this soul-searching reinforced the decision being made on the battlefield and confirmed it in the hearts of many once-enthusiastic Confederates.

As THE last sentence indicates, southern morale had an intimate relationship with events on the field of battle. The military power Confederates could bring to bear did not depend only on the number of soldiers in the field, the tactics and strategy employed, and the ability of the economy to support the military effort. Confederate power also varied in direct proportion to Confederate will. Thus it becomes difficult to consider the results of the war without discussing both the armies and the home front. To discuss either without the other is futile, for in a manner somewhat analogous to time and money, power and will are interchangeable. Sufficient will can compensate for serious deficiencies in power, whereas overwhelming power can force a successful conclusion when the will to achieve it is minimal. Certainly this is true when the power is military and the will is the national determination generated by morale. We know this relationship from our own recent history, if not from our daily lives; governments know it, or should know it, from the vicissitudes of their history.

Confederates knew of the relationship between power and will, but this knowledge did not always direct them to the logical conclusions. They focused their efforts almost totally on military operations and interpreted the prospects for their cause primarily in terms of the latest victory or defeat. Therefore, they effectively mobilized their economic resources in support of the war effort, constantly sought ways to use their manpower more efficiently and effectively, and attempted to avoid internal dissent. But the Confederacy neglected morale.

The Confederate leadership had little concept of mobilizing civilian opinion. Instead, it depended on military success to sustain the public will to attain victory and tended to define the problem of spirit and morale as one to be solved on the battlefield. Thus Confederates continually talked about military power and, to a lesser extent, economic power, and worked without ceasing to increase them. They also discussed will, but very often their concern went no further than that. Talk though they would about will—the morale, the spirit, the determination of the people back home—when Confederates made decisions they based them on military or at least economic considerations. Except for the obvious recognition that military successes would strengthen will, they left the latter to take care of itself.

Without overstating the point, it almost seems that the Confederate leadership looked upon will as a virtually inexhaustible resource that could not significantly increase except by victories in battle—although occasional fine speeches or stirring resolutions might do some good. On the other hand, they acted as if they could mine the will that did exist indefinitely and a sufficiency would probably remain. Many Confederates began to understand the incorrectness of this assumption only toward the latter half of the war, when losses at Gettysburg and Vicksburg, lengthening casualty lists, reconsiderations of the morality and expediency of slavery, and uncertainties about God's will in the conflict caused a great deal of southern soul-searching.

When victories became elusive and public spirit crumbled, generally Confederates could provide a solely military response, but this proved increasingly ineffective as the war lengthened. As a result, civilian determination continued its decline. Confederate decision makers only gradually came to understand the need to maintain will, prodded both by events and by the dissidents among them, who from the beginning, or at least since the reverses of early 1862, had pointed to the necessity to maintain, build, and restore civilian élan. Governors Zebulon Baird Vance of North Carolina and Joseph E. Brown of Georgia; Senators William Alexander Graham of North Carolina and James L. Orr of South Carolina; Representatives Henry S. Foote of Tennessee, Thomas C. Fuller of North Carolina, Williams C. Wickham of Virginia, and James T. Lamkin of Mississippi may have annoyed the Confederate administration, which had its attentions focused with equal narrowness and determination solely on the military challenges that lay ahead. Any opposition to military measures such as conscription, suspension of the writ of habeas corpus, or the impressment system posed by these mavericks took on the character of nuisance and sometimes even the taint of treason to determined Confederate bureaucrats, who saw the sole source of power in the barrel of a gun.

But the critics rightly emphasized—whether specifically or by implication—that in a total war military and civil policies and decisions differ little from each other. Furthermore, the population in arms may not serve exclusively at the front. It may, like the local militia, work in the field or shop one day and fight the next; or, like those engaged in agriculture in the backwaters of the Confederacy, it may never handle anything more lethal than a plow. Thus military decisions on conscription, habeas corpus, and impressment had a direct and obvious impact upon the civilians. When one examines Confederate history to determine the reasons for Confederate defeat, one studies both military and civilian decision making, for they amount to the same thing. A flanking movement in the Shenandoah, an assault at Shiloh, a retreat before Atlanta, or a withdrawal into Vicksburg were every bit as much civil decisions as they were military, even if the Confederate leadership failed to understand it.

This close connection between the civil and the military was not true in the North, at least not to the same degree, for the war led toward Union victory, the battles took place on someone else's territory, and

the country had sufficiently abundant resources of manpower and treasure to leave ample margin for waste and error or to compensate for a
lack of enthusiasm or flagging will. Many families could live relatively
normal lives, disturbed only by an empty chair at the table and sometimes distressing newspaper headlines.

No such normality could exist in the South, at least not after 1863,
for casualties, like defeats in battles and campaigns, had severe nonmilitary consequences. Both affected the morale of the home front as
well as that of the soldiers. Thus Confederates focused on military
operations and interpreted the prospects of their cause primarily on
the latest news from the battlefields. Even Jefferson Davis made this
mistake. When Joseph E. Johnston retreated before Atlanta, causing
his Union adversary grave concern, Davis joined the public panic in
seeing retreat as defeat, and he responded in a military way by replacing Johnston with the more aggressive John Bell Hood.

But except for such emotionally motivated military responses, the
Confederate government neglected morale; it had little concept of mobilizing public opinion. As David Potter, among others, has pointed
out, the Confederate administration made no serious effort to carry its
message to its own people in an effort to strengthen national will and
manipulate public behavior. Clement Eaton agrees but points out the
contrasting willingness and ability of the Confederate administration
to engage in an effective, well-organized propaganda campaign in Europe, the success of which was limited only by shortsighted and ineffective Confederate diplomacy. The obvious implication is that Confederates could have manipulated public opinion at home if they had
determined to do so. Instead of resorting to a propaganda campaign,
however, the Confederacy depended on military success to sustain the
public's will to attain victory, generally leaving the spirit and morale of
the Confederacy to the chances of the battlefield.[33]

Thus the student of Confederate defeat must never forget the essential unity between home front and fighting front. The Georgia militia
after Atlanta illustrates the point. Were they soldiers or civilians?
Whatever the legalities of the situation, in practice they were clearly
both, and the same held true for the masses of Confederates throughout the South—at least until they found themselves behind Union
lines, and even then many engaged in active hostilities. A study that

seeks to determine the causes of Confederate defeat, therefore, must never lose sight of the tight interrelationship of military and civilian decision making, though as a convenience to readers who like to penetrate the fog of war and who desire to understand the sequence of events more clearly than the participants, one must often adopt the organizational expedient of discussing military and civil affairs separately. Yet in the heat of the hour these amounted to the same thing, and Confederate will was the point at which the two came together.

When World War II began to go badly for Nazi Germany, propaganda minister Joseph Goebbels switched from optimism to pessimism and, by painting the consequences of defeat in the darkest hues, maintained the popular determination to fight on. The Confederates lacked much concept of systematically countering the effects of defeat until the last two months of the war, when public speakers in Richmond and declarations in Congress encouraged defiance of the enemy and rallied the people temporarily; but at that late date the stirring calls to arms accomplished nothing. Whereas World War II Germany, a small country assailed by millions of hostile soldiers, confronted insoluble military problems, the Confederacy, a huge country facing only a few hundred thousand armed enemies, had much cause to discount the consequences of lost battles and campaigns. But it did not.

Military events had significance for Confederates much greater than any particular battle or campaign warranted on its merits; they played too large a role in Confederate morale if only because the leadership made no concerted effort to tell the people otherwise. If Confederates lacked modern means to manipulate public opinion, they had means enough if they had thought to use them systematically. Of course, many leaders overestimated the importance of particular battles and campaigns. That many Confederates did not understand the power of propaganda, or did not use the knowledge as they should have if they did comprehend it, constitutes one of the points of this book.

Confederates constantly confused the role of the military power of their armies with that of the spirit and morale, the will, of their citizens. Often understanding something of the relationship, at least in theory, they nevertheless attempted time and again to attain on the battlefield what they lacked in morale. Although Vance, Brown, and others often seemed like scoundrels to military leaders and Richmond bureaucrats—and sometimes they were—they also were prophets. Such men deviated from normal Confederate policy and sought to maintain Confederate will by acting directly on the civilian population, rather than indirectly through another turning movement or frontal attack.

But overemphasis on the significance of military events flowed naturally from the halfhearted revolution in which southerners engaged. They did not declare, as the First French Republic had done in 1793, that

> henceforth, until the enemies have been driven from the territory of the Republic, the French people are in permanent requisition for army service.
>
> The young men shall go to battle; the married men shall forge arms and transport provisions; the women shall make tents and clothes, and shall serve in the hospitals; the children shall turn old linen into lint; the old men shall repair to the public places, to stimulate the courage of the warriors and preach unity of the Republic and hatred of kings.[34]

Like the French revolutionaries, Confederates conscripted their citizens and mobilized their economic resources, but, unlike them, southerners directed almost all of their revolutionary zeal outward toward adversaries in their bid for independence. They perceived Yankees as virtually the only opponents of their cause, focused their hopes and expectations on the military struggle, and did not, like their French and American revolutionary forebears, engage in ruthless suppression of internal dissent. Seeing northerners as their enemies, southerners generally failed to perceive dissenters and defeatists as opponents of independence in the way that American Patriots had viewed Tories or French Republicans had reacted against Royalists. The modest military actions against North Carolina and Tennessee Unionists did not compare with the military struggles against internal enemies in the American and French revolutions.

Like other soldiers in other wars, Confederate military leaders constantly attempted to answer questions of morale and spirit in military terms. When military successes eluded them or had no meaning, morale plummeted. Leaders often felt unsure of what to do next, except more of the same. Not knowing what to do after the fall of Atlanta, for example, Jefferson Davis sent Hood to Nashville and utter disaster. In the crisis of Atlanta, Davis had only a military answer. He toured Georgia, Alabama, and South Carolina for two weeks, during which he made a number of public appeals for renewed effort, but he did not follow up; he did not turn on the propaganda machine.

Davis at times did have some concept of the use of public appeals for propaganda purposes, for he had used the press extensively to promote himself and his ideas in Mississippi politics, and during the winter of 1864–65 he used the influence of his office to stir up public opinion favorable to the use of black soldiers. But though Davis and others in Richmond knew that will had importance, and they fretted and worried, they did not formulate policies that were directly calculated to improve the morale of the entire population in arms so that they could cope with momentary defeat. Vance and Brown, on the other hand, did just that by catering to the needs and desires of their people. As a result, they came into conflict with the authorities in Richmond.

Thus Confederates, though not really overlooking the problem of the home front, did not always define as enemies those who had lost heart or wanted peace, and when they finally did begin to think in such terms, the game had almost ended. "The malcontents, seizing on the restlessness consequent upon long and severe pressure," complained Davis, "have created a feeling hostile to the execution of the rigorous laws which were necessary to raise and feed our armies, then magnifying every reverse and prophesying ruin, they have produced public depression and sown the seeds of disintegration." But Davis and his administration had no policies either to suppress such malcontents or to regain their support beyond refuting criticism, wringing hands, and pointing fingers at those who had not thought and done as the leadership had wanted them to do.

By defining their revolution in constitutional terms with stress on state and individual rights, the Confederates found that constitutional constraints and legal scruples generally prevented their authorities from taking that drastic action against dissent which characterized the French and (to a lesser extent) American revolutions. When authorities did take severe action, they usually were responding to evasion of conscription laws, and they often acted without Davis's knowledge.

Lack of imagination precluded the other approach, a systematic appeal
to the public calculated to restore lost confidence and will. Davis identified the malcontents not as traitors but as "men of the old federal
school . . . who assume the guise of state rights men to sink the States
by the process of disintegration into imbecility and ultimate submission to Yankee despotism."[35]

Confederate authorities never squarely faced the problems of insufficient nationalism and crumbling morale. They diagnosed the problem, but military operations so occupied the center of the stage that
they virtually crowded out any systematic consideration of the crucial
significance of morale or of any direct measure to create nationalism
and the will to independence. For this reason, there can be no divorce
of military and social-political aspects of Confederate defeat; our discussion requires both.

ESSENTIALLY EQUAL to the armies of the North, or potentially so under
battlefield conditions, southern armies nevertheless in the end surrendered. The epitaphs written for the Confederate tombstone by contemporaries and historians each contain some truth, but they do not
explain why a would-be nation could establish a working government,
fend off enemy armies for four years, and then collapse. If supply met
essential needs, if we find that state rights or other internal dissent did
not significantly handicap mobilization for war, and if our investigation
should show that the Confederate military command displayed ample
competence, what interpretation would remain for a Confederate
failure following political, economic, and military success?

There is no little evidence available for the more satisfactory rationale, which we shall posit; our approach will be to show that most of
the frequently accepted explanations are not equal to the problem, and
then to offer more powerful solutions. One knows the answer is there,
somewhere—the Confederacy did not collapse without reason—and if
earlier interpretations are too weak, that only serves to prove that
historians have not yet isolated the critical, or proximate, cause. Key
questions of morale, willpower, guilt, and regret over the positive attributes of rejected decisions will prove the factors that best explain
Confederate behavior.

In short, our analysis will determine why southern nationalism
proved insufficient to achieve independence in the face of northern de-

termination to prevent it. Had the Civil War been an easy conflict, one that resulted in a rapid and thoroughly convincing victory with a minimum of bloodshed, the Confederate collapse obviously would not have occurred. But it was not an easy war. It dragged on, costing the lives of many of the strongest and finest young men. The long struggle dissipated southern economic strength and threatened the loss of racial control, eventually inducing some southerners to express a willingness to return to the Union in the mistaken notion that they might be able to retain slavery. Finally, the protracted conflict raised the specter of race war, which southerners long had believed would result if emancipation occurred.

So independence collapsed, and Confederates returned to the Union with a remarkably positive attitude toward making reunification work. Why? Although undefeated militarily, surviving severe economic pressures, and hindered but not seriously damaged by the consequences of the state-rights philosophy, they had suffered grievous wounds. The cumulative effect of Union military might, the ever-tightening blockade, a deteriorating economy, and internal dissension seriously affected the Confederate war effort. But none of these setbacks, nor all of them together, necessarily dictated defeat. The point is that the South could still have won, save only for the rapid diminution and ultimate death of morale, the will to win, during the last year or two of the war. The dynamics of giving up provide the key to why the South lost.

Toward the end, when the final result grew increasingly clear to all except the most sanguine and deluded, South Carolina Congressman William Waters Boyce wrote a long letter to Jefferson Davis strongly proposing new policies. We will discuss Boyce's ideas later, but his conclusion has relevance now. "A weak power engaged with a stronger power," he reminded Davis, "must make up in sagacity for what it lacks in physical force, otherwise the monuments of its glory become the tombs of its nationality."[36]

The lack of judgment that Boyce complained about lay in the leadership's confusion of military power and civilian will. Accordingly, Confederates pursued policies aimed at strengthening the military, but they neglected and even undermined public will. The weaker power, as Boyce pointed out, cannot afford to make such mistakes. Since we argue that internal dissension did not unduly disrupt the war effort, that the South displayed wisdom in the organization of its war production, that the power of the defense offset much of the North's advantage of superior numbers, and that the South displayed wisdom in its organization of war production, we must look elsewhere for the causes of Confederate defeat.

Confederate Senator Williamson S. Oldham of Texas offered an alternative explanation. An experienced politician and lawyer, Oldham in 1861 helped to lead Texas out of the Union over the objections of Sam Houston, the crusty pro-Union governor. Having made his decision for Confederate independence, Oldham served in the Provisional Congress and then in the Confederate Senate throughout that body's existence. Claiming to be a supporter of Jefferson Davis, Oldham nevertheless opposed conscription, suspension of the writ of habeas corpus, and martial law, and he logged a mixed record of support for the government's policy of impressment. Frequently on the losing side of an issue, the intractable senator stuck firmly to his principles—so much so that some critics thought him one of the obstacles to Confederate victory. Indeed, he was the sort of man Owsley and Donald blamed for defeat.

Oldham believed, for example, that the preservation of state rights was more important than the needs of the military and claimed to have been elected to the Confederate Senate for the purpose of opposing policies that tended toward centralization. Oldham was not, however, numbered among the fainthearted. He proposed a policy of burning the North's cities and its shipping facilities and pretended to know a foolproof way to do it; and, as the Confederacy approached defeat, he was one of the few congressmen to remain in Richmond until the adjournment of the last session of Congress. Then, three weeks before General Lee's surrender at Appomattox Court House, Oldham made his way back to Texas and subsequently into Mexico.

During his exile, first in Mexico and later in Canada, he pondered the question of why the Confederacy had lost, and after his return to Texas he tried to commit his ideas to writing. Oldham disapproved of Jefferson Davis's military strategy, strongly believing that Davis overemphasized the defense of Richmond and Virginia and underemphasized the West. But, Oldham admitted, defective strategy did not bring the ultimate disaster, nor did "the want of men and material resources to carry on the war." He recalled being a member of a joint House-Senate committee that served in January 1865 "to inquire into our present and future means of public defense." Congress considered the committee report in secret session, and apparently never printed it, so no official record of its contents exists. But Oldham claimed that after a thorough investigation, which included interviews with Davis, Lee, and various bureau chiefs, the committee "came to the unanimous conclusion and so reported, 'that we were in possession of resources, sufficient to enable us to carry on the war for an indefinite period of time.' "[37]

The stuff of war was available; the deficiency lay elsewhere. Oldham went on to deny that northern resources overpowered the South. He contended that military strength in November 1864 still stood on a par with that of the Union and believed that many former Confederates used the plea of resources simply because "such an excuse is flattering to one's vanity." He also denied that desertion or an obstructive Congress brought about the failure of the cause—state rights and internal dissent (as the historian would put it) did not produce defeat. Nor did it result from "want of patriotism, and selfishness of the people." These were symptoms, not causes.[38]

Rather, Oldham perceived other reasons why the South lost the Civil War. Continuing party divisions were important, for "men who had for years attached themselves to their parties and party leaders, who had for years, been taught by the latter to glorify the Union, as the greatest blessing. . . . could not in the course of a few days surrender up sentiments, they had entertained all their lives." Furthermore, the "federative power" of the government "was destroyed, and absolute despotic power, was conferred upon the executive and the military." Oldham exaggerated, but such measures as conscription, impressment, and suspension of habeas corpus alienated many Confederates, and instead of strengthening the government, they "weakened and paralyzed it." Thus, despite its control over the material resources of the South, the Confederacy could not "command and control its moral resources." By early 1865, when the Stephens-Campbell-Hunter peace commission reported Lincoln's precondition of Union for peace and pardon, many Confederates had accepted the inevitable. "Already conquered," Oldham remarked of the congressmen with whom he sat, "they were willing to accept the terms of the conquerors."[39]

Indeed, it becomes clear after reading Oldham's reminiscences that the erstwhile Confederate senator thought the cause of southern defeat was the flagging of Confederate spirit. The Confederate armies, he thought, were strong and almost equal to those of the Union "in all the elements of military strength *morale alone excepted*." Our assessments confirm that until 1865 the Confederate military indeed had the potential strength Oldham believed and that the basic cause of failure is found in his simple phrase: "morale alone excepted." The remainder of this book will explore the contributions of the components of Confederate military power and will examine the various causes for the deficiency in the vital element of morale. We will show why, in Clausewitz's terminology, the South lost its will to resist. The epitaph on the Confederacy's tombstone should read, "Died of Guilt and Failure of Will."[40]

In closing this introductory section, we should add two observations. First, we would like to make clear that our emphasis on the loss of southern will is not intended as a value judgment. With the perspective of more than a century to enlighten us, it is clear that the horrors of war had already become too great to comprehend fully and that extending the war would only prolong the folly of destruction and death, regardless of who might have won in the end. By late 1864, very likely earlier, those Confederates who argued for an end of war, even if that meant returning to the Union, did not include only the war-weary defeatists. Many among those who took that statesmanlike position may have lost their will, but they weigh more on the scales of humanity than those who would have fought to the last man.

Second, it will be apparent to many readers that much of our work is not new. To mix metaphors, we are not reinventing the wheel, but we do plow again some ground that has been plowed before, this time to prepare a new crop. This synthesis of previous scholarship, reinterpreted and added to our own ideas, is intended to provide some provocative ideas for future historians to challenge in their turn.

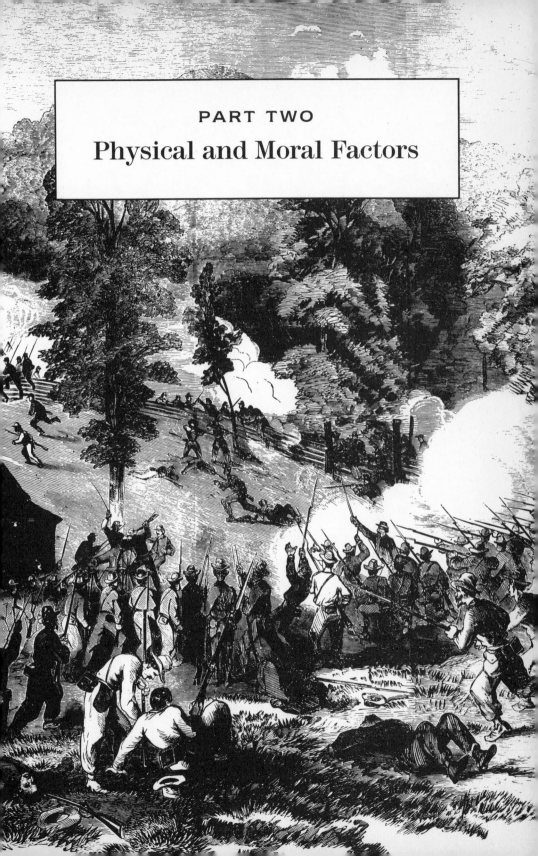

PART TWO
Physical and Moral Factors

The Confederacy began the war with many military advantages. The development of the rifle and other equipment for use by the contending armies markedly enhanced the power of the tactical defensive. The Confederacy's vast extent and the hostility of most of her people to the invader gave her an advantage which the numerically superior Union armies had little chance of overcoming. Nor did supply for southern armies present any serious obstacle because a rifle for each man and an artillery piece for each two or three thousand provided most of the weapons needed. A sievelike blockade, an effective mobilization, and successful creation of the needed establishments for manufacturing war material ensured an adequate, if not ample, supply for the Confederate forces.

But the Confederacy possessed less adequate spiritual resources. Many southerners had opposed secession, and some who had supported it had believed that it would not lead to war. Further, the South's nationalism had very shallow foundations, based, as it had evolved, largely on sectional differences created by slavery and on repeated claims grounded more on future hopes than present realities. And the South lacked the other factors usually fostering nationalism because it shared a common language and history with the Union. By placing George Washington, Thomas Jefferson, and even Andrew Jackson on its postage stamps, the Confederacy displayed how much history united rather than divided the contending sections. A mystical sense of unity never developed in the hearts and minds of the southern people.

Religion, another usual source of national difference, did not adequately distinguish the two regions either, in spite of some variations in the roots of their common denominations and the contradictory attitudes adopted toward slavery by the churches in each section. But relgion did provide a strong prop for southern morale because most

Confederates believed that God favored their cause and that, with His support, they must inevitably triumph. Religion thus provided a powerful source of the confidence most people felt at the prospect of a contest with a far larger, more populous, and richer adversary. During the first half of the war religion substituted in part for the Confederacy's deficient nationalism in providing the morale and motivation that were vital to such a desperate contest.

Chapter Two

Military Performance
and Possibilities

T O EVALUATE the military performance of the contestants in the American Civil War, and to determine whether the Union could have won by military efforts alone, the acknowledged experts on nineteenth-century warfare will provide the prime guide. The best-known among them in the 1800s, Antoine Henri Jomini, had studied the campaigns of Frederick the Great and Napoleon and had written detailed analytical histories of their campaigns to illustrate what he believed were certain immutable principles of warfare. In the 1830s he summarized these principles in a succinct book containing his recommendations concerning all aspects of war. More influential and better respected in the twentieth century, Jomini's contemporary Karl von Clausewitz also relied on military history and also drew his inspiration from the campaigns of Frederick and Napoleon. Clausewitz, too, explained his conclusions and recommendations in a major work, published posthumously in 1832.

These soldier-historians and theorists had participated in warfare under conditions essentially similar to those of the American Civil War, and they had studied it as well. Only the introduction of the rifle, the railroad, and the electric telegraph had altered the tactical and logistical conditions with which they were familiar, and these changes, though important, had not modified warfare enough to invalidate their judgments and prescriptions. Thus the works of Jomini and Clausewitz provide excellent authority for appraising the performance of Civil War leaders.

Organizing for a war that turned out to be far more extensive than anyone had expected, both Union and Confederate officials had to create European-scale war machines essentially from scratch. Clearly, considering the missteps of both, Americans of whatever section or persuasion lacked requisite knowledge for the awesome task. Even if some of the organizers did know a little of the theory of what they should be doing, actually carrying it out presented a problem of great magnitude. Among the more qualified, George B. McClellan had observed part of the Crimean War; Henry W. Halleck had read Jomini and perhaps Clausewitz as well as the other European theorists and had published *The Elements of Military Art and Science* . . . , which closely followed Jomini; and Irvin McDowell had been educated in France and in 1859 spent a year there on leave; but when put to the test all of these men proved unprepared for the tasks they faced. The less-experienced officers on both sides floundered even more. Of the officers in the United States Army who ever had commanded a unit even as large as a brigade, only one of them, Albert Sidney Johnston, was still young enough for active duty in the field.

To be sure, the Union did possess at the outset something of a military establishment, but the approximately fifteen thousand men available hardly met Antoine Henri Jomini's requirement for a "respectable" force, and even if, as he recommended, the Union could have doubled it by reserves, it still would have numbered only about 5 percent of the North's final war strength. Nevertheless the United States Army had directed its attention to providing the basis for wartime expansion and thus had fulfilled many of Jomini's prescriptions for preparedness. It had, for example, caused "the special arms of engineering and artillery to be well instructed" and had good systems for "clothing and equipment" and "for the commissariat, hospitals," and "general administration." But significantly, both the Union and the Confederacy shared in these elements of preparation; the Union retained the existing establishment and the bulk of the active personnel, but the Confederacy acquired key officers and used the previously developed methods. Upon these, the two sides built their armies and navies.[1]

Both sides also used the organization of command evolved before the war, but here the United States had failed to heed Jomini's injunction to provide either a "general staff" or "a good system . . . of directing the principal operations of war." Instead of a general staff that could plan, coordinate, and supervise the execution of orders, only one officer, the general in chief, in theory held command over the troops in the field. But he lacked power for he had no authority over the special staff or bureaus. These bureaus, which managed such essentials as transportation, food supply, engineering, and ordnance, worked directly under the secretary of war. Thus dual control existed that not only vested unwieldy power in the secretary but also deprived him of a coherent source of military advice and denied the soldiers any means of formulating unified recommendations.[2]

The Confederacy adopted the same organization, except that President Jefferson Davis, himself a former secretary of war and confident of his military ability, initially appointed no general in chief, relying instead on the adjutant and inspector general, whom he made the army's highest-ranking officer. This decision would have made sense as long as the South retained the defective old arrangement, but his adjutant and inspector general, Samuel Cooper, a sixty-one-year-old staff officer, could not provide the management and advice that a more energetic officer with greater field experience could have. Davis supplied much of this deficiency himself by drawing upon his own military education and varied military experience.

President Lincoln lacked Davis's military and administrative background, but in Winfield Scott he would have possessed the perfect general in chief had not the elderly warrior's seventy-five years borne so heavily upon him. Mentally alert, Scott found that his physical infirmities incapacitated him, and in the fall of 1861 he retired. But in any case the system made the general in chief an adviser only, with control of operations vested in the hands of the secretary of war; after January 1862, this was Edwin M. Stanton, an energetic and capable man, though militarily untutored. The Union badly needed a better command organization.

THE ENORMOUS forces that the North and South alike quickly mustered eclipsed the militia. Both sides created new armies essentially composed of civilians, a few of whom had experience in the regular army, militia, or Mexican War. The states raised these forces, which usually entered national service as regiments complete with officers from colonel down, all appointed by the state governments. Because of the small size of the regular army, Lincoln as well as Davis and their secretaries of war faced the critical task of appointing enough new general officers to command the brigades, into which the regiments must be formed, and the divisions, corps, and armies required for the management of the soon-to-be-mustered hundreds of thousands of men. This "selection of generals," wrote Jomini, was "most delicate," and "one of the most essential parts of the military policy of a state."[3]

Clausewitz had recognized that "in war men have so often successfully emerged in the higher ranks, and even as supreme commanders, whose former field of endeavor was entirely different." Agreeing, Jomini stressed that "the most essential qualities for a general will always be as follow [sic]:—First, *a high moral courage, capable of great resolutions;* secondly, *a physical courage which takes no account of danger.* His scientific and military accomplishments are secondary." But both Jomini and Clausewitz presumed that generals would be chosen from among the veterans of wartime military service. Davis and Lincoln could find few candidates whose moral or physical courage had been tested and even fewer who already had exhibited talent in war.[4]

Although Clausewitz stressed that "the simplicity of the knowledge required in war has been ignored," he believed that "no activity of the human mind is possible without a certain stock of ideas," and "for the most part these are not innate but acquired." Though he placed military knowledge second, Jomini agreed with Clausewitz on the importance of some military education, emphasizing that a general need not "be a man of vast erudition. His knowledge may be limited, but it should be thorough, and he should be perfectly grounded in the principles at the base of the art of war."[5]

Some of the more successful Civil War soldiers agreed with this professional assessment of the relative unimportance of military knowledge. A former merchant and brilliant Confederate general, Nathan Bedford Forrest found that the key to victory lay in "getting there first with the most," an emphasis on concentration most congenial to Jomini and Clausewitz. Professionally trained as a soldier, Ulysses S. Grant assigned the same subordinate role to military knowledge. His most recent biographer, William S. McFeely, contends that Grant "carried with him . . . an almost private joke. He had learned—or had somehow always known—how simple war is." This knowledge was a "colossal sick joke." Grant fully agreed that military knowledge was important, but it was not complicated. Writing in 1891, a former member of Grant's staff recalled the general's famous statement that "the art of war is simple enough; find out where your enemy is, get at him as soon as you can, and strike him as hard as you can, and keep moving on." Although this statement failed to characterize Grant's operations with the same felicity as Forrest's aphorism epitomized those of the Confederates, the European experts would have approved Grant's contention that "if men make war in slavish observances of rules, they will fail."[6]

But in selecting generals both presidents lacked time for an unhurried search, the war in progress demanding prompt appointments. Political requirements influenced choices in two ways. First, the country had a strong tradition of political patronage, and in filling government posts political considerations dominated. This custom had suffused the militia as well as the federal and state governments. Antielitism and the Jacksonian concept that public employment should be open to anyone augmented this convention. These attitudes were reinforced in military matters by a militia and citizen-soldier tradition as old as the first settlement of the country, and together they created a pervasive popular prejudice against graduates of West Point. Politicians especially valued military appointments because military glory previously had impelled four men into the White House. The second political factor, the need to use these prized appointments to bring all factions and interests together in support of the war effort, Davis understood and Lincoln comprehended completely.

Whereas Jomini disparaged "party spirit" in the selection of generals, Clausewitz would have understood it, "for it is policy that creates war."[7] In any event, Jomini and Clausewitz implicitly agreed that generals were made, not born, and that nothing prevented a politician with the necessary attributes, and with study and experience, from becoming a capable general.

The process of Union and Confederate appointments to general officer rank proceeded in much the same way. Each president divided the openings about equally between politicians and present or former regular army officers. Lincoln made some significant appointments of Democrats in an effort to rally more of the country behind the war effort. One of these, John A. Logan, a Stephen A. Douglas Democrat from Illinois, who had served as a lieutenant during the Mexican War, earned fame for his ability. Another Democratic appointee, Benjamin F. Butler of Massachusetts, became notorious largely for his military incompetence.

The Confederacy enjoyed greater success with its political generals because Davis, more than Lincoln, held them to the same standard of achievement as generals without political prominence. When a congressman from Confederate Missouri complained about one of the commanders appointed in his state, sneering at the man because he was a West Point graduate, Jefferson Davis coldly replied that because the Union in Missouri had replaced the politically popular General John C. Frémont, known as the pathfinder of the West, with a West Pointer, "the federal forces are not hereafter, as heretofore, to be commanded by 'pathfinders' and holiday soldiers, but by men of military educations and experience in war," and the South must follow suit.[8]

The Confederacy also adopted a better rank structure. Until 1864 the highest Union rank was major general because it seemed almost sacrilegious to appoint anyone to the next higher rank, lieutenant general, held previously only by George Washington, and in any event major generals cost less than lieutenant or full generals. The Confederacy early overcame this scruple and had both lieutenant generals and generals, all general officer ranks receiving the same pay. Promotion could then be made on merit and, though selection was far from infallible, it tended to leave the less capable, whatever their basis of appointment, at the lower of the four general officer ranks with the more able in command over them. Capable commanders had a particular significance because neither the Union nor the Confederacy ever possessed really adequate staffs. In Europe, good staffs had proven an effective method of compensating for mediocrity and even the incapacity of many commanders. It was, in fact, Jomini's concept that the staff should provide the brains while the commander provided the character and the moral courage to make the difficult decisions and adhere to them. Civil War generals had to furnish not only the character needed for command, but, often, most of the ability as well.[9]

The regular army boasted very little promising material. Virtually none of its officers had held important commands in the Mexican War, and few of them had any experience commanding a unit even as large as a thousand men. But they did possess some virtues: they had some knowledge of small-unit tactics, the army's logistic system, and the functioning of a military organization. By Jomini's standards the situation was not as bleak as it seemed, for "it is beyond question that war is a distinct science of itself, and that it is quite possible to be able to combine operations skillfully without ever having led a regiment against an enemy." Reading and Mexican War experience had supplemented the excellent educations of many West Point graduates and likewise had given many Civil War soldiers a grasp of two fundamentals, the primacy of the turning movement, agreed upon by Jomini and Clausewitz, and the tactical supremacy of the defense, especially when aided by entrenchments, a fundamental condition grasped only by Clausewitz.[10]

Many American regular officers had thus acquired, without Clausewitz's aid, the essence of his two main inculcations. In addition, many of them had the added requisites which Clausewitz found important in commanders. The intensity of the sectional controversy had made almost everyone aware of the "higher affairs of state" and "current issues," though the Union and its soldiers were divided over whether the war aims should include the abolition of slavery—but ironically, in the long run, so were the Confederates. Because most of the active officers on the eve of the war had attended West Point and served together in the small regular army, they tended to know a great deal about the "special virtues and defects" of the other former regulars who also occupied key positions. Their military experience had given them knowledge of such essential logistic factors as the ability "to gauge how long a column will take to march a given distance under various conditions." Finally, many of those given high commands initially, as well as others promoted later, had "an intellectual instinct which extracts the essence from the phenomena of life" or quickly acquired one by experience.[11]

This effort to extract the essence from military experience had more prominence on the Union side, where general officers faced the problem of overcoming the power of the defense. But most of the higher commanders on both sides demonstrated, either before or during the war, that they had thoughtfully and thoroughly analyzed the main issues of the art of war in their time.[12]

RELATIVELY EQUAL in ability and scanty experience, possessing similar ideas about logistics and strategy, familiar with the same administrative procedures, the generals of both sides prepared for battle. Only one side could win, and the student who attempts to determine why, despite this similarity in background, the generals of the South eventually lost, will have to answer many questions. But there are some very basic and obvious issues to deal with. And since the Civil War was, after all, an armed conflict in which thousands of basically decent men sought to kill thousands of other basically decent men, rightfully the initial questions posed should be military.

The military analysis throughout this book will address two basic questions, so obvious that they could easily be overlooked: Did the Confederacy conduct her military operations properly and skillfully? If so, would she have had an opportunity to win the war in spite of the North's superiority in men and material resources?

To answer these questions, we consistently apply the contributions of the two time-tested authorities on nineteenth-century warfare. Although many Civil War officers had some familiarity with Jomini, it is doubtful that many of them knew Clausewitz, whose book remained untranslated from the German until 1873 (there was no American edition until 1943). But to use these experts to evaluate performance and to determine the chances for success does not require that Civil War soldiers employed either of them as guides. They remain recognized authorities on nineteenth-century war, and the results of their lifetimes of study are the best sources of criteria for answering our two critical questions.

Although Clausewitz and Jomini wrote during the same period and each interpreted the Napoleonic revolution in warfare, their works contained significant differences. Clausewitz, in his very sophisticated *On War*, often exhibited a metaphysical tone and frequently assumed the reader's familiarity with Jomini and other theorists of warfare. More of a manual for commanders and war offices, Jomini's last work, his 1837 *Summary of the Art of War*, clung to the Enlightenment's idea of finding underlying, essentially geometrical, rules for warfare. But these two military historians expounded the general truths that they had learned from their thorough study of eighteenth-century and Napoleonic warfare. Much more unites their interpretations than separates them, for both men analyzed the causes of success and failure in the military operations of Napoleon's day, and they reached essentially the same conclusions.

Perhaps they disagreed most over the relative power of the offensive and defensive. Clausewitz regarded this as so fundamental a question that he essentially organized his treatment around the difference between the two. Over and over Clausewitz reiterated that *"the defensive form of warfare is intrinsically stronger than the offensive,"* and in his book he devoted three times as much space to defense as to attack. Jomini, on the other hand, regarded the offensive as strategically stronger and at least tactically equal to the defensive. But both disparaged a passive defense, agreeing that a defender who remained "passive and receiving all the attacks of his adversary will finally yield." And they both enjoined that the "defender must always seek to change over to the attack as soon as he had gained the benefit of the defense," a dictum to which Jefferson Davis, for example, paid lip service when he proclaimed his strategy to be "offensive-defensive." As Frank E. Vandiver has noted, this strategy was "designed to defend all the resources of the Confederacy and stockpile its strength" to "enable the country to maintain its armies and to counterthrust when chances and supplies permitted."[13]

Among their many areas of essential concord, perhaps the most significant for the Civil War was Clausewitz's and Jomini's advocacy of an attack on the enemy's flank or rear. Although Civil War soldiers tended to call all such attacks "turning movements," Clausewitz and Jomini distinguished two kinds, tactical and strategic. In a tactical turning movement, two armies stand face to face and one seeks to move at least some of its force around the opposing army to attack its flank or rear. In a strategic turning movement, the attacking army marches around to the far rear and places itself astride the communications of the defending army. This move often compels the defending army to fight to recover its communications and route of retreat. Then, if a battle ensues, the army that successfully had carried out a strategic turning movement would be on the more desirable tactical defensive. Clausewitz, in particular, saw that these maneuvers had become "a general law of the nature of engagements."[14]

Jomini preferred the strategic turning movement, the "system of modern strategy" in the "new era" created by Napoleon. He saw the opportunity for reaching the enemy's rear, where he "would have no other chance of escape than in forcing his way through your line." If Jomini had believed in the superiority of the tactical defense, he would have seen even more virtue in the strategic turning movement, for it compelled the enemy to assume the offensive to avoid being cut off from supplies and reinforcements. He disparaged the tactical turning movement, saying a general would "do better to employ strategic than tactical combinations" to seize the "enemy's communications while at the same time holding his own." He preferred the strategic because the tactical maneuver would only "dislodge" the enemy whereas the strategic would "ruin his army completely." Clearly, Jomini placed less stress on the capture and occupation of territory than T. Harry Williams believed.[15]

Clausewitz also stressed the turning movement, seeing that the use of this "most effective form" of attack was the "aim of every engagement." He also distinguished between the tactical and the strategic, but, unlike Jomini, gave more emphasis to the tactical, in which the attacker in battle attempted to turn the defender and the defender sought to prevent this by choosing a good position and having a reserve to turn or assail the flank of the attacker's turning force. Not sharing Jomini's admiration for the strategic movement to the enemy's rear, Clausewitz disparaged it as "not an invention of genius" and said that these "prize exhibits of the theorists" were "seldom found in actual war" because both sides "normally take precautions against them." But he did recognize the strategic turning movement's value on the defense when the attacker's communications were long and vulnerable; he further acknowledged its hypothetical merit when he emphasized that a decisive battle demanded "an enveloping attack or a battle with reversed fronts."[16]

The Civil War would prove both Clausewitz and Jomini correct about the ubiquity of the turning movement and substantiate Clausewitz's belief in the supremacy of the defense. After Clausewitz's death the substitution of the long-range rifle for the inaccurate smoothbore further increased defensive power. And most Civil War leaders were Clausewitzian rather than Jominian because most had learned from Professor Dennis Hart Mahan at West Point the strength of the tactical defense and the defensive value of field entrenchments, virtually ignored by Jomini but advocated by Clausewitz.[17]

Many changes in warfare before Napoleon's time benefited the South by making it easier to provide an army with effective weapons than it had been in the days of body armor, swords, and other hand-made weaponry. If equipping an army had involved great expense or had required substantial or sophisticated manufacturing capacity, the Confederacy would have had a distinct material disadvantage against the larger and more industrial North with its better-developed financial institutions and superb access to European resources. The widespread military adoption of the rifle just before the war also aided the South. The muzzle-loading rifle nearly completed the long chain of events which continually enhanced the power of the tactical defensive, and the Civil War became the first major war in which both belligerents equipped themselves fully with rifles.

In this war, as in any other, military success, Clausewitz stressed, would be measured by *"the political object of the war."* The Union had as its objective the complete suppression of the rebellion, the extinction of the Confederate States of America. Such a goal demanded a total victory and elicited the maximum possible resistance from the South. If the North were fighting, for example, over the fate of the border states of Missouri and Kentucky, the Union could have defined victory as the attainment of this limited goal. Southern resistance would have amounted to less for, as Clausewitz pointed out, "the smaller the penalty you demand from your opponent, the less you can expect him to try to deny it to you." And, of course, if the South attached more significance to its defeat than the North did to its victory, the Confederacy would make a greater proportional effort than the Union. Initially the South did make such an effort, and the Confederate public had a will strong enough to supplement many deficiencies in military power. When the South attached less significance to its defeat than the North did to its victory, Confederate morale would no longer match the task of maintaining public will at a level necessary for victory.[18]

Clausewitz noted that, depending on the political objective, the military means could range from "the destruction of the enemy's forces" to "passively awaiting the enemy's attacks." But for such a total political objective as that of the Union, Clausewitz recommended a campaign to destroy the enemy's armed forces, that is, to put them "in such a condition that they can no longer carry on the fight." The occupation of the enemy country and the destruction of its will to resist would follow.

But neither Clausewitz nor Jomini, who had more faith in the power of the offensive, had any recipe for success in waging a war that aimed at the total defeat of the enemy. Although both envisioned such a war, Jomini calling it an "invasion," they realized that such a decisive conflict would be rare, not only because political objectives seldom warranted so great an effort, but also because they knew the difficulty of attaining total victory. In fact, few historical models existed because, as Clausewitz pointed out, so many wars were limited or inconclusive that the majority are "so overwhelming as to make all other campaigns exceptions to the rule." Thus history provided few precedents from which they could derive a prescription for total victory.[19]

For a decisive campaign Clausewitz and Jomini agreed that the "forces must be adequate," "proportioned in magnitude to the end to be attained and to the obstacles to be overcome." But neither prescribed a specific ratio. They both felt that the size of the enemy's territory was perhaps as important as the size of the defender's armed forces. Clausewitz, who had participated in Napoleon's ill-fated 1812 invasion of Russia, gave this variable the most attention. This experience doubtless had helped him conclude that "a fairly constant ratio exists between the size of a force and the area it can occupy" and "the relationship between these two is permanent and fundamental."[20]

But Clausewitz did not establish this relationship, just as he and Jomini had failed to define the ratio between attacking and defending forces that they deemed adequate for a campaign aiming at the complete overthrow of the adversary. Clausewitz did, however, give a specific example of the forces he considered sufficient for a campaign against France. He hypothesized a war against France by Great Britain, Holland, Belgium, the Austrian Empire, Prussia, and all of the other German states. Their population would outnumber France's by two and a half to one, and they would place 725,000 men in the field. He assigned 50,000 Austrian troops to northern Italy and 25,000 British troops to coastal raids to immobilize about 60,000 French troops in coast defense. Deducting garrisons, 600,000 men were allowed for the principal campaign on the front from Switzerland to the English Channel.

He did not assign any force to France but, considering that the French regular army of that period numbered only 150,000 men, Clausewitz would hardly have expected that the French could manage to have more than 200,000, regulars and militia, to face triple their number on France's northeastern frontier.

He anticipated "one or more major battles," which, "with such superiority of numbers," would promise "decisive victory," the fall of Paris, and the advance of the allied armies to the Loire. At this point France would accept the peace conditions imposed by the allies. He did not define these conditions, but they clearly did not envision taking away French independence. A similar military defeat in 1871 compelled France to agree to a peace in which she lost the Alsace-Lorraine territory and paid an indemnity of five billion francs. Obviously Clausewitz had described a victorious campaign made possible by great superiority and an adequate ratio of the size of the force to the area it had to occupy. But he hypothesized political objectives more limited than those of the Union. He said nothing about what the military situation would have been if the allies had to advance south of the Loire, or if they desired to extinguish French independence. A three-to-one superiority and the immense force of 600,000 sufficed only to occupy about one-third of France; the campaign would have won only limited political objectives.[21]

This hypothetical campaign has instructive parallels with the Civil War. The frontier from Switzerland to the sea approximates the width of the state of Tennessee. The distance from the French frontiers to the Loire is about the same as that state's depth. Tennessee, Mississippi, Alabama, and Georgia together equal the size of France. The number of men Clausewitz proposed for this territory exceeds all Union forces in the field until 1865 and at least triple the number ever used in this area. In addition he hypothesized a numerical superiority of three to one, more than the Union had until 1865. Further, he implicitly assumed French qualitative inferiority because they would use some militia whereas the invaders could rely exclusively on regulars and well-trained reserves.

Surely Clausewitz's example shows that, had he lived until 1861 and studied the situation, he would not have believed any decisive campaign were possible for the Union, nor that the Union could conquer a country as large as the South: the Confederacy east of the Mississippi, alone, had nearly twice the area of France. He had said that Russia, admittedly much bigger, was "not a country which can be formally conquered—that is to say occupied," even by all of the states of Europe, including France. If the estimates are reliable, how else could Union forces successfully occupy the Confederacy, except by acquiescence of the population? One Confederate leader, Secretary of War George Wythe Randolph, believed such a conquest impossible. "There is no instance in history," he wrote at the beginning of the war, "of a people as numerous as we are inhabiting a country so extensive as ours being subjected if true to themselves."[22]

With some understanding of the power of the defense, the usefulness of turning movements, and other European ideas of warfare, Civil War generals went out to fight a war in which battles with significant results proved as elusive as Clausewitz and Jomini would have expected. But Civil War planners had more to consider than the role their armies would play. With extended seacoasts, mighty rivers, and an ocean highway for foreign supply, they also had to devote serious attention to naval affairs.

Chapter Three

The Impact of the Blockade

BECAUSE initial Union military planning recognized the impossibility of waging a decisive campaign against the Confederacy, Union General in Chief Winfield Scott had proposed a strategy proportioned both to the military resources available and to the actual political objective. He chose to take advantage of the western rivers, employing "twelve to twenty steam gunboats" and enough steam transports to carry sixty thousand men. With this combination he intended to drive down the Mississippi, expecting to have a small detachment on the river and another, larger force, inland cooperating so as to "turn and capture" all of the rebel river forts. He then envisioned "a cordon of posts on the Mississippi to its mouth from its junction with the Ohio" and "blockading ships of war on the seaboard." By keeping open the "great line of communication" of the Mississippi "in connection with the strict blockade of the seaboard," he would "envelop the insurgent States and bring them to terms with less bloodshed than by any other plan." Scott believed that a blockade would supply a key element in the grand strategy to defeat the new Confederacy.[1]

Scott's ideas illustrated that, in the Civil War, military and naval strategy went hand in hand. Communications often relied upon naval cooperation, and of course foreign supplies for both sides depended on the seas. Whether as blockaders or runners of the blockade, merchantmen or raiders, transports or river gunboats, ships had a key role to play. The effectiveness of that role, however, hinged on how well the generals and admirals, and the politicians, comprehended naval strategy and potentialities.

Perhaps the Union blockade best exemplifies the crucial role of the Union navy. Noting Scott's proposals and the extensive effort the North devoted to establishing and strengthening the blockade of the Confederacy's saltwater borders, historians generally have agreed that the major objective of the Union navy was the maintenance of an effective blockade; going one step further, they also conclude that the blockade succeeded sufficiently to be a major determinant of Confederate defeat. This conclusion follows naturally only if one assumes that results are always proportionate to efforts, for assuredly the blockade played a significant role in Union strategic thinking. Yet there is much evidence that the blockade was not as critical to Confederate fortunes as many historians believe.

On April 19, 1861, only six days after Major Robert Anderson's surrender of Fort Sumter, Lincoln proclaimed a naval blockade against the seceded states. Secondary objectives included the protection of American foreign commerce and the support of land campaigns. But the blockade as well as support of the army would necessitate combined operations, including landing troops on the coast. Secretary of the Navy Gideon Welles acknowledged these objectives in his annual report for 1861 when he affirmed Union naval strategy as follows:

1. The closing of all the insurgent ports along a coast of nearly three thousand miles, in the form and under the exacting regulations of an international blockade, including the naval occupation and defense of the Potomac river. . . .
2. The organization of combined naval and military expeditions to operate in force against various points of the southern coast, rendering efficient naval cooperations with the position and movements of such expeditions when landed, and including also all needful naval aid to the army in cutting intercommunication with the rebels and in its operations on the Mississippi and its tributaries; and
3. The active pursuit of the piratical cruisers which might escape the vigilance of the blockading force.[2]

Although the Union obviously implemented this strategy, its results are not so clear, and historians still continue to debate the Union navy's effectiveness. The blockade has become a highly significant issue simply because of the historiographic emphasis placed upon it; an impressive number of Clio's servants consider it a major factor in the Confederacy's eventual defeat. Allegedly the ever-tightening blockade gradually snuffed out the shipment of vital war material and necessities of life and impeded the export of cotton, the Confederacy's most acceptable collateral, to European ports. Furthermore, it supposedly stimulated economic chaos that finally shattered the Confederacy's will as well as its means to win.

In 1950 the venerable southern historian E. Merton Coulter wrote in *The Confederate States of America, 1861–1865*, that "without a doubt the blockade was one of the outstanding causes of the strangulation and ultimate collapse of the Confederacy," and in 1962 Rear Admiral Bern Anderson, in the best one-volume naval history of the war, stated that "without the relentless pressure of Union sea power . . . [economic disintegration] could not have been achieved. The blockade was the active instrument of that sea power, and it was one of the major factors that brought about the ultimate collapse and defeat of the South." Charles P. Roland agreed. "The silent grip of the Federal navy," he wrote, "grew ever tighter and the number of captures among blockade-runners steadily mounted. Still more significant, Southern ports were avoided altogether by the major cargo vessels of the world. By 1864 the blockade was strangling the Southern economy." Roland's statement implies the decisiveness of the growing power of the Union navy. From approximately ninety warships in 1861 the navy expanded to more than seven hundred by April 1865, clearly enough to close the 189 inlets and river mouths scattered along the more than three-thousand-mile southern coastline as well as to provide support for operations on the Mississippi River and its tributaries.[3]

James R. Soley, one of the first writers to emphasize the Union navy's role in defeating the Confederacy through the blockade, believed that "the number of prizes brought in during the war was 1,149 of which 210 were steamers. There were also 355 vessels burned, sunk, driven on shore, or otherwise destroyed, of which 85 were steamers; making a total of 1,504 vessels of all classes. . . . Of the property afloat, destroyed or captured during the Civil War, the larger part suffered in consequence of the blockade."[4]

No one can challenge the statement that economic welfare within the Confederate states had significantly diminished. A host of writers have described graphically the sufferings and hardships of civilians and soldiers, the impact these had on the means to continue the struggle, and, more important, on the *will* to do so. Students of the war overwhelmingly agree that this economic difficulty constituted a major factor in Confederate defeat. The real question, however, is the role of the Union blockade. Coulter, Anderson, Roland, Soley, and others notwithstanding, considerable evidence indicates that the blockade did not represent a major factor in the Confederacy's economic exhaustion.

The blockade certainly had economic strangulation as an objective. Did it fail to accomplish this goal because it was an ineffective, "leaky and ramshackled affair," as Frank L. Owsley contended? Some fifty years ago Owsley published his monumental study *King Cotton Diplomacy*. In a chapter entitled "The Ineffectiveness of the Blockade," Owsley evaluated the Union blockade in terms of the number of ships that eluded the blockaders, the increase in Confederate cotton exports, and the successful delivery of huge amounts of cargoes to the South. Although historians generally did not accept Owsley's conclusions, in later years other studies appeared that substantiated his work.[5]

Marcus W. Price's series of articles published during the 1940s and 1950s in *American Neptune* have been by far the most important in this regard. In his study "Ships That Tested the Blockade of the Carolina Ports, 1861–1865," he estimated that out of 2,054 attempts to run past the blockading vessels off Wilmington, North Carolina, 1,735 succeeded, or an average of 1.5 efforts per day, with 84 percent of them getting through. In a second article he analyzed the blockade of the Gulf ports. Between April 20, 1861, and June 4, 1865, according to his calculations, 2,960 vessels tried to slip through the blockade, a daily average of two. As with the Carolina ports, in 1861 very few vessels were taken. But in 1862 and 1863 the Union tightened the blockade. During that period the proportion of successful runs into and out of these ports amounted to 65 percent and 62 percent, respectively. He attributes the higher percentage of failures to the larger number of sailing vessels used in the Gulf. In 1864 and 1865, the picture changed dramatically, particularly in the number of steamers challenging the blockade. Nevertheless, in 1864, 87 percent, and in 1865, 94 percent of the ships that challenged the Gulf blockade got through. Although Price perhaps exaggerated his statistics on successful runs by including questionably fruitful so-called violations, he nevertheless clearly shows that the blockade contained many holes. It certainly proved ineffective at Wilmington, North Carolina, which became the most important port in the Confederacy for blockade-running. In a recent study, Richard E. Wood estimates that 230 runners entered that port in 1863–64 and fifteen more slipped in before the Union captured the port early in 1865.[6]

Frank E. Vandiver also recognized the inefficacy of the blockade. In a 1947 study of blockade-running through Bermuda, he wrote, "It must be apparent that the blockade was, from the Union point of view, far from a completely effective measure. . . . It is not too much to say . . . that the amount of supplies which did arrive through the blockade enabled the Confederate armies and people to carry on appreciably longer than would otherwise have been possible." More than thirty years later, in 1970, he remained convinced: "The task of sealing off the South with its vast coastline was super-human; not even the Federal navy could meet the challenge."[7]

A recently published study by Richard I. Lester, a British historian, agrees substantially with Vandiver. Both Lester and Richard Goff, the singular expert on Confederate supply, agree, however, that the Confederates might have won the war if they had broken the blockade. They imply that the Confederates could not create a naval force powerful enough to challenge Union sea power and to break the blockade. But the Confederate government never gave priority to challenging the Union blockade, a convincing argument, on its face, that the South did not find the blockade excessively damaging to its war effort. Because the Union considered the blockade its major naval strategy, many historians have simply assumed that its destruction was the major objective of the Confederate navy. As Anderson wrote, its presence "automatically made attempts to thwart that blockade the primary task of the Confederate Navy." This was not true. From the beginning Stephen Mallory, the Confederate secretary of the navy, viewed defense of harbors and rivers as the navy's major responsibility, which, of course, fitted in well with Jefferson Davis's overall strategy of defense.[8]

Nevertheless, Mallory did want to challenge the blockade. The Confederacy used cruisers such as the *Alabama* and *Florida* to assail

Union shipping in order to force the Federal navy to weaken the blockade by diverting ships for the protection of the commercial lanes. And
early in the war the secretary also ordered the construction of armored
vessels, both at home and abroad, to attack blockaders. But neither
effort proved successful. Depredations on the Union merchant marine
did not weaken the blockade, and Mallory's initial ironclad policy
failed. Only one armored ship built in Europe, the *Stonewall*, actually
reached Confederate hands, and it arrived too late to challenge the
blockade. Mallory's navy also tried to build within the Confederacy five
large ironclads capable of going to sea but completed only the
Arkansas and the *Virginia*, both of which proved unseaworthy.[9]

Therefore, historians generally regard the Confederate naval effort,
particularly the ironclad program, as a failure. They base this assessment on the erroneous assumption that the Confederates built ironclads to challenge the blockade and commissioned only a scant few. The
South laid down approximately fifty armored vessels but completed
and placed in operation less than half that number. With the exception
of the five initial vessels, however, Confederates intended the ironclads only for harbor and river defense.

Confederate officials wrote surprisingly little about the blockade in
their correspondence and exhibited more concern over its international implications than over the blockade itself or its effects on the
Confederacy. President Davis did not show much interest in naval affairs and generally left them in the capable hands of Secretary Mallory. Davis's few references to the blockade indicate concern from an
international point of view; he considered it a paper blockade, clearly
illegal, and thought other nations should ignore it. In January 1865 he
issued one of his few directives concerning naval operations when he
ordered the Confederate naval squadron at Charleston to attack Union
forces off the harbor—not because of the blockade but to try to prevent linkage between the warships and the approaching army of Major
General William T. Sherman.[10]

Even Mallory rarely mentioned the blockade in his reports and correspondence, and Secretary of War James A. Seddon premised his recommendations for foreign trade in strategic goods with the matter-of-fact
observation that "our staples can be exported and supplies introduced
with reasonable exemption from capture." Apparently, a substantial

number of Confederate officials did not view the blockade either as especially effective or as a serious threat. This does not mean that they ignored its existence, but they did not find that it produced sufficient damage to require a change in strategy. Students often assert that Confederate officials paid no attention to it during the early months of the war but that as its effectiveness increased, they became more concerned. In fact, Confederate officials were well aware that the South broke the blockade more frequently in 1864–65 than at any time previously. As late as March 1865, one newspaper editor yawned over the capture of Wilmington, the last open port, and told his readers that "we shall, no doubt, suffer considerable inconvenience," but denied that it would cause the Confederacy to succumb. "Our inventive faculties and mechanical skill will be quickened and developed, by necessity, to the supply of all our wants."[11] The editor's prediction of the future was a more accurate description of the recent past.

THE INDUSTRIAL revolution experienced by the Confederate states helps explain this almost blasé attitude toward the blockade. To have a chance to win, the Confederacy had to industrialize, and it did. No one has ever completely told the story of this transformation from an agrarian to an industrial economy, but in recent years several perceptive writers have examined aspects of it. In his biography of Josiah Gorgas, the Confederate ordnance chief, Frank Vandiver recounts success in developing an arms industry. Richard Goff does the same with the quartermaster stores, and William N. Still emphasizes the creation of a naval shipbuilding industry. Although the Confederacy did not obtain self-sufficiency, it made extraordinary progress. As Raimondo Luraghi, the most eclectic of this recent school, wrote, "Never before in history had anything like this been seen. A backward agricultural country, with only small, truly preindustrial plants, had created a gigantic industry, investing millions of dollars, arming and supplying one of the largest armies in the world."[12]

Clearly, although supplies from abroad were vital, the blockade did not cause the economic difficulties in the Confederacy. They resulted from internal problems such as interruptions of transportation and inadequate manpower resources, and, as we shall ultimately show, the collapse of the will to pay the price of achieving independence.

Although the Confederate government nationalized much industry, until early in 1864 it generally allowed blockade-running free reign. The evidence strongly suggests that during the first years of the war those involved in the blockade-running business were more concerned with bringing in goods that sold well than in meeting the needs of the war effort. In November 1864, only a few months before the final collapse, an official of a Wilmington, North Carolina, firm wrote to his agent in Nassau not to send any more chloroform because he was having difficulty selling it. The businessman requested perfume, "Essence of Cognac," because it would sell "quite high." Cargo manifests found in port newspapers and elsewhere suggest that this was not an isolated incident. As late as 1865 some southern newspapers still advertised civilian consumer goods that ships had brought through the blockade. Indeed, the importation of nonessentials created such a scandal that in February 1864 the Confederate Congress passed a law "to prohibit the importation of luxuries, or of articles not necessaries or of common use." This extensive list of prohibited commodities, too tedious to repeat, reveals the lucrative profits that southerners could earn by trading in unnecessary consumer goods instead of shipping war materials. Margaret Mitchell did not invent the Rhett Butler stereotype—it existed.[13]

Even in 1864, when the Confederate government finally established laws to regulate blockade-running, it required ships to reserve only one-half of their cargo space for government shipments. The enabling legislation became effective on February 6, 1864. The original bill, however, did not authorize commandeering half the space of blockade-runners. The House had voted down this provision during its consideration of the bill, although the president was allowed to prescribe regulations; Davis interpreted this law with utmost latitude.[14]

Davis justified his action in a message to Congress on December 20, 1864, contending that most owners of blockade-runners had allowed the government one-third of their cargo space even before the passage of the legislation and that since the profits of the blockade trade were "monopolized by foreigners," while the government alone bore the expenses of keeping ports open, it seemed only fair that the Confederate government should realize some of the profits by seizing a portion of the cargo space. Far from inhibiting foreign trade—except for a brief period when shippers tried to force relaxation of the regulations by curtailing their activities—these regulations seem to have had little or no effect upon the volume of trade, for in December 1864 Davis and Christopher G. Memminger, the secretary of the treasury, both maintained that the number of blockade-runners was still growing.[15]

Secretary of War James A. Seddon went further, claiming in early December 1864 that "the number of vessels engaged in running the blockade has steadily increased since the establishment of the regulations and is now larger than at any time before. Many new steamers are understood to be on the way to engage in the business." He underlined the ineffectiveness of the Union blockade by emphasizing that this stepped-up activity was taking place "though the stringency of the blockade is supposed to be constantly augmenting." Davis noted that the blockaders were making so much profit that the stocks of the trading companies were soaring in value.[16]

IN DESCRIBING efforts by the Union navy to enforce the blockade, historians usually emphasize the numerical increase in warships on blockade duty during the course of the war, suggesting that at some point the Union attained enough blockaders on station in southern waters to retard blockade-running significantly. Nevertheless, one recent study shows that, although the number of blockaders on the Wilmington station steadily grew, the number of blockade-runners captured or destroyed remained approximately the same.[17]

Squadron commanders constantly appealed for additional ships. Because of the shortage of vessels for both blockade duty and combined operations, the Union had to shift vessels from one point to another. Frequently the result was a noticeable rise in shipping at the port from which the navy withdrew blockaders.[18]

Union squadron commanders also encountered extremely difficult logistical problems that hindered their efforts to enforce a tight blockade. The use of steam-powered vessels theoretically increased efficiency, but vexatious problems of maintenance and supply largely offset the advantages. As early as 1862 the four blockade squadrons required approximately three thousand tons of coal per week, and the amount needed grew as the number of blockaders increased. A recent study by Robert Browning of the blockade off Wilmington clearly demonstrates that the inefficiency of the vessels deployed at Wilmington frequently and seriously weakened the naval force on that station, by 1863 considered the most important. Many blockaders had inadequate speed or poor seagoing qualities, especially in heavy weather. Blockading squadrons included many converted ships that could not operate at sea for long periods or carry their heavy ordnance without impairment of their performance. Too often they suffered breakdowns in machinery and had to leave their stations for long periods when the navy had no replacements to send. The writers suggest that repair time kept from one-third to two-fifths of the vessels constantly away from their stations. At one time the Wilmington station had ten of its vessels in the yards.[19]

Although the blockaders received some provisions and supplies while on station, they usually had to obtain coal and ordnance stores elsewhere. Beaufort, North Carolina, Port Royal, South Carolina, and Pensacola, Florida, became the most important supply depots for the various squadrons in the Atlantic and the Gulf. The depots, however, frequently ran short of coal, resulting in long delays before vessels returned to their stations. The coal shortage also affected cruising operations. In September 1863 Rear Admiral Samuel P. Lee, in command of the North Atlantic Blockading Squadron, wrote to the force commander off Wilmington: "You may find it expedient not to keep more than one of the little vessels moving about at a time, even at night."[20]

CLEARLY, CONFEDERATES could get whatever they wanted or needed through the blockade, if they wanted it badly enough. To do so, they had to regulate the trade by law or price, and they eventually adopted both methods. Davis complained of ruinous charges, as he did in other economic contexts; but had Confederates been willing to pay more for cargo space, they would have gotten more, and quickly. That they did not pay more, and that their own figures indicated that the blockade still remained relatively ineffective as late as December 1864, argues that they had sufficient domestic supply available to preclude the necessity of draconian measures to increase foreign supply. Private blockade-runners, whether grudgingly or not, did provide vast supplies, augmented by the eleven vessels that the Confederacy owned outright or in three-fourths share. Confederates struggled with the law of supply and demand, but in the end the law held firm, as Davis discovered in June 1864 when he refused to knuckle under to pressure to relax shipping regulations. The shippers came round; the price was right.[21]

The Union eventually stopped blockade-running, of course, but not by the action of the blockading fleets. If all stations suffered the same logistical problems and inefficiency among their vessels as the North Atlantic Blockading Squadron suffered at Wilmington, as seems to be the case, such difficulties seriously compromised the effectiveness of the entire operation. The Union most successfully hindered Confederate blockade-running with its army by capturing port areas and carving up the Confederacy into smaller economic units. The efficacy of the blockade off Galveston meant little after the fall of Vicksburg; the status of the port of Mobile had less consequence after Sherman's march to the sea. Of course, without the blockade the sea lanes would have been more open to Confederate trade; the presence of even an ineffectual blockading force certainly had some detrimental impact on Confederate supply. But clearly it did not have a decisive effect.

Thus the Union navy failed to interdict the flow of commerce in goods which market forces and the Confederate government deemed most valuable; the South did not lose the Civil War because of the blockade. The net was too loose to stop importation of many needed goods until the last port was closed in 1865. By then private and public industrial efforts had made the Confederacy less dependent on imports for products essential to the war effort.

Nevertheless, the blockade, the disruption brought to the southern economy by the demands of war, and the consequences of invasion did create economic difficulties for the home front. These hardships tested the morale and will of the people, qualities that necessarily rested in part on the intensity and extent of Confederate nationalism.

Chapter Four

Southern Nationalism

ARMED FORCES, the resources to sustain them, and a civilian population are not the only components of a military effort. Intangible resources also help a people wage a prolonged armed conflict, not the least of which is will, or morale. We contend that lack of will constituted the decisive deficiency in the Confederate arsenal. Some significant aspects of this problem, really a congeries of deficiencies, such as turmoil created by a sense of guilt and sin, will receive extensive treatment shortly. For now, it suffices to note that Confederates embarked on an enterprise demanding the utmost in teamwork, unity, and loyalty, without possessing these virtues in adequate degree. When the military effort began to falter, Confederates were unable to pick up the slack sufficiently to compensate for the loss of military strength. In basic terms, the Confederates lacked a feeling of oneness, that almost mystical sense of nationhood. They lacked a consensus on why they fought or what they stood for. The Confederate nation was created on paper, not in the hearts and minds of its would-be citizens. These deficiencies reflected a national will that did not equal the demands placed upon it.

The student of Confederate nationalism must make a distinction between two quite different kinds of nationalism. A number of recent historians, most notably Frank E. Vandiver, have emphasized the wartime development of a strong central government, which they consider a sign of Confederate nationalism. Using nationalism to denote a mode of government, usually in opposition to a state-rights style, these historians correctly point to the strong central government— one at odds with the notion of state rights, as many Confederates promptly and continually pointed out—that Jefferson Davis and other like-minded Confederates created to fight the war.

By the standards of the 1860s, the Confederates had a highly centralized and extremely powerful government, with a Constitution that had the potential for creating a stronger government than that of the Union in 1861. One need only think of the measures about which Jefferson Davis's opponents so frequently complained: conscription, suspension of the writ of habeas corpus, martial law, impressment, the regulation of trade and commerce, and, at the end, the recruitment of slaves as soldiers. Because of this high regimentation of the economy some scholars have labeled it "state socialism"—a label that few other historians care to dispute.[1]

This form of nationalism is a theme of Vandiver's study of the Confederacy. He believes that Davis personally created the Confederacy, although the creation "was not pleasant for a natural state righter, not easy for a man appalled by centralization." But Davis succeeded, believes Vandiver, who goes so far as to say that the southern president made the Confederate Constitution into a "revolutionary document" and "worked to build a sense in the southern people of a higher loyalty than state rights—a sense of Confederateness"—which admits that he jettisoned state rights in the effort to achieve victory. Davis himself tacitly confessed to having done just this, for at the end of war he complained that "malcontents . . . have created a feeling hostile to the execution of the rigorous laws which were necessary to raise and feed our armies. . . . Men of the old federal school are they who now invoke the laws of state rights to sustain a policy which, in proportion to the extent of its adoption, must tend to destroy the existence of the States of our Confederacy, and leave them conquered provinces."[2] Emory M. Thomas, a former student of Vandiver's, made one of the most forthright statements of this position. Thomas contends that nationalism was always present in the Confederacy but that the experiences of the first year of the war produced a revolutionary nationalism in which "national character grew to become more Confederate than Southern," a trend that continued as the war went on.[3]

Paul D. Escott's recent study of the failure of Confederate nationalism also provokes thought. Escott maintains that nationalism was there but that it failed to bring Confederate success because Jefferson Davis's policies alienated his constituency. Some policies, such as exemptions for overseers and conscription substitution, appeared to favor the rich, thereby antagonizing the middle and lower classes; other policies, such as those aimed at organizing a strong, centralized government, irritated segments of the planter class, which accused Davis "of trampling on the constitution and subverting the nation's purpose." This kind of nationalism, reflected in the powerful Confederate government, constituted a major element in enabling the Confederacy to fight as long and as effectively as it did. It is partly responsible for the prodigious struggle required to attain Union victory.[4]

ANOTHER KIND of nationalism, however, comes closer to explaining the breakdown of Confederate will and the perhaps predictable Confederate defeat. This nationalism does not refer to a style of government policy or economic organization but to the emotional bonds between citizens of the would-be nation. The problem, in a nutshell, is that the people of the South had no widely accepted mystical sense of distinct nationality. Some historians believe they have discovered such a nationalism, and this doubtless is what Vandiver and Thomas meant when they widened their definition of nationalism to embrace more than a mode of government, including also what they termed a "higher loyalty . . . a sense of Confederateness," and "a growing national character."

At this point we part company with the Confederate nationalists. We believe that the Confederacy functioned as a nation only in a technical, organizational sense, and not in a mystical or spiritual sense. An inadequately developed sense of nationalism hampered southerners in their quest for independence, as Kenneth Stampp points out in his provocative essay "The Southern Road to Appomattox." Only slavery gave the South its own identity, despite the efforts of some southern writers before the Civil War to pretend otherwise. Southern nationalism was, in Stampp's words, "that most flimsy and ephemeral of dreams." Many Confederates became Confederates not because they shared a sense of unique nationhood but because they had a mutual fear of a society without slavery and white supremacy. Whatever nationalism these southerners may have felt, it was not as strong as the fear of such a society. Many other Confederates had left the old Union with reluctance, for they had affection for the American past or understood the utility of the American polity, and they too could appreciate the attractive features of the rejected alternative. Thus when the Con-

federacy moved toward emancipation, its nationalism was insufficient
to maintain its war effort.[5]

IT CONFUSES the historian who desires to know why southerners lost
the Civil War to realize that many Confederates harbored conflicting
notions of why they fought. Although often true of countries at war,
such ambiguity was especially true of Confederates, perhaps more
than of any other fighting people. The Federals had a clearer idea; they
fought, by definition, for national unity, although they added the goal
of emancipation along the way. The southerners, however, experienced more confusion. Once the war came, they fought and mostly for
the South. But they had to justify the act. Confederates fought to
break away from a prior attachment, but this merely stated a fact and
did not provide a justification, a goal, or even a realistic alternative.
For some it was not even a desired alternative.

Some southerners supported their section because they had no other
choice. Indeed, the strength of Unionism in the South before the war
began, and even at its beginning, illustrates clearly that many Confederates fought for their independence as a second choice. Given the
alternative of remaining within a Union at peace or joining the Confederacy, people in vast areas of the South preferred the former. But
they never had the chance to make that choice. When Lincoln called
for troops after the fall of Fort Sumter and the war broke out, the
border state Unionists—a large enough group to force their states to
remain in the Union after the first wave of secession—felt betrayed.
They joined the Confederacy, for now they faced a different choice.

Because the option of remaining in a Union at peace no longer existed, these men were forced to choose between a Union at war or a
Confederacy at war, a narrow range of possibilities. As Jonathan
Worth, a leading North Carolina Unionist and wartime ally of Governor Zebulon Vance, noted, "Abolitionism and Secession were the only
commanders in the field—both . . . moved and instigated by the
Devil." Having to follow "one or the other we all enrolled ourselves as
true and liege vassels of secession."[6]

Although southern Unionism was not nearly so strong as Lincoln
and other northerners had hoped and believed, the delay of the upper South in joining the Confederacy strongly suggests the lack of

one of the key ingredients of Confederate strength—an adequately developed sense of nationalism. A bride who is the groom's second choice will not have a very attentive husband, nor will she make the best of wives. At the very time that Lincoln's actions were forcing the upper South into the arms of the states that had already seceded, some southerners still resented the choices they had to make. After Lincoln's call for troops, for example, one Tennessee newspaper complained of "the destruction by its own people of the greatest, the freest, the most beneficent and most powerful government ever known to man."[7]

Border state people found themselves in an especially difficult position. To side with the Union without knowing whether the Union would attempt to assert its authority in the departing South would place them in the position of treason to their state after secession; but if the Union acquiesced in secession, they would be left out on a limb. To whom, for example, would a Louisiana Unionist give his allegiance if the Union decided to let that particular erring sister depart in peace? But failure to choose meant that one could have no influence on events and might have to acquiesce in unwanted secession. Robert L. Caruthers, a Tennessee Union Whig, opposed secession until after Lincoln's call for troops. Then, like others, he went with his state. William Alexander Graham of North Carolina faced the same dilemma, writing after the war that he and other former Whigs "had ever been sincere & zealous adherents" of the Union, but finally "the only alternative left us, was the choice of the side we should espouse, when a favorable result to either, was to be little short to ruin to us." Ralph Wooster's modern work on the secession movement, to take only one example, indicates that in most southern states Unionism constituted a political force of some consequence until Fort Sumter, and in several states it remained significant even after the war began. The failure of four slave states to join the Confederacy exhibits the importance of Unionism.[8]

From the very beginning, the South was divided; even secessionists divided among themselves, and cooperationists were sometimes actually secessionists and other times Unionists. From the very beginning the southern monolith showed so many cracks that the notion of a widely shared sense of nationality becomes strained. Some Kentuckians preferred neutrality, and some North Carolinians called themselves Revolutionists. All southerners shared a fear for the future if outside forces disturbed the institution of slavery, and they lacked unanimity even on the significance of this issue.[9]

And yet, despite the internal divisions, southerners created an independent Confederacy. Steven A. Channing attempts to deal with this paradox by agreeing that the mere existence of the Confederacy must prove something. The real question remains whether that "something" constituted a distinctiveness amounting to nationality. Citing Kenneth Stampp on the negative side of the question and Eugene Genovese and Raimondo Luraghi on the positive, Channing rejects both points of view. He contends, instead, that Confederates had "an ideological core sustaining a latent cultural nationalism." Explaining this latent core, however, inevitably brings Channing back to the Negro presence, the equivalent of deducing the existence of a latent German nationalism in 1930 by the presence of Jews. Furthermore, the Negro presence did not have a nationalizing effect in much of the border region.[10]

Our argument does not deny that the black population provided, to paraphrase Ulrich B. Phillips, a central theme of Confederate history. It does deny that southern or Confederate nationalism resulted from anxiety, or even guilt, about the institution of slavery. That even those who trembled when they thought of the unchained slave did not agree on secession as a proper tranquilizer for their anxieties provides one of the strongest proofs of this contention. Some of these, the most practical of men, saw in the Union the bulwark of a stable society, without which any slaveholding community must collapse. James Lusk Alcorn of Mississippi, for example, denied that disunion would best protect slavery, a position typical of other Mississippi Unionists. As Percy Lee Rainwater noted, they "regarded secession as a doubtful remedy and as a hazard to the social order if it should lead to violent revolution." Marc Kruman observed the same reaction among North Carolina Unionists, who contended that secession would endanger slavery because secession would cause war, and "abolition would be the certain result of war." As it turned out, these North Carolina Unionists, caught in the middle, proved accurate prophets. Some of them even opposed secession on the ground that if the Confederacy reopened the slave trade it would ruin the value of slaves in North Carolina.[11]

In Washington, Elizabeth Blair Lee, whose brother Montgomery Blair soon entered Lincoln's cabinet, declared in January 1861 that she continued to hope the country could avoid civil war, "for it is so evidently a death knell to slavery in all those states who thro away the shield of our National Government—I cannot conceive the country so mad as to put themselves between the fire rear & front."[12]

This same anxiety existed throughout the South. Channing, the most able student of the South Carolina secession movement, sees anxiety as one of the roots of doubt for those who felt some hesitancy about immediate secession. Fearful of losing control over slaves, South Carolinians nevertheless chose secession, "yet that same fear was evoked by the turmoil which might accompany disunion." They took an uncharted course; some Confederates faced the future with unlimited and unjustified confidence, but others trembled with uncertainty. The former governor of Florida bitterly denounced the secessionists: "You have opened the gates of Hell," he predicted, "from which shall flow the curses of the damned to sink you to perdition."[13]

James Chesnut, Sr., for example, understood that for all the noise of the abolitionists, the Union was a great protector of slavery, just as many abolitionists had charged. "Without the aid and countenance of the whole United States," he remarked, "we could not have kept slavery. I always knew that the world was against us. That was one reason why I was a Union man. I wanted all the power the United States gave me—to hold my own." As one member of the Virginia secession convention reminded his colleagues, the civilized world opposed slavery, "and it is nothing but the prestige and power of the General Government now that guarantees to the slaveholder his right."[14]

Not only would the United States no longer use its strength to maintain slavery, it might use its power, as indeed it did, to undermine the institution. Furthermore, the geographic limits within which slaveholders had influence would contract when secession occurred. Jonathan Worth claimed that "slavery is doomed," for "with Canada in effect her [the Confederacy's] Northern border from the Atlantic to the Pacific—all hating us, it is madness to think of anything else only to cut the throats of the negroes or have our own throats cut." As North Carolina's *Daily Conservative* reminded its readers in 1865, Unionists had warned southern politicians in 1861 that leaving the Union "jeoparded the institution of slavery a thousand-fold more by secession, than by carrying on the contest under the old government."[15]

Indeed, the Union did protect slavery, and old Chesnut and others

like him apparently understood what one Illinois politician had to remind a Kentucky friend. On the slavery question, he warned, "You
ought . . . to appreciate how much the great body of the Northern
people do crucify their feelings, in order to maintain their loyalty to
the Constitution and the Union." Chesnut would have been taken
aback had he known that these were Abraham Lincoln's words, but the
future president was reflecting the feelings of many in his section who,
doubtful of slavery, nevertheless acquiesced in its existence for the
sake of the Union. In civil war, such northerners need no longer "crucify their feelings."[16]

Others, less pragmatic, had sentimental ties to the Union far more
difficult to cut than ties based on expediency or rational calculation.
When the final break came, with heavy hearts indeed such people followed their states away from the flag of their fathers. A. H. Kenan of
Georgia threw away the pen with which he signed his state's ordinance
of secession, and George T. Ward of Florida announced, "When I die I
want it inscribed on my tombstone that I was the last man to give up
the ship."[17]

Other people shared these sentiments, though most agreed that if
secession came they would go along with their states. In January 1861,
a backcountry Baptist minister wrote Zebulon B. Vance, then a United
States congressman, that "it is set Down that North Carolina is ces-
sion But if it is left to the people to say they will say Difernt . . . if
Division is the Result And the South has to set up for itself this people
is As true to the South As Any people that ever trod the Soil But let it
Be The Last Resort." In Georgia, a sense of unreality struck Benjamin
H. Hill, soon to be a member of the Confederate Congress: "Is it not
strange that we should fire cannons, illumine cities, raise bonfires, and
make noisy the still hours of the night with shouts over the destruction
of a government infinitely greater than Rome ever was!" Herschel V.
Johnson, Stephen Douglas's vice-presidential running mate in 1860,
felt equally downhearted. "I never felt so sad before," he wrote in his
autobiography. That such individuals frequently became enthusiastic
secessionists after Lincoln's call for troops in April 1861 does not
change the fact that the first hours of southern independence found
them in a distinctly doubtful mood, one that created an exceedingly
fragile basis for nationalism.[18]

Other Unionists found their loyalties equally torn. The *Nashville Republican Banner* claimed in August 1861 that Tennessee had stopped the secession movement. It had "declared against the abominable heresy, and determined to stand by the old Union," for Lincoln's policy seemed one of peace. After his call for troops on April 15, however, Tennessee Unionists "felt that they had been deceived—betrayed and outraged." They still believed that southern Unionists could have triumphed over the secessionists, but Lincoln's proclamation "knocked the blocks from under all of them, or nearly all. They had no ground on which to stand."[19]

Some other southerners, notably in west and north Texas and in the eastern mountains, were coerced into secession right from the beginning. With sympathy for the plight of such people, especially those of the mountains, Philip S. Paludan observes that they made their difficult decision to become secessionists often under the pressure of pro-secession neighbors, for "reasonable men not seeking martyrdom might [be wise to] become Southern patriots. For many among all classes there was little pleasure in being citizens of the new republic. . . . In such an environment it is not surprising that devotion to the Confederate cause was often not very deep." As Paludan observes, "Men who swore their loyalty to Dixie often swore, as one fellow put it, 'from the teeth out.'" Even members of the ruling elite harbored such attitudes, and, though they went along with their states, they never changed their minds on secession. Jeremiah Clemens was atypical in that he abandoned the Confederacy and went North before the end of the war, but as late as September 1862 he promised that he would "adhere to the Southern Confederacy more closely in storm and disaster than in sunshine and prosperity," even though he had never had "any extraordinary love for the Southern Confederacy. I was forced into it . . . by the action of my State."[20]

After the war began a considerable number of Confederates constantly referred to the conflict as one to protect their institutions, by which they principally meant slavery. But when the Confederacy itself considered the abolition of slavery such men felt betrayed, with consequences that had very significant effects. Not many Confederates openly spoke in 1861 of their desire for independence for its own sake. Jefferson Davis reminded his people that Confederates asked only "to be let alone," not a very sophisticated or inspiring reason for initiating secession and civil war.[21]

If they had been nationalists, those so-called southern nationalists would have looked upon their war as a true revolution—but not many of them did. In an offhand way Confederates often referred to their movement as a revolution, but they generally did not mean it in the same way as revolutionaries in other nations have meant it. The usage lacked fire; it was too casual to carry much ideological weight. When Georgia's Governor Joseph E. Brown used the word, admittedly he spoke with enthusiasm, but mostly in heated exchanges of opinion with Jefferson Davis, not with ringing conviction that Brown perceived himself playing a role in a truly revolutionary movement. Others were more equivocal. Howell Cobb said that what was most remarkable about the Confederate revolution was its conservatism, which some students might consider a contradiction in terms, and Alexander H. Stephens referred to secession as revolution in his "Cornerstone" speech, but Stephens had opposed secession. Davis used the word, but on at least one occasion he flatly asserted that "ours is not a revolution," for Confederates had merely "instituted a new government on the basis of those [inherited] rights. . . . We are not," Davis emphasized, "engaged in a Quixotic fight for the rights of man." If anyone played the role of fighter for the "rights of man," the Union did, and some historians contend that the North witnessed the real revolution.[22]

Whether the movement constituted a revolution was a disruptive question because southerners could not agree. In North Carolina, the Unionists, acquiescing in the inevitable, attempted to get the state to base secession upon the right of revolution, only to be heavily outvoted by the secessionist faction, which denied that secession involved revolution. If the South was attempting a revolution, it was one in which some of the leading revolutionaries renounced the very idea. "They did not believe there was any revolution in what they did," concludes Frank Vandiver about the Montgomery convention, for "revolution was anathema to them all." This position was logical for them because real revolution would threaten domestic slavery. Indeed, says Robert L. Kerby, the South lost the Civil War precisely because the leadership could not "admit that Southern independence could be achieved only by revolution." Such a paradoxical position provides a good indicator of a lack of nationalistic sentiment.[23]

Once the states had established the Confederacy, once the political machinery was set in motion and the society was functioning as normally as possible for a society under siege, so much internal opposition still existed that Confederate nationalism became more of a transitory emotion than anything else. Channing, aligning himself to some degree with Vandiver and to a lesser degree with David Potter, suggests that the creation of the government and the war that followed forged a core of prewar southern nationalism into Confederate nationalism. This conclusion, too, seems doubtful, except for a few members of an emotional and perhaps overexcited elite. Throughout the Appalachian chain of discontent, for example, analyzed so perceptively by Georgia Lee Tatum, lived vast numbers of ordinary folk who opposed the Confederacy from its very beginning, such as those in East Tennessee and western Virginia, or who came to oppose it actively within a few months or a year. As Philip Paludan has illustrated, these people often suffered directly and cruelly because of their lack of Confederate nationalism.[24]

Opposition, both political and military, emerged in other parts of the South as well. Surely one may question a nationalism felt deeply by so few and superficially by so many, especially when one considers that many loyal Confederates doubtless felt stronger allegiance to their region, state, locality, comrades-in-arms, or constituents than they ever did to a mystical Confederate nationality.[25]

Of course, the black population must be subtracted when one attempts to establish Confederate nationalism, for two different peoples occupied the same territory. Not only did black southerners have different goals from white southerners, but their presence in large numbers provided the most distinctive difference between the sections. Indeed, if the South had a distinctive nationalism in the 1860s, it was a black nationalism, probably unconscious, which white southerners would fight—as they did during Reconstruction—to avoid "Africanization."

No matter how one calculates, therefore, the Confederacy had a small number of true nationalists as a percentage of the total population—certainly not enough to carry the burden of a war in which the North heavily overmatched them. A latent core of true Confederates may have existed, but there was no "widespread determination to forge a Southern nation at all costs." And surely a losing war would not create more loyalty to such an abstract concept, especially when Confederates could look back and see highly desirable aspects in the rejected alternative—peace and Union.[26]

IT WOULD be unreasonable to expect Confederates to have developed sufficient distinctiveness from their northern brothers to evolve into a separate nationality. Grady McWhiney justifiably complains that too many writers "have tended to magnify the differences between Northerners and Southerners out of all proportion. In 1861 the United States did not contain . . . two civilizations." Any notion that the people of the two sections "were fundamentally different" is, says McWhiney, "one of the great myths of American history." He contends that historians have "ignored or minimized the common elements in the antebellum American experience." As Edward Pessen has pointed out, there were indeed differences between the sections, but "the antebellum North and South were far more alike than the conventional scholarly wisdom has led us to believe." After surveying an extensive literature, he concluded that "for all their distinctiveness, the Old South and North were complementary elements in an American society that was everywhere primarily rural, capitalistic, materialistic, and socially stratified, racially, ethnically and religiously heterogeneous, and stridently chauvinistic and expansionist." We could add more obvious similarities, which are so plain to see that they have become clichés. Very little separated them, not even including, for most people in either section, a greatly different view of their black countrymen. Racism was not much stronger in the South than in the North—its expression merely took different forms. The values the South shared with the North proved to be bonds, not wedges, and they were bonds that neither could escape.[27]

Most of all, these Americans, North and South, shared history; for the southerners did not have a distinctive sense of history. And shared history, one of the strongest bonds, sometimes overcomes even the powerfully divisive influence of language. David Potter's observation that Canada provides an illustration of two diverse peoples living in harmony without antagonism and disruption of national integrity has lost its appropriateness. But even in that instance, the linguistic dif-

ference, with all its accompanying cultural distinctions, has not by itself created serious internal stress within the last generation. It is of
equal importance that French and English Canada do not share the
same history. The Canadian (or American) experience may be contrasted with that of Switzerland, with its four languages and numerous
dialects, which nevertheless is held together by the adhesive of a common history. If one scratches beneath the surface of linguistic diversity
in a land of dissension, one will likely find historic diversity. If the
history has similarity, however, diversity of language may not have a
particularly strong influence in creating separate national feeling.[28]

In the United States, Confederates simply appropriated as their
own the history they shared with the Union and recreated it. One
could as reasonably suppose that the thirteen colonies had set out on
the path of separate statehood immediately on their founding as to
suppose that Confederates emerged with a complete nationality when
they fired the first shot at Fort Sumter. Early colonial history had
been British history. It took a century and more for the feeling of
unique experience to develop that we may call American nationalism.
Without its own distinctive past upon which to base its nationality, the
Confederacy appropriated history and created a mythic past of exiled
cavaliers and chivalrous knights that owed more to Sir Walter Scott
than to flesh and blood migrants from the Old World. The southern
objective, says Rollin G. Osterweis, "was not to alter the existing political organization, as in the case of the thirteen colonies, but to re-
draw boundaries that would conform to mythical but credited eth-
nographic needs." This was certainly the movement of an intellectual
elite, exercising a generous amount of wishful thinking.[29]

AND SO southerners did little, as Osterweis says, to change their polity.
They adopted their initial laws en masse from those of the United
States, and they wrote their Constitution virtually as a word-for-word
copy of the Federal Constitution, with only a few significant changes;
the Constitution underlined the lack of nationalism by implying the
right of secession. The several Confederate flags departed from the
design of the United States flag, but all included red, white, and blue
colors, with stars and bars in one form or another. Moreover, the great
seal also followed the Federal tradition, for it portrayed the equestrian
statue of George Washington erected before the Virginia legislative

buildings in 1857 (can one imagine the great seal of the United States portraying King William or Queen Anne?). The South's postage stamps and its currency, too, indicate to the modern historian the extent to which history was used to create a mythic past for Confederate use. Besides Jefferson Davis, Confederate stamps pictured George Washington, Thomas Jefferson, Andrew Jackson, and John C. Calhoun. A certain irony emerges here, for the inclusion of Jackson blots out the memory of his views in the nullification crisis of 1832, and Calhoun—the one true Confederate precursor—adorned a stamp that the Confederacy never used because rapid inflation rendered its low denomination inadequate. Jackson and Calhoun also appeared on some Confederate treasury notes.[30]

Confederate nationalists surely existed, but Confederate nationalism was more a dream than anything else. Simply to assert nationhood and to declare independence neither create nor reflect nationality. Nationalism is an elusive concept, and, as the emerging countries of the third and fourth worlds illustrate so well today, the creation of a new political entity does not necessarily mean that its citizens have a sense of unity or shared experience. Just the opposite is often the case, and in that sense, one might suspect that the United States today has not yet achieved a true sense of nationhood; how, then, could the South in 1860, or, for that matter, the North? If Confederates did possess a distinct nationality, it was one they shared with the North. Because country and nation are not the same, two separate countries may share enough of a common heritage that they may be part of the same nation—East and West Germany come immediately to mind, or better, the German and Italian states during the unification movements of the 1860s.

In confusing nationalism with sectionalism and exceptionalism, historians have created part of the problem. David Potter's essay "The Historian's Use of Nationalism and Vice Versa" reminds us that the North was not nationalistic simply by definition. Sectional considerations were strong on both sides of the Mason-Dixon line; perhaps the North rather than the South had strayed from American tradition and become sectional. Perhaps the majority in the North could manipulate the Union to further its sectional interests while the minority in the South could not. Frank L. Owsley had noted the same thing a quarter century earlier. Owsley charged that what historians have understood as nationalism was an "egocentric sectionalism" that was really only northern sectionalism "writ large." Nationalism cannot be defined by a simple head count.[31]

In much the same way that Potter and Owsley treated sectionalism, James M. McPherson deals with the question of southern exceptionalism. He, too, suggests that perhaps the North was different, not the South—that the North was the one "that departed from the mainstream of historical development." He points out that "the South's concept of republicanism had not changed in three-quarters of a century; the North's had," hence southern doubts about whether they were engaged in a revolution.[32]

Potter contends that efforts to find a *separate* culture in the South had been fruitless, although a *distinctive* culture did indeed exist. Much of this distinctiveness lay in the institution of slavery, which was so basic to their existence, most southerners thought, that they would fight to preserve it when it was threatened. As Potter points out, "The readiness with which the South returned to the Union will defy explanation unless it is recognized that Southern loyalties to the Union were never really obliterated but rather were eclipsed by other loyalties with which, for a time, they conflicted."[33]

Potter's discussion of loyalties goes right to the point, for a truly nationalistic movement will not be confused about where its loyalties lie. Yet this was a great source of Confederate confusion. Unionist and secessionist in 1861, returning easily to Unionism in 1865, southerners did indeed suffer a confusion of loyalties. Nowhere did this appear more than in the far West. Surely the idea of distinct southern nationalism breaks down in Texas. Americans who emigrated from the United States in the 1820s and 1830s settled there and became Mexican citizens. After the Texas revolution and the establishment of an independent republic, Texas became a state of the United States in 1845. In 1861 the state's allegiance switched once more, against the will of a substantial number of her citizens, and during the war some Texans threatened to leave the Confederacy and become independent again. Any nationalism in the Lone Star State was Texan nationalism, not southern or even American nationalism. In the East, on the other hand, South Carolina had as her most distinctive attributes her opposition to democracy (after 1828 it remained the only state in which the state legislature still chose presidential electors) and her propensity to get out on a limb, as the events of 1832 and 1850–51 demonstrated. Even other southerners sometimes had a difficult time taking South Carolina seriously. One of its leading citizens allegedly remarked after its secession that it was too small to be a nation and too large to be an insane asylum, and before Fort Sumter one Tennessee editor sarcastically referred to "that turbulent and mischief making little spot on the North American continent, known in the school geographies as South Carolina." To one Virginian, the Palmetto State was simply that "little impudent vixen."[34]

Surely, in their hearts many Confederates never truly felt the ties of a new nationality, though sectional interest may have stirred them. We find unconvincing those discussions that assume southerners developed a true nationalism that could transcend political boundaries or could exist without a political entity to shelter it. Avery Craven's *Growth of Southern Nationalism*, for example, says little about nationalism—he does not even list the word in the index. Craven does assert that the 1850s marked a period of changing relationships between the southern states on the one hand and the northern states and the federal government on the other, and that the Civil War "and the growth of Southern nationalism, which gives title to this volume, was largely a product of those relationships." This statement seems to indicate that southern nationalism had its basis in mutual distrust and dislike by the North and South. But instead of this negative emotion, nationalism means a positive affirmation of unity. Logically, therefore, Craven also mentions the pride southerners took in the accomplishments of the American nationality and concludes that by 1861 southern nationalism may not have been nationalism after all. The last chapters describe a section that felt itself compelled to leave the Union.[35]

In *The Idea of a Southern Nation,* a newer and more challenging study, John McCardell discusses the development of the concept in the nullification crisis of the 1830s, centering on the problem of slavery but examining also economic, religious, educational, literary, and political issues, and concludes that in each issue a feeling of separateness had developed by 1860. McCardell seems to equate nationalism with separatism; the two differ markedly, however, and if, as Craven believes, Confederates felt forced out of the Union, southerners could have

favored separation without being nationalists. Indeed, if the two phenomena are the same, the very strong resistance to secession in many
southern states, especially the border, would seem to justify the conclusion that nationalism amounted to no more than the ideological play-
thing of a segment of the elite. Even McCardell seems to have his
doubts; in his introduction he maintains that despite the growth of an
ideology of southern nationalism, "it is incorrect to think of Northerners and Southerners in 1860 as two distinct peoples" and that "the
majority of Southerners, probably even in 1861, still hoped that their
sectional rights could be maintained within the existing Union"; in his
conclusion McCardell argues that the strong state-rights position of
the southern nationalists had created tensions "that would produce a
new American nationalist ideology." This statement, the most able of
the southern nationalist case, seems in the final summation to support
much the same position argued in this chapter: that southern nationalism was not particularly strong and did not even include a majority of southerners. McCardell's thesis, in its essence, equates southern
nationalism with the desire of southerners to legislate for themselves,
not the same as a mystical sense of nationhood.[36]

David Potter reached some of the same conclusions as Craven and
McCardell in *The Impending Crisis*. Discussing the nature of southern
separatism, Potter detected the undeniable "spirit of southernism"
and thought of Edmund Ruffin and William Lowndes Yancey as genuine southern nationalists because they "had the vision of a South
united by shared distinctive qualities, and both seemed to care more
for the South as a whole than for their own states." This provides a key
to the question, and the Civil War historian would do well to recall the
number of times he has read the phrase "he went with his state," used
so often to describe the actions of leading Confederates. Vice-President Alexander H. Stephens thought of Georgia as his country, as Potter points out, and it is difficult to think that Jefferson Davis ever
cared more for the entire South than he did for Mississippi until after
he became president. Most leading secessionists saw southern nationalism merely as "bitterness against another country." The contrast
of men such as Ruffin and Yancey with other Confederates leads Potter
to conclude that southerners did not really desire a "separate destiny"
but rather "wanted recognition of the merits of southern society and

security for the slave system." The southern movement had "a strong color of nationalism," but the war did more to produce that nationalism than vice versa. Potter believed that southern nationalism supplemented, not replaced, Union nationalism by 1860 but that it lacked sufficient strength to unite southerners "in any commitment to southern nationalism, nor to a southern republic, nor even to political separatism." Instead, fear united them. In short, by 1860, North and South were, paradoxically, "separated by a common nationalism. Each was devoted to its own image of the Union, and each section was distinctly aware that its image was not shared by the other."[37]

Given the ambiguous nature of nationalism, the ambivalent conclusions that other scholars have reached on the subject, and the fragile nature of Confederate identity, we have little hesitation in expressing our serious doubts that the average Georgia plowman sensed a distinct nationality from the average Ohio plowman, even after the war began. That northerners and southerners had a past more common than distinct, however, does not alter the fact that some southerners attempted to pretend otherwise, but a pretend nationalism, or one newly discovered, will be of a thin and fragile variety that will bend and break under stress such as that imposed by a civil war.

We do not deny that the South was distinctive in a number of significant ways. But it seems clear that different though they might have been, southerners did not diverge so much from northerners as to constitute a different nationality. And the lack of national feeling explained the absence of sufficient will to counter the enervating effect on morale of military reverses or to compensate for the eventual decay of purely military power. The relative absence of reserves of national determination meant that military leaders had to conduct operations at a level of success above that normally necessary to meet military requirements per se so as to sustain morale. The failure of the people in arms to maintain a high level of determination placed too great a burden on the soldiers. But at the outset, a majority of southerners did not realize the deficiencies of their nationalism, and most, unaware of the odds they would ultimately face, trusted in God and looked with righteous confidence to the outcome of secession.

Chapter Five

Religion and
the Chosen People

T O ATTAIN VICTORY, the Confederates had to "fight united" and be consistently tenacious. They needed an intellectual and, better yet, a spiritual cohesiveness, and they had to have a clear vision of the hurdles that lay before them. These attributes they did not have, at least not in the quality and quantity sufficient to sustain them through a long, hard war. A strongly positive collective mind-set could have been nurtured, to be sure, but the results of the opening major campaign, the First Battle of Manassas, which ended with southern victory, provided no assistance for removing scales from the eyes of the overconfident young cavaliers or their equally unalert sires.

Jefferson Davis knew better, for he expected that the South would "be involved in that fiercest of human strife, a civil war," and the idea rightly filled him with horror; he recognized his would-be country's lack of means and, conversely, the great power of its opposition. Because Davis, and others like him, knew the demographics of the situation, they were not as ready to enter the lists as the young bloods who rushed to the new Confederate colors.[1]

Even men who should have known better, however, went willingly to war or urged others to do so, giving scant mind to the staying power of their own people and caring little about the absence of proper preparation. They stood at the brink of the unknown and jumped without adequate regard to what lay beyond. Why did they do it so resolutely and unsoberly; what explanation can there be for the South's mass psychology in 1861?

Emory M. Thomas has suggested that pre–Civil War southerners believed "themselves to be the last best hope of Western civilization." Those words have a familiar ring because they sound like Daniel Webster's remarks about an earlier generation, that of the newly born United States. And, too, they clearly reflect the views that Abraham

Lincoln held concerning the Union, though Lincoln was even more universal: he believed that the Union embodied the last best hope of mankind. And, assuredly, Lincoln was not alone in regarding the Union as an object of transcendent worth. Thus both northerners and southerners espoused related, and grandiose, perceptions about their mission in the world, although time and events had distanced their relationships.[2]

This common view of their significance in the world reflects basic similarities between North and South. But the regions had differences and, in spite of the same faith and denominations, religion constituted one of these. If will, or morale, supplies one of the intangible resources necessary to sustain a prolonged armed conflict, religion often proves a vital resource in maintaining will and morale. Unfortunately for the South, religion not only sustained morale, it also had the effect— eventually—of undermining it.

One important element of the distance between the churches was developed by Samuel S. Hill, Jr., in his 1979 Lamar Memorial Lectures, "The South and the North in American Religion." Hill and other religious historians in recent years have made truly exciting contributions, which affect interpretations of many areas in American history that some of us previously had viewed as being entirely secular. We agree wholeheartedly with Hill's statement that "given a new vision and boldness, concerning the unity of life in human society, the study of religion may take on unusual importance, inasmuch as both method and substance are inherently interdisciplinary."[3]

In constructing a model of southern religion, Hill builds upon, and then goes beyond, one posited by Emory Thomas. "It all had to do with race," Hill observed, and "by and large . . . slavery was as much an aspect of southern society as Thomas Jefferson, the city of Charleston, a rural way of life, and evangelical Christianity." Furthermore, as Thomas pointed out, to the degree that southerners developed anything resembling a national ideology, "the corporate Southern mind [became] comfortable with the potential for guilt that pervaded a life style largely grounded in slavery." This process, they both very well show, began in the southern churches.[4]

Indeed, as the most eminent and eclectic historian of the topic, Sydney E. Ahlstrom, has asserted in a Pulitzer Prize–winning book, the churches took a crucial part in the political events during at least the two decades preceding secession and Civil War. James E. Wood, Jr., a distinguished scholar and student of church-state relations, recently echoed this idea when he asserted that "at no time was organized religion in the United States more active politically than in the twenty years prior to the Civil War." Ahlstrom pointed out that "Bleeding Kansas had its Christian history," and—perhaps the most significant of any antebellum ecclesiastical development—all the churches, either de jure or de facto, divided eventually into separate northern and southern institutions. The Presbyterians, Methodists, and Baptists did it officially, but others followed suit, albeit in less formal manner. For example, although the Lutheran, Episcopal, and Roman Catholic churches remained officially undivided, the de facto existence of two sovereign nations at war separated them, at least for the duration of the conflict. And despite their official unity, "each contributed vigorous polemicists to both sides." The divisions were more fundamental than mere surface squabbles; the separate northern and southern versions of Christianity instead reflected differences in their environment and the necessity of one to cope with the fact of slavery.[5]

It is difficult to overestimate the role of the churches. According to William Warren Sweet, the dean of church historians for three generations, "There are good arguments to support the claim that the split in the churches was not only the first break between the sections, but the chief cause of the final break." He believed, too, that the churches provided a major part of the impetus for sustaining that rift. Once the churches split, religion supplied the glue that gave any internal cohesion to either section (or certainly to the South, Samuel Hill has agreed). "Nor were the clergymen repentant," Ahlstrom observed. His wide reading of sermons and tracts prompted him to conclude that such statements as the following, made in 1861 by the northern Methodist Granville Moody, were not extreme but typical: "We are charged with having brought about the present contest. I believe it is true that we did bring it about, and I glory in it, for it is a wreath of glory around our brow."[6]

Even the Roman Catholic church, in its own particular way, shared in this drama. That church had taken an official position during the antebellum period that slavery was not in itself sinful, and during the war, like all the other denominations, it "provided powerful champions of both causes." All eleven of the Roman Catholic bishops whose sees lay in Confederate states cooperated in behalf of the southern war effort, though, interestingly, none were native southerners.[7]

Paradoxically, dividing and yet not dividing, the Roman Catholic church much more pervasively than American Protestantism had come to grips with the concept that civil governments do not necessarily reflect eternal values nor serve as instruments in the attainment of God's will. Thus during the war a number of northern Roman bishops displayed the American flag in their cathedrals, and southern prelates to varying degrees espoused the Confederacy, and yet they had no problem regarding each other as Catholics still in communion. At the onset of hostilities, the bishop of Natchez ordered regular prayers for the southern officials rather than for those of the North; the bishop of Savannah held especially strong rebel sentiments; and the bishop of Richmond proved a most enthusiastic supporter of the southern cause: in addition to furnishing chaplains and detailing nuns as nurses, he promoted enlistments. But the Roman Catholics, though significant, were numerically minuscule compared to the mainline Protestants, for whom the war represented the playing out of a near-final element in God's cosmic design.[8]

Not only did the Protestant churches divide, North against South and vice versa, but southern churches assumed a large role in urging secession and, after the war commenced, many of the ecclesiastics went into combat, a large number as chaplains but a significant group as fighters. The latter's names are practically legion: Nathan B. Forrest's subordinate, the Reverend Major D. C. Kelley; R. E. Lee's artillery commander, the Episcopal priest William Nelson Pendleton; Stonewall Jackson's aide-de-camp, the Presbyterian minister Robert L. Dabney; others not as well known include the Reverend F. McMurray, who pastored a Presbyterian congregation at Union Springs, Alabama, until he took command of a company composed almost entirely of his church members; and Baptist minister H. A. Tupper, who served simultaneously as a line officer and a chaplain. The complete list is long, as W. Harrison Daniel reveals in his study: "At least one hundred and forty-one ministers of the Methodist Episcopal Church, South, served in the Confederate forces as soldiers and officers . . . [and] one Texas regiment had Methodist preachers for all of its officers." Furthermore, although southern churchmen did not universally approve the ordained clergy's entering combat service, Daniel found that "criticisms of such actions were mild."[9]

Of course, whenever one thinks of the fighting ecclesiastics, Leonidas Polk's name tends to head the list: the Episcopal bishop of Louisiana became a lieutenant general in the Confederate army. Polk, who had tried very hard to help initiate division in the national Episcopal church, declared in June 1861, "I believe most solemnly, that it is for . . . liberty . . . our hearth-stones, and our altars that we strike." His Anglican counterpart in Rhode Island, Bishop Thomas March Clark, however, challenged Polk's sentiments. Bishop Clark asserted that the North's was "a holy and righteous cause . . . God is with us . . . the Lord of hosts is on our side."[10]

These leaders of the Episcopal church made warlike statements in spite of their church's outspoken position of neutrality in the conflict. But Ahlstrom observed that "in other communions the language was even more self-righteous [and] volume after volume could be filled with the same bloodthirsty condemnations, the same prayers for aid from the Almighty, the same self-righteous benedictions." Only by accident, he asserted, did Julia Ward Howe's "Battle Hymn of the Republic," which she wrote during one sleepless autumn night in 1861, become singularly a northern war song, for "the literal content of her verses would not have prevented the Confederacy from adopting it." The churches rallied mightily, and at once, to support the war effort, particularly in the South. The Episcopal church of the Confederacy attracted much attention by bringing out a southernized version of the *Book of Common Prayer*, "but all churches," Ahlstrom concluded, "in effect, did as much." And the churches made prodigious efforts in behalf of the troops in the field and in support of noncombatants.[11]

In some sense the war was one between the churches of the North and those of the South. "The number of chaplains who volunteered was remarkably high," Ahlstrom found. "The Northern Methodist church alone provid[ed] nearly five hundred chaplains, the Southern Methodist and Episcopal churches about two hundred and one hundred respectively. Other churches, North and South, showed proportionate concern." And the feeling ran strikingly deep: when the Roman Catholic archbishop of New Orleans "called for volunteer Chaplains every Redemptorist and Jesuit in [the city] offered his service."[12]

BECAUSE WARS typically are uncertain, prudent people enter them only with hesitancy but, as with anything else, the way to diminish hesitancy is to deny the uncertainty and to proclaim the inevitability of desirable results. Afraid of what the end might bring, Americans on both sides calmed their apprehensions by asserting their confidence in a favorable outcome and grew in hardihood by the mutual sharing of opinions with those around them who repeated their slogans and assurances until many had repressed their doubts. So, in spite of knowing the bloody and unpredictable nature of war, especially a civil war, fire-eaters on each side attempted to persuade others, and thereby persuade themselves, that the outcome was certain and the end would be quick. Union fanatics receive no credit because their misgivings proved less congruent in the long run with their behavior than the misgivings of the Confederate fanatics. Both sides were heading for disaster, though the disaster was mitigated on one side and total on the other.

Outward appearances of southern confidence sprang from any of several sources. Given the uncertainties of this war and the well-known deficiencies in rebel resources, some early Confederates held their tongues and feared for the future, resolutely understanding the high probability that catastrophe was waiting in the wings. Others, who might share the same feelings, nevertheless could not afford to remain so reticent. Leaders such as Davis and Vice-President Alexander H. Stephens had to put on an optimistic front. Although they understood the possibility of failure, they could hardly admit it publicly. But most Confederates seem to have had less perception of the future and less understanding of what they did, and manifestations of their unrealistic bravado were not at all rare. The famous problem posed by a Confederate arithmetic text ("If one Confederate soldier can whip 7 Yankees, how many soldiers can whip 49 Yankees?") provides merely a single example.[13]

This reaction typifies the behavior patterns of people facing imminent disaster: they blot it from their minds, refusing to believe anything so awesome could happen. Thus some Confederates managed to convince themselves—not merely to assert but truly to believe—of the inevitability of victory. Leroy P. Walker, the first Confederate secretary of war, bragged with a confidence born of ignorance that there would be no war, that he would "wipe up with his pocket handkerchief all the blood shed as a result of the South's withdrawal from the Union." Even if war came, he himself would raise the Confederate flag over "Faneuil Hall in the City of Boston." Thomas R. R. Cobb thought that "the chances are decidedly *Against War,* there may be a little collision and much confusion, but no bloody or extensive war." In Tennessee, a former Unionist newspaper editor was positive that no one could "restore again, by a ruthless civil war, the Union which Washington and Jefferson constructed." The notion that the North might win the war amused a North Carolina planter, who informed his slaves that "if the North whups, you will be as free a man as I is. If the South whups, you will be a slave all your days." Upon his departure for the war, he told his slaves that he would "whup the North" by dinnertime. One of his slaves remarked that "it wuz four long years before he cum back to dinner. De tables was shore set a long time for him."[14]

Governor Joseph E. Brown of Georgia displayed even more naiveté. If war came, presumably including slave insurrection incited by the Union, the South would hold the trump card, he said, for "thousands of these Northern *white* laborers, who have suffered so much injustice at the hands of those, who have wrung from them the hard earnings of the sweat of their brows, might feel at liberty to require satisfaction for past injustice, and to assert the principle recognized in the South, that the true aristocracy is not an aristocracy of wealth, but of *Color* and of conduct. While their sense of justice might prompt them to assist the South against the aggressions of those in the North, who have denied equality to them, as well as to the people of the South."[15]

Although Governor Brown's opinions were extreme even for that day and place, his overconfidence was not unique. In December 1860 Edmund Ruffin, one of the few true southern nationalists, thought Yankees were too greedy to accept an expensive war; he still discounted any possibility of conflict as late as May 1861. Yankees were too cowardly, he thought, to invade the heart of Virginia. Even after the conflict had begun, he rationalized his mistaken predictions with the comforting notion that he would have been correct and there would have been no war if "submissionists" in the border South, including Virginia, had not encouraged northern action by creating the impression in the North that they were Unionists.[16]

Such bravado was widespread. In his memoirs, Jefferson Davis recalled that many Confederates hoped that secession "would so arouse the sober thought and better feeling of the Northern people as to compel their representatives to agree to a Convention of the States. . . . There were others, and they were the most numerous class, who considered that the separation would be final, but peaceful." Even as conflict developed, therefore, some still denied that it would occur or, once begun, that it would be long or serious. Davis noted in his recollections that most southerners thought even if war came, it would not last long.[17]

ONE MODERN study of disasters indicates that an individual who suffers anxiety because of "punitive self-condemnation" (that is, guilt) will tend to deny imminent danger because "it threatens to rouse unbearable alarm since real hazards assume the monstrous forms of his troubled fantasy. . . . If he suffers from intense guilt feelings and apprehension of punishment, when danger overtakes him he may be convinced that he is about to pay the extreme penalty for his sins. He is overcome with terror, face to face with death."[18]

Only in this last context do Mary Chesnut's outbursts against slavery in 1861 make sense, for even though she hated the institution she admitted that she enjoyed its benefits. "I wonder," she confessed privately, "if it be a sin to think slavery a curse to any land. Sumner said not one word of this hated institution which is not true. . . . God forgive us, but ours is a *monstrous* system and wrong and iniquity [sic]." "Slavery has to go," she admitted a few months later. "I hate slavery." Clearly Mary Chesnut felt a sense of guilt. And we suspect that she was far from alone, that this probably widespread guilt unconsciously compromised the initial determination of many Confederates and from the outset presaged the eventual defeat.[19]

The question of guilt has complexities that require special treatment, which it will receive at a later point. For now we need only say that religion had told slaveholders that it was not immoral to hold slaves, but it also told them that slavery could lead to sin. Slaveholders had obligations. Even the Bible had told them that; the master had a master, too, as Colossians 4:1 indicated. "Masters," the Scripture warned, "give unto your servants that which is just and equal; knowing that ye also have a Master in heaven." The master had to take proper care of his slaves, which meant respecting their humanity. The church made a strong enough impression on this issue to find its way even to the schoolbooks. "The sin of the South," claimed Mrs. M. B. Moore's *Primary Geography Arranged as a Reading Book for Common Schools,* "lies not in holding slaves, but they are sometimes mistreated." God would hold slaveowners "to account." Surely the church constituted a great mediator between master and slave, even though it supported the peculiar institution. Failure to meet Christian standards could subject a master to pangs of guilt, all the more because the church told him that in any event he was guilty of sin, a broad term that could cover everything from the condition of his birth to the sharp words he may have exchanged with a slave only a few minutes before. Church-induced guilt could easily be extended, say, to slavery or to a war to preserve slavery, especially after the Confederacy moved in the direction of emancipation.[20]

Most Confederates did indeed share a religious consideration. Religion further complicated their uncomfortable paradox: on the one hand it exacerbated and induced their guilt, while on the other, more and more it led them to act as they did. If guilt alone were not enough to sap morale, a pervading sense of ongoing sinfulness also was present, which added further doubts and created an atmosphere of religious fatalism: the South deserved any punishment it would receive. Individual initiative seemed somewhat meaningless because events lay in the hands of God. Of course, guilt and sin operated on northern Christians as well, but they did not carry the burden of slavery, they were not going against world opinion, and, especially as the war progressed, many felt the comfort of looming victory to help allay whatever doubts guilt and sin produced. Not so Confederates.

Although northern and southern Christians espoused similar forms of institutionalized religion that sprang from common origins steeped in Calvinism, differences between the two had evolved. Samuel S. Hill, Jr., has suggested that the work of Lewis Simpson in the literature of the colonial South reveals the early roots of this divergence, showing that "in contrast to the New England settlers' image of their errand into a wilderness, Southerners viewed their new habitat as a paradise." Thus "in Richard Niebuhr's classic typology," the South conformed to the "Christ *of* culture" pattern, whereas New England depicted the "very different" pattern of "Christ the *transformer* of culture"; in other words, "as far as religion . . . is concerned, South and North have had distinctive careers," even though both have been "inside the pervasive unity of a Protestant Christianity that is dominantly Calvinist."[21]

Hill sees the churches of the two regions as already "first cousins separated" by the time of the immediate postrevolutionary era, and both were evolving toward even greater separation, which became that of "third cousins alienated" by the post-Jacksonian period. "In the course of this evolution," he says, "the South became not only identifiable, distinctive, and self-aware, it was also on its way toward regarding itself as pure (purer than the North at any rate) and superior." Churches in both sections espoused millennialism in some form (looking toward eschatologic last days as imminent and desirable); indeed, as James F. Maclear so graphically phrased it, throughout the antebellum United States some form or another of millennialism was "so common as to be almost canonical." But, as Hill quotes William G. McLoughlin, "the white southerner felt that his region of the nation was already closer to millennial perfection than any other part of the country." The North was characterized by debate, turmoil, and schism, whereas in the South increasing religious homogeneity prevailed, which helped affirm the prevalent lifestyle.[22]

Increasingly over time, the lifestyle depended upon the continued existence of slavery, or so antebellum southerners typically thought. Slavery and Christianity were never in full harmony with each other, but religion in the South did much more to firm up the institution than to tear it down. During the seventeenth and eighteenth centuries southerners had considerable misgivings about Christianizing the slaves because traditionally in Western civilization only heathens were enslaved. But once they took that step, a particular form of Christianity for the slaves developed, which inevitably infected the Christianity of the southern whites as well.

Following the Second Great Awakening, which began during the 1790s, a widespread, literal acceptance of the Scriptures prevailed, from which proslavery thinkers within the church formulated treatises offering biblical support for the peculiar institution. One such work, by the Reverend Thornton Stringfellow, a Baptist minister in Virginia, became a best seller in the pre–Civil War South. The book seemed to help allay the vaguely troubled consciences of many southern Christians.

Whites in the South gave the slaves a form of Christianity that stressed humility, obedience to one's master, and contented acceptance of one's condition in life and put great emphasis upon reward in the hereafter. In addition, perhaps paradoxically, southern Christianity abounded with Old Testament theology (wherein God is all-powerful, totally just, and vengeful; He makes covenants with His people and rewards them richly but is not—as He would be manifested in the New Testament—particularly merciful). Antebellum northern Protestants had veered away from this interpretation, although the war jolted them back a bit. Thus in a Boston church on a fast-day morning, April 3, 1862, the minister's sermon proclaimed that "the Old Testament, in our current notions and sympathies has been almost outlawed from human affairs. . . . And now the days have come upon us, for which these strong-chorded elder Scriptures have been waiting."[23]

Unlike today, in the mid-nineteenth century Christians adhered to a widespread orthodox belief that had as a basic tenet the notion that God enters and intervenes in human history. It also seemed axiomatic to most Americans that the hand of God shaped all events because they implicitly believed that heavenly intervention in the Christian era occurred not only in the manifested divine person of Jesus Christ two millennia before but also in day-to-day events of their own time.

God rewarded, and He punished, and it behooved people to accept His will. But what was His will? Protestants in both North and South, especially after the war began, became convinced that His will was that their side be victorious. According to James H. Moorhead, the northern Protestant's "conception of history converted the Civil War into a crusade [wherein] the contest had to be pressed with unceasing vigor"; conversely, W. Harrison Daniel, author of careful articles on southern Protestantism during the Civil War, has found that "in numerous sermons the will of God was made synonymous with the cause of the Confederacy." As one Confederate private fervently prayed, "Oh, Lord, we are having a mighty big fight down here, and a sight of trouble; and we do hope, Lord, that you will take a proper view of this subject, and give us the victory."[24]

During the middle third of the nineteenth century, southern religious feeling was strikingly homogeneous. First, the Confederates in near unanimity were Protestant Christians, mostly Baptist, Methodist, Presbyterian, or Episcopalian, and the differences among these denominations were considerably blurred. Episcopalians, for example, tended overwhelmingly to be of the "low-church" variety and differed little from Methodists, who had only recently broken away from that denomination. Emory Thomas has found that this similarity was reflected in "camp meetings and interdenominational revival services, plus the ease and frequency with which Southerners attended services of various denominations."[25]

Furthermore, most southerners held to pervasive puritanical views. Although they might frequently rail mightily against the Puritanism "of their New England brethren," Thomas observed, still "they themselves had incorporated much of the Puritan heritage into Southern-style evangelical Protestantism." Likewise, "the hellfire-and-damnation emphasis of Southern Protestantism served as a kind of inverse support for the hedonistic aspects of the Southern life style" because "paradoxically . . . [their] deep consciousness of sin in this world and perfection in the next served as a bulwark of the Old South status quo." Thus this brand of Puritanism primarily homogenized and stabilized rather than induced change, and it injected an element of gloominess that mixed uneasily and unpleasantly with the more stereotypical "Southern gaiety." "It was no accident," Thomas observes, "that Unitarianism and transcendentalism attracted so few Southerners" because "southerners were not so optimistic" as to tend "to exalt humanity and to call it to perfection in this world. . . . They perceived reality as rooted in human frailty . . . [and] they accepted and even celebrated their humanity. . . . This was as true among Episcopalians as among Baptists."[26]

Theologically, although both northern and southern Protestants agreed that "God's greatest concern was to rescue alienated humanity from the consequences of the fallen state in both this life and the one beyond death," the northerner tended to view this process as operative within a large context, that salvation "would be of all as well as of each." For the northerner, society needed to be perfected; for the southerner, society, if already as perfect as man could make it, needed to remain stable while each individual worked out his own salvation.[27]

One of Ahlstrom's former students, James H. Moorhead, has argued brilliantly that northern mainline Protestants—Baptists, Congregationalists, Methodists, and Presbyterians (Old and New Schools)—believed devoutly that they indeed were seeing "the glory of the coming of the Lord," and further that the Union armies were hastening that coming, because the people of these churches perceived the Civil War as Armageddon.[28]

Reformation-era Protestantism generally had revived millenarianism, and the movement had spurred an eschatological revolution. But "in England this reawakened millennial consciousness acquired [a] peculiar intensity." The Puritans intertwined millenarianism with their beliefs concerning God's plan for America, believing themselves His new Chosen People and their new land His instrument for the ultimate conversion of the world. To be sure, similar thought was present among southern immigrants as well, but "it was from New England that [came] the most articulate statements of America's millennial role." By the time of the Civil War most Southern Protestant ministers only weakly adhered to millennialism, and many did not do so at all. The southern brand of this thought tended more toward what theologians call premillennialism (that is, that the return of Christ would occur before the millennium began and hence no particular human action was required to hasten the coming of the Kingdom). The majority of nineteenth-century northern Protestants, however, were postmillennialists, who believed that Christ would return at the end of the millennium and that God's people could do a great deal to hasten the course of history toward its inevitable destiny. Thus northern Protestants, albeit with cacophonic voice, variously articulated that "all was not well within God's new Israel" and that they needed to reform it properly before the Lord's return. Although northern Protestants might differ among themselves, and "the candidate for chief demon varied according to one's preference—Roman Catholicism, the slave power, abolitionism, Mormonism, or freemasonry"—they all displayed an amazingly united evangelical front, which consistently thrusted toward reform to make the country ready for God's final intervention. But the South's religious mind-set, unlike that of the North, induced an ironic, uneasy satisfaction with the present condition.[29]

Thus it should come as no surprise that religious differences also played a crucial role in the course of the Civil War. W. Harrison

Daniel's studies reveal that there existed "a close affinity, in the thinking of most Southerners, between patriotism and religious faith and duty." And, indeed, Sydney Ahlstrom believes that "for violence of statement and ultimacy of appeal, the clergy and the religious press seem to have led the multitude."[30]

Not only did the clergy in both North and South have large and regular audiences, but, contrary to the stereotypical characteristic of this age as one of little reading, especially in the South, the religious press spewed forth a vast array of tracts and periodicals. The Presbyterian pastor Moses D. Hoge, who personally shepherded hundreds of thousands of Bibles through the blockade, also brought in an undetermined number of tracts he had ordered printed in England. One Baptist chaplain, William E. Wiatt of the Twenty-sixth Virginia, provided "a veritable lending library." By the war's end, the Methodist papers alone were reaching four hundred thousand subscribers.[31]

Even more important, observes Ahlstrom, in this "age of great evangelical fervor, the clergy were the official custodians of the popular conscience. When the cannons roared in Charleston harbor, therefore, two divinely authorized crusades were set in motion. . . . The pulpits resounded with a vehemence and absence of restraint never equalled in American history." It was crucial and relevant to both North and South that God be and remain on their side.[32]

JEFFERSON DAVIS'S early proclamations of days of humiliation and prayer contained pro forma assumptions that God wore the gray. In May 1862 Davis converted to Anglicanism and was confirmed in Richmond's St. Paul's Episcopal Church, the "National Cathedral of the Confederacy" if ever there was one. Emory Thomas thought that in this conversion and in his proclamations President Davis "realized as a matter of personal piety and public policy that the Confederate cause required God on the Southern side." One year previous, in May 1861, Davis had claimed that "the manifest proofs of Divine blessing hitherto extended to the efforts of the people of the Confederate States of America . . . demand their devout and heartfelt gratitude," requiring them "to invoke the continuance of his favor." In October 1861 Davis thanked God for protecting and defending the Confederacy, acknowledged that victory belonged to Him, and prayed that He would "set at naught the efforts of our enemies, and put them to confusion and shame."[33]

But in addition to Davis, many other institutions and individuals also prescribed days of fasting, prayer, and humiliation from time to time. "The Confederate congress, state governors, ecclesiastical meetings, bishops, and sometimes army generals" either urged or ordered them, and typically, W. Harrison Daniel has found, "for these occasions ministers prepared 'war sermons' which could be used repeatedly, with slight revisions as conditions changed." Mary Boykin Chesnut noted in her diary that one such sermon "stirred my blood, my flesh crept and tingled. A red hot glow of patriotism passed over me. There was . . . exhortation to fight and die."[34]

Even with the knowledge that "God moves in a mysterious way, His wonders to perform," it still seemed likely that He favored the side of the righteous. Southerners long had examined themselves and their conduct in the light of Scripture, and most of them had concluded that they were the righteous and that slavery was correct, just as many of their northern counterparts had been persuaded by Scripture and by the preaching of northern abolitionist churchmen and their allies that the peculiar institution was sinful. If the institution was moral, so, too, was its protection, and, if forced upon the South, the resulting war as well. But if in an effort to win the war, Confederates themselves moved toward a policy of emancipation, they would be confessing doubt about the morality of slavery and—to many Confederates at least—they would be questioning the morality of the war and political system that were to save the institution.[35]

More recent history also served as a useful guide to God's preference. He did, of course, stand on the side of freedom, as white men interpreted freedom, and thus had given victory to the patriots in 1776. Surely He would not change in 1861; once again He would side with those who fought against despotism and for freedom, an idea that inspired confidence as long as southerners were persuaded, or could persuade themselves, that they and not the northerners represented that side. Southerners constantly saw the war as one for freedom, and they equated defeat with enslavement. "No alternative is left you," Davis warned his army, "but victory or subjugation, slavery, and the utter ruin of yourselves, your families, and your country."[36]

Davis was echoing the inculcations of the southern clergy. "Throughout the Confederacy," Emory Thomas found, "clergymen regularly delivered patriotic sermons to stir the blood of the faithful. Southerners were the 'chosen people' in these orations; Yankees were Philistines whom Jehovah would surely destroy in His time. In times of victory Southern arms were like those of Joshua; in the wake of defeats God was chastising and cleansing Confederates to prepare them for eventual triumph." W. Harrison Daniel observed that "denominational spokesmen reminded men of their patriotic duty to enter the army, and noted that for a man to remain neutral or silent was considered a crime 'just short of treason.'" Indeed, some clergymen assisted recruiting officers to garner volunteers by holding enlistment rallies in their church yards after Sunday morning worship services.[37]

But one should not presume that the clergy controlled or that they duped the people; if anything, they reflected rather than molded opinion. Daniel found that "most church spokesmen and denominational organizations" condemned "extortion, speculation, evading the draft, taking an oath of allegiance to the United States government, and possessing pro-Union sentiments . . . as sinful." One church in central Virginia expelled a family from membership because it hid a son from draft officials. The *Christian Observer* declared that for persons in areas invaded by federal forces to take a loyalty oath to the United States would be equivalent to becoming "an accomplice in murder." Southern clergymen who expressed pro-Union sentiment, as a few did, were usually removed from the pulpit by the congregation and perhaps even expelled from church membership.[38]

Even so, there still remained a lurking element of uncertainty, and at the war's beginning some Confederates found themselves "looking through a glass darkly." One southerner complained in 1861 that some of his compatriots claimed that "this is the darkness that precedes the dawn of malenium [sic], others say the judgement day is coming; I say, it is damn difficult to tell what is to be inaugurated." Fearing for the fate of the American experiment as his fellow citizens "are drifted into an unknown and tempestuous sea," a Tennessee editor warned that "an overruling Providence has a purpose to work but which finite minds may not anticipate." As late as July 1863, after the disasters at Gettysburg and Vicksburg, the cantankerous William W. Holden remarked that "if it should please Him to build up and perpetuate this new nation of Confederate States, He will do it; if not He will not do it.—that is all we know about it."[39]

Regardless of such uncertainty, however, it earlier had seemed incomprehensible to southerners that God would not side with the Confederate battalions. On the eve of secession the *Southern Presbyterian,* declaring for Christ, called upon southerners to decide current questions "by principles which depend so directly upon the Word of God." Translated into action, this meant that if the North did not give guarantees, but used force to oppose secession, the South should "throw the sword into the scales, and leave the issue to the God of battles." An Alabama minister concurred: "If we are right, and God is on our side, let us go forth fearlessly to meet the present crisis and conflict." There was no "if" about it, however, for "the Lord is with us," and he congratulated himself that his Christian and sectional duties so completely coincided. "We are . . . fighting not for ourselves alone, but, when the struggle is rightly understood, for the salvation of this whole continent," claimed J. D. B. DeBow. But if Confederates were not right and did not have God on their side, how could they go forth fearlessly? How, indeed, could they go forth at all?[40]

The South's religious views served as a trap for Confederate will. If, as Confederates said, God controlled events (and that would be difficult for most Christian southerners to deny) and victory was a sign of God's favor, then repeated battlefield successes would build morale and will by shoring up any wavering faith in the cause. By the same token, however, if the South began to lose battles, it could only mean that God did not side with the Confederacy, and if God sided with right, it would mean that the South did not have right on its side and God favored the adversary. God, then, had not chosen the Confederates, and it would be wrong for the South to continue to fight. This knowledge would inflict a devastating blow to morale. No one wanted to fight God; the fear that perhaps Confederates were doing so would surely knock out all the remaining props that held up Confederate will. When victories decreased and casualty lists lengthened, doubts about God's favor (never very far beneath the surface) began to arise and southern will weakened accordingly.

Such a confrontation between faith and reality might be avoided if the military power of the Confederacy were supported and supplemented with all the civilian willpower available. Thus southern congregations threw themselves into the war effort with a fervor that seemed to know no bounds in an effort not only to win the war but also to prove to themselves that God really *was* on their side. W. Harrison Daniel found, for example, that frequently Confederates would "manifest their patriotism by removing the carpet from the floor of the church and cutting it into blankets for the soldiers, by donating the church bell to be manufactured into armaments, and by contributing pew cushions for hospital beds." The various denominations pulled together with astounding unity, and for the war's duration "arguments of theology and polity were abandoned." Instead of damning each other, they might damn their northern enemies; and, although it occurred infrequently, some "denominational newspapers referred to Northerners as barbarians—modern-day Vandals, Huns, and Goths— who were seeking to gratify their 'hellish lusts.'"[41]

We have already noted the large number of ordained clergy who accepted combat duties; perhaps even more interesting, a number of chaplains threw themselves into the conflict, either occasionally to fight in a battle or otherwise to do something other than religious service. The subject has not yet received much study, but we know about enough of these men to conclude that their number and involvement could not have been inconsequential. Nicholas Davis, chaplain of Hood's Texas Brigade, had a reputation for his "military eye or prowess." Chaplains Andrew J. Potter and Randolph H. McKim displayed "a lust for battle," and Roman Catholic Chaplain James B. Sheeran deserves particular attention.[42]

Father Sheeran, a native of Ireland, had lived in the South for only three years before he joined the Confederate army as chaplain of the Fourteenth Louisiana. But he became, as Bruce Catton assessed, "one of the most dedicated of Southern patriots," who "detested the Yankee invader as hotly as any Confederate could." He called the Yankees "Lincoln's Bandits." They had been misled, Father Sheeran believed, because "some 20 years ago a few fanatics residing in New England began to preach in the name of Liberty and humanity doctrines subversive of our social and political edifice." This priest rarely passed an opportunity to speak at length with any Yankee prisoner he encountered, trying "to convert them, not to his own religious faith but to a realization of the justice and rightness of the Confederate cause."

Sometimes during battles he rounded up Confederate stragglers, formed them into firing lines, and, if he could not immediately find an officer to take charge, led them into combat himself. He wrote disappointedly of stragglers whose absence caused the Confederates to miss a charge when "the Yankees under McClellan could have been exterminated." One of his diary entries suggests the complexity of his motivation for his close attention to his ministrations, which he calculated would surely influence the war effort: "I had learned by personal observation," he wrote, "that no men fight more bravely than Catholics who approach the sacraments before battle." But, and this certainly must be emphasized, in spite of the foregoing Father Sheeran was not writing as a callous or hypocritical cleric; he genuinely practiced his faith, as a fair reading of his diary confirms. The point is that his piety and patriotism melded into one.[43]

Nor did northerners fail to manifest their share of indications that the war had religious undertones. The Yankees employed a female spy to monitor the movements of Reverend Hoge, the pastor who ran Bibles and tracts through the blockade, acted upon her information to capture some of his religious materials, and fired upon him, knowing full well the nature of his mission. And in 1861, when Jim Lane led a raid through pro-Confederate towns in western Missouri, "his chaplains even plundered furnishings for the churches in Lawrence."[44]

New England troops seem to have been especially vengeful toward Roman Catholics in the South. In Jacksonville, elsewhere in Florida, and in Georgia, they ravaged and set fire to Catholic churches. And "in Savannah, in spite of the bishop's protest, a general occupied a cemetery and did considerable damage when he converted it into a fortification."[45]

IN PART, then, the war was truly a struggle between the churches on both sides, and they contributed mightily to the maintenance of morale and the sustenance of steadfastness. Religion can inspire like no other force, and in America as in other cultures, war and religion might walk hand in hand, despite the teachings of Christ. The Old Testament frequently portrayed a God of war, who helped the Israelites defeat the Amalekites, Canaaites, and Philistines (in aggressive war, it might be added). Would He not do as much to destroy the Yankee (or Confederate) Philistines in these latter days? Just as some Christians might fight with unequaled bravery after taking the sacrament, others could be inspired by the proper application of the right theology. John Keegan notes that English troops received blessings and took communion before Agincourt and the Somme, for example. This "spiritual fortification" could calm a soldier's anxieties. "Indeed," says Keegan, "wherever the light of religion has not died out from armies, men seem to hunger for its consolations on the eve of action." The Christian Crusades and the Islamic jihad are further examples of religiously inspired war.[46]

In the Confederate army (and the Union army as well), it was not only on the eve of battle that spiritual consolation armed the soldier—and the civilian—for the tasks to come. "As its greatest social institution," James W. Silver correctly concluded at the end of his important little book *Confederate Morale and Church Propaganda*, "the church in the South constituted the major resource of the Confederacy in the building and maintenance of civilian morale. As no other group, Southern clergymen" contributed to and nurtured "a state of mind which made secession possible, and as no other group they sustained the people in their long, costly and futile war for Southern independence."[47]

But the same held true within the victorious North, for as Ahlstrom concluded, "a fervently pious nation was at war [and] men on both sides hungered for inspiration and peace with God. Dedicated men and women on both sides responded . . . with wide-ranging ministries. On both sides the soldier's sense of duty was deepened, his morale improved, his loyalty intensified."[48]

Thus piety provided an essential source of southern strength in victory and defeat, serving the will of the people in much the same way that factories and mines served the armed forces. Supported by their knowledge of the virtue of their cause, southern churches could strengthen the South's morale and energize its will. Religion played a greater role in the Confederate experience than in that of the Union because the South needed it more, for as military power ebbed away, the will of the people needed more and more reinforcement if the Confederacy was to survive. In a time of defeat, piety could do what military victories did in better times. "Perhaps," Ahlstrom concluded, "piety lengthened the war."[49]

If piety lengthened the war, would a lack of piety have shortened it? If victory or defeat is the criterion by which one measures God's role, the answer must be yes. But there is another way. Toward the end of the war, and after it, some southerners came to feel that the lost cause did not signify that God had abandoned His chosen people. Rather, they owed defeat and the changes that accompanied it to a merited punishment and a greater destiny, which they should not resist but welcome, "For whom the Lord loveth he chasteneth" (Hebrews 12:6).

We would not have qualified Ahlstrom's observation that piety lengthened the war, as did he, with "perhaps." Not only did piety lengthen the war, but the piety espoused by nineteenth-century Americans also had much to do with how the war was fought and—as we shall show in our final chapters—why the war ended as it did. The difference between mainline Protestantism in the North and in the South contributed to tipping the scales. The churches at first induced many persons on either side to dedicate themselves both vociferously and sacrificially to the struggle, but later in the war the situation changed significantly. Because of how they interpreted the war's course and how they related their perception of God's will to the onflow of events, northerners' religious mind-set spurred their allegiance to the war and its aims, even through the darkest periods of weariness with the struggle; southerners, conversely, became gradually convinced that God willed they should not win. As Charles Reagan Wilson has elaborated in his brilliant and stimulating book *Baptized in Blood: The Religion of the Lost Cause,* southern clergymen to the end remained the Confederacy's most important morale-builders, but even before the end some of them began seeking and formulating theological explanations for the South's defeat. The campaigns of the Civil War did not alone produce its outcome.

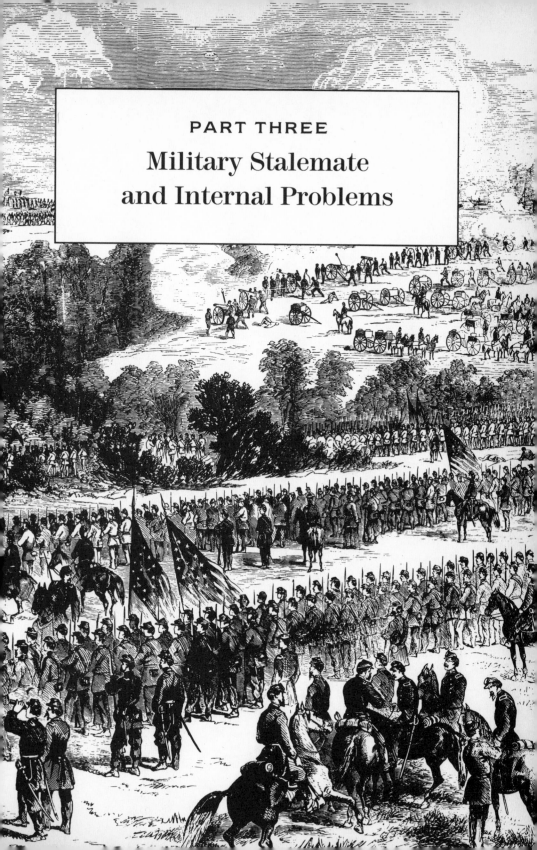

PART THREE

Military Stalemate
and Internal Problems

Both North and South relied on the products of the industrial revolution. They exploited the improved communications thus made possible to amplify the scale on which commanders could use Napoleonic concepts. Yet a military stalemate resulted.

In this context the Confederacy practiced a defensive strategy, one in harmony with its military situation and political objectives. Its conduct of operations depended on the good grasp of the European military tradition possessed by President Davis and his senior generals.

But the South also made imaginative use of the technological changes that had come since Napoleon's death. Railways and, to a modest degree, rivers provided the Confederates with a strategic mobility nearly equal to that of the Union. After almost a year of practicing a cordon defense with small forces posted to guard routes of approach by sea as well as land, the Confederates wisely organized their defense into a few major commands. Within these areas they employed the telegraph, the railroad, and the river systems to integrate their forces and concentrate them for defensive and counteroffensive purposes.

The rivers were even more important to Union communications than to those of the Confederacy; secure, efficient steam transportation by water supported most of the successful Union advances. After more than a year of trying to make headway on all fronts, the North concentrated its efforts in the West, with particular emphasis upon the Mississippi. Union armies exploited rail and water routes to advance into hostile territory. But instead of using rivers to concentrate in space, as did the Confederacy, the Union largely depended on the simultaneous advances of its armies to concentrate in time.

The Confederacy, too, relied on rivers for supply; and it used them as well to concentrate troops at points of suspected Union weakness,

Shiloh, for example. The South's reliance on maneuver exhibited very clearly its dependence on Napoleonic (or Jominian) inspiration. Thus it waged several dramatic campaigns based on surprise concentration by rail, which produced impressive, if temporary, successes.

These victorious campaigns and their consequences elevated and then depressed Confederate morale. Military results had great significance because southern people viewed the war as one of conventional military operations, rather than one they could win by patient exploitation of their advantages of size supplemented by national resistance. Because southerners could not envision a victory achieved by swallowing up invading armies, steadily diminishing them as they dispersed their strength to guard their imperiled communications, Confederates needed unequivocal, victorious battles to sustain their morale.

Thus military operations had to carry the burden of compensating for a lack of national feeling, which often led to local rivalries and petty jealousies that reduced the collective will of the people. Localities often picked up the slack by putting their own armies into the field and by seeing to the material needs of the distressed civilian population, thereby aggravating the problem by increasing the role of the states, which some Confederate leaders felt was already too large. But the crux was that not all of the South's citizens were dedicated to the goals for which the war was fought; many never became Confederate in heart.

In the long run, the comforts of religion also neutralized the will of the South. When affairs went poorly, southerners secured relief from the knowledge that God was active in human events. If the armies won victories, it proved that God was blessing Confederate efforts; if the armies suffered defeat, God was still at work, punishing His disobedient children. Either way, they rationalized the results as God's will. "If our people are true to themselves," wrote Reverend C. C. Jones, "by God's blessing the issue will eventually be favorable," although the "wickedness of our country" might create some difficulties.[1] Yet after four years the Confederacy's inefficiency, resignation, guilt, and lack of national feeling caused it to collapse.

The Confederacy's effective military performance had done much to sustain it thus far; it could have continued to do so. Despite the Union's increasingly sophisticated strategy, the United States could not overcome the obstacles of the inadequate numerical preponderance of its armies, the Confederacy's size, and the national resistance that required the occupation of hostile territory. For the Union to defeat the Confederacy, it needed more than military victories; as a corollary, if the Confederacy were to survive, it needed more than military power— it needed the strength that collective will could provide. The armies alone could not bring victory.

Chapter Six

First Blood

Within an air of unreality created by an amalgam of confidence, prayer, and some anxiety, both sides rapidly improvised armies after the fall of Fort Sumter in April 1861. The secession crisis and overconfidence of each assured that neither would think any more clearly about military problems than about political problems. Expecting that enthusiasm would provide the key to quick victory, both sides downplayed the need for military training. Symbols had importance, and national capitals are symbols of enemy power; thus it appeared logical to each adversary that the desired quick decision might be achieved by a prompt capture of the other's capital. Each placed its troops accordingly, concentrating to protect its own symbol while threatening that of the other.

Since the Confederates also sought to protect as much of Virginia as possible, they placed their army very close to Washington, menacingly and insultingly near, thought the Unionists. This situation led to a clamor from northern civilians and political leaders for an immediate offensive. But the unready Union forces had received practically no training, and General in Chief Winfield Scott's thinking harmonized with that of Jomini, who asserted that experience had "constantly proved that a mere multitude of brave men armed to the teeth make neither a good army nor a national defense." Nevertheless, in July 1861, General Scott allayed his misgivings and agreed to an advance by his green forces against what he knew to be equally untrained Confederates. Thus originated the campaign of First Manassas, the first major action of the war.[1]

This campaign contained many elements that proved representative of the Civil War. Both sides deployed on two opposing lines of operations. Outside of Washington, the Union army of Brigadier General Irwin McDowell and the opposing Confederate army, under Brigadier General P. G. T. Beauregard, used the same railroad. To the west, in the Shenandoah Valley, the Union army of Major General Robert Patterson drew its supplies from a spur of the Baltimore and Ohio Railroad while the opposing Confederate force, under General Joseph E. Johnston, held a position only twenty miles from the railroad in his rear. This short distance allowed wagons easily to bring the few supplies needed by the army of only twelve thousand men, camped during early summer in the rich farming country of the Shenandoah River Valley.

Each of the opposing armies had a "line of operations," that is, an axis of advance and retreat usually identical with the army's line of communication. This situation was governed, according to Clausewitz, by "Jomini's 'interior lines,'" "one of the main principles for the conduct of major wars." The employment of interior lines enabled a smaller force to "multiply its strength by rapid movement." Interior lines of operations permitted a general to "concentrate the masses and maneuver with his whole force in a shorter period of time than it would require for the enemy to oppose to them a greater force." The Confederates possessed interior lines of operations because the railroad network provided better communication between the armies of Beauregard and Johnston than it did between the Union armies of Patterson and McDowell. The terminology "interior and exterior" derives from the simplest form of this situation, illustrated in the following diagram:

```
                    Beauregard
   Patterson       and Johnston           McDowell
     USA      ---> <----  CSA     ---> <----  USA
  exterior line     interior lines       exterior line
```

The force in the middle, on the interior lines of operations, had the advantage because it could concentrate against first one and then the other of the opposing armies on the exterior lines.[2]

Successful simultaneous advances of both exterior armies in a coordinated movement would, of course, nullify this advantage. In fact, if countered by simultaneous advances, an effort by the armies with interior lines to concentrate against one opponent actually would work to their disadvantage. If, for example, in a case like that of the First Manassas campaign, all four armies had the same strength, say twenty thousand men, and the Confederates subtracted ten thousand men from one army and added them to the other, they would outnumber that army's opponent thirty thousand to twenty thousand. But against this three-to-two superiority, they would have left their other army with only ten thousand men to face twenty thousand, a more disadvantageous inferiority of one to two. Both Jomini and Clausewitz ignored these proportions and the consequent disadvantage of using interior lines when confronted by simultaneous advances.

The theory assumed that the interior forces would have better command and coordination than those on the exterior. The electric telegraph, a tremendous improvement over the previously used semaphore, praised by Jomini, enhanced coordination of the armies on both sides. Furthermore, the railroad had created many new lines of operations and interconnections among them.[3]

Jomini advocated interior lines for the offensive when, presumably, the interior forces would surprise the enemy and win a decision with the augmented force, while the diminished force retreated or otherwise avoided battle with the proportionately stronger oppponent. He assumed, however, that the outnumbered enemy force could not evade battle against the strengthened army on the offensive.

Interior lines also had excellent utility on the defensive because defenders could exploit them to reinforce a threatened army in the event of an enemy offensive on only one front. To carry out such a concentration required very good intelligence and rapid communication and movements, or the reinforcements would arrive too late to contest the enemy's initial advance. In July 1861 the Confederates chose to try this use of interior lines to reinforce their army threatened by the North.

Like the Confederate leaders, Union General Scott understood interior lines. When, in mid-July, he ordered McDowell to move toward Beauregard, he assured McDowell that, should Johnston seek to join Beauregard, there would be a simultaneous advance by the army in the Shenandoah Valley. With Patterson on Johnston's heels, the Confederate general could not aid Beauregard. But as it turned out, Scott did not get the performance he desired of Patterson, an elderly Pennsylvania manufacturer and a militiaman with experience in the Mexican War and War of 1812.

In advancing against Beauregard, McDowell based his plan on an envelopment, or tactical turning movement, such as Scott himself had employed in the Mexican War, a maneuver fully in harmony with the practice of Napoleon. Clausewitz strongly endorsed such attacks, insisting that "envelopment is the most natural form of attack, and should not be disregarded without good cause." Despite raw troops, the Federals had the proper organization and the men had received enough instruction to maneuver and carry out McDowell's plan to march a portion of his forces around the Confederate left, deploy, and attack the flank and rear of Beauregard's army. Beauregard also planned to turn his opponent's left. [4]

McDowell, with his husky, robust frame, was recognized as a serious, hardworking professional officer. Beauregard was in his early forties, small, vigorous, a graceful man who was faultless in dress and manner. Like McDowell, his professional reputation was exemplary. They were classmates at West Point, and afterward both had served with credit during the Mexican War and had reached the rank of major by the time the Civil War broke out. Both showed their West Point background in directing their troops to entrench, even though each planned to take the offensive. But the almost untrained troops and equally raw officers executed the operations ineptly.

McDowell's untrained army and untried organization did enjoy one advantage: its numerical superiority of about thirty thousand to twenty thousand. But McDowell lost this superiority when the Confederates not only made but succeeded in executing the proper responsive decision.

Aware on July 16 of McDowell's advance, Beauregard called for reinforcements. President Davis ordered both Theophilus Holmes from nearby Aquia and Joseph E. Johnston from the Shenandoah Valley to Beauregard's assistance. Because the telegraph provided prompt communication, the unopposed Holmes had joined Beauregard by the nineteenth; Johnston, sending cavalry under J. E. B. Stuart to distract and mislead the already confused and withdrawing Patterson, marched to the railroad, entrained, and had joined Beauregard with most of his army by July 20, the day before McDowell's attack.

On July 21, McDowell's flanking column of twelve thousand men began its advance. After stumbling around in the underbrush for several hours, they crossed Bull Run Creek and assaulted the Confederate positions astride Henry House Hill. At first the Union attack was successful, and the Confederates retired in some confusion. But reinforcements, including a brigade under Thomas J. Jackson, arrived quickly,

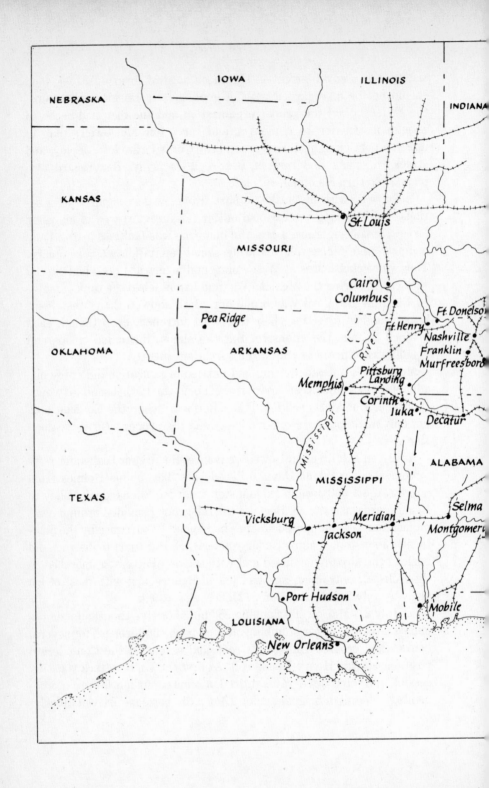

NEBRASKA

IOWA

ILLINOIS

INDIANA

KANSAS

MISSOURI

St. Louis

Cairo

Columbus

Ft. Donelson

Pea Ridge

Ft. Henry

Nashville

Franklin

Murfreesboro

OKLAHOMA

ARKANSAS

Pittsburg
Landing

Memphis

Corinth

Iuka

Decatur

Mississippi River

ALABAMA

TEXAS

MISSISSIPPI

Vicksburg

Meridian

Selma

Jackson

Montgomery

Port Hudson

Mobile

LOUISIANA

New Orleans

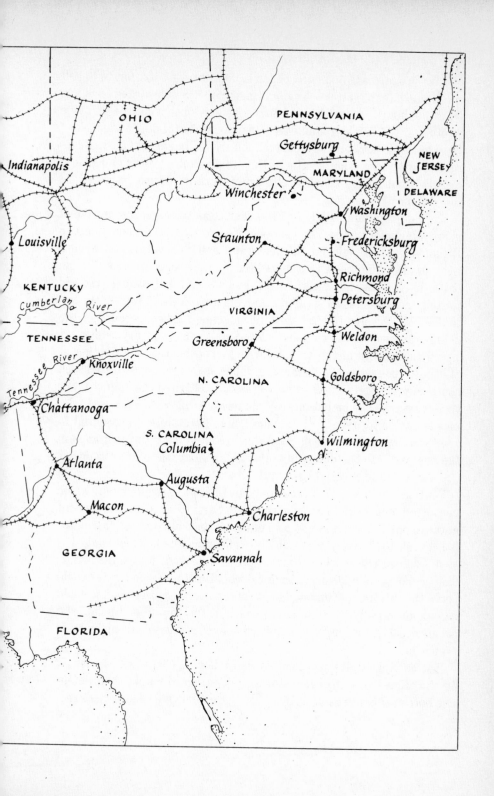

OHIO

PENNSYLVANIA

Gettysburg

Indianapolis

MARYLAND

NEW JERSEY

Winchester

DELAWARE

Washington

Louisville

Staunton

Fredericksburg

KENTUCKY

Richmond

Cumberland River

Petersburg

VIRGINIA

TENNESSEE

Greensboro

Weldon

Tennessee River

Knoxville

Goldsboro

N. CAROLINA

Chattanooga

S. CAROLINA

Columbia

Wilmington

Atlanta

Augusta

Macon

Charleston

GEORGIA

Savannah

FLORIDA

and Beauregard and Johnston began to concentrate their forces to halt the Union flanking attack. The fighting below the hill surged back and forth for hours. A newspaper correspondent observing the struggle wrote that the battleground was "a boiling crater of dust and smoke." Late in the afternoon the weary Union troops began to falter. Beauregard ordered a counterattack, the Union ranks broke, and before nightfall thousands of McDowell's army were in retreat back toward the Potomac.[5]

The campaign and battle of First Manassas were representative of many later operations. The Confederates, with direct connections to Richmond, had employed the telegraph and the railroad to exploit their interior lines and thereby effect a rapid concentration. In the battle itself both sides used entrenchments and had planned tactical turning movements. In spite of achieving surprise and seizing the initiative, McDowell's tactical turning movement failed because of the defensive power of the well-articulated nineteenth-century armies.

Although many of the troops carried smoothbores, the fighting at Manassas took place at a distance and, because horses constituted such conspicuous targets, no cavalry successfully charged the infantry. For these reasons the combatants had no need, as in earlier times, to deploy in order to have a continuous front, heretofore an essential to keep cavalry, or even enemy infantry, from getting through gaps in the line and into the defending infantry's vulnerable rear. Firepower now successfully covered gaps in the line.

Yet this new power of more rapid movement and deployment, which permitted McDowell to catch his opponent and to force an engagement at the enemy's disadvantage, also enabled the Confederates to counter it because their army was equally well articulated. They could not have avoided the battle without a precipitate and, for such raw soldiers, an especially disorganizing retreat. But the Confederates could parry the turning movement and avert disaster because they too could move men rapidly by road, concentrate at the threatened point, and deploy quickly, forming rough defensive lines rendered strong by their firepower.

Just as McDowell unconsciously had followed Clausewitz's formula for the offensive, so had Johnston and Beauregard fought their defensive battle without realizing that they were following Clausewitz's recommendation. Although they lacked the "substantial reserve . . . far to the rear" which the German prescribed, Johnston's forces arrived in time to fill this role and cover the "flanks against any wider and larger turning movement." Though Johnston and Beauregard essentially employed their reserve in a defensive manner, it did outflank McDowell's turning force much as Clausewitz intended when he enjoined "a subordinate turning movement, which is aimed at that part of the enemy's force that has executed the original envelopment." The battle fully justified both Clausewitz's faith in the power of the defense and, in that McDowell's attack failed, Jomini's preference for the strategic rather than the tactical turning movement.[6]

The battle resulted in a retreat of Union forces, the opposing armies now assuming essentially the same positions as before the battle. Clausewitz had foreseen the likelihood of such an outcome; in spite of McDowell's attack by a turning movement, First Manassas had essentially been what he termed "a battle fought with parallel fronts," the Confederates' minor "enveloping action" ceasing as soon as the northern forces retreated. Having noted that a battle with reversed fronts, when each army blocked the communications of the other, would prove decisive, Clausewitz believed that one with parallel fronts could not have an important result. In addition to these, he listed other conditions, each of which he believed would help preclude a decisive victory as well as prevent an effective pursuit. The Battle of First Manassas had all of these conditions. Without significant numerical superiority the victory would be less conclusive, and the pursuit would face serious handicaps unless it possessed a major advantage in cavalry. If, as was the case here, the winning army had vanquished only a part of the losing force, the defeated forces would still have available a large number of relatively fresh and unshaken troops to cover a retreat. Without any of these requisites the Confederates could not expect to accomplish more than they achieved.[7]

"Victory," however, "consists not only in the occupation of the battlefield, but in the destruction of the enemy's physical and psychic forces, which is usually not attained until the enemy is pursued after a victorious battle." Nevertheless, Clausewitz acknowledged the difficulty of pursuit and did not believe it could be effective unless it could begin on the day of battle. He would not have been surprised at the absence of pursuit after First Manassas, realizing as he did that "the winning side is in almost as much disorder and confusion as the losers," a condition that Jefferson Davis, for example, believed existed. But even though his forecast proved accurate, Clausewitz hardly could have imagined the great degree to which disorganization paralyzed both armies. This condition naturally resulted from the short time the armies had existed and the thoroughly amateur capabilities of almost all of their personnel.[8]

Almost all Civil War battles were characterized by the victor's failure to pursue. Even after the armies later became impressive organizations of well-led veterans, they still fought battles with essentially parallel fronts, and the victors usually lacked adequate cavalry or significant numerical superiority to pursue. Rarely did more than a fraction of the losing army suffer the heavy losses and the demoralization and disorganization of tactical defeat. Clausewitz noted difficult terrain as one more factor that would help prevent a decisive victory and hamper an effective pursuit. Since in the American Civil War the terrain was often rough or wooded, practically no battle ever met any of the conditions Clausewitz deemed essential for a formidable pursuit.[9]

The enemy's "psychic forces" could receive severe blows without pursuit, however, for Clausewitz did perceive one significant achievement that could be gained in a battle without pursuit—attrition, or "a reduction of strength relatively larger than our own." By this reckoning the Confederates gained a very modest victory: the Union forces in this defeat lost 2,708 men, less than 10 percent of McDowell's 28,000 men; but the Confederates, on the defensive, suffered even fewer casualties, barely 6 percent of their 32,000 soldiers. The First Battle of Manassas proved representative, and throughout the war the tactical advantage of the defensive almost invariably resulted in heavier casualties for the attacker than the attacked.[10]

The stalemate in Virginia—established, or at least confirmed, at First Manassas—continued into the spring of 1862, while both sides prepared their armies for the renewal of active operations in that theater. But the Confederate public saw in the victory at the Battle of Manassas and the halting of the Union advance confirmation of their confidence in victory if not of their belief that the war would be short.

But as the armies in Virginia faced each other, Confederate morale suffered a grievous blow when the Union attained dramatic successes in the West.

BOTH UNION and Confederate forces enjoyed good communications in the area between the Appalachians and the Mississippi. The Confederates relied primarily upon the railroad, and the Union depended largely on the Ohio and Mississippi rivers, giving the latter five major routes of possible advance into Confederate territory. Three lay along rivers, the Mississippi, the Tennessee, and the Cumberland. A railroad leading south from Columbus, Kentucky, and another from Nashville supplemented the three navigable waterways as routes of advance. But the Missouri River and the primitive railway network in Missouri together supplied better communications with Union forces west of the Mississippi than the rivers in Arkansas provided for their Confederate trans-Mississippi opponents. Confederates, however, enjoyed unity of command under an experienced regular officer, Albert Sidney Johnston, while Union forces lay divided between the competent regular Don Carlos Buell, commanding in central and eastern Kentucky, and the able Henry W. Halleck, also a West Point graduate, in charge from the Cumberland River west.

General Scott's plan had envisioned turning the Confederate positions blocking the Mississippi. The most important of these was a well-fortified and strongly garrisoned position at Columbus. To carry out a strategic turning movement against that stronghold, Union armies would have to advance along one of the good routes east of the river, for "the crucial question where two armies pass each other by" would be, Clausewitz emphasized, "whose lines of communications are the more secure."[11]

Such good communications had importance not only because of the South's sparse population and less intensive agriculture but because even good roads, then a rarity in the United States, could not provide the sole support for an army very far from water or rail transportation; wagon horses or mules consumed so much fodder that they could carry very little freight if the wagons had to carry nourishment for the horses. Even if the teamsters could find fodder along the route, transportation by wagon was so inefficient that it could supply only over short distances, and heavy use quickly wore out the available primitive roads even if rain did not sooner render them impassable.[12]

True, an army could live on the country, feeding its animals and men from supplies found in enemy territory or, for that matter, friendly territory. But an army not constantly on the move quickly exhausted the limited local supplies found in the sparsely settled South. A stationary army, like a city, must draw its supplies from a well-developed system of access to distant markets. An army dispersed over a considerable area could draw a significant portion of its subsistence from the countryside but still would have to depend in part upon more distant sources and, of course, could rely hardly at all on local sources for its munitions and equipment replacement. A moving army could sustain itself even in a sparsely settled country because it constantly entered untouched territory that yielded new sources of subsistence. For this reason raids did not require any supply lines, but operations aiming at permanent occupation involved changes of an army's base and characteristically necessitated water or rail lines rearward.

General Scott's plan did not envision a raid but a permanent occupation of the banks of the Mississippi with the occupying army based on the river's secure, efficient water communications. Tactical turning movements of Confederate positions on the Mississippi, like Columbus, Kentucky, could rely on the river for communications; a strategic turning movement would have to rely on the Tennessee, Cumberland, or railroad routes.

Confederates rightly recognized that the western streams constituted vulnerable arteries cutting deeply into the Confederacy's heartland, and the control and exploitation of the rivers did prove crucial to Union success in the West. Although historians have emphasized the role of railroads in bringing about the Union victory, in the West the rivers, not the rails, provided the key. "We are much obliged to the Tennessee which has favored us most opportunely," wrote Major General William T. Sherman to Rear Admiral David D. Porter. "For I am never easy with a railroad which takes a whole army to guard . . . whereas they can't stop the Tennessee, and each boat can make its own game." There was no practical limit to the capacity of navigable rivers to supply the Federal armies so long as the Union had sufficient vessels. One army supply officer calculated that an ordinary western river steamboat with a capacity of five hundred tons could in one trip carry enough supplies to subsist an army of forty thousand men and eighteen thousand horses for nearly two days.[13]

By 1860 nearly one thousand steamboats operated on the western rivers, and several hundred more were constructed during the war. Although an undetermined number fell under Confederate control, the overwhelming majority remained in Union hands. The achievements of Sherman, Grant, and other northern commanders in the West rested upon adequate supplies, and these depended, in turn, upon command of the rivers. The Union could not have established and maintained this control without an inland navy.

Early in the conflict, Union leaders realized the necessity of creating a naval force to assure domination of the Mississippi River and its tributaries. On May 18, 1861, Commander John Rodgers, the sometimes cantankerous forty-nine-year-old son of Commodore John Rodgers, received orders to report to Major General George B. McClellan at Cincinnati, Ohio, concerning the establishment of a "naval Armament on the Mississippi and Ohio to blockade all communication with the Confederate states." Since inland operations fell under army control, Rodgers's assignment rendered him subordinate to McClellan, a potentially touchy situation that caused surprisingly little friction. With the general's approval, Rodgers purchased and converted into gunboats three river steamers, the *Conestoga*, *Lexington*, and *A. O. Tyler*. These three small vessels constituted the beginning of what ultimately amounted to a powerful naval force on the western rivers. Following instructions, Rodgers also superintended the construction of several new vessels for operations on the Mississippi and its tributaries. On August 6, 1861, the government awarded a contract for seven boats to James B. Eads, a well-known St. Louis engineer.

A few days after the letting of the Eads contract, workmen made the final touches on two of the wooden gunboats, and on September 4 they made a brief sortie down the Mississippi River. Although these gunboats, *Tyler* and *Lexington*, possessed only partial crews of rivermen, a brief engagement occurred between them and Confederate batteries near Hickman, Kentucky, just north of the Tennessee border. Rodgers capably commanded the gunboats here, but this proved his only action in the West for shortly afterward, on September 6, 1861, Captain Andrew H. Foote relieved him.

Foote, a veteran of thirty-nine years in the navy, was deeply religious, described by one of his men as "a quiet unassuming gentleman, [who] feared no one but his God." In sharp contrast to his gentleness and devoutness, he acted aggressively toward the enemy. Like the sometimes individualistic Rodgers, Foote had excellent relations with the army officers with and under whom he worked, particularly U. S. Grant and John C. Frémont, to whom he reported for duty in September. Frémont placed under Foote's command all vessels "belonging to the entire floated expedition down the Mississippi River." His first objective was to complete the vessels under construction, including ironclads.[14]

On October 12, 1861, the Yankees launched the *St. Louis*, the first of the seven ironclads called "Pook turtles" after their designer, Samuel M. Pook. Within three weeks the remaining six appeared: *Cairo, Carondelet, Cincinnati, Louisville, Mound City,* and *Pittsburg.* Pook had designed wooden, flat-bottomed, light-draft, and low-freeboard center-wheelers measuring 175 feet in length. Each gunboat mounted ten eight-inch-shell guns. With slanted casemates covered with two-and-one-half-inch armor, one of their few weaknesses was vulnerability to plunging fire. They saw more service than any other class of river ironclads, fighting in numerous engagements from Fort Henry to Vicksburg and beyond. Other vessels, including two additional ironclads, *Benton,* converted from a snagboat, and *Essex,* converted from a ferryboat, a number of wooden vessels, and mortar boats, gradually augmented Foote's rapidly strengthening force. By mid-January 1862, Foote's naval force stood ready for active service. But by then Frémont no longer held his command; in November, he had issued an unauthorized edict emancipating slaves in Missouri and as a result had been replaced by Major General H. W. Halleck.

In Halleck, the Union commander on the Cumberland River and to the west, the navy possessed a good collaborator and a man who grasped the potential of the command of the rivers. Leaving the army as a captain in 1854, he had amassed a fortune in business and law before returning in 1861 as a major general. A studious officer who had won a Phi Beta Kappa key, he later published books on mining law, engineering, and the art of war. Though he cited Clausewitz in his book on the art of war, he had formed his ideas through a study of Napoleon and Jomini. But at West Point he had absorbed Professor Dennis Hart Mahan's teaching about the strength of the tactical defensive and the value of entrenchments.

While Halleck assimilated his command, Confederate General Albert Sidney Johnston, a much esteemed and experienced regular officer, deployed twelve thousand Confederate troops to defend the well-fortified river and rail center of Columbus, where they blocked two Union routes of advance, the Mississippi and the railroad running south to northern Mississippi. He posted his other major force, more than twenty thousand men, at Bowling Green, Kentucky, to oppose any advance by Buell over the railroad from Louisville to Nashville. At Fort Henry, artillery aimed toward the river blocked the Union navy's progress on the Tennessee, and guns at nearby Fort Donelson controlled the Cumberland River route. But the forts lay vulnerable to attack by land forces, for the combined infantry forces at both of them numbered only five thousand.

Meanwhile, General Scott had resigned as general in chief, and his ideas no longer dominated western strategy. Instead, the two separate Union western commanders, Halleck and Buell, each received pressure from Washington to advance. But control of the Mississippi no longer remained the focal point of Union strategic thinking. President Lincoln wished Buell to advance against the feeble Confederate forces in East Tennessee. Jomini would have disparaged such an operation, terming it a "diversion," which he criticized as usually "dangerous" unless political factors favored it; he did find such a move useful if the force would "receive strong support from the population among which it was sent." Such a diversion would belong "to political rather than military combinations," and indeed Lincoln's concern for the strongly Unionist population of East Tennessee helped prompt him to urge such a move. But primitive roads and heavy winter rains made Buell unwilling to undertake this advance in preference to his plan to thrust along the railroad from Louisville toward Nashville.[15]

Major General Halleck had his own plans. One evening during the Christmas season he dined with his chief of staff, Brigadier General George W. Cullum, and an old Mexican War friend, Brigadier General

William T. Sherman. Sherman recalled that "General Halleck had a map on his table with a large pencil in his hand, and asked, 'where is the rebel line?' Cullum drew the pencil through Bowling Green, Forts Donelson and Henry, and Columbus, Kentucky. 'That is their line,' said Halleck. 'Now where is the proper place to break it?' And either Cullum or I said, '*Naturally* the centre.' Halleck drew a line perpendicular to the other near its middle, and it coincided with the general course of the Tennessee River; and he said, 'That's the true line of operations.'"[16]

With adequate intelligence of Confederate dispositions, Halleck accurately discerned the weak point in the Confederate position and, urged by messages from Washington, prepared for an offensive on the Tennessee. Having already partially pacified Missouri, he could now use his rail and river communications to concentrate troops from Missouri for the blow against the weak Confederate center. In January 1862 he entrusted this river-borne offensive to Brigadier General U. S. Grant, commanding at Paducah, where the Cumberland and Tennessee emptied into the Ohio.

In the old army Sam Grant had a reputation as a drunkard and drifter. He reputedly left the army in 1854 because of his drinking problems and had done little better in civilian life. Nonetheless, Grant had impressed enough people that after the war came he received an appointment as a colonel of Illinois volunteers, and soon he was promoted to brigadier general. Grant was an unobtrusive, mild-mannered, colorless officer. A recent biographer admitted that "there is almost no glamour in the figure . . . he cannot be made into a Wellington or a Napoleon."[17]

Yet Grant was a relentless warrior and far from an ordinary general. Following Halleck's instructions, Grant with fifteen thousand men and Foote with seven gunboats moved south on the Tennessee, unleashing a combined naval and land attack against Fort Henry. With his own communications secure on the river, Grant followed Halleck's guidance and wisely sent one-half of his army to reach the rear of the fort, interrupt its communications, and trap the twenty-five-hundred-man garrison against the Tennessee River, which he controlled with his gunboats. Understanding the peril presented by this threat to his communications and realizing that his force was too small to attempt to stop Grant or to drive him back, the Confederate commander withdrew his garrison before Grant's overwhelming numbers could trap it. Fort Henry fell to Union forces on February 6, 1862. Again following Halleck's instructions, Grant promptly exploited his success by sending the gunboats upstream to break the Memphis and Ohio Railroad bridge over the river, thus protecting himself by cutting a major route of Confederate troop movements and supply.

Halleck had thus forced open a line of communications that enabled him to turn Columbus. He could not yet use it, however, because the Confederate force at Fort Donelson, whither the Fort Henry garrison had retreated, threatened the communications of an advance south. So immediately after capturing Fort Henry, Grant began marching toward the Cumberland, aiming at Fort Donelson, eleven miles away. While Grant battled roads deep in mud, Halleck frantically rushed him reinforcements of ten thousand men and pleaded for more from Buell, the quiescent commander to his east. Grant's slow and muddy march at last brought him to the river on February 12, near the fort, where the navy met him with reinforcements, gunboats, and supply steamers.

The Confederates responded to Grant's success by strengthening Fort Donelson with some troops moved from Bowling Green. But because the possibility of Grant's further success made the rebel hold upon Bowling Green so tenuous, the southerners also withdrew the remainder of their forces from that position, falling back over the railroad toward Nashville. The significant Confederate reinforcement at Fort Donelson, twelve thousand men, was now commanded by Brigadier General John B. Floyd, a former governor of Virginia whose ignorance of military affairs had not been remedied by undistinguished service as secretary of war in the late 1850s.

Albert Sidney Johnston, the Confederate theater commander, directed the outnumbered and inept Floyd to defend a position that had a river at its back. Though the guns of the fort succeeded in keeping the Union gunboats at bay, Floyd's position violated Clausewitz's "first and foremost" requirement for the security of his rear. His position "did not form a right angle with the direction of a nearby line of retreat." In fact, Floyd's position paralleled his line of retreat and, without consulting Jomini, the capable Grant did precisely what the Swiss authority recommended when he used his heavily reinforced army to surround the fort and Floyd's small force. Floyd was in a predicament foreseen by Jomini, "cut off" and having "no other chance of escape than in forcing his way through" Grant's lines. Realizing his peril, the untutored Floyd unknowingly followed the expert's prescription when he immediately threw "the mass of his forces" upon Grant's unentrenched army in an effort "to regain his proper line of retreat" to the east. Initially driven back, Grant counterattacked and recovered his line around the fort. The Confederates then surrendered the bulk of their forces on February 16, 1862.[18]

The fall of Fort Donelson secured the flank of the Union forces, which Halleck promptly ordered up the Tennessee River until they had moved as far south as the course of the river permitted. Though its strategic impact gave the battle at Fort Donelson its significance, Grant had attained one of the major tactical successes of the war. His own casualties in killed and wounded numbered slightly more than those of the Confederates, but his total casualties, including a few missing, amounted to only 2,832, 10.5 percent of his 28,000. Because of the capitulation, Confederate losses totaled 16,623, 79 percent of their 21,000 men.

Grant thus had virtually annihilated an enemy army by making the most of the opportunity to cut his opponent's communications by pinning him against a river. But in spite of Halleck's excellent strategy and good management, and Grant's energy and ability, Clausewitz had foreseen that such a victory could not have taken place without "*major, obvious, and exceptional* mistakes on the enemy's part," when the Confederate command divided its forces and placed Floyd's command where Grant could trap it so readily. Aided by Confederate ineptness, Grant and Halleck had accomplished the substance of Jomini's strategic turning movement.[19]

The Fort Donelson victory portended far-reaching consequences. The Confederates, as Halleck reported, now found themselves "completely turned on both sides of the Mississippi," and thus evacuated Columbus, "the boasted 'Gibraltar of the West.'" Not only were Halleck and Grant giving substance to Scott's strategy, but also Union control of the Cumberland and Tennessee rivers threatened Nashville's communications and forced the Confederates to evacuate the Tennessee capital. So in his operations, Halleck, a thorough student of Jomini and

Napoleon, had adhered to the United States Army's 1982 manual, *Operations*, when he attained surprise as he unconsciously followed the injunction "to avoid the enemy's strength and strike at his weaknesses."[20]

THESE EVENTS on the battlefield had immediate consequences on the home front. The Confederacy was one year old, and two forts and an army had surrendered under circumstances that seemed less than honorable, for two political generals had abandoned their commands at Fort Donelson and escaped south, leaving the unfortunate but responsible Simon Buckner to surrender to his old friend, Ulysses Grant. As might be expected, there were numerous recriminations, some expressions of doubt, and occasional confessions of inadequacy. Any northern overconfidence as a result of these actions would soon be dispelled; for the time being, however, there were those in the South who feared that the fate of the two forts presaged that of the Confederacy, especially when considered in the light of recent Union success in taking Roanoke Island on the North Carolina coast. "Events have demonstrated that the [Confederate] Government had attempted more than it had power successfully to achieve," wrote Davis in an obvious understatement. He felt the surrender at Roanoke Island was "deeply humiliating" but expressed the hope "that our reported losses at Fort Donelson have been greatly exaggerated."[21]

Confederate confidence naturally suffered, and internal rumblings mounted. Vocal and volatile Congressman Henry S. Foote, whose Nashville constituency was now in Union hands, attacked the secretaries of war and the navy, blaming them not only for the losses in Tennessee but for Roanoke Island as well. "Leave us now," he shouted, "and go to your own vocations; leave us; you have done us harm enough; go your way, you are utterly incompetent." Governor Joseph E. Brown of Georgia, however, issued a proclamation declaring that "the late reverses" showed "the absolute necessity of renewed energy and determination on our part." He demanded that the deficiency in firearms be remedied by the use of men armed with pikes. Exhibiting a civilian's often naive view of nineteenth-century warfare, he urged that pikemen advance "with a shout for victory" and "rush with terrible impetuosity into the lines of the enemy. Hand to hand, the pike has vastly the advantage of the bayonet." He asked whether, if five thousand men with pikes had charged "at the proper time, who can say victory would not have been ours at Fort Donelson?"[22]

So for most people optimism remained—Union victories had only destroyed overconfidence. Jefferson Davis's proclamation of February 20, 1862, reminded his fellow Confederates that they were "not permitted to furnish an exception to the rule of Divine government, which has prescribed affliction as the discipline of nations as well as of individuals." Faith had to be tested, and "the chastening which seemeth grievous will, if rightly received, bring forth its appropriate fruit." God still wore gray, but He might not always march in the Confederate battalions until they had been punished adequately for their iniquities, and each Confederate could decide for himself what those might be. Governor Joseph E. Brown of Georgia feared that the South's "constant successes" had "filled our hearts with vanity, and caused us to appropriate to ourselves a large portion of the glory that belonged to God alone. . . . The consequence has been that God has, for a time, withdrawn, kept his smiling face from us, and committed our enemies to triumph over us." The Virginia legislature accepted the setbacks calmly and urged Virginians to summon "new energies . . . until, with the blessing of God, we shall conquer an honorable peace, and finally establish our independence."[23]

Religion could explain that such a serious defeat did not necessarily show a lack of God's favor and thus help mitigate the blow to confidence and morale. And Confederate morale and will to continue the struggle depended heavily on military success and the support of religion because they had such tenuous support in Confederate nationalism. The spring campaigns would again tax that meager nationalism, for when Confederate military strength declined, sufficient compensating strength would not necessarily be found in the determination and will of the people.

The western defeats, which introduced realism, and the campaign of Manassas, which earlier had sustained unrealistic Confederate expectations, all conformed closely to the expectations of Clausewitz and Jomini. The military significance of these operations lies more in the ability of the victors to make the most of the weaknesses of the defeated than in the blunders of the defeated; on each side, important commanders had displayed a grasp of the art of war as understood by the experts and by their successes had, in a sense, validated the teachings of Jomini and Clausewitz. Such initial campaigns by inexperienced commanders provide little basis for assessing the adequacy of either Union or Confederate military performance, but the active campaigning of the spring would provide ample opportunity for exhibiting the competent professionalism of the military leaders on both sides as well as testing the adequacy of the training the troops had received and the courage of both soldiers and civilians.

Chapter Seven

Trial by Battle

T HOMAS BRAGG, Jefferson Davis's attorney general, never showed much optimism or enthusiasm for the Confederate cause. Like many former Whigs, especially fellow Tar Heels, when the military situation went poorly Bragg always tended to regret having rejected the alternative decision, and in early 1862 recent news from the army indicated that events were going unsatisfactorily indeed. Bragg was not one to throw in the towel; if he now harbored little enthusiasm, he did continue in desperation, the desperation of a cornered animal. He had foreseen the Confederate difficulties in the West and understood their significance; from his insider's position in the cabinet he saw the effect that severance of the line in Kentucky and the losses of Fort Henry and Fort Donelson had upon those who were more knowledgeable about military events than he. He complained in his diary that the Confederate army would be forced out of both Columbus and Bowling Green, and he perceived the Union advantage that derived from control of the Cumberland River. He observed both Secretary of War Judah P. Benjamin and President Davis, assessing them as gloomy and despondent. "It is idle," confessed Bragg, "to disguise the fact that we have latterly been luke warm and not fully alive to our danger." A few days later Bragg lamented that the southern people "cannot be induced to risk all & perhaps lose all, save their honor. The change is going on every day and our people have lost their enthusiasm."[1]

Bragg was prematurely disheartened. Soon after he spoke, Confederate soldiers were concentrating to meet the Union army in Tennessee and to deal it a powerful blow. The resulting conflict, Shiloh or Pittsburg Landing, although bloody, was not decisive. It did, however, unfold under such circumstances that both sides could interpret it as either a victory or a defeat, depending upon their psychological needs at the moment.

In retrospect, clearly the campaigns of the spring and summer of

1862 contributed to the stalemate, for they proved how difficult it was to destroy Civil War–era armies. The question at the time, had anyone known it, was whether stalemate would contribute most to Union victory by prolonging the war to the point that the Confederacy would lose simply because it had run out of resources and will, or whether stalemate would contribute to Confederate victory by proving to the world that the armies could suffer checks and wounds but would always survive to fight again. Decisive victories in this war would be few and far between. No matter how heavy the casualties one army could inflict, the other would always have the strength to survive. Further, the South's great size added to the potency of its defense, and because a stalemate had resulted and promised to continue, the ultimate reliance of both sides, especially the South, would have to be on the will of their people to continue the fight.

No conflict illustrates this observation better than the battle of Shiloh, in which more men died than in any previous battle on the North American continent—though worse battles were to come. Halleck had expected Confederates to counterattack against Grant's army, and when he had attained command over Buell in March 1862, he had ordered the bulk of Buell's forces to leave Nashville and to join Grant at Pittsburg Landing, far south on the Tennessee River. Anxious to control the Mississippi, Halleck did not concentrate his entire command on the Tennessee. He kept John Pope and an army of twenty-five thousand operating west of the Mississippi, working with the navy to capture the remaining Confederate strong points on the river, thus again adhering to the substance of Scott's plan, which called for permanent occupation of the banks of the Mississippi River. Believing that Grant's and Buell's forces would not be strong enough to resist a Confederate counterattack unless they united, Halleck ordered Buell to hurry and Grant to stand on the defensive and entrench.

Halleck's successful campaign had overwhelmed the Confederate center and deeply penetrated into Confederate territory. Divided by this movement and with both their Columbus and Bowling Green positions turned, Confederate forces fell back, abandoning much of Tennessee as well as all of their hold on Kentucky. Union troops advanced 150 miles in a month, something Clausewitz hardly would have believed possible, not only because of supply problems but also because he saw that the more distance involved the more the attacking army "is weakened—by the effect of marches and the detachment of garrisons." But the rivers and the steamers made this advance feasible. Neither Clausewitz nor Jomini envisioned the astounding success made possible by perceptive and energetic use of rivers. Halleck used modern gunboats and steamers to bring about a rapid and decisive Union advance.[2]

But the enemy also relied on products of the industrial revolution by employing the telegraph and the railroad to facilitate counterattack. The Confederates, led by Johnston's second in command, the capable Manassas veteran Beauregard, began concentrating all of the forces of the western department to strike Grant before Buell could join him. Beauregard ordered Major General Earl Van Dorn from Arkansas and Major General Leonidas Polk from Columbus. Johnston himself moved westward, first by road and then by rail, to Corinth, Mississippi, where Beauregard directed the concentration of all of the western forces. The concentration neatly fit Davis's offensive-defensive strategy, and he supported it by ordering five thousand men from New Orleans by river and rail and ten thousand from Mobile by rail. He even sought reinforcements from General Lee at Charleston. Thus the Confederates implemented a concentration that embraced the length and breadth of the Confederacy—from the Atlantic to Arkansas and from Kentucky to the Gulf.

Only Van Dorn in Arkansas lacked rail or water communications, and his failure to arrive until after the Battle of Shiloh resulted from his being far away in northwestern Arkansas, where he was losing the Battle of Pea Ridge. Despite Beauregard's energy and imperative orders from Richmond, the Confederates did not complete their national concentration of forces until after Buell had camped near Grant at the beginning of April. Halleck had won the race to concentrate on the Tennessee, but on the eve of battle Buell's army was seven miles downriver from Grant's, and Grant expected no attack.

Early on the morning of April 6, 1862, Confederates surprised Grant's unprepared army, catching the men at breakfast, unentrenched, with their commander away. Unable to turn an army with a river at its back, the Confederates launched an essentially frontal assault that lasted all day, the results of which again exhibited the resilience and relative invulnerability of highly maneuverable armies composed of troops largely armed with rifles. Though caught unaware and woefully ill-arrayed for battle, the Union soldiers fought well, and subordinate commanders, soon effectively coordinated by the imperturbable Grant, who had rushed to the scene, stayed the Confederate attacks. On the second day, facing 25,000 fresh men from Buell's army, which had joined Grant during the previous night, the Confederates withdrew successfully, in spite of potent attacks by the now numerically superior Union army.

The combatants in the hard-fought battle suffered immense losses, the Confederates sustaining casualties of 10,600, or 26.5 percent of their 40,000, and Grant 13,000, or 20.7 percent of his 62,700 engaged. The unforeseen onslaught and lack of much preparation help explain the large Union casualties even though they enjoyed the advantage of the tactical defensive on the first day. Using Clausewitz's criterion of attrition, victory belonged to the Union because it lost a smaller proportion of its force.

Although Grant had his back to the river and thus risked disaster if defeated, neither Clausewitz nor Jomini would have approved of the frontal attack at Shiloh. They would not have believed that a frontal attack against an enemy equal in strength with powerful reinforcements at hand would have had enough chance of success to warrant the gamble. Regarding speed and secrecy as the two requisites of surprise, Clausewitz would not have foreseen, in view of their slow and noisy approach, that the Confederates could have caught the Federals unready. But he would have anticipated that an unexpected attack would not decide the battle because tactical "surprise can never be *outstandingly* successful" and can rarely lead to "major results."[3]

Jomini would surely have been very pleased with the southern strategy. Substituting the railroad and the steamer for marching, the Confederates had sought "*to obtain by free and rapid movements the advantage of bringing the mass of the troops against fractions of the enemy.*" They had failed, of course, because Buell arrived. But in not making the defensive "passive" and by attempting to capitalize on the "opportunities of assailing the weak points of the enemy," they very likely would have earned his approbation, for Jomini gave great stress to attack by a concentration of forces against the enemy at his weak point. Clausewitz, on the other hand, gave little attention to this question, for he prescribed that "there is no higher and simpler law of strategy than that of keeping one's forces concentrated." With this view he doubtless would have had difficulty imagining the dispersal that preceded the Battle of Shiloh and that Jomini would have assumed to be characteristic. The Confederate concentration on the enemy's main force was, however, consonant with Clausewitz's teachings.[4]

The Battle of Shiloh proved a learning experience for all involved. Politicians and generals alike now realized that the war was going to cost far more blood and treasure than they had expected. Grant admitted that only after Shiloh did he abandon his expectation that the war would be short. After winning what he believed was a decisive victory at Forts Henry and Donelson, he was surprised that the Confederates not only did not give up but concentrated themselves and attacked. At that moment he "gave up all idea of saving the Union except by complete conquest." But this objective would have to wait, for, seeing his army exhausted, Grant confessed later that he "had not the heart to order the men who had fought desperately for two days" to pursue the retreating Confederates.[5]

GENERAL GRANT was in no position to put his newly established knowledge and policies to practice, for almost immediately after Shiloh Halleck journeyed from St. Louis and assumed personal command of the now almost fully concentrated armies of his vast department. Halleck joined Pope's forces from the Mississippi to his and, with more than one hundred thousand men, he faced Beauregard's army, barely half his strength even though belated reinforcements from Arkansas and South Carolina had just augmented it.

Never before having personally commanded more than a platoon, the energetic Halleck, on emerging from his office in St. Louis, became extremely wary and slowly, cautiously, used his superior numbers to threaten Beauregard's flanks and to force him gradually back toward Corinth. By now an experienced commander, Beauregard systematically protected himself, all the while seeking any opportunity to attack an exposed portion of the enemy's army. But Halleck kept his troops invulnerable for, true to his West Point training and the lesson of Shiloh, he entrenched at the end of each day's advance.

"Progress will be slower as troops increase in number," Clausewitz had pronounced, and, as if foreseeing Halleck's problems, had noted that "all plans and movements become [more] intricate and consequently everything requires more time. The attacker," with his large numbers, "is faced with the additional handicap that problems of supply make him spread out more than the defender, and, in consequence he always runs the risk of being overwhelmed by a superior force at some point." Halleck did not, however, spread out, even though he lacked a river or a railroad in the line of supply running to his rear. Instead, he corduroyed miles of road to ensure supply of his immense and well-concentrated army from its base on the Tennessee River.[6]

When Halleck at last confronted the Confederates before Corinth, Beauregard, though prudently entrenched, made a surprise withdrawal on the night of May 29–30, 1862. Under cover of darkness and sufficient noise, the moving locomotives and carefully coached men provided a convincing imitation of reinforcement rather than evacuation, thus misleading the Federals and facilitating an unmolested retreat south along the railroad.

Some northerners took heart at the capture of a Mississippi city at the end of the war's first year; others looked less sanguinely at the empty enemy fortifications. Ulysses Grant thought the victory "strategic," in that it gained control of the east-west railroad, but pointed out that "it was barren in every other particular." He expected "much unjust criticism" of Halleck's operation even though he himself realized that its "future effects will prove it a great victory." Sherman saw other benefits in the campaign. "I esteemed it a magnificent drill," he wrote in his *Memoirs*, "as it served for the instruction of our men in guard and picket duty, and in habituating them to outdoor life: and by the time we had reached Corinth I believe that army was the best then on this continent, and could have gone where it pleased."[7]

"Where it pleased" turned out to be both nowhere and everywhere. Halleck immediately began constructing massive fortifications around Corinth, indicating his estimate of the town's importance. He also established adequate communications by restoring the railroad from Memphis. Concluding that transportation difficulties, drought, and the unhealthy summer climate precluded an advance against Beauregard's army in northern Mississippi, Halleck assumed that Beauregard would suffer a similar immobilization. Expecting a stalemate at Corinth, Halleck promptly embarked on a new offensive when he ordered Buell to lead a large contingent eastward along the Memphis and Charleston Railway. By this movement, Halleck intended that Buell proceed rapidly to capture the key railway junctions around Chattanooga, thus cutting an important rail line connecting Virginia with Georgia and the Gulf to the south. Lincoln gave enthusiastic approval to this campaign because he had wished to break this important railroad and welcomed the initiation of his long-urged advance into loyalist East Tennessee. Buell's advance would also open a route of invasion toward Atlanta as well as place a Union army between Beauregard's army south of Corinth and Confederate forces in East Tennessee.

AS CORINTH fell and Buell's movement began, the campaign in Virginia reached a climax. But this major Union effort, quite foreign to General Scott's original anaconda strategy, had resulted from political realities and interaction among President Lincoln, Secretary of War Stanton, and George B. McClellan, McDowell's successor in command in Virginia.

General Scott's plan seemingly was succeeding in the West, where Halleck's advances were part of a pattern that included the fall of New Orleans to a combined navy-army expedition in April 1862 and the capture of Memphis and all Confederate positions on the Mississippi north of that important city in June. Only a small segment of the Mississippi remained in Confederate hands. But the other part of Scott's plan was not working. He had relied "greatly on the sure operations of a complete blockade of the Atlantic and Gulf ports." The blockade, however, was proving ineffective.[8]

The Union navy's acceptance of a blockade of the southern coastline as its major strategic responsibility made combined operations a necessity. For the blockade to be effective, the Union would have to establish bases for refueling and maintenance at selected sites along the southern coast. The adoption of steam propulsion made a close blockade somewhat more realistic than it would have been in the age of sail, but it created prodigious logistical problems. Guarding some three thousand miles of coastline with dozens of ports, inlets, and rivers required a huge armada. These vessels needed support facilities within a short cruising distance of their blockade station. Maintaining a close blockade proved much more difficult when the vessels had to leave their station periodically for fuel or repairs, particularly for steamers stationed along the South Atlantic coast and in the Gulf of Mexico.

The navy initially addressed these problems by a blockade board, or board of strategy, appointed by Secretary of the Navy Gideon Welles in May 1861. The board, which included representatives of the army, navy, and Coast Survey, prepared ten reports and memos which outlined hydrographic conditions along the southern coast, selected points to seize for bases, and advised an increase in the number of blockading squadrons.

At the beginning of the war the navy created two blockading squadrons, one in the Atlantic and one in the Gulf. The board recommended dividing each into two squadrons, making a total of four. Thus the Atlantic Squadron became the North Atlantic Blockading Squadron and the South Atlantic Blockading Squadron, the border between North and South Carolina determining their areas of operation. Meanwhile, the Gulf Squadron became the East Gulf Blockading Squadron and the West Gulf Blockading Squadron. The eastern squadron received the responsibility for all of Florida east of Pensacola, including the Atlantic coast and the Bahamas and Cuba. The western squadron blockaded Gulf ports west of Pensacola.

The board's concern for bases along the southern coastline resulted in expeditions to occupy Hatteras Inlet, North Carolina; Fernandina, Florida; Port Royal, South Carolina; and Ship Island, off the Mississippi coast. These operations were the genesis of the initial combined operations along the southern coastline.

Although the army had representation on the board and supplied units for these operations, no evidence exists that it looked at the expeditions' purposes as anything other than naval. Apparently the army had little interest in using the seized enclaves as beachheads to secure objectives inland. Major General McClellan evidently tried to interest the board in using these bases, especially those to be seized along the eastern seaboard, as staging points to attack key railway lines in the interior, but he had little success. Later, after his appointment as general in chief, McClellan would attempt to implement this concept.[9]

The seizure of Hatteras Inlet was the first sizable combined operation along the Atlantic coastline. The blockade board had recommended the operation, based upon information that Confederates were fortifying the inlet as a base for privateers. A small naval force under the command of Flag Officer Silas Stringham, a forty-two-year veteran of the navy, arrived off the inlet on August 26, 1861. After only one day of heavy bombardment the two forts guarding the inlet surrendered, rendering redundant the accompanying 860 Union troops under the command of Major General Benjamin F. Butler. Although the shelling of Port Royal received far more attention then and later, the heavy bombardment against the Hatteras forts clearly demonstrated the strength of naval gunfire against shore positions. As Bern Anderson rightly concluded, "This was an important action if only because it was the first of its kind."[10]

More than two months elapsed before the next operation along the coast. On November 4, Flag Officer Samuel F. Du Pont arrived off Port Royal, South Carolina, with a powerful naval force exceeding seventy vessels. Du Pont had assumed command of the South Atlantic Blockading Squadron in September, when the navy divided the Atlantic Squadron. Undoubtedly a major factor in the decision to appoint him to the command was that, while head of the blockade board, he had a major role in preparing the plans for the Port Royal expedition.

Du Pont, a member of a well-known Delaware business family, had the respect of his peers. An able though not aggressive naval officer, he would be highly lauded for his role in the Port Royal expedition. On November 7, 1861, his warships bombarded the forts guarding the bay for four hours and forced their surrender. The following day the first contingent of troops under Brigadier General Thomas W. Sherman disembarked and occupied the abandoned forts. As at Hatteras Inlet, these forts had fallen to naval gunfire. The navy considered the Port Royal expedition the first step in providing blockading vessels with repair and coaling facilities along the south Atlantic coast. The second step was the seizure of Fernandina.

The army, however, had other objectives. McClellan, by this time general in chief, had envisioned Port Royal as a stepping stone to a land attack on Charleston, Savannah, and the important railroad that ran between the two ports and linked the southeastern states with Virginia. General T. W. Sherman favored moving against Savannah.

Although it was reasonable to hope that these ports and the railroad might be seized immediately after Port Royal fell, for various reasons the army did not carry out the operations.

The navy had little interest at that time in an attack on Charleston or Savannah, planning instead to sink vessels loaded with stone to block the channels to the ports. Du Pont occupied himself with strengthening the blockade and gave only halfhearted attention to Sherman's efforts. Sherman's troops were thought to be unreliable, and he received no reinforcements. Nor did the navy furnish transportation to carry the troops from Sea Island to the mainland and provide logistical support. Finally, General Robert E. Lee assumed command of Confederate defenses in the area and began constructing defensive works along the river approaches to the ports and railroad. Although an expedition seized Fernandina in the spring of 1862, it would be the last successful joint effort of any size on the south Atlantic coast. The Union took Charleston and Savannah near the end of the war but from behind by land and not as a result of combined operations.[11]

Strategically similar activities along the North Carolina coast proved equally fruitless, although they enjoyed initial successes. In September 1861, General McClellan agreed to an expedition to capture Roanoke Island, North Carolina. Major General Ambrose E. Burnside, who may well have originated the plan (both he and McClellan claimed it), led the military force, which he had recruited and trained. Flag Officer Louis M. Goldsborough, who in September had replaced Silas Stringham in command of the North Atlantic Blockading Squadron, had charge of the naval part of the expedition.[12]

Goldsborough, or "Old Guts" as he was called by the sailors, was a well-known figure in the navy, partly because of his immense size, six feet, four inches in height, weight estimated at over three hundred pounds, and "red, red beard," and partly for what one officer called "his eccentricity in deportment." To junior officers "his manners [were] somewhat rough, so that he would almost frighten a subordinate out of his wits." Goldsborough, a competent officer, conducted the Roanoke Island expedition skillfully.[13]

Burnside, a West Point graduate from Indiana and a handsome, likable professional officer, was known for his magnificent sideburns. He was also unusually humble. Grant remarked in his *Memoirs*, "General

Burnside was an officer who was generally liked and respected. He was not, however, fitted to command an army. No one knew this better than himself. He always admitted his blunders, and extenuated those officers under him beyond what they were entitled to."[14]

McClellan, Burnside, and Goldsborough all had somewhat different objectives. McClellan wanted Roanoke Island as a base of operations from which the Union could move against the Wilmington and Weldon Railroad, but he needed naval cooperation to gain control of the sounds and the streams that led inland toward the railroad. Burnside agreed with this objective but also believed that the ultimate goal should be destruction of the Confederate forces in Virginia. To Goldsborough the island would provide a base to blockade the important interwater route to Norfolk. He realized the importance of the sounds, the Dismal Swamp, and the Albemarle and Chesapeake canals to Norfolk and southeastern Virginia.

On February 7, 1862, some ten thousand troops under Burnside's command joined Goldsborough's force of seventeen shallow-draft gunboats in assaulting Roanoke Island. Under the protective fire of the Union warships, the troops landed in waves similar to the pattern later employed in the Pacific during World War II. In addition to providing the assaulting troops with fire support, Goldsborough's active vessels defeated a small force of Confederate gunboats and bombarded two forts until they were effectively neutralized. Two days after the initial landing the army had secured the island.

The expedition only partially realized its objectives. The Union occupied a large part of eastern North Carolina but did not seize the railroad until William T. Sherman's troops did so in the spring of 1865. McClellan's abandonment of the Peninsula campaign resulted in Burnside's recall to the Army of the Potomac, and, after that, the Union never stationed enough troops in eastern North Carolina to mount any serious threat to the railroad. Union forces never tried to exploit Roanoke Island for military operations in southern Virginia other than a small raid to the Dismal Swamp Canal. Its seizure did, however, contribute to the blockade effort, particularly in the North Carolina sounds, and was a factor in the Confederate evacuation of Norfolk.

In the Gulf of Mexico, the blockade board had selected Ship Island as the potential site of a naval base. The navy chose this narrow sand bank, several miles off the Mississippi coast, because of its situation on the interwater commercial route between Mobile and New Orleans. From the Union navy's point of view it was an ideal location for maintaining blockaders and as a staging area to attack both ports. Although the Confederates had fortified and garrisoned the island with more than eight hundred men, in September 1861 they evacuated it. It then became an important logistical base for the Gulf Blockading Squadron and its successors, as well as the jumping-off point for Union operations to seize the passes to the Mississippi River and New Orleans. Like Hatteras Inlet, Port Royal, Roanoke Island, and other enclaves, Ship Island became an important blockade base, but the mere occupation of these points did not ensure the success of the blockade.

EVEN IF the blockade had been very effective, it would not have equaled the task of crippling quickly so large and nearly self-sufficient a country as the Confederacy. More important, the Union had adopted measures inadequate to bring the South "to terms" when these terms were extinction. Thus Scott's strategy would not suffice in view of the Union's war aims and the potency of the South's determination. Indeed, no strategy could succeed until one element of this equation—Union war aims or Confederate determination—was altered.

The amount of blood shed in the Civil War was proportional to the goals of the two sides and their will to achieve them. Had this been an ordinary nineteenth-century war between two independent European countries, doubtless it would not have gone on so long. But when one contender has the goal of obliterating the other, the will of the other to resist is increased beyond what it would be if the cost of defeat were merely the loss of a province here and an indemnity there. By the same token, the government that seeks to extinguish its opponent has a more formidable task in some respects than the opponent has. For that government, not faced with extinction, the alternatives to total victory are reasonable and hence easier for the people to accept. To keep the people up to the mark becomes difficult. In 1862 the Union goal was reconstruction, and the government would not, could not, accept anything less.

The Union had, therefore, no choice but to aim at a decisive war, whether or not its resources matched the task. Clausewitz's prescription for a decisive war was to aim at the enemy's "center of gravity," or source of strength. In the case of his own campaign against France, he identified two centers of gravity, Paris and the army. He expected to defeat the French army and in the course of the campaign capture Paris, thus overcoming both. The Confederacy presented no such simple problem: Richmond was in no way analogous to Paris, the Confederacy had several major armies, and the South had many centers of gravity. To seize control of the Mississippi, opening it to Union commerce and dividing the Confederacy, certainly would strike a blow at one source of the enemy's strength, and the necessary attack on the major army defending it would provide another blow. Similarly, the Confederate capital and the army defending it offered two more centers of gravity. Buell's movement toward Chattanooga and the railway between Virginia and Atlanta created the possibility that Buell could advance into the populous and important state of Georgia. The conquest of Georgia and the breaking of the communications between the Atlantic and Gulf states certainly would be a blow at a center of gravity, even if Buell met no Confederate army on the way.[15]

The Union, of course, made no conscious decision to aim at these centers. The traditional importance and prestige of the Mississippi guaranteed that it would be an objective, and the proximity to Washington of a Confederate army and the Confederate capital meant that Richmond and the army defending it would, for domestic political reasons alone, also be a Union objective.

To REPLACE McDowell after the defeat at Manassas and to head Union forces in the important Virginia theater, Lincoln appointed George B. McClellan, who had conducted successful operations in mountainous western Virginia. Like the other generals on both sides, McClellan lacked any previous higher command experience, although he had graduated from West Point and, in addition to his service in the Mexican War, had had the opportunity to observe the French and British armies in the Crimean War. Like Halleck, he had left the army in the 1850s and established a successful business career before returning as a major general in 1861. McClellan, young, in his early thirties, handsome, and brilliant, had graduated second in his class. "Little Mac" was probably the most popular commanding general with the rank and file during the war. He instinctively knew how to appeal to the common soldiers, and they responded, even the hard-bitten veterans.

> For McClellan's our leader; he is gallant and strong
> For God and our Country we are marching along.[16]

sang the Army of the Potomac in the winter and spring of 1862. At West Point he had thoroughly learned Professor Dennis Hart Mahan's doctrine of the power of the defense and was a devotee of the turning movement. Capturing the imagination of both the public and his army, McClellan enjoyed several months of exemption from public or official pressure to advance against the Confederate army near Washington. Believing in thorough preparations, he used this time for training his rapidly growing force, the Army of the Potomac.

Meanwhile, Lincoln had learned much about the art of war. That southern railway lines between Virginia and Tennessee were shorter than comparable northern lines of communication impressed Lincoln and his secretary of war. They became obsessed with the Confederates' ability, using these interior lines, to transfer troops much more quickly from one army to another than the Union possibly could. After thinking about this problem for nearly a year, Lincoln developed a concept identical to Clausewitz's "rule" or "elementary law of war," the "unification of forces in time," which would enable the Union to neutralize the interior lines that permitted Confederates to unify their forces. In the winter of 1862 Lincoln adopted the strategy of simultaneous advances. Though often flawed in execution, this Clausewitzian unification of forces in time, rather than space, remained basic Union strategy throughout the rest of the war. Lincoln had so clear a concept that he readily could have used Clausewitz's words for the strategic "law of simultaneous use of forces" and written, as did Clausewitz: "If concentration is to be achieved, at least in terms of time, the offensive must be launched from every practicable point at once."[17]

But simultaneous advances proved difficult to achieve in practice. General McClellan stressed training for his army and kept his plans secret even after Lincoln, in November 1861, had given him the added duty of replacing Scott as general in chief. Increasingly, the public demanded action, but winter came with the army, still near Washington, observing the nearby Confederates. Pressed by public opinion for immediate action, Lincoln at last ordered simultaneous advances for the winter. Halleck would move, though impelled in part by a rumor of reinforcements coming from Virginia to the West, rather than by Lincoln's order. But McClellan could not move, immobilized by muddy roads and a dispute with Lincoln and Stanton over strategy that arose from Lincoln's and Stanton's natural belief in a direct offensive against Joseph E. Johnston's well-entrenched army near Washington. McClellan emphatically objected to this plan and at last revealed to the president his own intentions for a Virginia campaign.

When he presented his plan to Lincoln, McClellan argued against the president's suggestion of directly attacking Johnston's army. McClellan stressed that the results of any victory following a direct attack on Johnston's forces "would be confined to the possession of the field of battle, the evacuation of the line of the upper Potomac, & the moral effect of the victory—important results it is true, but not decisive of the war nor securing the destruction of the enemy's main army." "When we have gained the battle," he pointed out, "the question will at once arise 'What are we to do next?'" He insisted that the likely sequel of such a frontal victory, a push toward Richmond, would enable the enemy to "dispute our advance, over bad roads, from position to position." McClellan thus not only shared Clausewitz's belief in the indecisiveness of parallel battles but had even raised Clausewitz's question about these battles: "Every attacker, therefore, has to ask himself how he will exploit his victory after the battle."[18]

For the Union situation in Virginia, Clausewitz's recommendation would have been that "if, for instance, the main object is the enemy's capital, and the defender has not taken up a position between it and the attacker, the latter would be making a mistake if he advanced straight on the city. He would do better to strike at the communications of the enemy army and its capital and there seek the victory which will bring him to the city." McClellan proposed exactly this strategy, wishing to use water communications for a surprise turning movement by landing at Urbanna on the Rappahannock River. From there he was unclear as to whether he would aim at Johnston's communications, thereby following Clausewitz's prescription, or try to capture Richmond while Johnston's army was away.[19]

But fundamentally McClellan's ideas harmonized with Clausewitz's.

If the battle were to yield prisoners and artillery as well as enemy killed and wounded, Clausewitz insisted that the "strategic circumstances" would have to provide for "threatening the enemy's rear and protecting one's own." As the advocate of the strategic turning movement, Jomini also surely would have approved McClellan's plan, for he stressed the need *"to strike in the most decisive direction,*—that is to say in the direction where the consequences of his defeat may be most disastrous to the enemy."[20]

Reluctantly President Lincoln acquiesced. But in early March 1862 Johnston, realizing his vulnerability to just such a strategic turning movement, protected himself by falling back to the line of the Rappahannock. Nevertheless, McClellan did not hesitate for he had ready an alternate plan, which would threaten the Confederate capital by using the water route to move to the Peninsula between the York and James rivers. He could expect to move rapidly up the Peninsula because his control of both rivers would enable him to force the Confederates back by threatening waterborne turning movements against their rear. His easy advance would take him all the way to the vicinity of the Confederate capital, where he would enjoy a good water line of communications. He could, however, expect to face well-entrenched Confederates, who would have every possible advantage of fighting on the defensive.

Seemingly McClellan would only have transferred the stalemate from the vicinity of Washington to that of Richmond. This change would, of course, give a significant psychological advantage to the Union, but what other success did it promise? The Union would have to besiege; but such a siege could not starve out the city because its extensive rail network could readily supply both the city and its defending army, a network McClellan could not possibly interdict from his Peninsula position. But the Union forces could conduct a traditional siege, digging diagonal trenches to provide protected approaches, and they could demolish the Confederate defenses systematically with vast quantities of artillery. This form of warfare the engineer-trained West Point graduates understood entirely and McClellan knew perhaps best of all, for he had observed the successful Anglo-French siege of the Crimean city of Sebastopol.

The Union could expect to win such a campaign of matériel, just as the

French and British had prevailed over the Russians after an eleven-month siege. Moreover, McClellan correctly believed that the Confederates would feel compelled to respond to this menace to their capital by taking the offensive against his army on the Peninsula. McClellan would then have gained one of the principal advantages of the turning movement, forcing the enemy to assume the tactical offensive against his prudently selected and prepared position. Of course, victory would give him no chance to trap the Confederate army, but even Napoleon had entrapped enemy armies on only two occasions.

Although both Clausewitz and Jomini would have approved of making the enemy's capital the objective, they would have disparaged attacking it without having first defeated the enemy's army. But Johnston parried any effort to reach his rear and McClellan expected to be able to besiege Richmond. Clausewitz nevertheless would have seen merit in McClellan's plan. The prospects for the siege were bright because McClellan had all of Clausewitz's requisites for success. McClellan would have excellent communications and, if "most sieges fail for lack of equipment," McClellan's ample supply of the proper artillery guaranteed success. Clausewitz would also have recognized the strategic situation McClellan could create, for although Clausewitz believed that "such cases" were "so rare" that he would not list the situation among his "concepts and principles," he did recognize that an attacker might "occupy a strong position in the hope that the defender would attack him there." He also realized that a siege could force the defender to "take the offensive to break up the siege."[21]

But McClellan's strategic concept eluded the Union civilian leaders, conditioned as they were to conceiving of warfare as frontal battles. Yet the civilians knew that, except for the amphibious operations that had secured blockade bases on the North Carolina coast, Union forces had carried out no active military operations in the east since the Battle of Manassas. They realized the political necessity that McClellan do something about the rebel army still at the gates of the nation's capital. Clausewitz would have understood what the public wanted. A battle, followed by the withdrawal of the enemy, had appeal. The retreat following a conflict "is the only element that affects public opinion outside of the army; that impresses the people and the governments." When McClellan's movement to Fort Monroe caused the enemy to fall back toward Richmond, McClellan provided the retreat, but, lacking the battle first, it did not meet the public's needs.[22]

Lincoln and Stanton had difficulty understanding why their capital would be safe while McClellan was fighting on the York-James Peninsula, and they insisted on a large garrison for Washington. Because the distances were small and his communications short and secure, McClellan could reach Richmond before Johnston could exploit his interior lines to capture Washington and return in time to save Richmond. But McClellan had failed to explain satisfactorily to Lincoln and Stanton why few Confederate generals, least of all McClellan's cautious adversary, Joe Johnston, would trade a temporary capture of Washington for the permanent loss of Richmond. Lincoln therefore withheld McDowell's corps from McClellan and used it to protect the capital.[23]

Because public perceptions played such an important role in the Civil War, the respective governments did not have the freedom to adopt the strategy they would have liked, as the misgivings of Lincoln and Stanton about the protection of Washington by troops on the York-James Peninsula indicate. Therefore, they had to consider each movement in terms of what the people would think, a consideration that occurred more often to Lincoln than to Davis. It was precisely because will was so important to eventual achievement of the government's goals that public opinion had to be consulted, as Clausewitz had indicated. Thus capitals became an important objective, whether there was any intrinsic reason for them to be so or not. Civil War leadership had always to keep in mind that a great victory, perceived by the public as a defeat, would actually be a defeat because it would tend to undermine rather than support the public will.

A MENACE to the naval superiority upon which his plan completely depended almost thwarted McClellan's offensive. Before the war was even a year old, Confederates sought to apply modern naval technology to compensate for their deficiencies in conventional arms. Indeed, the guns facing Fort Sumter had barely cooled when Confederate Secretary of the Navy Stephen R. Mallory wrote in an oft-quoted report: "I regard the possession of an iron-armored ship as a matter of the first necessity. . . . If we . . . follow their [the United States Navy's] . . . example and build wooden ships, we shall have to construct several at one time; for one or two ships would fall easy prey to her comparatively numerous steam frigates. But inequality of numbers may be compensated by invulnerability; and thus not only does economy but naval success dictate the wisdom and expediency of fighting with iron against wood." That same day the Confederate Congress appropriated $2 million for the purchase or construction of ironclads in Europe.[24]

Although the Confederacy eventually contracted for several powerful armored vessels in England and France, these initial efforts failed. Secretary Mallory then determined to build ironclads within the Confederacy. In the middle of July 1861 the Confederate navy decided to convert the frigate *Merrimack* at the navy yard in Norfolk into an armored vessel (later commissioned the *Virginia*), and six weeks later it awarded contracts for the construction of two ironclads to be built at Memphis, Tennessee. Two other vessels were contracted in New Orleans. Mallory optimistically believed that these armorclads could operate on the open sea as well as on inland waters and could challenge Union blockaders. The secretary's optimism was ill founded. Only three of the vessels became operational, and none proved capable of going to sea. The *Virginia*, however, proved an effective warship in the confined waters of Hampton Roads and became a serious threat to McClellan's plans.

On March 8, 1862, the *Virginia*, the first of the Confederate ironclads to engage in combat, steamed into Hampton Roads and there destroyed two Union warships and dispersed the transports assembled to support McClellan's campaign. On the following day the Confederate ship returned to the Roads, determined to complete the destruction of the Union flotilla. There followed one of the most dramatic naval engagements in history: the USS *Monitor*, which fortuitously had arrived the night before, challenged the *Virginia*. For several hours the two protagonists fought it out, and at the end both withdrew, little damaged.

The engagement had far-reaching consequences. The *Monitor's* impressive showing produced such an intense enthusiasm in the North that a "monitor craze" swept the Union. From then until the end of the war the Union navy concentrated on building monitor-type vessels, eventually more than thirty. Ironically, the Union navy, which ob-

The Confederacy's Permanent National Seal. Surrounded on the seal by symbols of a bountiful and blessed agricultural Eden, George Washington was revered by the Confederates as the father of their country. (Courtesy of the Museum of the Confederacy at Richmond, Virginia.)

The equestrian statue of George Washington at Richmond, Virginia. The same image of George Washington as appears on the Confederacy's National Seal stands larger-than-life between St. Paul's Episcopal Church and the capitol building designed by Thomas Jefferson. (Photograph attributed to Andrew J. Russell.)

Antoine Henri Jomini, the great military theorist and disciple of Napoleon Bonaparte. Many scholars have incorrectly blamed Jomini's writings for engendering the supposedly faulty "place-oriented" strategies of innumerable Civil War generals.

Karl von Clausewitz, perhaps the greatest of all modern military theorists. Our approach in this book has been to assess the Civil War generals by measuring their thoughts and actions against the prescriptions of Clausewitz and Jomini.

Lee and His Generals, a painting by George B. Matthews. This fanciful gathering, of course, never took place. But it is a good, and long a popular, rendering of what many Lost Cause enthusiasts might regard in a vein somewhat akin to Leonardo da Vinci's *Last Supper*. (U.S. Signal Corps photograph 111-BA-2013, in the National Archives.)

"STONEWALL" JACKSON.

LONGSTREET.

STUART.

R. E. LEE.

MORGAN.

JOE. JOHNSON.

BEAUREGARD.

Facing page: Generals of the South, a collage of card portraits. These romanticized portraits appeared widely on cards not unlike those later found in packages of bubble gum—or the "holy cards" at times quite popular among Roman Catholics. Some partisans used these cards as Christmas greetings or even tree decorations. (Courtesy of the Chicago Historical Society.)

Postage stamps of the Confederacy. The Confederate government issued fourteen different stamps. The likeness of Jefferson Davis appeared on eight of them, making his image readily recognized throughout the entire South (one surprised soldier, on unexpectedly coming face-to-face with the President, stammered, "Oh! You look so ——— much like a postage stamp"). The other great "Southern Americans" depicted on stamps are Andrew Jackson and Thomas Jefferson on two each; George Washington and John C. Calhoun—the earlier ideologist of secession—on one each.

Field post office at Falmouth, Virginia. Mail was, to be sure, important—even vital—to those on either side. Note here, too, the woman postal worker. Both the North and the South employed hundreds of women in the mail service, another watershed of the Civil War era. Many of these women were the wives of postal workers who volunteered or were drafted for military service. (Courtesy of the Chicago Historical Society.)

viously had to assume an offensive strategy, adopted as its principal ironclad a vessel that was basically defensive in nature and generally inefficient as an aid in the navy's two primary responsibilities, blockade and combined operations.

While the Union ironclad building program after 1861 emphasized monitors, the Confederate program changed from an emphasis on offensive operations by challenging the blockade to one of defense. The apparent unseaworthiness of the *Virginia* and the ironclads built in New Orleans and Memphis, the lack of adequate facilities and qualified technical expertise, the belief that powerful armorclads could be obtained in Europe, and, most important, the growing threat to the Confederacy from invasion and combined assaults all contributed to this change. From 1862 until the end of the war the Confederate naval construction program concentrated on small, shallow-draft, harbor-defense armored vessels. Approximately forty were laid down and half were completed.

The immediate consequence of the *Virginia-Monitor* engagement also altered McClellan's campaign. From a naval standpoint the clash constituted a victory for the *Monitor* because the *Monitor* saved the Union vessels in Hampton Roads. The momentary strategic results for land operations, however, favored the Confederacy, which had effectively blocked McClellan's approach to Richmond via the James River. The Union general had expected that his naval support would permit him to use the James as a primary line of communications and to use both it and the York River to protect his flanks. The *Virginia*'s control of the James forced him to shift his line of communications to the York. He also lost much of his naval support when Flag Officer Goldsborough decided (with McClellan's approval) to "watch and neutralize the *Merrimac* [sic]" to prevent the Confederate armorclad from threatening McClellan's operation.[25]

Until early in May 1862 a virtual stalemate prevailed between the Union and Confederate naval forces in the Hampton Roads area. Neither side was willing to risk its armored vessel. On May 3, General Joseph E. Johnston, in command of Confederate military defenses on the Peninsula, noted McClellan's advance up that marshy neck and ordered the abandonment of Yorktown and Norfolk. Eight days later, because her base of operations was being evacuated and her draft was too deep to ascend the James, the Confederates destroyed the *Virginia*. With Norfolk in Union hands and the Confederate ironclad eliminated, the James River lay open. On May 11 Goldsborough ordered the *Monitor*, the ironclad *Galena*, and three wooden vessels to steam up the river toward Richmond. Four days later at Drewry's Bluff, eight miles below the Confederate capital, Confederate defenses repulsed them.

Although the Union navy's initial sortie on the James River did not succeed, McClellan's Army of the Potomac continued to advance slowly up the Peninsula, reaching the Chickahominy on May 20, 1862. The navy convoyed transports up the York and Pamunkey rivers, carrying reinforcements and supplies, and as the Confederates fell back in the face of the Union invasion, gunboats began easing up the James. By the end of May the Union navy enjoyed control of the James as far as City Point, near the entrance to the Appomattox River. While the bloody two-day engagement at Seven Pines (Fair Oaks) was being fought, Confederate engineers were strengthening the barrier and supporting works at Drewry's Bluff.

MEANWHILE, MCCLELLAN'S strategy was working as he had designed it. He proceeded very deliberately against limited opposition. The Confederates had made no determined effort to hold the Peninsula because Union naval superiority and troops on transports posed a constant threat of a turning movement by water. When McClellan's army reached the outskirts of Richmond, the Confederates believed the menace to their capital so great that they felt compelled to attack, thus validating McClellan's strategy.

In that first attack, at the end of May in the Battle of Seven Pines, the Confederates attempted to annihilate two exposed corps of McClellan's army. The still inexperienced Johnston and his three subordinates bungled a good plan, though McClellan's absence from the battlefield resulted in the Union army's failure to offer coordinated resistance. The outcome of the essentially frontal battle again demonstrated the relative invulnerability of the contending armies. The Confederates, on the offensive, suffered about six thousand casualties, 15 percent of their force, whereas the Union losses amounted to about five thousand, 12 percent of those engaged. In stopping the Confederate assault, the Union army won the biggest engagement yet fought in the East; but because neither side retreated, and the armies ended in the same position as before, the result did not satisfy the Union public.

Even though his plan was working, McClellan became more and more pessimistic and, apparently losing his concept of the operation, he came to believe that he must attack the Confederate fortifications rather than receive their assault in his well-entrenched position. Clausewitz was familiar with a commander who could "in the peace of his room far removed from danger and responsibility, arrive at the right answer. . . . But beset on every side with danger and responsibility he will lose perspective."[26]

PRESIDENT DAVIS, detailing his military chief, Lee, as the wounded Johnston's successor, still faced the task of preventing the Union from besieging the Confederate capital, an operation he expected would inevitably succeed. While McClellan was approaching Richmond, the Confederates were waging a triumphant campaign in the Shenandoah Valley. This fertile farming region, watered by the Shenandoah River, lay between the main Appalachian range on the west and the single ridge of the Blue Ridge Mountains on the east. Here the Confederates had a small force commanded by the brilliant and combative Thomas J. "Stonewall" Jackson. His small army had the aid of the forces posted to cover the railroad that connected Richmond and the Valley. As McClellan moved to the Peninsula, Jackson took the offensive in the Valley, a diversion that Clausewitz would have approved.[27]

After beginning with an unsuccessful attack on a superior force, the reinforced Jackson distracted the attention of the Union command by skillfully using interior lines to defeat one Union force approaching from the west and then to drive another north from the Valley and across the Potomac. Diverting their attention from Richmond, Lincoln and Stanton saw an opportunity for Union troops to reach Jackson's rear. They thus engaged in an attack that ignored "the strict logical necessity of pressing on to the goal," which would have seemed to Clausewitz "like an idler who strolls through a campaign and takes advantage of the occasional bargain that comes his way."[28]

But because the capture of Jackson's now substantial force would have been quite a bargain, Lincoln not only directed forces from western Virginia toward Jackson's rear, he also sent in the same direction part of the troops near Fredericksburg that were cooperating with McClellan. Barely slipping between the forces approaching his rear from east and west, Jackson then turned on his pursuers and defeated first one and then the other. A state of equilibrium returned to the Valley, and Jackson was, by the ninth of June, available for further action.

IN JUNE Lee and Davis considered sending Jackson additional troops to relieve the pressure on Richmond by having Jackson cross the Potomac, thus further distracting Lincoln's attention and diverting Federal troops from the Peninsula. But Lee and Davis decided instead to concentrate against McClellan. As in the Shiloh campaign, the Confederates employed the telegraph and the railroad to take advantage of their interior lines for a counterstroke to drive back the enemy. Reinforcements that Davis had ordered to Richmond arrived from the Carolinas and, at the last moment, Jackson moved stealthily by rail from the Valley. This exploitation of interior lines would have warmed Jomini's heart. Clausewitz, too, would have approved, for "where the weaker side is forced to fight against odds, its lack of numbers must be made up by the inner tension and vigor," which, he wrote, when "combined with a wise limitation in objectives, the result is that combination of brilliant strokes that we admire in the campaigns of Frederick the Great."[29]

In prescribing for the defense, the U.S. Army's 1982 field manual on operations paraphrases Napoleon with approval, saying that "the entire art of war consists of a well-planned and exceptionally circumspect defense followed by a rapid, audacious attack." Joe Johnston's retreat to Richmond had provided the circumspect defense; Lee planned to provide the assault. At Shiloh, Sidney Johnston had effected "concentration," achieved "surprise," and displayed "audacity," all qualities demanded of the offensive by the manual. But in striking an enemy army with its back to a river, he had failed to make one of the manual's desired "well-conceived attacks against weakness," engaging rather in one of the "force-on-force battles of attrition" disparaged by the army's doctrine. Instead, the manual points out that "envelopment avoids the enemy's strength" and that "destruction is most practical after the enemy has been turned out of a position."[30]

Lee, too, knew this, and he planned to force McClellan to retreat by a tactical turning movement that, by threatening McClellan's communications with his base on the York River, would force him either to withdraw or to attack the Confederates. The turning force, Jackson's eighteen thousand men from the Valley, would advance in the rear of McClellan's north flank. Independently of whether Richmond was truly menaced, Clausewitz would have endorsed such a counterattack because "within the limits of his strength a defender must always seek to change over to the attack as soon as he had gained the benefit of the defense." Of course, he realized it was *"a risky business to attack an able opponent in a good position,"* and "it would be stupid to attempt it" if "he can get his way without assaulting" entrenchments. Lee adopted the obvious means of avoiding McClellan's entrenchments, the method indicated by Clausewitz: "Maneuver the defender out by threatening his flank." Though Jomini would have preferred a strategic turning movement, he, too, would have seen merit in Lee's projected counterattack. But Clausewitz's preference for the tactical turning movement gave Lee's plan more affinity for Clausewitz than for Jomini.[31]

When the attack began in late June 1862, however, not only did the inexperienced Lee and his primitive staff bungle almost as badly as had Joe Johnston at Seven Pines, but even the seasoned and usually brilliant Jackson performed badly; the competently conceived and promptly executed concentration and turning movement became a fruitless series of battles consisting of strong frontal attacks against a weak flank of McClellan's army.

At the end of June McClellan decided to transfer his base to Harrison's Landing on the James River, where the navy could provide better assistance. A naval flotilla under Commander John Rodgers provided fire support for McClellan's troops as they took up positions at Malvern Hill on June 30, 1862, and there on July 1 fought the last of the Seven Days' Battles. The Peninsular Campaign was over, although the participants did not know it.

In the following weeks the Union Navy Department heavily reinforced the flotilla. By the middle of July twenty-three warships including ironclads had concentrated on the James between City Point and Drewry's Bluff. By that date Captain Charles Wilkes had taken command of the James River Flotilla, which then constituted an "independent division" of the North Atlantic Blockading Squadron. Although the navy was preparing for a renewed attack on Richmond by combined forces, such a move did not materialize. On July 26, army headquarters ordered McClellan and his army back to the defenses of Washington. During the first two weeks in August units of the James River Flotilla covered the withdrawal of McClellan's force as it retired across the Chickahominy and back to Fortress Monroe and Yorktown. The flotilla then returned to Newport News, where it disbanded on the last day of August. Rowena Reed rightly concluded that "no Civil War campaign better demonstrated the superior advantage of water communication than the Peninsula operations."[32]

McClellan effectively exploited naval support in gaining control of the Peninsula, and, without a navy, the Confederates could not challenge Union control of the James. The *Virginia* had been destroyed, additional ironclads were still uncompleted, and the wooden vessels in the James River were too few and too weak. From its base in Hampton Roads the Union navy continued to maintain control of the rivers flowing into the Chesapeake Bay. Unchecked by Confederate gunboats, which remained above the obstructions at Drewry's Bluff until 1864, Union naval vessels made only occasional sorties up the James River.

THESE SEVEN days of battle caused McClellan to retreat and send panicky telegrams to Lincoln and, in turn, forced the alarmed Lincoln to order reinforcements from the Carolinas, from Halleck in the West, and even from the militia in faraway Massachusetts. Nevertheless, by using his water base on the coast, McClellan had reached the enemy's rear and threatened something the enemy thought vital—his capital. In this way, McClellan had compelled the Confederates to attack him twice and so could combine the strategic offensive with the advantages of the tactical defensive. As a result of their two assaults, Johnston's at Seven Pines and Lee's in the Seven Days' Battles, the Confederates had lost more than twenty-six thousand men, nearly 30 percent of their available force, whereas, fighting on the defensive, the Federals had lost slightly more than twenty thousand men, only about 20 percent of their forces engaged.

McClellan's strategy had worked, but did he win? By the criterion of attrition, he certainly did. In his march south to the James River he had left behind no artillery or other "trophies" to symbolize his defeat, and in his retreat he had sacrificed very little of the territory he had gained. Though he did not acknowledge it, however, he had given up his intention to besiege Richmond, and his own morale had suffered severely. Thus by Clausewitz's indicators, the advantages were about equal. But the northern public had no question as to who had won. Acutely aware of this, Lincoln commented that McClellan's "half-defeat" seriously depressed the public's morale in spite of Halleck's Union armies' "clearing more than a hundred thousand square miles of country" in the West. McClellan had thus failed to deliver both his own objective and the military victory in Virginia, so politically necessary for the Lincoln administration.[33]

The Seven Days' Battles constituted a victory for the Confederates also because they had denied McClellan his objective and pushed him back thirty miles from Richmond. Not for the moment, at any rate, did the Confederate leaders need to fear a Sebastopol-type siege whose withering fire of overwhelmingly superior artillery inexorably would demolish their defense until the city fell or was literally laid in uninhabitable ruins. Yet the immense losses involved in his victory made Lee wary of battles and reassured him of the wisdom in his original intent to force McClellan back by threatening his communications. Having graduated from West Point before Professor Mahan's time, Lee and Davis did not share McClellan's respect for the power of the tactical defense. But the Seven Days' Battles educated them rapidly and, like Clausewitz's interpretation of Frederick the Great, "realizing that even victories cost too much," they quickly resolved to avoid battles if possible and to fight on the defensive.[34]

If the leaders on either side had realized that the armies were stalemated, perhaps they would have attempted earlier to influence the enemy's public opinion and willpower. As things stood in midsummer of 1862, however, Confederate victories had little meaning except for their effect on morale and for possession of the battlefield when the fighting stopped because the price was fearfully high. As Mrs. Chesnut put it: "Shiloh was a victory—if Albert Sidney Johnston had not been killed. Seven Pines—if Joe Johnston had not been wounded." So many young men had died; such victory "does not seem to soothe the sore hearts." Jefferson Davis's proclamation of the previous February, when hopes were high, now reflected fully his admonition that God was testing Confederate "faith and perseverance . . . and the chastening which seemeth grievous will, if rightly received, bring forth its appropriate fruit."[35]

The campaign in Virginia and that of Shiloh exhibited Confederate mastery of the use of interior lines to concentrate against invading forces. Their exploitation of the railway and the electric telegraph to carry out these concentrations across an unprecedented expanse of territory was a major innovation in warfare. Although Europeans had employed railways for troop movements and supply, they had yet to use them to execute such concentrations as had characterized the campaigns of Frederick the Great and Napoleon. With the aid of the railroad and telegraph the Confederates had magnified greatly the scale of these operations, carrying out concentrations over hundreds of thousands of square miles in North America that marching men had earlier conducted in areas of only tens of thousands of square miles in Europe.

Though the Union had made much less use of these new resources for rapid concentration of troops, Federal commanders, especially Halleck when he reinforced Grant before Shiloh, clearly grasped what the Confederates could do and sought to guard against it. The Union innovation consisted of the brilliant use of the strategic and logistic potential of the rivers and the Chesapeake Bay, a potential much augmented by the speed and carrying capacity of the steamer and the combat power of the armorclad gunboat. The Union did not neglect railways nor the Confederates the rivers, and both relied on steam power on rivers as well as on rails to supply their huge armies.

In battles the Union forces had the advantage because at Seven Pines, the Seven Days' Battles, and the first days at Fort Donelson and Shiloh they were on the tactical defensive. The Confederates had to rely on the tactical offensive if they were to reap the fruits of their use of the railroad for concentration. Only in this way did it seem possible to drive back the enemy, recover lost territory, and so regain access to the matériel and manpower resources overrun by initial northern successes. Such a strategy had disadvantages, however. To the extent that Confederates went on the offensive, as they did at Shiloh and the Seven Days, they would suffer more casualties by giving up the advantage of the defensive. Since civilians almost always perceived the fortunes of their country in terms of the battlefield and, more specifically, who retreated and who did not, McClellan's retreat before Lee's attacks in the Seven Days confirmed the Peninsula campaign as a victory that elevated southern morale and depressed northern spirits; Halleck's slow advance after the Battle of Shiloh even encouraged Confederate perception of that conflict as a victory and affected morale accordingly. So the conclusion of these first large-scale military operations worked to sustain Confederate motivation to prosecute the war.

In such a state of affairs, Confederates might find justification in going over to the offensive, especially if that strategy had the bonus of entering enemy territory, fighting on his ground, and subsisting off his crops. Whatever they might gain by conquest, however, they might lose in manpower and matériel. Careful forethought would be necessary to ensure that the results of counteroffensives would be worth their cost, for, when the army finally retired to secure better supply or to protect its communications by moving closer to its base, the Confederate public would perceive the retreat as a defeat. The result would be a loss of military power, but under such circumstances that an easy augmentation of will would not provide compensation.

The blood lost in the forthcoming Antietam and Perryville campaigns (September–October 1862) would be difficult to replace, and the ever-lengthening casualty lists would underline the tactical supremacy of the defense and the vital importance of maintaining the morale and will of the civilian population.

Confederates were lulled into some degree of overconfidence at this point, or they never would have advanced into the North in the fall of 1862. They were misled by faulty intelligence about the degree of support they might find for the Confederate cause in the two Union slave states of Kentucky and Maryland. It seems likely that they were also fooled by the ease with which they had defeated the Union army once again in a return engagement at Manassas.

Chapter Eight

The Politics of Dreams

T HE FREQUENT REPETITION of Clausewitz's dictum that war is an
extension of politics has turned the dictum into a cliché. The repetition of the phrase, however, does not diminish the appropriateness
of its application to the campaigns of the fall of 1862, when Confederates attempted to exert military pressure for a political purpose, using
military success to undermine Union morale in the hope that another
state or two might join the South or go its own way. All wars have at
least some political aspects, especially those which Jomini termed "national wars." Civil wars after all often have the character of national
wars, too, and in many of them at least one people risk their independence. In a sense the Union as well as the Confederacy risked its independence in 1861–65; one did not have to be particularly foresighted to
see that a Confederate victory inevitably would change the Union's
character and even might destroy it by encouraging further fragmen-
tation of the truncated remainder.

Indeed, the South hoped for such an outcome, and her early policy
aimed toward it. Some historians have speculated that in the beginning many Confederates actually had hoped for a re-creation of the
Union—on their terms. Kenneth Stampp discusses this possibility in
his thoughtful essay "The Southern Road to Appomattox," suggesting
that "for many Southerners secession was not in fact the ultimate
goal" but merely a way to negotiate a rearrangement of the old Union.
We find some tempting but fragmentary bits of supporting evidence
here and there throughout the literature of the secession movement,
including the frequently quoted statement of Thomas Reade Rootes
Cobb that the South could make better terms for itself under the Confederate Constitution than under the United States Constitution. The
Confederate Constitution would have allowed such a reconstruction,
for it provided that new states could be admitted into the Confederacy
by a two-thirds vote, a provision evidently aimed not only at the slave
states still in the Union but also at the states of the old Northwest.[1]

Most likely, however, the Confederates did not hope so much for reconstruction under a new flag and constitution as for a further division of the United States between the Northwest and the East. On February 22, 1861, the Provisional Congress passed "a bill to declare and establish the free navigation of the Mississippi River" in an attempt to calm the fears of Union states bordering that river and to drive a wedge between the interests of New England and the Middle Atlantic states on one hand and those of the old Northwest on the other. Agreeing to this policy, Jefferson Davis signed the bill into law three days later. Only two weeks thereafter, the southern Congress ratified this policy, while acting in its capacity as a constitutional convention, by establishing the process for admission of new states by a two-thirds vote. That this provision was put into the Constitution reflects the anticipated potential and very special meaning it had for the Confederate leadership.[2]

THE CONFEDERATE strategy in late summer and early fall 1862 therefore comes as no surprise. With one eye cocked toward the Northwest and the other carefully examining the apparently anomalous situation of two Union slave states, Maryland and Kentucky, the Confederate leaders amused themselves by dreaming of a politico-military offensive. The possibility of exploiting northern internal discontent and turning it to southern advantage especially fascinated them. Flushed with successes that began with the Seven Days' Battles and anticipating further victories, the Confederate Senate passed a resolution on September 12, 1862, calling upon President Davis to direct his commanders to reaffirm free trade on the Mississippi River wherever "they approach, or enter, the territory of the United States bordering upon the Mississippi River, or the tributaries thereof."[3]

Both the political aspects of the war and authorized incursions into Union-controlled territory that had clear political implications interested Jefferson Davis. Indeed, Frank Vandiver refers to the 1862 thrust into Maryland as "part of the biggest, most comprehensive political campaign attempted by the Confederate government" and hints that at that late hour some Confederates thought they might yet "detach a Yankee state or two from the Union." Acting upon evidence of northern internal discontent and vague reports of a "Northwest Conspiracy," Davis sought to undermine enemy morale even further by successful advances into both Maryland and Kentucky by Generals Lee, Braxton Bragg, and Edmund Kirby Smith.[4]

Once established in enemy territory, Davis wished these victorious generals to issue proclamations informing the inhabitants that the South fought not for conquest but for self-defense, reaffirming the Confederacy's commitment to free navigation of the Mississippi River, and calling upon individual northern states to "secure immunity from the desolating effects of warfare . . . by a separate treaty of peace." Even if this maneuver did not shake the allegiance of the Northwest, perhaps these military operations, by bringing war to the doorsteps of Union voters for a change, would persuade them to vote for less resolute candidates. The catch, however, was that the operations would have to produce tangible military results.[5]

The most obvious measure of success would be defeat and destruction of a Union army, which would break the stalemate. Such a victory was unlikely under the conditions of the 1860s, although the South could aim for other, more feasible goals. In both the East and the West, Confederate commanders wished to feed their men and animals on the enemy's ground, to tap a new resource of potential recruits, and to afford "the people . . . an opportunity of liberating themselves." Even if these accomplishments proved elusive, Confederates could at least annoy and harass Union forces and spoil their offensive plans.[6]

THE CONCEPT of the base provides the readiest means of understanding the movements made by the Confederate army in Virginia to realize the leadership's visions, as well as the actions and capabilities of the Union army. In the spring of 1862 General McClellan had used his command of the Chesapeake and the rivers of eastern Virginia to turn the Confederates back to Richmond. By the same token, Stonewall Jackson had campaigned successfully in the Shenandoah Valley. When McClellan reached the vicinity of Richmond, the Confederates had considered reinforcing Jackson so that he could cross the Potomac and menace Washington. This strange situation, in which each side had the potential to turn the other, not only characterized operations in Virginia for the remainder of the war but also provides an excellent illustration of the military thinkers' notion of a base.

The concepts of interior lines and the base were, Clausewitz wrote, the "two main principles for the conduct of major wars" which had been developed in his time. Originated at the end of the eighteenth century by Heinrich Dietrich von Bülow, the concept of the base appeared in the writings of both Clausewitz and Jomini, the latter employing it to explain strategic turning movements. Bülow conceived of an army's base as a line and placed great stress upon its breadth. A broad base provided more routes of supply and retreat than a narrow one. Several routes of retreat protected an army from being turned and having to fight its way back. He diagrammed the narrow base, with the dashed vertical line indicating the line of supply and route of retreat (Figure 8.1). He also diagrammed the broad base, with the dashed lines indicating the possible routes of supply and retreat (Figure 8.2). Clearly, the army with the broad base is less likely to have a turning movement block its retreat or to be forced to take the offensive in battle to recover its communications.[7]

Jomini used this concept to create a geometrical abstraction of the strategic turning movement. For successful turning movements an army required a two-sided base. He diagrammed such a base as shown in Figure 8.3. An army could base itself anywhere along the two sides of this right angle. Such a base facilitated a strategic turning movement because the turning army could advance around the defending army's right and base itself in its rear, as diagrammed in Figure 8.4, D standing for the defending army and A for the attacking army, and dashed lines for communication to a base.[8]

If army A turned army D, it would follow the solid line of march shown in Figure 8.5, relying on the new dashed line of communications.

Thus army A could retain a line of communications while cutting army D's, which had importance because a movement without communications would put both armies in the same predicament, as Figure 8.5 indicates. Without the base on the right of the diagram, army A, in cutting army D's communications, would have placed army D on its own communications, and both would be in the same situation, deprived of communications. Whichever army ran out of supplies first would have to take the offensive to return to its base or retreat by making a wide circuit around the opposing army. But with the two-sided base, army A would have the assurance of supplies while cutting

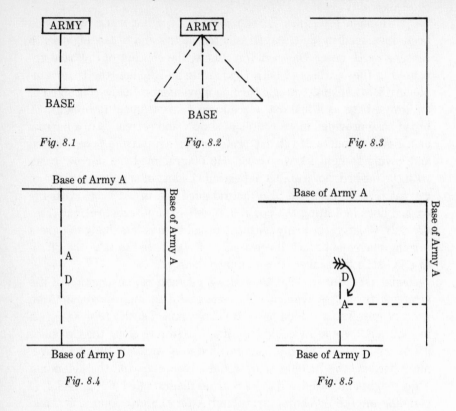

Fig. 8.1   *Fig. 8.2*   *Fig. 8.3*

Fig. 8.4   *Fig. 8.5*

off army D's and forcing army D either to retreat to avoid being turned or, if turned, take the tactical offensive to recover its supply line.

Bülow's and Jomini's geometrical conceptions and illustrations would be a needless complication did they not so well correspond to the situation in Virginia and help explain three years of operations in that theater. The Union base was two-sided, as shown in Figure 8.6. The Baltimore and Ohio Railroad and the canal along the Potomac provided a base for an advance of Union armies anywhere along the northern side of the map; Union naval superiority and transports in the Chesapeake Bay provided another base along the right side of the map that enabled the Union army to base itself on any of the navigable rivers, the Potomac, Rappahannock, York, and James. Thus the Union armies could move into the rear of any Confederate force near Washington, easily turning the Confederate right, as McClellan had done in his 1862 Pen-

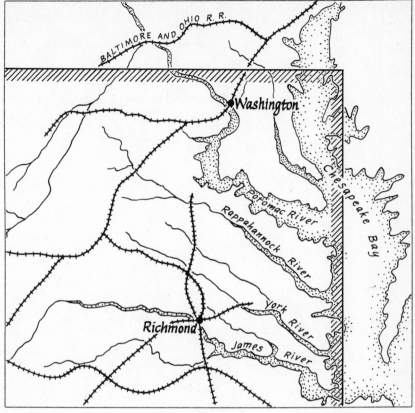

Fig. 8.6

insula campaign and as Grant and Meade were to do in their 1864 campaign from the Wilderness to Petersburg.

But the Confederates also had a two-sided base (Figure 8.7). Richmond and the Virginia Central Railway provided one base, from which
the Confederate army could operate anywhere between Richmond and
the Shenandoah Valley. And the railway also furnished excellent communications to the Valley, which itself provided most of the elements
of another base because of its rail connections to Richmond and
Lynchburg, the fine road that traversed it, and the abundant crops of a
fertile general farming region. Confederate armies could easily use
their base to turn the right of Union armies south of Washington and

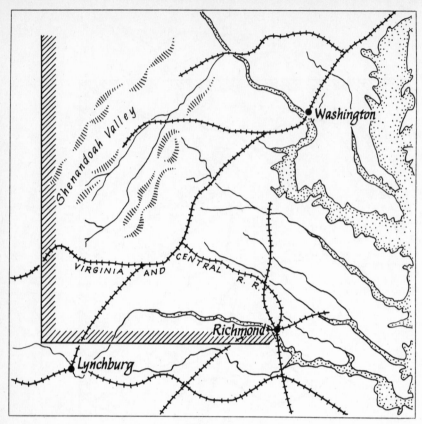

Fig. 8.7

pass into their rear as far north as Pennsylvania. They exploited this capacity to turn the Union right in the critical Gettysburg campaign of 1863, the Mine Run campaign of 1863, and General Early's operations toward the District of Columbia in the summer of 1864. They also used this strategic ability in the campaign of late summer 1862, from Second Manassas to Antietam.

Thus with each contender having a two-sided base, the campaigns in Virginia consisted of three years of inconclusive seesaws of turning movements in which each side tried, but neither decisively reached the rear of the other. This mutual advantage placed a premium on good generalship. Fortunately for the Confederacy, in assigning Lee to command the army opposing McClellan, Davis selected someone who not only well understood the opportunities presented by the Confederacy's two-sided base in Virginia but who also had the skill, boldness, and leadership ability to make the most of it.

Just before appointing Halleck general in chief in July 1862 and while McClellan remained immobile on the Peninsula, Lincoln had called another successful general from the West, John Pope, previously one of Halleck's western subordinates. Lincoln now placed Pope in command of the new fifty-thousand-man Army of Virginia, which he and Stanton had concentrated southwest of Washington.

The new commander got off to a bad start. In a statement issued to his troops shortly after taking over, he tactlessly compared the eastern armies unfavorably with those in the West, "where we have always seen the backs of our enemies." Halleck knew of Pope's boasting and its effect on the rank and file in the eastern armies, but he worried far more over the strategic dispositions of Pope's Army of Virginia encamped near Washington, McClellan's Army of the Potomac in defensive positions near Richmond, and Lee between them, enjoying interior lines.[9]

Immediately Halleck and the very able quartermaster general, Montgomery C. Meigs, made an urgent visit to McClellan on the Peninsula. They found him pessimistic and unwilling again to take the offensive against Richmond unless he received substantial reinforcements. Though certain that McClellan greatly overestimated the enemy's numbers, Halleck discerned a serious menace in the Union's strategic situation. He realized that unless the Confederates perceived that McClellan threatened Richmond with a siege, they would have the liberty to exploit their interior lines to attack either McClellan on the Peninsula or Pope near Washington.

So the new general in chief promptly ordered McClellan to evacuate the Peninsula and bring his army north to support Pope. Halleck, realizing that Pope's weaker and unentrenched army constituted the obvious Confederate objective, warned Pope to be cautious and not to advance until McClellan's army was at hand. Halleck's anxiety increased because he knew Pope from the Corinth campaign and was keenly aware of his limited capacities as a field commander.

Lee analyzed the situation very much as Halleck did but, in addition, saw that Pope's army threatened the Virginia Central Railroad, the Confederate line of communication with the Shenandoah Valley and important for strategic and logistical reasons. Still fearful of being forced back to Richmond and into the siege he dreaded, Lee felt concern for supplies that came from the area south of the Rappahannock. These considerations led Lee to exploit his interior lines again to concentrate quickly against Pope, while McClellan slowly carried out his evacuation of the Peninsula. After a preliminary engagement, Lee brought virtually his entire army north into a position before Pope.

Lee's strategy, like that planned for the Seven Days' Battles, called for Jackson to execute a turning movement to threaten the enemy's communications, thus forcing a withdrawal. But this time Lee wished to avoid battle, relying on the menace to Pope's communications to force that general back to the vicinity of Washington, thus liberating northern Virginia without a fight. In late August Lee directed Jackson, with half of his army, to march around Pope's western flank while Longstreet, with the other half, fixed Pope's attention on his front. Even though Lee intended Longstreet to follow Jackson's corps promptly once it had passed Pope's flank, Lee necessarily planned to divide his army.

Clausewitz would have seen "hazard" in such a move and would not feel that it was justified without significant numerical superiority unless the enemy had exhibited a "loss of impetus," such as McClellan had done on the Peninsula. Jomini would have agreed in disparaging such a division of forces, but undoubtedly would have put his finger on part of Lee's inspiration, for he believed that what might be "hazardous in the presence of Frederick, Napoleon, or Wellington might have entire success against a general of limited capacity." Lee counted not only on Pope's limited capacity but also on Jackson's generalship and on the tactical power of the defense, recently exhibited so clearly in the Seven Days' Battles.[10]

Clausewitz explained the hazard involved in splitting Lee's forces: the "danger lies in that division itself, for the enemy has the benefit of his internal lines and can thus bring superior numbers against any individual part of his opponent's force." And Pope tried to do just that, falling back and concentrating against Jackson. But Jackson moved his army into a strong position and, though he did not entrench, arrayed his men behind a railroad embankment. Pope's frontal attack at the end of August had little chance of success against Jackson's ably led veteran corps.[11]

While Jackson successfully fought the defensive battle in his advantageous position, Lee approached with Longstreet's corps. Unwilling to risk an attack, Lee sought to relieve the pressure on Jackson by a new turning movement, this time using Longstreet's corps. A grand flanking assault resulted when Lee realized that Pope, unaware of Longstreet's presence, was continuing to attack Jackson. Lee then hurled Longstreet's men into the fray but, even though he had half of his army virtually at right angles to Pope's, Lee failed to destroy the enemy force. The maneuverability and defensive power of Pope's troops enabled him promptly to redeploy, cover his exposed flank, and withdraw in the night.

Unlike McClellan, Lee was naturally combative and, though wishing only to force Pope back, remained ever alert to any opportunity again to attack him advantageously. The originally unintended battle itself contributed to the success of the campaign because Lee's casualties amounted to a little over nine thousand against sixteen thousand sustained by Pope. Since the Confederates had about forty-eight thousand men and the Union seventy-two thousand, Pope suffered losses proportionately, as well as absolutely, higher than Lee's. Compared to total manpower resources, however, the attrition balance stood slightly against the Confederates.

The demoralized Pope fell back to Washington's defenses. But, again, the lack of favorable conditions did not permit a destructive pursuit. The battle added a great deal to the prestige of Lee and precipitated the reassignment of Pope to the command at St. Paul, Minnesota, where, though he would have to cope with Sioux Indians, he would be far from any Confederates.

Lee, on the other hand, confidently and immediately sought to repeat his triumphant maneuver by again passing west of the main Federal army in early September. He could then cross the Potomac River, advance into the slave state of Maryland, and break the Baltimore and Ohio Railroad, one of the Union bases, threatening vital Federal interests and compelling the Army of the Potomac to fall back over that river to conform to his movement.

In this advance Lee relied on his Shenandoah Valley base, planning a line of wagon transportation from Winchester, Virginia, through Harpers Ferry into Maryland. He intended, of course, to support his army primarily by living on the Maryland agricultural region during the harvest season while his quartermasters and commissaries gathered the crops in Virginia which would feed his army during the following winter. With such key items as ammunition, salt, and coffee brought by wagon, he could remain in Maryland through most of the fall. But eventually, having exhausted the resources of the region, he would have to return to Virginia and reestablish contact with rail communications for the winter. Clausewitz believed that such an operation could provide "protection for one's own territory" as well as "yield food-supplies." Such pieces of territory "are usually held temporarily, for the duration of the campaign, to be abandoned in the winter." Like Lee, he foresaw that this kind of occupation could "be achieved without major engagements."[12]

The confident Lee thought the movement especially promising. Confessing that his army lacked adequate preparation for such an advance, he nevertheless thought the opportunity too good to lose. The movement west and even farther north would not endanger Richmond, for the Union army would be busy coping with Lee's forces. Lee had such zeal for his plans that he took the unusual step of moving without Davis's clear permission, informing the Confederate president, "I shall proceed to make the movement at once, unless you should signify your disapprobation."[13]

Established in Maryland, Lee would occupy a flank position, threatening the flank and rear of any Union advance toward Richmond. "By crossing east of the Blue Ridge," Lee informed Davis, "both Washington and Baltimore would be threatened, which I believed would insure the withdrawal of the mass of the enemy's troops north of the Potomac." Even if forced back into Virginia, Lee intended to occupy a location that would either place him on the flank of the Union army if it moved on Richmond or give him a favorable situation with good communications to Richmond in case the Union Army of the Potomac should attack him. In this way he could protect Virginia and spend the fall in a place from which he could be driven only by a frontal assault. In expecting to remain so long unmolested north of the Potomac, Lee apparently counted on the reluctance of Union generals to make a frontal attack.[14]

Like other Confederate leaders, Lee saw political advantages in this favorable logistical and strategic position, and they had played a part in his calculations. With his army in Maryland during the Union's fall congressional elections, he believed northern peace candidates would benefit from the resulting impression that the North could not subdue the South, thus undermining the will of the North to continue the war. Successes by Bragg and Kirby Smith in Kentucky would multiply the effect; if they failed, Lee reminded Davis, Bragg's forces could be "advantageously employed" in Virginia.[15]

On September 2, Lincoln, apprehensive over Lee's victory at Second Manassas, so close to Washington, gave McClellan the task of coping with Lee's new movement. Still immensely popular with the army, Little Mac soon absorbed Pope's short-lived Army of Virginia into his own Army of the Potomac and began to conform his movements to those of Lee. In addition to McClellan's army, the North had a twelve-thousand-man garrison at Harpers Ferry, at the head of the Shenandoah Valley, which had provided an important link in the cordon protecting Maryland and the Baltimore and Ohio Railroad.

Owing to rugged terrain, which made Harpers Ferry a potentially strong position, Lee could not easily follow what Clausewitz would have recommended—"by-pass the strong position and pursue his own designs"—because the garrison posed a threat to his rear and the position presented an obstacle to communication with Maryland. Lee therefore decided to leave half of his army to attempt the capture of Harpers Ferry while he remained in Maryland with the other half. This plan seriously divided his forces, but Lee did not have much anxiety because he knew McClellan had resumed command and was counting on that general's usual caution and excessive deliberation of movement.[16]

Having luckily captured some of Lee's orders, however, which revealed Confederate plans, McClellan moved his eighty thousand men with unaccustomed speed. At first Lee had decided to withdraw across the Potomac because his dispersed army was unready for battle. When he learned, however, that Jackson had overcome an inept defense and had captured Harpers Ferry and its garrison, Lee decided instead to concentrate and fight. McClellan thought surely he could beat "Bobby Lee," knowing his intentions, even though Lee enjoyed the tactical defensive. Thus the Union attacked all day on September 17, 1862, in a series of five successive assaults along Antietam Creek on the north side of the Potomac. Lee had not entrenched before the battle for he did not subscribe to Dennis Hart Mahan's doctrine of field fortification.

The result was bloody. One of McClellan's corps commanders reported that "every stalk of corn in the northern and greater part of the field was cut as closely as with a knife, and the slain lay in rows precisely as they had stood in their ranks a few minutes before. It was never my fortune to witness a more bloody, dismal battlefield." It contained so many bodies that, in one veteran's recollection, a man could have walked through it without stepping on the ground.[17]

Without a particularly strong position, Lee's seriously outnumbered and hastily concentrated army of 45,000 beat back McClellan's attacks with difficulty and, though on the defensive, suffered slightly heavier casualties, 13,700 to 12,500. But if the 12,000 Federal prisoners captured at Harpers Ferry are also counted, the total losses in the campaign were about proportional to the strengths of each side. In a precarious position, with his immobile army unable either to supply itself by foraging or to obtain supplies by rail, Lee climaxed what was essentially a raid by withdrawing into Virginia. Though Lee had been tactically successful in resisting McClellan's attacks at Antietam, the retreat, foreordained yet premature, proved that the Union had won the battle; thus the benefits in political and public morale redounded to the North.

General Lee had announced to the people of Maryland that he came to enable them to overthrow a "foreign yoke," but he had admitted to Jefferson Davis that he did not "anticipate any general rising of the people in our behalf," although he hoped to gather a few recruits and some subsistence. Nevertheless, Lee had used the opportunity to play the politician, proclaiming to Marylanders as Davis had commanded. He also advised Davis that the time was right to recommend to the United States government that it acknowledge the independence of the Confederacy. Lee thought that, coming at a time of advantage, and before battle, the North could not construe the suggestion as a confession of weakness; Union rejection would prove that it, not the Confederacy, was responsible for continued war. In that event, "the proposal of peace would enable the people of the United States to determine at their coming elections whether they will support those who favor a prolongation of the war, or those who wish to bring it to a termination."[18]

Instead of damaging Union morale by a Confederate victory, Lee instead withdrew and provided the Union with its first major eastern victory in which the rebels had retreated. Instead of using the military situation as an excuse for the Confederacy to call for peace, Lee's withdrawal had provided Lincoln with the springboard for his preliminary Emancipation Proclamation, issued September 22, 1862, and seriously dampened any Confederate prospects for diplomatic recognition by European powers. Although the war now completely changed character, Lee had accomplished his strategic aim and part of his logistical objective by halting his withdrawal immediately south of the Potomac. Here he subsisted his army far from central Virginia and still threatened the flank and rear of any Union advances south from Washington.

IN THE West, meanwhile, the military situation had changed dramatically in July 1862 as soon as Lincoln had called Halleck to Washington to become general in chief. Since Halleck avoided appointing a new western commander in his place, the Union organization reverted to two separate commands, Grant's and Buell's. Halleck controlled these armies from Washington and continued to press Buell for a more vigorous advance eastward along the Memphis and Charleston Railroad. Buell had made substantial progress, though he had had to abandon the repair of the railroad from Memphis and now drew his supplies from Nashville and Louisville along the railroad running south to Decatur, Alabama.

But instead of pushing forward rapidly as Halleck desired, Buell stopped. Already harassed by guerrillas, he halted in August, when cavalry raiders interrupted his communications in the first major application of what became a fundamental and most effective Confederate defensive strategy. Adequately supplemented by the activities of guerrillas, cavalry broke the fragile rail lines in Buell's rear, burning bridges and trestles and tearing up track. Without rail communication and out of reach of the river steamers, Buell refused to advance farther in such sparsely settled country with only primitive roads for supply.

Winfield Scott had believed cavalry to be obsolescent because its battlefield charges had lost most of their value, and hence he had resisted raising much cavalry for the Union armies. Jefferson Davis, on the other hand, had served in the dragoons on the frontier, and some of his senior generals had served in the cavalry; accordingly, these Confederate leaders favored mounted forces. Their cavalry soon equaled the Union's in numbers and exceeded it in effectiveness as it developed a major role in raiding Union communications.[19]

Under the leadership of such renowned officers as Turner Ashby, Wade Hampton, John Morgan, Joseph O. Shelby, J. E. B. Stuart, Earl Van Dorn, and Joseph Wheeler, Confederate horsemen earned the respect of their enemy. Sherman wrote that southerners "are splendid riders, first-rate shots, and utterly reckless. . . . They are the best cavalry in the world." This respect, however, did not reach a responsive chord with the Confederate infantry. As Bell Wiley wrote, "Whenever a cavalry unit rode by a group of infantrymen, the latter would almost invariably turn loose a flood of invective and derision." One footsore veteran supposedly said that the mounted service steered so clear of dangerous combat as practically to constitute a life insurance company. And another one remarked that the cavalry "never will fight. I think it is useless to have them in the Army eating rations." But these commentators failed to grasp the paralyzing effect their cavalry had on Union movements when working in conjunction with guerrillas to break Union rail communications.[20]

Although Jomini failed to grasp the ineffectiveness of cavalry on the battlefield, he well understood its role in raiding enemy communications. Also pointing out that militia made "excellent partisan soldiers" for raiding operations, he realized that "it is certain that a numerous cavalry, whether regular or irregular, must have a great influence in giving a turn to the events of a war. It may excite a feeling of apprehension at distant parts of the enemy's country, it can carry off his convoys, it can encircle his army, make his communications very perilous, and destroy the *ensemble* of his operations. In other words it produces nearly the same result as a rising *en masse* of a population, causing trouble on the front, flanks, and rear of an army and reducing a general to a state of entire uncertainty in his calculations." Two cavalry raids on his vulnerable rail communications had indeed reduced General Buell to a "state of entire uncertainty," just as Jomini would have anticipated. Although Clausewitz did not stress the cavalry's role, he, too, would have realized the significance of raids on communications, the enemy's vulnerability to them, and their effectiveness in "cooperation with disaffected subjects," who, of course, abounded in Buell's rear.[21]

Raids led by the brilliant Nathan Bedford Forrest and the daring John Hunt Morgan had broken Buell's communications. But another factor had helped stop Buell, one which Jomini would have understood and which boded ill for the Union cause. Jomini would have called the Civil War a "national war," which he defined as war "waged against a united people, or a great majority of them, filled with a noble ardor and determined to sustain their independence: then every step is disputed" by guerrillas, "the army holds only its campground, its supplies can only be obtained at the point of a sword, and its convoys are everywhere threatened." The large forces necessarily diverted to protect communications, supplies, and personnel menaced by guerrillas made Jomini very pessimistic. "Under these circumstances" the decisive campaigns of "a war of invasion become very difficult, if not impossible." The tasks to attain victory increased for not only must the invaders destroy the defending armies, but "the country should be occupied and subjugated."[22]

Clausewitz agreed with Jomini about the difficulties of winning a national war, and he also saw that guerrillas needed the support of regulars, which Forrest's and Morgan's raiders provided. He listed other conditions important for guerrilla success:

1. The war must be fought in the interior of the country.
2. It must not be decided by a single stroke.
3. The theatre of operations must be fairly large.
4. The national character must be suited to that type of war.
5. The country must be rough and inaccessible, because of mountains, or forests, marshes, or the local methods of cultivation.

The South possessed all of these characteristics for successful guerrilla warfare as well as men "used to hard, strenuous work," if not privation; these factors would be partially neutralized in the Civil War by a feeling that was less than national. Indeed, in some areas of the Confederacy, such as western Virginia, western North Carolina, and especially eastern Tennessee, the "national" feeling of the inhabitants was for the Union, and it was the Confederacy that was embarrassed by disruptive guerrilla operations. Clausewitz did not consider population density a factor in such warfare; a "scattered distribution of houses and farms" rather than a population concentrated in villages helped the national resistance, as did poor roads and a "disproportion between the invading army and the size of the country." Thus Clausewitz's assessment was as essentially pessimistic as Jomini's.[23]

Both raiders and a national resistance by guerrillas played a part in what would have posed a serious problem in any case. Jomini had stressed that "deep lines of operations . . . are always dangerous in a hostile country," a situation aggravated by the need of Union quartermasters and commissaries to bring large quantities of supplies from the rear, it being "quite impossible" to subsist an army in a country as sparsely populated as the South. Clausewitz emphatically agreed, almost exactly describing Buell's difficult situation "at the end of a victorious campaign," which had conquered West and Middle Tennessee, "when lines of communication have begun to be overstretched. This is especially true when war is conducted in an impoverished, thinly populated and possibly hostile country. . . . Often the finest victory has been robbed of its glory as a consequence of this problem."[24]

Actually Clausewitz realized that a force-to-space ratio like that in the Civil War meant that raiders could be effective in any case, even against communications at a right angle to the front. Civil War conditions fully met his other criteria for vulnerability—long communications exposed for a long time in hostile territory.[25]

Jomini briefly referred to the means of protecting communications threatened by raiders and guerrillas. He believed there should be depots in towns fifteen to thirty miles apart, except "where the population is hostile" when "they are most necessary and should be most numerous." He prescribed small garrisons for these depots and "movable detachments passing continually between the army and the base." This method envisioned guarded convoys of wagons moving from depot to depot. Railways presented somewhat different problems because the numerous flammable wooden bridges and trestles required special protection. But the Union adopted the substance of Jomini's plan of protection and therefore required significant forces to protect the long railway lines supplying Buell's motionless army.[26]

The Confederates meanwhile did not realize how successful their guerrillas and cavalry had been in completely halting the main Union offensive in the West. Therefore, they planned a counteroffensive with their principal western army. With the advice of Beauregard, whom he had replaced, General Braxton Bragg, the capable but very abrasive new Confederate commander, undertook in July 1862 to use the railroad to counter Buell's already almost-neutralized menace to Chattanooga. Bragg planned to do this by carrying out a strategic turning movement on a vast scale to threaten Buell's communications. This offensive with half of his Mississippi army, also embodying the concept of the concentration of dispersed forces against a weak line, employed, of necessity, the circuitous railway route from northern Mississippi south to Mobile, north to Atlanta, and thence farther north again to Chattanooga. Bragg, with his excellent management providing supplies along the route, expedited the transfer by ordering the garrison at Mobile to move immediately to Chattanooga, to be replaced by the last troops to leave northern Mississippi. In this way he established a "pipeline" for moving men from Mississippi to Tennessee.

In Tennessee, Bragg's forces, over half of his original army in Mississippi, joined those of Major General Edmund Kirby Smith's Department of East Tennessee for a march into Kentucky. Moving rapidly, unexpectedly, and in coordination with Kirby Smith's march upon Lexington, Kentucky, Bragg planned to threaten Buell's supply, the railroad to Louisville, and force his retirement. This operation would be a strategic turning movement of the kind Jomini admired, for Bragg might gain a position athwart Union communications, where he could force Buell to attack him. But Bragg did not initially intend this outcome. Instead he began his advance without any precise strategic plans.

NEVERTHELESS, EXPECTATIONS for the western campaigns of Bragg and Kirby Smith matched the hopes for Lee's simultaneous march into Maryland, and all had the same goals. Bragg, for example, believed that Middle Tennessee and Kentucky were ripe for the picking, because, as he wrote, the inhabitants "have found that neutrality has afforded them no protection" and they "have become intensely hostile to the enemy." With "arms and support" the populace would surely rally to the Confederate standard, for "the country is aroused and expecting us." For his part, Kirby Smith believed that "politically, now is the time to strike at Kentucky," and he proclaimed "a general amnesty for all past offenses" to East Tennesseans in the Union army—a step he would not have taken unless he had some hope that the region eagerly awaited the Confederate embrace. Like Lee, however, Kirby Smith placed considerable emphasis upon logistics. Finding himself in southeastern Kentucky and short of necessities, he felt that he had best advance on Lexington and take what he needed in the fertile Blue Grass region. He also hoped to raise additional recruits and wished to divert the attention of Buell from Bragg's movements; nevertheless, he would be content with solving his supply problem.[27]

Of course, politics could not be far from anyone's mind, regardless of the supply situation. The Kentucky delegation to the Confederate Congress urged upon Bragg and Davis the need to advance so as to secure the services of the "large proportion of the young men [who] will at once join our army," a question they examined in the light of its "political aspects" of an overthrow of Union government in the state. Although Kirby Smith became somewhat doubtful on this point when he discovered that southeastern Kentucky still felt hostility toward the Confederacy, he harbored greater hopes for the interior. After turning the Union position at Cumberland Gap in August 1862 while Lee fought the Second Battle of Manassas in Virginia, Kirby Smith entered Kentucky and, at Richmond, surprised and captured a large party of Union recruits. By the beginning of September he had occupied Lexington and the rich Blue Grass region.[28]

In a separate advance Bragg moved north on a route parallel to Kirby Smith's but west of him and close to Buell's army, which used the Louisville and Nashville Railway for its communications. "Kentuckians," proclaimed Bragg on September 14, 1862, "I have entered your state with the Confederate Army of the West, and offer you an opportunity to free yourselves from the tyranny of a despotic ruler." Thinking that they were responding positively, he appealed to Richmond for arms for the men who were "flocking" to the Confederate standard.[29]

Though concerned about Kirby Smith, Buell focused his attention on Bragg, whose route of march clearly aimed at his rear. But Buell did not hurry his entire army north to protect his communications because he feared that, if he did, Bragg might suddenly turn west, capture Nashville, and so reconquer Middle Tennessee. Buell's deliberately slow withdrawal enabled Bragg to reach Buell's rear and place his army on the Louisville and Nashville Railway. But Buell did not intend to try to recover his communications by attacking Bragg. Instead he waited, well supplied at the depots along his railroad. Bragg, on the other hand, had to live off the country, where he found but scant food for his men and animals.

Unlike Lee in Virginia, Bragg had no two-sided base, and he lacked enough wagons to draw supplies from a distance. So Buell easily outwaited the overconfident Bragg, who very quickly had to march northeast to join Kirby Smith in the Blue Grass, leaving open Buell's route of retreat to Louisville. The entire campaign was shaping up as a Confederate fiasco. As long as the Union controlled Nashville and the railroad back to Louisville, the Confederates in Kentucky remained mere raiders, who, like Lee in Maryland, would have to withdraw before winter, if not sooner expelled by Union military action.

Nor did the campaign augment Confederate manpower. Men did not rally to the rebel flag. Quite the reverse. In mid-September one of Bragg's subordinates noted that when Bragg issued conscription orders the countryside was thrown into a "feverish state" and thousands of men fled to the mountains or to Union lines. Kirby Smith also noted the reluctance of Kentuckians to be liberated. He had arms to issue but garnered few men to receive them and concluded that "their hearts are evidently with us, but their blue-grass and fat-grass are against us." Bragg himself soon realized the futility of his proclamation and his hopes, admitting that now he too had arms but no takers and complaining that new recruits did not equal half his losses. "Unless a change occurs soon," he told Richmond, "we must abandon the garden spot of Kentucky to its cupidity." In language less colorful but of the same import as Kirby Smith's, Bragg told Adjutant General Samuel Cooper that "the love of ease and fear of pecuniary loss are the fruitful sources of this evil." "Enthusiasm is unbounded," he wrote a week later, "but recruiting at a discount; even the women are giving reasons why individuals cannot go."[30]

Although the strategic turning movement by Bragg and Kirby Smith had not forced the enemy to fight at a disadvantage, nor gained much, it had succeeded magnificently in relieving the apparent threat to Chattanooga, and it had turned Buell all the way back to Louisville. The Confederates spread their forces out in Central Kentucky, temporarily supplying them sufficiently. This achievement was short-lived, however, for Buell immediately moved out of Louisville with a strongly reinforced army, and Bragg, after an inconclusive battle at Perryville, October 8–9, 1862, withdrew from Kentucky via Kirby Smith's route and ultimately based himself at Murfreesboro, Tennessee, on the railroad south of Nashville. Here the Union army, based on the same railroad running southeast from Nashville, stymied him.

Meanwhile, Confederate forces from Mississippi sought to advance into Tennessee in an effort to follow Bragg's instructions to aid his campaign by a move on Nashville. But they met Grant's army, which Halleck had left standing on the defensive in northern Mississippi. In the first engagement, at Iuka, Grant tried a maneuver much like Lee's in the Second Manassas campaign. Though he failed to reach the Confederate rear, he did send the rebels scurrying southward. In their second attempt the Confederates reached the rear of Corinth, held in force by Grant's subordinate, the excitable but determined William S. Rosecrans, "Old Rosey" to his admiring soldiers. Ironically, their attack on Corinth's rear brought them against what had been the Confederate front when Beauregard had resisted Halleck the previous spring. Rosecrans effectively used Beauregard's old entrenchments and beat off the Confederate assaults, inflicting serious losses.

After this second defeat, the Confederates withdrew, but Grant did not press southward. As with Buell after Perryville and McClellan after Antietam, Grant found that the lack of supplies in the country to be traversed precluded a prompt follow-up of a victory. The significance of the fall battles was limited to the retreat of the defeated, the attrition resulting from the conflicts, and the political effects of the engagements. The military situation remained essentially in a stalemate.

JOMINI HAD foreseen this indecisive outcome. He did have some faith in the frontal assault, especially if the attacker was strong enough to combine it with a tactical turning movement, but the outcome of frontal battles, relying on "main force," would depend, he thought, on the "relative numerical superiority, the morale of the two armies, and other circumstances with reference to which no fixed rule can be given." But victories in such battles would be "indecisive" if "*attacks were made in front*" and the victor did not pursue the defeated. Buell's fight at Perryville, like McClellan's at Antietam, had relied on essentially frontal attacks. Grant's forces had been on the defensive against frontal assaults at Corinth. So, as Jomini had foreseen, frontal attacks without pursuit yielded little but attrition and the retreat of the enemy.[31]

Clausewitz, who gave greater emphasis than Jomini to the importance of battles, believed that the "degree of a victory" depended upon whether it turned the enemy, whether "rough or hilly country" diminished the impact of the victor's numerical superiority, and whether the victor possessed more or better cavalry. At least two of these inhibitors characterized most Civil War victories because rolling and forested terrain predominated on southern battlefields and tactical turning movements usually failed. Clausewitz did believe, however, that a "significant superiority in numbers . . . will suffice to assure victory however adverse the other circumstances." But because the Union forces rarely enjoyed as much as a two-to-one numerical preponderance, few battles met Clausewitz's criteria for decisiveness, and fewer battles had much impact beyond attrition.[32]

Without pursuit, thought Clausewitz, "no victory will be effective," the "importance of the victory" depending on the "vigor of the immediate pursuit." But he believed that superiority in cavalry was essential to the pursuit and, without it, "the effects of the pursuit are lost, and with them some important results of the victory." The introduction of the rifle after Clausewitz's death deprived cavalry of even more of its combat effectiveness against infantry, diminishing the significance of having stronger cavalry. More important, almost until 1865, the Federal forces lacked predominance in cavalry.[33]

Thus the Union enjoyed the numerical superiority in infantry which, if adequately concentrated, would suffice to assure success but lacked supremacy in cavalry to exploit defeat of the enemy even if the rifle had not nullified much of the potential of cavalry in pursuit. Thus clearly

Clausewitz forecast that Civil War battles would have no more than the very limited significance they did in fact have. Lacking ability to win total victory in battle or to conduct an effective pursuit, Union forces had to occupy the enemy's territory. This meant they had to contend with the nearly insurmountable problems of operating over long lines of communication in a thinly populated but hostile and huge country as they conducted a national war without decisive numerical superiority against adequately armed and competently led Confederate armies. Great victories or the capture of enemy armies therefore continued to be improbable unless, as at Fort Donelson, the enemy made serious mistakes.

Just as their difficulties matched Clausewitz's perceptions, so too Union plans closely followed his prescriptions. To seek a decision against the enemy, Clausewitz suggested an advance "with the utmost speed" to destroy the enemy's main forces with as few decisive battles as possible. Lacking sufficient numerical preponderance or an adequate ratio of force to the Confederacy's large area, the Union, though aiming at Confederate centers of gravity, had to follow his proposal for pursuing less ambitious objectives. Although most campaigns were limited, thought Clausewitz, in truth they fell "between the two poles." For such restricted campaigns Clausewitz recommended conquering territory, supply depots, and fortresses, which the invader could secure without battles. There might be battles, too, victories "for the sake of trophies, or possibly simply of honor," which would raise the army's prestige. The Union public, seeing war in terms of decisive battles like Yorktown and Waterloo, demanded just such engagements, and a victory in such a contest would, Clausewitz foresaw, "lend a semblance of superiority. It satisfied the vanity of the general, the court, the army, and the people, and thereby in some measure the expectations that are always pinned on an offensive."[34]

Lincoln, understanding the military realities as seen by the generals but also comprehending the public's yearning for dramatic results, found himself caught between the two. He appreciated the favorable impact on public opinion of the victories of September and October 1862, coming, as they did, on the heels of menacing Confederate raids into Kentucky and Maryland.

IN BOTH East and West, therefore, the Confederacy's grand designs of the August to October 1862 campaigns failed, except for the temporary gain of subsisting in enemy territory. The Federal elections of 1862 were a setback to the Republican party, but not decisively so; for example, Ohio and Indiana gave only slim majorities to Democrats, and, though the Democratic margin of victory was greater in Illinois, it became clear that the Northwest had no idea of detaching itself from the Union. The inauguration of a new Confederate governor in Kentucky, who was immediately forced to flee, hardly constituted adequate political compensation for all that trouble.

In the long run, therefore, the political benefits of these campaigns redounded to the Union. The check at Antietam caused British statesmen to pause and then delay indefinitely possible recognition of Confederate independence. Most important, Lincoln's issuance of the preliminary Emancipation Proclamation changed the character of the war. Conversely, it upset many Unionists, especially in the border states, and encouraged some Confederates to fight with more determination than before. Even the staunch East Tennessee Unionist T. A. R. Nelson announced that whereas he had opposed dissolution of the Union because the resulting war could lead to the overthrow of slavery and because secession was unconstitutional, now, exercising the right of revolution, he supported the Confederacy because of the "atrocity and barbarism" of the Emancipation Proclamation. He noted that "the race is not always to the swift nor the battle to the strong . . . it cannot in the nature of things be possible that a just God will prosper the efforts of a man or a Government which has hypocritically pretended to wage war in behalf of the Constitution but now throws off the mask and sets it utterly at defiance."[35]

The proclamation, however, actually stood the war on its head. The Confederates no longer appeared before the world, and themselves, as champions of national self-determination; instead, they were forced to assume the character of suppressors of individual self-determination. Southerners now appeared to the Western world as quintessentially espousing an institution that most of the rest of Western civilization had come to despise and had renounced. They were on the moral defensive; the guilt over slavery and war which some had felt in 1861 now afflicted more southern consciences than before and forced profound reexamination of southern war goals, with consequences that became apparent toward the end of the war.

For the time being, in October 1862, Confederates could only be sure that they had not met the main political purpose behind their invasions of Kentucky and Maryland. They had not detached the Northwest from the Union, the Federal elections of 1862 had not brought victory to an antiwar faction, and neither the border states nor many of their citizens had taken the opportunity to enlist under the stars and bars. This latter point had great importance, in the West at least. Jefferson Davis contended after the event that only "the expectation that the Kentuckians would rise en masse with the coming of a force which enabled them to do so . . . justified an advance into that State. . . . That expectation," he acknowledged, "has been sadly disappointed." In the future he would not likely authorize such expeditions. The experience had been disappointingly instructive to Confederate planners and generals, who had been full of confidence only two months before.[36]

When Bragg had entered Kentucky and issued his fruitless proclamation, he had told Kentuckians that if they preferred Federal rule, "show it by your frowns and we shall return whence we came." Kentuckians had frowned, no doubt induced both by the implied threat of Buell's army and by suspicion of Confederate staying power; and Bragg and Kirby Smith, equally prodded by Buell's reinforced army and the conflict at Perryville, returned from whence they had come. Kentucky remained safely within the Union for the remainder of the war.[37]

In the first year and a half of the conflict Union forces had aimed at many of the objectives Clausewitz prescribed, including "the occupation of important towns, fertile agricultural areas, or disaffected districts," such as East Tennessee, "which can be seduced into revolt," and of course Scott's plan and Union campaigns aimed to "disrupt communications." The Confederate forces also unconsciously followed Clausewitz's recommendations, adhering to his prescriptions for the defense, taking advantage of the obstacles presented by terrain, employing fortifications, and making the most of the support of the public in a national war. Initially, the inexperience of both armies aided the

Confederates, for, as Clausewitz noted, ill-trained troops were "better suited to the defense than to attack."[38]

Clausewitz had listed four alternatives for the defender: (1) deep retreat, (2) passive defense and "direct cover," (3) active defense, including counterattack, and (4) strategic turning movement. In the West, for example, Halleck's offensive had forced the Confederates to make a deep retreat into the interior of the country. But Clausewitz thought a deep retreat should be a last resort, and, of course, the Confederates agreed.[39]

Actually the Confederate use of the strategic turning movement as a means of defense fully vindicated Clausewitz's view. Lee, explicitly, and Bragg, as his strategy evolved, planned to use the turning movement to force the enemy back without conflict. As it worked out, both fought essentially defensive battles and returned to positions at least as far advanced as their starting points. Each campaign had enabled them to subsist briefly in the enemy's country, and each occupied the enemy throughout the excellent fall campaigning season. Threats to the communications of two Union armies had forced them back and protected Confederate territory for a campaigning season, major defensive accomplishments for the weaker Confederate forces.

Clausewitz's recommendation for resisting a campaign such as the Union's to occupy southern territory would have intended that the Confederates should "draw the utmost benefit from waiting." He would have advised that the defender "cover the country by spreading out forces" and "interpose his force quickly by means of flank marches wherever his extension is not wide enough." The Confederates followed this plan successfully in Virginia, and Sidney Johnston had attempted it with less success in the West. If the attacker pierced this defense, Clausewitz would have advised that "there would still be time for the defender to concentrate his forces." But Sidney Johnston did not concentrate adequately at Fort Donelson, for Grant and Halleck were not to be "stopped by a moderate sized but strong post" as vulnerable as that which Johnston established at Fort Donelson. Only at Shiloh did the Confederates concentrate in a futile effort to recover their lost defensive line.[40]

An alternative to this system of defense by "direct cover" was,

Clausewitz explained, "additional reliance on mobility, active defense, and even offensive measures," including "attacking the enemy in flank or threatening his rear." Lee and Bragg followed this style of defense with their strategic turning movements in September and October 1862. But earlier the Confederates had failed to honor Clausewitz's injunction to avoid "any unfavorable engagements." In spite of the surprise attained, the frontal attack at Shiloh does not fit Clausewitz nor does Joe Johnston's attack at Seven Pines or that at Corinth. Lee's effort to turn McClellan during the Seven Days' Battles was laudable in intent if bungled in execution, and, of course, the defensive battle of First Manassas turned out well. Beauregard's retreat before Halleck and Bragg's avoidance of battle in Kentucky, especially his withdrawal from the field at Perryville, met Clausewitz's warning to avoid battle; Lee's intent only to turn Pope back and his successful attrition at Second Manassas also conform to Clausewitz's model. The results at Antietam might have been better if Lee's orders to his troops had followed Clausewitz's injunction that "the art of intrenchment must come to their assistance." By the fall of 1862 the Confederates were more often trying to avoid battle or remain on the defensive and thus their strategy harmonized much more with Clausewitz's ideas.[41]

Even though he stressed the defensive and prescribed economical methods for its conduct, Clausewitz always looked to the offensive, and it animated all of his ideas. Confederate strategy followed these prescriptions, for the Confederates were, as Clausewitz would have desired, also "on the alert *for a chance to strike a favorable blow*" as "a necessary complement to the defense as a whole, to be used at times when the attacker takes things a little too easily and lays himself wide open at some points."[42]

Particularly in Middle Tennessee, the Confederates had followed Clausewitz's second offensive injunction, "action against the enemy's lines of communication." In both the East and the West the Confederates employed "raids and diversions into enemy territory." On a very large scale, both Bragg's Kentucky and Lee's Antietam campaigns constituted a diversion, "an attack on enemy territory that draws off the enemy's forces from the main objective." Both campaigns effectively diverted the Union, although the result was disappointing because of the apathetic response of Kentuckians and Marylanders to this Confederate attempt at "cooperation with disaffected subjects of the enemy." Thus the Confederates, like their adversaries, substantially adhered to the ideas of Clausewitz and Jomini for prosecuting defensive war under very favorable conditions, the attacker coping with long lines of communications, the huge spaces in relation to the forces available, and an inadequate numerical superiority to achieve a decisive victory.[43]

Confederate generals in the West came to rely on raids. This method of defense, one Clausewitz would have prescribed and Jomini would have regarded as virtually invincible, forced Union commanders to allocate a third, and more, of their forces to defending their communications. So it is hard to criticize either contestant for failing to wage the war according to the rules set down by the authorities.

But the successful exploitation of their advantages of geography and national resistance did not produce sufficient achievements to sustain Confederate morale and determination to fight on to victory, nor was skillful handling of Confederate troops successful enough to prevent the course of military events from sapping Confederate strength and testing Confederate will more than that of the Union. Although momentarily elated by the dramatic advances of Lee and Bragg, the Confederate public received no permanent lift from the early fall campaigns, for the Confederate people perceived as defeats the retreats that Clausewitz and Jomini could have foretold. Few grasped the strategic and logistic benefits of these raids—for that is all they amounted to, in the end—seeing them rather as failed invasions.

THE UNION army owed much to the navy. Halleck and Grant's victories at Fort Henry and Fort Donelson and subsequent advance far up the Tennessee River depended on the river for supplies and the navy for critical support, as did McClellan's Peninsula campaign; on the other hand, General Buell's advance in Tennessee, deprived of rivers for supply, succumbed to Confederate cavalry raids. Gunboats guarded the transports and even provided artillery support for Grant's army at Shiloh. Union warships contributed less, however, on the Atlantic and the Gulf, waters with which navies usually had more identification. The fleets did impede Confederate trade, but to do more, they needed the help of the army. But on the coasts the army did not give as much help as it might have, and the leaders of coastal operations rarely displayed either the vision or cooperation that had characterized operations on the inland waters.

So command of sea and rivers could not give the Union victory any more than could the army's preponderance on land. Despite northern military and naval superiority, therefore, Confederates by fall 1862 were still not convinced that time was against them. Most southerners agreed that their situation was difficult, and some thought desperate, but they agreed also that the question over which they fought was still an open one. Lincoln's Emancipation Proclamation, which had the eventual effect of increasing northern manpower because it logically led to the use of black soldiers, seriously concerned southerners. Many Confederates considered it an open invitation to the slaves to slay their masters, which it was not; others welcomed the proclamation, for they believed the threat of a new society that it contained would convince Confederates of the need for a more determined resistance, and, for a time, it probably did.

More significant, the proclamation opened the way for the use of black soldiers and more effective use of black labor. Further Union advances permitted and encouraged the disaffection of the black third of the Confederate population and allowed its employment in a military capacity. The flight of the slaves provided tangible military benefits to the Union, while depriving the Confederacy of much of its labor and sapping its morale and will. Had Lincoln issued the proclamation at any other occasion than a Union victory, it could have had no such effect, for it would have been seen as the last gasp of the expiring Union. By providing the Union with a victory just when Lincoln needed it, the Confederacy had allowed the slave issue legitimate partnership with the issue of Union. Thus, in the long run, the proclamation, linked with other factors, proved a detriment to the southern war effort and weakened the resolve of the people. The proclamation placed the South on the moral defensive before the opinion of the Western world and made it difficult to maintain that the intent of the war was merely to achieve independence for southerners when that meant slavery for blacks. Later on, when the outcome of the conflict grew exceedingly doubtful, the prospective new society would force Confederates to reconsider the alternatives to war and slavery and eventually to accept, if not to welcome, those other options.

Chapter Nine

The Union Navy
and Combined Operations

A S WE HAVE SEEN, land operations had important political consequences, but so did naval operations. Although these operations
were less important in the South's defeat than those on land, they did
produce potent indirect results. For example, the Union navy helped
to exacerbate internal dissension that often involved state-rights arguments. The navy enabled Federal troops to establish themselves
around the Confederate periphery, to stab into the interior to threaten
the railroad along the Atlantic coast, and to play a major role in bisect-
ing the country along the line of the Mississippi River. These gains
occurred while the Army of the Potomac and the Army of Northern
Virginia seesawed back and forth over the same scarred patch of Virginia between Richmond and Washington. Each time the navy assisted
the army in establishing an enclave, threatening a coastal railroad, or
cutting off a segment of the Confederacy, reverberations occurred in
Confederate politics. State governors were concerned about the defense of their states and thought the central government paid insufficient attention to local defense. The Federal navy had a direct negative
effect on the relations of individual states to the Confederate government.

CLAUSEWITZ HAD proclaimed that armies incapable of a decisive
campaign should attack important cities, agricultural areas that might
provide bountiful supply, and regions where they suspected the population might be unsympathetic to the governing authorities. He had
also foreseen that engaging in at least a few political battles could have
importance for prestige or morale. This view was logical, and, without
having read Clausewitz, Union army commanders directed their
troops against the Confederacy's fortresses, population centers,
breadbaskets, important depots, and areas of Union strength, such as

East Tennessee. Since many of the fortresses, population centers, and depots were located on or near the coast, close collaboration with the navy in combined operations became essential to Union success.

McClellan's campaign on the Peninsula had illustrated clearly the navy's potential, for the Baltimore and Ohio Railroad and the Chesapeake and Ohio Canal provided one base to the north and the navy in the Chesapeake Bay and adjacent rivers created another base to the east. Although cooperation usually left something to be desired, the combined operations against New Orleans, Fort Henry and Fort Donelson, and along the Mississippi River until the capitulations of Vicksburg and Port Hudson, also show the successful use of naval forces in conjunction with the Union army. But combined operations did not always bring success. Along the saltwater coasts cooperation was minimal; the army typically proved less than enthusiastic. The mixed results often culminated only with the capture of the objective not via combined operations but by the approach of massive Union forces from the rear, making the objective no longer strategically important, as at Savannah or Charleston.

If the coastal operations fell short of hopes harbored by some naval planners, it was not for lack of effort by the navy or absence of soundness in the concept of combined operations. Indeed, early in the war on the East Coast the idea proved itself tenable, although a skeptic might say that the Union owed those successes primarily to weakness of the Confederate effort. But even if that were true, it did not hold true on the western rivers, where combined operations prevailed against determined Confederate resistance.

NEW ORLEANS was the first important Confederate port to fall to Union combined operations. Flag Officer David G. Farragut's orders to command the West Gulf Blockading Squadron in January 1862 informed him that he should consider the opening of the Mississippi River and the seizing of New Orleans as his major objectives.

Farragut, sixty years of age when the Civil War broke out, had served in the navy forty-nine years. A native of Tennessee, he was the adopted son of Commodore David Porter. Perhaps the most capable naval officer on either side, Farragut based his superb tactics on an analysis of his shortcomings and those of his opponent. Lashing of weaker vessels to the sides of more powerful warships, as he did at both New Orleans and later at Mobile Bay, for example, was a brilliant innovation. He grasped the limitation of land fortifications in naval actions, and on the Mississippi River and Mobile Bay he used this tactical understanding successfully. He carefully prepared his thorough operational plans. Finally, he was extremely energetic and aggressive.

Plans called for combined operations to secure the opening of the lower Mississippi and the capture of New Orleans. The army commander, Major General Benjamin F. Butler, raised a ten-thousand-man force to cooperate with the navy in the Gulf of Mexico. Butler was a political general, that is, one who was appointed because of his influence and connection. Halleck remarked that "it seems but little better than murder to give important commands to such men as . . . Butler"; and a Confederate general referred to him as "a harmless menace." Nevertheless, Butler would survive a number of military embarrassments only to serve in Congress, run for president, and hold an appointment in the administration of President Grant.[1]

Early in April Farragut's squadron of seventeen vessels entered the mouth of the Mississippi River. On April 19, Union mortar boats opened a heavy bombardment upon Fort Jackson and Fort St. Philip, located some seventy miles below the Crescent City. Five days later the warships passed the forts and, after defeating a small Confederate river flotilla, reached New Orleans. The city surrendered without resistance. In the meantime Butler's troops, supported by the mortar boats, forced the forts' surrender and finally reached the already occupied city on May 1. The fall of the largest port in the Confederacy was a severe blow, not only to its economic well-being but to the morale of the people at large. It was the first major urban center captured by Union forces, and it fell with insignificant opposition.

ALTHOUGH FARRAGUT next wished to attack Mobile, Alabama, which ranked second to New Orleans in importance as a Gulf port, the Navy Department decided to delay that operation until the Union had secured and established control along the Mississippi River as far upstream as Vicksburg. Early in May 1862 Farragut sent seven of his vessels up the river and followed shortly afterward in his flagship, the *Hartford*. Eighteen hundred troops under Brigadier General Thomas Williams accompanied his warships.

Farragut's vessels ascended the river without opposition, forcing

the capitulation of small river ports along the way. The initial attempt
to take Vicksburg, however, failed, largely because the naval commander badly underestimated the number of troops needed to seize
the town. In late May the combined force retired downriver, Williams
and his men remaining in Baton Rouge while Farragut went all the
way to New Orleans. But in June 1862, under orders from Washington, Farragut returned to Vicksburg. With the support of mortar
boats and General Williams's troops, reinforced to thirty-two hundred
men, he unsuccessfully attempted to pressure the port into surrendering. Aware by now that a winning assault on Vicksburg would require
considerably more troops than were available, Farragut prudently
sought additional reinforcements.

On June 29 Flag Officer Charles H. Davis, in command of the Mississippi River Flotilla, received a message from Farragut requesting his
assistance. The flotilla was at Memphis, which it had forced to surrender early in the month. The capture of Memphis had culminated
five months of impressive operations by the Mississippi River Flotilla,
which had started in February with the combined assaults on Fort
Henry and Fort Donelson.

During the following hundred days, Union forces using the Tennessee and Mississippi rivers as highways penetrated deep into the
Confederate midland. As Union troops and gunboats moved along the
Tennessee toward Corinth, combined forces also descended the Mississippi. While Union forces fought at Shiloh, Island Number 10, located where the Kentucky-Tennessee state line struck the river opposite Missouri, surrendered to Union military and naval units. On
April 13, Flag Officer Foote's gunboats arrived above Fort Pillow, and
for more than a month the Union warships and troops under Major
General John Pope attempted to capture it.

On May 9 a festering wound forced Foote to relinquish his command,
and the able Captain Charles Henry Davis replaced him. A New Eng-
lander and a Harvard graduate, Davis was a quiet and deliberate naval
officer who had a reputation for being something of an intellectual.
Despite suffering a defeat at the hands of a small Confederate river
flotilla the day after taking over from Foote, Davis used his vessels
effectively not only against Fort Pillow but later to assail Fort Randolph. By early June Davis's ships approached Memphis and captured

that city on June 6 after his vessels had defeated the Confederate River Defense Flotilla. From there the gunboats proceeded down the river to join the oceangoing warships of Farragut's squadron.

Farragut had hoped not only to acquire the support of Davis's gunboats but additional army units as well. But these were not forthcoming, and other troubles also came in mid-July. The river was falling, malaria afflicted and weakened General Williams's force, and an embarrassing incident occurred when the Confederate ironclad *Arkansas* ran through the combined naval force anchored above Vicksburg. Farragut thus decided to abandon his effort to take the city. Leaving gunboats to support Williams's soldiers in Baton Rouge, Farragut, promoted to rear admiral after his victory at New Orleans, returned to the Crescent City.

Poor cooperation between the army and navy and gross underestimation of the number of troops needed to secure Vicksburg caused the failure of this and several other expeditions sent to capture that key city. Accordingly, Vicksburg remained in Confederate hands a year longer than it might have. Nevertheless, by late summer of 1862 Union naval forces effectively controlled most of the Mississippi as well as many of its tributaries. The absence of Confederate naval opposition contributed to this result. With the destruction of the *Arkansas* in August 1862 the Union removed the last serious threat by a Confederate warship in the West. Although the southerners completed another ironclad, the *Missouri*, at Shreveport on the Red River and converted a few river steamers to gunboats, none of them ever posed much of a threat and the Union retained control of the western rivers.

WITHOUT AN adequate naval force to challenge the Union naval activities, the Confederates could resort only to guerrillas. The partisans frequently fired upon various vessels, but they rarely stopped any, except when they could bring artillery into play. Confederate guerrillas gained some success on the narrow streams flowing into the Mississippi, but the only notable achievements occurred near Johnsonville on the Tennessee River and on the White River in Arkansas. In the fall of 1864 near Johnsonville several batteries of artillery under the command of Major General Nathan B. Forrest destroyed four gunboats and damaged a fifth. In June of that year on the White River a small Confederate force ambushed and captured the steamer *Queen City*.[2]

Confederate guerrilla activities, however, did not seriously endanger Union control of the rivers. During most of 1863 and 1864, for example, some six or eight light-draft "tinclad" steamboats provided adequate protection for the scores of transport vessels that steamed securely in convoys up and down the Tennessee and Cumberland rivers. From January 1863 until the river became too low for navigation in June, the navy convoyed 400 steamboats and 150 barges on the Cumberland to Nashville without the loss of a single ship.[3]

The Mississippi Squadron duplicated this impressive accomplishment. From the fall of 1863 until the spring of 1865, the squadron's size averaged approximately eighty vessels, ranging from light-draft "cottonclads" to ironclads, not a large force considering the thousands of miles of river that it had to patrol. The coastal blockading squadrons had many more ships; in October 1864 the North Atlantic Blockading Squadron alone comprised approximately one hundred vessels. Yet despite the limited number of gunboats available, the Union navy not only maintained effective control of the western rivers but cooperated with the army in combined operations.

On October 9, 1862, forty-nine-year-old David Dixon Porter assumed command of the Mississippi Squadron with the rank of rear admiral. Porter, a mere lieutenant the year before, had been elevated over more than eighty officers—commanders, captains, and commodores—to become the second admiral ever in the United States Navy. To his mother, Porter wrote, "How proud my old Father would be if he could see me an Admiral. . . . It seems somewhat like the Justice of Providence who takes this method of mortifying them for their treatment of my Father." His father, Commodore David Porter, had been one of the most controversial officers in the United States Navy, a man who, as his biographer wrote, was courageous, intelligent, and dedicated, and at the same time impulsive, hot-tempered, conceited, "somewhat vicious, and finally paranoiac." The younger Porter took after his father in many respects.[4]

The new admiral was so ambitious and self-confident that frequently he irritated his seniors as well as many of his peers. One newspaper correspondent wrote that he was "vain, arrogant and egotistical to an extent that can neither be described nor exaggerated." He had no compunction about undercutting his fellow naval officers, even including his brother by adoption, David Farragut. Yet the perceptive Union Secretary of the Navy Gideon Welles recognized under the pretentiousness a man who combined daring with "great energy, great activity and abundant resources." Porter was intelligent, enterprising, and an extremely competent, if not brilliant, officer.[5]

Porter's two greatest assets for Union naval operations on the western rivers were his organizational ability and his understanding of combined operations. Porter's relationship with army officers was mixed. He disliked political generals such as Banks and Butler but got along well with old regulars like Grant and Sherman. Grant admired him and in his *Memoirs* compared him to Lord Nelson. Porter was chagrined, however, that Grant gave the army more credit than the navy for certain operations. But Porter was by far the most successful officer in the Union navy in joint operations. John Milligan writes in *Gunboats down the Mississippi* that during the Vicksburg campaign "Porter was largely responsible for . . . harmony."[6]

Upon taking command, Porter made crucial changes, and after Vicksburg fell, he reorganized the entire squadron. The most important part of the new organization was the division of his command into districts, with subordinates in charge of each and a number of vessels to patrol their designated areas. He first tried this decentralized policy on the Mississippi River and later extended it to the Tennessee, Cumberland, and other streams under his jurisdiction. Generally, the policy proved effective because he gave his well-selected district commanders the necessary authority to carry out their responsibilities.

Porter rarely interfered with his district commanders, spending most of his time at his headquarters in Cairo, Illinois. From the fall of Vicksburg until October 1864, when he left to take over the North Atlantic Blockading Squadron, he made only one extended cruise in southern waters. Then, in the spring of 1864, he personally led the naval force that ascended the Red River to cooperate with the army of Major General Nathaniel P. Banks. Porter's organization remained in effect even after Rear Admiral Samuel P. Lee relieved him in October.

It is difficult to determine the importance of Porter's district policy in Union naval control of the rivers, but the evidence strongly suggests that it was effective and efficient. Porter's flexibility enabled Admiral Lee to reinforce the patrols on the Tennessee River, when in 1864 the Confederate army under General John B. Hood threatened Nashville and Middle Tennessee. Union Major General George H. Thomas attributed the "demoralization of Hood's army leading to its destruction in December, 1864, to the cooperation of naval units on the Tennessee River." Undoubtedly this Union control of the western rivers played a major role.[7]

As long as Union armies could depend on secure, efficient water transport, they had success, dramatic in the beginning, steady and dependable later, but when they were beyond the reach of the navy and water transport, the armies encountered severe difficulties. Although naval operations in the West were as difficult as those along the Atlantic seaboard, they were far more important. Whereas the blockade had little effect on the war's outcome, naval control of the western rivers enabled Union armies to gain and maintain control of the heartland of the Confederacy. The Comte de Paris, a French observer with the Union armies, correctly noted after the war, "We shall always find . . . that whenever the Federals were supported by a river, their progress was certain and their conquest decisive." Given this causal relationship, it is clear that the Union navy delivered some important blows to Confederate power and will and provided an ingredient essential to Union success in the western theater of war.[8]

IN CONTRAST, Union sea power was not as effective in its efforts to control the Gulf or eastern seaboard through either a blockade or the capture of the key port cities. Three of the major southern ports, New Orleans, Norfolk, and Galveston, fell in 1862, though less than a year later Confederate forces recaptured Galveston. The other ports—Mobile, Savannah, Wilmington, and Charleston—remained in southern hands until 1865.

Leaders on both sides regarded Charleston, the "Cradle of the Rebellion," as dear because of its symbolic importance, and as such it was a major point of contention. Both Union Secretary of the Navy Welles and his capable assistant, Gustavus V. Fox, felt confident that a sufficiently powerful naval force, even without army assistance, could capture the port. Earlier successes at Port Royal, Hatteras, and in the West had convinced both of them that a naval bombardment could overcome land fortifications. They were also certain that ironclads, particularly monitor types, could run past the forts and intimidate the city into surrendering by threatening bombardment.

Rear Admiral Du Pont, in command of the South Atlantic Blockading Squadron, had strong reservations about such action, however, and favored instead a combined operation. Nevertheless, under pressure from Washington he reluctantly agreed. On April 15, 1863, seven monitors, along with the ironclads *New Ironsides* and *Keokuk*, attacked Charleston's Forts Sumter and Moultrie. After an engagement of slightly less than two hours' duration, Du Pont's battered vessels had to withdraw. The attack's failure illustrated to Du Pont and other naval officers that monitor-type vessels, with their small gun batteries, lacked adequate firepower for bombarding well-situated land fortifications. In the attack on the forts, the combined batteries of the monitors' guns fired only 139 rounds. As Du Pont wrote Welles, "I remind the Department that ability to endure is not sufficient element wherewith to gain victories, that endurance must be accompanied with a corresponding power to inflict injury upon the enemy." Despite this criticism, monitors continued to be the backbone of Union offensive operations.[9]

After 1863 the navy grudgingly accepted Du Pont's conviction of the tactical necessity of combined operations to take Charleston. The navy worked out a plan with the army whereby troops under the protection of naval vessels would occupy Morris Island, a small sand spit within firing range of Fort Sumter. From this position Union artillery might destroy the fort, allowing the warships to enter the harbor and force the surrender. During the months that followed the Union took Morris Island and reduced Fort Sumter to rubble, but for various reasons was unable to secure the port until 1865.

In July 1863 Rear Admiral John Adolphus Bernard Dahlgren replaced Du Pont. A gunnery expert known not only for his inventions but also for his political influence, Dahlgren was a favorite of President Lincoln. The president had put him in charge of the naval force at Washington though he held only the rank of commander and later promoted him to rear admiral without consulting Secretary of the Navy Welles. Dahlgren coveted command of the Charleston naval force and had pleaded for it, but not until Du Pont asked to be relieved did he receive it.

Dahlgren had served in the navy for more than two decades, but he had seen almost no combat. Nevertheless, he stoutly believed, wrongly, that his ships could take Charleston. Frustrated by lack of cooperation from the army, which assigned low priority to Charleston; by the Confederate defense network around the harbor and the elaborate obstructions blockading its entrance; and by delays in acquiring the additional monitors that had been promised, Dahlgren and his vessels on the Charleston station spent the remainder of the war furiously bombarding fortifications and positions and chasing blockade-runners but could not enter the harbor until near the war's end. Confederates finally abandoned the city on the night of February 17–18, 1865, faced by units of Sherman's army approaching from Georgia. On the following morning the *Canonicus*, leading a group of other monitors from Dahlgren's squadron, finally dropped anchor in the harbor.

The fight for Charleston took longer than it should have. The army had not shown much interest in combined operations there when they had been most feasible, just after the fall of Port Royal in November 1861. Momentary advantages had passed, and the army allowed opportunities to evaporate and the Confederates to fortify. The naval effort to capture the city without significant assistance from the army proved fruitless; worse than that, as Admiral Bern Anderson put it, "the siege of Charleston, in which the city was vigorously and resolutely defended, in the end proved to be a great waste of Union resources. . . . Union naval forces were squandered for no real gain."[10]

Admiral Dahlgren finally came to understand the futility of an attempt to capture the city by the navy alone, and when it fell at last, he sent hearty congratulations to Sherman. "Your campaign was the final blow, grand in conception, complete in execution." Thus Charleston fell, captured neither by direct naval action, as Secretary Welles had hoped, nor by direct military action; and it was no longer worth the price paid. As Sherman explained in December 1864, by then the city was "a mere desolated wreck, and is hardly worth the time it would take to starve it out."[11]

Less than two months earlier, Sherman's troops had captured Savannah by more direct action. Like Charleston, the Georgia port had held out against joint Union army and navy operations for more than two years. As early as the fall of 1861 plans existed for combined forces to attack Savannah, but that assault never materialized. Union troops did occupy Tybee Island, capture Fort Pulaski, and make unopposed reconnaissance forays along the coast and inland streams in the port's vicinity, but the army never provided enough troops to mount a serious effort against the city. Naval vessels assigned to the Savannah station blockaded the inlets leading to the Savannah River, occasionally patrolled the maze of streams that connected the inlets, and bombarded Confederate positions. In turn the Confederates built a series of fortifications and established a small naval force with ironclads to guard the port, but Union forces rarely challenged them. Admiral Du Pont regarded combined operations against Savannah as too risky, and Dahlgren never even considered the idea. Savannah fell to Sherman's troops on Christmas Day 1864.

As at Charleston and Savannah, Sherman's pressure from inland was a major factor in the fall of Wilmington, North Carolina, the last major Confederate port on the eastern seaboard. Wilmington had enormous value to the Confederacy; after the capture of Norfolk early in 1862, it was the closest port of any size to Richmond and the Army of Northern Virginia. By the summer of 1863 it had become the single most important center for blockade-running.

Because of peculiar geographical conditions along the North Carolina coast, the Union found it almost impossible to blockade successfully the mouth of the Cape Fear River, which connected the port with the Atlantic. Two navigable entrances led to the Cape Fear: New Inlet and Old Inlet, separated by Smith's Island, located directly in front of the river mouth. Jutting out into the Atlantic about twenty-five miles from the southeast corner of the island was Frying Pan Shoals. In addition, the Confederates had managed to erect unusually strong defenses. Fort Caswell guarded the southwest point of one entrance, and Fort Fisher, considered by many to be the most powerful fort in the Confederacy, guarded the northeast point of the other. The only feasible way to seal off Wilmington was by an amphibious assault.

Although in 1861 the Union blockade strategy board had recommended the seizure of Wilmington, the project remained low in priority until 1863. Rear Admiral Samuel Lee was the first commander of the North Atlantic Blockading Squadron to emphasize the port's importance. His predecessors, flag officers Stringham and Goldsborough, had considered the capture of the principal forts and towns in the sounds region of North Carolina more important. Commenting upon this policy, in 1863 Lee lamented to Welles: "Loadstones instead of stepping stones to progress. . . . The easy capture of Fort Macon gave us the possession of Beaufort Harbor; thus we had all the seacoast of North Carolina, except Wilmington, the capture of which was as easy then as difficult now. . . . But the complete acquisition of the seacoast was abandoned in the favor of the sound towns."[12]

One of his subordinates described Lee, a Virginian, as courteous, modest, retiring, careful, and conservative; another, on his staff, called him solemn and serious. Secretary Welles considered him "careful, and circumspect almost to a fault, but while vigilant, he has not dash and impetuous daring." Lee could not tolerate indiscretion or inaccuracy in his official correspondence, hence his reports were "written and rewritten . . . altered in phraseology and not in meaning, signed and sealed, reopened and reread, criticized and discussed, repunctuated sometimes to a wearisome minutiae." Lee had a difficult time delegating the routine details of his squadron, hence he spent much of his time grappling with problems concerning repairs, assignment of ships and personnel, fuel, provisions, and the like. He never believed that he had enough ships or the cooperation of a military force powerful enough to attack the forts guarding the river.[13]

Although more than once the navy urged seizure of the forts by amphibious assault, until late in the fall of 1864 the War Department showed little interest. The army was far more desirous of taking Goldsboro and cutting the railroad through there or seizing Charleston as a base to move inland. Despite the army's scant enthusiasm, the navy proceeded with plans to attack the forts. Secretary Welles decided to replace Lee, but his first choice, Farragut, turned down the appointment. The choice then fell upon Rear Admiral Porter. That able officer assumed command of the North Atlantic Blockading Squadron on October 10, 1864, and, with enthusiastic support from the general in chief of the army, immediately began to assemble a powerful fleet to attack the forts.

Porter had the task of preparing the way for a landing by a sixty-five-hundred-man force headed by Major General Butler, but Porter and Butler did not cooperate well; the situation worsened because the two leaders held joint command, neither possessing final authority. On

Christmas Eve 1864, firing more than twenty thousand shells, Porter's fleet bombarded Fort Fisher. Porter claimed that the fort sustained extensive damage, but in reality it suffered very little, as the first Union troops ashore wryly discovered when they approached the relatively unharmed walls. Butler, in an unusual instance of military sagacity, therefore refused to attack, ordered his troops back to their transports, and the day after Christmas returned them to Norfolk. Porter furiously complained to General Grant about Butler's action and requested the organization of a second expedition. Grant agreed and assigned Major General Alfred H. Terry, with instructions to cooperate with Porter and to regard him as the commander of the operation.[14]

By the beginning of 1865 Grant had become interested in seizing the fort so he could better support Sherman's invasion of the Carolinas. Sherman's troops would need supplies, and the Cape Fear River was navigable to Fayetteville, a hundred miles upstream.

On January 12, 1865, Porter's fleet again loomed off Fort Fisher. Forty-four warships, including several ironclads that closed to within seven hundred yards of the fort, opened a devastating and deliberate fire on selected targets. On the thirteenth and fourteenth under the fire of Porter's guns Terry's eight thousand troops landed. On Sunday, January 15, two thousand sailors and marines waded ashore and attacked the seaward face of the fort while Terry's troops assaulted from the land. Although the seaward strike failed, it diverted attention from Terry's columns, which broke inside and captured the fort. Within a few days the Union also captured Fort Caswell, and Confederate troops evacuated Wilmington.

Authorities generally agree that the second Fort Fisher operation was one of the most brilliant, if not the most brilliant, amphibious operation carried out during the war. It surely constitutes the best performance by a naval force in such an operation. From the navy's point of view the Fort Fisher operation had real significance. Its capture and that of Caswell finally closed Cape Fear to blockade-runners. For the army, however, the operation meant very little until an additional twenty thousand men arrived, took Wilmington on February 22, and thus established a base for that force and for Sherman's army when it entered North Carolina soon after.[15]

On April 12, 1865, three months after the fall of Wilmington, Mobile, Alabama, the last major port east of the Mississippi, surrendered to Union forces. Yet nine months earlier the port had ceased to have importance. In August 1864 Admiral Farragut had led a fleet of four monitors and fourteen wooden vessels into Mobile Bay. The fleet had successfully passed the forts defending the bay and then had defeated the small Confederate squadron therein. Farragut's victory effectively sealed the port. If adequate troops had accompanied this naval force, the Union could have taken Mobile after the surrender of the forts guarding the bay's entrance. The Confederates had fewer than four thousand troops in the partially completed fortifications, yet the army felt it could not commit the necessary troops until early 1865. The army then agreed to provide substantial reinforcements to take Mobile and move inland toward Montgomery and Selma in cooperation with General James H. Wilson's cavalry raid, but the war ended before the operation against the inland cities could take place. Nevertheless, for four months, January to April 1865, some forty-five thousand men under General E. R. S. Canby cooperated with naval units of the West Gulf Blockading Squadron under Commodore Henry K. Thatcher to clear the Confederates from the small forts and fortifications guarding the approaches to Mobile. Although ultimately successful, the occupation of the port had no military significance. Mobile surrendered a few days after Montgomery and Selma had fallen to Union cavalry. Its capture occurred exactly four years after the firing on Fort Sumter and three days after Lee surrendered the Army of Northern Virginia.

NAVAL OPERATIONS, especially on the western rivers, contributed directly and greatly to the destruction of Confederate military power and conquest of important territory. Although residents of the Confederate interior might ignore the naval presence unless their homes were located along important navigable streams, in coastal and adjacent river areas Union warships caused considerable anxiety because their unexpected arrival might cause the capture of a town or the closure of a port. Even when its operations were unsuccessful, the existence of the Union navy created tensions for citizens within proximity of navigable water. The naval power thereby contributed to the dissolution of Confederate power and will. Even threats that had little intrinsic military significance had an impact on the morale of the people directly affected. In the West the arrival of the Union fleet, or only a single ship, often created an umbrella under which lukewarm or needy Confederates could engage in an illegal cotton trade with the North, send money back and forth across the lines, or even provide for their individual safety by seeking the protection of Union forces. More often, Confederates fled from the Union presence and went deeper into the interior. In either event, the movement of refugees was demoralizing to the refugees themselves and to those around them. Moreover, both the rivers and the enclaves established along the coast with naval support served as objectives for runaway slaves and, when blacks were admitted into the Union army, they served also as recruiting depots. In short, the navy placed on the doorstep of many southern communities a reminder that the war could affect them personally, not just the soldiers on distant battlefields. Once the war began to turn against the South, the naval presence could be a deadening, morale-sapping reminder of what might lie in store for the entire South.

Although Union land forces made relatively little use of their positions in Atlantic ports or inlets to raid the railroad that paralleled the seaboard between Richmond and Savannah, their ability to threaten the railroad, together with the actual or implied menace to Wilmington, Charleston, and Savannah, also caused the Confederates much anxiety. To protect the ports and the railroad Confederates applied their pipeline concept and used the railroad to transfer forces along the coast. If, for example, they believed Charleston threatened, they could order troops south to the city from a point farther north, while simultaneously ordering other troops to that point from a location even farther north. In this way, Charleston would receive reinforcements from Wilmington, while men from farther north replaced those at Wilmington—and so on up the line to Richmond, which had actually given up some troops. Charleston thus gained forces far more quickly than if it had to await the arrival of reinforcements directly from Richmond.

When the Confederates augmented these defending troops with local forces raised by the states, they further integrated local defense with national. Adequate local defense along the coast played an important part both in sustaining civilian morale in these regions and in defending nationally important ports and the railway along the Atlantic coast. State forces and Confederate regulars long had cooperated in this effort, and in 1863 the Confederacy systematized this joint effort and sought to strengthen it by requiring states to provide such troops. By 1864 they became partly national forces, called reserves, with an experienced Confederate general officer to command them in each state. Composed of men in exempt occupations and those too young or too old to take the field, these troops proved effective at manning fortifications, thus releasing regular soldiers to join the main armies. Thus coast defense came to depend even more than before on local resources, and these local defense forces made a more significant national contribution than heretofore.

What else did these successful Union coastal operations achieve? They had as their principal objectives the closure of important ports and establishment of bases to move against Confederate transportation and industrial facilities inland. The Union did not accomplish these goals. With the exception of Norfolk and New Orleans, captured in 1862, no major Confederate port was taken and held until 1865, and even then no port was captured as a result of direct naval action or siege. Of the five seaports taken in the last six months of war, Savannah, Charleston, Wilmington, Mobile, and Galveston, land forces seized two from the rear and two fell indirectly as a result of pressure from the rear.

It seems that the Union missed valuable chances to deal severe blows to the Confederate war effort. But in 1861 neither side had well-organized land forces available and the Union navy had expanded little from its peacetime strength. The Union had greater opportunities because the Confederates had not erected the fortifications that later protected their ports. But at this stage of the war the Confederates posted a higher proportion of their forces to guard the coast than they did later. In early 1862, when he ordered ten thousand men from Mobile and Pensacola to Tennessee, President Davis confessed "the error" of his "attempt to defend all of the frontier," both coastal and inland, and planned, but did not carry out, the drastic step of "abandoning the seaboard" to save Tennessee by concentrating men for the Shiloh campaign. The Union would, therefore, have faced comparatively greater land forces had an early attempt been made against coastal cities.[16]

A Union concentration against the coast, earlier or later, would have brought a rapid response, especially along the Atlantic, where the security of the coastal railroad always caused the Confederates much anxiety. But this same railroad would have facilitated rapid concentration of troops to contest the Union landing force; and just as the Union would have diverted forces from the main armies to the coast, so also would the Confederates. In a contest against such landings, the Confederates would have had the advantage of more rapid concentration because their ports all had telegraph communication whereas the Union squadrons, lacking wireless, would have had to depend on dispatch boats for communication. By 1864, when the Union concentrated most of its soldiers to support the simultaneous land advances, the Confederacy could do likewise because the newly organized reserves assumed a greater role in coast defense.

Thus it is not easy to predict what outcome a greater Union effort would have had, and it is clearly presumptuous to assume the easy capture of many ports. If, however, the Union had succeeded early in eliminating ports captured or closed later, the blockade would have been strengthened significantly; but in view of the Confederate ability to improvise, the quantity of consumer goods brought in throughout the war, and the relative Confederate independence of imports in the latter part of the war, it seems unlikely that a more effective blockade would have broken the military stalemate or seriously affected the capabilities of the Confederate armies. Of course, a tighter blockade would have increased civilian hardships and further depressed morale and taxed the Confederacy's nationalism. But greater Union military success on other fronts would also have had a depressing effect on morale and, in addition, would have deprived the Confederacy of resources because the Union would dominate more of the South's territory. It is, therefore, difficult to hypothesize the results of more intense Union naval activity along the coasts.

Even so, Union combined operations played an important role. Despite poor cooperation between the services, the wrong kind of ironclads, and the failure to exploit initial advantages, the soldiers and sailors together did what neither could do alone—they successfully brought the war to the coastal areas of the South long before the major Union armies were able to do so. They tied up Confederate troops, diverted scarce resources to building and equipping fortifications, and caused Confederates a great deal of anxiety. And the naval victories and threats had unexpected political consequences, helping to ignite tempers and deepen differences on issues that cut to the core of the Confederate raison d'être and causing southerners to ponder again questions of secession, independence, and state rights.

Chapter Ten

State Rights and the
Confederate War Effort

T HE RELATIONSHIP of naval operations to local defense, and specifically of local defense to the problem of Confederate-state in-
teractions, requires special attention; and we also need to give some
consideration to the historian most responsible for the state-rights interpretation of Confederate defeat. If the South lost the Civil War because it did not have the will to win, one reason, surely, was the internal dissension caused by the state-rights controversy. So thought
many historians of an earlier generation, following a thesis demonstrated most prominently by Frank L. Owsley, who contended, as we
already have noted, that the Confederacy "Died of State Rights."

No one would deny the disruptive effect of the conflict generated by
differing notions of how best to preserve liberty and to organize southern society for the war effort. Many Confederates became upset over
the controversy between the Confederate government and the states
on the question of local defense. Owsley asserted, for example, that in
the fall of 1861 Georgia's Governor Joseph E. Brown danced "a frantic
jig up and down Georgia . . . accusing the Confederate government of
gross neglect" because of "the exposed condition of Georgia's coast."
Owsley maintained that during the following spring North Carolina
kept a large force of state troops to meet the threat of seaborne attack
and that by the fall of 1862 North Carolinians resented the conscription of state troops, which the Tar Heels believed had "left the state in
the lurch in the matter of coast defense."[1]

Some present-day historians would agree that the state-rights controversy hindered the war effort, although they believe it was seldom
as vital as Owsley and other historians of his generation claimed. Others point to mitigating factors and declare that state rights often constituted only a symbol of deeper difficulties, and some of these histo-

rians even assert that state rights had positive aspects that actually assisted the Confederate war effort. We think that there is much to be said for both of these views and especially those of the latter group. Our own studies have led us to conclude that on balance the discord generated not only was not a decisive factor in Confederate defeat, but that it was, instead, an advantage in the war.

Owsley placed great emphasis on the number of soldiers committed to local defense, and he accused Governor Joseph Brown of Georgia in particular of hoarding men and weapons and of arranging the exemption of a multitude of local officials from conscription. Governor Brown and others were guilty of these charges, but it is easy to overestimate the effect. As we pointed out in Chapters 6 and 8, the railway and the telegraph permitted the Confederates to integrate local with national defense. State forces provided a valuable reinforcement for the Confederate armies, often replacing them in coast defense duties, while also allowing the men in these essentially militia forces to continue to work in vital occupations for much of the time. Appendix I deals in greater detail with Owsley's thesis about local defense.

Of course, the state-rights problem revolved around more than local defense, as Owsley's book attempted to show. Still, this fortuitous juncture in our discussion of Union naval success and local defense affords us a logical springboard for our attempt to come to grips with this most persistent of the interpretations allegedly explaining Confederate defeat, state rights. Surely one could not expect that the establishment of scattered, small, and lightly held enclaves of Union strength along the Confederacy's Atlantic coast would lead to severe internal stress in addition to whatever difficulties the somewhat less than successful blockade created. And yet, as our discussion of naval affairs already has indicated, there is evidence that this was the case.

In *The Rebel Shore* James M. Merrill suggests that the early naval attacks brought fear to the hearts of southerners, who came to know that Yankee sea power "could strike swiftly, mercilessly, and without warning against Confederate shores." Reacting as one would expect, Confederate civilians fled to the interior and pleaded for better defense of their coasts. Merrill contends that "the theory that states' rights were responsible for the ultimate collapse of the Confederacy began when southern governors balked at dispatching men, arms, and ammunition to the Virginia firing line in order to protect their own sea-coasts." This intransigence, Merrill points out, set up internal conflict, for Confederate officials had to choose between moving troops from the coasts and strengthening their armies, or leaving them where they were and exposing the armies and the states they defended. The former choice could lead to competition with state governors for men and supplies, as citizens pressured their governors to place local defense above the needs of the entire Confederacy.[2]

Certainly it would be an oversimplification to attribute the Confederate state-rights movement solely to the early successes of the Union navy, nor did Merrill intend such an implication. His purpose was to examine the development and use of amphibious strategy and tactics, and he was content to put forward only this significant suggestion. Yet Merrill's remark must be noted, for he reminds us that local defense involved questions of resource and manpower allocation and that incursions into the Confederate interior by bodies of Union troops was not the only reason local defense became an issue.

Governor Vance, for example, faced a difficult problem in maintaining morale in North Carolina. Individual liberty was very important in the minds of white North Carolinians. "They believed," Marc W. Kruman wrote, "that the white man who was deprived of his liberties was just as much a slave as the black bondsman. Black slavery was only the most extreme example of the condition of slavery." "If checks were not placed on the power of rulers," Kruman continued, "they would concentrate power in their hands and use it to destroy the liberties of the people. Therefore, the people needed specific safeguards for their liberties. First, they demanded that civil power always be supreme over military power. . . . The strength of the military necessarily increased during wartime. . . . Therefore, Conservatives argued that it was 'necessary to hold in check that propensity which war is always likely to bring forth.'" "A strong state government," North Carolinians believed, constituted "the second safeguard of the people's liberties. It could serve as a buffer."[3]

Regardless of their political persuasion, North Carolinians resisted conscription, Kruman noted, because they rightly believed that their state already had provided more than its share of soldiers. But "more important . . . was the fear that conscription represented the first

step toward military despotism," a fear the Confederate Congress also
aroused when it authorized the suspension of habeas corpus and Davis
issued a series of implementing proclamations. With the subsequent
arrest of some North Carolinians, Tar Heels also developed "apprehension about the independence of the state's judiciary." Such wor-
ries were not just chimeras, for in mid-1863 Secretary of War James A.
Seddon seemed to threaten the judicial process by blaming desertions
of troops from North Carolina on state courts, which were said to have
declared conscription unconstitutional. Seddon asked Governor
Zebulon Vance to intercede. But Vance believed that an independent
judiciary was "the only hope of freedom in times of passion & of violence" and declined Seddon's request.[4]

These fears, plus the cumbersome and unpopular substitute laws,
also contributed to a growing uneasiness on the part of North Carolinians that led many of them to issue calls for a convention to allow the
state to "act in her sovereign capacity to defend herself." But the crux
of Kruman's case stresses that historians have been incorrect in seeing
the movement as an effort to achieve a reconstruction of the Union.
The evidence, he says, indicates the contrary, that "many Conservatives were trying to extricate themselves from an almost inextricable situation. They wanted to protect their freedom and seek an honorable peace, *but in the Confederacy.*" Vance and others worked against
the calling of such a convention "because they believed that it would
lead to reconstruction rather than to an honorable peace," and they
tried to find other ways "to preserve the rights and liberties" of the
citizenry.[5]

As Kruman concluded, "The anxieties of North Carolinians and
other white southerners were paralleled in the North, yet the contours
of dissent in the two regions differed." Furthermore, one might justly
add, so too did the response on the part of officials who tried to counter, or cater to, that dissent, because the northern discontent was
tempered considerably by the existence of viable, legitimate opposition in the form of the Democratic party, which had much realistic
hope of effecting great change in the Union by ousting Lincoln and his
party in 1864. At the least, they had a chance to force moderation of
Republican policies by threatening resurgence at the ballot box, as
happened in 1862, when Democrats picked up approximately thirty

seats in the House of Representatives. Lincoln had to take account of a powerful, organized opposition, of which Governor Horatio Seymour of New York is only one outstanding example. The Union president had to tread warily in the path of these opponents; he also had to watch his own Republicans carefully, for they often expressed as much discontent with him as the Democrats did, if for different reasons. James G. Randall and David Donald observed in their classic synthesis that "it would indeed be hard to name any faction in the fall of 1862 that was pleased with Lincoln." As Donald remarked elsewhere, Lincoln's ability to remain in office despite this opposition indicates the president's outstanding political ability.[6]

In his essay "Jefferson Davis and the Political Factors in Confederate Defeat," David Potter pointed out the significance of this very important political difference between the problems of Lincoln and Davis. Supposing that long years in a sectional minority protecting slavery with "legalistic safeguards . . . may have impaired the capacity for affirmative and imaginative action on the part of the Southern leaders generally," Potter suggests "that the Confederacy may have suffered real and direct damage from the fact that its political organization lacked a two-party system" to give legitimacy to opposition. Political parties channeled discontent and new ideas in the American system, but without parties the Confederacy lacked an institutionalized way to influence policy from outside the government. Not surprisingly, men such as Governor Vance resorted to state-rights tactics—what other avenues of protest lay open to them?[7]

Arthur Schlesinger, Sr., long ago pointed out that almost every state had used state sovereignty at one time or another to protect its interests, employing the theory as a political shelter; nevertheless, he believed the argument "artificial," somewhat like the shelter "that a Western pioneer seeks . . . when a tornado is raging." Lewis O. Saum observed that "as is the case with aspirin for a headache, a state rights position is taken at need, and a shelter makes sense when a tornado threatens." In the same way, state rights made sense to Vance and others facing similar problems.[8]

It is significant, in this regard, that not only did Davis not have parties to contend with, but Vance in North Carolina did, for there Union Democrats and Whigs had coalesced into the Conservative party, opposing a Confederate party made up of the remaining Democrats and a few Whigs. "North Carolina Conservatives," Kruman observes, "were . . . left with two unsatisfying choices. A small portion moved unwittingly in the direction of disloyalty to the Confederacy and reconstruction of the Union; the larger portion was left to complain bitterly and impotently of the threat to their freedom."[9]

This last point is important, and it needs to be emphasized here, lest we tend to fall into the trap of going along too closely with Owsley's line of argument. Time and again the Confederate government overruled state objections to violation of state-rights principles; if the states had been getting their way, they would not have had so much complaint to voice. State-rights protesters had very little success, which caused controversy unless their immediate goals coincided with those of the Confederacy. The frequency of their objections indicated frustration rather than disruption. For example, except for the coastal areas, North Carolina was relatively safe and undisturbed for most of the war. It was, however, "more susceptible to the demands of the Confederate government than other states." Thus three states, including North Carolina, paid two-thirds of the levy under the tax-in-kind and made other contributions in like measure. And though Vance and Governor Joseph Brown of Georgia appear to be the most notable obstructionists in Owsley's reckoning, we should remember that their states nevertheless gave generously to the Confederate war effort. The *Official Records* indicate, for example, that Georgia and North Carolina together furnished about 42 percent of the conscripts and volunteers from east of the Mississippi River after the passage of the original draft law of April 1862.[10]

And, as the Davis administration's successes with these difficult governors suggest, "the confrontations," David A. Scarboro argued in a 1979 article, "demonstrate the various ways in which problems in Confederate-state relations were resolved. They show that negotiation played a far larger role than confrontation."[11]

The negotiations and the revealing manpower figures may provide a key to the proper understanding of the Confederate war effort. How can one accuse Georgia and North Carolina of damaging the war effort when they contributed so much to it? Indeed, there is good reason to believe that the state-rights controversy did not constitute a net loss to the Confederacy and that it was, on balance, an asset. Historians have sometimes let the colorful characters involved in the controversy blind them to a clear understanding of what those characters did when they were not arguing with other Confederates. Far from damaging Confederate staying power or subtracting from Confederate will, state rights put into action was very likely an important reason why power and will lasted as long as they did.

Governor Vance stands out as a good example of the positive aspects of state-rights theory and practice, for he interposed himself between the state and central governments in an effort to mitigate the more dire recalcitrance that might otherwise have resulted in North Carolina. A well-liked pro-Union politician before the war, Vance was elected governor of North Carolina in September 1862 while serving as a colonel in the army. The Confederate party, which he ousted, had proved unpopular because of the early reverses at Hatteras and Roanoke Island and widespread objections to secession in the first place. Vance received his nomination from the Conservatives, mostly former Union Whigs, led by William W. Holden, a Raleigh newspaper editor who had remained a Unionist until the Fort Sumter incident and who then had become a secessionist. But by 1862 Holden had lost his enthusiasm for the cause. He apparently hoped to achieve control of the North Carolina government through Vance and then move toward a separate peace. But Holden clearly misjudged Colonel Vance. To the great surprise of some of his supporters, Vance not only promised to support the war but actually did so.

The circumstances of his election as a protest candidate, however, plus his contentious nature, labeled Vance as an obstructionist through the remainder of the war—and much of the historiography that followed. To the extent that Vance did not willingly follow Davis's lead, he was indeed an obstructionist, at least from the point of view of the Confederate government. But, as Clement Eaton has pointed out, Vance, and Joseph E. Brown as well, were under tremendous pressures from constituents, most of whom in Vance's case had not been original secessionists and many of whom were thoroughly tired of the war and the hardships it brought them. One constituent asserted his confidence that Vance would defend the state, "that is, that you will do all in your *power to cause the Confederate Govemt* to do it, for it is the duty of the *Confederate Govemt* to do it—We have done our duty as a State—and as a State we should be equally defended." A poor woman begged him to do justice to nonslaveholders and informed him: "We are a desolate and ruined family for extortion [high prices] runs so hie [sic] here we cannot support our family" if her husband were called into service; "I trust," she concluded, "you will hold the rane in your own hands and not let the confederate congress have the full sway . . . we trust in god and look to you for some help." Faced by such appeals, what was a conscientious governor to do?[12]

And sometimes Vance got what he wanted from the central government. In recent investigations of the specific issues of conscription, exemption, salt production, impressment, and shipping regulations as matters of dispute between the governor of North Carolina and President Davis, David Scarboro discovered that time and again "the Confederacy made concessions when Governor Vance was able to persuade the administration that to do so would either be of practical advantage to the war effort or would be politically expedient. Where he failed to do this, the state's claim usually received short shrift." And whenever "Davis refused to offer any concessions the governor backed down."[13]

If Jefferson Davis thought Vance was a problem, he should have paused to consider what William W. Holden or someone like him would have done to the relationship between the president and the governor. Thus governors like Vance headed off and to some extent pacified more serious internal discontent than any they created. The proof came, in Vance's case, when the man who originally had promoted his candidacy became so dissatisfied with Vance that he ran against him in 1864 as leader of a faction of antiwar activists within the Conservative party. Many of those men later showed their discontent with the Confederacy by becoming Republican leaders after the war. Supported by subversive groups such as the Heroes of America, an anti-Confederate secret society, Holden and his followers wanted the state to call a convention and negotiate a peace without regard to the other Confederate states. Paul Escott recently expressed the view in a communication to the authors of this study that the purposes of such a convention—should one have been held—are even clearer in Georgia than in North Carolina. For in Georgia, "the leaders of the movement were at least very concerned about following correct form and procedures. Holden did not always make such a pretense." Holden received a great deal of attention with his claim that it was a "rich man's war and a poor man's fight," but his following proved significantly smaller than that of Vance, and Holden never got into power until after the war had ended, when President Johnson appointed him provisional governor. Vance beat Holden and his peace platform by a four-to-one majority, saving Davis much greater trouble.[14]

Vance was more a symptom than a disease, and in any event he sometimes took a strong anti-state-rights stand (judged in the North Carolina context) that must have risked his following among some of the localistic voters. In November 1862, for example, news from the Tar Heel state was "distressing," reported ultrapatriotic John Beauchamp Jones, a clerk in the Confederate War Department, who noted in his diary the amazing rumor that "but for the influence of Gov. Vance, the *legislature* would favor reconstruction!" And the following spring, when the decisions of a local judge rendered his own authority uncertain, Vance asked Davis to call out the North Carolina militia for the purpose of capturing North Carolina deserters from the army. Far from arguing by mail, Vance was acting in a spirit of wholehearted cooperation, asking Davis to use his authority in an area where Vance found his own in dispute.[15]

If some of the forces engaged in such tasks as protecting the coast or guarding salt production may have been redundant, the number of Confederate troops shielding against menaces to rear areas was minuscule compared with the Union's commitment to similar tasks. The Federal armies, on the average, devoted about one-third of their forces to safeguarding communications from guerrillas and cavalry raiders. And for the most part the Union had to commit its regular forces to these tasks of guarding railways and the like for it found too much difficulty organizing a reliable militia in essentially hostile territory. Union local defense for these purposes absorbed far more troops, relatively as well as absolutely, than the Confederacy ever devoted to its local defense responsibilities.

Much of the state-Confederate antagonism had its origins in the operations of the Union navy on the Confederate seaboard. Owsley made frequent reference to this defense problem. But the governors took meaningful steps to meet the difficulties involved in protecting their exposed coasts, and the joint effort of the central government and the states helped to prevent the Union navy from continuing the successful expeditions it had conducted in the first part of the war. This was only one part of the way in which local defense aided the Confederacy, and local defense constituted only one of the methods in which the states aided the southern war effort.

Paul D. Escott recently looked afresh at the state-rights thesis, among other issues, in his *After Secession: Jefferson Davis and the Failure of Southern Nationalism.* Although we do not agree with all of his conclusions, his book is an impressive piece of penetrating scholarship. Two chapters in particular interest us here: "The Debate over Centralization" and "Leadership and Loyalty—Jefferson Davis, Joseph E. Brown, and the Common People."

Confederates wrestled mightily over the definition and form of their political values and goals. Davis, though undoubtedly a state-rightist, did not believe his position was incompatible with support of an operative federalism or with the existence of a strong central government. While Davis had to struggle against those who disagreed, Escott contends that "on the whole he won," but "the victory was not without cost." For example, Davis lost some of the support he previously enjoyed from state-rights advocates among the planter class, and these became opponents.[16]

But the significant point is that the war effort forced Davis and his government to face problems that transcended any that even the United States had dealt with in the past. There never had existed the "unified national army under central direction" that the South needed and created. Not unnaturally, the state governors balked from time to time at some of the centrally directed military operations and maneuvers. But did they thereby necessarily undermine the war effort? Escott thinks not and proceeds to argue his case by explaining just how much revolutionary centralization did take place despite protests. This phenomenon, sometimes called Confederate nationalism (incorrectly, we believe), caused far-reaching change in administration and a quickened pace of economic development. We do not refer here to the nationalism involved in a mystical sense of nationhood or of shared loyalties, but rather to that which characterized the development of styles of governing and uses of power, in either the public or private sectors—a sort of organizational nationalism, intended to promote centralization and uniformity, and not necessarily loyalty or brotherhood.[17]

Recent historians did not invent this centralization, though it has become a major point of discussion only within the last ten years. Contemporary Confederates perceived it and railed against it with little success, as Escott noted. Senator Louis T. Wigfall of Texas, for example, opposed the establishment of a Confederate supreme court because the uniformity imposed by John Marshall on the old Union taught Wigfall that supreme courts could destroy localism. Other senators also resisted legal centralization, with the result that the Confederacy never established such a court, although its Constitution had authorized one. Even the building of railroads aroused apprehension, and in February 1862 ten members of the Provisional Congress entered a protest in the *Journal of Congress*. They objected that such construction would undermine state authority and that the South did not need them "because armies and munitions and military supplies have been, are now, and probably always will be mainly transported by other means." Most important, however, was the extensive power granted the president to make contracts for construction, to ignore "vested rights" of corporations, and to "adopt any course he may choose for making a railroad between the points designated. . . . The wishes of States, the vested interests of States in other roads, corporate rights, rights of private property . . . all are made to fall before the fiat of the Executive." Power, a power that could be exercised uniformly, was what frightened these traditionalists.[18]

RICHARD D. BROWN has addressed the problem of state rights in his provocative work on modernization. He noted that "secessionists rejected the idea of national uniformity, celebrating instead state and local sovereignty. In their rhetoric, uniformity became a monster." They looked backward "to an earlier, more traditional republicanism." In the North, on the other hand, men believed that "national uniformity . . . required enforcement at gunpoint." In the generation before the war, the North was "propelled . . . further toward modernity," while the South moved "toward a fuller commitment to a traditional outlook." And yet, as Brown explains, "the war was a modernizer of immense proportions for both sides . . . . Both North and South took long steps toward integrating local and supralocal experience." One of these steps, in the Confederacy, led to changes in the labor system, as southerners hired slaves for use in newly developing industries. Indeed, the entire course of Confederate economic change illustrates Brown's point.[19]

As early as the 1930s some perceptive students noted such changes, most prominently Louise B. Hill, who examined the efforts of the Confederate government to impose uniformity on foreign trade and pronounced the result "state socialism." And in 1950 E. Merton Coulter discussed the work of Josiah Gorgas, head of the Ordnance Bureau, who organized Confederate munitions manufacturing. He also noted the actions of the Confederate Congress and executive, which loaned private contractors money to meet start-up costs and limited the profits these government-sponsored enterprises could make. They required factories producing goods that were needed in both the public and private sectors to sell as much as two-thirds of their output to the government. This regulation and others as well were enforced by Confederate control of required manpower through conscription and exemption laws and by control of necessary rail transport, without which goods could neither be made nor marketed. Using manpower and transport as a club, the government encouraged a widespread development of war industry—sulfur, nitre, powder, clothing, shoes, and the like—that was "remarkable for a region which had long frowned on manufactories." The enthusiasm for industrialization went beyond wartime exigencies, thought Coulter, and created interest in postwar economic growth as well.[20]

Despite Coulter's relatively positive evaluation of Confederate industrialization, in 1954 Clement Eaton contended, contrary to the beliefs of today's most prominent students of Confederate history, that although the blockade "should have stimulated the growth of Southern manufacturing plants," it did not do so because too many southerners hoped the North would lift the blockade. Yet Eaton, too, remarked on the efforts of the military to produce its own shoes, other leather goods, and clothes, and of the government to channel industrial expansion by its control over manpower and transportation. The Confederacy, he said, found it necessary to "invade" the economy and abandon laissez-faire. Charles P. Roland also noted the accomplishments of General Gorgas and the Ordnance Bureau, and like Coulter he underlined the importance of the expansion of private industry, the Tredegar Iron Works especially. Just as Coulter had, Roland discovered wartime enthusiasm for postwar industrial expansion.[21]

This interpretation of Confederate economic change was not widely accepted or discussed until the 1970s. Frank E. Vandiver, for example, pointed to the increasing uniformity (the word is ours) imposed on Confederate industry. With splendid success, Josiah Gorgas took over procurement of munitions: powder, lead, cannon, shot, shell, carbines, rifles, and pistols. The same pattern was repeated elsewhere; quartermaster officers took over textile factories, the Medical Department absorbed laboratories and operated distilleries, and private companies were subjected "to subtle management techniques" as government "supervision came in thin disguise." In May 1863 a new Confederate law permitted "the War Department to seize and manage railroads, regulate freight schedules, and interchange rolling stock." At last the imposition of uniformity on the transportation system gave some chance of logic to railroad management.[22]

In his 1966 Walter Prescott Webb Memorial Lecture, Vandiver had summed up this institutionalization of the South (Brown would have said modernization). "Necessity worked its own miracles in Dixie," he declared, calling attention to the new factories, mills, laboratories, and the like that furnished the needs of the soldiers so effectively "that by 1864 the Confederacy had become an industrial state." This transformation, thought Vandiver, was "the most important fact about the wartime South . . . because it changed forever the agricultural nature of the section." Vandiver, Gorgas's biographer, logically became one of the first to see the institutional significance of Confederate economic development.[23]

One of Vandiver's former students, Emory Thomas, has taken a similar position, first in a path-breaking, marvelously provocative, and insightful little book, *The Confederacy as a Revolutionary Experience,* and later in *The Confederate Nation, 1861–1865.* In the latter Thomas discusses the industrial concerns owned by the Confederate government, the ones stimulated by it, and the economic controls imposed by the government. He emphasizes the centralization involved "because time and the South's laissez-faire heritage precluded the development of a broadly based socialized industrial economy." He agrees that Confederates produced an impressive, indeed "phenomenal," industrial establishment, despite some understandably conspicuous failures in the course of a "military-industrial revolution," "a pragmatic response to the demands of industrial war."[24]

Despite these hints and suggestions over the years, it took an Italian scholar to codify and elaborate data his American counterparts had at their fingertips for a decade and more and to present the familiar facts sufficiently developed for our purposes. Although no one has told the full story of Confederate industrialization and economic intervention, in 1978 Raimondo Luraghi demonstrated what many students of the Confederacy had observed and some had come to believe. Despite the lack of a wide literature on the issue of Confederate economic development, many students had come to an often unspoken agreement that the Confederacy had experienced a remarkable industrialization. Thus Luraghi's *Rise and Fall of the Plantation South* became the first scholarly work to do justice to an amazing, even magnificent, achievement—the industrialization of the Confederate South. He argues more extravagantly than Thomas did, but his work merits close examination. In his chapter titled "Forced Industrialization through State Socialism" Luraghi rightly asserts that "this sector of Confederate history is, indeed, far from being well understood." A forced industrialization of revolutionary proportions took place, and indeed it was carefully managed and assertively created.[25]

The capital to accomplish this revolution was scrounged out of almost nothing. And despite being called upon to make prodigious sacrifices and to accept monumental changes, "all in all, the planter class showed a remarkable patriotism and understanding of its duties," even anticipating the central government in perceiving the need to nationalize foreign trade.[26]

Luraghi explains, "The Confederate government acted immediately to nationalize the whole productive power of existing manufactures. . . . [And] following the Tredegar [Iron Works], practically every other existing industry was put under contract by the government." But the government also engendered the formation of new industry by providing help through loans for "50 percent of setting up expenses and advancing as much as one-third of the value of the contemplated output." In addition, "such industries were allowed to produce only for the government," and the profits were limited "to keep prices on a reasonable level." Soon the Confederacy advanced to fixing the prices of goods made by its contractors.[27]

Two important tools strengthened the Confederacy's hand in this process: conscription, which allowed the exemption of skilled workers, and the imposition of public domination over rail transportation. Thus the Richmond authorities could force obedience from industrialists by denying them the manpower or transportation they required. This regulation even extended to wool carding because "the government had all the factories under its control."[28]

After gaining control of the thirty-nine furnaces in the South, the Confederacy provided money to build more. It created the amazing "giant Augusta Powder Works at Augusta, Georgia. The buildings . . . were taken and the land around them purchased . . . [to establish] the largest nationally owned factory system in the world to that time." The Augusta factory was the most impressive of the many publicly owned concerns that produced nitre, lead, rifles, shoes, buttons, and other items.[29]

Meanwhile, the navy contracted with existing shipyards for shipbuilding and repair and established new yards, most of them government-owned. A shortage of machinery forced the navy to buy foundries to produce engines and parts, propellors and shafts. A large, fully adequate rope walk was established at Petersburg. But the most extensive naval industry, the Selma Cannon Foundry, which had proved unprofitable to its owners, was purchased and transformed into a naval heavy ordnance works that cast more than a hundred cannon. The navy had almost thirty installations, including shipyards, ordnance plants, machinery works, and a powder mill.[30]

All this government-induced and controlled activity turned the cities where it occurred into large industrial centers. "Among the most remarkable of such industrial cities was Richmond . . . [but] Augusta, Georgia, was truly a 'Confederate city,'" as were Columbus, Atlanta, Macon, and Selma. Very significantly, says Luraghi, "had the Confederacy lasted a little longer, coordination of national productive activities in such centers would have brought more and more planning and centralization." He may well be right, especially if the theoretical prolongation of Confederate existence had been during wartime, with its accompanying pressures for centralization, rationalization, and institutionalization. Then the Confederacy would have been an even better illustration of Richard D. Brown's concept of uniformity and modernization.[31]

Even though this industrialization had a narrow base and depended on the Confederate war effort for its market, it reflects a vigor and resource much at variance with the traditional image of a government trammeled by state rights. Although it would be extreme to claim that the Confederacy developed the value system and habits of mind of northern industrialization, it would not be too much to say that some individual southerners did and that further industrial development and modernization would have occurred if the South had won the war. Unfortunately for the South, defeat and the turmoil of Reconstruction discouraged both native capital and outside investment, hence wartime development proved to be a false start except, for example, at places like Richmond, where the Tredegar Iron Works had done a thriving business even before the war.

WITH the tremendous growth of control over the economy, nationalization of industry took place in conjunction with exploitation of free and slave labor and with the practice, when necessary, of impressing needed supplies from farmers, producers, or owners. A special bureaucracy reached into each state to regulate the process. This system, too, caused discontent among the governors and citizens. Manufactured goods such as wagons or harnesses, slave labor, and food and forage were the items most frequently impressed. Farmers always claimed they received too little for the goods government agents forced them to give up, and the agents suspected each farmer of being a speculator who thought more of his pocketbook than of the welfare of the army. Protests were voiced in Georgia and North Carolina, as one might expect, but also in other states. Governor Thomas H. Watts of Alabama, for example, complained about the way impressments were made. Even when done "by considerate officers," the practice was "odious to the sense & feelings of the People." But officers often were demanding, taking more than citizens thought necessary and at prices that, to the producers, seemed confiscatory. Watts, a former Confederate attorney general, warned the War Department that if the Confederate bid for independence failed, it would be because of "acts of tyranny by our own officers." Impressment was creating "opposition to the Government and our cause," he warned, and he urged Secretary of War James A. Seddon "to consider well the disastrous policy of harassing the producers . . . or else the consequences may be serious."[32]

Some Confederates even thought impressment was an unconstitutional attack on private property rights. Nevertheless, the practice continued and became a major source of government income—and of public disaffection. In its effort to mobilize the economy, as in some other activities, the Davis government sometimes did exceed its constitutional prerogatives. Escott mentions, for example, that the Constitution required that a census be taken before taxes be levied but "boldly Davis argued that the government had a duty to disregard that provision. . . . War had made a census impossible." And, in truth, a census was impossible. How, in December 1863, the Confederacy could have counted all its alleged citizens, including those in the vast areas outside effective control, defies understanding. That Davis's action in this instance justly may be regarded as bold tells us much about Davis and more about the Confederacy; Davis's extended argument of the obvious on this point reveals a punctilious regard for the proper procedures of government. Curtis A. Amlund delineates other instances in his unfortunately too thinly documented but useful book *Federalism in the Southern Confederacy.*[33]

Escott, who on the whole denigrates Davis's conduct in forging nationalism, credits him not only for realizing that local loyalties had a proper place within the Confederacy but also for seeking to use these loyalties in a positive way. "Davis regarded himself a strict constructionist," noted Escott, but within a context of a "federal pattern," which was, he hoped, "removed from northern influences."[34]

Indeed, Davis was a state-rights man; he had been one before 1861 and so he remained in 1865. As president of the Confederacy, he naturally viewed problems from a different perspective than he had when a senator and from those of his governors. But basically Davis sought to maintain state rights within a federal system much like that of 1789; in the Civil War context this meant getting free of the old Union, which had become increasingly more centralized and uniform. To his adversaries within the Confederacy, however, state rights was a more negative idea that meant getting free of all centralization except within their own states, which might become as centralized and uniform as they wished. Both viewpoints were state-rights-oriented in their assumptions about the nature of proper government and in their motivations; they differed in their definitions of effective state-rights government and how best to achieve it.

Despite his troubles with Governors Brown and Vance, Davis managed to win most of his struggles with the internal governmental structure on both the national and state levels. Conscription is a major case in point: a revolutionary principle, it met test after test in many of the state courts. Although Davis doubtless felt much apprehension while the deliberations proceeded, even the Georgia supreme court ruled that the draft was constitutional, whereas the Pennsylvania supreme court rejected the Union draft as unconstitutional. But not only "as he predicted" did Davis win "all his court tests," the decisions also met with hearty popular approval, indicating, Escott correctly perceived, that "Davis did not stand alone against his critics."[35]

Occasionally adversaries such as Governor Brown successfully defied Davis, but their actions had less impact than may appear at first glance. Referring to Brown's withdrawal of the Georgia militia from active duty with the Confederate army in September 1864, Escott believes that "Amlund's study cogently argues that these potential troops would not have changed the outcome of the war." Amlund contends that the Confederacy was too far gone for the withdrawn troops to make any difference. Although perhaps true, we believe it is more to the point that these troops were performing essential service in both conducting local defense and raising provisions and that when the need was greatest, they would have been available.[36]

In his chapter "The Debate over Centralization," Escott also claimed that state rights constitute something of a red herring. As Thomas B. Alexander and Richard E. Beringer have shown with respect to Confederate congressmen, Escott asserts even more broadly that typically officials at any level of government "took many limitations of states' rights in stride and reacted strongly only when many constituents were involved." Rather than being a malignant disease that brought about the Confederacy's downfall, state rights, Escott concludes, "became a useful tool for any politician who wanted to rise on the falling fortunes of the South." Manifestations of opposition to the Confederacy on the grounds of violated state rights thus constituted a safety valve for anger fed by resentment, discontent, and fear of ultimate failure by the government. We are reminded of Lewis O. Saum's argument that just as storm cellars and aspirin have their proper emergency uses, so, too, do state rights.[37]

Clearly, state rights failed substantially to inhibit Confederate development of "organizational" nationalism, that is, centralized control and uniformity. State rights did not hamper economic control and mobilization any more than it restrained such military nationalism as conscription. And state action in raising troops, throughout the war as well as initially, contributed more to the Confederate war effort than it subtracted.

IN HIS chapter "Leadership and Loyalty—Jefferson Davis, Joseph E. Brown, and the Common People," Escott builds part of his argument for *After Secession* upon the excellent doctoral dissertation by another former Frank Vandiver student, John Brawner Robbins. Indeed, Escott proclaims Robbins's dissertation as "a necessary corrective to the view that states' rights caused the defeat of the Confederacy." Escott reasons that "for the first time in their experience," during the Civil War "the yeomen became dependent upon government," and, "although strident opposition to Davis' policies arose, on the whole people accepted his leadership and the government's assumption of major new powers"; moreover, "many southerners [even] wanted the central government to go further and undertake more responsibilities than it already had."[38]

Curtis Amlund and Robbins both emphasized that the Confederate Constitution had created a very powerful central government, capable of positive action and not just negative obstructionism. But despite its specific strengths, such as the inclusion of a "necessary and proper" clause, "most students of Confederate government" have persisted in following Owsley's lead and thus have continued to view "the constitution as a clear-cut and concise embodiment of state rights thinking." Confederates, it is reasoned, created their strong government unintentionally. This conclusion, however, seems most unlikely. Every politically active Confederate was a walking constitutional commentary. Southerners had argued the United States Constitution so long and so thoroughly and had listened so intently while others did the same that to assume they did not understand the nature of the government they created seems to us absurd. Robbins would agree, for he asserts that the very term "state rights" probably meant something different—or larger—to Civil War–era southerners than it has to subsequent students. It would seem, Robbins said, that southerners employed this term "to stand for the preservation of a way of life which included localism, individualism, agrarianism, and the protection of their peculiar institution."[39]

Owsley attempted to underpin his state-rights thesis with allusions both to the Confederacy's halfhearted and intermittent suspension of the writ of habeas corpus and to the resistance and resentment manifested when it was suspended. Robbins devotes an entire chapter to the subject. At the outset it is necessary, Robbins observes, to realize how zealously southerners "guarded against any undue intrusion in their life by the national government." Davis "framed his program of Confederate nationalism in consideration of . . . [the] traditions" highly valued by southerners, "constitutional guarantees of law and liberty," which induced them "to be extremely sensitive to any threat of arbitrary arrests or martial law."[40]

Robbins cites an instance of protest by Governor Thomas O. Moore of Louisiana in which the governor, "having called the Confederacy to task," "presently assured Davis that he intended an attack neither upon him nor upon his direction of the war effort." But because such a hesitant and critical attitude existed, "Davis carefully sought," Robbins asserts, "to achieve a balance between Confederate and state governments. He resisted attempts to declare a general suspension of the writ throughout the Confederacy and endeavored to preserve both liberty and law in all parts of the country."[41]

The debates of September 1862 "demonstrated that the opposition to suspension of habeas corpus sprang from a concern to maintain civil authority and from a desire to subordinate the military to civilian government." In *State Rights*, Owsley makes much of the spectacular resistance to suspension in Georgia during the spring of 1864 led by the

"Georgia triumvirate" of Governor Brown, Vice-President Alexander H. Stephens, and the latter's brother, Linton Stephens, as an example of the weakening of the Confederate government because of a devotion to state rights. "But there is," Robbins reminds us, "another side, for not all were in opposition." Even the Georgia senators, Herschel V. Johnson and Benjamin H. Hill, who had opposed the suspension, acquiesced in the action, trusted Davis, and rebuked their disruptive Georgia friends.[42]

"Greatest support for suspension in the second Congress," wrote Robbins, anticipating the general conclusion of Alexander and Beringer, "came from regions which had been overrun by the enemy. Opposition centered in the newly elected delegations from Georgia and North Carolina," the states still enjoying the greatest degree of interior status. "As a constitutionalist, Davis naturally sought a constitutional solution" and thus believed that he should ask Congress for each specific granting of suspension. Congress failed to grant Davis as much power to suspend the writ as he had requested, but the contention that the reason for this denial was congressional respect for state rights, as Owsley testified, "is even more questionable" than the idea "that the failure to gain this power substantially altered the course of the war."[43]

Owsley argued this point in *State Rights*, but as Robbins noted, quoting from William M. Robinson, *Justice in Grey: A History of the Judicial System of the Confederate States of America*, "There is ample evidence that the army did not permit itself to be wholly checkmated in the handling of disloyal and suspect cases simply because it was denied the more effective modes of dealing with them under martial law." Thus, Robbins concluded, "State rights played an insignificant role in the debate on habeas corpus. Those who defended the doctrine of state rights, for the most part, merely played on the lowering morale of a war weary people facing defeat and the end of their dreams in order to advance personal political ambitions." This overstates the case somewhat, for other Confederates, who were opposed to conscription, used the unpopular suspension of the writ of habeas corpus as a safe way to attack the military draft, for, between the two, suspension was clearly more unpopular, and the writ was sometimes used to undermine conscription. As Senator Albert G. Brown remarked,

"The country should not be lost because of the opinion of every petty judge, authorized to issue a *habeas corpus*. . . . It would be bad to have it said, after we were in our graves, that our liberty had been lost whilst we were struggling over petty constitutional questions." These fears may have been exaggerated, but they were nevertheless real. Moreover, many Confederates who opposed conscription were not obstructionist in their state-rights opposition to the measure. Conscription broke with the American tradition; yet, Robbins observed, "Southerners, for the most part, greeted conscription more calmly than their foes across Mason and Dixon's line; certainly no bloody draft riots such as those in New York City occurred any place in the Confederacy."[44]

Even members of Congress who so firmly espoused state-rights doctrines that they hesitated to allow measures to pass that unduly strengthened the central government often tended to see the necessity of conscription and reasoned it to be "within Congress' constitutional power to pass the law." Most state-rights congressmen objected to the conscript law primarily because of the form it took; rather than rejecting the idea of compulsory service out of hand, they made alternate proposals. A Senate proposal by James L. Orr of South Carolina, for example, would have authorized the president to establish a quota for each state, "deduct therefrom the number of soldiers now in service," and requisition governors for the remainder; if a state failed to meet its quota, the president would call out that state's militia. In its final form, however, the original law made an adequate "concession to state rights" by requiring "that conscripts 'shall be assigned to companies from the State from which they respectively come.'" The wisdom of the provision reflects in the unfortunate results precipitated when the provision was not fulfilled.[45]

That the Union long delayed conscription, continuing instead to rely on states to raise troops, seriously diminished the effectiveness of her armies. Whereas Confederate conscripts usually reinforced existing veteran units, most northern states formed their recently enlisted soldiers into new companies, so their veteran units shrank in size and freshly raised regiments often composed almost exclusively of green men were sent into battle. A year or more was needed for these novices to acquire the effectiveness of the comparable Confederate or-

ganization in which veterans and conscripts were integrated. Thus
state prerogatives in the North reduced the Union army's combat effectiveness while national action in the South maintained the quality of
the Confederate land forces. But Congress's provision assigning draft-
ees to companies from their own state undoubtedly eased the conscripts' integration into their units.

Robbins admitted that Governor Brown of Georgia engaged Davis
"in a long, legalistic dispute on the nature of Confederate government
and the unconstitutionality of conscript laws," thereby establishing
himself as "the foremost gubernatorial critic of conscription." But
someone was bound to be foremost; Brown enjoyed playing that role,
and he did not sway any major segment of the country, or even of his
own state, to massive defiance of the law's operation. One editor called
Brown's position "ridiculous." "The Governor," said J. Henly Smith in
a letter to Vice-President Stephens, "was a 'cranky and very unsafe
man—governed as much by vindictiveness and other bad impulses as
by patriotic or correct views.'" Other critics, too, voiced their disagreement with Brown.[46]

The governors' reactions to the conscript legislation are better illustrated by John Milton of Florida and John Gill Shorter of Alabama than
by Joseph Brown. Even the governor of South Carolina, that ancient
hotbed of state rights, was pacified after his early objections to the
exemption law that accompanied the conscript legislation. "A strong
letter" was enough to do the trick, and "conscription functioned
smoothly in the state until the last years of the war." Davis argued
with Governor Francis Pickens that if the president were wrong, the
proper mode of redress was not defiance of Congress but appeal to the
courts. "The Confederate courts, as well as those of the State," Davis
noted, "possess ample powers for the redress of grievances whether
inflicted by legislation, or Executive usurpation." South Carolina
would be embarrassed if it defied a law that was subsequently upheld
in the courts, meanwhile subjecting the state's citizens to punishment
for its violation.[47]

Davis's faith in the courts was not misplaced, generally speaking.
Significantly, and damning to the state-rights thesis, "in practice the
greatest support for conscription came from courts, usually state
courts," in contrast to resistance in the North. The state courts tested

and affirmed the law's constitutionality, and they addressed questions concerning "the relation between state and Confederate governments. On both problems judges rendered decisions favorable to the nationalist viewpoint." To be sure, there were exceptions; not surprisingly, the most important one was a judge in North Carolina, Richmond M. Pearson, who "thwarted the operation of conscription in the Tarheel State by issuing writs of habeas corpus to free men held by Confederate conscript officers. [But] his obstructionist tactics became so great [i.e., pernicious] that even Governor Vance hoped to check his influence."[48]

Robbins's analysis indicates that Owsley's interpretation was faulty, for "engaging in a life or death struggle, many willingly extended to the Confederate government direct coercive power over individuals." And "in supporting conscription they demonstrated that Confederate leadership was equipped to face the reality of modern war." In 1880, General Emory Upton praised the Confederacy for adopting conscription. It had served a national purpose because it explained "for all time, the meaning and extent of the power to raise and support armies. Appalled, but not unmanned, it rose to the occasion . . . treating the principle [of state sovereignty] as a dead letter." Upton's praise was overgenerous, but what some choose to call nationalism, and we choose to call centralization and uniformity, decisively undermined the operation of state rights and autonomy, even though lip service was still paid to the old ideas.[49]

GIVING SERIOUS consideration to the common folk's support of the Confederacy, Paul Escott states that, although "ideology meant less" to the masses, it does not follow that they felt markedly different from either their elected leaders or the upper classes. "Their prime need," Escott continued, "was immediate economic assistance, and they did not hesitate to seek or accept it whenever it was offered. Indeed," he asserts, "a majority of the common people may have welcomed and even desired an aggressive expansion of the central government's role." These southerners sent thousands of letters to their central government. Most of the writers had a specific problem that they wanted the government to do something about; a few even "revealed something about the people's political values and showed that some ordinary southerners wanted the Richmond administration to ignore states' rights."[50]

In a more recent article considering only North Carolina, Escott dealt with how very hard the war hit the populace. North Carolina was "a small-farming state; 72 percent of its white citizens had no slaves to do the essential work of raising food." Yet the state contributed more men in proportion to its population than any other. In an "initial burst of regional loyalty," many thousands of Tar Heels volunteered, and then—because the state stayed securely under southern control for so long—the Confederacy drew heavily upon it. "The state provided more conscripts than any other"; approximately 125,000 of its male citizens served at some time or another, more than its entire military population because of the service of overage men and underage boys.[51]

The masses complained variously about shortages, the substitute law, the law exempting the overseers of twenty or more slaves, and inflation. Davis was not unaware of nor insensitive to these problems, but he took no action to solve them because of "the continual atmosphere of military crisis. Often . . . the pressing needs of the army . . . aggravated the problems of the poor." But "without the support of the common people the Confederacy could not survive," and as the war went on, the central government failed to fulfill their requirements.[52]

The majority of Confederates had very real needs, as Owsley emphasized in a 1926 article, "Defeatism in the Confederacy." He stressed that by 1863 "enthusiasm had disappeared from great sections . . . and was rapidly dying among the soldiers. . . . By 1865 a complete collapse was impending, even had the Confederate army remained undefeated." He began his exposition by focusing on the upcountry regions, where "hope of an ultimate settlement" and "lack of economic interest in slavery and sectionalism" from the first had induced in the populace there either coolness or outright opposition to the Confederacy. Once the war began, however, many of these people had sided with the South because "they disliked 'Yankees' and feared Negro equality . . . and were stung to great anger" by Lincoln's "invasion." Significantly, Owsley thought that "the up-country people could easily fight a ninety-day war . . . but not a war that lasted over several years. Anger and enthusiasm are too transient to serve as a basis of war."[53]

But in his article Owsley did not stress the uncertain bases of Confederate nationalism. Rather, he examined closely the factors that sapped the will to win, seeing the primary cause of the "defeatist psychology" in "the suffering of the soldiers and their families." He noted that "the raids of the enemy and the occupation of the country also added tremendously to the destitution of the people. Frequently this destitution was made more appalling by the terror-stricken women and children fleeing back into the Confederate territory where they were without homes, food, or any means of support save what the charity of others almost as poor might offer."[54]

In support of this conclusion he cited enemy "robberies, rapes, arsons, and plundering," as well as "depredations of every description, broken open smokehouses and stables and stolen meat, forage and horses" and "breaking up of furniture." Owsley's Confederate source believed that as a result of these devastations, the "feeling of the inhabitants, especially those who have heretofore been neutral or Union in sentiment, is now strong for the southern cause. The depredations of the enemy has [sic], I think, been beneficial to the cause." A Union general, whom Owsley quotes, must have reached the same conclusion, for he proposed to curb this activity by hanging perpetrators if necessary.[55]

Owsley does not discuss the allegations that these ravages were counterproductive, although such incidents often are. But his point about the morale-depressing effects of terrorist activity is well taken. Whether such devastations lower morale and engender defeatism depends on the duration or repetition of the hardships and the prospect of relief from them. Of course, strong nationalism or a feeling of distinctiveness from the invader do much to fortify endurance in the face of enemy action. In earlier wars, for example, Christians displayed greater fortitude in withstanding terrorism by infidels or heretics than they did when people of an essentially identical religion sought to intimidate them. Owsley's reference to good combat performance by a Union regiment composed of white Alabamians illustrates this point.

If some southerners fought on the enemy side, many more must have been lukewarm to the Confederate cause, and, after their indignation at the depredations subsided, their thoughts may well have turned toward peace.[56]

Experiencing Union destructiveness, as distinguished from reading and hearing about it, influenced few Confederates, for most lived far from the scene of active campaigning. But Owsley does not rely on the direct or indirect effect of enemy action to explain defeatism. He stresses the economic suffering of many citizens, showing that by mid-1863 speculation and rising prices had severely hurt poorer consumers and turned their minds to thoughts of peace; by this date, there were organized tories even in South Carolina. Many families were left destitute by the enlistment or conscription of their menfolk. Certainly the soldier's pay did not suffice, with inflation escalating prices, particularly for salt, an absolute necessity in that era. But the Confederate government did a great deal to solve or at least to alleviate its salt-supply problems. A vast array of supportive officials evolved to help with coordination and distribution, and through government efforts salt was often "parceled out to the families according to need, with preference given to indigent soldiers' families."[57]

The Richmond bread riots of April 1863, repeated that spring in Atlanta, Columbus, Salisbury, and High Point and in September in Mobile, bear testimony to real deprivation in the eastern portions of the Confederacy. Even in the countryside disorders erupted because of a shortage of food; the paradox of an agricultural society able to feed and supply its soldiers but not always its citizens was dramatically apparent. Paul Escott found much support in North Carolina for Owsley's position on the effects of destitution on the morale and will of the people. In that state 20 to 40 percent of the home-front population needed food and poor relief. "Eventually," wrote Escott, "both state government and the Confederacy became involved in relief efforts, but the evidence leaves little doubt that they were not equal to the challenge."[58]

Disaffection caused by the government's inability to meet the citizens' needs contributed to an organized peace movement in the South. Peace societies, Owsley says, "began to show great strength by 1863."

"The 'Peace Society' of Alabama," he writes, even "claimed that information furnished by it to the Federal armies resulted in the surrender of Vicksburg and the defeats around Chattanooga."[59]

Owsley observed that the operation of the conscription act and its exemptions also caused hard feelings and reinforced the discontent fostered by enemy action and economic deprivation. He stressed the effect of hardship on the home front on soldiers, believing that men deserted whenever they "received letters from home, depicting such terrible conditions and at the same time telling of able-bodied speculators who should have been in the army." The results, as he poignantly put it, were that "the morning sun often shown upon an empty tent, the former occupant of which was far on his way back home, presenting his cocked musket as a furlough, to any who questioned his going." Owsley sketches the problem convincingly. The suffering caused by disorder, destitution, inflation, and inadequate relief had defeated many of the poor up-country people, some of them at an early date, and caused them to withhold their support for the continuation of the war. This "defeatism," Owsley concluded, "had sapped and mined the moral foundations of the South . . . and by 1865 a complete collapse was impending, even had the Confederate army remained undefeated. . . . The will to war had been broken by causes other than military defeat."[60]

Owsley does not directly address the question of the vigor of Confederate nationalism, although he does note its comparative weakness in the up-country region; instead, he stresses the reasons why it decreased and defeatism and the peace movements emerged. Basically, the hardships of a war economy and the almost inevitable inequality among individual contributions to the conflict depressed home-front morale, and this feeling, communicated to the troops, along with the operation of the conscription act, helped foster desertion and loss of morale in the armies.

Stanley Lebergott agrees with Owsley's interpretation and quotes with approval General Joseph E. Johnston's belief that in "the last year of the war a soldier's pay 'would scarcely buy one meal for his family. . . . Soldiers of the laboring class were compelled to choose between their military service and . . . their duties to their wives and children. They . . . left the army and returned . . . to support their families.'" Impressment of supplies, Lebergott adds, "concentrated on the easiest targets—farms run by soldiers' wives, who," Johnston argued, "'wrote that it was necessary that he [the soldier] return to save them from suffering and starvation. Such summons . . . was never unheeded.'"[61]

The privation and sense of injustice on the home front exercised a tremendous attraction to draw men from the ranks. But for the first three years of the war, soldiers resisted this call surprisingly well. The activities of the state governments must have provided one cause for their persistence with the colors.

IN THE absence of sufficient aid from the Confederate government, the states were the logical agencies to step into the gap and provide succor to the suffering families of private soldiers and poor folk. Charles W. Ramsdell's classic study *Behind the Lines in the Southern Confederacy* provides a thumbnail sketch of the myriad activities that the states undertook to relieve the trying condition of their people. These steps "involved an unprecedented extension of political authority and control," Ramsdell believed, and pointed to the record. In 1863, for example, Mississippi appropriated $.5 million to relieve the families of poor soldiers, and North Carolina spent $1.5 million. Georgia allocated $2.5 million for direct relief, $.5 million for salt, $100,000 for cotton and wool cards, and $6 million for "indigent dependents." Louisiana set aside $5 million for pensions, and Alabama appropriated $4 million for destitute families of soldiers. Early relief efforts had often been under local control, but by 1864 the states had taken over most of the task "in the interest of greater efficiency and a more equal distribution of the burden," and both taxes and grants made from those taxes began to be levied and distributed in kind instead of in cash because of the difficulties with the currency. The in-kind system was awkward, but it was required by the disordered state of Confederate finances. This arrangement tells us much about the condition of the Confederate economy in 1864 and goes far toward explaining why relief programs were necessary.[62]

In all of this activity, no state stood ahead of Georgia. Her governor, Joseph E. Brown, was in the forefront of governors resisting policies of the Richmond government, and he led his state to a similar premier position in its activities related to the war effort. Much of the state's energy went to aid the poor, especially those dependent on the fighting men, as Paul Escott has clearly shown in his superb 1979 Southern Historical Association paper, "Serving Two Masters: The Political Acumen of Georgia's Joseph E. Brown."

Governor Brown also deplored the raising of large quantities of cotton, a misallocation of resources, as Stanley Lebergott has shown, resulting from planters looking to their pecuniary gain rather than the needs of a war economy. The governor tried to restrict the growing of cotton to concentrate production on the foodstuffs needed by the common people. With the same objective he "waged a relentless war on distilleries" to conserve grain for human consumption.[63]

The state of Georgia, for example, arranged for its own stocks of salt, which it supplied free or at low cost to the poor. But "soldiers' wives and widows and the parents of dead soldiers" had priority in this distribution. Governor Brown also advocated many other measures to aid the fighting men, including tax exemptions for the poorer soldiers and a one-hundred-dollar payment for the family of each of these men in the armed forces. The state also provided food to the indigent, including more than one hundred thousand bushels of corn in 1864.[64]

In turning the "state government into an effective relief agency," Brown and the legislature raised taxes and enlarged the budget tremendously, spending in 1863 an amount in excess of all state appropriations for the decade of the 1850s. Inflation accounted for some, but far from all, of this increase. Most of the budget went for welfare and military expenses.[65]

In addition to raising armed forces to protect the state, Georgia did much for the war effort by assisting its men in the Confederate army. To meet their needs the state purchased at home and abroad such necessities as blankets, clothing, and medicine, eventually chartering ships that ran the blockade with state-owned cotton and returned with goods for the state. The governor could point with pride in 1864 to the appropriation of "$10,000,000 to feed and clothe the suffering wives, and widows, and orphans, and soldiers, and to put shoes upon the feet and clothes upon the backs of soldiers themselves, who are often destitute."[66]

By 1864 Georgia's military expenses accounted for over 43 percent of state expenditures and welfare activities for over 51 percent. Although counties equipped volunteers, the bulk of their increased outlays went for welfare. The motive behind this public spending and support of soldiers' families was the desire to diminish desertion. Fearing that if the soldiers became "demoralized," defeat would result, Governor Brown said: "Let our soldiers know that their loved ones at home are provided for." Thus more than half of the state's war-related expenditures went for welfare and even more of the counties' outlays. Of course, soldiers also received direct aid from the state government.[67]

Georgia helped pay for these expenditures by borrowing, reducing nonmilitary costs, and levying a progressive income tax that helped shift the tax base from proportional to progressive and redistributed purchasing power. Brown believed that because the "poor have generally paid their part of the cost of this war in military service, exposure, fatigue and blood, the rich, who have been in a much greater degree exempt from these, should meet the money demands of the Government." Therefore, Brown intended that Georgia's wealth would be taxed as heavily as necessary to provide for the needs of the soldiers and their families.[68]

North Carolina did as much for its troops and exceeded Georgia's total of eight thousand men kept out of the Confederate army. But depriving Confederate service of such a large number of men did not represent a total loss to the war effort. Often, when governors sought an exemption for an individual, they responded to a request such as that made to Governor Brown in behalf of a blacksmith whose neighbors supported his appeal because they stood "in grate need of a smith to repair their plows to prepair their lande for a small grain crop." Of course, many of these exempts served in the militia, and their civilian occupations help explain Brown's great anxiety to furlough them during the expected period of inactivity in 1864 after the fall of Atlanta.[69]

On balance, Georgia's contributions toward winning the war seem to have greatly exceeded the losses resulting from obstruction and keeping more men out of Confederate service than necessity probably warranted. And if Georgia's attempts, like its obstruction, surpassed the norm for the other Confederate states, still its contributions show what other states did in a lesser degree to support the home front as well as local defense and the armies. Meanwhile, the central govern-

ment was not without a share of compassionate and sensitive officials
who did their individual bits to provide relief for some segments of the
populace.[70]

Thus the common folk, the backbone of the South, felt tremendous
deprivation and, though the Confederate government tried at several
levels to alleviate the situation, its efforts proved inadequate to meet
their needs. Georgia's spectacular example of state aid endeared the
governor to the common folk, for the "southern yeomen were not as
ideological as the planter class and they supported Brown not because
he was fighting for states' rights but because he was standing up for
their interests." As Escott notes elsewhere, "Many states rights controversies in the latter part of the war actually had their origin in
welfare." In their "simple desire to relieve their hard-pressed citizens," he concluded, "state leaders found themselves opposing the
programs of the central government." Because Brown, Vance, and
some other governors achieved a measure of success in meeting the
welfare needs of their constituents, the war effort was strengthened,
not undermined, and the positive aspects of state rights became more
apparent.[71]

IN THE light, therefore, of the careful analysis of a number of scholars,
Owsley's state-rights thesis does not carry the weight long attributed
to it. The development of centralization and uniformity within the Confederacy and the revolutionary changes that were wrought are far
more significant phenomena from our point of view than the state-
rights ideas to which so much lip service was paid. There was a state-
rights sentiment, yes—especially vented in rhetoric that provided a
needed release of tension and a rallying point for a political opposition
deprived of the legitimacy of party division.

Meanwhile, conscription, adopted by the Confederacy more than a
year before the Union enacted a comparable measure, proved effective.
This policy helps explain why the Confederacy mobilized a higher percentage of its total population, slave and free, than did the North and,
unlike the North, maintained its strength in a way that did not dilute its
combat effectiveness. The Confederacy supplied and equipped these
large armies and kept its railroads going, albeit with steadily declining
efficiency. The Confederate Constitution was strong enough to sanction

these effective war measures. And even when there were manifestations of state-rights-motivated resistance to government practices, their impact was not serious, much less devastating. Though the national military effort circumscribed state activity, it did not impair the vigor of the state governments, which still could and did make many valuable contributions that directly and indirectly aided the war effort.

Historians generally have been negligent in treating this phenomenon, often regarding state rights from an exclusively negative point of view. Perhaps the reason for this attitude is that state rights in their own time often have been used as a political tool to block social change. Or they may be reacting to the use of state rights to justify noninterference with the institution of slavery in the generation before the war. The idea has therefore acquired the same reputation as the institution it was used to protect, which is as logical as equating Lewis Saum's aspirin or storm shelter with a headache or tornado. That a remedy may be used for questionable ends, however, does not affect its legitimacy nor should it color historians' evaluations of its potency. Just because the idea had positive aspects in the Civil War does not necessarily mean it would provide a suitable tool with which to meet twentieth-century crises. One must analyze the issue in the Civil War context, applying it to the government of people who were used to being governed by a light hand. When the antebellum American turned to government at all, it was usually to the state government. Americans of all sections and parties believed in the general principle of state rights; they differed only in its particular application. "Died of State Rights" must be chiseled off the Confederate tombstone.

Chapter Eleven

Union Concentration
in Time and Space

S TATE RIGHTS was not a decisive factor in the Confederate defeat and even had the positive effect of assisting the war effort by using abilities and resources at the state and local levels to supplement the work of the central government. At times of crisis, recriminations and fault-finding between the two levels of government were to be expected. On the whole, however, if the Confederacy could not match Union resources, it came close enough to prevent northern armies from achieving their objectives. Since the Confederacy did not die of state rights or any of its corollary problems, we must look elsewhere to explain Confederate defeat. Unless Confederate military performance had deteriorated, or the Union had found some way to overcome its inadequate ratio of force to space, the Confederacy could expect to continue to prevent its opponents from achieving any decisive success. The stalemate would continue.

But the campaigns had more than military significance for the Confederacy. Confederate morale and the South's imperfect, fragile nationalism depended on apparent military success for critical support. To sustain morale, the Confederacy's armies had to win victories in battle and prevent the loss of small but necessarily symbolic pieces of territory. Of course, we must take into account the perversity of a symbol. If both sides believe that a symbolic victory or patch of earth is a real objective, it becomes a real objective.

In the spring of 1862 the Union armies of Halleck and McClellan had made simultaneous advances (concentration of forces in time, as Clausewitz called them). After repelling the fortuitously concurrent diversions of Lee into Maryland and of Bragg, Kirby Smith, Price, and Van Dorn in the West in the fall of 1862, Halleck and Lincoln planned a new coordinated offensive. Simultaneous advances seemed particularly important because Halleck and the president were convinced that Confederate use of interior lines had caused Union defeats. Many Union soldiers falsely believed, for example, that reinforcements from Beauregard in Mississippi had fought with Lee in the Seven Days' Battles. The Confederates had, however, made vigorous and intelligent use of their railroads in the First Manassas, Seven Days, Shiloh, and Kentucky campaigns. Some of their lines of communication between theaters were much shorter than those of the Union, the railroad from Richmond to Chattanooga being the most important. But another key connection, the route from northern Mississippi through Mobile to Chattanooga, far exceeded in length the Union rail and water routes between these two major lines of operations. Further, without adequate maintenance, Confederate railways deteriorated. Worn rails dictated slow speeds, and slow speeds had the same effect as greater distances.

But the South did not need to have interior lines of operations, that is, to have better railroad interconnections than the North had, to move troops from a quiet theater to reinforce a menaced army. Surprise could substitute for interior lines. Jefferson Davis's often active and strategically intelligent direction of the South's war effort employed Confederate railroads to obtain concentration in space.

Lincoln and Halleck again wisely applied the principle of concentration in time, that is, simultaneous advances, in the fall of 1862. Unlike the situation in the spring, however, the Union now had three main lines of operations, Virginia, Middle Tennessee, and the Mississippi, in addition to those along the coast. But President Lincoln and General in Chief Halleck stressed the land frontier of the Confederacy, and in December 1862 Halleck made a strong but not entirely successful attempt to coordinate the advances of the armies in these three main theaters. The other feature of the fall strategy, a deliberate plan to concentrate in the West with special emphasis on opening the Mississippi River, resulted from Halleck's influence and Lincoln's response to the obvious midwestern concern, reflected in the fall elections, that the Union gain control of that symbolically and commercially important river.

Lincoln and Halleck would have been happy to have McClellan make a forward move immediately after the Battle of Antietam, before the other armies were ready. But McClellan's difficulties in supplying and reequipping his large force reinforced his reluctance to advance directly against Lee. McClellan saw the strategic situation just as Lee did; he knew instinctively that Lee's two-sided base threatened his army, for Lee had not only Richmond and the vital Virginia Central Railroad as one base to the south, but, thanks to rail and road connections, he had the Shenandoah Valley and its abundant crops as a second base to the west. From this Valley base Lee threatened the flank and rear of any Union advance on Richmond. As he explained to Stonewall Jackson in November, when the Union army already was moving toward Fredericksburg, "Your remaining in the valley was based upon the supposition that, by operating upon the flank and rear of the enemy, you might prevent his progress southward." For this reason McClellan felt that he must move directly on Lee's army because to thrust toward Richmond would expose his own flank and rear.[1]

Lincoln and Halleck emphatically disagreed and pointed out to McClellan that he, too, had a two-sided base, the Chesapeake Bay side of which could supply him if he moved toward Richmond and Lee's critical Virginia Central Railroad. Lincoln wrote McClellan, beginning his letter by quoting from Jomini: "Again, one of the standard maxims of war, as you know, is 'to operate upon the enemy's communications as much as possible without exposing your own.'" Attempting to persuade McClellan that he could turn the Confederate army, Lincoln explained that Lee's route to Richmond "is the arc of a circle, while yours is a chord." Lincoln then dwelt on the advantage of McClellan's two-sided base: "The chord-line, as you see, carries you by Aldie, Hay Market, and Fredericksburg; and you see how turn-pikes, railroads, and finally, the Potomac by Aquia Creek, meet you at all points from Washington." Had Lincoln been encouraging McClellan to march all the way to Richmond, he could also have pointed to the Rappahannock and York rivers as sources of supplies and extensions of his base.[2]

In late October McClellan finally began to move his Army of the Potomac forward, not to outrun Lee to Richmond but to threaten his communications and force him from his position. But immediately after the fall elections of 1862, Lincoln replaced McClellan, the cautious Democratic idol, and chose instead the experienced and successful but inept Ambrose E. Burnside. Burnside at once began for the first time the straightforward fighting advance so ardently desired by such combative civilians as Secretary of War Stanton. Burnside's advance and his use of the communications in eastern Virginia for a base vindicated Lincoln and Halleck's belief that Lee's position in the northern Shenandoah Valley had not interdicted an advance directly on Richmond. Lee originally had surmised that the Federals again would use McClellan's Peninsular strategy and advance south of the James River. By early November the shape of events was becoming clearer. Soon Lee became certain that the Union objective was Fredericksburg, and on November 22 he informed Richmond that Burnside's forces had arrived on the opposite side of the Rappahannock at Fredericksburg.[3]

Lee confessed that he had no idea what Burnside intended to do there, but he reasoned that if Burnside changed "his base of operations" to the James as had McClellan, "the effect produced in the United States would be almost equivalent to a defeat," because the public demanded the direct, fighting advance which McClellan's more sophisticated strategy had denied them. Lee therefore expected Burnside to attempt a move from Fredericksburg to Richmond, which he accordingly sought to obstruct. Davis agreed with Lee's assessment for, as the president pointed out to Lee, McClellan had lost his command because of his hesitant movement from his Potomac base, and "it is hardly supposable that his successor will fail to attempt the movement."[4]

The results could have been predicted even before the battle occurred. Attempting to continue his direct advance on Richmond, Burnside met Lee's army on December 13, 1862, in a most disadvantageous position for Union fortunes. Apparently believing he faced only one wing of Lee's forces, he actually attacked all of Lee's army, head-on. Burnside lost about 12,500 men compared to only 5,300 for the Confederates. This Union frontal attack, like that of Pope against Jackson's corps at Second Manassas, failed utterly.

Lee had every excuse for optimism as this battle approached, yet he remained circumspect even as the advantage grew. He believed that "we must make up our minds to fight with great odds against us." He therefore denied a request to reinforce Wilmington from his army, instead expressing the wish that his own army might be doubled. He regretfully concluded that additional troops for North Carolina must come from that state itself. This latter remark not only illustrates Lee's prudence but also seemed to justify the suspicions of men such as Governor Vance. Lee's caution had the effect of reinforcing Vance's demands for North Carolina's control over her own local defense and thereby contributed to the feeling of isolation and neglect that helped to sap the will of the Tar Heels.[5]

Although Burnside's bungling produced this colossal Union failure, many Union generals thought that politicians, who saw war in terms of battles and did not understand the power of the tactical defense, had ordered it. These generals believed, with Clausewitz, that such "blind aggressiveness would destroy the attack itself, not the defense." Despite the drubbing he received, Burnside at least proved the indestructibility of Civil War armies.[6]

BURNSIDE'S ATTACK had been the first conflict in the Union's simultaneous advances scheduled for December 1862. The second took place in Tennessee. Here, too, Lincoln had changed generals, replacing Don Carlos Buell because the victor of Perryville, like McClellan, seemed addicted to overly thorough preparations. Lincoln playfully diagnosed this as a disease, which he called the "slows," and replaced Buell with William S. Rosecrans, who, like Burnside, had achieved success in an independent command. Rosecrans also believed in thorough preparation, but he had ample justification in taking such pains in view of the interruption of the Louisville and Nashville Railroad by Confederate raiders and guerrillas.

Like Burnside, Rosecrans believed in the possibility of a decisive, essentially frontal battle. At the end of December, after accumulating adequate supplies, the new commander, a courageous and hard-drinking Democrat with theological interests, advanced directly on Bragg's army at Murfreesboro. The Confederates were expecting the move and the impending battle. Kirby Smith reported that Rosecrans was "enterprising" and his force "underestimated," but he expected Bragg to give a good account of himself. Though each commander planned to attack the other's right, Bragg attacked first, on December 31, 1862, and the surprise he attained, together with his concentration of superior numbers, rather than turning the enemy, enabled him to drive back the flank of Rosecrans's army through a 90 degree angle. Nevertheless, the power of the defense and the maneuverability of the armies allowed Rosecrans to defend his peculiar position, though he had clearly lost the battle.[7]

But Rosecrans was either too obtuse or too optimistic and determined to realize that the Confederates had defeated him, and he refused to retreat. In this case Rosecrans's obstinacy had its rewards, for, after several days with the armies facing one another, Bragg lost his nerve and concluded that he, not Rosecrans, had lost the battle. Bragg therefore retreated, inspired, perhaps, by Rosecrans's deception. The latter brought empty railway trains in at night with troops on hand at the station to cheer, thus simulating the arrival of reinforcements. Rosecrans occupied Murfreesboro on January 5, 1863.

The armies remained unshaken by the immense losses in this hard-fought battle, proving again—as if proof were still needed—that Civil War armies could not be destroyed. Each side lost about twelve thousand men, 31 percent of the Union army and 33 percent of the Confederate. Bragg fell back thirty-six miles to the next town on the railroad, where he took up a position he would hold for the next half year. Rosecrans made no effort to pursue Bragg's unshaken, veteran army. Like most Civil War battles, this was a case of the "beaten force being able to rally only a short distance away without its situation changed at all." Even more than usual, the explanation lay "in the fact that the superiority won in battle was not enough to drive its impact home," as Clausewitz would have put it.[8]

But in view of the more ample Union manpower, more such battles, with essentially even losses, would have been advantageous to the North. Other than casualties, the psychological impact was the main significance: the Confederates retreated at Murfreesboro and, therefore, had given Lincoln a much-needed political victory and Rosecrans a temporary reputation as a successful and combative general.

The two armies in Tennessee faced each other during the winter and spring of 1863, and, though constantly urged again to attack Bragg, Rosecrans spent his time improving the capacity of his communications and supply arrangements. He ensured their security against raiders and guerrillas, worried about another Confederate diversion into Kentucky, and tried to cope with the vastly superior cavalry force that the Confederates had concentrated against him. This cavalry force not only menaced the vulnerable railroad connecting his army with the Ohio River at Louisville but controlled the countryside, helping the Confederates supply themselves. And by circumscribing the area of Federal foraging, the powerful Confederate cavalry made Rosecrans even more heavily dependent upon the fragile railroad.

And yet the psychology of the Murfreesboro campaign damaged southern morale. Indeed, Confederates not only acknowledged Rosecrans's enterprising nature but confessed to overconfidence themselves. Both Bragg and Joseph E. Johnston had relied excessively on winter weather to hinder enemy action and on "the want of such enterprise heretofore by the enemy" in East Tennessee, and it seems logical that such a fatal attitude would have applied in the generals' assessment of their chances in Middle Tennessee as well. In any event, Confederate consternation was plain. Johnston regretted that Bragg had fallen back "so far," attempted unsuccessfully to get Bragg's cavalry to force Rosecrans into retreat, and was chagrined to note that Bragg was not beaten back, but rather "fell back . . . on hearing that the enemy was re-enforced." Seeking to aid Bragg, Johnston faced a dilemma. Just before the Battle of Murfreesboro, the president had ordered troops from Bragg's army to Mississippi; so Johnston queried Davis as to "which is the most valuable, Tennessee or the Mississippi?" Such questions are confessions of despair. They ask, in effect, what do we choose to lose? General Bragg even sent an anxious appeal all the way to General Beauregard in Charleston, asking for assistance from that quarter. The Creole general had his own problems with coast defense, however, and not only gave no aid to Bragg but asked Bragg for aid in the form of captured guns. And here we might add that Bragg's request was symptomatic of a Confederate tendency to look to the coast for assistance when the interior was in need; Bragg's appeal may have made much sense to him, but it would have made little sense to the governor of South Carolina. Clearly the situation in the West was desperate.[9]

BUT THE view from the Union's side was at least as gloomy. Of Lincoln and Halleck's three concentrated, simultaneous advances planned for

December 1862, one had failed completely in Virginia, a second had only accidental and dubious success in Middle Tennessee, and the third, along the Mississippi River, seemed to be as unrewarding as the campaign in Virginia, though less bloody. Grant's campaign against Vicksburg had preceded Rosecrans's costly but modest victory, and it seemed to lead to no positive results. Strongly reinforced for a push down the Mississippi to capture the Confederate stronghold, Grant determined on dual advances. One force under William T. Sherman would move on the river; the other, under Grant, would advance along the railroad toward the rear of Vicksburg's river-oriented defense. Grant thought these two forces would mutually support each other and that his own would turn Vicksburg's defense by cutting the railroad to Jackson.

The offensive proved a dismal failure. Grant had to abandon his own advance in mid-December when a raid by Confederate cavalry under General Van Dorn destroyed his depot at Holly Springs, even capturing Mrs. Grant's horses and burning her carriage; another raiding force, under the incomparable Nathan Bedford Forrest, had also broken his railroad farther north at Jackson, Tennessee.[10] For the time being Van Dorn's success spelled the doom of Grant's move. Cut off from reliable communication with his base, Grant fell back. Sherman also retreated, for his waterborne attack failed in the rugged and fortified terrain north of Vicksburg, when, on December 29, 1862, his force of 25,000 lost 1,776 men in an unsuccessful assault at Chickasaw Bluffs. The 13,800 entrenched Confederate defenders lost only 207 men. Sherman had had little choice but to make a frontal attack, for his water line of communications led directly to Vicksburg and, amid swamps and obstructed bayous, led nowhere else.[11]

Lincoln and Halleck's simultaneous advances, which menaced all major rebel armies, had worked to prevent Confederates from reinforcing one threatened theater from another, unmenaced area. In fact, an effort to do just this had helped the Union when President Davis had taken a strong division from Bragg before the Battle of Murfreesboro and sent it to Mississippi, where much of it arrived too late to contest the advance of either Grant or Sherman.

But the failure of the triple offensive, plus the backlash against the final Emancipation Proclamation of January 1, 1863, caused Union morale to suffer. The reverses sustained by the Republican party in the fall elections two months earlier seemed but the beginning of the consequent misfortune. On January 3, 1863, Governor Oliver P. Morton of Indiana warned Secretary of War Stanton that his state legislature intended "to pass a joint resolution acknowledging the Southern Confederacy, and urging the States of the Northwest to dissolve all constitutional relations with the New England States. The same thing," he added, "is on foot in Illinois." Lincoln's concern deepened when General John A. McClernand told him that he had heard citizens in Illinois shouting hurrahs for John Morgan, Jefferson Davis, and Stonewall Jackson.[12]

Iowa was also in a demoralized condition. Shocked by the emancipation policy and encouraged by their party's success at the polls the preceding November, Democrats held numerous peace meetings throughout the state in January 1863. Governor Samuel Kirkwood, fearing "an outbreak of the disloyal," asked for five thousand arms and authority to raise two or three regiments to intimidate "unscrupulous men [who] are organizing and arming for the purpose of resisting a draft," many of whom were evidently active in the Knights of the Golden Circle. It is no wonder that Lincoln said, as Orville H. Browning recorded in his diary, "The Almighty is against us, and I can hardly see a ray of hope."[13]

The events of late 1862 and early 1863 caused a temporary rise in Confederate morale, and Bragg initially had reported the Battle of Murfreesboro as a victory. Early in the new year, Secretary of War James A. Seddon reported to Davis that the army was "fully equal, if not superior, in all the elements of strength to what it has been at any previous period in the war." Pointing to the disasters of early 1862, Seddon summed up the year as one in which the armies were "not conquered, or repelled, but diminished by their own successes"; the salvation of the Confederacy lay in the valor of its army and more particularly in the Conscription Act. The results, said Seddon, could be seen in the victory at Fredericksburg, from which the Union army had "slunk away amid storm and darkness"; the "gallant repulse" of the Union's combined action at Vicksburg; and, writing before he learned of Bragg's retreat, the "decided victory" of General Bragg at Murfreesboro.[14]

When, on January 12, 1863, the Confederate Congress convened for its new session, Davis concluded in his message that the first two years of Confederate history "affords ample excuse for congratulation and demands the most fervent expression of our thankfulness to the Almighty Father, who has blessed our cause." Confederates, said Davis, "have added another to the lessons taught by history for the instruction of man; . . . they have afforded another example of the impossibility of subjugating a people determined to be free" even in the face of superior numbers or resources. John Beauchamp Jones, the rebel war clerk, gloated over the recent news and purred to his diary that it affected "the spirits of the people . . . and we have a merrier Christmas than the last one." The initial news of a victory at Murfreesboro was so good, said Jones, it "caused even enemies to pause and shake hands in the street." This resurgence of Confederate will was even visible to the North. William T. Sherman, once again before Vicksburg in March 1863, informed the governor of Ohio that "the South to-day is more formidable and arrogant than she was two years ago." Despite low morale on one side and high morale on the other, the situation remained in stalemate.[15]

IN THEIR response to the Union drives, the Confederates, except in Bragg's offensive battle, had adhered to Clausewitz's prescription for the defense. Lee had not avoided conflict, but his very strong position at Fredericksburg had made the attrition of his victory favorable to the Confederacy. Sherman's defeat at Chickasaw Bluffs had the same effect, and the Confederate commanders had stopped Grant's advance exclusively with raids against rail communications and Grant's "great depot of provisions and munitions," as Jomini would have called it.[16]

Fully sharing Clausewitz's and Jomini's conviction about the vulnerability of long lines of land communication, Grant, having water communications and thus more active than the rail-dependent Rosecrans, directed his attention to a means to turn the right, or northern, flank of the Vicksburg position without counting on the railroad. He refused to use the railroad again because Confederate cavalry had just proven its vulnerability. Grant therefore relied on water communications and combined operations with naval forces in his long and ultimately futile attempts to turn Vicksburg via a route through the bayous and swampy waterways north of the city. Grant's efforts to avoid dependence on the railroad reveal the real dimensions of the Union problems in conquering the Confederacy, obstacles that became clearer as operations in the West settled into a winter stalemate.

Confederate communications ran through friendly country where their forces were not usually short of supplies because, as Clausewitz would have anticipated, they had "been able to stockpile in advance." The larger size of the Union armies proved a handicap, for "an army's dependence on its base increases in intensity and scale with any increase in the army's size." Clausewitz had emphasized this problem with a metaphor: "A mere sapling is easy to transplant, but the taller it grows, the harder this will become." Thus "the longer the war remains static, the more important the problem of subsistence will become." But again this condition bore more heavily on the larger Union army, which, being "in enemy territory," had fewer communication routes and was able to rely only on the "roads on which it advanced in the first place." It must improve its "essential lines of communication" by installing "its own administration and must do this by the authority of its arms." This meant establishing garrisons throughout occupied territory to enforce its authority against the hostile populace and protect its communications, "everywhere exposed to attacks by an insurgent population."[17]

"These difficulties are particulary great," according to Jomini, "when the people are supported by a considerable body of disciplined troops. The invader has only an army: his adversaries have an army, and a people wholly in arms, and making means of resistance out of everything, each individual of whom conspires against the common enemy; even the noncombatants have an interest in his ruin and accelerate it by every means in their power." In his rear the invader "holds scarcely any ground but that upon which he encamps; outside the limits of his camp everything is hostile and multiplies a thousandfold the difficulties he meets at every step of the way."[18]

General William T. Sherman experienced in West Tennessee and northern Mississippi exactly what Jomini described, and in many other occupied areas the situation was comparable. Sherman found, in a land where "every house is a nest of secret, bitter enemies," that, though Union "armies pass across and through the land, the war closes in behind and leaves the same enemy behind." He pointed to the basic constraints within which the Union had to operate. "We are forced to invade," he wrote the governor of Ohio during the Vicksburg campaign in March 1863, and "we must keep the war South until they are not only ruined, exhausted, but humbled in pride and spirit." But he warned, "Our lines of communication are even threatened by their dashes, for which the country, the population, and character of the enemy are all perfectly adapted. The whole male population of the South is armed against us, and we ought to outnumber them—we must outnumber them if we want to succeed, and the quicker the better." The conclusion, to Sherman, was obvious: "Since the first hostile shot the people of the North have had no option; they must conquer or be conquered. There can be no [middle] course." This was "no longer an open question; we must fight it out. The moment we relax, down go all our conquests thus far."[19]

The Confederates did well because they had excellent cavalry and understood how to use it. The initial emphasis on cavalry and a high proportion of recruits familiar with horses assured high quality. Because the United States had a strong mounted infantry tradition, Confederates, trained in this tradition, understood well that cavalry while mounted could not fight infantry. Throughout the Civil War, cavalry on both sides functioned as mounted infantry, riding to battle but dismounting to fight as infantry. In this way, with their superior mobility as compared with marching infantry, they had something in common with twentieth-century aircraft in that they used their strategic mobility to reach the enemy's rear and, momentarily concentrating their forces, attacked the enemy's communications. Their initial supremacy enabled this action; it was as if the Union, with more powerful ground forces, was attempting to invade a country that had a stronger air force.

Most of the principal southern military leaders had experience on the frontier, where cavalry had developed techniques for coping with mounted native American raiders. Jefferson Davis, for example, had been a lieutenant in the dragoon regiment established in 1833. He understood well this use of mounted men, for he had advised President Polk in 1848 that "horses are in my opinion no more than transportation to Riflemen, giving celerity of movement but necessarily to be left in rear of any field on which Riflemen are to be brought into action."

Davis therefore had the experience to understand modern mounted operations.[20]

Major General Edmund Kirby Smith, also a former cavalryman, had dispatched the first of the major western raids, the two in the summer of 1862, which halted Buell's advance on Chattanooga. The Confederates were fortunate in finding able soldiers to carry out their raids. All had "presence of mind" and were "bold and full of stratagems," qualities Jomini would have deemed important in such leaders. John S. Mosby, a Virginia lawyer, operated very effectively as a partisan in Virginia, and John H. Morgan, a Kentucky merchant, devoted a good deal of time to raids, largely in Kentucky. Finally captured, he did not always heed, as did Mosby, Jomini's wish that such leaders avoid "useless danger."[21]

Most important and effective as a cavalry commander was former Memphis plantation owner, real estate broker, and slave trader Nathan Bedford Forrest, who proved to be a brilliant soldier and an audacious and almost invariably successful raider. He enlisted as a private and finished the war as a lieutenant general. In his forays into West Tennessee he recruited his forces, adding men from the pro-Confederate population as well as horses on which to mount them. The disposition of Grant's forces during his move against Vicksburg in the early spring of 1863 indicates the seriousness of the menace of raids by Forrest and others and of the strenuous efforts to meet them. Grant's army before Vicksburg numbered thirty-six thousand men; that of his rear area commander, headquartered at Memphis, numbered sixty-two thousand.

The Union had avoided many of the troubles caused by guerrillas and cavalry raiders by using gunboats on the rivers. In fact, the rivers had provided the foundation for the initial Union successes, which had forced on the Confederates a method of defense Clausewitz called deep retreat, or withdrawal "into the interior of the country." The long, vulnerable lines of supply and the forces needed to guard them exhausted the "momentum of the attack," and the invader perished "by his own exertions" in coping with "the sheer problems of existence" so far from home.[22]

But the navigable rivers and the powerful gunboat fleet had saved the Union advance along the Tennessee and Mississippi from these

problems. Whenever Union armies, such as Buell's
had to leave the river, they faced these difficulties a
emy's withdrawal into the interior, added to the rai
nications, constituted what Clausewitz called the
For this strategy the South had three "favorable circum
sparsely cultivated area," a people who were "loyal and warlike," and,
in its hot summers and damp and muddy winters, "severe weather
conditions." Clausewitz's equation would be altered, however, if the
people were no longer "loyal and warlike," as was increasingly the case
as the war wore on.[23]

Even Jomini, the apostle of the power of the offensive, would have
believed that such a resistance as the Confederacy employed would, in
the mountains of Switzerland, enable a "disciplined force" to "hold its
own against a triple number." The South's forests, bad roads, and vast
extent certainly constituted a worthy substitute for Switzerland's
mountains. That logistical difficulties had halted Buell and Grant and
immobilized Rosecrans seemed to confirm Jomini's and Clausewitz's
views about the virtual impossibility of conquering a country the size
of the South. But once again, if the equation were altered by a less
favorable manpower ratio between the contending armies, a decline in
skill, or—and this is a key point—an undermining of morale, the results might be different.[24]

Both Clausewitz and Jomini, then, understood the need for a loyal
citizenry possessed of strong morale, at least when the enemy was
operating in one's own territory. But this sine qua non posed a serious
problem for Confederates. Some had harbored little enthusiasm for
the future from the very start; by mid-1864 even the government's
loyal supporters carried debilitating burdens of guilt, fear, and war
weariness that diluted morale and rendered Confederate determination too weak for a successful defense of the southern government and
way of life.

Occupying Confederate territory, protecting it from raids like those
led by Forrest and Morgan, and covering rail lines absorbed enormous
Union resources. For example, in January 1863 against 13,000 Confederates who menaced northern Mississippi and West Tennessee, the
Union posted 51,000 men to cover railroad tracks and the routes of
advance of potential raiders. About 56,000 men protected Kentucky,

✓est Virginia, and the line of the Baltimore and Ohio against the contingent threat of 15,000 Confederates. Including the garrison of Washington and troops deployed by both sides in Missouri and Arkansas, 190,000 Union troops, more than a third of the Union total in the field, defended territory and communications against the threat of 43,000 Confederates, about one-sixth of all those available. As the amount of captured territory increased and communications lengthened, this situation could only grow worse for the Union. The Confederates, aware of this potential advantage, continued to dedicate a part of their cavalry to raids that menaced the Union army's logistical tail and disturbed political conditions.

FOR A decisive war Clausewitz had placed exclusive stress on battles: "Battle is the one and only means that warfare can employ" against the enemy for "destroying his armed forces." He did envision the fall of a capital as possibly decisive but only if the capital were very significant and the enemy's armed forces quite weak. As a rule, however, and certainly in the case of the Confederacy, "total victory" over the enemy required the "destruction of his armed forces" with "the occupation of his territory only a consequence."[25]

Some Confederates fully understood this Clausewitzian concept. Senator Williamson S. Oldham, for example, deplored squandering Confederate resources to defend the vulnerable capital and urged the evacuation of Richmond and the reestablishment of communication with the trans-Mississippi West. He concluded, at least in postwar hindsight, that the Confederacy should have avoided "crushing battles." Instead, he advocated attacking small federal units as they dispersed over the large area of the Confederacy. Oldham sensed that extensive occupation of the South could be, as Clausewitz implied, a greater source of grief for the attacker than for the defender.[26]

Total conquest required sufficient superiority in numbers, skill, and morale and an adequate ratio of force to space. If these were not available, Clausewitz would have expounded no means of attaining any victory adequate to the Union's total political objective. Nevertheless, he did occasionally allude to another method of winning, and this method the Union implicitly pursued. He realized that "the fighting forces are meant to protect their own territory and to seize the enemy's: it is the territory, on the other hand, that sustains them and keeps restoring their strength. Each then depends on the other." Understanding that the armed forces and their country "give mutual support and are of equal value to each other," Clausewitz pointed out the primacy of the armed forces because, "while they interact, they do so with a difference. If the forces are destroyed—in other words, overcome and incapable of further resistance—the country is automatically lost. On the other hand, the loss of the country does not automatically entail destruction of the forces," a point that Oldham, for one, well understood. Clausewitz realized, of course, that this was true only in the short run.[27]

Clausewitz noted that giving up part of a country's land and resources during a withdrawal into the interior ultimately would weaken the defender because it would involve the forfeiture of magazines and depots as well as the production of the country. If the country were rich enough, it even could support the attacker's army, enabling him to "live at the enemy's expense"; this had been the objective of Lee, Bragg, and Kirby Smith in the late summer and fall of 1862 in the campaigns into Maryland and Kentucky which had led to the battles at Antietam and Perryville. In the case of these brief incursions, however, the "additional wealth" gained might "not be enough to meet the additional outlay" caused by the campaign. But for an invading army, capture of part of the enemy's "territory and resources" would "reduce his national resources" and place time on the invader's side. "If the conquered areas are important enough, and if there are places in them vital to the areas still in enemy hands, the rot will spread, like a cancer, by itself; and if only that and nothing else happens, the conqueror may well enjoy the net advantage. Time alone will then complete the work" because the enemy's armed forces gradually would weaken.[28]

In planning a blockade and seeking, by control of the Mississippi, to divide the Confederacy, General Scott had recommended just this approach. Scott's strategy of exhaustion of the enemy's resources by blockade, division, and conquest of territory remained the Union's implicit policy. It had enjoyed brilliant initial success when Halleck and Grant exploited the western rivers; it collapsed when Grant, Buell, and Rosecrans depended on rail communications. These failures led, after a season of intense military activity, to a stalemate during the winter of 1863 on what had become the four major fronts in the war. Without adequate north-south communications in Arkansas, that theater continued to remain relatively quiescent. In Virginia, as in Tennessee, the opposing armies lay inactive in winter quarters.

Lincoln and Halleck gave priority to the West, however, reinforcing Kentucky with a corps from Virginia but stressing the Mississippi by increasing Grant's strength and also directing an expedition from New Orleans up the river. For the time being, however, their concentration resulted only in Grant's ineffectual pursuit of various schemes to find water communications to supply a turning movement against Vicksburg on the north.

Lincoln and Halleck also devoted much of their intellectual energy to solving the problem of operations in Virginia. They did not believe that a siege of Richmond would inevitably succeed; rather, they saw a siege as presenting the well-entrenched Confederates with an opportunity to economize on men in the defensive, enabling them to spare troops to reinforce other armies or to use their Shenandoah Valley base to threaten a raid across the Potomac.

Thus Lincoln and Halleck decided to change their objective. They would no longer attempt to reach Richmond but would use the Army of the Potomac to keep Lee well away from Washington and wait for him to make a mistake that would permit the Army of the Potomac to attack him with advantage and hurt his army. They looked to the West, particularly to Grant, for their important achievements.

Davis, lacking a general in chief or a strong headquarters staff, wisely decentralized through four regional commands: Lee in Virginia and North Carolina; Beauregard in South Carolina, Georgia, and Florida; Joseph E. Johnston in Tennessee, Alabama, and Mississippi; and Kirby Smith in the trans-Mississippi. This command organization gave these senior and experienced generals substantial forces coupled with maximum autonomy in their employment and placed on Davis and his headquarters minimal demands for strategic intervention from Richmond. After November 1862 Davis relied heavily on his capable new secretary of war, James A. Seddon, a planter and former congressman, who had quickly acquired a firm grasp of the essentials of strategy and logistics.

Lincoln and Halleck again wished for simultaneous advances for the spring of 1863, but they could not persuade Rosecrans to advance. The Tennessee commander appeared to them to have contracted a case of the "slows." But to Rosecrans caution seemed only sensible in the face of the menace to his rail communications and the vastly superior cavalry force that Johnston had concentrated against him. In spite of urging, he waited, accumulating supplies and improvising cavalry by mounting infantry on mules.

IN VIRGINIA a new man headed the Army of the Potomac, Joseph Hooker, one of Burnside's subordinates and a capable corps commander who had actively sought the post. Joe Hooker has been aptly characterized as a hard-boiled soldier. Along with McClellan he was popular with the enlisted men, partly because he looked like a good general and partly because he rebuilt his army's morale during the winter. He reformed the commissary and quartermaster services, and, as Bell Wiley wrote, "Whatever they thought of Hooker's other qualities, soldiers highly approved his competency as a provider." His real test as a commander, however, occurred on the battlefield.[29]

In the last few days of April 1863, General Hooker took the offensive against Lee, trying to turn his left flank, reach his rear, and compel him to attack to recover his communications. Hooker picked an opportune time to attack, when a major part of Lee's army was in southeastern Virginia, principally to relieve Lee's critical supply situation along the Rappahannock.

Lee, concerned to preserve his communications with the fertile Shenandoah Valley, posted himself to protect the Virginia Central Railroad, also covering as much of the subsistence area north of Richmond as possible. For these reasons, and to avoid the still-dreaded siege of Richmond, he determined to hold his line of "permanent defense" on the Rappahannock. In addition to these military reasons, he had a political motive to avoid yielding any territory close to the Confederate capital: he hoped, by a successful defense of all Confederate territory, to discourage the northern public and promote the continued growth of the northern peace movement.[30]

Hooker employed his two-to-one numerical superiority to force his way across the Rappahannock on April 28–29, 1863, and pierce Lee's defensive line in an advance that turned the Confederate army on the west. Lee, instead of falling back to the North Anna, the next river line, made a determined, skillful, and costly, but successful, effort to hold the line of the Rappahannock. "In such a battle," Clausewitz explained, "the attacker's turning movement, intended to give his attack a better chance and his victory a greater scale, is countered by a subordinate turning movement, which is aimed at that part of the enemy's force that has executed the original envelopment." Lee attempted precisely this maneuver and succeeded in turning Hooker, attacking the turning force in the flank. Had Hooker been as imperturbable and optimistic as Rosecrans had been at Murfreesboro, however, the Union army could have remained south of the river and claimed a victory because it had advanced. Hooker's retreat back across the river on May 5 signified that he had lost the Battle of Chancellorsville. Lee had held the river line but at frightful cost—12,700 casualties compared to 16,800 for the Union army, 21 percent of his army against 15 percent of Hooker's. Again the armies proved indestructible, and again the stalemate continued.[31]

MEANWHILE, to the West, Grant at last succeeded in turning Vicksburg and reaching its rear, where he could cut the city's rail communications to Jackson. Abandoning his effort to turn Vicksburg on its northern flank, he had improvised a road and water line of communications on the west bank of the Mississippi and moved south of the city. The navy provided the key to Grant's campaign because on the night of April 16, 1863, it succeeded in conveying quartermaster transports safely below the Vicksburg batteries. The navy thus not only allowed supplies to be moved south of Vicksburg but also provided protection to the transports that ferried Grant's army to the east bank and brought other supplies across from the west bank.

Grant had marched his army southward past Vicksburg on the west side of the river, and the navy had ferried him across, completing the process by April 30. Pushing away the small Confederate force resisting him, Grant then proceeded northeastward. He next moved against Vicksburg's communications, while relying on wagon transport from the river for some supplies and on the abundance of that fertile, unforaged region where food and fodder crops had, to a considerable extent, supplanted cotton, and local poultry and cattle furnished his need for meat. In the words of the United States Army's new operations manual, which uses this campaign as an example, Grant had "turned the Confederate defenses and put the Union army within reach of the enemy's rear area."[32]

A position in Vicksburg's rear would improve Grant's communications because he could regain contact with the river and yet be east of Vicksburg, the objective he and Sherman had tried in vain to reach the previous December. From this site he could interrupt the rail communications between Vicksburg and Jackson, forcing John C. Pemberton, the Confederate field commander, either to attack Grant's defensive posture to recover his communications or to move the bulk of his army away from Vicksburg. In either event, the advantage would lie with Grant.

But the Confederates were rushing troops to the scene by rail, and Joseph E. Johnston, the department commander, arrived to assume personal direction of these forces accumulating at Jackson. Faced now by two armies, the far larger one under Pemberton near Vicksburg and a small but growing force under Johnston at Jackson, Grant took advantage of his interior lines. Concentrating against the smaller threat, Grant sent two corps to attack Johnston while he kept the third corps west of Jackson to hold back Pemberton should he advance. The two attacking corps easily took Jackson and pushed Johnston's little force away to the north. Grant then capitalized on his interior line of operations, concentrating two of his corps against Pemberton, while the third, under Sherman, remained temporarily near the Mississippi capital to keep Johnston at bay. Sherman not only held Johnston but destroyed the industry in the city and, more important, wrecked the railroad eastward, thus depriving Johnston of rail communications for supply should he attempt to advance westward. Meanwhile, Pemberton, inexperienced in field command, had remained in paralyzed inactivity halfway between Jackson and Vicksburg.

When Grant moved against Pemberton, the Confederate general made a brief stand in the Battle of Champion's Hill on May 16, 1863; but Grant pushed him back. Then, contrary to his orders, the demoralized Pemberton retreated into Vicksburg, which Grant surrounded while at the same time reestablishing his communications with the river. Though President Davis reinforced Johnston with troops from Tennessee and South Carolina, Grant, likewise heavily reinforced by

Halleck and Lincoln, remained on the defensive except for one abortive assault on Vicksburg's powerful fortifications. Johnston, too, remained relatively inert despite orders from Secretary of War James A. Seddon directing him to relieve the city. "It is an error," Robert G. H. Kean, in charge of the Bureau of War, wrote of Seddon's order in his diary. Kean, having read in a book of Napoleon's maxims that a "general should not obey against his own judgement" was so troubled by Seddon's order and Napoleon's rule that he urged John A. Campbell, the assistant secretary of war, to show the book to Seddon. But Johnston, short of wagons and with a destroyed railroad between him and Vicksburg, did not take the offensive against Grant's army.[33]

Grant therefore enjoyed the fullest tactical advantage of the defensive which his successful turning movement had given him. Having interrupted Pemberton's communications and still on an interior line between the paralyzed Pemberton and the inert Johnston, he was on the strategic offensive and the tactical defensive. He exploited this situation with entrenchments against the trapped Pemberton, and with Sherman posted between Vicksburg and Jackson, with what Clausewitz called "an army of observation," to defend against Johnston. His new line of communications along the Mississippi, guarded by gunboats, provided complete security. He had only to wait until Pemberton, trapped against the river obstacle and exhausting his supplies, surrendered thirty thousand men on July 4, 1863.[34]

General in Chief Halleck, congratulating Grant on his campaign, wrote: "In boldness of plan, rapidity of execution, and brilliancy of results, these operations will compare most favorably with those of Napoleon about Ulm." The Ulm campaign, when Napoleon reached the rear of the Austrian army under the inept General Mack, exemplified the strategic turning movement from which Jomini had derived his ideas and which he had cited to illustrate his point.[35]

Grant's turning movement illustrated "the system of rapid and continuous marches" which, Jomini said, "multiplies the effect of an army" and, in seizing interior lines and concentrating his forces first against Johnston and then Pemberton, Grant brilliantly embodied their "successive employment upon points where it may be important to act, to bring superior force to bear upon fractions of the hostile army." In this way he was able "to prevent the parts of the enemy from concentrating or from affording each other mutual support." Clearly Jomini would have agreed with Halleck and seen that Grant's campaign epitomized the sense of Napoleon's "system of modern strategy," the purport of which Jomini had attempted to capture in one part of his "fundamental principle of war." Grant had succeeded in his aim "to throw by strategic movements the mass of an army successively upon the decisive points of the theatre of war and also upon the communications of the enemy as much as possible without exposing one's own."[36]

In his analysis of Civil War military operations T. Harry Williams clearly overlooked how closely Grant's Vicksburg masterpiece conformed to Jomini's vision of the strategic turning movement, a concept he had drawn from Napoleon's campaigns. In accord with Clausewitz's judgment as to the rarity of such maneuvers, the Civil War witnessed only two of Jomini's favorites, but Grant executed both of them, at Vicksburg and at Appomattox at the end of the war.

Of course, Grant needed Pemberton's blunder of retreating into Vicksburg to give him Pemberton's army as well as the city. Thus, as Jomini and Clausewitz would have pointed out, to "bury an army . . . simply to retard a siege would be folly" and since "famine" caused the surrender of Vicksburg, the large force there "hastened rather than retarded the surrender." Even if the presence of the army had prolonged the resistance, the defender had "to pay for this advantage with the loss of the defending force," one of the three main field armies of the Confederacy. Jomini believed that Napoleon's success at Ulm owed much to the incapacity of Mack, the Austrian commander, when he commented that "a general may attempt with a Mack as an antagonist what would be madness to do with a Napoleon." Grant also acknowledged Pemberton's contribution to his success by referring to him as his "best friend." It all proved, once again, how difficult it was to capture entire armies. In this case, as at Fort Donelson, however, the feat was accomplished with the aid of an inept opponent.[37]

FOLLOWING THE fall of Vicksburg and the withdrawal of Johnston's army east of Jackson, Halleck removed troops from Grant to conquer more of the trans-Mississippi. The concentration against this region, though sound in that Halleck intended for it ultimately to release additional troops for operations in the East, had the effect of presenting the Confederates with no threat on the Mississippi line. The Confederates took advantage of this Union inactivity to give active consideration to a plan long advocated by General Beauregard for concentration against Rosecrans's army, the weakest of the three main Union armies east of the Mississippi.

Lincoln and Halleck did not, however, perceive Rosecrans's army as weak. They threatened him with removal from command if he did not make a simultaneous advance against Bragg and, in May, when Grant at last took the offensive in Mississippi, they explained to Rosecrans how propitious was the time to attack: President Davis had weakened Bragg's army to reinforce Johnston's Vicksburg relief army at Jackson. Rosecrans, still trying to improve his cavalry and concerned about his communications, had not completed his preparations. But Rosecrans also pointed out that the rebels would act in accordance with the relative value they placed on Tennessee and Mississippi, and, as we have seen, Johnston posed that very question directly to Davis. Rosecrans feared, he wrote Halleck, that an early movement on his part would force Confederates to conclude that they could aid the cause in Mississippi only if they rapidly abandoned Tennessee; this move would place "their whole force at once back to a position from whence they could send much heavier detachments south, and wait our progress over obstructed roads and destroyed railroads, which we would be obliged to repair." In other words, Rosecrans thought he was aiding Grant simply by maintaining a strong position where he was, thereby holding Confederate troops as far away from Grant as possible.[38]

It was not until the end of June 1863, therefore, that Rosecrans at last began his offensive against the weakened Bragg at Tullahoma. But although the Federal commander had been obstinate about moving, he proved optimistic once in motion. "Old Rosy" was popular with his troops and, undeceived as to the possibility of a decisive frontal battle, he had an excellent plan to spare them the casualties of another Murfreesboro. Distracting Bragg by a feint to the west, Rosecrans carried all his supplies and marched rapidly, moving his entire army around Bragg's right. Bragg, his communications threatened and facing the likelihood that Rosecrans's army actually might reach his rear, did not attack Rosecrans; instead, he retreated rapidly all the way back to Chattanooga on the south bank of the Tennessee River, where he settled on July 7, 1863. Without a battle, Rosecrans had, in a little over a week, advanced four times as far as he had after his victory at Murfreesboro. The Union army now stood very close to Chattanooga, where lay heavy industry and railroad connections to Atlanta and Virginia.

With pride, Rosecrans reported his achievement in turning Bragg out of his entrenched position and completing the conquest of Middle Tennessee. But Secretary of War Stanton, known as a believer in marching forward to attack the enemy directly in battle and skeptical about maneuvers and strategy, seemed to ignore Rosecrans's triumphs. Miffed, the general expressed hope "that the War Department may not overlook so great an event because it is not written in letters of blood." Clausewitz would have agreed: such maneuvers were "obviously preferable to pointless battles—victories that cannot be exploited," such as Murfreesboro.[39]

Meanwhile, Confederates in the East still stood on the defensive, although not for long. Lee's belief that the enemy Army of the Potomac would soon advance again conditioned his planning. Lee did not realize that Lincoln and Halleck viewed Virginia as a theater of secondary importance, had little hope of a successful attack on his army, and did not wish to push him back to Richmond and besiege the city. This last possibility Lee not only expected but dreaded because he doubted that the Confederate supply organization then could provide adequately for his army.

Lee would have preferred not to defend the Rappahannock River again but knew he must do so to cover the Virginia Central Railroad leading to the Shenandoah Valley and to protect his supply region north of Richmond. But his commitment to stand along that line deprived him of room to maneuver. In casualties the Battle of Fredericksburg had proven the value of the Rappahannock defensive line; the Battle of Chancellorsville had shown it to be a liability.

Jomini urged that a general not "make the defense passive: he must not remain in his positions to receive whatever blows may be given by his adversary." Clausewitz's injunction also fit Lee's situation after the Battle of Chancellorsville. "Once the defender has gained an important advantage, defense as such has done its work. While he is enjoying this advantage he must strike back, or he will court destruction. Prudence

bids him strike while the iron is hot and use the advantage to prevent a
second onslaught. . . . Whenever a victory achieved by the defensive
form is not turned to military account, where, so to speak, it is allowed
to wither away unused, a serious mistake is being made." Davis concurred in "the disadvantage of standing still" and regretted "that any
advantage should have been lost by delay."[40]

Lee therefore decided to use his Valley base to turn Hooker back; he
also wished to "create an apprehension for the safety of their right
flank and the Potomac," in the hope of diverting Federal troops from
the "line of their operations in the South." As he had the previous fall
in the Antietam campaign, he also planned to supply his army from
untapped resources in the North, leaving most of Virginia to be
gleaned for winter needs. He certainly expected to have to fight a
battle if he crossed the Potomac, but, unconstrained to defend a particular line, he could select a strong position and let Hooker come to attack him. And so in early June 1863, Lee moved into the Valley and
northward in a raid that by month's end had carried him across the
Potomac and into Pennsylvania.[41]

But Lincoln, adhering after Chancellorsville to his and Halleck's belief that the best strategy in Virginia was to wait for an opportunity to
catch Lee at a disadvantage, had been content for Hooker to "keep the
enemy at bay, and out of other mischief, by menaces and cavalry
raids." Lee's advance, however, changed his mind. He wrote Hooker:
"I believe you are aware that since you took command of the army I
have not believed that you had any chance to effect anything until
now." And now he urged Hooker to move against Lee's army because
it had left the protection of its entrenchments and the Rappahannock
River line.[42]

In entering Pennsylvania, Lee had moved more than one hundred
miles by road north of Winchester, at least triple Grant's distance from
the Mississippi when he had engaged Pemberton. Lee had no prospect
of drawing supplies from such a distance even had Winchester been a
Confederate railhead. But, like Grant, he entered a fertile region, previously unforaged. In his position in central Pennsylvania Lee did not
threaten any Union communications because the Army of the Potomac
had conformed to his movement and kept to the east of him. Hooker
had no military need to respond to Lee's raid at all, other than keeping

between Lee and the seaboard cities. But Lincoln and Halleck viewed the situation as the opportunity to hurt Lee's army for which they long had hoped and waited. Lincoln had wished to move the Army of the Potomac west and south of the Confederate force to block Lee's line of retreat and, in effect, turn him, but this proved politically unfeasible because it would have left Harrisburg, the Pennsylvania capital, unprotected. Therefore, instead of trying to trap Lee, the Army of the Potomac moved north, keeping east of him.

At the end of June Lincoln and Halleck selected a new commander, the capable George G. Meade, whose appointment had been rumored since Hooker's late fiasco. Meade had "been long enough in the war to want to give them [the Confederates] one thorough good licking before any peace is made, and to accomplish this," he wrote, "I will go through a good deal." Having received the chance to administer that "licking," the careful Meade reconnoitered a defensive position southeast of Gettysburg, which had at its back a rail line running to Baltimore. With this position in his rear he then pushed forward toward Gettysburg, where he would find most of Lee's army.[43]

Against the wily and cautious Meade, Lee would have to attack or withdraw. Meade proved very slow and circumspect in initiating an assault, thus forcing the Confederates to wait for battle, but to remain concentrated because the immediate presence of the Army of the Potomac would have further complicated Lee's supply by requiring that he gather from a smaller area than if he remained dispersed. Furthermore, he was already hampered by the activities of the Pennsylvania militia and other ill-trained troops in the vicinity, who had circumscribed his foraging. He could not wait; Meade could.

Lee anticipated this necessity by concentrating against and assailing a fragment of Meade's army. Each side then rushed men to Gettysburg until both armies were fully concentrated by the end of the second day of battle. Lee had more than seventy thousand and Meade at least eighty-five thousand effectives. On the offensive, the Confederates had pushed back the Union forces, but the Federals did not retreat far. On the third day both armies faced each other when Lee, uncharacteristically, made a frontal attack that failed disastrously.

The Battle of Gettysburg, July 1–3, 1863, cost the Confederates twenty-eight thousand men, more in three days than in all of Lee's previous purely offensive conflict, the Seven Days' campaign. His losses amounted to 33 percent of the men available at the outset of the operation. Meade also suffered enormous losses, twenty-three thousand men, but these numbered only 20 percent of the larger body of Unionists available at the beginning of the campaign. On the fourth day, though neither side moved, Lee perceived no choice but to withdraw. Unlike Rosecrans at Murfreesboro, he could not wait until Meade retreated because he had no railroad to the rear of his position, whereas Meade was within ten miles of a spur of the Pennsylvania Railroad.

Lee's army was seriously hurt, but it was by no means destroyed. Lincoln, who had regarded the Gettysburg campaign as the long-awaited opportunity to hurt Lee's army, felt terrible frustration at Lee's escape. He was amazed that Union movements seemed intended "to cover Baltimore and Washington" rather than "to prevent his crossing [the Potomac] and to destroy him." In his retreat Lee backed up against a flooded river, but Meade made no attack, and Lincoln believed he did not "appreciate the magnitude of the misfortune involved in Lee's escape . . . the war will be prolonged indefinitely." Especially with Lee well entrenched, Lincoln probably much overestimated the possibility of a successful attack just then, and yet he was correct in grasping Clausewitz's warning that "whenever a victory achieved by the defensive form is not turned to military account . . . a serious mistake is being made."[44]

In his disappointment the president overlooked the successful aspects of the campaign—Lee's army had suffered very serious losses and the strategy of waiting for Lee to make a mistake had worked. Nevertheless, from Lee's point of view the campaign also had enjoyed considerable success. Believing that he would have faced a determined Union effort to cross the Rappahannock, he thought that his Pennsylvania raid had disrupted that campaign. Although he had not remained in Union territory as long as he had hoped, he had for some time supplied his army at the enemy's expense, although not to the degree he had hoped. At least in some measure he had met both of the objectives of the campaign.[45]

IF LINCOLN was chagrined over the results of the Gettysburg campaign, he felt great satisfaction at the outcome of the concentration on the

Mississippi that he and Halleck had engineered. But the Union gains from the opening of the Mississippi were more symbolic and political than militarily substantial. The stalemate only appeared to be broken. The loss of transit between East and West hurt Confederate supply not at all; the two parts of the Confederacy long had been logistically separate.

To Confederates, then, the loss of the Mississippi was largely limited to diminished prestige and a psychological defeat; the enemy had cut their country in half and badly damaged military and civilian morale. True, the Union gained in substance the use of the river for commercial navigation and easy access to the Red River for any advance into Louisiana; but the Union also acquired a liability—more territory to be guarded. Instead of Confederate troops protecting Vicksburg, Union troops now had to stand duty there. The Union army had to defend a long frontier between Memphis and Baton Rouge against raiders, and individual snipers could fire on passing steamboats. Although the Mississippi afforded secure passage of military supplies, normal traffic faced harassment and required defense, if only because of the traditional importance of Mississippi River commerce and the prestige of having opened the river. After the fall of Vicksburg the Union employed at least fifteen thousand men along with gunboats of the Mississippi squadron to defend nonmilitary commerce on the river.

The Confederacy's loss substantially would have equaled the extent of the Union's gain had it not been for Pemberton's gift of the thirty thousand men of his army. But the tangible achievement of gaining control of the important river became a major source of improved Union morale, a sign that the Union armies again were making progress in subduing the South. Conversely, it became a source of damaged Confederate morale. "Confederate loyalties," Lawrence N. Powell and Michael S. Wayne wrote in 1983, "softened and crumbled even more as news of Union victories began piling up and ultimate defeat loomed increasingly likely." After Vicksburg, the situation worsened: "As the Confederate government proved less able to protect its citizens, they in turn proved less willing to give their government loyalty."[46]

ON JULY 12, 1863, R. G. H. Kean, the head of the Confederate Bureau of War, made a doleful entry in his diary. "The week just ended," he wrote, "has been one of unexampled disaster since the war began. Besides the surrender of Vicksburg and the retreat of Bragg behind the Tennessee river, which opens the whole Southwest to the enemy who now have two powerful armies opposed to two feeble ones, it turns out that the battle of Gettysburg was a virtual if not an actual defeat. . . . All accounts represent this as the most sanguinary battle yet fought." In addition, the Union mounted its combined-operations attack against Charleston and Fort Wagner, military organization seemed defective, and the manpower available under the conscription laws was almost all allocated. Kean tersely concluded: "We are *almost exhausted*."[47]

The events of Vicksburg, July 4, Gettysburg, July 1–3, and Tullahoma, July 7, caused many northerners to breathe more easily than they had only six months before. And by the same token, it gave Confederates a most serious pause. Secret organizations raised their heads, dissenting politicians began to scheme for office, and hitherto stout hearts began to harbor misgivings for the future.

The fate of Vicksburg was perhaps inevitable, given Grant's skill and Pemberton's ineptitude. In any event, at Vicksburg and Tullahoma, trouble went out looking for Confederates. The distressing setback at Gettysburg, however, occurred because Confederates themselves sought trouble, and found it. Passive in Mississippi and Tennessee, they were the active architects of their fate in Pennsylvania. Although in turning Hooker back rather than awaiting his expected advance, Lee adopted a shrewd defensive strategy, he overlooked its potential impact on morale. Once Lee reached Pennsylvania, to withdraw without battle would look like a defeat; to give battle and then withdraw would still look like a defeat. Either way, Lee's raid was doomed to be perceived as a defeat by the Confederate public unless he had been able to destroy the Army of the Potomac—a most unlikely eventuality.

The result of Confederate failure to reckon the cost properly was that, when the inevitable withdrawal came, Confederate will was damaged more than it would have been if Lee had merely remained quietly in Virginia and let the Union do the attacking. Coming at about the same time as Vicksburg and Tullahoma, the news of Gettysburg served only to thicken the gloom of the southern people. The South had not paused to count the cost when Lee marched north, and when he returned it would be difficult to compensate for the military consequences of his operation—and of the Vicksburg and Tullahoma defeats—by an augmentation of will. Morale was seriously affected by the defeats of July 1863, a fact reflected in the fall 1863 elections to the Confederate Congress, when two-thirds of the freshmen selected had been men who opposed secession in the crisis of 1861. This is not to say that the Confederate armies were no longer able to achieve success on the battlefield. But it is clear that Confederates could no longer count on military success to sustain their will. The ponderous hammer blows of military activity could not answer subtle psychological questions about public morale.

Yet Confederates had prevented northern armies from achieving their ultimate objectives during the winter of 1862–63 and the spring that followed. The events of July 1863, moreover, required a reevaluation of the situation; any fair-minded assessment had to conclude that internal dissent had not caused these reverses. Furthermore, analysis of the military situation in the summer of 1863 would reveal that Confederate arms were still effective, and the Confederacy had lost only a small proportion of its vast territory. Considering the South's defensive military and political objectives, the Confederacy continued to enjoy success.

So the Union concentration in time and space improved its situation only marginally and, as it turned out, only temporarily. In spite of Rosecrans's advance, the Confederacy still had a foothold in Middle Tennessee and controlled East Tennessee. The attack on Charleston had failed, and Union control of the Mississippi did not seriously harm Confederate supply. The fall of Memphis a year earlier had cut the major links between the Confederacy's two parts, and each had functioned as a self-sufficient entity ever since. They continued to do so until the end of the war, with occasional shipments of critical supplies sneaked across the river. Lee's campaign into Pennsylvania had fulfilled some of its objectives, and his army and Meade's spent much of the remainder of the year in a quiescent state north of the Rappahannock. The campaign had again exhibited the insuperable difficulties the North faced in trying to conquer such a large country. The stalemate continued.

The South had suffered a serious manpower reduction through Lee's heavy casualties in the Battle of Gettysburg and Pemberton's surrender, even though Grant had paroled Pemberton's army. But between June and December 1863 the total manpower on the Confederate rolls declined less than 9,000, from 473,058 to 464,646, a reduction of less than 2 percent. Conscription and volunteering had brought enough new men to the armies almost to make up the losses sustained in the summer and fall campaigning. But the number of men present with their units had decreased from 307,464 to 277,970, a decline of 30,000. This toll reflected an increase in the proportion absent from 35 percent to 40 percent and certainly indicates a rise in desertion. These figures reflect discouragement and diminution of the will to continue the struggle. As one young officer informed his father, "The men can't be prevented from deserting when they think there is no prospect ahead for getting home," and he added soberly that "among the deserters are some of the bravest men of our army. . . . Our leaders do not seem to think that the *morale* is as great a portion of an army, as Napoleon thought." Obviously, defeats in the field had severely taxed the Confederacy's flimsy nationalism.[48]

And even the top leadership began to entertain doubts. Robert E. Lee assured Jefferson Davis that he was "not in the least discouraged nor . . . [has] my faith in the protection of an All Merciful Providence, or in the fortitude of this army . . . [been] at all shaken," and Davis acknowledged that "it is not for man to command success, he should strive to deserve it, and leave the rest to him who governs all things." Confederates were reassessing their positions and, like the prophets of old who warned the Israelites to place their faith in God, men like Davis and Lee were trying to do just that. But modern men are most likely to assert such eternal truths when the more ephemeral ones seem to be dissolving; Davis and Lee seemed to be trying impotently to overcome their justifiable, real, and growing fears.[49]

And yet the Confederacy lasted almost two more years; the stalemate continued, the decision of battle was by no means yet certain, as we can see so clearly in hindsight, and within a few months the fortunes of war seemed to turn once again. The Confederacy still had large forces in the field, and the Union army had only barely penetrated the southern heartland; after more than two years of war Union land and naval forces had tamed the Mississippi River, but Tennessee was not yet secure, the Carolinas, Alabama, Georgia, and Florida were hardly touched except along the coasts, and much of Mississippi was still safely intact. Most of the trans-Mississippi West also remained beyond the scope of Union control. If Pickett's charge at Gettysburg was the high-water mark of the Confederacy, as has been frequently asserted, it took an amazingly long time for the flood to recede.

In the remaining twenty-one months the army still fought, the economy became more self-sufficient, and the administration of government became more centralized and uniform; the willpower of the southern people seemed to suffer the most, and at this early date it seemed to flag no more than did that of the northern people. Nevertheless, from July 1863 onward internal will became an ever more important indicator of declining Confederate strength; at the very moment that the South needed to stiffen its will to compensate for an overall decline in military fortunes, that will became less reliable. Internal dissension caused by state-rights issues induced some of this slippage of morale, although the positive aspects of state rights balanced the difficulties that this philosophy of government created.

One could say much the same of religion, for it too encouraged doubts about southern institutions and behavior, while at the same time seeing God's favor in the ability of Confederate arms to confront northern armies successfully. Yet military affairs in July 1863 caused Confederates to approach the question of God's support in a new way. As the success of Confederate arms became more elusive, southerners came to ponder God's role in the war, and they concluded that God was punishing or, at the very least, testing them. In time, Confederates would go further than this, concluding that, since victory depended on God's favor, the deteriorating military situation could mean only that God had not smiled on the cause; if this were so, then defeat was inevitable. It was not a cheering prospect.

Chapter Twelve

The Battle Is the Lord's

SOUTHERN ARMIES had suffered serious reverses at Vicksburg, Tullahoma, and Gettysburg in July of 1863, and these in turn had a decided impact upon the will to win of the Confederate civilians. The loss of control over more of her territory had no particular consequence for the South, or should not have, except insofar as territory was symbolic of a country's ability to maintain its sovereignty over all of its claimed domain. Unfortunately for the South, her people claimed that lost territory was more important than in truth it was; accordingly, its loss had a greater negative impact on the country than it should have had, and fear and foreboding stealthily crept in to take over the corners of Confederate hearts and minds, left vacant as morale and will withered away.

As other people have done in times of disaster and stress, many Confederates turned to religion for guidance. Evangelical Christianity had taught them that God operated in human affairs and had assured them that He was on their side—the side, they claimed, of liberty. Thus piety had lent moral strength to the armies, who, like the patriots of 1776, fought not for slavery but against slavery and for liberty. Religion also sustained and magnified the will of the people to see this struggle through to the end.

When victory eluded one's grasp, however, religion showed another face, and Christians both North and South came to wonder whether the war was a punishment or perhaps a trial to test their worthiness. In either case, they could appease God; but if the course of the war was still unfavorable, it would be a sign that God's will was not what Confederates had hoped it was. Events such as Vicksburg, Tullahoma, and Gettysburg forced Confederates to reexamine the war and their own consciences, for in July 1863 it was not difficult to conclude that alternative decisions—Union and peace, for example—had attractive features that a long war with an uncertain outcome did not have. And if the South was fighting for liberty, and the means used to fight that war seemed to subvert liberty, why bother to fight at all?

Thus defeatism crept slowly into the hearts of large numbers of Confederates. As they pondered the mysterious ways of the Lord, some of them looked North and saw the massive resources available to the Union cause and wondered whether they had not been tempting fate when they entered the contest. More efficient use of southern resources and the proper strategies could compensate for northern abundance; nevertheless, many Confederates doubtless compared themselves to David taking on Goliath.

This parallel was instructive and comforting, for it would seem to prove that God did not always side with the strongest battalions; rather, He espoused the cause of those who, like David, served the Lord. And, as we have already noted, Confederates liked to believe that they walked rightly with the Lord. The language of Jefferson Davis's early proclamations asking his fellow southerners to celebrate days of humiliation and prayer suggests widespread presumption that the Heavenly Father unquestionably supported the Confederacy. President Davis noted that "it hath pleased Almighty God, the Sovereign Disposer of events, to protect and defend the Confederate States hitherto in their conflict with their enemies, and to be unto them a shield." The Georgia legislature agreed with Davis's automatic assumption that God and the Confederacy walked side by side. Its resolution of November 1862 called upon the people "to unite at the throne of grace to invoke the continuation of His Divine Presence and protecting Providence" and to acknowledge the practical demonstration of "the presence of Almighty God, and His protecting Providence in the many hard fought battles, and glorious victories over our common enemies." The positions of the president and the legislature had considerable logic in 1861 and 1862, when, although the Confederacy had suffered some defeats, it had also won victories and Confederate armies still had undiminished strength.[1]

But by the middle of the war one reasonably could question the assumption that God wore gray. Although assuredly He still daily entered into human affairs, the *North Carolina Christian Advocate* found no proof "that God had always been on our side, or that he operates *actively*, in this controversy at all." The *Advocate* suggested that

God may even have left both sides "to the control of Satan" because of their failure to appreciate "the great blessings He conferred on us under the first revolution." In reply, another religious paper restated the basic suppositions: God never withdraws from a conflict but always chooses one side or the other; the only exception would be "when, in the origin and progress of the war, *each party to the conflict is equally guilty.*" Fortunately for the South, such a situation did not exist in this instance, for the *Fayetteville Presbyterian* concluded that "if God is not for us the Confederacy is in much worse condition than we had ever imagined it to be." But the Georgia legislature also believed that God continually entered human history and, moved by "our national calamity and distress," urged the people "to humble themselves before God, and with penitence for our past sins, national, social and individual; and with an honest, earnest desire to obey His laws; implore through the merits of our Saviour, His forgiveness, and plead for wisdom to guide us."[2]

These quotations indicate the mental struggle that Confederates underwent as they tried to reconcile their hopes and their religion with the costs and prospects of the war. By mid-1863 the casualty lists had grown far longer than anyone on either side had dreamed possible, and victory seemed much more distant than it had the summer before.

EVENTS HAD not gone nearly so well as faithful Confederates thought they should have, and these troubled rebels were determined to understand why that had happened. Religiously oriented southerners, which included most of them, believed that they could turn to their Bibles for answers. David had killed the giant Goliath, but the Lord had chosen David. Throughout, the Old Testament drove home the lesson that when Israel remained faithful to God, she prospered; when calamity came upon her, she suffered proper punishment for sin. The prophets repeatedly had emphasized this lesson; they also promised that when God's people returned to their proper allegiance, He would bless them again. So if God's support of the Confederacy seemed not so certain as it once was, the Bible pointed both to the reason and the remedy. Like Israel, Confederates had gone astray; but like the chosen people of old, all would be well if they returned to the fold with rekindled faith in Him.

James W. Silver pointed to these basic suppositions in his study *Confederate Morale and Church Propaganda*. "In the middle of the nineteenth century," he wrote,

> it was generally conceded that the great influences in life were of a religious nature. The primary purpose of existence with most people was eternal salvation. Therefore, it was deemed essential that the individual should conduct his everyday affairs in harmony with the wishes of a just and stern God. . . . Because of the limited industrial resources of the South, the success of the Confederacy depended on the degree of intestinal fortitude developed by the man on the street and on the farm. He needed to identify himself as a member of God's chosen people and his country as a fulfillment of the destiny of history.[3]

These assumptions could only lead to the conclusion that, if the Confederacy was losing the war, people were not conducting their "affairs in harmony with the wishes of a just and stern God."

In an earlier day of victory, the *Daily Lynchburg Virginian* had noted the moral of all this. Early successes had made obvious the work of "the hand of the Great Ruler of the Universe." "Who can question these manifestations," the editor exulted, "or doubt that the Lord of Hosts was with us?" The armies of Israel enjoyed success as long as they trusted in God, but when they forgot Him, then "bitter waters were given them to drink." "Let us not arrogate to ourselves," the editor continued, "the glory that is due to the Lord of Hosts. His hand is in all this." But this optimistic statement was issued ten months before the Battle of Gettysburg and the fall of Vicksburg.[4]

After the fortunes of the war had turned, events taught the identical lesson but with a different tone. Following Sherman's capture of Atlanta, the same editor took his text from the book of Judges, saying that Joshua defeated the Midianites because of his loyalty to the Lord. "Perhaps," this editor warned, "we are suffering chastisement for the same reason that it was once visited upon the once favored people; nor can we, with a true faith in the Divine Record, and an humble trust in that gracious Being who controls our destinies, doubt, that when 'the altars of Baal' shall be thrown down, and the people turn humbly to the source of all help, deliverance will come."[5]

History had taught its lessons. The southern clergy, says James W.

Silver, and, we should add, the laity as well, had "developed an infallible formula. Every Confederate victory proved that God had shielded
His chosen people and every defeat became the merited punishment of
the same people for their sins." And when faced with defeat, Confederates had not far to look to discover sins that could serve as a ready
explanation, including "violation of the Sabbath, intemperance, dema-
goguery, corruption, luxury, impiety, murmuring, greed and avarice,
lewdness, skepticism, 'Epicurean expedience,' private immorality, ill
treatment of slaves, profanity, a proud and haughty spirit, speculation, bribery, boastfulness, and the 'sin of all sins,' covetousness." God
had smiled at First Manassas, Second Manassas, Fredericksburg, and
Chancellorsville, but He had frowned at Gettysburg, Vicksburg, and
Tullahoma. After these battles there flowed forth "an avalanche of
sermons stressing the sins of the Confederate people." "Apparently,"
remarked Silver, "it never occurred to anyone that He might have
been a disinterested or even a disgruntled spectator."[6]

Ironically, some of the clearest and most poignant statements of this
particular religious mind-set came not from southern pens but from
that of Abraham Lincoln. Possessed of a keen sense of the tragic ironies of life and of the problems involved in discerning God's will, Lincoln
much more eloquently articulated such thoughts than could most
Americans of his time, including his Confederate counterpart. "From
the beginning," Lincoln told a group of visiting clergy shortly before
the victories of July 1863, "I saw that the issues of our great struggle
depended on divine interposition and favor." In an early memorandum
of uncertain date, apparently written for his eyes only, Lincoln noted
the inevitable, resultant religious tension that he later wrote into his
Second Inaugural Address. "The will of God prevails," Lincoln assumed, apparently in September 1862, and both sides claim

> to act in accordance with the will of God. Both *may* be and one *must* be
> wrong. God can not be *for*, and *against* the same thing at the same time.
> In the present civil war it is quite possible that God's purpose is some-
> thing different from the purpose of either party—and yet the human
> instrumentalities, working just as they do, are of the best adaptation to
> effect His purpose. I am almost ready to say this is probably true—that
> God wills this contest, and wills that it shall not end yet. By his mere
> quiet power, on the minds of the now contestants, He could have either

saved or *destroyed* the Union without a human contest. Yet the contest began. And having begun He could give the final victory to either side any day. Yet the contest proceeds.[7]

The following March Lincoln's proclamation of a national day of fasting called upon the nation and its people "to own their dependence upon the overruling power of God, to confess their sins and transgressions, in humble sorrow, yet with assured hope that genuine repentance will lead to mercy and pardon." The war, proclaimed Lincoln, "may be but a punishment, inflicted upon us, for our presumptuous sins." Despite His blessings, "we have forgotten God. . . . It behooves us then, to humble ourselves before the offended power, to confess our national sins, and to pray for clemency and forgiveness." And after the victories of Gettysburg, Vicksburg, and Tullahoma, Lincoln called upon the people "to render homage due to the Divine Majesty, for the wonderful things He had done in the Nation's behalf, and invoke the influence of his Holy Spirit" to transform the rebels, guide the government, console the victims, "and finally to lead the whole nation, through the paths of repentance and submission to the Divine Will, back to the perfect enjoyment of Union and fraternal peace." But Lincoln also understood that God's purposes, whatever they might be, "are perfect, and must prevail, though we erring mortals may fail to accurately perceive them in advance. We hoped for a happy termination of this terrible war long before this; but God knows best, and has ruled otherwise."[8]

Lincoln's deeply moving ideas, and the moving idiom in which he wrote them, contends Cushing Strout, indicated the Union president's "deepening sense of a providentially guided historical process that brings man to judgement through a great crisis in human affairs." Lincoln felt that God was involved in the war for the Union, but he sought a deeper meaning in the conflict. He came to feel, says Strout, that he was "part of a drama whose script he did not himself write, but he was not yet sure of his own role in it or of the full meaning of the story." As Lincoln moved toward his decision to issue the Emancipation Proclamation, he also moved toward the fatalistic view that the war was a providential means of freeing the slaves.[9]

That God acted in history to bring man to judgment was a belief that many southerners could easily accept, though they would have been surprised to know that this was also Lincoln's view; that the war was the instrument of Providence to free the slaves, some southerners began to suspect toward the end of the war. After the war, however, many former Confederates accepted this notion also.

Others shared Lincoln's fatalistic musings. In June 1864, after the bloody assault at Cold Harbor, southern editors copied with keen satisfaction an item they found in New York's *Spirit of the Times*, which lamented that "we are almost led to believe that God not only is not with us, but against us. . . . And why should He be with us, base, groveling, and corrupted as we are? We are not with Him! We are a godless, conscienceless, religionless people."[10]

Considering the divergences that had separated the churches, the religious thought of North and South displayed striking similarities; for each saw its own region as the legitimate "new Israel." Each side operated from the same beliefs, seeing victory as a sign of God's favor, defeat as a sign that the people had strayed from Him and thus had lost favor, and the war itself as a lesson to all. As Bertram Wyatt-Brown noted in his study of southern honor, "Resignation to God's will, faith in the literal word of scripture, and a sense that the 'fratricidal' war was a divine visitation upon the land for the sins of all Americans were common opinions among the religious folk of the time."[11]

Many southerners expressed early in the conflict the idea that the war constituted a divine affliction shared by both sides. In his November 1861 inaugural address as governor of Georgia, Joseph E. Brown uttered his confidence in the future, thanked God for past victories, but declared that "the Ruler of the Universe has determined that the pride of both sections of the old Union shall be humbled and that they shalt be punished during this strife for national wickedness in high places, as well as for individual transgressions."[12]

But victory belonged to the righteous. After Confederate victories at Second Manassas and Richmond, Kentucky, in August 1862, Jefferson Davis proclaimed a day of prayer and thanksgiving, inviting his people "once more to his footstool, not now in the garb of fasting and sorrow, but with joy and gladness." Clearly, then, "the Christian patriot . . . cannot overlook the hand of God in this war" and would surely "believe that God is for us and with us . . . notwithstanding our man-

The blockade-runner *Ad-Vance*. Originally the *Lord Clyde*, this blockade-runner was acquired by the state of North Carolina in 1862 and was renamed in honor of the wartime governor. She made eleven successful trips between Bermuda and Wilmington. (Courtesy of the North Carolina State Department of Archives and History.)

Deck view of the steamer *Hudson*, which was the first blockade-runner captured by the North. (Courtesy of the National Archives.)

Governor Zebulon Vance of North Carolina. Vance was an intelligent and innovative politician, who often clashed with Jefferson Davis. (Courtesy of the North Carolina State Department of Archives and History.)

President Jefferson Davis. Varina Davis claimed that this photograph was the only wartime portrait taken of her husband. Davis's haggard visage reveals some elements of his rough-edged personality. (Courtesy of the National Archives.)

Facing page: Thomas W. Higginson's regiment of Negro troops, South Carolina. This was the first, and one of the most famous, of the black regiments. These pioneers left a lasting legacy in American military history. Their compassionate white colonel later proudly wrote of their exploits in his *Army Life in a Black Regiment.* (Courtesy of the National Archives.)

Company E of the Fourth U.S. Colored Infantry at Fort Lincoln, Virginia. The sharp-looking orderliness of this outfit reflects the impact of training and experience. By the last months of the war, there were as many black troops in the Union army as there were men then on duty in the entire Confederate army. (Courtesy of the Chicago Historical Society.)

The Confederate blockade-runner *Robert E. Lee.* (Courtesy of the Library of Congress.)

Anti-Lincoln, pro-McClellan campaign poster. Southerners took gleeful delight in the North's hard-fought wartime presidential election, and hoped for a McClellan victory—which many believed might bring the war to a favorable end. (Courtesy of the Louis A. Warren Lincoln Library and Museum at Fort Wayne, Indiana.)

Field headquarters of the U.S. Christian Commission. Every corps and division in the Federal army had a unit of the Christian Commission. This group raised over $4 million; it offered care for the sick, spiritual consolation, and field chaplaincy services—erecting hundreds of chapel tents and distributing many thousands of Bibles, hymnbooks, and other printed religious matter. (Photograph attributed to Alexander Gardner.)

Church service at Camp Cass, Arlington Heights, Virginia. Some rather elaborate accessories were available for the celebration of this Mass. Protestants, who of course were much more numerous than Catholics, typically gathered underneath huge brush arbors for preaching and for praising the Lord. (Courtesy of the Chicago Historical Society.)

Poplar Grove Church. This log edifice was planned and built by the Fiftieth New York Volunteer Engineers. Various army chaplains and visiting clergymen were invited to officiate at services. After the war there were efforts to move the building to Central Park in New York City. (Photograph attributed to Alexander Gardner.)

The Confederate Powder Works at Augusta, Georgia. (Courtesy of the Library of Congress.)

ifold and grievous sins." The "repentant, humble people, devoutly acknowledging the justice of the punishment He has brought upon them," would find that their faith would make them invincible. The events of July 1863, however, forced Confederates to reassert some of their basic assumptions. The editor of the *Memphis Daily Appeal* (by then published in Atlanta) saw the fall of Vicksburg as "the heaviest blow of the war," and with the news from Gettysburg he confessed that "it is difficult to discover any escape from the present unpleasant dilemma" unless all the people rose up to drive away the enemy—which, of course, they did not do.[13]

But perhaps the people could appease God. A letter in the *Milledgeville Confederate Union* a month after Vicksburg, Gettysburg, and Tullahoma stated the case simply: "We need the favor of God. Without it, we perish. God is angry with us for our sins. Hence the war itself, and hence the reverses of this summer." President Davis led the way. On July 25 he announced "a day of fasting, humiliation, and prayer," appealing to the public "to take home to our hearts and consciences the lessons" taught by recent reverses. "Our successes on land and sea," he warned, have "made us self-confident and forgetful," and "love of lucre [has] eaten like a gangrene into the very heart of the land, converting too many among us into worshippers of gain and rendering them unmindful of their duty . . . to God." Confederates must "receive in humble thankfulness the lesson which he has taught in our recent reverses."[14]

The following fall, after more defeats, but after more victories as well, the states issued proclamations of similar import. Governor Brown of Georgia led the way, declaring a day of fasting, humiliation, and prayer and asking other states to do likewise, in the belief that if God saw "a whole nation on its knees, fasting, in deep humility, and penitential confessions," He would "strike terror and dismay into the hearts of our enemies." Other states followed Georgia's example. The Alabama legislature recommended that southerners humble themselves, be penitent, "obey His laws, [and] implore through the merits of our Saviour, His forgiveness, and plead the wisdom to guide us." The Mississippi legislature expressed confidence in the leadership of Jefferson Davis, its native son, and asked God, for the sake of Jesus Christ, to forgive sins, protect soldiers from disease and battle, and save the people, while the "people acknowledge our dependence on Him who holds the destinies of nations in His hand." Florida also called for a day of fasting, humiliation, and prayer for early December 1863.[15]

These public prayers implied that the people could placate and supplicate the God of the Confederacy. Enough fasting, sufficient prayer, and ample confession of guilt would surely persuade Him to make His presence felt in a more positive way. One newspaper editor noted the truth of this notion in September 1862, for when events had turned against the South, Confederates had turned in humility and trust to God, beseeching Him to "turn away his wrath. . . . And lo! What a change has been wrought in our fortunes," for victory had come at Second Manassas and Richmond, Kentucky. "Never was there a greater deliverance vouchsafed to any people"; yet the day before the publication of these thanks to the God of the Confederacy—before the writer could have known of the event—General Lee had fought the Battle of Antietam and was even then retreating from Maryland.[16]

As DEFEAT approached, and God had not vindicated the cause, such logic could lead to only one conclusion: Confederates had not been true to themselves or God, or else God's support would have brought more positive results. The wife of a Georgia preacher spoke for many when she cried out in 1863, "How long will this awful conflict last? And to what depths of misery are we to be reduced ere the Sovereign Judge of all the earth will give us deliverance? It does appear that we are to be brought very low. May the Lord give us such true repentance and humility before Him as shall turn away His wrath and restore his Favor, through the merits and intercession of our Divine Redeemer!" "If it was not for the supporting hand of God we must give up and die," she wrote in her journal in December 1864. Her brother confessed the same religious mind-set, acknowledging his belief that "without special divine interposition we are a ruined people." The *Raleigh Daily Progress* agreed and urged that the war must end: "We are for peace, because, with an implicit faith in Divine teaching, we believe that the sins of nations as well as of individuals will overtake them, and that God will avenge himself on this American people, if this unnatural, fratricidal butchery is suffered to go on." A North Carolina politician expressed equal fatalism. Although he believed the South must fight on, he acknowledged that "no human foresight can tell what the end of our troubles will be. Whither we are drifting none can divine. How long we will be compelled to suffer the great God can only tell."[17]

With encouragement from the master class, antebellum southern Christianity, distinctly emphasizing Old Testament themes, had helped slaves to accept their bondage; now the wheel had turned, and the same religion helped southern whites accept the possibility of defeat because the victory that would have signaled God's favorable judgment on the Confederacy had proved elusive. The unforeseen and unpleasant side effects that came in the wake of war doubled the Confederate dilemma. Not only did the judgment of God seem to place Confederates in an uncomfortable position, but so did the actions of other Confederates. That war would cause death and a certain amount of dislocation came as no surprise; but that it would affect the system of government took many southerners unaware. The *Daily Lynchburg Virginian* observed: "We dared a revolution, and provoked a war." Southerners thus easily could conclude that "everything now must be sacrificed to success, because anything is preferable to defeat."[18]

But not everyone agreed with the opinions of this anonymous writer because not everyone thought of defeat as the greatest of horrors, and many who did think so did not believe that any and all sacrifices were necessary, or even helpful, in avoiding it. The price of victory, if they could achieve victory, was going to be infinitely higher than most of the Confederates of 1861 had bargained for. As this realization was driven home, the citizenry showed a natural resentment. A Georgia newspaper set the tone: "We are learning by bitter experience," its editor remarked, "that hotspurs and demagogues are unfit to govern a country. Such men brought us into trouble, and seem to be incapable of taking us out. They were suffered to lead the country in 1861, and none of the blessings which they predicted have been realized, while most of the evils apprehended by more considerate men have come to pass."[19]

Clearly, some Confederates felt betrayed. One of these, Governor Vance of North Carolina, agreed substantially. He remarked early in 1864 that, before they tried secession, the people had understood it "as completely as an abstraction could be understood." Angry because in 1861 he and his fellow Unionists had faced a choice between two undesirable alternatives, he reminded North Carolinians that "we were promised it should be peaceable. What is the result? Fie, it has been anything else. It has involved us in a war that has no parallel upon the pages of history." The search for scapegoats proceeded to the very end. "Many of the leaders of the present revolution," wrote a Virginia editor just before the final curtain, "were greatly at fault at the beginning. They seemed to have no conception of the magnitude of the work they were undertaking. They were self-deceived and misled the people. Consequently, the masses were not prepared."[20]

And the sufferings abounded, reported almost daily by newspapers, private letters, and personal experience. Sometimes impressment officers took more than the people reasonably could give and left them destitute. Other times Confederate irregulars or even regular soldiers committed such outrages on citizens that many plain folk feared them as much as they feared the Yankees. Inflation created devastating inroads into the standard of living of the middle and lower classes, and some citizens who lacked sufficient daily bread thought their more fortunate neighbors delayed in coming to their assistance. These problems, and others, sketched by Charles W. Ramsdell in his thoughtful commentary about life behind the lines, give evidence that despite faith, or perhaps for lack of it, the costs of war went beyond the ability of the Confederacy to pay.[21]

Hardships depleted a morale no longer so well sustained by religion. If many Confederates began to question whether they deserved victory, religion had ceased to provide the same confidence it had supplied two years before. So military defeat not only depressed morale but, by raising a question about God's favor, sapped the support religion had given to morale. And in the absence of strong nationalism and distinctive differences between southerners and the invaders from the North, the South's will to keep on fighting badly needed the support of religion and military success.

Whether more realistic expectations of the future in 1861 would have made a significant difference in 1864 remains another question, but nevertheless the expectations of 1861 led to inevitable disappointments, especially in the face of assurance that God would favor the cause unless His people proved unworthy. That Confederates did not deserve victory seemed a logically inescapable conclusion and requires examination of the thought processes that caused Confederates to question their goals, institutions, personal worthiness, and, eventually, even the war itself.

WHAT MECHANISM translated these very real problems and attitudes into a decisive defeatism? It was not simply that morale was undermined but that despite the insurmountable problems apparent to most Confederates by the end of 1863 or early 1864, the war effort continued. Ironically, even as the people's enthusiasm for war diminished, their commitment to it increased.

North Carolina provides a useful microcosm to examine this paradox for, as Owsley observed, it had become one of the major centers of discontent with the war and the Confederate government. It also supplied an exceedingly large number of men and a great deal of matériel to the Confederate army, and not merely because of demographics or geographical location. Governor Vance, a Unionist in 1861, argued toe-to-toe with Davis and resented the war. But he also fought bravely on the battlefield, then administered his state in such a way as to use state-rights theory to bolster the war effort. Other North Carolina conservatives felt much the same way. All of them, said the *Raleigh Daily Conservative*, "were opposed to the breaking up of the old government." As late as 1864 such men still thought that "to remain in the old government and labor to restore it" would have provided the best way to correct the errors into which the federal government had fallen. Nevertheless, the newspaper advised Confederates to stay with their new government because it was the only one they had and they were sworn to defend it. But this unenthusiastic endorsement shows an utter lack of Confederate nationalism. The editor concluded that the South must fight on, for the enemy stood at the door: "Look steadily at him and drive him from our soil, but never forget that our rulers at home need watching at the same time." What held true for North Carolina, by extension, also held true for any part of the Confederacy afflicted by defeatism, except areas like East Tennessee and West Virginia, whose people had never abandoned Unionism, which remained a potent force even after the secession decision.[22]

To most modern Americans these attitudes may not seem paradoxical, but they seemed so to many Confederates. Certainly Jefferson

Davis never comprehended Vance or others like him. Neither, for that matter, did those who wished to halt the war on the basis of reconstruction understand Vance—men like William W. Holden, for example. Actually, the militant Confederates and the pro-peace groups perceived Vance differently, and neither correctly. Furthermore, even in our own time historians have continued to show confusion over Vance's motives and goals, as we already have seen.

Perhaps the social psychological theory of cognitive dissonance can help to make sense of this strange behavior. The theory sheds some light on the ways people make decisions, why they cling to inappropriate choices, how they reduce tension between urgent courses of action and contradictory reality, and the obstacles they must overcome before eventually they can change decisions. The conservative North Carolinians, for example, provide examples of "the frequent observation that the less rational a reason you had for doing something, the more you will defend and justify the fact that you did it." The theory explains, further, why people act in ways that may seem irrational or self-defeating to today's historians. This approach may help us to understand why Confederates fought to preserve an institution that bothered the consciences of many of them, how casualty lists increased psychological tension, and the way an unsuccessful war and the change of war goals combined with religious views to undermine fatally the Confederate war effort. Having embarked on a course designed to protect slavery by establishing separate independence, many southerners acted in a fashion that seems to have prepared them to accept defeat.[23]

Sometimes contradictory or self-defeating behavior results from cognitive dissonance, which we may summarily define as the perception of contradictory information. Dissonant perceptions lead to "psychological discomfort" in decision making, just as hunger leads to physical discomfort. In both instances an individual seeks to reduce discomfort by whatever action he deems appropriate. He eats if he feels hungry; he examines and reexamines his information if he suffers from cognitive dissonance. In the latter instance, he evaluates information in such a way as to justify his condition, plans, hopes, activities, or beliefs. In a negative sense, he unconsciously seeks to fool himself and may even attempt to defeat his own goals. In the words of psychologist Leon Festinger, who developed the theory, cognitive dissonance "centers around the idea that if a person knows various things that are not psychologically consistent with one another, he will, in a variety of ways, try to make them more consistent." Festinger clarifies the concept by the common-sense observation that a person standing in the rain without getting wet would be puzzled because he would receive dissonant information (rain, yet dry), which would motivate him to reduce the resulting discomfort by trying to comprehend how such contradictions could occur. In the absence of a satisfactory and logical explanation, such as a raincoat or an umbrella, the victim of dissonance may need to resort to an unsatisfactory and illogical solution, although, if that explanation effectively reduces dissonance, it will not seem bizarre or illogical to him.[24]

Simply because an individual knows of some alternative information or course of action does not ordinarily create a dissonance problem. The mechanism comes into play to the degree that a given decision contains an emotional investment. The greater the emotional investment, the greater the commitment to the decision; the greater the commitment, the greater the dissonance created when the decision turns sour; the more inappropriate the original decision becomes, the greater the dissonance, and the more effort the victim makes to reduce the discomfort of conflicting knowledge. To justify one's choice of a dress or shirt presents an easy task, but to justify human bondage, rebellion, war, a change in war goals, or death confronts people with severe problems. Such decisions could, and did, create understandably severe postdecision dissonance. Under the pressure of cognitive dissonance, southerners equated bondage for slaves with freedom for themselves; rebellion against the nation became loyalty to constitutional ideals; war became a means of achieving honorable peace; changes in a war goal from preservation of slavery to independence became a restatement of an old desire simply to be let alone; and death became life, at least in the hereafter. Such contradictory justifications could cause confusion for outside observers, although historians familiar with the truespeak and double think of an Orwellian era should have little difficulty seeing the reality behind the smoke screen of sincerely believed rationalizations. When a decision might have, or already has had, an important influence in one's life, the situation becomes ripe for the creation of severe dissonance that must be reduced.

The knowledge of the attractive features of rejected alternatives creates such dissonance. Memory of roads not taken and choices not made may cause the decision to frustrate and disturb the individual, especially when he has a strong emotional commitment to it and when rejected alternatives have features that look more attractive than they did at an earlier time. But because he has already made the decision, he must justify it, no matter how desirable the rejected alternatives may seem. Having made a bad bargain, he must hug it all the closer; having made his bed, he must sleep in it. By the middle of the Civil War most Confederates had become fully aware of the advantages of the repudiated choices. Especially among original Unionists, peace and Union looked extremely alluring by 1863; but the South had not taken the road of no war, no casualty lists, and Union. Rather, southerners had decided to protect their autonomy and institutions, by force, as it turned out. The more aware of the attractive features of the rejected alternatives Confederates became, the higher their postdecision dissonance and the greater the necessity for them to justify the choice they had made.

They could accomplish that unconscious task—reducing dissonance and justifying choices—in several ways. Southerners could deal with dissonance by distorting their perceptions, filtering out new and disturbing knowledge so that they could no longer perceive any conflict of dissonant information. The militant secessionist, for example, might convince himself that all Republicans were "Black Republicans" and, like John Brown, wished to see servile insurrection with all the bloodshed and horror that implied. Events actually reinforced this perception, for the Emancipation Proclamation convinced many Confederates that the North sought a servile insurrection. And if one became convinced of that, then certainly he fought on whether or not he originally had favored secession. Such people could not turn back because the threats to their well-being had become even more serious than in 1861. This resolution of cognitive dissonance created a commitment that augmented or substituted for deficient Confederate nationalism in prolonging determination to continue the war.

Southerners could also reduce dissonance a second way, as the discussion at the beginning of this chapter illustrates: they could add new "knowledge," perhaps by emphasizing that the disasters of this unhappy war, and indeed the war itself, were, somehow, the unfolding of the will of an omnipotent God, and they could not, and should not, avoid God's designs; many Confederates would have agreed with the editor who claimed that "the terrible convulsions which have been witnessed in this land for the last two years . . . have been permitted by Him for some wise, it may be inscrutable purpose."[25]

Altering one of the two elements, either by revising one's beliefs or changing one's decision, provided a third way to reduce inconsistency between knowledge and behavior, that is, dissonance. Some amended their knowledge (beliefs) and discovered that the war to preserve slavery actually had become a war for independence, and always had been, a tack that Confederates increasingly adopted as it became apparent that slavery would become a casualty no matter who won. Other Confederates varied their behavior (decisions) by subtly attempting to renounce their decisions. They contended that they had forced the Union to accept constitutional limitations, that they had vindicated southern honor, and hence they could envision an acceptable peace without the military victory that their comrades demanded. These people became the true peace advocates, some even convincing themselves that timely reconstruction could preserve slavery. In early 1865, for example, Senator William Alexander Graham of North Carolina pondered whether "reunion, by which ten States may defeat the proposed [thirteenth] amendment to the Constitution, & retain slavery be not preferable to the triumph of his arms, and the subjugation of every thing to his power." Others in this category agreed with the Virginia newspaper editor who concluded simply, and logically, that "if the South is to be abolitionized in the end, it would have been far better for us to be abolitionized in the beginning."[26]

As a later chapter will emphasize, the Confederates in the second and third categories, afflicted by feelings of religious fatalism, guilt, sin, betrayal, and futility, became the point men in the movement that eventually sapped Confederate will.

Group behavior also contributed to reduction of postdecision dissonance. Individuals sharing similar beliefs could control new information. Mutual discomfort brought relief through the social support of one's leaders, followers, or comrades, who, because they had the same beliefs, mitigated doubt and reinforced one's original conclusions by adding the new information that one had companions facing the same difficulties. Doubtful decisions took on new validity because social sharing of attitudes bolstered the legitimacy of the original decision.

In an area where southerners had undertaken secession only with great reluctance, such as North Carolina, for example, people frequently used another way to reduce postdecision dissonance caused by the knowledge that they had opposed secession but had nevertheless accepted it and supported the war that resulted. They asserted, as did M. S. Robins, the editor of the *Daily Conservative*, that the South had to pursue the unwanted war as a matter of principle. Reminding his readers that "many of us battled faithfully against the causes which brought on this war," he washed his hands, or reduced his dissonance, by the Pilate-like remark that "the crime of bringing it on does not rest on our heads." But he faced a decision already made that he must render acceptable despite the attractive alternatives of peace. "What then," Robins wrote in surprise and shock at the very idea of ending short of independence the war he and his fellows had opposed, "shall we, after having spilt so much blood, sacrificed so many lives and so much treasure, in defence of the eternal principles of right, shall we back down? Never! Never!" He denied that the South had entered into war to maintain the right of secession. Rather than this nonsense, he asserted that "we are fighting for Southern equal rights and Southern property, and nothing else, or the whole affair is a kink or a mith [sic] in the brain of a madman." He not only accepted the unwise decision but glorified it despite his knowledge, indeed his active support, of earlier, more attractive alternatives. Committed to the decision and bolstered by the social support of his fellows, Robins maintained as late as December 1864 that conservatives still believed secession a mistake but that they must stick by the Confederate government because it constituted "the only government they've got, and because they are sworn to defend it."[27]

Robins and others with the same view reduced their dissonance in a way that may seem strange to some historians today—they hugged an acknowledged evil all the closer to their hearts because it was their own—but they used their arguments to convince others and in so doing managed to persuade themselves. In this way, groups clung to ideas—slavery, unsuccessful war, the chimera of independence—long after they had become inappropriate. "After being exposed to evidence of one's senses which unequivocally demonstrates a belief system to be wrong," notes Leon Festinger, "people tend to proselyte more vigorously for the belief system." They ignore new and incompatible information: hard-line Confederates, for example, who were firmly committed to the decision for secession and war, reduced dissonance by changing information—claiming that they fought the war for independence, or southern rights, or whatever—rather than by changing behavior and giving up the fight.

Thus, and to anticipate ourselves somewhat, by 1864 many Confederates were willing to surrender slavery if to do so would help attain independence; more and more southerners claimed that they had sought independence all along. They substituted war goals, discussed more extensively below, as postdecision dissonance subjected Confederates to the discomfort caused by the knowledge of the attractive features of the rejected alternative—hence the anguish and guilt over an unsuccessful, bloody war for slavery. But most Confederates continued to spurn the rejected alternatives, Union and peace, until shortly before the final collapse, as they reduced discomfort by creating "an increase in the desirability of the chosen alternative and a decrease in the desirability of the rejected alternative." Hence the constant clatter about an honorable peace, meaning peace with independence, and the fear that defeat meant subjugation, which would in turn mean slavery for the losers. Emotional investment is an important component in the creation of the psychological discomfort of cognitive dissonance; dissonance increases in proportion to the importance of the problem, as people "try to justify a commitment to the extent that there is information discrepant with that commitment."[28]

Faced with the realization that they might not merit God's favor or, after a prolonged and costly struggle that they might have made the wrong choice in seceding, many Confederates found ways to resolve the resulting dissonance. But the very fact that many of them faced dissonance indicates the weakness of their original resolution. Moreover, a determination to fight on based on the product of dissonance resolution provided a very feeble substitute for a will based on strong nationalism with deep roots in the past or important cultural or linguistic distinctiveness from the enemy.

SOUTHERNERS HAD to add a new element to their mental equations when unwanted by-products of their war efforts accentuated postdecision dissonance. Not only did they have to reckon with God and the northern army, but they were hindered by other Confederates. Many a Confederate might have discovered that he was his own worst enemy. For example, the issues involved in the establishment of centralization, uniformity, and internal control shocked, amazed, disillusioned, and angered significant segments of the southern community. The mobilization of both men and resources necessary to wage war successfully proved a good deal more rigorous than Confederates ever had dreamed, creating postdecision dissonance over and beyond that caused by the mental and spiritual traps of religious fatalism and the increasing size and success of the Union army.

Suspension of the writ of habeas corpus for varying periods of time, martial law with ever-present provost marshals to enforce it, impressment of supplies at less than market prices, and conscription had not been part of the original bargain. No one had expected such unpleasant side effects when the states marched out of the Union. At the end of the war one politician echoed the disillusion of many of his fellow Confederates, remarking with magnificent understatement and sarcasm, "Secession seems not to have produced the results predicted by its sanguine friends. There was to be no war, no taxes worth prating about, but an increase of happiness, boundless prosperity, and entire freedom from all Yankee annoyance." But instead the war brought conscription, destruction, and infringement of civil liberties.[29]

As he often did, Governor Joseph E. Brown of Georgia well articulated the resulting discontent. Brown objected violently to the suspension of the writ of habeas corpus for its alleged infringement upon state sovereignty. More to the point, he said suspension was "not the constitutional liberty which so many Georgians have died to defend," for it gave the president the powers of a monarch. Conscription provoked Brown's displeasure even more. When Georgia entered the "revolution," "we [little] supposed . . . that the person of the freeborn citizens of the respective States would be regarded and claimed, while at home in pursuit of their ordinary avocations, as the vassals of the central power, to be like chattels, ordered and disposed of at pleasure." "At one fell swoop," Brown asserted, conscription "strikes down the sovereignty of the State, triumphs upon the constitutional rights and personal liberty of the citizens, and arms the President with imperial power." Ironically forgetting that the South was fighting this war more to prevent some men from becoming free than to ensure that others would remain free, Brown, shortly before the end but before he had given up all hope of victory, announced to the Georgia legislature that conscription had transformed the people's war into "the Government's war, and he was no longer a free man but the slave of absolute power. This was not the freedom he set out to fight for." Thousands of other Confederates agreed, he thought, and, "feeling that they wore the collar of power upon their necks, have left the army without leave."[30]

Others besides Brown vehemently objected to the conscription law. Texas Senator Williamson S. Oldham declared that the Confederate government had no power to conscript without the consent of the states: "This was not circumlocution; it was the theory of our government." C. C. Herbert, one of the Texans in the House of Representatives, supported Oldham and warned that "it would not do to press the conscription law too far upon the people. If it became necessary to violate the Constitution . . . he would be for raising in his State the 'lone star' flag that had twice been raised before." Reuben Davis of Mississippi (no relation to Jefferson Davis) thought conscription a mark of slavery, telling his colleagues in Congress that "he had rather be a 'naygur' than a victim of the Conscription Law." Confederates frequently maintained that they were "demanding only to be let alone." Many Confederates could understand that well enough. But Philip S. Paludan's observations on this point about the mountain people applied to many other southerners as well. "Fighting for the right to be left alone," he wrote, "was a cause mountaineers could rally round. Being compelled to fight for that right—well, a man did not have to be very sophisticated to smell something wrong with that."[31]

This centralization of power and imposition of uniformity ran contrary to the goals Confederates originally had sought to achieve by war. It put the legitimacy of the war effort in doubt and heightened the tensions created by postdecision dissonance. Even the goals of the war seemed to have changed, the rules of the game being altered in mid-course. Given the pressures of the war, this power evolved logically, but it ran against the grain of many Confederates nevertheless. Conscription, for example, increased Confederate strength by bolstering the armed forces, but it also had the compensating deficiency of undermining Confederate morale. Vice-President Alexander H. Stephens, resenting conscription, suspension of habeas corpus, and impressment, vented his frustration to Senator Herschel V. Johnson. Stephens did not wish to build up opposition to Jefferson Davis; rather, his feelings for Davis were "akin to suspicion and jealousy." Stephens wrote that his "hostility and wrath (and I have enough of it to burst ten thousand bottles) is not against him, or any man or men, but against the thing—the measure and the policy which I see is leading us to despotism." Stephens's objective was not to inaugurate a counterrevolution but "to keep the present one . . . on the right track."[32]

Other men expressed similar feelings in a more moderate but equally determined manner. Independence with centralized power, thought Governor Brown of Georgia, "would be very little better than subjugation, as it matters little who our master is, if we are to have one." Three months later he wrote, "If this is the sort of independence for which we are fighting, our great sacrifices have been made but to little purpose. The recognition by foreign powers of the independence of our rulers and of their right to govern us, without the recognition of our rights and liberties by our rulers, is not worth the blood of the humblest citizen. We must gain more than this in the struggle, or we have made a most unfortunate exchange."[33]

Brown was really asking again why the Confederacy was fighting at all; he saw clearly enough that he did not have the same reasons many other southerners had, which led to the inevitable conclusion that many soldiers had given their lives in vain. James L. Orr, a South Carolina senator, referring to the suspension of habeas corpus and the vast numbers of provost marshals enforcing martial law on the civilian population, feared that the executive was subverting the civil power and demanded that "the legislature should put a curb on the unbridled will of military power" to avoid "despotism." Referring specifically to Orr's comments, Richard C. Puryear of North Carolina claimed that Orr also reflected the opinions of North Carolinians, who were "willing to fight and die for liberty" but "never will wear the chains of a foreign or Domestic tyrant." If people did not resist, "then we shall be fit subjects of Slavery," he added, "and it matters not whether our Master be a Northern or Southern Tyrant." Congressman James T. Leach of North Carolina expressed equal concern. "The rapidity with which our dangers seem to accumulate, and the fearfull [sic] consequences that are likely to grow out of them to ourselves and to our posterity," he noted, "should engage the serious attention of every christian patriot and statesman; the earnest inquiry is, what shall we do to stay the hand of a military despotism more to be dreaded than death itself?"[34]

These were the problems Brown and others talked about. If southern sacrifice resulted in despotism, then the war had produced nothing, indeed worse than nothing, for remembering the desirable features of the rejected alternative of peace, some Confederates could not accept a road to independence that violated their ideas of the fundamentals of a free government. At the end, almost as a political postmortem, the *Daily Conservative* complained that the leaders had not consulted the popular will at the inception of the Confederacy or in its management and asked rhetorically, "Have not the people been rather led or driven, instead of leading?" Fighting, they thought, for freedom, all too many southerners felt disillusionment with the despotism they believed to be emanating from Richmond. This supposed tyranny resulted not only in internal dissent—which, in itself, did not always do harm—but also in strength-sapping discouragement and suggestions about future policy that did not always accord with official administration ideas. Appalled by centralized power and the length, bloodshed, and probable outcome of the war, they looked ever more regretfully at the attractive features of rejected alternative decisions.[35]

In a famous letter to Jefferson Davis, written as the curtain began to fall in October 1864, South Carolina Congressman William W. Boyce urged the president to bolster the fortunes of the peace faction of the Democratic party in the North by indicating a willingness to have all the states convene for the purpose of discussing peace. Not only motivated by a desire to end the war, Boyce also hoped to avoid Confederate despotism. "Well," he wrote Davis,

> we have been at war not quite four years, and what is the result? Is not
> our Federal Government in the exercise of every possible power of a na-

tional central military despotism? Suppose there were no States, only provinces, and unlimited power was conferred upon you and Congress, what greater power would you exercise than you now do? . . . Indeed if you were appointed Military Dictator, what greater powers could you exercise than you now do?

If you tell me that they [the powers] are necessary, I reply, that is precisely my argument. My argument assumes and requires that necessity. It is plain that our government exercises the powers of a central despotism. . . . The truth is, that the Government at Washington has not dared to exercise power on the grand scale that our Government has.

The only way to avoid that despotism, thought Boyce, lay in escaping wartime centralization by securing a lasting, harmonious peace.[36]

One of the operating assumptions behind the thinking of Vance, Stephens, Brown, Boyce, and others was the very practical one that if the war inevitably resulted in despotic rule, the reason for fighting was nullified. If one believed in the desirability or inevitability of restrictions upon self-government, he could have had them without leaving the Union. Some southerners had used the fear of subjugation to powerful central authority to justify secession in the first place; to go through a bloody war and come out at the same point hardly seemed worth the effort. Idealistic motivations also affected attitudes. The Confederate elite, even those supposedly responsible for the alleged despotism, were truly dedicated to constitutional order. As David Donald points out, throughout the war Confederates believed in and pursued constitutional liberty as they understood it, and in many respects Davis infringed less upon the liberties of the people than did Lincoln. But some Confederates apparently believed deeply that unless they could preserve the spirit as well as the letter of their Constitution, they had made a mistake to secede and fight. A game won by cheating would bring only a hollow victory. "This is the peoples' revolution," declared Congressman John P. Murray of Tennessee, "and they will tolerate no subversion of their ancient liberties. . . . [I have] never understood that political doctrine that teaches that in order to get liberty you must first lose it, nor the paradox that in order to be healthy you must first ruin your physical constitution."[37]

These statements make it easier to understand why Confederates overcame their misgivings and fought to keep their slaves, for the sanctity of property was one of their tests of liberty. This feeling increased as casualty lists lengthened, for the emotional investment in the lives lost made it unthinkable to let go of the institution for which those lives had been sacrificed. When, finally, the Confederacy moved to emancipate slaves, the unthinkable had occurred, and a furious negative reaction arose among those who had always thought that the protection of property rights in slaves, not independence per se, was the goal for which they had initiated the war. This last twist will be discussed thoroughly at a later point. For now, it is sufficient to understand that emancipation was a perfectly logical step for the Confederacy to take if the war continued to drag on, bleeding the South of her best young men. At the same time, it was equally logical for other Confederates, who had thought much about slave property in 1861, to feel betrayed when they were told in late 1864 and 1865 that slavery was expendable. And behind these thoughts were the promptings of religion, which seemed to provide a clear indicator that for some reason God was not smiling on the Confederate cause.

As early as 1863, therefore, many Confederates were doubting whether their prospects justified their efforts, whether the end justified the means. Men such as Davis, of course, never had doubts. Despite heavy sacrifices of blood and treasure, Davis believed that "the prize for which we strive, freedom and independence, is worth whatever it may cost." He did not mention individual freedom, for Confederate centralization did not circumscribe his activities. The masses of southern voters, however, thought differently. Trying to get themselves out of the trouble into which their leaders had led them, they cast about for alternatives. No one had forced the southerners to secede. They had had an alternative, and if either decision would result in despotism, why indeed had they rejected the Union? Some disillusioned conservatives recognized one reason: the people had never sanctioned the course of the politicians, "but when the ball of revolution had received such momentum, it could not be stopped." No one had consulted the popular will, and the people had become "the dupes of demagogues and partizan tricksters who have carved out for them and forced them to execute." If that were true, men were dying for no good reason.[38]

No longer was it possible to renounce secession itself. Multitudes of

Confederates did the next best thing and attempted to resolve their dissonance and seize whatever remained of the rejected alternative by renouncing secessionists. In the 1863 elections many secession Democrats lost their seats to Union Whigs. North Carolina, an extreme example, replaced a delegation in the House of Representatives that was 60 percent Democrats with one composed of 90 percent Union Whigs. In the entire Congress about half the secessionists and half the Unionists won reelection; the new congressmen, however, were two-thirds Unionists, and many of the reelected secessionists won their seats by votes from refugees and the army, for these congressmen represented districts in which normal political process had become impossible because their constituents lay outside effective Confederate control. This election did not reflect a true peace movement, for the winners, with a few exceptions, warmly supported the war effort. But they had opposed the decision of 1861, had consented to it only with reluctance, or had at least warned of the dangers to come, and they represented a desire on the part of many Confederates to "turn instinctively to those old leaders, who foretold their present situation, for counsel and instruction."[39]

The election of 1863 not only reflected an attempt to reduce postdecision dissonance by partially renouncing the decision makers of 1861, it also indicated popular perceptions of Confederate prospects. The people seemed to feel that if the previous leadership had blundered in getting the South into a war and then could not achieve victory, perhaps those who had had sufficient farsightedness to oppose the secession movement might have more success in the conduct of the war. During 1863 this became an important consideration on all sides, as prospects for an early peace faded and hopes of victory dimmed. Even if one expected defeat, he fought on, because whether one gave up and submitted or suffered subjection in defeat, the result came out the same—reunion. Many preferred the latter because reunion through defeat "would at least save us our honor," whereas reunion through negotiation would not. So Confederates continued to fight, to preserve honor if nothing else, even though "the prospect of success is not more than flattering; indeed, all things considered, it is gloomy and forebodes evil."[40]

The confrontation between faith and reality forced Confederates to look to the future with much anxiety as the erratic but increasingly successful course of the Union army gradually crushed the will of the citizens. Required more and more to doubt that they were on God's side, or God on theirs, they had to reexamine themselves and their religion to see whether war and slavery were compatible in either a religious or a social-political sense. If they were not, perhaps God's grace could once more be assured by reforming slavery, or even eliminating it. Piety lengthened the war at this point by assuring southerners that God would not abandon them, although He might well punish them for their transgressions. Piety was not lost, nor faith either; but many Confederates became less certain of what God's will might be in this conflict. The Lord's will, once so obvious, had now to be searched out and the ways of God and man reconciled as best they could.

As military power declined, civilian will, now undermined by the doubts of religion, could no longer supplement the force of arms. As will slowly expired, so too did the military strength of the Confederacy. In spite of the discouraging outlook, however, the Confederacy fought on, some Confederates even retaining hopes of eventual victory. And truly these hopes did not lack a foundation, for northerners also were becoming war weary and southern arms continued to inflict heavy losses upon attacking Federal armies. The final question, therefore, still remained in doubt over the winter of 1863–64. Many Confederates agreed that their large army gave them the power and even the duty to fight on, at least until their means of resistance became inadequate to achieve independence—which clearly had not yet happened. Only then would they resign themselves to their fate, to " 'accept the situation' and make the best terms in our power." With an effort of will, therefore, Confederates not only continued to fight, but with such success that multitudes of northerners still could not confidently forecast the eventual outcome of the conflict.[41]

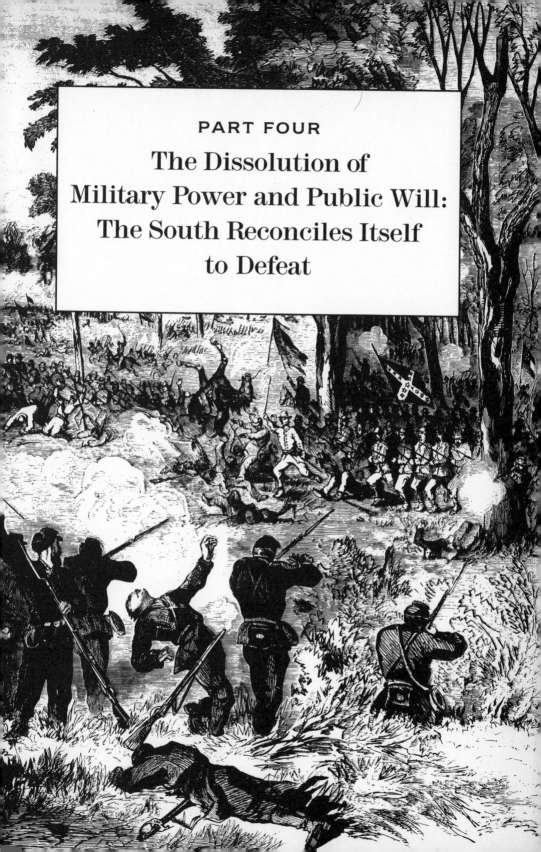

PART FOUR

The Dissolution of Military Power and Public Will: The South Reconciles Itself to Defeat

It long has been easy for the student of the Civil War to conclude that the high point of Confederate fortunes came in the middle of 1863 and that the retreat at Tullahoma, the surrender at Vicksburg, and the defeat at Gettysburg marked a decided reversal of Confederate fortunes; but this was not so obvious to contemporary Americans on either side of the Mason-Dixon line. The Confederate army by no means stood defeated after 1863, and neither did the citizenry.

To be sure, the situation had deteriorated considerably. The last large-scale, interdepartmental, offensive concentration of southern troops occurred in the late summer and fall of 1863, and it led to the Confederate victory at Chickamauga. After that, Confederate armies, though not abandoning counteroffensives, made no other comparable effort. Union attempts to engineer concentrations in time had succeeded, virtually completely in December 1862 and partially in the spring of 1862 and 1863. In 1864 the Union attempted a concentration in time once again and achieved its best synchronization. The armies of Grant and Sherman moved successfully, leading to the military climax in the march to the sea, the siege of Petersburg, and ultimately the breaking of the stalemate and the surrenders at Appomattox and Durham Station.

The defeat of the Confederacy did not, however, constitute a military achievement. The quashing of Confederate arms occurred because Confederates chose not to mobilize their home front as well as they had their fighting front. They allowed the essential element of will to atrophy under the discouraging events of the last year of the war. Searching for means of increasing the strength of the armed forces, the Confederate leaders tried new recruitment schemes and amended their manpower system. In the end, however, the only way they could think of to strengthen the army was by recruiting black soldiers. As so often throughout the war, military questions received only military answers.

To be effective, black soldiers had to have an appropriate reward, and that could only mean emancipation, which some southerners thought denied the very purpose of the Confederacy. Conflict over this issue further reduced popular morale, which was already shaken, for even those who assented to Confederate emancipation as a last resort had now to face the fact that the Confederacy was playing its final card. Victory now became the impossible dream because not enough Confederates willed independence hard enough or long enough to win.

In the end, however, though perhaps ironically, the South perceived that she too had her victory. From the ashes of military defeat, former Confederates discovered a new freedom in the removal of slavery, yet managed nevertheless to hold fast to some of the advantages that the dead institution had provided. As they looked back at the crisis of 1861 from the vantage point of the postwar generation, white southerners came to agree that they had never fought for slavery at all, but for their own honor and the rights of their states. Since the war had destroyed neither, but, rather, the war and the reconstruction and reconciliation that followed had confirmed both, they could point to their own significant victory. For the surviving veterans, the conflict became the perfect war because both sides could claim triumph.

Chapter Thirteen

The Last Campaigns

To MILITARY REVERSES the Confederates always found military answers. When the armies encountered defeat, the response was to compensate by a future victory. Although the armies sought such a victory to recover lost territory and resources, counteroffensives also served to enhance morale diminished by the preceding reverses. This relationship between military action and morale exhibited itself particularly well when the Confederacy mounted a large offensive after the loss of Chattanooga, East Tennessee, and the crucial western railway from Richmond to Atlanta. And this campaign in September 1863 came close on the heels not just of the fall of Chattanooga and Knoxville but of the discouraging summer defeats of Tullahoma, Gettysburg, and Vicksburg. If one could overlook the actual military motivations, one could believe that the Confederacy had inaugurated the Chickamauga campaign to elevate the morale that was depressed by previous reverses.

And in fact the Confederates did rely far too much on military successes to sustain will and confidence. For a time, successful offensives could restore some measure of national feeling. But the Confederacy had a basic problem of depleted civilian will that ultimately it could not overcome. One answer to the gradual decline of Confederate military strength would have been to supplement military strength with increased civilian determination. A good public information program might have had value, although we cannot expect nineteenth-century men to think in twentieth-century terms. But it is not too much to expect that the Confederate leadership would see that home-front difficulties could not necessarily be solved by increasingly expensive battlefield victories.

The southern governors had understood this problem and had used their state governments to meet the material needs of their people, lest the destitution into which the war had forced them cause morale to crack so completely as to shatter the war effort. Another victory in Virginia would not fill an empty stomach in North Carolina or plant the crops in Georgia. Governors Vance and Brown, and others as well, had understood that; Davis did, too, but was unable to turn his attention away from the battlefields long enough to give proper attention to civilian problems. And it became necessary to adopt military strategies that did not contain within them the seeds of home-front discouragement. General Lee's two incursions into the North, Antietam in September of 1862 and Gettysburg in June of 1863, had the fatal flaw that when he retreated—and it was inevitable that he must—the retreat would be perceived as a defeat and southern will would be damaged accordingly.

THE IMPORTANT Union victories of July 1863 did not inaugurate a steady decline in Confederate fortunes. Indeed, the fortunes of war turned rapidly in the opposite direction, but first another advance by Rosecrans's army, this time into Georgia, further diminished southern hopes.

After Tullahoma, Rosecrans planned to maneuver Bragg back still farther by turning the Confederate flank once again and threatening the rebel rear. Strategically the move resembled Rosecrans's previous campaign, but, since he intended that it should take place after the fall of Vicksburg and during the period of Union inactivity in Mississippi and Virginia, Rosecrans asked Halleck for a movement by Grant to keep Johnston from aiding Bragg. Not only did the appeal come too late, for Johnston already had sent reinforcements to Bragg, but Halleck, intent on the trans-Mississippi, did not order any distracting activity by Grant's much-shrunken army. Rosecrans, however, did receive his requested simultaneous movements by the long-inert Union forces in Kentucky, the command of which had passed to Burnside.

In spite of pressure by Halleck to follow up his Tullahoma success with an uninterrupted advance, Rosecrans had to delay his movement for six weeks while he repaired his railroad, accumulated supplies, and waited for the corn to ripen, all necessary because again he would move his entire army around Bragg's in a deep turning movement against the Confederate general's communications. With no base such as that which Lee had in the Shenandoah Valley, the Federal army again would be out of touch with its own communications, depending, as in the first advance, on what the army could carry with it, on living off the country, and on what wagons could bring by a circuitous route through rugged country over bad roads. Rosecrans was ready on August 16.

Again distracting Bragg, this time by moving one corps toward Chattanooga and bombarding the city, Rosecrans succeeded in moving his other three corps over the unfordable Tennessee River and around Bragg's west flank. This move so threatened Confederate communications that Bragg forfeited Chattanooga to the Federal troops on September 9 and fell back to protect his railroad in north Georgia. Though his inadequate cavalry failed to supply him with information, Rosecrans felt confident that Bragg was withdrawing all the way to Atlanta. Meanwhile, Burnside had advanced from Kentucky and taken Knoxville on September 2, also cutting the railroad from Virginia to Atlanta. Far from retreating, however, Bragg was repeating previous Confederate strategy, when, as Jomini would have expressed it, "the whole theatre of operations may be considered as a single field upon which strategy directs the armies for a definite end." As if they were following Jomini's and Clausewitz's precepts, Confederates sought to take advantage of their interior lines and the enemy's temporary inertia to "be more closely concentrated" and to employ "mobility" to compensate for being the "weaker side."[1]

Though they lacked interior lines because their troops had to move in roundabout fashion over a rickety transportation system, the Confederates achieved strategic surprise when they exploited their railroads and rapidly assembled the most far-flung concentration since Shiloh. When they abandoned the East Tennessee line of operations, the army opposing Burnside there moved to unite with Bragg, and they were joined by most of the remainder of Johnston's infantry, which was sent forward to north Georgia. President Davis earlier had sought a part of Lee's army to reinforce the West but had run into an example of what Clausewitz called a commander's feeling of "proprietary right" over all of his troops and the usual objection "to any part being withdrawn for however short a time." Nevertheless, on September 9 Davis ordered the bulk of Longstreet's corps, nearly a third of Lee's infantry, to join Bragg. Rosecrans, commanding the smallest of the major Federal offensive armies, was perhaps the only Union commander to confront such superior numbers in a major battle during the war; he had fifty-eight thousand men to face an enemy concentration of seventy thousand. The Confederates were making such a powerful response not only because they wished to counteract Rosecrans's success but also because they already had become convinced that Tennessee presented a promising opportunity for an offensive.[2]

Turned from his Chattanooga position, Bragg was, as Clausewitz would have analyzed such situations, "forced to fight an offensive battle and to forego the further benefits of *waiting, of a strong position, and of good entrenchments*, etc." To compensate for these disadvantages, Bragg had substantial reinforcements. But Bragg moved slowly, and Rosecrans, suddenly realizing his danger, succeeded in concentrating his army, which had been widely dispersed in order to pass through the mountains.[3]

As the battle of Chickamauga developed, Rosecrans countered Bragg's plan to overlap his north flank and the Confederates therefore resorted to frontal assaults. One of these assaults, a strong one under Longstreet at midday of September 20, achieved an overwhelming triumph because Rosecrans had inadvertently left a hole in his line. With the right of his army collapsed under this attack, Rosecrans lost his usual determination and, unlike his imperturbable behavior at the battle of Murfreesboro, concluded that he had lost the battle. After a successful resistance for the remainder of the day by his north wing under stolid, capable Major General George H. Thomas, his army withdrew to Chattanooga, September 21–22, 1863.

The tactical victory of the Confederates meant that their relative losses were not as heavy as the tactical offensive typically dictated; they lost fewer than 18,500 to more than 16,000 for the Union army. As a result of winning this encounter, Bragg could take up a position on the south side of the Tennessee River, where he could compel a further Union retreat because his position cut the railroad from Nashville to Chattanooga. Without the railroad, Rosecrans would be unable to bring in enough supplies. Nevertheless, the demoralized Rosecrans clung to Chattanooga and the gains of his second strategic turning movement. He had again demonstrated the defensive power of a Civil War army, not only to resist attack but also to maneuver so as to survive even a major breakthrough in its line of battle. Bragg, on the other hand, had shown the recuperative power of Civil War armies. Having suffered defeat but a few months earlier and having just been turned out of two positions, he now gained victory, and the winners of the earlier battle and maneuvers huddled in fear and want behind their defenses. Both armies demonstrated by their indestructibility the difficulty of achieving decisive results on the battlefield, even when, as in this case, one commander blundered seriously enough to present an open gap to his adversary.

The Confederate concentration for the Battle of Chickamauga had caused great concern in Washington and precipitated a counterconcentration that called for men to fight in Georgia from Grant's army and from as far away as Minnesota. But none of these troops arrived until after the battle. In addition, Secretary Stanton emphatically insisted on reinforcing Rosecrans with men from the Army of the Potomac. Lincoln and Halleck resisted this idea because they saw more opportunity in an attack by Meade against Lee. Since the Confederate transfer of Longstreet to Tennessee had weakened Lee more, proportionately, than it had strengthened Bragg, they believed they had now found the moment for concentration in time through an advance by Meade. But Meade reported that Lee and the defensive power of his weakened army was still too strong. He did not see how he possibly could hurt Lee; so Lincoln and Halleck acquiesced in Stanton's plan to send two corps from Virginia by rail to reinforce the besieged Rosecrans.

Confederate strength around Chattanooga soon diminished, when, on November 4, Bragg sent a major part of his army, Longstreet's corps, toward Knoxville in East Tennessee to resist Burnside's army from Kentucky. Bragg wished to reestablish there the Confederate line of operations that he had abandoned so as to have the maximum concentration for Chickamauga. Though this Confederate move aroused apprehensions for Burnside's safety and for the security of the occupation of East Tennessee, which the Union finally had liberated, the Union command sent no troops to aid Burnside as long as Bragg beleaguered Chattanooga.

By now Lincoln had lost all his remaining faith in Rosecrans, and he combined Rosecrans's and Burnside's departments with Grant's and placed all three in the new Military Division of the Mississippi, to be commanded by Grant. In turn, Grant replaced Rosecrans with the reli-

able George H. Thomas and went in person to head the forces concentrating near Chattanooga. Grant immediately infused energy into
the improvement of the supply lines and, at the end of November 1863,
after Sherman's corps had joined him from Mississippi, carried out a
series of operations, the battles of Lookout Mountain and Missionary
Ridge.

In these contests Grant, with sixty-one thousand men to forty thousand Confederates, took the offensive against Bragg's entrenched
army, succeeding in one major frontal attack in driving the demoralized Confederates well back into north Georgia. Grant thus raised
Bragg's siege of Chattanooga and consolidated the gains Rosecrans
had made by his September turning movement. These dispositions
continued all winter, with Longstreet and Burnside facing each other
near Knoxville and Grant opposing Bragg's army in north Georgia.

Meanwhile, when Meade lost two corps in September to reinforce
Rosecrans, Lee took the offensive in early October 1863 to prevent the
Union from sending more of Meade's men west. Using his characteristic turning movement, Lee again passed to the west of the Union
army and forced Meade back to Washington by threatening his communications. But Meade stayed ahead of Lee and entrenched near the
railroad, where Lee, without a railroad and unable to disperse so as to
live on the country, fell back, reaching his rail communications along
the Rapidan by November 7. Meade followed, but slowly, because he
had to rebuild the railroad destroyed by Lee's advance.

Then, under pressure from Lincoln and Halleck to strike hard at
Lee, shortly after Thanksgiving Day, Meade and his entire army
turned Lee's position on the east, only to find his move detected and
Lee's army well entrenched on Mine Run, at right angles to his old
position. Low on supplies and at some distance over bad roads from a
railroad, Meade then withdrew north across the Rapidan on December
1–2 just before Lee sought to drive him back with a counter turning
movement that advanced into the vacant Federal positions. Thus
Meade and Lee concluded operations in Virginia in 1863 and settled
into winter quarters, again confirming the stalemate in that theater
and the virtual impossibility of Meade's superior army catching Lee at
a disadvantage and hurting him. Halleck was exasperated; Lincoln,
proving more realistic, accepted the situation philosophically.

BUT AGAIN the lesson was in the ease with which the fortunes of war swung from one side to the other. At Chickamauga Bragg raised Confederate hopes from the bleak outlook of the previous July, only to suffer disappointment again at the battles of Lookout Mountain and Missionary Ridge. But in Georgia and Tennessee in the West, and in Virginia in the East, the end of 1863 saw a significant stalemate, with opposing armies watching each other warily.

In his message at the opening of the fourth session of the First Congress in December 1863, Jefferson Davis confessed that the South had suffered "grave reverses" over the preceding seven months and that these setbacks had caused considerable discouragement, but he also observed that morale soon stiffened. Despite serious losses in 1863, the Confederacy proved at Chickamauga that the war would not end very soon. Also, in spite of the fortunes of the battlefield, the problems of the blockade, relatively inferior economic development, and some decline in morale, the Confederacy remained strong enough to prevent significant deterioration of its military position. Indeed, southern armies won other victories that year, although less dramatic. Confederates repulsed the Federals in Texas, Louisiana, and at Charleston, as well, and otherwise held them at bay in the major theaters of war. With some justice, Davis asserted that "the Army is believed to be in all respects in better condition than at any previous period of the war." Indeed, the Confederacy had retained the capability not only to preserve its own existence but in doing so to threaten its adversary's determination to continue the struggle.[4]

As to the Union victories in 1863, on the other hand, the psychological impact of the loss of such a strategic geographical feature as the great river compounded by the loss of Pemberton's army and Union victory at Gettysburg could, to invoke Clausewitz, "make the enemy collapse with exhaustion or, like a wounded bull arouse his rage." The formidable concentration for an offensive at Chickamauga clearly indicated that the Confederacy was not ready to collapse with exhaustion or depleted morale. Indeed, the Confederate chief of ordnance, General Josiah Gorgas, noted in his diary that Bragg's defeat was not disastrous and that "the chief loss is after all in the self-confidence of the Army." Thus the Union's achievements of 1863 only amounted to limited successes.[5]

In two and a half years of warfare Confederates had followed closely Clausewitz's prescription for the defensive, except for Pemberton with his egregious blunder of losing his army at Vicksburg. Each Confederate general had sought "to keep his territory inviolate, and to hold it for as long as possible." In Tennessee the Union had driven back the Confederate armies, conferring on them the benefit of the strategy of withdrawal into the interior, and the Confederates had taken advantage of this situation by striking at "the enemy's lines of communications" and carrying out "raids and diversions" in Bragg's Kentucky campaign. And Lee's position after the Battle of Antietam fulfilled a similar mission for "he did not hope to hold it, still less to make it a base for a further advance, but as a sort of outwork."[6]

Confederate attacks on the enemy "main force" where conditions seemed "favorable" had less success because neither of the offensive battles of 1863 had military results proportional to their cost in casualties. Clausewitz counseled that "where the weaker side is forced to fight against odds, its lack of numbers must be made up by the inner tension and vigor that are inspired by danger. . . . If an increase in vigor is combined with a wise limitation in objectives, the result is that combination of brilliant strokes and cautious restraint that we admire so much in the campaigns of Frederick the Great." Frederick had not confined himself to the defensive, but "he always regarded offensives solely as a better means of defense." After seven years of war, Austria made peace, convinced "that their forces could not on their own outweigh the genius of the king." Confederate strategy displayed many characteristics in common with Frederick's, and their offensives were neither more frequent nor more costly.[7]

The heavy Confederate casualties at Gettysburg, Chickamauga, and Vicksburg meant that the Union had gained much through attrition in 1863. For the 1864 campaign, the Confederacy tried to make good most of these losses by conscripting seventeen-year-old boys and men aged forty-six to fifty. The older men would tend to lack the physical attributes for extended soldiering and were therefore to be used, with the seventeen-year-olds, for local defense. The army also gained recruits by curtailing exemptions, but it is doubtful whether this added many men. The effect of taking the boys and the older men, even temporarily, could be disastrous for a local community and no doubt contributed to a resentment of Confederate authority and the decline in civilian morale.

UNION STRATEGY became more sophisticated when Lincoln added a political dimension that Clausewitz and Jomini would have approved. On December 8, 1863, the president announced a plan for reconstruction of the Union that made it easy for separate states to establish governments that Lincoln would recognize and receive back into the Union. Except for abolition of slavery, Lincoln's plan did not penalize the seceding states, although it did punish certain classes of rebels, excluding them from the privilege of taking an oath of loyalty. Further, the provision that loyal state governments could be reestablished when 10 percent of the qualified voters in the state voluntarily took the prescribed oath suggests Lincoln's lenience and political sagacity.[8]

The terms seemed easy enough, yet some northerners opposed them on that very ground. Confederates displayed mixed reactions. Although they were virtually unanimous in rejecting Lincoln's amnesty, the reasons for that rejection varied. Some simply were amazed at Lincoln's presumption of eventual victory, warned that "Lincoln has counted his chickens," and questioned the chance of a "successful hatching" in the face of the three hundred thousand men the Confederacy had under arms. Others thought it would tend to increase the Confederate war effort by stimulating determination to avoid defeat. The will to win would be increased, and the South would add one hundred thousand men to the army as a result. A clerk in the War Department, John Beauchamp Jones, thought it an "electioneering document," and Robert G. H. Kean, head of the Bureau of War, called Lincoln's proclamation "an able and crafty paper" and thought the 10 percent provision was designed to promote class antagonism by "divid-[ing] the lower orders from those in positions of power." Some southerners thought it incredible. "We have only to confess that we are felons needing to be pardoned," protested one editor, "that we are cowards . . . that we are fools . . . to kiss the hand dripping with the blood of our kinsmen." Others held it up to ridicule. William Porcher Miles, a South Carolina congressman, thought it best "to treat Mr. Lincoln and his amnesty manifesto with silent and unmitigated contempt. The whole thing was too weak, so puerile, that it would only meet with the derision of the civilized world." Congressman Henry S. Foote of Tennessee labeled it "truly characteristic" of the "imbecile and unprincipled usurper, who now sits enthroned on the ruins of constitutional liberty."[9]

Lincoln had hoped that his measures would help build Unionist strength in such partially reconquered states as Louisiana and Tennessee. If they succeeded, they would have contributed toward diminishing civilian resistance and guerrilla warfare in occupied areas. Jomini, having served with the French in their struggle against the Spanish national resistance to Napoleon, reached the same conclusions and explicitly prescribed political measures for combating guerrilla warfare. He recommended that the invader "calm the popular passions in every possible way, exhaust them by time and patience, display courtesy, gentleness, and severity united, and, particularly, deal justly." Lincoln's liberal plan of reconstruction certainly met Jomini's prescription fully, and Clausewitz's, too, in his only political suggestion, "treating the population well."[10]

But many Confederates saw Lincoln's amnesty proposal not as a way for uncertain Confederates to get out of a difficult situation as gracefully and as easily as possible, which it clearly was, but as an attempt by Lincoln to impose a despotism. Southerners had resisted change, and rather than allow the attractive features of the rejected alternatives—peace instead of war, Union in place of secession—to dictate their course, they supported their resolve to secede, and, inadvertently, to fight, by interpreting the new information contained in Lincoln's declaration in such a way as to support their original choice or at least to make a change of selection impossible. Thus southerners interpreted Lincoln's 10 percent plan, which might have created severe postdecision dissonance, in such a way as to prove the undesirability of reunion with a government that circumvented the principle of majority rule. From the northern point of view, as few as 10 percent of the voting population of the rebel states would be able to rescue the South and return it to the Union without further penalty save the abandonment of slavery; from the southern point of view, however, that same small 10 percent could dictate the course that the other 90 percent would have to take. Seizing upon this latter as truly indicative of Lincoln's intentions, and viewing it from the standpoint of the republican tradition of majority rule, they refused it.

The provision in Lincoln's reconstruction program that prescribed the abolition of slavery confirmed that the Confederacy would have to fight to retain its original war aim. But many southerners had felt increasingly uncomfortable with the preservation of slavery ever since the Union had made its destruction an objective, one which world opinion approved. Though the interpretation of Lincoln's 10 percent proviso as antidemocratic helped southerners resist the attractiveness of Lincoln's nonpunitive offer of reconstruction, this point of view, which reduced dissonance for some, did little or nothing to strengthen the Confederacy's waning resolve.

Lincoln's political program could aid the Union war effort when and if southerners accepted the terms of the amnesty, but the Union's military solution was not working well. The blockade remained only a serious nuisance and the conquest of the Mississippi had conferred no significant military or logistical benefit. The prospects for the conquest of additional territory were bleak because the Union had exhausted its water communications. It had taken about a year and a half to advance the one hundred airline miles from Nashville to Chattanooga and another half year to consolidate the gain. This did not augur well for additional western advances using rail communication. An advance in the East had even bleaker prospects, for Lincoln and Halleck had not planned any serious effort in Virginia for a year.

BUT UPON General Grant devolved the task of determining the strategy for 1864, and he would try a new approach to break the stalemate. Grant's success at Chattanooga confirmed his reputation, not just as the premier Union general but as one of sufficient standing to receive the rank of lieutenant general, previously held only by the revered George Washington. In the winter of 1864 Congress established the rank, and in March Lincoln appointed Grant to the position. As the senior officer he automatically became general in chief. In actual function Grant became chief of staff to Lincoln, and Halleck became Grant's chief of staff, continuing his duties of operating the very effective army headquarters which he and Stanton had built.

In anticipation of his new assignment, Grant already had envisioned a strategy for the 1864 campaigns, conceived out of his experience of the war as well as his collaboration with the brilliant and imaginative William T. Sherman. Like virtually every other Civil War general,

Grant by the end of 1863 perceived that the destruction of an enemy army in battle was practically impossible. Though he twice had captured entire Confederate armies he remembered the difficulty and how much he owed to the ineptitude of his opponents. Grant also had long been convinced of the almost insuperable obstacles to supplying the Union armies over great distances by railroad. Confederate raiders and guerrillas were too formidable. The strategic consumption caused by the use of troops to guard the railroad eventually would absorb so many men as to stall the advance. The Union armies encountered the same problems in occupying territory. Guerrillas and raiders made it hard to control the country, and occupation required an enormous number of soldiers. The Union already employed a third of its soldiers garrisoning territory and guarding communications.

It seemed as if the Union could not deprive the Confederacy of its armies by destroying them in battle, capturing them as at Vicksburg, or occupying the country on which they depended for support. Grant proposed to solve this quandary by making it unnecessary for the Union armies to rely heavily on railroads and impossible for the Confederate armies to do so. He planned to use water communication where available, but he placed his primary reliance on raids, which required no communications at all.

Grant intended to use armies, not just cavalry, for raids aimed at breaking Confederate railroads. In one sense he copied, then expanded upon, the enemy's strategy; in another he reverted to the strategy of earlier times, when armies attempted to win a favorable peace by invading the enemy's country and living at his expense through contributions and looting. But the industrial revolution had given Grant a new objective, the railroads upon which depended the Confederacy's armies and war economy.

Grant, who had spent the winter of 1864 planning, originally wanted to rely on water communications to initiate two landings on the coast, one on the Gulf of Mexico at Mobile, Alabama, and another in North Carolina. He intended the force at Mobile to march inland up the Alabama River and cooperate with another army, under Sherman, moving southward from Chattanooga toward Atlanta. These two armies would break the Confederacy's remaining east-west rail connections. The proposed army of sixty thousand men landing on the North Carolina coast had the objective of raiding inland to break the north-south railways before approaching Wilmington from the rear and capturing it.

These operations, together with that planned for Virginia, truly would have placed the Union on exterior lines because the South's railway network connected all of Grant's objectives. Since Grant, like Lincoln and Halleck, planned simultaneous advances, there would be concentration "at least in terms of time," which Clausewitz had explained and Lincoln had grasped early in the war. In March of 1864 Grant explained his plans to Sherman. "As soon as the season would permit," Sherman recalled, Grant planned that "all the armies of the Union would assume the 'bold offensive' by 'concentric lines' on the common enemy, and would finish up the job in a single campaign if possible." Jomini, normally a proponent only of interior lines, believed in such a "concentric" attack on exterior lines "in the case of a considerable numerical superiority" and when there was "no danger of being beaten separately by a stronger enemy." But it is unlikely that either Clausewitz or Jomini would have approved of Grant's campaign because he aimed neither at Confederate armies nor at the conquest of Confederate territory. Instead he planned to strike at the enemy's communications.[11]

Heinrich Dietrich von Bülow, the originator of the idea of the base, was one authority who might have approved. Though Clausewitz had relied on Bülow's theory of the base, he dismissed the remainder of his work as dealing "with minor matters only" and believed his opinions "can hardly be counted as practical rules." Except for paying some implicit attention to Bülow's theory of the concentric advance, Jomini, like Clausewitz, also had ignored all of Bülow's ideas except the base. But Bülow had ideas much like some of those which T. Harry Williams attributed to Jomini in that Bülow disparaged battles and his prescriptions aimed at the conquest of territory.[12]

Bülow, who died early in the nineteenth century, published several military works. The principal idea in his most basic, *The Spirit of the Modern System of War*, depended on the hypothesis that armies did not live on the country but received all of their supplies from the rear. Although he understood the falsity of this supposition, he nevertheless built his geometrical and somewhat abstract system of strategy on it. Thus he developed a theory in which the contending armies should have as their only objective the enemy's supply lines. But his fundamental premise and the strategy deduced from it, unrealistic for the Europe of his time, did fit remarkably well the conditions of the American Civil War. "A general," he wrote, "should make his own magazines, and the safety of his lines of convoy, the principal object of his operations, rather than the army of the enemy itself." Thus, "in offensive war, making movements around the enemy, and alarming him for his supplies, is a much surer way to compel him to fall back, than expelling him by main force out of his position; for he would soon find another, where he would be firm again." The Union armies' dependence on railways for a farther advance in the West thus fit Bülow's hypothesis well.[13]

Bülow also grounded this recommendation on his realization of "how indecisive these general engagements are in the modern system of war." He had noted that "a defeat is of much less consequence in the modern system of war, than it was among the ancients." He observed that "modern battles never weakened an army to such a degree, but that it may be ready for a fresh attack a few days later." His skepticism about the significance of battles certainly fit the conditions of the Civil War and conformed to Grant's confidence that he could safely risk operating on exterior lines.[14]

If Grant, in fact, had been applying Bülow's ideas, as, of course, he was not, he would have seen that their logical extension in the railway age would be not only to strike at the communications of a particular army but to expand Bülow's principle to aim at the railway network that bound the South together. In relying on raiding armies operating on exterior lines, Grant would have found comfort in another of Bülow's conclusions: "It is always possible to avoid battle, by not suffering the enemy to approach too near." Bülow believed so strongly in the possibility and necessity of avoiding battle and had such faith in the superior efficacy of an attack on the enemy's communications that he laid "it down as a principle, that when an army is obliged to fight a battle, it has certainly committed some previous fault against the present rules of war."[15]

This idea so infuriated Clausewitz, who stressed the importance of battles, that he ridiculed Bülow as a soldier who regarded "battle as a kind of evil brought about by mistake—a moribund manifestation to which an orthodox, correctly managed war should never have to resort." In justice to Bülow, it must be noted that Jomini and, particularly, Clausewitz had perceived the difficulty of pursuit and the improbability of a battle that destroyed the enemy army, which the Civil War's experience confirmed. Bülow, on the other hand, stated the general case of battles that produced killed and wounded and a short retreat. He simply ignored the possibility of a battle with an effective pursuit.[16]

In developing his interpretation of Civil War generalship, T. Harry Williams overlooked the correspondence of Grant's strategy of raids against enemy communications with those of the pedantic German theorist Bülow. When, following Grant's directions, Sherman carried out two great raids over hundreds of miles in hostile territory with only one offensive battle, a small one at Kennesaw Mountain, he approached in spirit Bülow's ideal of winning without fighting. Williams erroneously attributed this concept not to Bülow but to Jomini. But Jomini, who had introduced the term "logistics," had too realistic an understanding of how armies lived on the country to have adopted Bülow's necessary assumption of dependence on supply lines; the railway age had made this supposition relevant, and Grant had devised his own version of Bülow's premature insight.

As the unconscious executor of Bülow's ideas, Grant aimed primarily at the two railroads that passed through Georgia, linking Alabama and Mississippi with South Carolina, and the two lines that joined South Carolina to Virginia. Raids by armies with infantry and engineers could do a more thorough job of destruction than raids by cavalry, if only because they had more manpower. Living on the enemy's country, the raiding army also would consume food and fodder that otherwise would be available for the Confederate armies. In addition, Grant wished to destroy arms works, foundries, textile mills, and other installations that contributed to the Confederate war effort. These raids would deprive the Confederate armies of their support without the necessity of Union occupation of more Confederate territory.

This strategy had, of course, something in common with that of the Confederates, who consistently used cavalry to raid Union communications. Clausewitz had recommended counterraids, "sending a force of equal strength to raid an equivalent area of the enemy's country," but Grant's plan differed in that he intended in part to use armies for this task and to substitute these raids for further attempts to conquer territory. Of course, the strategy of raids and the strategy of conquest of territory both had the common objective of attacking the enemy's supplies, thus crippling his armies by means of deprivation. Grant made this strategy clear to Sherman in early April, directing him "to get into the interior of the enemy's country as far as you can, inflicting all the damage you can against their war resources." General Franz Sigel in West Virginia and others were to participate in this concentration in time by keeping other Confederate armies busy enough so they could not be shifted to areas of greater need. "In other words," concluded Grant, "if Sigel can't skin himself, he can hold a leg whilst some one else skins." Grant's strategy had a parallel in the strategic bombing in World War II, in which bombers attacked enemy factories and railroads to deprive enemy armies of the essentials to keep fighting. Strategic bombing also included the element of killing and terrorizing civilians, which Grant did not include in his strategy, although in practice it sometimes had that effect.[17]

Grant's strategy was old-fashioned in the sense that it reverted to that of earlier times, when the ratio of force to space did not suffice for belligerents to aim at the territorial conquest of their enemy. Instead, they raided enemy territory, living at enemy expense and carrying off booty. The Battle of Poitiers in the Hundred Years' War, for example, occurred when the French overtook a booty-laden, raiding English army and forced it to fight. Such a strategy of raids had, of course, far more limited political goals than the Union's and was on a minuscule scale compared to Grant's.

GRANT'S 1864 campaign did not equal his ambitious plans because neither of his projected raids from the coast materialized. The force that he intended to attack Mobile, Alabama, and advance up the Alabama River went instead up the Red River in Arkansas, where it suffered defeat and then endured delay so it could extricate the accompanying fleet, which had been trapped by falling water. Lincoln and Halleck vetoed Grant's recommendation for a coastal landing in North Carolina to break the north-south railways, raid the eastern portion of the state, and capture the important port of Wilmington. They objected because they lacked the sixty thousand men the project required and, more important, because it conflicted with their strategy for dealing with Lee's army in Virginia. They could not help but see Grant's proposal as another way to use the coastal base to take Richmond rather than, as Grant intended it, a crippling blow against Confederate supply.

For the 1864 campaign only Sherman's army was left explicitly aiming at the enemy's railroads, and Sherman was to begin his operations with a conventional campaign to capture Atlanta. After that, he intended to carry out a raid against the other east-west railroad by marching to connect with the navy either on the Gulf or the Atlantic at Savannah. Sherman's task would be more difficult because no Union army from Mobile would menace, with a concentric advance, the rear of the Confederate army opposing Sherman in north Georgia.

Grant left the operation of the Washington headquarters to Halleck, his chief of staff, and decided to accompany Meade's army. This arrangement enabled Grant to devote virtually his full energies to the campaign against Lee, not only because of Halleck and an excellent general staff but because Grant's plan for Sherman would "determine the object of the campaign, the nature of operations," as Jomini would have put it. And Grant carefully avoided "the presumption to indicate the manner" in which Sherman "should maneuver to attain this object." As general in chief, Halleck had practiced a similar style of command, and Grant found it very congenial. With Sherman in command between the Appalachians and the Mississippi and Halleck providing coordination of supply and reinforcements and coping with the difficult situation west of the Mississippi, Grant felt free to pay full attention to Virginia.[18]

He had a dual task in the campaign against Lee. Strategically the Union still was making its main effort in the West, which had implied accepting stalemate in Virginia and not besieging Richmond. But the transfer of Longstreet from Virginia and the South's subsequent victory in the Battle of Chickamauga had been a traumatic experience for the Union. The strategy of raids from concentric lines, involving concentration in time rather than in space, required careful coordination. The Union army in Virginia must occupy Lee so closely and continuously that he could not spare any reinforcements for the West to help Bragg's successor, Joseph E. Johnston, oppose Sherman. In late April Grant explained to Lincoln that, although he must commit many troops to protect Union-held territory, they could do so "just as well by advancing as by remaining still" and that by advancing they could also prevent the enemy from detaching troops from that front for use elsewhere. "Oh! yes, I can see that," replied Lincoln, using the same analogy Grant himself had written to Sherman earlier that month. "As we say out West, if a man can't skin he must hold a leg while somebody else does."[19]

Grant also had a political task in the campaign in Virginia, one which fortunately conformed to this strategic objective. The northern public counted on the new lieutenant general to take on Lee, the South's best general, who had threatened Washington and twice raided north of the Potomac. The public, Lincoln's critics, and many soldiers both expected and demanded such action. Northerners had come a long way since 1861, when they thought only of capturing cities, and the simplistic slogan "On to Richmond" accurately represented the depth of their military thinking. At last realizing that they could not brush aside rebel armies as many citizens had expected McDowell to do at Manassas in 1861, they focused their concern upon decisive battles, which like Waterloo they saw as the means to victory. Now many believed that cities could come or go; the essential factor in making war was the enemy army. Thus one soldier wrote that "the capture of Richmond has been harped on too long. It is an old fogey idea. We are after Lee's army—nothing more, nothing less. The life of the Confederacy is in its moving columns and it is our task to beat it out. It matters little whether its death rattle issues from Richmond." Such people had not yet thought as far as Grant had, however, and did not yet understand that if the armies themselves were virtually indestructible those armies still relied on communications and supply. If these could be denied, the army, to say nothing of the cities it protected, would be vulnerable. But most people still conceived of the coming campaign as a contest of champions fighting battles in which the loser retreated, "the only authentic proof of victory," Clausewitz believed, which "impresses the people."[20]

To occupy Lee and give the public its yearned-for victories, Grant planned concentric movements, which, adventitiously, followed Jomini's prescription. Lines of operations, wrote Jomini, "should be *interior* if the forces be equal, or *exterior* in the case of great numerical superiority." This Grant had, for the army opposing Lee outnumbered him about 118,000 to 64,000. While Lee faced Meade's army west of

Fredericksburg, the more than thirty thousand men under Benjamin F. Butler would ascend the James River, where they would land almost in Richmond's rear. This army easily could overwhelm the small Confederate contingent near the Confederate capital, cut its rail communications to the south, and, if not take the city, at least beleaguer it by occupying the south side of the James. To save Richmond Lee would have to rush reinforcements from his army, enabling Meade, against his much-weakened opponent, to push rapidly south, cutting the railroads north of the city and either forcing its evacuation or beginning a siege that would sever almost all of Richmond's communications.[21]

BEGINNING ALMOST simultaneously with Sherman in north Georgia, in May 1864, Grant and General Benjamin F. Butler moved forward, while small Union forces also advanced in western Virginia. Grant's basic strategy provided that Meade would turn Lee by marching around his eastern flank. Lee sought to prevent this move, and the armies met in a densely forested region called the Wilderness. The terrain nullified numerical superiority, and Grant's progress was arrested in bloody engagements on May 5–7, 1864. He promptly moved east and south in another effort to get around Lee. But the Confederates headed him off at Spotsylvania, and during the next two weeks the armies dug in opposite each other. By this time Grant learned that General Butler had failed, even though he had surprised the enemy and landed his army easily.[22]

Confederate officials, however, also had plans for the James River, aiming to regain the lower Peninsula and Norfolk, but they had waited until their naval force on the James was powerful enough to challenge Union control. By March 1864 they had three ironclads ready and cut a passage through the Drewry's Bluff barrier. But before they could launch the combined operation, Butler's troops, supported by gunboats, ascended the river to take up positions at Bermuda Hundred, several miles above City Point. Soon some thirty-two thousand men, the Army of the James, supported by four monitors, an ironclad, and a large number of wooden gunboats, had concentrated on this section of the river. Butler then vacillated while Confederate troops arrived from North Carolina under the command of the experienced and energetic General Beauregard. Having stopped Butler's fainthearted offensives, Beauregard counterattacked at Drewry's Bluff, May 16, 1864, and drove Butler into a bend in the James River, bottling him up with entrenchments.

Butler had directed his advance up the James, one part of Grant's strategy for 1864, toward Petersburg. The plan failed because Grant entrusted the command to Butler, a Massachusetts politician with little experience in field command. Grant misjudged Butler because the political general showed he knew *"how to arrange a good plan of campaign"* but proved, during the campaign, that he lacked Jomini's other requisite for a general, knowledge of "how to carry it to a successful termination." Although Butler did not achieve his objective, his army nevertheless joined supporting naval units of the North Atlantic Blockading Squadron to prevent Confederate reoccupation of the Peninsula. In June, when General Grant shifted his army from north of Richmond to south of the James, these units successfully blocked Confederate naval efforts to interfere with his movement.[23]

Control of the James River by the Union navy constituted a major factor in the inability of the Confederates to retake the lower Peninsula and the port of Norfolk. It also provided an artery of supply, which ultimately contributed to the fall of Richmond.

His plan for a rapid advance on Richmond at once stymied by Butler's ineptitude yet made possible by the presence of the North Atlantic Blockading Squadron, Grant resolved on a frontal attack to push Lee directly backward toward Richmond, to placate the public, and possibly to gain a significant victory in battle. He began a series of assaults against the Confederates at Spotsylvania on May 10. But against entrenched, well-led, rifle-armed veterans, Grant's skill and numerical superiority were of no avail. Repeated strikes in mid-May failed at Spotsylvania.[24]

After ten days' bafflement around Spotsylvania, Grant again turned Lee, this time with more success. Once more passing the Confederate army's eastern flank, he moved halfway to Richmond before the skillful Lee reached his front, dug in along the North Anna River, and brought his advance to a halt on May 23. Avoiding another attack, in late May Grant again exploited his two-sided base, turned Lee on the east, and reached a position at Cold Harbor, east of Richmond, where he could draw his supplies from some of the same sources McClellan had used in 1862. Before this time, Grant's supply arrangements had been almost equally simple because he could avail himself of his base on the Rappahannock River, connected with his army by wagon transport. "The vicinity of the sea," Jomini would have pointed out, "is invaluable for the transportation of supplies; and the party which is master on this element can supply himself at will."[25]

Failing even in his goal to appease the public with dramatic victories, Grant nevertheless was succeeding in his strategic mission to engage fully the attention of all Confederate forces in Virginia and North Carolina. But his operations, which resulted in heavy casualties, not only failed to give the public any clear-cut victory but also presented him with no alternative but to besiege Richmond. Grant proposed to do this from south of the James River, where he hoped to cut most of the Confederate capital's direct rail communications with the states to the south. Before he made this final turning movement to reach the city of Petersburg, south of Richmond, he made one last frontal attack at Cold Harbor in search of elusive victory. This ill-advised effort on June 3 found the Confederates well entrenched, and the Union forces lost almost seven thousand men in less than an hour. Confederate losses amounted to less than fifteen hundred. The total casualties in the campaign were proportional to the forces engaged, each side diminished by about 50 percent of its initial strength. Union morale probably suffered more than Confederate morale because Union soldiers acutely felt the futility of assaulting entrenched positions. The heavy casualties not only disenchanted the northern public with battles but also hurt President Lincoln's reputation with both the people and his own party. Victory seemed as far away as ever. To many, Grant appeared to have done no more than hopelessly reach McClellan's 1862 position. War weariness had become critical for both the North and South. Morale on both sides would depend a great deal on whether the Union could achieve a victory the public could appreciate.

In the last act of this campaign, Grant skillfully conducted a surprise turning movement against Petersburg, but a determined defense by General Beauregard from June 15 through June 18, 1864, prevented him from capturing the city. Beauregard fended off inept Union attacks until Lee sent reinforcements. Both sides then dug in and a trench-warfare stalemate continued for the next nine months. The rickety Confederate supply organization managed to feed both Lee's army and the Richmond population during this siege, despite Union raids on the railroads. Because the Confederates now had the advantage of a fully entrenched defense, Grant concluded that Lee possessed twenty-five thousand more men than he needed to protect Richmond and Petersburg and therefore prudently telegraphed Sherman to beware of reinforcements coming from Virginia.

Grant correctly appreciated that Lee could spare a substantial force but erred as to where Lee would employ it. Initially diverting troops to Lynchburg to repel a Union raid, Lee again exploited his Shenandoah Valley base by sending north an entire corps under the eccentric but talented General Jubal A. Early. In the first part of July Early crossed the Potomac into Maryland, where his raid caused a great commotion, especially when he paused near Washington before falling back to the Valley. Grant diverted two corps to strengthen Washington, but they could not prevent Early later in July from again raiding across the Potomac and reaching Pennsylvania.

Grant then placed the capable and energetic Philip H. Sheridan in command of nearly fifty thousand men assembled at the north end of the Shenandoah Valley to resist Early's scant twenty thousand. In September and October 1864 Sheridan seized the offensive and, winning three battles, which helped to depress already depleted Confederate morale, drove Early far southward. Both sides then diminished their forces in that theater. This campaign had little effect on the operations in the Richmond-Petersburg area, where Grant attacked sporadically, usually in abortive efforts to cut Confederate communications. Sheridan's campaign did, however, have a political effect in the North. It ensured the protection of Washington, and it assisted the Republican party in the fall elections. Grant confessed in his *Memoirs* that he was "much relieved" after Sheridan's victory, for "the administration was a little afraid to have a decisive battle fought at that time, for fear it might go against us and have a bad effect on the November elections." Far more than most generals on either side, Grant always understood the political nature of the war. Union morale had suffered a shock when General Early had raided to the outskirts of Washington in July 1864, but such threats would no longer be possible.

"This decisive victory," wrote Grant, "was the most effective campaign argument made in the canvass."[26]

SHERMAN'S 1864 operations against Johnston paralleled Grant's against Lee but with several important differences. First, Sherman did not have to win battles, for the public had no such expectation of him. Second, he had to move more slowly than Grant because he lacked water communications, possessed only one base, and had to rebuild and fortify the railroad as he advanced. Third, just as Grant feared that Lee might detach troops to reinforce Johnston, Sherman felt a similar but less acute apprehension that Johnston might send men to strengthen Lee. And, unlike Grant in the early stages of his campaign, Sherman had no hope of a distraction in Johnston's rear; that had been the goal of the aborted Mobile landing.

Sherman's operation, like Grant's, well could have been based on Bülow's observation that "there is no position, however well it may be protected against an attack in front, however well chosen it may appear to cover the country you have to guard, from which you may not be very quickly expelled by the maneuvers of the enemy on your flanks, particularly if he be superior in forces." Sherman began his campaign with a superiority of almost one hundred thousand to Johnston's fifty thousand, an ample number to maneuver the Confederate army back to Atlanta just as Grant had turned Lee back to Richmond.[27]

The careful and thorough Sherman began his campaign on May 7 with a very wide turning movement by McPherson's army, about one-fourth of Sherman's consolidated force. That excellent plan, conducted by a competent general, came close to reaching Johnston's communications, but the Confederate general withdrew quickly enough to cover them, though forced to abandon Dalton, Resaca, and other points in the process. The timely arrival on May 13 of a reinforcement of thirteen thousand men from the Mississippi, the bulk of the infantry of the Department of Mississippi and East Louisiana, aided Johnston. Had Grant's proposed Mobile landing taken place and the projected twenty-five thousand men then been advancing north from Mobile, these forces from Mississippi undoubtedly would have been engaged in opposing that offensive. Instead, the Confederates were free to concentrate troops from the Mississippi line of operations on the north Georgia line of operations. Even so, with one hundred thousand men, Sherman still possessed ample numerical preponderance to continue his campaign of turning movements to force Johnston back.

Successively, Sherman faced and turned elaborately entrenched Confederate positions at Allatoona Pass, Marietta, and the Chattahoochee River, against which he deployed his own men in entrenchments similar to those of Johnston; both the astute Sherman and the wary Johnston probed for weakness without finding any. The weather alternated between hot and rainy as Sherman rebuilt his railroad and in a period of less than two months carried out the five major turning movements that forced Johnston back toward Atlanta. In all of these operations only one battle occurred, a small one at Kennesaw Mountain on June 27. Here Sherman attacked Confederate entrenchments, in part to show Johnston that he could not rule out an attack and so must man his lines well. Sherman lost only three thousand men and Johnston barely eight hundred, the difference illustrating the power of the entrenched defense.

Johnston, undermined by his own corps commanders and by his usual secretiveness about his plans, failed to allay genuine fear in Richmond that he would continue to retreat indefinitely. Like Grant, who had to win victories because the public expected and needed them, Johnston also needed victories. The administration in Richmond was hostage to the notion that successful battles allowed one's own troops to advance and forced enemy troops to retreat. Confederate armies still had much strength, however, and Johnston was touted as one of the best generals in the Confederacy, second only to Lee. At the beginning of May the Confederacy had enjoyed no major victories since Bragg's at Chickamauga in September 1863. Thus public expectations were almost as high and demanding of Johnston as they were of Grant, and both commanders were confidently expected to satisfy the needs of their country for a morale-boosting victory. These victories were to have not only the spiritual result of raising each public's morale but also the political effect of influencing the forthcoming Federal elections of 1864. In the case of Union victories the connection would be obvious, helping to persuade the voters that the end would not be far off if only they continued to support the war effort.

The effect of a Confederate victory on the Union elections would have been a little more subtle. Larry E. Nelson has pointed out that Davis sought to demonstrate to the Confederate public that the 1864 political campaign would exacerbate the internal problems of the Union. Protests against emancipation, the draft riots, and separatist tendencies in the old Northwest "might result in election of a [presidential] candidate amenable to Confederate independence," although Jefferson Davis tried to prevent southern expectations from becoming unrealistic. Northern war weariness also was applying pressures for peace on Abraham Lincoln, many Confederates thought, and the best way to increase this pressure was to win military victories. All these forces increased pressure on Johnston, just as political necessity had done to Grant. Southern hopes of influencing the election of 1864 rested on Johnston's ability to stop Sherman, but a Confederate force that always retreated could not halt that Union general. "Undoubtedly," says Nelson, "the Federal election was among the welter of considerations that led to the removal of Johnston and the appointment of Hood to command the army." Davis had urged his people that "only significant Southern military success could influence Northern sentiment," but in the end the effort was beyond Confederate abilities and Davis was criticized by some Confederates for relying on military success to apply political pressure, instead of using political means to do so. The outcome of the affair, of course, was more beneficial to the Union than to the Confederacy.[28]

This is one of the few times, perhaps the only time, that Davis consciously aimed his military plans to satisfy the requirements of civilian opinion. It offers an intriguing suggestion of what he might have done on other occasions and opens the unanswerable question of what effect such efforts might have had if they had been adopted at a time of more hopeful Confederate fortunes.

Because Johnston seemed always to retreat, which did not bode well for victory, many influential southerners urged his replacement. When Johnston refused to give Davis full information of his plans, even to indicate when and where he might attack Sherman, Davis felt that step was necessary. On July 17, 1864, Davis gave the command to John B. Hood, who promptly attacked Sherman on July 20, 22, and 28 in the costly battles of Peachtree Creek, Atlanta, and Ezra Church. On each occasion Sherman's well-entrenched veterans repulsed the assault. Sherman's casualties, about six thousand men, numbered much less than half of Hood's, whose much smaller army of fifty-one thousand could ill afford such losses.

Hood, a tall, lean Texan, had graduated near the bottom of his class at West Point; his courage and boldness were unquestioned, however. He had a meteoric Civil War career, rising from captain in 1861 to general in command of one of the two most powerful Confederate armies. He paid tragically for his courage, losing an arm and leg in combat. By 1864 he was physically and emotionally drained, and as Thomas L. Connelly cogently concluded, "simply did not have the character that was required" to command an army.[29]

Clausewitz admired boldness. "In a commander a bold act may prove to be a blunder. Nevertheless it is a laudable error." But he described another kind of boldness as well, one "governed by superior intellect [that] is the mark of a hero. This kind of boldness does not consist in defying the natural order of things and in crudely offending the laws of probability." Hood's attacks did offend the laws of probability by challenging the established supremacy of the entrenched defense and thus began wearing away the strength and morale of his own Army of Tennessee; he had defied "the natural order of things" with bold moves that were not, under the circumstances, signs of a "superior intellect." He would not have won Clausewitz's approval.[30]

After a month of preparation outside of Atlanta, Sherman moved his army south of the city and severed its communications, forcing Hood to evacuate. Sherman occupied Atlanta on September 2, 1864, blocking one of the key east-west rail lines. He gave his men a rest, but Hood, watching from a few miles away, devised a new and more sophisticated offensive. After he and President Davis had conferred, Hood embarked on a campaign that amply illustrated the applicability of Bülow's theories to the railway age.

Bülow believed that "the best manner of covering a country lying behind . . . is to fall upon the flanks of the enemy advancing, and by this bold movement to change defense into an attack. At all events the most absurd conduct would be to wait for him in a defensive position." Lee had followed this specific philosophy after the Battle of Chancellorsville in conceiving his Gettysburg campaign. The same idea also underlay his Second Manassas and Antietam campaigns and Bragg's campaign into Kentucky. But Bülow was more emphatic: "I boldly draw the rule," he wrote, "which is entirely new, never wage a defensive war, properly so called, but to change it speedily into offensive, by the simple act of falling upon the flanks of the enemy, and attacking his rear."[31]

Less than a month after the fall of Atlanta Hood did precisely this. He marched west and north of the city, menacing Union communications and drawing Sherman and the bulk of his army north, back toward Chattanooga. Hood could remain in this area indefinitely because he had a line of communications from Rome, Georgia, southwestward into Alabama, a flank position that Johnston had ignored in his retreat. But when Hood advanced, this line of communications furnished him with a base similar to Lee's in the Shenandoah Valley. Moreover, Sherman lacked any base comparable to that provided by the Chesapeake Bay and the Virginia rivers. He was now compelled to face Hood with his line of communications parallel to his front, a situation which Bülow, Jomini, and Clausewitz all would have agreed presented a serious danger.[32]

Perhaps more significant than Hood's good base was his wise decision to avoid Sherman's army and confine his activities to menacing Sherman's communications. This strategy, too, accorded with Bülow, who had written not only that "a battle may always be avoided" but that "the best thing an army can do, and particularly when it is weaker than the opposed forces, is to attack the flanks of the enemy, unless it means fighting altogether, and to confine itself to maneuvering against his supplies."[33]

According to Clausewitz, the truth of Bülow's generalization depended primarily on the ratio of force to space and also on whether the defender had withdrawn into the heart of his country. Drawing on his experience of the French campaign in Russia in 1812, Clausewitz commented that "in a country as immense as Russia, two armies could play a regular game of tag with one another." Although the region in which Sherman and Hood played tag was much smaller than Russia, their armies were puny in size compared with the huge forces used by Napoleon and the Russians in 1812. Hood had ample space in which to keep out of Sherman's way, to keep in touch with his sources of supply, and yet to threaten Sherman's communications. Clausewitz could also have noted a similar disproportion between the size of armies and the space in which they operated in the South in the last years of the American Revolution, where they could have observed a comparable game of tag being played by Nathaniel Greene, Daniel Morgan, Lord Cornwallis, and Lord Rawdon.[34]

Thus in October 1864 the contending forces found themselves locked in an entrenched stalemate in Virginia and in another deadlock based upon marches and countermarches in north Georgia. West of the Mississippi the situation differed little, the Union having just repulsed a raid by General Sterling Price that went east to the outskirts of St. Louis, Missouri, and as far west as the Kansas border before Union troops defeated him and forced him back to Arkansas. In more than three years of war the Union had divided the Confederacy along the Mississippi River, captured key cities, and operated in every one of the Confederate states, while the Confederacy had captured no Union cities, except temporarily in Kentucky, and had operated only in the border states of the Union, leaving the others totally untouched. And yet the Union had conquered completely only one Confederate state, Tennessee, and had taken two and a half years to do that. It was not until September 1864, forty months after the firing on Fort Sumter, that Union troops had occupied Atlanta, located in the heart of the Confederacy. This military stalemate carried a potentially significant impact on political affairs. Well might Confederates expect that the snail's pace of Union conquest would so discourage northerners that they might be willing to turn to a peace candidate in the 1864 elections.

But Confederates did not look upon these signs of defensive strength and gird their loins to continue the battle indefinitely. The political significance of this attitude was clear. Before the fall of Atlanta, it appeared to the weary Union that the war was likely to drag on for several more years, unless by some stroke of good fortune the Confederacy simply collapsed, which did not seem likely. The fall of Atlanta changed the entire complexion of events, for Sherman had provided a needed victory—expected more from Grant than from him—that indicated the beginning of substantial progress. As a result, in 1864 the Union voters reelected the administration.

On the Confederate side the fall of Atlanta produced exactly the opposite effect. Desertion rates, already serious, now multiplied as the needs of destitute families at home were reinforced by a soldier's presumption of the inevitable outcome of the war to persuade him that there was no more point in risking his life for a lost cause. It was no longer possible to augment military power by the strength of national will, nor was it possible to stiffen civilian determination by exciting victories on the field. The basic purposes of government are to protect lives and property, but as casualty lists lengthened, the letters from home grew more urgent, and the Union armies seemed more aggressive, it became clear that Confederate armies were doing neither. Why, then, a Confederacy? Thousands of soldiers and civilians asked themselves that question and concluded that "their interests could best be protected by rejoining the Union": accordingly, they waged war with less enthusiasm than heretofore. After Atlanta, the bottom was about to drop out of the Confederate tub.[35]

And yet the Confederate armies could still pack a stunning punch, if properly directed, even if they could not, by themselves, bring the war to a victorious close. But Confederate victory had never depended on military successes; a national resistance in a vast, thinly settled country would have sufficed. Such a war, however, the South was no longer prepared to wage.

CLAUSEWITZ'S ANALYSIS of military operations had described such an outcome, and he would have said it resulted from the Union lacking sufficient force for a decisive campaign against the powerful Confederate armies, especially in such a vast country as the South. And Clausewitz would have been correct for the right reasons because both parties had followed his prescriptions, albeit unconsciously. Realizing the futility of seeking decisive battles, Union generals on the offensive had sought to occupy Confederate territory. On the defensive, the Confederates had sought to protect their territory and, in so doing, had used all of Clausewitz's methods. For the most part they had relied on natural obstacles and entrenchments to cover their territory and had effectively interposed their "forces quickly by means of flank marches." In fact, by using the railroad and telegraph to integrate all fronts and constantly to concentrate and reconcentrate their forces, the Confederates provided textbook examples of the application of the products of the industrial revolution to strategic maneuver.[36]

Confederates had been equally telling in employing the active means of defense by "raids and diversions into the enemy's territory," by attacks on his lines of communication, and preeminently by use of the strategic turning movement as a means of defense. The Confederates had also remained consistently "on the alert *for a chance to strike a favorable blow.*" They had frequently created their opportunities by concentration and had often attained a measure of strategic surprise. Tactically these blows left much to be desired, and too often the battles involved essentially frontal attacks; but the Union army also suffered from the same difficulty in translating into practice the tactical turning movement favored by Clausewitz and understood by many Civil War generals. The southern defensive effort received powerful assistance from the national character of the war and the guerrilla warfare that it engendered. Confederates made the most of this situation by their strategy of cavalry raids against Union communications, which harmonized adequately with the activities of the guerrillas. And so the war continued in the stalemate that Clausewitz would have anticipated.[37]

Although both Clausewitz and Jomini owed a debt to Bülow, they would doubtless have been surprised how the railroad had made Bülow's principles applicable to campaigning in the stringent logistical environment of the American South. Grant had no specific plans for coping with Hood's strategic turning movement and sudden reliance on a strategy akin to that advocated by Bülow. But, adventitiously, Grant's strategy of raids became the perfect antidote; now he was ready for Sherman to begin his raid to the coast.

In this operation, Sherman no longer would have any communications to protect or for Hood to threaten. In the middle of November 1864 Sherman therefore abandoned Atlanta and his northward line of communications and led an army of more than sixty thousand men on the long-projected raid to the coast. He marched to Savannah, Georgia, but he created such ambiguity about his route that he had no difficulty avoiding the meager forces available to oppose him. His army moved rapidly, easily living on the country. It destroyed in its path anything of value to the Confederate war effort but concentrated on the major east-west railroads, accompanied by an engineer regiment specially equipped to destroy them.

Southerners had looked anxiously to the Union presidential election, hoping for Lincoln's defeat as a sign of the failure of the enemy's determination to triumph over the Confederacy. But hardly had the northern electorate disappointed them by reelecting Lincoln when Sherman commenced his campaign, and it further eroded the South's will to continue the struggle. Thus Sherman's Georgia raid was a political as well as a military maneuver, and it was aimed as much at Confederate morale and will as at her railroads and granaries. Before he began his raid, Sherman noted that if he held his communications, he would "lose a thousand men monthly," without any appreciable result. He resolved therefore to begin implementing Grant's raiding strategy and "make the march and make Georgia howl." The object was not only to destroy resources needed for the Confederate military effort but also to " illustrate the vulnerability of the south. They don't know what war means; but when the rich planters of the Oconee and Savannah see their fences, and corn, and hogs, and sheep vanish before their eyes, they will have something more than a mean opinion of the 'Yanks.'" This was a deeper thrust into the heartland of her territory than the Confederacy had yet experienced, and it would mark a complete change from only two months before, when the Confederate interior had seemed virtually invulnerable to large-scale Union operations. It would also have a corresponding effect upon the people's will.[38]

SHERMAN'S MARCH presented the Confederates with a serious dilemma. Hood had his main Confederate force in northern Alabama, far in Sherman's rear, and would have little chance to overtake him. Instead of opposing Sherman, Hood decided to march into Middle Tennessee while Sherman moved toward the coast. This odd spectacle of two armies marching away from each other into the other's territory had occurred during the American Revolution and had more than once characterized operations during earlier times. In similar operations in previous wars the military forces also had lacked sufficient strength to dominate the relatively large area in which they operated.

But as Hood headed north toward Nashville, he planned not a raid but a reconquest of Middle Tennessee. Clausewitz would have expressed skepticism of such a strategy, asking whether a permanent or temporary occupation would "really be worth the cost of the operation. . . . An offensive of this type is not always appropriate to make up losses elsewhere" because "in general one tends to lose more from occupation by the enemy than one gains from conquering his territory, even if the value of both areas should be identical." But the regions did not have equal value because Middle Tennessee could not possibly contribute as much to sustain Confederate armies as the railways in Georgia, severed by Sherman, had provided throughout the war.[39]

Not only in strategy but in other ways Hood's and Sherman's campaigns differed significantly. As a raider, Sherman had the goal and the opportunity to avoid the enemy's army. But Hood, aiming to conquer territory, had to engage Union forces in his path. The advantage of the defense belonged to the Union, which Sherman counted on when he left in Tennessee a large but motley contingent under command of the careful George H. Thomas. And Hood seemed determined to help the Union make the most of its advantage. After first turning back the Federal army opposing him almost to Nashville, on November 30, 1864, he made a costly frontal attack against his entrenched opponent at Franklin, Tennessee. Hood had an army roughly the same size as that of his opponents, but the power of the defense proved decisive as Hood lost 15 percent of his force, including six generals killed or mortally wounded. His capable adversary, the seasoned John M. Schofield, withdrew even though he had resisted Hood's attacks successfully and his casualties numbered barely a third of his opponent's. Schofield fell back to Nashville, where he joined Thomas in well-entrenched positions protected from turning movements by the Cumberland River, patrolled by Union gunboats.

In freezing weather Hood reached the outskirts of Nashville and waited before the city, unable to move against Thomas's superior and amply supplied army. Thomas would normally have done nothing except let the bad weather and inadequate supplies complete the destruction of the enemy army. But Hood's advance to a position not occupied by a Confederate army since early 1862 created a sensation in the North, and it was not counterbalanced by any news from Sherman, whose march cut him off from communication with army headquarters. Lincoln insisted on an attack, and on December 15–16

Thomas, in an essentially frontal battle, easily drove Hood's already demoralized army into northern Mississippi. Superior in numbers, morale, and cavalry, Thomas conducted a damaging pursuit. Discredited and disgraced, Hood resigned as commander; his army had lost so heavily in numbers and morale that it effectively had ceased to exist.

MEANWHILE, BACK in Georgia, Sherman's raid had reached the Atlantic coast near Savannah on December 13, enabling him to make contact with the South Atlantic Blockading Squadron and force Confederates to evacuate Savannah, which permitted him to establish a new supply line. At one time Grant had wanted Sherman to base himself on the Savannah River and advance toward Augusta, Georgia; but he and Grant now decided on a second raid, north through South Carolina into North Carolina. Sherman's route would allow him to break the Charleston-Atlanta railroad again as well as cut both north-south rail lines between South Carolina and Virginia. Because Confederates were concentrating to oppose Sherman and this raid would bring Sherman toward Lee's army in Virginia, Grant prepared for Confederate use of interior lines to concentrate against Sherman. Wanting Sherman to have a supply line so he could remain stationary and hold his ground, Grant sent Schofield with part of Thomas's army by rail and water to land on the North Carolina coast, take Wilmington, and establish a line of communications with which Sherman could connect if necessary.

Fort Fisher fell to a combined assault in the middle of January 1865. Schofield's XXIII Corps reached the North Carolina coast on February 9 and, along with the troops of Major General Alfred Terry, occupied Wilmington eleven days later. The Union force, some thirty thousand effectives, then prepared to move up the Cape Fear River and secure Fayetteville for Sherman's approaching army.

Having at last achieved the North Carolina raid he had projected a year earlier, Grant also finally realized his objective of having an army land at Mobile and march north into Alabama. A force of almost forty thousand men from the trans-Mississippi embarked on this campaign soon after Schofield landed in North Carolina.

By the winter of 1865 Federal efforts to improve the cavalry at last had created a well-led, efficient force, numerically superior and better armed than its Confederate counterpart. Grant used this force to make several minor and two major cavalry raids, which supplemented those by three different armies. Both major raids began in March. One, under James H. Wilson, moved from Tennessee into Alabama and captured Selma, an important war industrial center on a rail route connecting Georgia and Mississippi. The success of this maneuver preempted the work of the slow-moving force at Mobile. The other raid, under Sheridan, went from Winchester, Virginia, through Virginia to the army near Richmond. Sheridan's raid successfully disrupted Richmond's rail and canal communications with the western part of Virginia. By the end of March Sheridan had completed his destructive raid and had joined Grant at Petersburg, the army from the trans-Mississippi was besieging Mobile, the Selma cavalry raid was in full swing, and Sherman and Schofield had united in North Carolina after Sherman had beaten off a feeble attack at Bentonville on March 19–21 by a small Confederate army under Johnston. Grant was clearly attaining the object of his raids, to "leave the rebellion nothing to stand upon."[40]

The strategy of raids had carried the major burden of breaking the stalemate. On April 1 Grant sent Sheridan's cavalry and two corps of infantry in what Jomini would have called a "great movable and temporary" detachment "to compel your enemy to retreat to cover his line of operations." Sheridan reached the rear of the Petersburg defenses and, defeating the Confederate forces opposing him at Five Forks, so threatened Lee's communications that the Confederate leader carried out his long-contemplated withdrawal from Richmond the next day. His line of retreat lay along the railroad running southwest, but he had to begin by marching due west because Sheridan's detachment moved southeast of him, heading westward. Lee faced a perilous situation, which Grant made the most of, strengthening Sheridan and giving him what Jomini would have described as the mission "to take possession of an important point upon the communications of an enemy already retreating." Thus at Appomattox Court House Sheridan's detachment blocked Lee's withdrawal and forced Lee to surrender his army, which he did on April 9, 1865.[41]

LONG SIEGE lines, like those around Petersburg, reappeared in future wars and characterized almost all operations on the western front in

World War I. The high ratio of force to space in that war made them almost inevitable, just as had the large Union and Confederate concentrations around Richmond. But the combatants had such substantial forces that entrenchments soon covered the frontiers, providing no opportunities for turning movements like Grant's last campaign. That siege and Grant's Appomattox campaign provided an opportunity for the elderly Jomini, who studied the Civil War closely, to make a prescient comment. Noting that the long, entrenched lines of the Richmond-Petersburg siege might reappear in the future, he showed his approbation for his favorite maneuver when he asked: "But will they terminate in as brilliant a victory as that obtained by General Grant?"[42]

Thus Grant again carried out the strategic turning movement favored by Jomini, and like that at Vicksburg, it forced the capitulation of the enemy army. Rosecrans had attempted this manuever, and Lee had used it to drive back Pope, but only Grant had carried out campaigns comparable to Napoleon's of Marengo and Ulm. In formulating his interpretation of Civil War military strategy, T. Harry Williams failed to note both the conformity of Jomini's precepts to Napoleon's practice and how Grant, doubtless unknowingly, had successfully followed Jomini and emulated Napoleon. Williams also did not see how much Grant's greatest successes resembled in concept the practice common to both Union and Confederate generals and thus how much Jomini and Napoleon agreed and how uniformly their essentially identical ideas permeated the campaigns of generals on both sides.

Grant's brilliant campaign, and the strategy of raids, however, did not end the war. The Confederacy had lost long before, when its armies had melted away during the fall and winter. On December 31, 1864, the proportion of men present with their units had declined to less than 50 percent, a major decrease from the more than 60 percent with their units six months before. The loss of Atlanta and Sherman's march, combined with Lincoln's reelection, severely crippled Confederate will to win. Military events had marked and helped to undermine the southerners' commitment to their new nation.[43]

Yet in December 1864, with Sherman's army confined to the Savannah area, Union forces had almost completely evacuated Georgia, holding little or no more of the state than they had when Sherman began his campaign in May. The situation differed little in Alabama, though the Union navy had closed Mobile Harbor; and in Mississippi the Union had not acquired much new territory since the fall of Vicksburg, though Union forces had conducted several raids since the fall of the city on July 4, 1863. In the vast Confederate area west of the Mississippi no substantial territorial changes had occurred in 1864, and Price's raid into Missouri had created a serious commotion in that state.

So, except for broken railroads and the damage done along the path of Sherman's raid and the smaller diversionary spring and summer raids in northern Mississippi, the Union did not leave much evidence of Sherman's crucial campaign and its concomitant operations. Except in Virginia, the Confederacy had lost little territory since May, and even there the Union had added only a small portion of the state to the area it dominated. But Grant's raiding strategy had not aimed at acquiring more of the Confederacy and, in any event, such a strategy could not control territory. But even breaking the key trunk-line railways in Georgia did not have an immediate effect on Confederate logistics, for the main Confederate armies continued to receive needed supplies.

So to Confederates the military situation in December 1864 should have appeared far from hopeless. By one of the most important measures of military success, loss of territory, they had suffered very little military adversity. Nevertheless, the Confederates had exhausted their morale and will to win. Their deficient nationalism no longer equaled the task of continuing the struggle, and the desertions of the soldiers, which had accelerated in the last months of 1864, continued apace into 1865. And these desertions reflected not only the soldiers' discouragement but a similar collapse in civilian dedication to the cause. In the end the armies dissolved in spite of vast areas of unoccupied, and even unmolested, territory and military alternatives that still were open. Southerners had waged war skillfully, but victory had eluded their grasp.

Grant's strategy of raids had provided a useful solution to the military stalemate. But a broken stalemate means only that military activity becomes more fluid; it does not dictate the defeat of one side or the other. Even when the Union armies accepted the surrender of the Confederate armies, the latter had still other alternatives open to them.

The capitulation of the Confederacy was but a symptom of the triumph of defeatism throughout the South. Few southerners wished to continue the fight. Slavery was gone, state rights appeared to be gone, soul-searing casualty lists indicated the loss of many young men, and even God seemed to be against them. "O, God," prayed one Confederate in the summer of 1864, "wilt thou not interpose Thy strong arm to stop the bloody strife? Wilt Thou not hear the prayers of Thy people who daily say, Lord, give us peace?" But the depression of the people and their desires for peace deepened after the fall of Atlanta and the start of the siege at Petersburg, and by 1865 morale was beyond recovery. The armies had not yet surrendered, but the people were beaten. A Richmond editor correctly pointed out in January 1865 that the disasters suffered by Confederate arms were not worse than earlier setbacks, but he noted that "the people have been more depressed by them than they ever were before" because now they were expecting peace. Statesmen were talking of peace, believing that the people would give up the "chimera of Independence" if they could be "restored to their rights of the Union." The contest was over. "Our people *are* subjugated—they are crushed in spirit—they have not the heart to do anything," wrote one Confederate congressman, "but meet together and recount their losses and suffering." There were still those who felt the Confederacy could not lose if the people made up their minds to accept nothing but independence on their own terms and "to make any sacrifice which may be required." But the days of sacrifice were over.[44]

All that remained was to contemplate the struggle, to ponder the meaning it may have had and the lessons God may have intended to teach, to learn to bear one's burdens, and to consider the attractive features of the alternatives rejected in the great decision of 1861. The Civil War disappeared from the battlefields, except for the monuments that future generations erected. It remained, however, in the hearts and minds of the people, which is the most enduring feature of flimsy and romantic Confederate nationalism.

Chapter Fourteen

God, Guilt, and the
Confederacy in Collapse

I N 1862 the Confederates ultimately had halted the Union spring advances and followed them with the counteroffensives of Lee's Second Manassas and Antietam campaigns as well as Bragg's Kentucky campaign. In 1863 they had responded to Union spring offensives, including the very successful one at Vicksburg, with counterattacks in Lee's march to Gettysburg and Bragg's victory at Chickamauga. In 1864 the pattern had repeated itself, with Federal onslaughts followed by Early's two crossings of the Potomac and Hood's turn of Sherman and subsequent advance on Nashville.

Formidable resistance still remained possible for Confederates, but they failed to repeat the pattern of previous years with any counterattack in 1865. Only in part did military events cause this failure. In the East during 1864 Lee had avoided taking the initiative in tactical assaults. He had employed his Shenandoah Valley base to use Early's corps to menace Washington and Maryland without Early's initial involvement in any battle. Ultimately Early fought three battles, attacking in two of them. Certainly Lee had followed fairly faithfully Jomini's and Clausewitz's prescription for an active defense and, by not involving his main army in an offensive battle, Clausewitz's injunction to avoid such conflicts. In the West Johnston had followed the same policy as Lee, but Hood assailed his opponent in four battles with his main force, three essentially frontal. These combats, together with the defeat at Nashville and the resulting disastrous retreat, virtually destroyed the Confederacy's important western army. Hood's departure from the circumspect Clausewitzian recommendations seriously diminished Confederate military strength in 1865.

The outcome would have differed had Hood's movement on Sherman's communications worked. In his operations immediately after the fall of Atlanta Hood did avoid battles or even any contact with Sherman's main force. This course halted Sherman in north Georgia while he and Hood played a game of tag. Hood's army, diminished but not yet seriously depleted in numbers or morale, still measured up to the task. Earlier, Confederates conceivably might have stopped Sherman before he reached Atlanta if they had had recourse to the cavalry raids that had worked so well in 1862. Joe Johnston had advocated just this response by forces from northern Mississippi under the formidable Forrest, but, distracted by expeditions from Memphis organized by Sherman, President Davis had chosen not to employ Forrest's men for this purpose.

In any case, Grant's intention to use raids would have defeated either means of breaking Sherman's communications because Sherman was not irrevocably committed to capturing Atlanta before beginning his march to the sea. And Sherman's movement toward the coast caused Hood to counter with his Nashville campaign, raising the question of the contribution to Confederate defeat made by the innovative Union strategy and whether Grant's plan rather than Hood's loss of the Army of Tennessee may have provided a military reason that precluded a Confederate campaign in 1865.

Grant's way of war, though differing in objective from any envisioned by Clausewitz or Jomini, fit well with the evolution of Union strategy along lines anticipated by Clausewitz. For total defeat of an enemy he had prescribed *"the destruction of his armed forces and the conquest of his territory,"* pointing out that "the destruction of his armed forces is the most appropriate action and the occupation of his territory only a consequence." But Clausewitz would have known as well as the Union commanders that they lacked adequate superiority to destroy the South's armed forces. Instead, Union leaders adopted as their objective the "necessary evil," to "occupy land" before defeating the hostile armies.[1]

Clausewitz had seen value in ways "to influence the enemy's expenditure of effort; in other words, how to make the war more costly to him." Casualties inflicted in battle and conquest of territory provided two obvious means, but he noted three others all relevant to this discussion: *"the seizure of enemy territory; not with the object of retaining it* but in order to exact financial contributions, or even to lay it waste"; giving "priority to operations that will increase the enemy's suffering" with the essentially political object of increasing his desire for peace; and finally, outlasting him, "using *the duration of the war to bring about a gradual exhaustion of his physical and moral resistance.*" Clearly, in such a war it was unlikely that one army could annihilate the adversary's physical existence; it was necessary to lay siege to his spiritual-moral resources.[2]

The Union had followed all of these prescriptions. Yet through its successful resistance, the Confederacy relied more than the Union did upon the strategy of wearing out the opponent's will to win. In a sense Grant's strategy made irrelevant the continuance of Hood's army in its old form. It had recovered from defeat, heavy casualties, and retreat after Shiloh, Murfreesboro, and the battles at Lookout Mountain and Missionary Ridge. That it did not display the same resilience after the Battle of Nashville and could not, as in the past, replace its casualties illustrates how much its morale and faith in victory had changed. But the army owed its loss of effectiveness as much to the collapse of Confederate morale as to Hood's generalship.[3]

Although the Confederate supply organization still provided the essentials for the South's forces in April 1865, it could not have continued much longer with the mainline railroads broken and Wilmington, Charleston, Savannah, and Mobile completely closed by capture. At this late date a raid north was hardly feasible for Lee, with his animals debilitated and his men's physical and spiritual condition weakened by inadequate rations, distressing news from home, and doubtful notions about the Confederacy's ultimate prospects. No western concentration of troops could be created to conduct a major raid, for Davis had transferred the remains of the Army of Tennessee east to resist Sherman. Moreover, Wilson's cavalry raid to Selma and the readiness to raid northward of the powerful landing force at Mobile would have imposed on a reinvigorated Army of Tennessee, had one existed in the West, the same logistic constraints that hampered Lee in the East. And without functioning trunk-line railways, the Confederacy probably could not have kept its men together and could not have made a frontal resistance against any advance by the major Union troop concentrations.

To campaign in 1865 the main Confederate forces would have had to withdraw into the interior, closer to their sources of supply, and disperse into smaller groups. This strategy would increase the availability of food and fodder but would not have worked as well to connect with sources of ammunition, weapons, and shoes. Because of the simplicity involved in equipping and sustaining mid-nineteenth-century armies, however, the Confederates still would have remained formidable. John Shy notes that "when the Confederacy gave up, its main armies had been destroyed, its people were tired, and its resources depleted." But "continued military resistance . . . was possible and was seriously considered at the time." The Confederacy still possessed important advantages, considering that "the vast spaces, rural economy, and poor transportation system of the South were ideal factors for an effective large-scale resistance movement along guerrilla lines." Under such conditions, Shy contends, "the South could have been made virtually indigestible for a Federal army." He believes that the Confederacy had the weaponry and manpower to continue effective resistance; he also believes Confederates had retained the will to resist, but that is unlikely. Still, given sufficient weapons and a handful of men with the will to use them, a Confederate remnant could have created no end of difficulty for the Federal government after Appomattox and Durham Station.[4]

No longer opposed by major concentrations of force, the Union army would then have had the task of occupying the entire Confederacy. The area then rendered defenseless by Grant's strategy of exhaustion would have been enormous, for until then the Union actually had conquered only a small part of the South. And in moving to occupy a vast land defended only by small, dispersed forces Grant might have opened himself to serious difficulties. Clausewitz and Jomini surely would have anticipated that Union armies would feel most acutely that they were engaged in a national war in which "a people enthusiastic in its political opinions" rushed "to meet the enemy in defense of all it holds dear." When, in a national war, the defeated withdrew into the interior, defenders employed as a "last resort" the guerrilla warfare of a "general insurrection." In this way they could mobilize new strength, "not otherwise available" until that time. Jomini, who had fought against such a resistance in Spain, knew how formidable it could be: "The whole country is the scene of hostilities."[5]

Jomini described a war in which the invader "holds scarcely any ground but that upon which he encamps; outside the limits of his camp every thing is hostile and multiplies a thousandfold the difficulties he meets at every step." The defenders enjoyed an overwhelming advantage because "each armed inhabitant knows the smallest paths and their connections; he finds everywhere a relative or a friend who aids him; the commanders also know the country, and, learning immediately the slightest movement on the part of the invader, can adopt the best measure to defeat his projects."[6]

The invader would be almost helpless against the guerrillas, for "without information of their movements, and not in a condition to send out detachments to gain it, having no resource but in his bayonets, and certain safety only in the concentration of his columns, [the invader] is like a blind man: his combinations are failures; and when, after the most carefully-concerted movements and the most rapid and fatiguing marches, he thinks he is about to accomplish his aim and deal a terrible blow, he finds no signs of the enemy but his campfires." And "while like Don Quixote, he is attacking windmills, his adversary is on his line of communications, destroys the detachments left to guard it, surprises his convoys, his depots, and carries on a war so disastrous for the invader that *he must inevitably yield after a time.*"[7]

Jomini had noted three methods of defense—the traditional, employing a regular army; a regular army doubled by the addition of a trained national guard, which he favored; and a "spontaneous uprising" of the people who waged guerrilla war against the invader. He believed the second method, coupled with retreat, would vanquish invaders by requiring detachments to garrison territory and would suffice to provide an adequate national defense. Though Confederates lacked a regular army, they had followed Jomini's prescriptions by creating a large force based on conscription; and until 1865 events had fairly faithfully followed his forecast.[8]

But in 1865 the Confederates, prevented by Grant's strategy from keeping their forces concentrated any longer, may well have had to depend heavily or almost exclusively on guerrilla warfare. Jomini called this a "war of extermination" and considered it to be a "last resort," not only because he believed regulars and a national guard would provide an adequate defense but because he saw guerrilla warfare as unnecessarily expensive. Having seen such a war firsthand in Spain, he knew that the invaders retaliated with savagery and "by way of reprisals" committed "murder, pillage, and incendiarism throughout the country." These "consequences are so terrible that for the sake of humanity we ought to hope never to see it."[9]

Many Confederates would doubtless have agreed with Jomini, for they had formed traditional armies for their defense rather than relying on guerrilla warfare of a popular uprising. Jomini saw a force of regulars augmented by militia as a "mean between these contests between people and the old regular method of war between permanent armies." Believing in the sufficiency of his system of regulars and militia, Jomini had written: "I sum up this discussion by asserting that, without being a utopian philanthropist, or a condottieri, a person may desire that wars of extermination may be banished from the code of nations and that the defenses of nations by disciplined militia, with the aid of good political alliances, may be sufficient to insure their independence."[10]

Jomini restated this point in a way that has misled many readers as to his view of warfare: "As a soldier, preferring loyal and chivalrous warfare to organized assassination, if it be necessary to make a choice, I acknowledge my prejudices are in favor of the good old times when French and English guards courteously invited each other to fire first,—as at Fontenoy,—preferring them to the frightful epoch when priests, women, and children throughout Spain plotted the murder of isolated soldiers." Readers, failing to note that Jomini wrote of the fate of Napoleon's soldiers in Spain, that he supported the kind of warfare Napoleon waged and was making a choice between two undesirable extremes, have taken this statement to mean that he advocated some species of pre-Napoleonic warfare. But as a soldier he wished to avoid assassination at the hands of "priests, women, and children" and to fight a war as he understood it rather than a guerrilla war for which he believed the main weapons were political. Nevertheless, he saw guerrilla warfare as a "last resort," before which the invader must "inevitably yield."[11]

Union generals shared Jomini's aversion to guerrilla warfare and feared that the Confederates, who had employed it in Union rear areas, might rely on it even more in 1865. Grant's recurring nightmare in the last days and weeks of the war was that Lee's troops somehow would succeed in eluding his grasp and escape to the mountains to continue the fight by means of guerrilla warfare. General Sherman, too, displayed special concern. After Lincoln's assassination he arranged his first ill-fated settlement with Joseph E. Johnston for the specific purpose of neutralizing the surrendering army so "that the dispersion and disbandment of these [Confederate] armies is done in such a manner as to prevent their breaking up into guerrilla bands." Otherwise, he feared, "we shall have to deal with numberless bands of desperadoes." Joseph E. Johnston cooperated with Sherman because he, too, worried about that possibility.[12]

The Union commanders need not have feared an expansion of guerrilla warfare. Little did they realize that, after a long war against such a determined opposition, the spiritual underpinnings of Confederate resistance had almost melted away. The Confederates lacked enough nationalism to continue a conventional defense, much less have the motivation to engage in an ongoing guerrilla war. This is not to deny, however, that there might be issues so deeply felt that southerners would resort to partisan warfare to assert their interests; it is just that Confederate nationhood was not one of them.

Like many leaders on both sides, Johnston and Sherman did not look favorably upon guerrilla warfare; most professional soldiers in the nineteenth century felt the same way. The Civil War had generated enough such hostilities already. The internal war in Missouri saw a few hundred pro-Confederate guerrillas holding down several thousand Union troops, and similar activities had taken place in Kentucky and Tennessee; Sherman himself had had to contend with the problem when he commanded in Memphis in 1862.[13]

The Confederates' refusal to consider the guerrilla alternative may be a major reason why the South lost the Civil War. At the very least, it is certain that if they had adopted such a strategy in 1865 the Union would have had a much larger job on its hands than the one it had just concluded. Robert L. Kerby sees the decision to fight as a *"de facto nation-state waging conventional war"* as one of the critical Confederate decisions, and he contends that the South should have waged the contest along the lines of the national liberation movements of a century later. The southern failure, believes Kerby, was that it fought the wrong kind of war, that it should have staged a protracted guerrilla war of liberation "to wear down the enemy's capacity and will to resist" before engaging in conventional war. Some contemporary southerners agreed. J. D. B. De Bow, for example, called upon Confederates to "sacrifice . . . military punctilio," make ready for the "partisan skirmish," and "prepare for guerrilla war." But there were relatively few such men.[14]

That Confederates did not fight a war of liberation is not necessarily because it is a twentieth-century model. They were familiar with the example of Spain in the Napoleonic Wars and with their own scattered guerrilla activity. But waging the contest in that way would have given the war more of a revolutionary character and so have made it vary from the constitutional model with which southerners had begun their struggle. It is also possible that southerners did not want independence badly enough to resort to such extreme measures, that they did not equate their devotion to a cause by the amount of someone else's blood they were willing to shed for it. But it may also be that, despite the atrocities that occasionally marked the conduct of both sides in the Civil War, Confederates were too civilized and valued humanity too highly to engage in such bloody encounters. Guerrilla wars are particularly messy, and it was clear that many leading Confederates were too humane to inflict the requisite bloodshed and terror on either their enemies or fellow southerners.[15]

So, in spite of almost perfect circumstances for it, the Confederacy did not resort to a general insurrection. Such warfare, which inevitably involved poorly controlled and disciplined troops and even irregulars, could lead to actions that contravened the laws of war. The sack of Lawrence, Kansas, in August 1863 by Confederate irregulars under William C. Quantrell exemplified this when Quantrell's men killed 150 citizens and destroyed $1,500,000 in property. Although most leaders and many followers on both sides had their moral sensibilities numbed by atrocities, mistreatment of prisoners, occasional terrorism, the rare rapes that did occur, deliberate destruction of civilian property not of direct military use, and the like, there were some things most of them did not wish to do and other things some of them would not do. The frequent hesitancy of soldiers in the ranks to fire on enemy sentries is one example, and this hesitancy was codified by Federal military law.

Thus the Union issued rules of warfare that may not always have been obeyed, but at least they set a standard against which any soldier's conduct might be measured. Lincoln's rules for war were written by Francis Lieber and promulgated by the War Department as General Orders No. 100, April 24, 1863. Soldiers, warned Lieber, "do not cease . . . to be moral beings, responsible to one another and to God." This maxim was important. "Wanton" violence, unauthorized destruction, pillage, sacking, "rape, wounding, maiming, or killing" of enemy civilians were prohibited, and the sanctions were severe: "A soldier, officer or private, in the act of committing such violence, and disobeying a superior ordering him to abstain from it, may be lawfully killed on the spot by such superior." Even the enemy's combat soldiers were protected, for "outposts, sentinels, or pickets are not to be fired upon except to drive them in, or when a positive order, special or general, has been issued to that effect."[16]

Confederates also felt the weight of moral responsibility. There were acts that some of them regarded as absolutely improper, even if to refuse to do them might hurt one's chances for ultimate victory. To be sure, soldiers on both sides often overcame their compunctions, sometimes without much difficulty. But we cannot help but recall with bemused interest the outcome of an 1863 incident when certain Confederate scouts had fired upon some of Sherman's troops while the poor victims were bathing. "I gave orders that this practice must be discontinued at once," the commander of these Confederates reported to his superior, "also all similar ones at variance with the useages [sic] of civilized warfare." As one of the authors of the present study observed, "the war still retained a touch of chivalry—and cleanliness." An air of civilized sincerity permeates an order that George W. Randolph, Confederate secretary of war, issued to General G. J. Rains prohibiting the use of land mines—an order the likes of which no present-day general in any army is likely to issue. "It is not admissible in civilized warfare," wrote Randolph,

> to take life with no other object than the destruction of life. Hence it is inadmissible to shoot sentinels and pickets, because nothing is attained but the destruction of life. It would be admissible, however, to shoot a general, because you not only take life but deprive an army of its head.
> It is admissible to plant shells [i.e., land mines] in a parapet to repel an

assault or in a road to check pursuit, because the object is to save the work in one case and the army in the other.

It is not admissible to plant shells merely to destroy life and without other design than that of depriving your enemy of a few men, without materially injuring him.[17]

The reaction of General Joseph E. Johnston reflects this same scruple when, after the abandonment of Richmond, fleeing Confederate President Davis was unwilling to surrender without terms and was unwilling to disband the army. Johnston refused to follow the president's orders, believing "that it would be the greatest of human crimes for us to attempt to continue the war; for . . . the effect of our keeping the field would be, not to harm the enemy, but to complete the devastation of our country and the ruin of its people." Accordingly, Johnston worked with Sherman to achieve an orderly surrender of his army. But Johnston also showed that he realized how high the cost of such a national resistance would be and that a war of extermination would ensue.[18]

People who, like Johnston, might have been expected to be sympathetic toward irregular warfare on the part of the defeated southerners, also worried that guerrillas sometimes degenerated into mere bands of outlaws. Even in lesser extremes, guerrillas did not always have the same views as government officials as to the identity of the enemy. This confusion could, and sometimes did, result in internal warfare, a fratricide, in which Confederate civilians feared their own guerrillas as much as they did the Union army. The mountain hollows in the Appalachian chain of discontent provided frequent tastes of partisan warfare. As Philip S. Paludan has shown, it was a vicious circle. The irregulars created trouble, or threatened to, and the regulars were sent to punish them; but exactly who were the enemy? The innocent as well as the guilty suffered, leaving scars that could remain for a generation or two. Examples in our own time also illustrate the potential for mass disorder and indiscriminate killing. In Yugoslavia during World War II, Marshal Tito's Partisans often fought General Draja Mikhailovitch's Chetniks and vice versa, when both supposedly were engaged in fighting Nazis. And in the 1980s the Afghan guerrillas fight not only the Russian occupation forces but each other as well.[19]

One should not discount the possibility that guerrilla warfare for the purpose of achieving independence would have done more long-run damage to Confederate society than it would be worth, and that on top of the disorder already inflicted by regular warfare. Many southerners had opposed secession in 1861 because they understood that the Union was actually the best protector of slavery. Slavery was almost gone by March 1865, but the Union still had a similar role to play. Given the racial attitudes of the North, a reunited country was perhaps the best guarantee of white supremacy. Whether successful or not, a prolonged guerrilla war presented the specter of a population of former slaves slipping all remaining bonds of social control and would inevitably involve black participation in some form. Southerners had just gone through enough of that experience not to want to try the experiment again.

Just before Appomattox the opportunity for extensive guerrilla warfare still remained. General E. Porter Alexander, chief of artillery of Lee's first corps, proposed that Lee's remaining troops "take to the woods and bushes" and return to their states to support the various governors in attempts to get the best possible terms from the Yankees. As Alexander recalled the conversation, however, Lee foresaw the consequences. The escaping troops "would be without rations and under no control of officers. They would be compelled to rob and steal in order to live. They would become mere bands of marauders." The outcome would cause even further devastation to the South, and Alexander confessed shame for his proposal. In a 1902 address for Alumni Day at West Point, Alexander thankfully remembered that Lee had avoided a protracted guerrilla war such as the recent Boer War in South Africa. Thus instead of withdrawing to the interior, as Sherman feared, the main Confederate armies simply surrendered.[20]

But the concerns of Lee and Johnston, and the obsessions of Sherman and Grant, were justified in 1865 for, as Kenneth Stampp and Carl Degler have reminded us, guerrilla war did indeed break out, not in 1865 when the government and regular forces of the Confederacy collapsed, but during the years of Radical Reconstruction, spurred by the government's policy of black equality. The effect of the policy did not surprise Sherman; Grant, too, had premonitions of trouble, for he feared that the use of black troops on occupation duty would provoke guerrilla activity.[21]

But when Lee and Johnston surrendered, Confederates—however

unhappy—did not take to the hills with their guns. They faded away instead to their homes or looked to new futures in the West or in other countries, while the Confederate dream dissolved into a misty sentimentalism. To be sure, that dream was revived periodically, on Jefferson Davis's birthday or Memorial Day or a host of other occasions, over the next several generations—especially as long as any of the war veterans remained alive. But by our own time—and it has long been a fait accompli—the dream has blurred into a standard of individualism and regional ethnicity, a standard so vague that when it is displayed—as indeed it frequently is, on bumper stickers and belt buckles and at certain college football games—it is little better understood than is the South itself as it is portrayed in television situation comedies.

So the guerrilla resistance that Lee, Johnston, Grant, and Sherman feared came not in the war but in the postwar period. Only then did southerners feel strongly enough to resort to secret conflict and civilian resistance to oppose Federal policy. Militarily, it has significance that southerners possessed far fewer resources relative to Federal authority in the Reconstruction period than they had during the war. But the South nevertheless lost the war and won the Reconstruction because "the North, in spite of its great physical power, lacked the will to prevail," just as the South had lacked the will in 1864 and 1865.[22]

THROUGHOUT THE war, each side had sought to gain political leverage to manipulate its adversary when military pressures did not suffice to bring him to heel. Thus the Confederacy had looked with great hope to the 1864 Union presidential elections. Larry E. Nelson recently examined this Confederate *realpolitik*, noting that both Davis and his internal opponents saw the Union election of 1864 as a unique opportunity for the Confederacy. Though they differed in their prescriptions to capitalize on this occasion, most Confederates agreed that they needed to mobilize Union discontent and undermine Union will sufficiently so that voters would select a peace candidate to replace Lincoln.[23]

This strategy suggests a secondary purpose. Although Nelson does not emphasize the point, he implies that if the Confederacy missed the opportunity and if the Union did not select a president who might accede to southern ambitions, however defined, the event would rejuvenate the South's war effort by demonstrating that the Confederacy could end the conflict short of total defeat only by all-out efforts on the battlefield. For example, Josiah Gorgas noted in his diary that Lincoln had been reelected "by overwhelming majorities." The North was determined to crush the Confederacy, and he concluded that "the War must go until this [northern] hope is crushed out and replaced by desire for peace at any cost."[24]

A December 1864 resolution of the Alabama legislature expressed the thought that the reelection of Lincoln indicated "a fixed determination to subjugate us or destroy us, and not permit any honorable peace to be made." Many drew this conclusion, which meant that those who had once favored reconstruction were no longer justified in doing so. One had to fight because one had no alternative other than submission, which would be dishonorable. Subjugation, thought Senator Herschel V. Johnson, "would at least save us our honor." Between the choices of reconstruction and extermination, Alabama legislators and many other Confederates believed they preferred extermination.[25]

They drew a reasonable conclusion, if the fear of the Florida legislature had any substance. There lawmakers announced that the election results indicated the North's determination to wage a war not only for emancipation and arming of the slaves but also for confiscation, destruction, murder, arson, and degradation of the white race. Thus the Confederacy could conserve honor, to say nothing of independence, only by force, and not by negotiation. As Davis put it, "Do you not know that the only way to make spaniels civil is to whip them?" The success of Confederate political machinations, southerners came to understand, depended upon the battlefield. Unfortunately for the Confederacy, Lincoln's reelection, which caused real discouragement in the South, indicated that the Union electorate, heartened by the fall of Atlanta and Sheridan's victories in the Shenandoah Valley, agreed with their president. The fate of the South depended upon the battlefield as never before. But for many southerners Lincoln's reelection dashed their hopes of victory, and they became increasingly willing to abandon the struggle.[26]

Of course, the Union was playing politics also. We have already mentioned the political effects of Lincoln's emancipation and amnesty proclamations. Now, in late 1864, the Union was turning to a closer integration of military and political means to achieve the desired end. In that sense Grant's strategy of raids indeed had political implications, for its ultimate objective was to cause a political change of course in the South by removing the military props from the Confederate policy of independence. But the means, Sherman's and other raids, had an immediate impact that preceded, even precluded, their effect on the supply of Confederate armies. From this time on, every time a southern governor or legislator mentioned the possibility of a convention of the states to negotiate peace, he was manifesting a small measure of the political success of Grant's strategy.

Lincoln, always conscious of political factors, believed that his loss of the 1864 election would likely spell defeat for the Union, and to secure that election he applied pressure on his commanders to allow troops from Indiana and other states that did not permit voting in the field sufficient furlough to leave their posts and return home to vote.[27]

The Union also was trying, implicitly at least, to outlast the South. The Union had occupied little territory and, except with the help of Floyd, Pemberton, and Hood, had little success in destroying Confederate forces. The raids, however, especially Sherman's, would hurt the Confederacy and, to some degree, would increase the suffering of civilians. And Sherman saw the political significance because his raid would "demonstrate the vulnerability of the South, and make its inhabitants feel that war and individual ruin are synonymous terms." Sherman attempted to use his march through Georgia politically, and it, in turn, exemplified the strategy of raids. He had earlier sent word to Governor Brown that if the governor would withdraw Georgia troops from the Confederate army, he would "spare the State," confining his troops to the main roads and paying for his provisions. "It would be a magnificent stroke of policy," he wrote an interested Lincoln, "if we could, without surrendering principle or a foot of ground, arouse the latent enmity of Georgia against Davis."[28]

Sherman saw his march as "another way," to quote Clausewitz, "to increase the likelihood of success without defeating the enemy's forces." An operation that had *"direct political repercussions"* could have a decisive effect. Sherman believed that "if we can march a well-appointed army right through his territory, it is a demonstration to the world, foreign and domestic, that we have a power which Davis cannot resist. This may not be war but statesmanship. . . . If the North can march an army right through the South, it is proof positive that the

North can prevail in this contest." He hoped, as Clausewitz expressed it, "to overcome the enemy's will," because his raid, "operating upon the minds of the sensible men," would convince southerners that "victory was impossible." Sherman's thought also paralleled Clausewitz in his view that in "destroying the enemy's forces . . . nothing obliges us to limit this idea to physical forces: the moral element must also be considered."[29]

Although Clausewitz did not predict success for these methods, he and Jomini would have believed that the South encompassed an area too large for the Union to conquer with the forces available, especially when opposed by a national resistance. Still, Sherman's raids dramatized the South's vulnerability. "If the enemy is to be coerced," wrote Clausewitz, "the hardships" imposed "must not be merely transient—at least in appearance. Otherwise the enemy would not give in but would wait for things to improve." Regardless of whether the Union destroyed the enemy's armed forces and occupied its territory, it could not win "so long as the enemy's *will* has not been broken." Sherman's raids aimed at the enemy's will because they seemed to make the Confederates "literally defenseless or at least" made that "danger probable."[30]

Vulnerability, suffering, and the apprehension that these conditions would continue indefinitely discouraged all southerners, not merely the population exposed to Sherman's raids. As prospects for victory dimmed, "the desire for peace on either side will rise and fall with the probability of further successes and the amount of effort these require." But as Clausewitz always stressed, war is not "*something autonomous* but always an *instrument of policy*." And policy provided the key because, "since war is not an act of senseless passion but is controlled by its political object, the value of the object must determine the sacrifices to be made for it in *magnitude* and also in *duration*." By 1865 the Confederacy had lost its will for sacrifice, of whatever degree or period.[31]

When the Congress came to Richmond for its last session, in November 1864, the Confederacy had little hope of outlasting the Union; only a most extraordinary event could have changed the course of the war. Most Confederates seemed to have realized this, although they did not necessarily admit it openly. Ever since the fall of Atlanta two months previous, "a Southern nightmare had materialized." Cast about as they would, they could find no way to revive their fortunes. Whatever the future, whatever the duration of the war, southerners came to acknowledge that they could not envision a favorable end. There was no reservoir of national determination to fall back upon when the military no longer possessed the power to sustain itself by military means alone. The time had come when the struggle would depend almost totally on the will of the people in arms. But by the winter of 1865, the people were too demoralized to provide the supplementary strength that they had provided in the past.[32]

IN THE closing months of the war the military and psychological bases of Confederate defeat became closely intertwined. The fall of Atlanta, Sheridan's victories, and the impact of the strategy of raids starkly brought home to Confederates that God did not support their side, at least in the ways they previously had believed; clearly, if He had preferred them, the fortunes of war would have favored the South. Facing defeat, southerners felt compelled to reconcile the ways of God and man. They could do this by changing the perception of God, which led to the conclusion that perhaps He was not on the Confederate side after all. They could also manipulate God by appeasement, supplication, and prayer. If these efforts did not work, however, the only way to reconcile man to his God was for man to change his perceptions of himself. This led to self-examination that obliged Confederates to confess that God punished them for not being in step with His ways. "Can we believe in the justice of Providence, or must we conclude that we are after all wrong?" asked Josiah Gorgas. "Such visitations give me to great bitterness of heart, and repinings at His decrees. It is apparent that we are not yet sufficiently tried," he confessed, for he saw the hand of God directly punishing the people for not being in step with His ways. His people had the duty to confess their sins, accept His punishment, and invoke His blessing. "If repentance, humiliation and faith were unfeigned," then He would prosper southern arms and the war would go well.[33]

If they were sincerely to repent, Confederates had to determine wherein their sins lay. As they searched for examples of their apostasy, many of them came to conclude, even if grudgingly, that the difficulty lay in the institution of slavery. Northern Protestants had long since reached this conclusion, for ever since the Emancipation Proclamation and the subsequent movement toward enacting the Thirteenth Amendment they had made the war one to end slavery and had seen northern arms prosper thereafter. Thus, as Moorhead has observed, "to an unprecedented extent, the war had broken down distinctions between the sacred and the secular, endowing the arms and policies of the Union with religious significance."[34]

Thus the strategy of raids not only vindicated and intensified by reinforcement the Protestant religious convictions espoused by each side but also forced the South to reconsider its own domestic institutions. The Confederates' religious views predisposed them toward this conclusion. They saw God's hand in history and believed events would reflect His will. By late 1864, therefore, God's will was becoming apparent; His people had the task of accounting for and adjusting to it. "What have we done," asked Gorgas, "that the Almighty should scourge us with such a war—so relentless and so repugnant. . . . Is the cause really hopeless? Is it to be abandoned and lost in this way?"[35]

SINCE THE discomfort created by the dissonant knowledge of alternative decisions surely caused great pain, it took much thinking to reduce it and accept new ideas of the Confederate future. Some southerners could not envision and accept even the possibility of defeat, so understandably painful the prospect loomed. At the end of March 1865, one Confederate expressed his "unshaken faith in the ultimate triumph of that cause" and confessed himself "provoked and annoyed that any human being, who had *faith in God*, should doubt." Others felt equally certain of the outcome, even on the brink of defeat. The editor of the *Lynchburg Virginian* thought that the side devoted to "right and justice, against wrong and oppression," inevitably would win, and concluded that, since the Confederacy had right on its side, "if we . . . do not falter, we must succeed." A Georgia congressman agreed. God would never "desert a cause so pure and just as ours." "I do not see, but I feel," said Senator R. M. T. Hunter, "that there is a righteous God in Heaven, who holds our destinies in his hand, and I do not believe He will allow us to be cast down and the wicked to prosper."[36]

Many southerners had expressed similar sentiments at an earlier period of the war, but by 1865 patience with God's slow process was wearing thin. "It is time for thee, Lord, to work," reminded the

Lynchburg editor. God was clearly putting His people to the test. Jefferson Davis believed this, and so did others. Josiah Gorgas thought that God sent afflictions "to assure us of our strength," but he also observed that "even those whose faiths remain unshaken find it difficult to give a reason for their faith."[37]

For most Confederates, however, after the fall of Atlanta and the reelection of Lincoln, and certainly after Sherman's march to the sea, the time had come to face the inevitable. Their religious views made this process easier. Their brand of Christianity and the religious fatalism they espoused allowed them to overcome more easily than otherwise the dissonance created by the knowledge of the attractive features of rejected alternatives. God's will became a psychological bridge to the acceptance of defeat. Confederates reminded their countrymen that they "must walk by faith, as well as sight," for it was "not vouchsafed to mortals to control events that own a higher Power. There is a divinity that shapes our ends." For whatever reason, God might be punishing southerners. In any event, He was making His displeasure known. We cannot deny, said a refugee editor from Tennessee, "that we are mere instrumentalities in the hand of Omnipotence." In such situations, one must necessarily rely on a merciful God.[38]

Reliance on God meant repentance of sin. Southerners fully realized that they had shortcomings. God had punished them and would continue to do so "until the whole people shall have repented of their sins in sackcloth and ashes," for they "have sinned grievously." Here the clergy had a vital role to play. A Richmond editor called upon the preachers to "preach until every man thinks the Devil has gotten into his pew, and is chasing him up to the corner of it." The clergy, rigidly scrupulous and ambitious, proved only too ready to respond and thundered attacks on such vices as alcohol, sexual pleasure, merrymaking, and gambling, among others. Obviously, some ministers were using the war for complex ends, to promote the church, or their version of it, rather than the Confederacy; nevertheless, most clergymen preached that a "return to Christ" would bring victory. Others pointed to the apparent manifestation of God's wrath and complained that people had not learned the obvious lesson. Rather, they had been "driven away from God's commandments" at a time when they ought to be learning to submit to His will. The Episcopal bishop of Virginia, John Johns, asserted that God's displeasure resulted from the collective guilt of all southerners, and he expressed amazement that God had not punished His people sooner and more drastically.[39]

Psychologists emphasize the role of guilt in shaping behavior. This emotion would have equal importance in any age, for Christians believed, and still do, in the omnipresence of sin. Bishop Johns gave voice to this belief, but what sin or sins so oppressed Confederates as to cause God to spread His wrath over the people? Some thought God might be punishing southerners for extortion (charging high prices) or violation of His commandments. Others looked to other sins. In his study *Confederate Morale and Church Propaganda*, James W. Silver points to the role of slavery and touches upon the two aspects of the institution that caused Confederates to ponder. Many thought the institution inherently wrong; but even if it were right, the people did not administer it according to God's will. The institution itself, plus failure to respect slave marriages, to encourage sabbath worship among slaves, to provide religious instruction to slaves, or to protect them from unkind masters, clearly involved sins that led to God's condemnation. Thus the Roman Catholic bishop of Savannah called upon the South to make slavery "conform to the law of God" because He would not bless "a state of things which would be a flagrant violation of His holy commandments." Such perceptions sometimes resulted in an effort to reform slavery, as discussed, for example, by Bell I. Wiley, who noted the efforts of some Confederates "to humanize the institution, and to bring it up to 'Bible standards.'" Some reformers contended that the war was a punishment, not for slavery but for the South's "refusal to cleanse slavery of its abuses." More important, as a consequence of this guilt, some southerners even questioned the entire institution. This questioning had a close relation to the problem of morale and to Confederate nationalism, for slavery constituted the major difference between North and South. If Confederates lost confidence in its legitimacy, sooner or later they would lose confidence in their country as well.[40]

The South had seceded because many southerners thought that the Lincoln administration made slavery unsafe within the Union. The Confederates fought for a separate nation based on slavery, their political objective, and the strength of the Confederacy's will to make a long, strong resistance could, Clausewitz would have believed, "only be gauged approximately by the strength of the motive animating it." The motive animating the Confederates determined how much military success the Union must achieve, for "if the enemy is to be coerced you must put him in a situation that is even more unpleasant than the sacrifice you call on him to make."[41]

But Lincoln realized that military success did not constitute the only variable, for he understood Clausewitz's point that "the smaller the penalty you demand from your opponent, the less you can expect him to try to deny it to you." Lincoln's peace terms, in the form of his reconstruction plan, asked nothing from the South except the extinction of slavery. Insisting on no political or economic penalties, he invited the states back into the Union to resume their places as if they had never left it—except that they must give up slavery. He even invited them back with increased strength in the House of Representatives because, with slavery obliterated, the three-fifths compromise would become moot, enabling the South to count its entire population.[42]

Thus the issue of peace, like the issue that precipitated the war, revolved around slavery. To know whether slavery had enough strength as a political object to enable the Confederacy to outlast the Union, it is necessary to realize that slavery had changed since 1860. In the Union slave state of Maryland, for example, the price of slaves on the Eastern Shore in 1864 was barely 20 percent of the 1860 figure in spite of wartime inflation. This depressed market obviously reflected a belief in the doom of slavery, even in a state not affected by Lincoln's Emancipation Proclamation. Union forces had freed slaves in the occupied Confederate areas and enlisted tens of thousands of them in the Union army. Raiders already had emancipated many more who followed the infantry when it left. On one occasion Sherman measured the blacks who accompanied his raiding army in miles.[43]

"Wars," Clausewitz wrote, "must vary with the nature of their motives and of the situations which gave rise to them," and "the original political objects can greatly alter during the course of the war and many finally change entirely *since they are influenced by events and their probable consequences.*" Just as the Union had added the extinction of slavery to its original war aim of preservation of the Union, so too had the South altered its concept of the political goal of the war.

The changed prospects of slavery gave hope to some of its secret opponents and caused second thoughts among many of its unthinking or passive supporters, just as the course of the war must have discouraged those who had not believed that secession would bring war. After all, Clausewitz had realized that "the same political object can elicit *differing* reactions from different peoples, and even from the same people at different times."[44]

Kenneth Stampp has reiterated the close relationship of morale and slavery in a challenging attempt to solve the puzzle of the breakdown of Confederate will. He suggested what he believes to be "a partial explanation of Confederate defeat." In an essay entitled "The Southern Road to Appomattox," Stampp advanced the admittedly controversial thesis that enough slaveholders and other southerners had doubts about the morality of slavery and hence the validity of the Confederate cause to undermine southern commitment and help ensure defeat. Accepting David Potter's argument that Confederate failure resulted largely from the failure of its politicians and political system, Stampp asks why southern politicians—who had shown so much able leadership in the generations before the war—should suddenly prove incapable of providing the leadership necessary for achieving independence. Rejecting Frank L. Owsley's notion that state-rights doctrine had much to do with the outcome, agreeing with David Donald that the Confederates lacked self-discipline, and nodding toward Bell Wiley's thesis of the decisiveness of internal disharmony, Stampp sums up the Confederate problem, correctly, we believe, as "weakness in morale." A country with resources equal to or inferior to those of its adversary can conquer only if it possesses superior morale, but this the Confederacy lacked because of "uncertainty about the South's identity, of the peculiar circumstances that led to secession and the attempt at independence, and of widespread doubts and apprehensions about the validity of the Confederate cause." Stampp believes that the fact of slavery, which had caused secession and war, made Confederates uneasy. Southerners had "to soft-pedal the very *cause* of the war," making it "a considerable disadvantage as far as its moral position was concerned."[45]

Building on these observations, Stampp proposes the hypothesis that many Confederates lacked deep commitment to the cause and that, unconsciously, "the behavior of some suggested that a Union victory was quite an acceptable result." The failure of a true southern nationalism to develop partially caused this paradoxical conduct; only slavery gave Confederates a common and distinct identity, for most of the attributes that southerners shared with each other—language, religious values, and history—they also shared with northerners. Pointing out that some southerners had favored secession only to force negotiations for a favorable restructuring of the Union (one suspects that Stampp overestimates the number of those who took this ambiguous position), Stampp concluded that these Confederates found themselves "fighting for an independence they had never sought" and "may well have turned now unconsciously to reunion through defeat" to regain their true national identity.[46]

That, in defeat, the South managed to jettison the burden of slavery provides a second, more important reason for its paradoxical behavior. Believing, as we also do, that a significant number of southerners never truly convinced themselves of the positive good of slavery, Stampp agreed with an argument posited by Charles G. Sellers, Jr., that the inconsistency between maintaining bondage and at the same time promoting liberty bothered them. We would add that the dissonance between Christian precepts and the administration of slavery was also bothersome. Although not universally true, guilt, from whatever variety of sources, tormented enough consciences to influence collective behavior and provide a margin of shattered morale that led to Union victory. Stampp notes one convincing proof of this thesis: "the readiness, if not always good grace, with which most Southerners accepted the abolition of slavery." In doing so, they abandoned the elemental cause of the war and the emblem of their nationalism.[47]

Kenneth Stampp hardly stands alone in detecting an undercurrent of guilt in southern thought on slavery. Thomas Jefferson trembled for his country when he reflected that "God is just . . . [and] his justice cannot sleep forever." Mrs. Chesnut's prayer on the eve of the Civil War, "God forgive us, but ours is a *monstrous* system and wrong and iniquity [sic]," forthrightly confesses her afflicted conscience; her overseer believed that most southern women were abolitionists at heart, "and hot ones, too." And yet, though Jefferson and Chesnut were not alone, at the same time multitudes of southerners seem to have felt no apparent guilt whatever. The writings of modern historians reflect this dichotomy. In 1949, Rollin G. Osterweis remarked that the "guilt complex over slavery . . . is as difficult to prove as it is to establish" and suggested that "this hypothesis of the guilt complex" reflected "some projection of twentieth-century standards."[48]

Wilbur Cash saw an Old South driven by defeat, shame, and guilt to justify itself by romantic make-believe. Charles G. Sellers, Jr., made perhaps the most straightforward statement of the hypothesis when he contended that "the paradox of the slaveholding South's devotion to 'liberty'" provided "the key to the tragedy of southern history." When white southerners demanded freedom for themselves without acknowledging that others had similar rights, they engaged in "a disguised protest against, or perhaps an escape from, the South's daily betrayal of its liberal self." Bell I. Wiley believed that Confederate internal dissension came from feelings of guilt about slavery and that this consciousness of culpability became an ever-heavier burden as Confederate defeat approached. Robert Penn Warren believes that just "as there had been a crypto-unionism in the Confederate psyche, so there had been a crypto-emancipationism, or at least a deep moral, logical, and economic unease," and Carl Degler notes that "emancipation was not accompanied by the kind of emotional resistance that a challenge to deeply held values can be expected to call forth." The clear implication is that emotions were shallow because southerners were, on the whole, happy to be rid of slavery.[49]

Perhaps the best discussion of slaveholder guilt is by James Oakes. We do not necessarily agree with the thesis of Oakes's complete work, but he provides a useful discussion of the relationship of religion and slavery that makes some salient points. Evangelical religion, says Oakes, was taken seriously by slaveholders, and it led them into inevitable feelings of guilt over their ownership of other human beings. Like other white southerners, slaveholders had been caught up in the revival movement of the late 1700s and the years that followed. Its influence was so strong that "slaveholders often remembered the conversion experience as a central event in their lives, one which informed all subsequent thought and action." The evangelicals believed that God controlled "all events on earth, and man was helpless before His powers." Despite God's power, however, the state of man was wretched because of sin, which "was so prevalent in the world that only universal human degradation could explain it." From this point it was an easy logical jump to conclude that all men were equally degraded and from that conclusion to reason further that all men were equal before God. Evangelical Protestantism also rejected the quest for material wealth, which was characteristic "of a sinful covetous world." "Within the context of a slave society," says Oakes, the attack on materialism "served as a psychological medium through which masters expressed their misgivings about bondage. They complained repeatedly about the 'difficulty of serving both God and Mamon.'" Evangelical religion influenced slaveholders "to bring their ethical convictions into line with their daily practices," a difficult task that never was fully accomplished. The resulting psychological tensions, Oakes believes, were mitigated by the notion that slaveholders were responsible only to God. This reasoning had the convenient effect of justifying slavery and denying the arguments of the abolitionists; it also had the disturbing effect of underlining "the masters' fears that they would ultimately be judged by God for their behavior as slaveholders." The result, as one may well imagine, was psychological turmoil in which slaveholders (and, by implication, other evangelicals as well) questioned their beliefs, confessed the weakness of their faith, and made "startlingly frequent declarations that when they died they would go to hell." For slaveholders death and slavery were related, he explains, "for their conduct as master was subject to God's judgement at death." But secular culture "pressured the slaveholders to behave in ways their religious convictions told them were wrong and sinful." Not all owners felt the same degree of guilt, to be sure. But "few escaped it entirely," concludes Oakes, "for the elements of psychological conflict were intrinsic to slaveholding culture."[50]

On the other hand, James L. Roark thinks few slaveholders felt any sense of remorse about their property, except, perhaps, women, who "may have had special empathy for slaves because they subconsciously recognized the parallels between their positions, one as slave and the other as 'Southern lady.'" Eugene D. Genovese goes even further, expressing surprise at the very notion that planters had such feelings:

Did substantial numbers of slaveholders feel guilty about holding slaves? There is no evidence that they did . . . and it is difficult to see why they should have. . . . If some historians choose to be impressed by the evidence that some planters, accepting the moral standards of bourgeois society, felt guilty about slavery, others may be permitted to be impressed by how many did not, for their failure to display a sense of guilt demonstrates just how far they had advanced toward alternative notions of morality and social order.

James Brewer Stewart agrees, at least for the nullification-era generation. Instead of "spasms of racial guilt," South Carolina's nullifiers were motivated by a desire "to fend off malevolent forces which eroded patriarchal independence and threatened to destroy white domination and therefore all social order."[51]

Despite these sweeping statements rejecting the guilt thesis of Stampp, Cash, Sellers, Wiley, Oakes, and others, it seems obvious that it existed—not for all planters, certainly, but for many, perhaps even most. One need not prove, and probably could not prove, that either guilt or its absence predominated among southerners, whether slaveholders or not. Stampp's argument, to which we subscribe, simply states that however many slaveholders felt the pangs of conscience, the number was large enough to have a far-reaching effect upon the Confederate war effort.

We discuss Stampp's hypothesis at length because it seems to us to go a long way toward explaining why Confederates lost a war that they had every chance of winning; but he rightly admits that he offers only a "partial explanation." Building on Stampp's suggestion, we offer a more complete and, we hope, more satisfactory explanation for the result of the Civil War. Perhaps we can provide in addition some notion of the psychological mechanisms that operated upon usually unconscious desires among Confederates to produce a fearful yet consoling resolution of their problems.

We argue that many southerners did feel guilt over slavery and thus unconsciously looked to a Union victory and emancipation as desirable outcomes of a disastrous war, as Stampp suggests. Clearly this sentiment served as a self-fulfilling prophecy, causing southerners to accept past and current defeats in such a way as to encourage future defeats as well. We would add further, however, that these Confederates, and many other southerners as well, came to believe that God willed that slavery should end, and from that point they logically progressed to a sense of guilt over the war itself, a guilt that could only increase as both the war and the casualty lists grew longer. Still others had their crisis of conscience when it became apparent that the South would lose the war, and these souls were joined by others who had become greatly disillusioned when Jefferson Davis and other members of the Confederate leadership abandoned the earlier war goal of preserving slavery by proposing to arm and emancipate slaves. All of these negative attitudes together amounted to enough to provide the margin of Union victory, especially when reinforced by the religious fatalism that permeated the South's brand of Christianity.

This is not to say that a significant number of southerners consciously desired defeat. But many of them had unconscious inclinations in that direction, and defeat would have its rewards. For some, the loss of slavery would be a favorable outcome, if the collective behavior of the postwar South is any indication. Few southerners ever admitted a desire to restore slavery, but thousands confessed relief that war had destroyed the peculiar institution. The loss of slaves would make defeat less fearsome and hence easier to accept. By the same token, defeat would mean the end of a war that most of them had not wanted. In defeat, Confederates could recapture the clear advantages of the rejected alternatives, Union and peace, thereby reducing the postdecision dissonance between their knowledge of the horror of the war in which they were engaged and their knowledge that the South had had other, more attractive alternatives in 1861.

A nationalism based on an institution about which many southerners felt guilt could not sustain the Confederacy past the losses and disappointments of late 1864. And with military reverses inducing many to believe that God did not favor their cause, religion, which had originally buoyed up Confederate confidence, not only no longer supported morale but even inspired in some southerners a fatalism about defeat. When Confederates read in their Bibles the verses that assured them that "there is none righteous, no, not one. . . . For all have sinned, and come short of the Glory of God," they saw the inextricable connection of religion and guilt. So strong was the relationship of the two concepts that both of them must constitute key words in the lexicon of those who would isolate the causes of the Confederate defeat.[52]

God played a vital role in Confederate fortunes, and southerners therefore offered prayers daily to enlist His favor to the cause. But what happened when these supplications did not work? Their failure posed grave dangers to the southern peace of mind. As defeat came, the dissonance between the supposed knowledge of God's favor and the knowledge of imminent defeat created great psychological discomfort. Like any dissonance, this discomfort would have to be reduced. One could not achieve psychological harmony, at least not in 1865, by maintaining that Confederates actually were winning the war. Memories were too vivid, information too recent and reliable, casualty lists too long, and destruction too great for such mental legerdemain, although it did occur, apparently, in the postwar years. The impending loss of the war did not, therefore, lend itself to psychological manipulation.

One could, however, reduce the dissonance between defeat and God's will by denying the existence of God or by altering one's vision of Him. For example, one could retreat into deism, which held that God might exist somewhere but did not intervene directly in human affairs. Some southerners became receptive to this idea, believing that if the cause failed, "they would lose all faith in a prayer-answering God." Most, however, could not accept this solution as a way to reduce dissonance because they truly adhered to the basic assumptions of a conservative and orthodox Christianity.[53]

Only one way led out. Those who concerned themselves with religious matters could finally reduce cognitive dissonance only by the cognition, or "knowledge," that the loss of the war proved that God, if not actually against the South, at least was not acting positively for the South. Thus, one Confederate confessed to his diary the anguish of his heart and the loneliness of an abandoned soul: "I fear that God has ceased to work miracles. He certainly seems now to be on the side of our oppressors. We are in our last struggle, & without his almighty aid the Southern Confederacy will cease to exist in the next four months. . . . While our enemies insultingly exalt over the glorious battle fields where our greatest defenders died in vain." He wrote in May 1865, when the only Confederate armed forces still in the field were those of the Trans-Mississippi West. But he still called upon God: "O thou Almighty Ruler of Nations . . . be now our Sword & Shield! . . . O come to our help and deliver us." But if it were true that God was "on the side of our oppressors," and this seemed the only logical conclusion, it could result only from Confederate guilt about something, and what more logical sins to feel guilty about than slavery, war, and a failure to remain true to Him? Believers did not find this a comfortable position, and it led to the ultimate conclusion that if the South truly were guilty of these sins, then defeat provided the logical, fully deserved, and absolutely inevitable outcome. No struggle could prevent an adverse result if God had entered human history and had determined the outcome; rather, the people must accept the result as an aspect of God's wisdom and submit to His punishment in the hope that it would bring them to His mercy.[54]

By the same token, northerners could and did see in looming victory evidence of God's approval, though war weariness appears to have affected both sides in stringent measure until the last part of 1864. A new hymn, written on the eve of the conflict, had great popularity among Union troops all during the war:

> Stand up, stand up for Jesus,
> The trumpet call obey;
> Forth to the mighty conflict
> In this His glorious day.
>
> Stand up, stand up for Jesus,
> The strife will not be long
> This day the noise of battle;
> The next the victor's song.

One Union clergyman graphically proclaimed a downfall for "the Dagon god of the South." Northern Protestants generally believed the Cavalier civilization of the South had the most intense guilt and that God was using the Civil War as a means to punish both sides for not having themselves stamped out immorality. But assuredly, after He had completed the punishment of both, the North would be victorious.[55]

Lincoln himself noted the obvious: both sides "read the same Bible, and pray to the same God; and each invokes His aid against the other." Perhaps, mused Lincoln in his Second Inaugural Address in March 1865, God willed the war as punishment for slavery, a position that southerners began to accept. If so, the war likely would continue until

He completed the punishment because "the judgments of the Lord, are true and righteous altogether."[56]

Southerners could not object to Lincoln's logic; the conclusions, however, bothered them. Certainly Lincoln could more easily call attention to the obvious, for by March 1865 most people knew the Union would win; if God marched with the victors, then the Federals did not need to examine their consciences too deeply, for God had justified their actions by the results. Radicals such as George Washington Julian could proclaim after the killing had ended that the war had been not only an effort to save the Union but also "a grand and final battle for the rights of man, now and hereafter" and that "God would never smile upon our endeavours till we accepted it as such." And if success measured the brightness of God's smile, He had indeed smiled on the Union by late 1864. To the same degree that Federals could exalt their self-righteousness and spur themselves to greater efforts because they were winning, Confederates had to confess their sins and prepare to sacrifice their will to the will of God because they were losing.[57]

Lincoln also illustrated the emotional involvement that comes with long casualty lists. The Gettysburg Address dedicated the nation to continue the task that the dead had begun: "that from these honored dead we take increased devotion . . . that we here highly resolve that the dead shall not have died in vain." Union officer and future president James A. Garfield agreed, living in the hope that "the thousands who have fallen on the bloody field, or have gone to the silence of death in the terrible fever wards of the hospitals, will not have died in vain." Other northerners felt the same emotional investment in the war that Lincoln and Garfield felt, for in death many had paid a high price. For the Union the result repaid the cost; but Confederates could see by late 1864 and early 1865 that their dead *had* died in vain—unless . . . unless they could salvage something of consequence from defeat. Some could find value in the end of slavery, or the saving of honor, or the maintenance of a particular notion of constitutional order, or even white supremacy.[58]

One sees in the behavior of many Confederates the working of this hopeless struggle to avoid the logical consequences of their beliefs and to reduce dissonance. Thus, in 1864, Governor Vance sincerely proclaimed his belief that it constituted an "impiety to suppose He will let us be conquered by such a cruel and wicked race as the Yankees, if we only prove true to ourselves." A Raleigh, North Carolina, newspaper had given Vance and others the social support necessary to maintain such views just two months later. "The God of nations," announced the *Daily Conservative*, as if it had just received a direct revelation, "will, sooner or later, and in His own way, vindicate their cause, in the eyes of the nations of the Earth, and to this [sic] dismay and ruin of their enemies."[59]

Another paper earlier had reflected unease at the thought of the masses of dead and of God's judgment and urged the South to fight on. "To entertain the thought of giving up the struggle in which we are engaged, before the accomplishment of the object which we have in view," it warned, "would be to prove false to ourselves—to our brethren who lie slaughtered on many a gory field, to our country, to the interest of civilization and humanity, and to those who are to come after us." Most important, "it would also indicate a want of faith in God which would merit the severest punishment that could befall us." The writer who composed and accepted this commentary reflected a defeatist mentality. For to stake victory on God's favor, justly conferred, confessed that if victory did not come it would fail because God had not conferred His favor, and, more ominous, would lead to the inevitable conclusion that the South had not merited that favor. In true circular fashion, this logic could only lead back to the further confession that the South did not deserve God's favor, and, if it did not, sin and guilt were the reasons. Guilt over what? Slavery, the war, the long casualty lists, although every orthodox Christian undergoing the punishment of defeat could search his heart and find other reasons as well. With this logic, such individuals eventually would become more than ready to bow their heads to accept the defeat that seemed to be God's will. One must fight on to prove that God favored the South; conversely, when it became apparent that God was not with the South, one had better not fight on. Such thinking would encourage southern efforts when the armies were triumphant, for victories meant God was with the South; but these attitudes would have the opposite effect when casualty lists lengthened and the Confederate record was one of defeat and disaster. In effect, the people's piety, which once led them to support the war so strongly, had become a dubious asset. The course of battle created doubts about God's favor, and southern will was diminished as a result.[60]

Thus Confederate will was no longer a power that could supplement military might. Rather, the little that remained was not aimed at prolonging the war but at ending it and finding some lasting meaning in the experience. At the very end Mary Chesnut made note of a formerly fiery preacher who obviously acknowledged this Christian logic, for, now chastened, he advised his listeners "to cultivate a submissive spirit." Not surprisingly, even Jefferson Davis changed his tone. His proclamation of humiliation, fasting, and prayer of March 12, 1864, quoted congressional confession of "the chastenings to which we are being subjected" and acknowledged "that our sins as a people have justly exposed us to his chastisement," one "administered by a Fatherly hand for our improvement." By the end of 1864, Davis's tone had become more penitential. He called upon the southern people "to accept, with fervent submission, the chastening of his all-wise and all-merciful providence," admitting that "our sins have merited and received grievous chastisement." In January 1865 Davis issued his last proclamation seeking God's favor, and it was—appropriately, in view of the state of Confederate affairs—even more humble. He urged Confederates "to bow in humble submission before his footstool, confessing our manifold sins, supplicating his gracious pardon, [and] imploring his divine help."[61]

Evidently God guided affairs only according to His plan. Feelings of sin and guilt naturally provoked a fear of punishment and provided an obvious and ready answer to those who questioned why God had let such evils occur. The outcome of the war constituted heavenly punishment, which must not be resisted but accepted with Christian humility because God ordained it. And because He ordained it, the punishment—for slavery, for making war, for shedding blood—was fully justified. Perhaps only the pure in heart could gain victory, although any true Confederate might doubt this conclusion if he gave a moment's thought to the despised Yankees. With typical fatalism, Confederate Senator Herschel V. Johnson, who had been reluctant to leave the Union in the first place, detected "a sort of undefined notion that God . . . is permitting us by our own folly to work out the emancipation of our slaves." The Reverend John Jones echoed this sentiment. He, too, came to believe that God was "intruding to make us willing to relinquish slavery by feeling its burdens and cares."[62]

As James L. Roark observes, it was "likely that some plantation folks saw in the destruction of slavery the fiery cleansing of sin." Thus Dolly Burge, a Georgia planter's wife, resigned her cares "into God's hands. If the South was right, God would give it victory; if slavery was wrong, 'I trust that He will show it unto us.'" Confederate Brigadier General Frank Paxton also reflected this fatalism, resigning himself to God's will with the comforting thought that "we are in the hands of a just God, who will give us peace when we deserve it." And one of Jefferson Davis's friends recalled after the conflict had ended that he had felt during the war as if "the end was being shaped for us, and not by us." "We are not permitted," wrote Davis himself in another proclamation, "to furnish an exception to the rule of Divine government which has prescribed affliction as the discipline of nations as well as of individuals. Our faith and perseverance must be tested, and the chastening which seemeth grievous will, if rightly received, bring forth its appropriate fruit." What one southern lady said after the war could apply just as well to the thoughts of thousands while southern commitment and will weakened and the war drew to its close. The war and emancipation were, she thought, "just like one of the great changes, revolutions, that we read about in history. It all had to be, I should think, and so there must be there is a Providence in it; it must be for the best, in some way."[63]

Chapter Fifteen

Coming to Terms
with Slavery

SOUTHERNERS HAD RETREATED into religious fatalism as the Civil War drew to a close and their country and their dreams collapsed. Not only had the Confederacy lost its bid for independence, which its would-be citizens would confine thereafter to their hearts; in the process, they had lost slavery, an object that northerners and southerners alike agreed was worth fighting over. Indeed, so desperate had the situation become in the last months of the war that the Confederacy had sought to gain foreign support, to strengthen its depleted armies, and to outbid the Union for black manpower by proposing to emancipate its slaves. Confederates had been required to ponder the purposes of the war and come to terms with the destruction of slavery and the disintegration and surrender of its armies.

SOUTHERNERS WERE not particularly surprised when the government impressed slaves for use in military construction or mobilized them to serve as cooks, laborers, teamsters, nurses, and the like with the armies; some Confederates, however, were dubious about any military use of the black population for fear that it might lead to their use as soldiers. These doubters were correct. The surprise, shock, and furious opposition with which some Confederates met the proposal to use slaves as front-line soldiers, and then to emancipate them, is a good measure of the despair to which other Confederates felt the course of the war had driven their country. Eventually the question had become no longer one of policy or even of the proper place of blacks in Confederate society. By late 1864 the problem had become terrifyingly simple. Confederates had to decide whether to use slave soldiers and perhaps avoid defeat, or whether to reject the proposal and lose for certain unless they resorted to the national resistance of guerrilla warfare. The reaction of individual southerners would depend upon which of two war goals they valued most highly—independence or the maintenance of slavery.

By itself, the proposal to use slaves in a combat role in the Confederate army betrayed desperation, especially when one considers the earlier thunder of rage and threats of death that Confederate leaders issued when Lincoln made his proclamations of emancipation and the Union began to recruit black soldiers. In September and October 1862, several congressmen proposed to counter the preliminary Emancipation Proclamation by killing all captured Union soldiers. "The time had arrived," cried Senator Gustavus Adolphus Henry of Tennessee, "when we should declare a war of extermination upon every foe that puts his foot upon our soil. . . . We should meet a foe of the character that menaces us, under the black flag, and neither ask nor receive quarter from this day henceforward." In May 1863 congressmen had roared defiance once again, and this time they enacted their emotions into law. Confederate forces should not treat white officers of black troops as prisoners; instead, they were to "be deemed as inciting servile insurrection, and shall, if captured, be put to death, or otherwise punished at the discretion of the [military] court." The Confederates should deal with black soldiers themselves in accordance with the law of the state in which they fell captive.[1]

But as the war wore on Confederates became more aware that shortages of manpower might force the South to move in the same fateful direction as had the North. Contemplation of the possibility of a decision to use slaves in their armies brought the South face to face with an issue that cast doubt on one of its fundamental assumptions. For if one must surrender a goal, one must invent a new one to replace it, else, as in this case, hundreds of thousands of comrades had died for nothing, and the weight of those departed souls could be crushing for the survivors who had a conscience. By 1864 the course of the war had forced Confederates to think the unthinkable.

In January 1864, General Patrick Cleburne proposed to his fellow general officers of the Army of Tennessee that the South employ blacks as soldiers. The country faced a grave situation, Cleburne thought. After three years the Confederacy had "spilled much of our best blood," but the "fruits" of struggle "have slipped away from us and left us nothing but long lists of dead and mangled." Demoralization, desertion, and apathy were growing within the army at a fearful rate. Furthermore, slavery had become a source of military weakness because Confederates in the battle zones took the Union oath to protect their property and because the slaves themselves often provided valuable information to the enemy. So Cleburne and thirteen of his division officers concluded that the time had come to "commence training a large reserve of the most courageous of our slaves, and further that we guarantee freedom within a reasonable time to every slave in the South who shall remain true to the Confederacy in this war." If he had to choose between slavery and independence, the practical Cleburne preferred to give up the former to save the latter. The plan would work, Cleburne thought, because then slavery no longer would present an obstacle in the path to European recognition and moreover, it would remove the incentive for slaves to join the Union army.[2]

The proposal apparently constituted the first formal discussion of the topic within the Confederate leadership, although many persons— both leaders and general public—had heard the subject discussed privately. One congressman had proposed emancipation (although in connection with recognition, not slave soldiers) as early as May 1863, and many declared him crazy for his pains. Considering the emotional investment that southerners had in slavery, accentuated by their sanctions against Union emancipation and Union black soldiers, and increased now that the casualty lists had reached an extended length, it is not surprising that anyone who questioned slavery was considered crazy, for such ideas were both frightful and explosive.[3]

Shrinking from the possible consequences of public knowledge of Cleburne's recommendation, therefore, Jefferson Davis suppressed it. Davis had good reason for anxiety concerning the question of slave soldiers, for, as Cleburne implied, the slave must receive an appropriate incentive for him to perform as an effective soldier. Emancipation was the only suitable reward, and that raised ticklish questions of racial adjustment and the horrifying question of war goals, the reasons so many had gone to war in the first place. That Davis kept Cleburne's memorandum to himself does not mean he did not think about it or that the idea had not already occurred to him. Davis admitted after the war that early in the conflict he would have considered such an idea "preposterous." But he also confessed that when he had suggested the use of blacks as teamsters and laborers, he had thought the experience would be useful in case the South should ever need them under arms.[4]

By the time the last session of the Confederate Congress convened on November 7, 1864, many saw black soldiers as the only possible alternative to capitulation. But for fear of public opinion, the issue had to be soft-pedaled. In his opening message to Congress, Davis stated, "I must dissent from those who advise a general levy and arming of the slaves for the duty of soldiers." He continued, however, with the ominous warning that "should the alternative ever be presented of subjugation or of the employment of the slave as a soldier, there seems to be no reason to doubt what should then be our decision."[5]

Using the moral and popular authority of his office in a way he never had before and never would again, Davis floated trial balloons and encouraged his administration to join him in hinting to other influential people that the country had to consider arming the slaves. Davis generated the public pressure that pushed him and Congress into a policy decision—although it was too late to affect the outcome of the war. Had he been so alert to the possibility of shaping public opinion before November 1864, Davis would no doubt have made his task easier, if not more successful.

Be that as it may, in the fall of 1864 many Confederate leaders, editors, clergymen, and army officers agreed with Davis. Immediately a number of congressmen supported the trial balloon with enthusiasm, while official policy, and indeed the secretary of war, was still denying that the administration contemplated the use of black troops. Secretary of State Judah P. Benjamin was writing letters encouraging journalists and politicians to discuss the question and pressure the people and government to move in this fearful direction, and Jefferson Davis was supporting the proposal in private. Using the example of his experience in leading his own slaves against a band of armed, white intruders on his lands, Davis contended that blacks would make good soldiers. Years later he recalled that he had warned a senator who hesitated to make the difficult move that if the Confederacy lost, "there should be written on its tombstone, 'Died of a theory.'"[6]

This issue, then, forced fundamental reconsideration of the entire Confederate position. The arguments of Cleburne, Davis, and their supporters in the leadership took the practical side of the question. Support came from all over the Confederacy. In Mississippi editors split on the question, but as early as April 1863 one of them had urged the people "to make any and every sacrifice which the establishment of our independence may require. . . . Let not slavery prove a barrier to our independence. . . . Let it perish!" Congressman Warren Akin of Georgia underlined the dilemma:

> I can only say it is a question of fearful magnitude. Can we prevent sub-jugation, confiscation, degradation and slavery without it. If not, will our condition or that of the negro, be any worse by calling them into service.
>
> On the other hand: Can we feed our soldiers and their families if the negro men are taken from the plantations? . . . If I were convinced that we will be subjugated, with the long train of horrors that will follow it, unless the negroes be placed in the army, I would not hesitate to enrol [sic] our slaves and put them to fighting.[7]

Senator George Graham Vest of Missouri reached the same conclusion by the same reasoning. "It is a very difficult question," he wrote Governor Thomas Reynolds, "but in our condition I can see no reason for hesitation." Since the Federals were already using black soldiers, the Confederacy faced the question of whether to "let them fight against us or make them take up arms in our interest." General Josiah Gorgas, who was close to Davis, made similar admissions in private. "The time is coming," he confessed, "when it will be necessary to put our Slaves into the field and let them fight *for their freedom.*" Emancipation would result, but independence might necessitate the surrender of slavery anyway. In the fall of 1864, Gorgas thought the entire country was moving rapidly to that position. He was correct. The plain folk joined in pressuring the government. The arming of the slaves, admitted a Georgia farmer as he tried to prod the government into action, constituted a "last resort" if the country were to avoid subjugation. "I see but one alternative left us," an anonymous writer told Howell Cobb, "and that is to fill up our army with negroes. I have no doubt but they can be made as good soldiers as the population our enemies are importing from Europe. . . . If you do not put them in the field they will very soon be taken from us and made to take up arms against us." "Some think that our soldiers would not be willing to have

negroes placed in the army [but] if Gen. Lee would say that it is necessary there would be but few objections."[8]

Indeed, by January 1865 General Lee did think as Cobb's correspondent hoped, and he used the same practical argument for the same
practical end. "I think," he wrote, "we must decide whether slavery
shall be extinguished by our enemies and the slaves be used against us,
or use them ourselves at the risk of the effects which may be produced
upon our social institutions. My own opinion is that we should employ
them without delay." Lee added that "the best means of securing the
efficiency and fidelity of this auxiliary force would be to accompany the
measure with a well-digested plan of gradual and general emancipation." When Lee's feelings became known, many expressed approval,
as if his endorsement had made it safe for others to discuss this most
difficult question.[9]

Some Confederates, however, felt that Lee's support for emancipation amounted to a betrayal of the Confederacy. With a remarkable
simplification, Robert Barnwell Rhett, Jr., claimed that "the whole
question is one—JOHN C. CALHOUN vs. DANIEL WEBSTER and ROBERT
E. LEE" and concluded that the good general, "noble gentleman and
accomplished soldier that he is," knew more about military than civil
affairs. In thinking Lee a secret emancipationist, Rhett did not miss
the mark very far. After the war Lee told the Joint Committee on
Reconstruction that he thought Virginia would fare better if she could
"get rid of" the black population. "That is no new opinion with me,"
the general noted. "I have always thought so, and have always been in
favor of emancipation—gradual emancipation."[10]

A month after Lee expressed open support for arming slaves, one of
Davis's correspondents warned that even though God sanctioned slavery, the institution weakened the country in the war, and further, that
"the teachings of Providence as exhibited in this war dictate con-
clusively and imperatively that to secure and perpetuate our independence we must emancipate the negro."[11]

Any plan to use slave soldiers clearly must include emancipation, as
men on both sides of the question realized. Thus the issue of slave
soldiers led inevitably to questions of economic interest and racial adjustment. R. G. H. Kean noted in his diary that congressmen from the
occupied areas were more in favor of arming slaves than were those

from the rest of the country and that the planter interests strongly opposed it.[12]

Indeed, most supportive legislators represented areas either occupied by the Union army or in danger of occupation; such congressmen would have more urgency behind their opinions and a greater desire to fight with no holds barred, while, at the same time, the situation of their districts shielded them from constituency pressures that other congressmen had to consider. They also represented areas that had fewer slaves than most of the deep South. Congressman Warren Akin of Georgia sadly observed that people "give up their sons, husbands, brothers, & friends, and often without murmuring, to the army; but let one of their negroes be taken and what a houl [sic] you will hear. The love of money," he concluded, "has been the greatest difficulty in our way to independence."[13]

The economic issue should not be overemphasized, for many southerners realized that in the postwar adjustment they could control black labor, as we shall note below. The question of racial adjustment, however, did set many Confederates' heads to spinning. Back in 1861, a few perceptive southerners had thought of the Union as a guardian of slavery and contended that their property had greater safety in a sometimes hostile Union than it would in an independent country of their own. Such men now looked like prophets, for the Confederacy had raised the awful specter of the breakdown of social controls that the South supposedly escaped when it left the Union. After the war, Congressman Edmund S. Dargan of Alabama reminded President Andrew Johnson that he had often told Johnson that he had "never seen the day" that he would not "have preferred the abolition of slavery if the two races could have been separated the one from the other." But the races were not separated, not yet at least, and southerners gave free rein to their fears. Congressman James T. Leach of North Carolina thought arming slaves "would make a San Domingo of our land." Some Confederates were so frightened that a few began to think of returning to the Union as a way of retaining slavery.[14]

This notion seemed as strange to some Confederates as it does to us today. In the summer of 1863 an Alabama newspaper editor saw such people as deluded fools, and the next winter Governor Vance viewed as "lost to reason" those who thought reconstruction would save slavery.

By early 1865, however, some Confederates had let wishful thinking get the best of them. A Virginia editor commended Senator William Alexander Graham of North Carolina for taking a stand with those who did not "labor under the hallucination" that if the South lost the war it would lose all its property. Indeed, Graham and others believed that voluntary return then, in January 1865, would save the peculiar institution and perhaps secure other concessions as well. Much impressed by the discussions that the Stephens-Hunter-Campbell peace commission had had with Lincoln and Stanton, Graham began to consider "whether reunion, by which ten States may defeat the proposed [thirteenth] amendment to the Constitution, & retain slavery be not preferable to the triumph of his arms, and the subjugation of every thing to his power." Jehu A. Orr, congressman from Mississippi, agreed with this view, so naive at this stage of events, that slavery might yet be saved. In his memoirs he claimed that in spring 1864 he and several other representatives and senators drew up a resolution "looking to the re-construction of the Union, in which the institution of slavery was to be secured by a compact with the Government of the U.S." Orr also recalled that during a visit to Richmond in January 1865, Francis P. Blair, Sr., had stated that the Union might consent to gradual emancipation, taking thirty-one years, if the Confederacy agreed to reconstruction.[15]

But the partisans of arming the slaves triumphed during this "debate on emancipation," as Robert F. Durden calls it. After initial rejection, the bulk of the southern leadership gradually moved toward acceptance of the idea. It became policy in March of 1865, just before the end, by a combination of law and executive order. Southerners approached the question from two directions, one idealistic and the other practical. The idealists were those who always had doubted the institution or who had come to feel some pangs of guilt about slavery; they also included those who saw the hand of God at work as the South lost the war and slavery with it because He did not will that the South should win. The stress of war allowed them to bring their misgivings into the open. They included people like Mrs. Chesnut, always an undercover abolitionist of sorts, who eventually thought that the elimination of slavery had enough value to compensate for a failure to win independence.[16]

Those who may have doubted the institution but who argued for emancipation and the arming of the slaves on the grounds of practicality joined the idealists. Anything that would assist the war effort they considered acceptable, and if Confederate blacks could have more use free than slave, these southerners saw little reason not to change their minds about the proper role of blacks in southern society. Together these two groups had sufficient strength and influence to translate their ideas into Confederate policy, forcing a wrenching decision upon their countrymen.

The emancipation issue profoundly disturbed many southerners. Slaves armed like their masters might become the equal of their masters, and thus "a war for the freedom of the white man [would become] a struggle for the freedom and equality of our slaves." The newly freed slaves would not have intellectual parity with whites, some Confederates claimed, and they lacked trustworthiness when influenced by liquor and lust. Many whites displayed sexual fears. Governor Vance called for opposition to the proposal so as to avoid Negro officers on the streets insulting white women by their very presence. "What say our women?" queried a private citizen in North Carolina. "They can but execrate it. Will North Carolina submit?"[17]

THE ISSUE of slave soldiers and emancipation went beyond the merits of the question, however, for it forced Confederates to evaluate the goals of their war effort. But as they began to consider what they were fighting for, they noted that ideas on the subject varied. If the southerners' war effort suffered seriously from lack of broad support when the war went badly, part of the reason may lie in the confusion over why they were fighting in the first place. And this confusion inevitably created some dissonance because it implied that southerners had made the decision for secession not only with insufficient knowledge of what lay in store but also with inadequate understanding of why they had made it at all. It put the legitimacy of the 1861 decision into doubt and thereby strengthened the appeal of the alternative decision not made.

Back in 1860–61 the issue had seemed clear. Southerners talked then of slavery and, to a lesser extent, of racial adjustment and state rights. They had not said very much about independence per se or about honor. Although many advanced different arguments from time to time, and in a complex problem such as this probably no two people thought the same, from the start a large part of the Confederate elite pointed to slavery as the cause of armed conflict. Robert Hardy Smith, a member of the Provisional Congress, wrote in 1861 that "the question of negro slavery has been the apple of discord" and that "we have dissolved the late Union chiefly because of the negro quarrel." Only a few contemporaries would have disagreed—in 1861.[18]

In his famous "cornerstone" speech given just after his inauguration as vice-president of the Confederacy, Alexander H. Stephens not only asserted that slavery "was the immediate cause of the late rupture and present revolution" but also claimed, using biblical metaphor, "that slavery, subordination to the superior race, is his [the Negro's] natural and moral condition" and that "the stone which was rejected by the first builders is become the chief stone of the corner." In this he echoed Robert M. T. Hunter, who had stated on the floor of the United States Congress in 1859 that the Union was like an arch, "and the very keystone of this arch consists of the black marble cap of African slavery; knock that out, and the mighty fabric, with all that it upholds, topples and tumbles to its fall." In December 1860 Hunter wrote about the "insane war upon slavery" that he thought the North was waging and predicted "general civil war" if the government should try to coerce seceding states to remain in the Union.[19]

Henry S. Foote, a leading Tennessee Unionist, former governor of Mississippi and longtime antagonist of Jefferson Davis, also thought the impending war was caused by slavery. No believer in the "abstract right of secession," Foote feared the destruction of the South if the sections did not make some adjustment before "Abolition shall become firmly seated in the high places of power"; he had opposed the possible appointment of William H. Seward to Lincoln's cabinet because "the great leading object of his life as a public man has been to undermine and to crush the system of domestic slavery existing in the South." Reuben Davis of Mississippi took a somewhat different view. He found the principles of the Republican party "subversive of the constitutional compact between the States," but believed the basic problem was the slavery controversy and northern "fanaticism"; as a member of the House Committee of Thirty-Three, he therefore attempted to safeguard southern property rights in slaves.[20]

Even Jefferson Davis, who always emphasized the constitutional aspect of the cause of the war, underlined the northern threat to the security of property in slaves. He implied, furthermore, that if the Union did not enforce the Fugitive Slave Law the South would be justified in withdrawing from the Union—all of which reads like a threat to break up the Union over the issue of slavery. By the same token, Davis's farewell address to the Senate in 1861 not only emphasized constitutional questions but also complained of attacks upon the "social institutions" of the South. In his opening message to the second session of the Confederate Congress, April 19, 1861, Davis continued his constitutional complaints, but he also emphasized the passage of "a persistent and organized system of hostile measures against the rights of the owners of slaves," the efforts of "fanatical organizations" to foment slave rebellions, the attacks upon slaveowners attempting to recover fugitive slaves, and the creation of a political party that sought to render "property in slaves so insecure as to be comparatively worthless."[21]

In an address to the people issued at the end of the first Congress, in 1864, J. L. M. Curry (the reputed author) reminded his fellow Confederates that the South seceded from a Union hostile to southern institutions and formed a new government based "on the proper relations of labor and capital"—not, we may note, on proper Federal relations or a reformed constitution. As late as February 1865, the *Charleston Mercury* admitted that the South started the war to preserve slavery. But under the pressure of a failing war effort, the South eventually abandoned the institution even though it had constituted a major, some would say *the* major, precipitating factor in the coming of the war.[22]

If the Confederacy needed more soldiers to achieve its goals and if slaves provided the only major source of new soldiers, and if the army would need emancipation to motivate those slaves to fight on the side of the Confederacy, those southerners who believed the states had seceded, established the Confederacy, and gone to war to save slavery would suffer a severe dissonance problem. Not yet able or willing to resolve that psychological conflict by changing their decision, that is, giving up the war effort, some southerners mitigated their dissonance by changing their information instead, claiming that they were not waging the war to protect slavery but to achieve independence. By contending that they had not fought the war to save slavery, such southerners made it easier for their comrades to push for emancipation and the arming of the slaves.

As Robert F. Durden indicates, the question of goals helped force many Confederates to decide what they valued most, slavery or independence. Before 1864 one could fight for both. By the summer and fall of 1864 it became an either-or proposition; Confederates could not achieve both goals but might still achieve one. "We are fighting first for our liberty and independence," a Georgia preacher warned his son, "not for our interests." Herschel V. Johnson claimed further that the South had two goals, for he added good government to the aim of independence. In the last days of its existence, the Congress of the Confederacy called upon the people to keep their goals in mind, for the object of the war was independence. Those who thought otherwise fell into error, for "slavery, so far as the action of Virginia was concerned, had nothing to do with it." Remarkably, many people believed this argument, so far had some Confederates gone in resolving the dissonance created by the attractive features of the rejected alternative. But the war involved more than independence, for many Confederates fought to maintain white supremacy. Although few Confederates wished to admit it, white supremacy brought the question back to slavery because the peculiar institution provided the way in which white southerners preserved white supremacy and maintained racial adjustment along the lines they desired.[23]

Not surprisingly, the discovery that the South was not fighting for the purpose that many Confederates originally believed raised resentments and reopened old arguments. Had they not created the Confederacy to save slavery? Who had advocated independence in 1861 without linking it to slavery in some way? Many southerners found the implications of these questions profoundly disturbing. Their politicians had rejected reconciliation and pursued secession, which had the "natural consequence" of war for the maintenance and potential expansion of slavery. Now some people were asserting that the fight was for independence instead. Those who had provoked war to preserve slavery in the western territories were not even able to preserve it in the southern states. No wonder the rejected alternatives began to look more attractive, as some southerners who had not favored secession and war logically asked why, if the South could abolish slavery so it could continue the war, it could not do so to end it? More to the point, why could not the South have acquiesced on the territories question and other slavery issues and avoided war in the first place?[24]

But if the Confederacy freed its slaves, it would be denying its own history. If not for slavery, why did the South fight? Some Confederates had always contended that state rights constituted the heart of the problem, and others who asserted that they fought to check the encroachment of an all-powerful central government now joined them. This notion eventually had almost universal popularity in the postwar South, but Confederates reached the state-rights thesis by either of two routes, neither of which excluded the other. First, there were some southerners who had looked to the incompatibility of Yankee centralization and southern autonomy during the secession winter of 1861 and others who had come to that idea later on. Second, there were those who accepted the same issues as the first group but extended the struggle against centralization to include Confederate centralizers as well as those of the North. These true state-rights men, examined earlier, wondered why the South had established its own modern, centralized state if it was waging war to escape centralization.

This debate posed a relevant and upsetting question, and many resisted the change in war aims. A North Carolina editor reminded his readers that the South was not fighting to affirm the right of secession. That, he said, was nonsense. Rather, the South fought for property as well as for equal rights. Saying otherwise questioned the propriety of the war. Governor Brown had to remind Georgians of their recent history. "Some persons in authority," he noted, "seem to have forgotten that we are fighting for anything but independence." If they truly had that goal for the war, then "the whole struggle is in vain"; as Brown pointed out, southern states had had independence under the old government. If, therefore, they fought for independence, "our sacrifices have been made but to little purpose." He agreed that the war was waged for "our *rights* and our *liberties*," but he defined these to include slavery. Another Georgian complained that whenever the South departed from the doctrine of state rights, it betrayed the Revolution, admitting "that we broke up the Union upon false issues." The question contributed to the hostile feelings that some Confederates had for their central government. Like conscription, suspension of habeas corpus, and impressment, the emancipation issue brought up the question of "our rights and our liberties." If slave property were confiscated, even under such a pleasant-sounding word as emancipation, it would be one more indicator of the despotism that the Davis government had established. In making this proposal, it seemed to some southerners that Davis was grasping for ever greater power, and therefore he had to be resisted as a matter of principle. These fears could arouse much anxiety. Whether one fought for slavery or state rights seemed to make little difference in 1864 and 1865. The policy of the Confederate government—under the guise of necessity, to be sure—subordinated both of these goals to emancipation and centralization. But war, emancipation, and despotism seemed to be a poor exchange for the privileges that southerners had enjoyed in the Union before the war. Nevertheless, many Confederates had a difficult time trying to avoid posing the question: Why should the fight go on?[25]

They should continue the war to preserve honor, said some. The recent work of Bertram Wyatt-Brown should remind us how important honor was to southerners. It involved not the bleating of a braggart so much as a standard for the conduct of life. It comes as no surprise, therefore, that when Confederates talked of honor they did not mean pride so much as moral integrity, personal bravery, Christian graciousness, deference to and respect for others, and self-worth, recognized by their peers. Most southerners held these values as important considerations, not only in the settlement of the war but also in daily life. It was no small thing, therefore, to fight for honor. The impediment was that honor had come to be all there was left to fight for; slavery was about to go, by the action of the Confederacy itself. Independence had become just as precarious by 1865. Some Confederates thought the South itself had destroyed state rights, and all believed that they would lose it for certain if the Union triumphed. By the process of elimination, therefore, honor became important as never before.[26]

But a second impediment sprang from the particular demands for an honorable peace, by which most Confederates meant a peace that did not entail reunion. By definition, therefore, Confederate defeat must result in a dishonorable peace, the compromise of honor. A peace with reconstruction would have to be rationalized in some way, until it appeared compatible with honor. Southerners most sought to avoid humiliation—loss of honor—and many of the Confederate dead were sacrificed to honor rather than to any realistic hope of victory. If surrender and honor could be reconciled, however, southerners could accept defeat more easily. In the long run, honor provided a justification that Confederates thought made the war worthwhile, and a fierce resistance was one way to preserve honor. Thus after the war, a South Carolinian salved his damaged ego, claiming that "there is no humiliation in our position after such a struggle as we made for freedom from Yankees." There were other consolations, including martyrdom and the memory of one's "superhuman struggles and sacrifices," but honor included these.[27]

The unexpected lengths one would go to avoid or postpone defeat furnished one sign of a stout, fierce resistance. Slave soldiers and emancipation surely fit that criterion, for who in 1860–61 would have guessed that the South would ever voluntarily give up the very institution that had created the turmoil of the 1850s and the war of the 1860s?

The choice was made easier by the logic of desperation, the humiliation that would accompany defeat, and the realization of slavery's probable doom no matter what decision the South made. Gradually southerners realized that if the hated Yankees succeeded in nothing else, they had delivered a mortal wound to the peculiar institution. Under such circumstances one could be very practical in advocating the arming of the slaves for, as Mississippi Congressman John T. Lamkin pointed out, one might as well favor black soldiers, with emancipation as their reward, since the slaves would have freedom whether the Confederacy won or not. "And to tell you the plain truth," he wrote his wife, "I dont [sic] care whether they are or not. . . . Slavery is played out." Congressman Akin's wife put the same ideas more strongly: "Every one I talk to is in favor of putting negroes in the army and that *immediately.* . . . I think slavery is now gone and what little there is left of it should be rendered as serviceable as possible."[28]

The psychology of fear, resignation, and projection were clearly operating here; often describing defeat as subjugation to slavery and despotism, Confederates would secure protection by using slaves for soldiers. Mrs. Akin and Congressman Lamkin could more easily think the unthinkable by telling themselves that slavery had reached its end in any event. Hence to use slave soldiers, with the likely promise of emancipation as their reward, was giving up nothing that had not been lost already. Fear also played its part—not only fear of defeat but also fear of large numbers of blacks out of social control. This, the question again of racial adjustment, would be solved in a grisly way, perhaps, if blacks went into the army. The thought that if the South put blacks to fighting some would die mollified Congressman Akin's wife. If that were not done, "there will soon be more negroes than whites in the country and they will be the free race. *I want to see them got rid of soon.*" A Virginia newspaper urged its readers to conquer their prejudices so that the war would not destroy the "flower of the country." As for the slaves, "surely they are good enough for Yankee bullets."[29]

But what does surrender of a basic war goal mean? The proposal generated some disturbing conclusions, which became more disturbing as the policy became more widely advocated. For if slavery was a cause of war, then if the South placed slaves in the army and emancipated them, there was no reason, some Confederates thought, to continue the war. In March 1865, a Mississippi newspaper editor was enraged by the proposal to put slaves in the army and emancipate them. Rather than support such a policy, "we shall advocate an immediate peace upon the best terms that may be attended to us." Emancipation would be "a total abandonment of the chief object of this war," and state rights would be lost with it. "Why fight one moment longer," he asked, "if the object and occasion of the fight is dying, dead or damned?" Why indeed? And he was by no means the only disillusioned Confederate to ask this question. A month later, John W. Brown, a Union Whig of Camden, Arkansas, mourned that putting slaves in the army made "a dangerous experiment and will fail in the results anticipated." It was, as he pointed out, "giving up the principles upon which we went into the War." Fearing the worst, he reached the obvious conclusion: "We had better make terms while we can, than to persist in a cause to the utter destruction of our men, and their families, and all we have and then have to submit at the last." In Virginia, the editor of the *Lynchburg Republican* thought that "if our people are not capable of vindicating their title to property in negroes, then they ought to quietly surrender the question, stop the war, abolish slavery, and confess themselves eternally disgraced."[30]

In turning their backs on slavery, "giving up the principles upon which we went into the war," southerners also gave up that which most fundamentally distinguished South from North. They were denying the basis of whatever nationalism they had at a time when the Union had attained impressive military successes. This denial and defeat, combined with faltering support from religion, not only resulted in soldier desertion and civilian defeatism but also made many Confederates feel betrayed.

And what of those who agreed to secession only reluctantly, who left the Union for no other reason than to preserve slavery? Would they not feel a particular sense of betrayal when their leadership performed the bait-and-switch tactic that pushed the South toward emancipation? And would not many who had had more positive views of secession join them? To ask the question answers it. North Carolina Congressman Josiah Turner, Jr., thought the policy "made our subjugation inevitable." He felt it "would teach him [Turner] to take sides with the enemy. When the President arms the slaves he seals the doom of the Confederacy; he may then speak to the undertaker, and write its epitaph."[31]

North Carolinians seemed particularly upset. One editor, scoffing with surprise, thought the idea "farcical, if not down right derangement"; later, ready to quit the war, he bitterly noted that southern politicians had assumed the "extra-Constitutional position that each State had the right to separate from the common government. . . . Now mark you," he wrote, "all this was done *for the preservation and perpetuation of slavery.*" Clearly revealing his sense of betrayal, he went on to claim that "sober men . . . are ready to enquire, if the South is willing to abolish slavery as a condition of carrying on the war, why may it not be done, as a condition of *ending the war?*" Governor Vance asserted that the proposal to arm and emancipate slaves would "surrender the entire question which has ever separated the North from the South, would stultify ourselves in the eyes of the world, and render our whole revolution nugatory—a mere objectles [sic] waste of human life." William W. Holden, by now a bitter enemy of Vance, agreed with this assessment. Unlike Vance, who saw no alternative but to fight on, Holden saw the change of policy as a reason to give up and underlined his views in an early 1865 editorial in which he labeled the emancipation and slave soldier proposal "a confession of subjugation. It surrenders the great point upon which the two sections went to war." William Alexander Graham, Confederate senator from North Carolina, concurred. When General Lee advocated enlistment and emancipation of slaves, Graham threw up his hands in despair. "With such wild schemes and confessions of dispair [sic] as this," he wrote, "it [is] high time to attempt peace." Governor William Smith of Virginia justifiably and anxiously informed his senate that North Carolina strongly opposed the idea of slave soldiers and that "one of her Senators has declared that if the policy should be adopted by the Confederate Government his state would regard the institution of slavery as abolished and having gone into the revolution for its preservation, she would no longer have a motive to continue the struggle."[32]

For many Confederates, the implications of slave soldiers and emancipation were much more disturbing than merely questioning why they had gone to war and whether they could, or should, drop out. Independence could be sought for its own sake, an alternative that Paul D. Escott emphasizes, but after defeat, which now seemed close at hand, that goal would be ashes. Or they could seek refuge in the concept of honor, but that was clutching at straws.[33]

The southern attitudes enumerated above reinforced each other, added converts to the unconscious acceptance of the bitter pill of defeat, and increased the taste of dust and ashes in the mouths of some of the most determined and valiant Confederates. The history of the twentieth century and the American experience of the last twenty years are convincing reminders that an unsuccessful war, no matter what the reasons for failure, provides one of the most powerful influences motivating a people to reevaluate its goals, attitudes, and opinions. For as the war drew to a close in the latter half of 1864 and on into 1865, what had the South to show for its efforts, its bloodshed, and its commitment except long casualty lists, depleted coffers, and the loss of slavery? If some pretended to fight on solely for independence, white supremacy, or honor, they did so because nothing else remained to fight for. It provided their answer to the haunting question, why fight at all?

On a much more fundamental level, however, the dual questions of slave soldiers and emancipation concerned racial adjustment and thus transcended practicality. In the face of clear evidence to the contrary, some, but by no means all, Confederates maintained that slaves simply could not, and would not, fight. A people obsessed for generations with the fear of slave rebellions now pondered whether blacks would fight.

This issue brought into doubt what southerners had long believed about black people and thus led to some disquieting conclusions. Blacks had a role to play, southerners had long thought, but not that of a soldier. To argue that blacks could fight, but probably would not fight for the Confederacy, seemed logical enough. Thus Congressman Henry C. Chambers remarked that Confederates could promise the Negro a home, "but the Yankee said he would give him a home and the right of property. The President can offer him no motive which the enemy cannot easily counteract by offering him a higher one." But Chambers went on to claim, despite the evidence furnished daily by the Union army, that "the negro cannot be made a good soldier. The law of his race is against it."[34]

Others echoed this conclusion. Congressman Thomas S. Gholson maintained that "you cannot raise and educate slaves to become soldiers" and emphasized the issue of racial adjustment by pointing out that "you can not fight white and black in the same army, without putting them on the same footing." Howell Cobb got to the heart of the question: arming slaves was "the most pernicious idea that has been suggested since the war began," for "if slaves will make good soldiers our whole theory of slavery is wrong." John M. Daniel, wartime editor of the *Richmond Examiner*, remarked to his readers (November 8, 1864) that "we surrender our position whenever we introduce the negro to arms. If a negro is fit to be a soldier, he is not fit to be a slave; and if any large portion of the race is fit for free labor—fit to live and be useful under the competitive system of labor—then the whole race is fit for it." With devastating logic, Daniel pointed out that if the South rewarded the black man with emancipation for service in the army, then, contrary to what southerners had contended, "his freedom is therefore a boon—it is a better state—a natural good of which our laws deprive him and keep him from." Robert Barnwell Rhett, Jr., came to the same conclusion:

> But if the slavery of the Confederate States be not the best condition for the negroes amongst us—if they are fit for freedom and manumission be a desirable improvement in their political *status*—an improvement which they may claim as a reward for service—then the justification heretofore set up for holding them as slaves is false and unfounded. Then is the base of our institution but shifting sand, and the superstructure, unable to support the beating of the winds and the waves, must fall.[35]

Governors Vance and Brown made the same judgment and expressed it in remarkably similar language. Brown told his state legislators that if God had created blacks for slavery, then He did not intend that they serve as soldiers, for "whenever we establish the fact that they are a military race, we destroy our whole theory that they are unfit to be free." Both concluded that "when we arm the slaves we abandon slavery." These Confederates did not then proceed to the conclusion that slave soldiers should bring equality. Rather, they would deny equality by denying slave soldiers.[36]

The manpower problem and the issue of slave soldiers were not the only features of the Confederate emancipation issue. In January 1865, Jefferson Davis had sought to secure diplomatic recognition of the Confederate government and help in breaking the Union blockade by sending Duncan F. Kenner, a Confederate congressman and one of the South's largest slaveowners, to Europe. Kenner's mission, which was kept secret at the time, was to propose to the governments of Great Britain and France that a bargain be struck whereby the Confederacy would be recognized as a legal and actual government. In return, the Confederacy would emancipate its slaves to meet the strong objections that some Britons and French had to slavery.

The fact of Jefferson Davis's proposal is startling enough, for taken with the slave soldier proposal it indicates the desperation to which the course of the war had driven the Confederacy, and it also reflects an unusual flexibility of mind on Davis's part. But the result of the mission was negative. Upon his arrival in Europe, Kenner had made contact with James M. Mason, the Confederate envoy to Great Britain, and

John Slidell, the Confederate representative to Napoleon III of France, and told the surprised diplomats of Davis's policy. After some hesitation, in March 1865 Mason spoke with Lord Palmerston, the British prime minister, on the question of recognition. He did not explicitly offer emancipation but hinted at it broadly enough that Palmerston knew well enough what was on Mason's mind and gave Mason to understand that emancipation would have no effect on British policy. Slidell had a similar interview with Napoleon, who told Slidell politely but firmly that he would not recognize the Confederacy unless Britain did also and that in any event French policy toward the Confederacy had never taken slavery into consideration. This response was a surprise to some Confederates. Howell Cobb, for example, had argued against the use of black soldiers, urging the government to "yield to the demands of England and France and abolish slavery, and thereby purchase their aid."[37]

Kenner returned to Richmond and reported his lack of success to Davis, who, doubtless less naive than Cobb, probably expected the result. Because the mission was carried out in secret and few people outside the inner circles of government knew about it at the time, it has only a minor role here, for it had little effect upon the morale and will of the Confederacy. Nevertheless, the Kenner mission is important as a major initiative in Confederate foreign policy and for illustrating both Davis's commitment to independence and his desperation in the final weeks of the Confederacy's existence.[38]

ATTEMPTING TO fend off defeat thus required Confederates to undergo a radical change in their thinking, as suggested in an earlier chapter. Some among them added new knowledge to their beliefs, emphasizing that the outcome of the war fulfilled God's will. Others, and the groups are by no means mutually exclusive, altered their beliefs, discovering that their war to preserve slavery actually constituted a war for independence, a revision of goals that had taken some Confederates by surprise. Some who reduced the dissonance between their knowledge of the original Confederate war goal (to preserve slavery) and their knowledge of the new Confederate war goal (to achieve independence) felt betrayed; others felt renewed, at least until their religious views intruded. Still other Confederates had felt they could abandon the war effort because they had preserved their honor by the losing fight and because, whatever the outcome of the war, they expected to be able to maintain white supremacy. However different the assumptions and modes of thought, all these lines of logic led to the eventual acceptance of defeat. There was another prominent view: if guilt over slavery had the importance we believe, then many Confederates could accept defeat, indeed embrace it, not in spite of the end of slavery, but on condition of its demise.

Beyond that, however, the weakening of old assumptions about slavery often led to individual anguish that betrayed a guilty conscience. Was the South waging a conflict over a questionable institution? If so, not only must the Confederates bear the blame for slavery itself, they must also bear the burden of the blood shed to protect it. This raised the stakes, for the question stood as an indictment of the past as well as the present. Emancipation would become a confession that the South had "for 80 years, or more, been guilty of fostering an institution which was wrong."[39]

No thoughtful Confederate could allow himself to reach such conclusions without suffering anguish of heart and mind about the basis upon which southern society rested and about the men who had died to sustain it. L. Q. C. Lamar, for one, had "never entertained a doubt of the soundness of the Southern system until he found that slavery could not stand a war." Mrs. Chesnut, who confided opinions on so many subjects to her diary, had confessed her unease over the war and the lengthening casualty lists after only a year of fighting. Would success repay all that blood? "After all, suppose we do all we hoped. Suppose we start up grand and free—a proud young republic. Think of all those young lives sacrificed! If three for one be killed, what comfort is that? What good will that do. . . ? The best and bravest of one generation swept away! . . . But those poor boys of between 18 and 20 years of age . . . they are washed away, literally, in the tide of blood. There is nothing to show they were ever on earth." By 1863 she had become even more distraught, commenting about the sour remarks of newspaper editors who made the maimed and wounded soldiers "think that all this is for nothing—that they are wounded and die in vain." And Chesnut clearly feared that the dead had sacrificed themselves uselessly because in January 1865 she and her friends grieved over their dead with the bitter thought that "their lives had been given up in vain. . . . What a cohort would rise to view if thoughts took shape. Splendid young life sacrificed—in vain."[40]

Others came to similar conclusions. A North Carolina editor declared as early as July 1863 that he stood for peace because, among other reasons, "there has been enough of blood and carnage, enough of widows and orphans, heart broken mothers and sorrowing fathers." Another editor declared in 1864 that the "Courts of Heaven resound with one great prayer; the supplications of a sorrowing people for the return of *peace*. Weary with blood and slaughter, surfeited with tears and suffering, appalled at the dire calamities which war has inaugurated, the heart of the nation pants for relief." A few months later he offered more pointed warnings. "The Rubicon is passed," he wrote, and one could not retrace one's steps and give up the war. Still, he had never favored secession in the first place, so he comforted himself with the thought that "the crime of bringing it on does not rest upon our heads."[41]

Although this particular editor also asserted that it was necessary to fight until victory to justify the loss of so much blood and treasure, other Confederates had doubts. "God forbid," said Congressman James T. Leach, "that I should ever endorse the last man and last dollar principle unless from dire necessity; the idea alone is enough to freeze the blood of humanity in the heart of any Christian." After the conflict ended, some of Mrs. Chesnut's friends "were talking of a nation in mourning. They were deploring the glorious young blood poured out like rain on the battlefield. For what?" they asked. And she added some lines from Sir Walter Scott that indicated her own misgivings: "Never let me hear that brave blood has been shed in vain. No. It sends a roaring voice down through all time."[42]

Even the Georgia legislature reflected some of this feeling. Although it blamed the war and its prolongation on the Union, it nevertheless believed that the "guilt of its continuance" would rest on both governments and both peoples unless the state and central governments of the two sides used "their earnest efforts to put an end to this unnatural, unchristian and savage work of carnage and havoc." Although the legislature also concluded that full prosecution of the war must accompany peace overtures to the Union, nevertheless the key word here is guilt—clearly Georgians felt concern about the moral implications of what they were doing and admitted officially that they could be responsible for some of the resulting evils.[43]

When the Confederate leadership changed southern war goals from slavery to independence in late 1864 and early 1865, it heightened this combination of resentment, guilt, and disillusion. As the ultimate outcome of the Confederate debate on emancipation became clear, remorse and anger struck many reluctant Confederates, for the government's policy created dissonance. Such people could no longer reconcile their country's action (wage war to save slavery) with its object (give up slavery). They would have to change either action or object. Until such a change occurred, the resulting dissonance produced severe discomfort, reflected in attempts to prevent emancipation and the arming of slaves and efforts to prove the primacy of other war goals. But finding guilt a difficult emotion to overcome, at Christmas 1864 many Confederates regretted "this hellish work at which angels weep" and reminded each other that a restoration of the Union months earlier could have saved slavery and precious lives as well.[44]

In March 1865, as the Confederate government finally ended the debate over black soldiers, Virginia's Senator Robert M. T. Hunter revealed the stress in the minds of many Confederates when he futilely attempted to block the movement. When Congress made the decision to enlist slaves, it would call into question the decision of 1861 and make the alternative rejected then look attractive now. It would acknowledge, Hunter said, that "we were wrong in denying to the old Government the right to interfere with the institution of slavery and to emancipate slaves." Why, then, had the South seceded and provoked the war? And why did that war continue, for, as Hunter pointed out, to continue the war under such circumstances amounted to "an abandonment of this contest." Robert Barnwell Rhett, Jr., revealed his distress when he reminded Confederates that South Carolina left the Union because of the slavery issue and that "slavery and independence must stand together. . . . To abandon our most essential institution is to abandon and give up that very thing for which we began the fight." Hunter drew the most disturbing conclusion: if slavery caused the war (Hunter had believed in 1860–61 that it did), and if the Confederacy had abandoned the war goal of preservation of slavery, how could it justify the loss of so many lives to save it? How could one justify one's emotional investment and the expenditure of so much blood and treasure? "If this is so," cried Hunter, "who is to answer for the hundreds of thousands of men who had been slain in the war? Who was to answer for them before the bar of heaven?"[45]

Orthodox Protestant Christians would have a difficult time with that question, and some clearly found the answer more disturbing than they could admit. They saw more than betrayal of Confederate war goals; they felt also a betrayal of the deep voice of a disturbed conscience. As Martin Luther had written more than three centuries earlier, "This is the worst of all these ills, that the conscience cannot run away from itself, but it is always present to itself and knows all the terrors of the creature which such things bring even in this present life. . . . [The] greatest of all these horrors and the worst of all ills is to have a judge. . . . For this is the nature of a guilty conscience, to fly and be terrified, even when all is safe and prosperous, to convert all into peril and death."[46]

Most Christian southerners read their Bibles and believed them. They had read many times those portions that seemed to justify slavery, but they had read other portions that seemed less supportive, including the book of Hebrews (10:31), which reminded them that "it is a fearful thing to fall into the hands of the living God." Who could blame Confederates for growing troubled? If blacks could fight, they must be unfit for slavery; but who could fault southerners who tried to avoid that conclusion (the logic of which placed their souls in jeopardy) by insisting that blacks would not be effective in combat? This last hope for Confederate victory would therefore be a false hope, and the South had to accept defeat with all its horrors, both real and imagined, or else avoid it by last-minute, superhuman effort. Who could censure those who therefore claimed that constitutional issues, or the desire for independence, or the need to uphold honor had caused the war, not slavery? For to answer Hunter's question, one must justify the bloodshed by inventing a new war goal, else those multitudes in blue and gray had died for nothing.

Perhaps this need for vindication helps to explain the South's stubborn and increasingly shrill excuse for continuing slavery despite the undercurrent of guilt and increasing defensiveness that runs throughout the antebellum period, through the war, and into the generation beyond. Perhaps the theory also helps to account for the appeals to abstract ideals of liberty and republicanism as southern behavior became, in the words of Charles G. Sellers, quoted earlier, "a disguised protest against, or perhaps an escape from, the South's daily betrayal of its liberal self." Perhaps this also reflected the Shakespearean saying about those who protest too much.[47]

Early in the twentieth century, W. E. B. Du Bois noted the effect of such attitudes. "Deeply religious and intensely democratic as are the mass of the whites, they feel acutely the false position in which the Negro problems place them. . . . The color line is a flat contradiction to their beliefs and professions." These words had as much truth during the Civil War as when Du Bois wrote. A sense of sin, accompanied by a feeling of guilt and a fear of imminent punishment, forced the answer to those Christian believers who asked the inevitable question, why did God let this happen to me? From some Confederates the answer was that defeat was a just punishment—punishment for the sins of slavery, of making war, of pride—take your choice.[48]

The time came, therefore, when the force of events plus the power of guilt overwhelmed the reasoning of those who sought to maintain slavery. They argued that they did not really like slavery; that regardless of the outcome of the war, the institution would end; that if they acted with skill they could still retain white supremacy and the benefits of slave labor without the slave system; and that in any event they were better off without it. Thus by the end of the war Confederates had begun to raise black regiments, with the implied promise of emancipation. In the face of war, of runaways, of black soldiers in the Union army, and of increasing difficulty in getting slaves to work, southerners could reduce the psychological discomfort caused by dissonant, alternative policies about slavery only by turning to new arguments, thereby adding new cognitive elements. Having taken warnings of war and catastrophe with insufficient seriousness, such people became more penitent and responsive to the fate the future might have in store for them. Thus, as Kenneth Stampp noted, "The readiness, if not always good grace, with which most Southerners accepted the abolition of slavery." For example, Henry S. Foote declared in 1866 that few intelligent southerners "would now resuscitate this defunct system if they had it ever so much in their power to do so" and predicted that the South would "be far better off in time to come *without slavery* than *with it*." A young Georgian became convinced that slavery "was the greatest drawback" to the South and that "with its abolishment a new era has begun for us and that in our apparent destruction we will yet find our salvation and ultimate independence." Slaveowners who had felt a sense of unease if not actual guilt over slavery also had their reward. "When at last, they lost the profits and conveniences of slavery," says Stampp, "they won the chance to live in peace with themselves and with their age. It was not a bad exchange." Other southerners were relieved, eager, and hopeful because they would no longer have to support slaves they did not need.[49]

For some southerners fatalism supplied the new cognitive element. "All things work for good for those who love the Lord," said the tradition. For the South, this became an interpretation of history. If the war destroyed slavery, said the *Milledgeville Confederate Union*, it would not happen because of the wrong of slavery but because of "the moral relaxation and depravity" of southern society, or perhaps because the slaves had had the benefits of Christian protection long enough and could now return to Africa to spread the Word. In either event, the result "had to be," for Providence directed affairs.[50]

Many found the destruction and suffering of the South equally mystifying: "I never question the wisdom of God in permitting them," wrote one southern lady a generation after the war, "but I pondered upon them, and have never yet reached their unfathomable depths." Thomas L. Connelly and Barbara L. Bellows point to the inevitable conclusion. By the end of the war, which seemed to show that God did not side with the South, some southerners came to the frightening conclusion that they were estranged from their Creator, Who had rejected His people. If so, why placate further for victory or slavery or anything else. One need only accept one's fate and get right with God once again. This idea represented a vital mainspring of Confederate acceptance of the verdict of the battlefield and made it easy for men such as William C. Rives suddenly to "accept without hesitation or reserve the constitutional amendment already made for the extinction of slavery—a consummation long & anxiously sought, though in a dif-

ferent mode & by other agencies, by many of the wisest & most il-
lustrious citizens of my own state."[51]

For others pragmatism provided the new element. They correctly
foresaw that the South would be able to keep white supremacy and
most of the benefits of the slave system. In the summer of 1865 a Georgia woman argued that the South could abandon slavery because state
laws still would permit whites to control the black population. As an
official of the Freedmen's Bureau in Richmond told the Joint Committee on Reconstruction in 1866, Virginians preferred blacks to remain
free, and they would not reenslave them if they had the chance: "I
think they would prefer to hold him by their laws, &c., in a situation
which would be slavery in effect but not in name, so as to have the
benefit of his labor without the responsibility of supporting him." In
1868 a South Carolinian "even maintained that the Civil and Criminal
codes could make blacks more completely slaves after emancipation
than they had been before." A former Confederate officer agreed. The
South could recover all it had lost, he thought, "save slavery and even
that will come again under another name." Aspects of proslavery
thought were not erased by the war, and some traditional ideas about
race "retained their validity. . . . To say that emancipation transformed the southern world," writes George C. Rable, "is true but misleading." Even J. D. B. De Bow agreed slavery ought not to be
restored even if it were possible, but the labor system after emancipation was not free labor as northerners understood it: "However pro-
fusely southerners might welcome emancipation, many unconsciously,
and a number both consciously and publicly, looked back longingly on
the former glories of plantation slavery." But the institution itself was
dead. Confederate defeat left behind much windy rhetoric but few re-
grets either at the end of the war or in the years that followed.[52]

Some southern whites could even rationalize black suffrage. Henry
S. Foote advised the South to sustain the freedman's rights "in order
to rescue the white millions of the South from a state of permanent
degradation" (that is, from northern vengeance and carpetbag government). As late as 1869, one of former Confederate Congressman James
Lyons's correspondents advised Virginians to acquiesce in universal
manhood suffrage because only then could they get universal amnesty

"and, thus," he wrote, "put ourselves in a condition to control the slaves—is it not the least and best of all the evils submitted to us?" To accept blacks at the polls would strengthen conservatives and perhaps gain concessions on other points—enfranchisement of all former Confederates. It "may be an evil," wrote one Virginian in New York City, "but White Suffrage here can hardly be esteemed a blessing since this great city is ruled and governed by Poverty, Vice and Ignorance."[53]

Seeking to confront their difficulties in a practical way, southerners relinquished slavery but not racism. Events proved the correctness of the views of those who said that they could control black labor just as well without slavery. Peonage, contract labor, convict leasing, and lien laws served to perpetuate involuntary servitude well into the twentieth century. The South, writes Daniel A. Novak, "had a metamorphosized slave psychology. It had simply adapted its laws to meet the formal structures of the Civil War amendments, in order to retain as much of its old rules of labor control as possible." As Pete Daniel wrote, "Out of the ashes and ruins of the Civil War the shadow of slavery once more crept over the South." Peonage, he noted, "practically reinstituted slavery." As late as the 1920s "all too many planters . . . continued to regard blacks as private property." Henry W. Grady's well-known statement, long after the war, that "the South found her jewel in the toad's head of defeat," was merely coming to a logical conclusion. All had happened for the best because "the shackles that had held her in narrow limitations fell forever when the shackles of the negro slave were broken." "The free negro counts more," Grady added, "than he did as a slave."[54]

But problems still remained. If the South had gone to war because of slavery, white supremacy, the desire to be independent, the wish to preserve honor, and state-rights constitutionalism, but slavery was abandoned, racial control put in question, and independence lost, then it became all the more necessary to justify in other terms the horror of war, the loss of blood and treasure, and the humiliation of defeat. Only honor and state rights remained to soothe hurt feelings by serving as war aims that had been attained by Confederate arms, even though southerners actually had compromised those as well in their effort to keep the Confederacy alive. Nevertheless, more southerners became convinced after the war than before it that they had fought the honorable fight to preserve the Constitution of their fathers from the subversive attacks of Black Republicanism and even from some would-be nationalists within the Confederacy. For most, this soon became the new cognitive element that reduced the psychological discomfort caused by knowledge of alternative policies on slavery. They soon forgot the strong central government—a government at odds with the notion of state rights in its actions if not in its rhetoric—that they had created to fight that war; they also promptly forgot their own decision for emancipation, their high desertion rates, and the suddenness of Confederate collapse.

Chapter Sixteen

State Rights,
White Supremacy, Honor,
and Southern Victory

I N THE FACE of Union success on the battlefield that threatened both
the institution of slavery and the independence of the Confederacy,
and under the threat of internal policies that also threatened slavery,
Confederates were forced to rethink the decisions of 1861. They succeeded in reducing the dissonance between their goal of preserving
slavery and the realization that they would have to emancipate their
slaves by discovering that they had not embarked on secession and
war to preserve slavery or white supremacy at all, but rather to secure
independence. Likewise, during the conflict they had thought about
the centralized government they had created and concluded that they
were fighting less for state rights than for independence and honor and
that any means justified the attainment of those ends. But in the process of this rationalization, Confederates could not help but examine
the attractive features of their rejected alternatives. Moreover, they
could not undertake this national introspection at leisure but were
forced to do so under the pressure applied by advancing Union armies.
Religiously oriented Confederates also felt pressure because they saw
the military situation as God's punishment, perhaps for the sin of slavery, or for the war and its casualties, or for any other sins of which the
people were guilty. This self-examination resulted in a mind-twisting
reorientation of Confederate thought in which guilt and necessity interacted to produce a temporary synthesis that resolved much of their
dissonance.

The synthesis did not last long because Confederate independence
became a forlorn hope by late 1864, and southerners abandoned the
goal completely at Appomattox Court House, Durham Station, Cit-
ronelle, and New Orleans. Once again Confederates had to resolve the

dissonance between their goals and the results. A sampling of the literature of self-justification of the postwar generation reveals that they did not have difficulty with this resolution. Southerners reduced dissonance in several ways, and as they did, slavery and independence both became afterthoughts; southern goals and southern accomplishments became nicely congruent by a process similar to that which occurred when Confederates substituted independence for slavery.

By the end of the war in the spring of 1865, many Confederates had therefore come to accept a new world-view that was more compatible with the reality of the last few years than their old world-view had been. Having fought a war for slavery, they surrendered it unwillingly to Confederate policy and later willingly (though not graciously) to Union policy, for they were coming to the conclusion that they would be able to control black labor just as well without the peculiar institution as with it. Having fought a war for independence (although some Confederates thought this a secondary consideration), they abandoned that goal, too, for they could win independence only by continuing a disastrous war in which God evidently favored their adversary. Confederates had also fought for local control of racial adjustment—meaning white supremacy—and state rights, but the Freedmen's Bureau, the Thirteenth, Fourteenth, and Fifteenth Amendments, and the quest of former slaves for equality seemed to put white supremacy in doubt. And state rights had been compromised by the threat of an all-powerful government first of the Confederacy and then of the Union.

Honor, however, remained, for it was an inward feeling of self-worth, supported by integrity, bravery, and social deference, that enemy armies could damage but could not destroy. Yet former Confederates eventually claimed to have secured all three of these goals: state rights, white supremacy, and honor. How had they been able to do that?

First, one must recall that southerners possessed and enjoyed state rights, white supremacy, and honor before the war. These three features of southern society were as closely intertwined after the war as they had been before it. In the institution of slavery white southerners had ensured their supremacy over their black countrymen, and state rights were supposed to guarantee the maintenance of this supremacy. Any northern violation of southern rights or attack on slavery tended to place southerners in an inferior position, and hence they felt that their honor was infringed upon. Not to uphold the southern position on slavery was therefore dishonorable. The result was that politicians in the antebellum South had competed with one another to prove that they were "sound" on the slavery question but that their opponents were not. This, in turn, reflected on the opponents' sense of honor, and they replied with the charge that it was the other fellows who might compromise the peculiar institution. Thus "the politics of slavery became the politics of the South." William J. Cooper, Jr., characterizes the interrelationship of slavery and honor as one in which "protecting slavery meant considerably more than merely defending their [southerners'] peculiar institution. Protection meant guaranteeing control over their own destiny, a destiny inextricably caught up in slavery. Loss of control meant jeopardizing their freedom and independence, and southerners knew better than anyone else that loss of freedom and independence led to slavery, to a status of abject dependency and subordination. For southerners their institution of slavery was also inseparably intertwined with their sense of honor and equality. . . . Southerners believed the institution of slavery honorable."[1]

If "white supremacy" is substituted for "slavery," the analysis fits the postwar period just as well as it fits the antebellum era. Postwar southerners did not vie for glory on the slavery question, but the candidate who could convince the voters that he was "sound" on white supremacy but that his opponent was not would win the election.

Thus as southerners attempted to regain their sense of control and autonomy, they sought nothing that they had not already had just a few years before. Independence, however, was different. One could say that southerners enjoyed independence within the Union, but this was not exactly what Confederates had wanted. The strike for independence was therefore an attempt to achieve something new, which they had not possessed before. Thus independence had become the direct object of Union military action, as had slavery. But it never had been a purpose of the Union to destroy southern honor, although many northerners were delighted to see the "chiv" taken down several notches. There were some people among the Union leadership who would have destroyed state rights and white supremacy if they could have, but they never had sufficient support either from the people or from the politicians. White supremacy and state rights meant almost as much to northerners as to southerners, as illustrated by postwar political controversies over civil rights for blacks and the general agreement that government must not be too strong. Yet there was discontinuity here. Southerners might doubt that state rights would be viable in the future, and when they saw black soldiers on their streets, they might question whether white supremacy could be maintained. They might feel dishonored because they had been defeated in war. To assume that because these three elements were present in the antebellum South, therefore they could not be real goals in the war, however, is to read history backward, whereas southerners had to live it from day to day. The war did threaten state rights and white supremacy, if not honor, and it was perfectly reasonable for Confederates to set their sights on the maintenance or reestablishment of these threatened characteristics of their culture.

It is a question of perceptions, similar to the situation when an army retreats even though it may have won a tactical or strategic victory. If the people perceive retreat as defeat, it will be defeat, at least in a sense, and will affect morale accordingly. By the same token, if southerners perceived that their social and political systems had been put in jeopardy, or their honor had been questioned, they would act accordingly. And Lincoln's election did seem to threaten southern feelings of self-worth in overexcited and sometimes paranoid, parochial politicians. Furthermore, Lincoln was perceived to be a threat to slavery—that was what secession and war had been all about—and he seemed to threaten state rights as well because the Federal government, if it had a mind to tamper with slavery in the states, could not do so without trespassing the bounds of state rights as southerners understood them. The southern achievement of these goals was therefore a real accomplishment, not simply a return to the status quo ante.

How, THEN, had former Confederates managed to claim state rights, white supremacy, and honor as their victory?

In the first place, they reduced the psychological discomfort created by the knowledge that they had gone to war to preserve slavery but had not achieved that goal by adding a new cognitive element consistent with the reality created on the battlefield. Just as they dis-

covered independence to be the real goal during the struggle, former
Confederates began to understand after their defeat that all along
they actually had fought for state rights. Even the centralizers and
modernizers, forgetting the wartime system they had created, made
this assertion, as if stating a truth always understood, merely requiring mention to gain universal belief. It seemed axiomatic—independence had not constituted the main issue of the conflict after all, or
even slavery, but state rights.

Jefferson Davis believed this as much as anyone else. Righteously
proclaiming state rights in the postwar period, he forgot the "nationalist" Davis who led a powerful Confederate government and who
is so well portrayed in the publications of Emory M. Thomas and Paul
D. Escott. During the fighting, as Escott points out, Davis had talked
state rights even as he attempted to promote centralization and modernization in his pursuit of independence. In frustration and anguish,
Davis had asserted in 1865 that "malcontents" deliberately seized upon
the discontent created by a hard contest and "execution of the rigorous
laws that were necessary" to victory and, invoking state rights, have
"sown the seeds of disintegration."[2]

Hence the secondary war goal, the maintenance of state rights, not
only outlived the debacle but was actually revived by defeat. One
would think that, as in the case of slavery, Confederates would abandon a doctrine that had proved so unprofitable, and that, like slavery,
they had admitted to be a cause of an unsuccessful struggle.

A number of historians have noted this curious phenomenon. In his
examination of the Confederate movement for emancipation, Robert F.
Durden contends that a major element of the "southern apologia" for
the hostilities "was the emphatic denial that the South's primary aim in
fighting was the preservation of slavery. Liberty, independence, and
especially states' rights were advanced by countless southern spokesmen as the hallowed principles of the lost cause." Steven A. Channing
concludes that South Carolinians saw the war as a necessary risk and
felt secession presented the only practical way to avoid the destruction
of the peculiar institution. Constitutional arguments merely provided a
convenient smoke screen. "After the war," however, South Carolinians
"came forward to clothe the traumatic failure of the movement in the

The Shirley House during the Vicksburg siege. The grimness of war is reflected in the scarred grounds of this stately house, used by one of the Union generals for his headquarters. The picture also shows the beginning of "Logan's Sap," a tunnel dug by the Union under the Confederate siege defense. (Courtesy of the Chicago Historical Society.)

Ruins at Columbia, South Carolina, 1865. Myths long held that all of Columbia, like Atlanta, had been wantonly burned by the order of William T. Sherman during his infamous march to the sea. Recently, Marion B. Lucas has brilliantly argued that only about one-third of Columbia burned, and even that part burned more as a result of an "accident of war" than of Sherman's inhumanity. (Courtesy of the Chicago Historical Society.)

Ruins at Charleston, South Carolina, 1865. Union troops perhaps did show a special tinge of vindictiveness at Charleston—where the war's shooting had first begun. (Courtesy of the Chicago Historical Society.)

Overleaf: Concert of the Advance Guard, a painting by A. De Neuville. It has not seemed to matter much that the artist probably had the Franco-Prussian War in mind: to Southerners, this sardonic scene represents a "violation" of the South's sanctity and integrity. The emotional impact of Sherman's thrust could not more poignantly be depicted than by this representation of "a squad of Yankee invaders, amid the ruins left by battle, further defiling one family's possessions." (Reproduced from the photogravure by John S. Chavalier.)

Confederates Under Fire at Petersburg, a watercolor by W. L. Sheppard. This 1886 artwork, based on a wartime sketch, depicts the terror in the trenches during the war's longest siege. Bruce Catton observed that such artworks sometimes "put a strange pastoral tint on the grimmest battlefield"; but he also remembered that during his Michigan boyhood the Catton household's set of *Battles and Leaders* was immensely popular with every Civil War veteran in the area. (Courtesy of the American Heritage Picture Collection.)

Confederates Spiking Guns at Appomattox, a watercolor by W. L. Sheppard. Here the artist has vividly conveyed the resolute sadness, and the grim tasks being performed by Lee's bedraggled veterans as the end drew near. (Courtesy of the American Heritage Picture Collection.)

Two decorated veterans on their way to the seventy-fifth anniversary commemoration of the Battle of Gettysburg. Two badge-emblazoned ancient warriors reminisce about the glory of yesteryear, and the war wherein above all else the North had preserved the Union—and the South had retained honor. (Courtesy of the Chicago Historical Society.)

Memorial Hall at New Orleans, Louisiana. Once the National Headquarters of the United Confederate Veterans and now the Confederate Museum, this building also has been a repository of archival and museum mementos, and the home of the Louisiana Historical Association. It was here that Jefferson Davis lay in state after his death. Note the building's resemblance to a church. It even has stained glass windows, one of which is dedicated to Father Abram J. Ryan, the "poet-priest of the Confederacy" who composed the lyrics: "Furl that Banner, softly, slowly! Treat it gently—it is holy." And gently, indeed, they did. The building is, perhaps, the principal "cathedral" of a "religion," the civil religion of the Lost Cause. (Courtesy of Glen R. Conrad, editor of *Louisiana History.*)

misty garments of high constitutional rights and sacred honor."
Clement Eaton noted with agreement the observation of John W.
DeForest, a Union officer, that the southerners he had met in South
Carolina ignored slavery as a cause of the conflict, maintaining instead
that constitutional issues had brought on the crisis. Kenneth Stampp
points out the prevalence of such views. After the surrender southern
whites "denied that slavery had anything to do with the Confederate
cause, thus decontaminating it and turning it into something they could
cherish." He suggests that they may have done this to avoid the guilt
over slavery long held by many slaveholders. James L. Roark denies the
guilt but sees the same result. True enough, before the war, and during
it, many southerners thought slavery so basic to their system that they
fought to preserve it. "But after the war," Roark notes, "planters could
often be heard to argue that the Confederacy was founded on other
principles—liberty, independence, and especially states' rights." Roark
contends that this behavior "is evidence of a nearly universal desire to
escape the ignominy attached to slavery in the postwar period"; consequently, southerners argued the constitutional point instead.[3]

But why and how did the switch take place?

To be able to live with himself, and to avoid loss of honor, a man had
to feel that he had made worthwhile and proper efforts, else he would
once again fear the bar of heaven, as Senator Hunter had in regard to
slavery. How did he reconcile defeat and death with the knowledge of
his own responsibility for bringing on the conflict in the first place?

So ingrained were feelings of guilt, betrayal, and regret at alternative decisions that they lasted beyond 1865. Years later, many Confederates could justify their actions and make sense of the results only
by reference to the goal of state rights. The morality of slavery, so
often asserted in the antebellum and war eras, did not relieve the psychological discomfort of the postwar generations. For many former
Confederates, proslavery defenses crumbled so immediately and so totally after the fighting ended that such an argument would no longer
have been respectable. Early in the struggle Mrs. Chesnut had asked,
"What are they fighting for," if not slavery? Back came the reply: "For
Southern rights, whatever that is!" So they had recourse to a proper
constitutional doctrine of state rights, which, when mixed in varying

proportions with white supremacy and honor, reduced their dissonance in three ways.[4]

First, southerners could change one of the two conflicting elements
that created the dissonance. Thus most southerners came to deny that
slavery had caused secession. Reuben Davis blamed fate, not any person or event. "Rather," he wrote, "it was the inevitable consequence
of a great current of popular passion, resistless in its force, and sweeping everything before it." When a northern newsman discussed the
question with delegates to the South Carolina constitutional convention in September 1865, his head fairly spun with the various explanations he received. "It is already a question how the state got into Rebellion," wrote Sidney Andrews:

> "Disunion was born in the parishes," said an up-country delegate. "The
> political leaders carried us out," said one merchant to me. "The Rebellion
> came from the people," urged a man who had been a colonel in the Rebel
> army. "We went out to save slavery," argued Delegate [James L.] Orr.
> "We went out for State rights," responded Delegate Dunovant. "The
> woman tempted us, and we did eat," answered delegate Summer. . . . "I
> begin to wonder, after all," said the mayor of one of the back cities, "if
> there was any real occasion for us to go to war." "You never'll get us into
> another war till we know exactly what it is about," remarked a Columbia
> merchant in my hearing.

In a similar manner, General James Longstreet reputedly declared
after Appomattox Court House that he would not fight again unless he
clearly felt it necessary. Even during hostilities disillusioned questioning of the conflict occurred, reflected, for example, in a pathetic entry
in J. B. Jones's diary. "Oh for peace once more," he wrote. "Will this
generation, *with their eyes open*, and their memories fresh, ever go to
war again?"[5]

These last few statements portended danger; they confessed that
the South had sacrificed lives for no particular reasons or for reasons
no one understood. Therefore, it became necessary to justify that horror and erase that uncertainty; but one could not do so by mere hero
worship or battle accounts. Southerners needed something to be *for*
that would mend damaged self-respect, not just something to be

against. They required this not only for the self-respect of the veterans and their civilian comrades, but to ensure that future generations would interpret the war with proper respect for those who had served. In their speeches to former soldiers, Confederate veterans constantly repeated this theme, so often in fact that it is clear these orators meant and fully believed what they said. "We fought for the Constitution," declared one. "We went to war . . . to save the Constitution as we read it," asserted another. The shift of arguments from the vulnerable slavery issue to the abstract principle of constitutionality was, says Howard Dorgan, "immensely helpful to the apologists. They could defend abstract principles without a close examination of actual societal practices protected by these principles." The future would have to understand that the South had not taken up arms to save slavery.[6]

The argument therefore shifted: if the South had not fought for slavery, it had fought for state rights, constitutional government, and honor. These arguments constituted a basic theme in the social support that Confederate veterans provided one another. The points meant just as much to former Confederate civilians, of course. Thus in November 1866, the formerly militant *Charleston Mercury*, run by Robert Barnwell Rhett, Jr., quietly mewed that differing theories of government had caused the war. Rhett, Sr., once a fire-eating secessionist congressman, maintained in 1867 that secession occurred "on account of one cause only—the usurpations of the Northern States. . . . When . . . this whole instrument lost its character, and, from a limited Government, the Government of the United States was clearly lapsing into a limitless despotism, the Southern States seceded." Former Senator Williamson S. Oldham agreed:

> Whatever false or incidental issues were raised during the war to arouse the passions, influence the judgement, and control the actions of men, there was, in fact, but one great paramount question between the parties, and that was, whether the Constitution of the United States created a government for a single political society, and consolidated the pre-existing communities composing the several States into one great political family—or whether each State constituted an independent political sovereignty.

Oldham dismissed slavery as merely a "subordinate" issue.[7] Virginia's Senator Robert M. T. Hunter, who had talked about both slavery and state rights before the war, had somewhat different ideas in 1876. He admitted that slavery "was cause enough to have produced such a result." But "fear of mischief far more extensive" presented the real problem. Southerners, he wrote, "determined to make a holocaust of all that was dear to them on the altars of war sooner than submit without resistance to the loss of liberty, honor and property by a cruel abuse of power and a breach of plighted faith on the part of those who had professed to enter with them into a union of justice and fraternal affection." Given the alternative of losing constitutional rights as they understood them or "armed resistance," southerners chose the latter.[8]

Henry S. Foote also emphasized state rights, believing that the Union had broken up because of an attempt "to avoid the imaginary danger of consolidation." Reuben Davis looked at events from a somewhat different perspective. In his memoirs he wrote of a "combination" formed to destroy slavery and emphasized that "this was held to be an infraction of that voluntary compact which held the States together. . . . Nevertheless," he recalled, "whichever might be the right interpretation of the Constitution, I was in favor of war if necessary to secure our rights."[9]

In a biting attack, lost-cause apologist Albert T. Bledsoe admitted that the "unjust treatment of the slavery question, by which the compacts of the Constitution" were "grossly violated," provided one basic reason for secession. But the title of his book, *The War between the States, or, Was Secession a Constitutional Right Previous to the War of 1861–65?* clearly showed that in 1866 Bledsoe thought the constitutional question bore the greatest responsibility. Long after the war former Confederate Congressman J. L. M. Curry took the argument further back into history. The conflict "originated in the convention which framed the Constitution." Slavery merely presented "the occasion, the incitement, which developed widely divergent, fundamental differences as to the character and functions of the Federal Government."[10]

These men, Rhett, Oldham, Hunter, Bledsoe, Curry, and others, had much support. Alexander H. Stephens spent his early postwar years cranking out in two volumes a deadly dull defense of the Confederacy, titled *A Constitutional View of the Late War between the States*. Slavery no longer supplied a cornerstone. Now the war "had its origin in *opposing principles*, which, in their action upon the *conduct of men*, produced the ultimate collision of arms." These conflicting principles "lay in the organic Structure of the Government of the States. . . . The contest was between those who held it [the central government] to be strictly Federal in its character, and those who maintained that it was thoroughly National. It was a strife between the principles of Federation, on the one side, and Centralism, or Consolidation, on the other." Stephens mourned the loss of constitutional liberty and asserted that these governing ideas merely collided over the question of slavery. The idea still circulated a generation after the end of the war.[11]

Jefferson Davis's memoirs, written twenty years after the conflict began, also supported the view that a problem of constitutional interpretation caused the conflict. Confederates, said the erstwhile president,

> fought for the maintenance of their State governments in all their reserved rights and powers, as the only true and natural guardians of the inalienable rights of their citizens. . . . This overthrow of the rights of freemen and the establishment of such new relations required a complete revolution in the principle of the government of the United States, the subversion of the State government, the subjugation of the people, and the destruction of the Union.

The slaves were legally free and the Union back in one piece when Davis wrote, yet he contended that the war had subjugated men and destroyed the Union. And one should understand that he sincerely believed this argument. Davis reduced his postdecision dissonance by confessing that, although the South had not won, it should have. Davis and others who shared his views, excessively proud of the Confederacy and their roles in it, fell into the class proudly labeled "unreconstructed." It was such individuals who established and ran the historical societies, veterans' organizations, and cemetery associations. Like Davis, they reduced their postdecision dissonance by claiming that the South should have won, even if it did not. Their societies and journals excused Confederate errors and quarreled over minor points.

"Exposed to evidence" of their senses, "which unequivocally demonstrates a belief system to be wrong," people like Davis, J. William Jones, and Jubal A. Early tended "to proselyte more vigorously for the belief system." The literature of the lost cause is full of examples. To such former Confederates, it was "still not yet two o'clock on that July afternoon in 1863, the brigades are in position . . . and Pickett . . . waiting for Longstreet to give the word and it's all in the balance. . . . *This time. Maybe this time.*" As for Davis, to the end of his life he actually believed state rights was the basic issue involved in the coming of the Civil War.[12]

Even in their popular fiction southerners of the postwar generation declined to accept the embarrassment of defending slavery. Writers, like politicians, saw slavery as only incidental, a pretext for controversy. They believed in the doom of slavery and thus asserted that the South fought on other grounds, those of constitutional doctrine. States had a constitutional right to secede; this right had not been employed to preserve slavery but to protect southern rights.[13]

If southerners denied that slavery caused the hostilities, they nevertheless accepted racial adjustment, or white supremacy, as an important precipitating factor. The conflict did not result in the immediate triumph of white supremacy, of course. On the contrary, it seemed to deal a powerful blow to the notion, at least temporarily and on the surface. Although southerners castigated Yankee "Puritans" for attempting to interfere in their affairs, the South did not attempt to restore formal slavery. In the post-Reconstruction period, however, white southerners did impose their ideas of proper racial adjustment by means which, though short of declared rebellion, nevertheless often involved guerrilla violence that enabled them to pass important post-Reconstruction legislation restoring white supremacy.[14]

Southerners found a second way to use honor and state-rights doctrine to reduce dissonance by pointing to the positive results of the war and defining them primarily in terms of honor and state rights. One hardly would think that from the southern viewpoint such a war could have a positive outcome. Bluecoats occupied the South, carpetbaggers and scalawags controlled legislatures, slavery had vanished, and war had killed or crippled an entire generation of manhood. Postdecision dissonance obviously existed. The rejected alternative, not seceding, had tempting features after Appomattox that historians easily can imagine if they are willing to use a counterfactual proposition. Nevertheless, James D. Bullock, writing from his voluntary exile in Liverpool, stoutly maintained that when the "score is made up" it would include nothing about the war to cause shame.[15]

Shame stood in opposition to the honor Confederates had wished to preserve. If they could avoid shame, they would maintain honor. The secession crisis was caused not only by fear of northern interference with slavery. It also involved honor, for to submit to northern aggressions on their private property would violate southerners' honor. If they would maintain honor, they had to oppose the shame of subordination to any man, much less to northern Black Republicans. Thus honor had helped to provoke war. "The inhabitant of the Old South," writes Bertram Wyatt-Brown, "was not inspired to shed his own or another's blood for the right to own slaves. . . . A close reading of Southern rhetoric on the eve of the war should make clear the fact that white Southerners were certain their cause was justified by that prehistoric code [of honor]." But valorous performance in war, even a losing war, was not only honorable in itself but would lend an aspect of honor to the resulting peace. To preserve honor, therefore, Confederates had to avoid the shame of Yankee arrogance, or easy capitulation, or black equality, and they had to fight. Indeed, the seeming totality of defeat had intensified feelings of honor, for even when all else seemed lost, honor remained, and the politics of personal honor, constitutionalism, and racism survived the war and continued well into the postwar era.[16]

Southerners therefore continued to display vigilance in preserving any legitimate rights that seemed to be threatened. An unsuccessful attempt to safeguard rights did not entail as much shame as refusal even to try, and the more determined the conflict that resulted, the more honor that accrued to the defeated victim. One Confederate glimpsed the possibilities of this balm for the wounded pride in April of 1865. Searching eagerly for some silver lining, he scanned the political and military sky but did not find an encouraging view. "To me all is dim, dark, impenetrably so, except so far as the ruin of our Southern country is concerned. And what have we gained . . . ?" In despair he went on to note that "we are told there is hope, & a little longer strug-

gle, a few more lives laid down, a few more hardships endured, &
then—what then? 'And there's the rub.'" He found all this very dis-
heartening, but, seeing the outlook not totally dark, he acknowledged
that "our soldiers have won honor."[17]

Honor would not seem to constitute a sufficient reason to go to war,
but in the soft light of the postwar years the jewel of honor and self-
respect shone ever brighter. A South Carolina planter reflected this
notion in May 1865, when he claimed that "there is no humiliation in
our position after such a struggle as we made for freedom from
Yankees." The statement proved that in defeat the South could—and
did—preserve honor. This removed one of the impediments to peace.
No longer did one have to define a peace with honor as a peace with
independence. Honor per se provided prize enough, especially if coupled with white supremacy and the preservation of state rights. Honor
had made the sacrifice worthwhile. It had to, for the end of slavery and
of independence made it necessary that other goals bear the burden of
justification. As one former officer apologetically explained, a rebel
"has but his misfortunes and honor left to him." This romantic notion
has captured some historians. Charles W. Ramsdell, for example,
agreed that the Confederacy may have been doomed, but the people of
the "Lost Cause" won his admiration, for "they went on to the tragic
end, aware of what was impending, without faltering. For that they
will live, with honor, throughout history." That Confederates went on
without faltering is doubtful, as Ramsdell's own analysis proves; but
the victory of honor became part of his own particular mystique of the
Civil War.[18]

Thus Confederates came to believe not only in the rightness of going
to war but also that the struggle merited all the economic and emotional investment the South had put into it. And the social support of
their fellows aided them in this conclusion. They arrived at this justification simply because no one likes trifles; they had to convince themselves of the importance of the reasons they fought.

But more subtle reasons existed as well. One of Jefferson Davis's
correspondents, discouraged by the political outlook in 1874, took the
position that "we demanded nothing but our rights, and were right in
demanding them." Many others in the postwar generation voiced similar notions. In his inaugural address as commander of the United Con-

federate Veterans in 1904, former Lieutenant General Stephen D. Lee not only asserted that "the South fought for liberty and the right of self-government as guaranteed in the Constitution" (that is, state rights) but also claimed honor by contending that "the world is richer and better, purer and greater for the tragic story of forty years ago." "Without the shedding of blood," he reminded his ancient comrades, "there is no redemption."[19]

Former Confederate General E. Porter Alexander's view differed only slightly. State sovereignty and the right of secession "may have been wisdom for that [nineteenth] century," but governments, like nature, must adapt to new conditions, and under modern conditions of national commerce the "'inspired wisdom' of the previous century had now become but foolishness." Few people had then held such Darwinian concepts of politics. But the men of the 1860s had held certain views of liberty, and "it would not be liberty if we could not secede whenever we wished to," Alexander added. The South would have displayed cowardice if it had not resisted. And, he claimed, "posterity should be grateful for our having forced the issue and fought it out to the bitter end." The South had not shed blood in vain. It had created a legacy of devotion, memories, and inspiration for future generations, which, "in the furnace of our affliction, have made a worthier race"; moreover, "in the heat of battle" the bonds of union "were cemented in blood." Thus was honor preserved.[20]

In 1887, former Confederate General Henry R. Jackson had put the matter more boldly. "The people of the South," he said in a public address,

flew to arms not to perpetuate but to imperil their peculiar institution— not to save, but to sacrifice property in defense of honor—nay, to sacrifice life itself rather than tamely submit to insolent wrong. For the right to govern themselves, bequeathed to them by their fathers, they were prepared to immolate all. The principle for which they fought—the only principle of government expansive enough to meet the requirements of advancing civilization . . . was American born. Sun of the modern as compared with the ancient civilization . . . it rose in the west, and now mounts the western firmament red with the blood of Confederate heroes—moist with the tears of Confederate widows and orphans. Eastward shall it continue to roll, carrying with it the blessed light of the

Christian civilization all round the globe. And so surely as it moves it shall bring the day of a final triumph, to be decreed by the mind and conscience of men to time-tested faith. In that triumphal procession Abraham Lincoln shall not move as the rightful President, but Jefferson Davis, the so-called "traitor" leader of a so-called "lost cause". . . . In that silent but majestic march will move "the Confederate States of America," each wearing her truth-studded crown of sovereignty untarnished.[21]

Jefferson Davis agreed with this reasoning, reducing his dissonance by the conjecture that for victory a "cause should be righteous but also that it should be righteously defended." As to the merit of some of his co-defenders he had his doubts. But they must have had enough virtue because he questioned whether the Confederate cause had truly failed and concluded that the results showed "that we were more right than even our own people generally knew."[22]

If the South could salvage honor from an unsuccessful war, it could also preserve it by recalcitrance in the face of what southerners perceived as a vengeful Reconstruction. If they went along with northern demands in the Reconstruction amendments, for example, southerners would imply acceptance of northern values. To avoid such unmanly conduct it thus became the part of honor to resist. The possibility of black citizenship and suffrage undermined a southern honor that depended on a sense of racial superiority. For Radicals to impose their version of Reconstruction on a people with these racial attitudes was a markedly different case from southern acceptance of Reconstruction without resistance. One Georgia politician complained that if he had to eat dirt he preferred "to be compelled to do it," rather than be "invited to it as a desirable meal."[23]

But by the end of Reconstruction and the compromise following the Hayes-Tilden election of 1876, Federal control in matters most important to southerners—race relations and the distribution of political power—had ceased. The Radical Republicans had passed from the scene, and northern Republicans as well as Democrats freely conceded to the southern states their right to dismantle as much of Reconstruction as they pleased, except the Thirteenth Amendment.

Thus southerners who argued that they had fought the war for state rights and white supremacy could point to this situation as evidence of victory. And they could argue that this victory had, in a sense, a greater magnitude than the one for which they had fought from 1861 to 1865. Not only did the North now concede southern rights but it had itself accepted the state-rights philosophy for which the South had battled. The war had not merely brought victory and restored honor to the South but had given enlightenment and benefits to the nation as a whole.

During Reconstruction Confederates who had not sufficiently satisfied their honor by a resort to war to assert their rights could easily assert them by means of peacetime politics. They needed only a recalcitrant frame of mind and a sense of honor that defined honor only in terms of success in getting what they wanted or manly resistance in battling what they did not want. Because southern ideas ultimately prevailed in the Reconstruction experiment, southern pride eventually had satisfaction after the war, if not during it. Not only had they preserved state rights and white supremacy but honor as well. Such people reduced postdecision dissonance by increasing the attractiveness of the chosen alternative. And because honor remained intact, indeed even augmented in strength, generations after the war could hazard the conjecture that perhaps the lost cause had not been lost after all.

This idea added a new cognitive element, the third way in which former Confederates reduced the dissonance between the knowledge of defeat and the knowledge that their own doctrines had brought on an unsuccessful war. In his discussion of the conflict between the alternatives of postwar collaboration and intransigence, William B. Hesseltine emphasized the "compromise by which the 'results of the war' could be shared by Northerners and Southerners alike." This compromise increased the attractiveness of the chosen alternative. It employed state-rights theory and the concept of honor to alter the equation by denying that the South had lost the war. True, Lee surrendered to Grant, but as a number of Radicals noted during the latter phases of Reconstruction, often it did not seem that way at all. "The South surrendered at Appomattox," complained Albion W. Tourgée, but "the North has been surrendering ever since." Even on the supposed losing side, a sufficient number of positive results existed to justify a suspicion that victory had not gone exclusively to the larger battalions.[24]

Former Confederate Congressman John Vines Wright was numbered among those who took this position, who increased the attractiveness of the chosen alternative, and therefore claimed some measure of victory for the South. Stephens had said that the South left the Union, not to destroy the constitutional principles of its government but to preserve them. Wright took this observation one step further. His remarks epitomized the compromise that shared the "results of the war." Wright lamented the conflict and the dangers through which the country had passed and expressed the hope that the experience would serve as a warning for the future. But then he went on to assert that the "North went to war to preserve the Union. The South went to war to preserve the Constitution. Through the madness of the hour both might have been destroyed. In the mercy and wisdom of Almighty God both were preserved."[25]

Wright did not lack for companions. Speaking for the clergy, Randolph McKim contended that the Confederates had fought for self-government, which state rights now protected, and "that the Northern armies saved the Union, while 'the armies of the South saved the rights of the States within the Union.'" Other former Confederates held similar views. Referring to resurgent Unionism and the struggle of both North and South for white supremacy and constitutional principles, Edward A. Pollard contended that the South "had not lost her cause, but merely developed its higher significance." Clearly Jefferson Davis agreed with Pollard. The cause, he informed Lucius B. Northrop, longtime comrade and former Confederate commissary general, was "'buried deeply' but 'not lost.'" Northrop agreed, as did other Davis correspondents, one of whom contended that the abolitionists had constituted the real rebels and that they still feared state rights.[26]

The argument lasted into the twentieth century. Walter Neale, a last-ditch defender of the lost cause, told his comrades of the Eighth Virginia Regiment in 1910 that since the victors fought for union, only the right of secession was lost. All others remained. Each state "fought that her sovereignty might be hers for ever, and each was assured that never should her sovereignty be placed in jeopardy. Thus the defeated countries [as Neale referred to the states] were victorious in defeat." James D. Bulloch, former Confederate naval agent in Great Britain, went further. Since no constitutional amendment denied secession, that right remained. In short, the South, too, could claim her victory. She had not lost the lost cause, after all. "With their old frame of reference shattered," writes Jack P. Maddex, many Confederates—like Edward A. Pollard—could rest content that the "Confederacy had stood only for white supremacy and constitutional limitations. As long as white men governed by limited powers, they might trust that the essence of their 'Lost Cause' remained with them. In time they might forget that they had ever believed in, and loved, plantation slavery."[27]

Much of this compromise lives on; white southerners still claim their share of the victory, although white supremacy is no longer respectable, especially since the civil rights movement of the 1960s. And neither does the notion of honor have the strength it once had, though insofar as it does survive it probably has more strength in the South than in the North. But state-rights constitutionalism still is an important concept today, with adherents not only in the South but throughout the country. The traditional conflict between state and Federal authority continues to be a basic theme in American politics.

Only in the South, however, does today's constitutionalism link to the events of 1861–65. There the views of Wright, Pollard, Davis, and Neale survived generations of solid South politics and remain with us today. "While we did oppose each other, section against section, in a bitter and bloody civil war," observed Jerry L. Russell, the Arkansas editor of the *Civil War Round Table Digest*, "our nation and its form of government was not destroyed . . . but rather strengthened and given a sense of national identity. . . . The American form of government . . . was tested in the furnace of civil war and it withstood that test." Indeed, Russell points out, the test continues because the issues, including state rights and Federal encroachment, still live with us. Russell's perceptiveness was unsubtly underlined by a 1979 article in a suburban Houston newspaper, concerning the local chapters of the United Daughters of the Confederacy. One of the members concluded an interview with the remark that "they [Confederates] weren't fighting to preserve slavery. They were fighting for States' Rights. But I don't suppose we're ever going to get the textbooks changed until they're printed someplace else besides Yankeeland."[28]

THE DEMANDS of war had forced Confederates to compromise their war goals. State rights were compromised first, not without formidable internal opposition, as the Confederacy created a modern, centralized state to manage efficiently an exacting war effort. Slavery went next, destroyed by Union policy and the actions of the slaves themselves but also by Confederates' desperate last-minute gamble to keep the independence movement alive. But the decision came too late, and the South lost independence too. What, then, had Confederates fought for? The loss of slavery and the failure of independence seriously threatened white supremacy, the policy of determining the terms of racial adjustment by the dictates of the southern white population. Southerners did, however, expect to play an important role in determining the future nature of this accommodation even though the war had turned out unsuccessfully. The outcome also menaced honor, but even during the war Confederates managed to salvage this goal by their determined resistance.

To fight for honor, and to emerge from the war scarred but with honor largely intact, represented no small accomplishment. For most Confederates, however, it did not suffice, and they sought to resurrect other goals as well. In time they restored white supremacy by both legal and illegal means, but this too was not enough to meet their needs. They did not regain slavery, nor did they exhibit much desire to have that institution restored, for with renewed white supremacy dictating the terms of race relations they did not seem to have much need of it. The South regained state rights in the compromise of 1876–77 and in the process used it to bolster honor still further and to resume southern direction of race relations. In turn southern independence was substantially restored, albeit within the Union. The death of chattel slavery, along with the surrender of dreams of separate nationhood, allowed the South to claim victory, in partnership with the North, while state rights, white supremacy, and honor proved that the South had not fought in vain. Vanquished only on the field of battle (and over the years they even explained away this defeat), southerners could claim victory in partnership with the Federals. When men like Congressman Wright claimed victory for both sides, they were reporting an aspect of reality that evaded the understanding of most northerners but nevertheless constituted an important part of the Civil War settlement. Nor were they promoting new ideas. Rather, the compromise ratified thinking that dated to the war years.

It may seem to require amazing mental agility to conclude that the Confederacy had won victory. Yet if one takes as one Confederate goal the self-respect of a people, as another goal the preservation of the notion that Americans anywhere had a constitutional right to deal with their own people and institutions as they desired without outside interference, and, as a third, the desire to exercise that right in respect to their own black population, one has only to look at the century between the first and second Reconstructions to see that Stephens, Davis, Wright, and the others were correct. The South had indeed preserved its view of the Constitution, white supremacy, and honor. After the unsuccessful struggle to preserve slavery and achieve independence, southerners had returned to the constitutional issue. If the war was lost over slavery and independence, the peace was waged— and won—for state rights, white supremacy, and honor. In this way, the South could claim "a moral, if not a military, victory," conspiring with historians "to prove that no one—no white man at least—had really lost the Civil War."[29]

PART FIVE
Epilogue

Confederates sacrificed much to achieve nationhood, and many persons would argue that it is unrealistic to hypothesize that with greater effort southerners could have won their independence. But that seems to say that Confederate defeat in the Civil War was inevitable, and like most historians we have an aversion to the claim that great events have inevitable outcomes, as if the participants were mere puppets controlled by some unseen hand.

We believe assuredly that the Civil War did not have an inevitable outcome, for the Confederacy almost won. At several points Union determination faltered, and in 1863 and much of 1864 it seemed a reverse race, in which the adversaries competed to see which of them would first become so absolutely war weary that it would be willing to accept the other's war goals. Not until the autumn of 1864, with the fall of Atlanta, Lincoln's reelection, and Sherman's march to the sea, did the events of the war take on even a shadow of inevitability.

Thus it stands to reason that at several points Confederates could have reversed the trend of events. How? Not, most likely, by direct, conventional military means because Civil War armies created a military stalemate by their virtual immunity to destruction, and the large size of the theater of war made operations indecisive. What the Confederates needed for victory was a collapse of the Union home front, induced most likely by the continued stalemate of the armies and the effects the resulting casualties would have had upon civilian morale. Through most of the war, the possibility of a collapse of the Union home front had every bit as much likelihood as disintegration of the Confederate home front. And if, by April 1865, Union morale had not collapsed, an unconventional military strategy still presented a viable alternative for the Confederates, although it would have created more domestic turmoil, especially among the black population, than Confederates wanted to see. Nevertheless, guerrilla warfare was by no

*means impossible for the South in 1865. But the South lacked a cred-
itable nationalism that would encourage such extreme measures, and
Confederates decided instead to give up the war and return to the nationalism of the Union; moreover, peace, the attractive feature of the
rejected alternative to war, looked very good to a people bloodied by
four years of combat. Indeed, it could be a measure of humanity that
Confederates were willing to quit before they achieved independence.*

*Confederates quickly came to terms with the collapse of the indepen-
dence movement, not joyfully, often with great resentment, but they
came to terms. And they did so quickly enough and sufficiently to
expect a proper share in the governing of the United States only eight
months after the fall of Richmond and General Lee's surrender at
Appomattox Court House.*

*Confederates could come to terms with defeat so quickly because
they never had much sense of distinct nationality (the Union was
"home") and because they did not lose everything in the defeat. They
lost independence, but they could reclaim another form of independence within the Union. Southerners had lost slavery, but they still
could control the labor force. Confederates had struggled for other
goals that were implied in 1861 but seldom mentioned explicitly until
the courts of the war had turned against them. And after the war,
when the dust had settled, former Confederates could claim that they
had fought successfully for state rights, white supremacy, and honor.*

*In the dark days of World War II, after the fall of France, Antoine de
Saint-Exupéry expressed in moving, poetic prose what it meant to
have national honor compromised in defeat and the feeling that bound
Frenchmen together at that sad point in their history. "We dwell in the
rot of defeat," he explained, "yet I am filled with a solemn and abiding
jubilation, as if I had just come from a sacrament. I am steeped in
chaos, yet I have won a victory." In defeat, Saint-Exupéry's victory
was that he felt a comradeship with his countrymen that he had not
felt before, one that bears some analogy to the feelings of many former
Confederates eighty years earlier: "Since I am at one with the people
of France, I shall never reject my people, whatever they may do. I
shall never preach against them in the hearing of others. Whenever it
is possible to take their defence, I shall defend them. If they cover me*

with shame I shall lock up that shame in my heart and be silent. Whatever at such a time I shall think of them, I shall never bear witness against them."[1]

If "France" is deleted from these words, what remains is the comradeship of a lost cause, of a people in arms, defeated but not crushed, humbled perhaps but not humiliated. Such a spirit encourages a people to rise again and, in the Confederate context, permits some understanding of the lost cause mentality. More united in defeat and the subsequent Reconstruction than in their brief independence, Confederates seemed to forge a distinctiveness after the war that they had not had before or during it. Perhaps that helps to explain the curious yet successful attempts to salvage some elements of victory—state rights, white supremacy, and honor—from the failure of independence.[2]

Chapter Seventeen

Why the South Lost

THE IMMEDIATE popular response to the question posed by this
book and this chapter is usually that the North overwhelmed the
South with its great numbers and resources. The Union possessed
more than twice the population of the Confederacy, and the South endured an even greater disadvantage in military population, for the
South included four million slaves, excluded from direct military participation on the Confederate side. But though numbers were certainly
important, the inherent advantages of defense, illustrated by the virtual impossibility of destroying an enemy army unless it had an incompetent commander, required a greater disparity before the size and
resources of the Union could explain Confederate defeat.

Many Confederates agreed that numbers or resources did not provide
the margin, although they disagreed on what did. General Beauregard,
for example, claimed that "no people ever warred for independence
with more relative advantages than the Confederates; and if, as a military question, they must have failed, then no country must aim at
freedom by means of war." "The South," Beauregard asserted, "would
be open to discredit as a people if its failure could not be explained
otherwise than by mere material conquest." To Beauregard, the Confederates did not owe their defeat to numbers but to faulty strategy and
the poor leadership of Jefferson Davis, who attempted to defend all
Confederate territory, thus dispersing Confederate strength and for-
bidding adequate concentration.[1]

Some historians of our own generation agree with the thrust of
Beauregard's remarks, though finding different flaws in Confederate
military leadership. Clement Eaton, for example, aligned himself with
T. Harry Williams, both of them maintaining that despite northern
superiority in men and resources, the South had a good chance of
success until Gettysburg and Vicksburg. "The chance was lost,"

says Eaton, because Davis "made the dubious decision of allowing [Lee] . . . to invade Pennsylvania instead of sending strong reinforcements from his army to defeat Grant at Vicksburg." But the ultimate cause of Confederate defeat, according to Eaton—and in agreement with a number of other historians cited earlier—was a loss of the will to fight. Both sides suffered from this problem, but after July 1863 it was worse for the South. Southerners' "morale rose and fell with victory and defeat, and also with their estimation of the northern will to persevere." At this point we should recall the biting comment of Confederate Senator Williamson S. Oldham, who maintained that the argument of numbers flattered one's vanity but that the Confederacy had everything it needed to fight in 1865, "morale alone excepted."[2]

But the Confederates did lack morale, and their morale was sapped by uncertainty about their war aims. To fight to be left alone, as Davis and others put it, did not prove very inspiring. Most Confederates thought the war was fought to attain security of slave property and autonomous government, with independence as merely the means by which they would achieve the desired end. But the growth of power of the central government compromised autonomous government, and the exigencies of manpower policy and foreign policy jeopardized slave property. The authorization for enlistment of slaves in the army and the proposal to grant them freedom as a result of their service reflected a Confederate alteration in war aims whereby the means became an end. Secession to protect slavery had, ironically, led to a war by the end of which the Confederacy would arm slaves and even offer them their freedom. But in denying the original motive for the establishment of a separate country, the Confederacy undermined the fundamental basis of its tentative nationalism and deprived many of its citizens of their motive for continuing the conflict.

Lincoln's Emancipation Proclamation made it difficult for Confederates to feel entirely at ease with their assertion that they were fighting for liberty. It aggravated the misgivings of those who long had harbored quiet doubts about slavery and made many others even more uneasy about their isolation in a world in which the great powers of Europe, now joined by the United States, sought to extirpate slavery. Many southerners felt guilt over the institution or at least unease about their position. Thus, as the struggle drew to a close, the commit-

ment to slavery of many southerners withered in the face of the contradiction it created and under the weight of world moral disapproval,
which some Confederates felt acutely.

The change in the Confederacy's explanation for secession and war
shows the seriousness of the cognitive dissonance created by the problem of slavery. To consider it merely a contest for the proper interpretation of the Constitution was to deny recent historical fact, but
the constitutional question offered a far more comfortable explanation
for the sacrifice of so much blood and treasure than the protection of
slavery had. But to reject slavery as the cause for secession eliminated
the characteristic that most distinguished the North from the South.
Common history and language united the sections and so, too, in a
lesser and more complex sense, did religion; only slavery truly separated them. By the end of the conflict many southerners had denied
the basis of their distinctiveness and of their nationalism. Without a
sufficiently distinctive history to undergird their weak sense of nationality, Confederates created their own mythic past to support the
notion that the war was the logical outcome of a controversy over state
rights, not slavery.

In any case, slavery had provided a very slender foundation for a
distinguishing nationalism. When southerners' allegiance to slavery
faltered, no ground for distinctiveness would remain. This lack of significant difference from the Union even applied to the emerging constitutional explanation of secession and war. Those who came to see
state rights and a decentralized government as the cause for which
they fought were very often the same people who denounced the centralized despotism of the Davis administration. Why, many asked,
fight against one centralized government only to preserve another?

Thus the course of the conflict quickly exacerbated the weakness in
the southern sense of separate identity and in the original cause of
secession. Frank Owsley remarked that "the up-country people could
easily fight a ninety-day war . . . but not a war that lasted over several years. Anger and enthusiasm are too transient to serve as a basis
of war." What he said of the up-country people could reasonably have
been said of the low-country people also, even though they, in fact,
displayed much greater allegiance to the cause. But neither, as it
turned out, had enough deep and enduring support for the struggle.[3]

In fact, considering their fragile and insecure nationalism, one could almost ask what induced southerners to make such a powerful and prolonged resistance? Certainly the climate of opinion, which for two decades had reflected a consciousness of divergence between the sections and a hostility to Yankees, had much to do with magnifying grievances and strengthening the feeling of separateness. The churches contributed powerfully to fostering this climate of opinion, but they, too, like slavery and limited government, failed as the conflict wore on. In the same way that slavery was removed as a motive for continuing the struggle by the understanding that it was doomed regardless of who won, and development of centralized Confederate government mitigated state rights as a source of motivation, so, too, religion ceased to sustain Confederate morale and confidence in victory. Defeat in battle and loss of territory cast doubt on whether God truly favored the Confederacy and, for those who concluded that God did not, the cause seemed hopeless. The devout had no motive to keep struggling against God's will. A powerful prop initially, religion thus became a source of weakness in adversity.

As Confederates pondered the religious meaning of the Civil War, especially in the last dark months, they questioned why God had failed them. Southerners answered that question in various ways, most of which related to sin and punishment. But in identifying God's will with their own affairs on earth, Confederates unconsciously had been expanding their faith to the point that they created—in effect—a civil religion.

It is beyond the scope of this book to apply the concept of civil religion to the events of the Civil War. It is sufficient to our thesis to note that an American civil religion existed and that it was profoundly related to American nationalism. We suspect that it was also related to vague notions of Confederate nationalism. In his elemental study *Nationalism: A Religion*, Carlton J. H. Hayes has written about nationalism as a religion of sorts. Primarily a historian of the modern Western world, Hayes touched only lightly upon the American Civil War. But he did suggest that in addition to the primary nationalism of the United States, there were two others—the embryonic secondary nationalism of the Confederacy and the tertiary nationalism of the lost cause.[4]

Our point is that the latter two never developed into the potent nation-building and nation-sustaining force that American nationalism, however weak or strong, eventually became. While Confederate nationalism, such as it was, crumbled away during the Civil War, American nationalism developed further and eventually emerged in the postwar period with Abraham Lincoln as its chief apostle, and he has been its figurehead ever since. As one historian remarked at a scholarly program commemorating the bicentennial of the American Revolution, in the American mind "Washington is but a monument, while Lincoln *lives*." (It is no accident, we suspect, that the highway signs directing motorists to the Springfield, Illinois, exits give directions to the "Lincoln shrines.")[5]

But what is it that makes Lincoln an American saint? We think Edmund Wilson in his essay "The Union as Religious Mysticism" correctly answered the question. Essentially, Lincoln himself "came to see the conflict in a more and more religious light," but beyond that there was a particular "interpretation of its meaning, that—influenced, of course, himself by the 'climate of opinion,' of the North—he fixed in the minds of the Union supporters." And as Martin Marty phrased it recently, "Lincoln did forge and use a new political religion for union," and thus Lincoln provided the North with an asset that the "Confederacy was missing." Was the American civil religion necessary for northern victory in the Civil War? Possibly not, but in all likelihood Kenneth S. Kantzer is correct in his characterization of American civil religion as "the cement holding our nation together."[6]

And what of the South's civil religion, however embryonic: did it not exist? Yes, but only in embryo; it was aborted before birth. The reason is because its mother could not carry it to term: the philosophical and religious underpinnings of the Confederacy were not spawned in an atmosphere of nationalism but in one of racism and fear. And when at last it became obvious that even Confederate victory could not have resulted in a satisfactory continuation of white supremacy through the maintenance of slavery, white supremacy had to be nurtured in other ways. In a secular sense, this was done by salvaging the extant social structure in the nationalism of the lost cause, but the process also had its religious history because much of it occurred within the churches. Within those potent and significant institutions, a virile response to the Confederacy's change in war aims was forged.[7]

Owsley's thesis "that the Confederacy collapsed more from internal than from external causes" certainly could find strong support in the embryonic nature of Confederate nationalism and the debilitating effects of southern civil religion in the face of God's apparent disfavor. But Owsley's original hypothesis, the crippling effect of state rights, does not, upon closer examination, suffice.[8]

The tangible effects of state rights, as distinguished from the rhetoric, had little negative effect on the Confederate war effort. Even the total number of exempted men was small in relation to the Confederate armies, and most of them made significant economic contributions, served in local defense forces, or both. The protection of ports and the production of such important items as salt had an importance that military authorities and President Davis both recognized, and state local defense forces therefore contributed materially to this effort. Further, state endeavors to supply and equip local defense forces and to meet the needs of their own men in the Confederate service provided a major supplement to the national war effort. State uniforms and blankets did not come from stocks accessible to the Confederate government; rather, they constituted an addition to the total available. If Governor Vance in truth had ninety-two thousand uniforms at the end of the war, as he claimed, they did not belong to the Confederate government but were an addition to the total stock of uniforms in the Confederacy, a supply made ready by the state's funds, enterprise, and concern for its fighting men. On balance, state contributions to the war effort far outweighed any unnecessary diversion of resources to local defense.

State-rights attempts to obstruct the Confederate government by resisting conscription or the suspension of habeas corpus, for example, also had a negligible effect. State rights in writing and oratory provided a rallying cry for opposition that already existed in any case. Just as in England under the early Hanoverians the association of the Prince of Wales with the group out of power showed the opposition's loyalty to the king and dynasty, so an appeal to the universally accepted notion of state rights provided a legitimacy to the opposition and protected it from accusations of disloyalty during a struggle for national existence. Thus state rights made a political contribution, one probably necessary in the absence of organized political parties.

In view of the rhetoric of state rights and the long, disputatious correspondence between Governor Brown and the Richmond government, Frank L. Owsley made a natural mistake in choosing state rights as the internal cause of Confederate collapse. But in placing the blame on disunity caused by state rights, he did not show that military causes inadequately explained defeat. Considering the still continuing flow of books and articles about Civil War military operations, he displayed wisdom in avoiding a topic on which he would have had difficulty securing agreement. But in view of the harmony of Clausewitz and Jomini on the relevant strategic variables, it is possible to use them effectively as authorities to provide a fairly firm basis for settling the military questions about the Confederacy. Their essential consensus says that an invader needs more force than the North possessed to conquer such a large country as the South, even one so limited in logistical resources.

In making this judgment Clausewitz and Jomini assumed a national resistance. This the Confederacy made, so far as its limited national will permitted, as the Union's difficulties protecting its railroads from guerrillas amply attest. Sherman's complaint about invading a country populated by the "meanest bitterest enemies" illustrates the strength of the national opposition that the Union armies initially confronted.

Clausewitz and Jomini also assumed a competent defense. Using their principles and criteria, the South clearly provided an excellent army, very capably led. Examples of Confederate bungling, such as Pemberton's losing his army at Vicksburg or Bragg's ineffective campaigning, are counterbalanced by Burnside's fairly reliable mismanagement and the pessimism and slow execution of such generals as McClellan and Buell. Both sides wasted lives in frontal attacks, sometimes because they knew no better and other times because commanders and their subordinates lacked the ability or experience to catch their opponent at a disadvantage.

Since the Confederate army clearly did not have a significantly worse command than the Union forces, Clausewitz's and Jomini's strategic variables of space and supply must control. In view of the experience of the operationally superior French armies in Spain and Russia, one must respect their sophisticated conclusion from appropriate historical experience as well as their authority as experts on the kind of war the Union and Confederacy fought. They might well have added the American Revolution to their example of the virtual impossibility of overcoming a national resistance in a vast space without overwhelming forces, and Jomini did include it in his list of national wars.[9]

T. Harry Williams said Jomini preached cities and territory, rather than enemy armies, as the objective in military operations. If this was the case, and it certainly was not in the instance of the strategic turning movement which Jomini liked so well, it proved a realistic doctrine for both armies. Jomini's fondness for the strategic turning movement does fit with Williams's idea that Jomini favored maneuvering over fighting. As to Williams's idea that Jomini advocated one big effort at a time in a single theater, the precept of the use of interior lines to concentrate on a single line of operations also fits Williams's interpretation. The Confederates practiced this strategy successfully in the Shiloh and Chickamauga campaigns and on a lesser scale in the Seven Days' Battles. The Union did the same after the battles of Lookout Mountain and Missionary Ridge and in a different way by their earlier concentration on the Mississippi. But the Union relied more on concentration in time, advocated by Clausewitz, as well as on Jomini's concentration in space.

Williams and some other historians in this country seem to have misunderstood Jomini enough to overlook his essentially Napoleonic viewpoint and to attribute to him some of the views held by Bülow and others in an essentially pre-Napoleonic tradition. Williams also noted a differential effect in Jomini's influence on each combatant that is hard to discern in the West Point officers, many of whom served apprenticeships under Winfield Scott and Zachary Taylor in the Mexican War.

Thus both armies seemed to have followed Jomini while they fairly consistently, though unconsciously, responded to Clausewitz's perception of the difficulties of executing decisive campaigns in view of the power of the defense, the lack of overwhelming numerical superiority, and the huge extent of the Confederacy. Clausewitz, who had considerable knowledge of the French campaign in Russia, stressed the obstacle of the size of an invaded country, whereas Jomini, who had served with the French in Spain, predicted most clearly the trouble Confederate guerrillas caused the Union invaders. These difficulties, foreseen by the authorities and present in abundance in the Civil War, adequately explain the slow progress of Union armies. It is not necessary to look to Jomini, or elsewhere, to find a reason for the protracted character of the Civil War.

In spite of Lee's blunder in attacking the Union center on the third day of the Battle of Gettysburg, and Grant's seriously mistaken assault at Cold Harbor, they and the majority of other generals on both sides adhered more to Clausewitz than to Jomini in their recognition of the power of the defense. Grant best exemplified Jomini's ideal with his victories at Vicksburg and Appomattox, but the failure of other generals to achieve similar successes justified Clausewitz's observation that such maneuvers rarely would succeed. And the ideas of Bülow proved not archaic but ahead of their time, though not because of the author's foresight. Unconsciously, Hood used them in a manner approved by Clausewitz, as did Lee in his Second Manassas, Antietam, and Gettysburg campaigns. Grant's strategy of raids also had an indirect relation to Bülow's concept of attacking the enemy's communications rather than his army.

Thus we have difficulty following T. Harry Williams in discriminating between Jomini's possible influence on either side or seeing Jomini as a potential inhibitor of action on the part of Union or Confederate generals. That Jomini and Clausewitz have so little difference in their prescriptions and that Jomini had more faith in the offensive makes it hard to single out Jomini as hampering offensive action or as an advocate of a pre-Napoleonic form of warfare when no authorities so classify Clausewitz.

So Confederate military competence that capably managed its armies and consciously, and skillfully, used cavalry raids to aid guerrillas in destroying Union supply lines provided the means of validating Clausewitz's and Jomini's judgment about the impossibility of the Union attaining its strategic objective by military means if faced with a determined, unremitting national resistance. If, then, the Confederacy had the means to resist military conquest, one must find the cause of defeat within. If state rights was not this cause, what alternatives are there to the thesis of insufficient nationalism as the internal cause of defeat?

In spite of the blockade and the steady decline of the railways, Confederate supply did not fail. After each apparently catastrophic shock, such as the closure of communication with the trans-Mississippi or the loss of key railroad lines, the ramshackle Confederate logistic organization, displaying an amazing resilience, continued to make adequate provision for the armies. The accumulation in Richmond during the winter of 1865 of a week's reserve of rations for Lee's army illustrates the South's capability. Lee still had this reserve available in early April, in spite of the earlier closure of Wilmington, the presence of Sherman's army in North Carolina, and Sheridan's devastating raid against supply and communications northwest of Richmond. The Confederacy provided its armies with food and clothing, albeit often in barely adequate and sometimes inadequate quantities, and with a sufficiency of weapons and ammunition. And all the while it kept a higher proportion of the population under arms than did the Union.

As Stanley Lebergott has shown, the Confederate Congress did not prohibit the export of cotton, a measure many believed would bring intervention on the South's behalf by France and the United Kingdom in an effort to save their cotton textile industries. This failure, like the failure to restrict cotton planting during the war, reflects a lack of appreciation of the nature of total economic mobilization and a concern for the pecuniary interests of the growers of cotton. But the production of so much cotton between 1861 and 1865 (the 1864 inventory equaled twice the exports during the war) also indicates a debilitating confidence in a short conflict and an early return to unimpeded cotton exports. Significantly, the 1862 cotton crop was the second largest on record.[10]

But the production of too much cotton and not enough food crops, like the decline in railway service and the constraints of the blockade, severely affected the home front, already heavily taxed through inflation and diminished in manpower because of the needs of the army and of war production. These costs and hardships, like the casualties in battle and the gloom occasioned by defeats, depressed civilian morale. Many of the deficiencies of Confederate supply affected civilians more than the armies and aggravated hardships inseparable from such a bloody and costly war. And the depressed morale of the home front communicated itself to the soldiers through newspapers and the Confederate postal service, which continued to function throughout the war in spite of numerous obstacles, including a constitutionally mandated requirement that postal expenses not exceed postal income.

The defeats, shortages, reduced standard of living, and change of war goals, as well as the war's length, obviously placed a severe strain on the Confederates' dedication to their cause. The high degree of dependence of Confederate morale on military events meant that setbacks on the battle front usually had a significance far beyond the military importance of the loss of a battle or a fragment of territory. A succession of defeats and territorial losses, though not representing militarily consequential conquests of the South's vast land area, worked steadily to depress morale and confidence in victory. With fewer such military disappointments and less hardship for civilians, or with a shorter war, Confederate nationalism, weak though it was, would have equaled the demands placed upon it and might well have developed real strength after the war; in any case, a greater measure of nationalism during the conflict certainly would have enabled the Confederates to resist longer.

In addition, planters felt alienated from a government that seemed to threaten their privileges and property and, in spite of the exemplary relief efforts of Georgia and North Carolina, and the similar, if not so extensive, measures in other states, the yeomen, too, felt disaffection with the Confederacy. Both planter and yeoman paid economically for the immense war effort, but too many yeomen lived too close to the margin of existence not to feel the hardships acutely; the costs of the war deprived them of the means to meet their basic needs, or threatened to do so. At the same time they felt that, with such perquisites as the exemption of the overseers of twenty slaves and the right to purchase substitutes for military service, the rich did not bear their fair share of the burdens. Paul Escott stressed that throughout the struggle the planters gave primacy to their own rather than national interests. He points out that "a selfish and short-sighted ruling class had led its region into secession and then proven unwilling to make sacrifices or to surrender its privileges for independence." These class differences in the demands of the war effort created another drain on the limited supply of Confederate nationalism.[11]

But the resulting decline in commitment to the struggle did not begin to affect the war effort very seriously until after the middle of 1864. Then soldiers began to leave the army in increasing numbers. The fall of Atlanta in early September and Sheridan's victories over

Early in the Shenandoah Valley, victories that significantly improved Lincoln's chances of reelection, also signaled the beginning of a marked rise in desertion from the Confederate army. Soldiers left not only from discouragement at these defeats but also from a realization that Union victories increased the likelihood of Lincoln's continuation in office and his policy of prosecuting the war to victory. As the fall elections confirmed this apprehension, the augmented stream of deserters continued unabated. The soldiers were voting for peace with their feet, and the few disaffected conscripts sent to the Confederate army probably hurt morale and effectiveness more than their small numbers could have added to its strength. By the early spring of 1865 the Confederate armies east of the Mississippi had shrunk to barely half their size the previous August.

Adventitiously, Grant's strategy began to play some part in this Confederate decline soon after the Union presidential contest of 1864, when Sherman marched from Atlanta to Savannah, breaking railways, destroying factories, stripping the countryside of slaves, and subsisting an army of sixty thousand men on the country. Sherman perceived the effect of this devastation on southerners when he wrote that his march would show the falsity of Davis's "promise of protection. If we can march a well-appointed army right through his territory, it is a demonstration to the world, foreign and domestic, that we have a power which Davis cannot resist." He believed that there were "thousands of people abroad and in the South who will reason thus: If the North can march an army right through the South, it is proof positive that the North can prevail in this struggle." But Sherman's raid occurred well after the exodus from the army began. His raids through Georgia and later into the Carolinas only reinforced a discouragement that already had begun to manifest itself in a dramatic rise in the desertion rate.[12]

Since Lee's army and the other main armies remained sufficiently supplied until the end of the war, one reasonably can conclude that Grant's military strategy influenced the outcome of the conflict but did not determine it. The Confederacy's forces dwindled and surrendered before Grant's raids could deprive them of supplies. The strategy of raids had, of course, considerable political and psychological significance, reinforcing the effect on southern will of the defeats of September and October and the return of Lincoln to the Executive Mansion.

In any event, Grant's strategy alone could not have won a war against a people sufficiently determined to maintain their independence. Grant aimed only to break up the Confederacy's main armies by severing the railroads that connected them to their supplies of food, shoes, uniforms, weapons, and ammunition. He provided no means of dealing with these armies should they disperse and thereafter continue offering organized resistance as units ranging in size from a division of several brigades down to independent companies. These units would have dominated the country, reducing Federal control to the immediate vicinity of the Union armies, as Jomini had learned in Spain. Such forces, aided by guerrilla activity, could have found some food and other supplies in the country they controlled and secured more from the invader's always vulnerable supply columns.

But Confederate armies surrendered rather than dispersing into small but formidable groups, and the soldiers went home for the same reason that many had already deserted—they did not want an independent Confederacy badly enough to continue the struggle, and they placed the welfare of their loved ones ahead of the creation of a new nation. But even if they had wished to continue, slavery would have inhibited the usual war waged by small units and guerrillas against invading armies. Indeed, many slaves already had become sympathizers and recruits for the Union. The same bitter experience of Santo Domingo might have come to the South, just as southerners always had feared.

As old Confederates resolved their dissonance in one way or another, they indicated directly or indirectly that what Ulrich B. Phillips called the central theme of southern history inevitably had dictated their actions. Whether pro-Union or prosecession, in favor of the war or opposed, pushing for peace or desiring to fight to the bitter end, willing to accept Radical Reconstruction or challenging it, white southerners had "a common resolve indomitably maintained—that it [the South] shall be and remain a white man's country." The South could give up slavery with more relief than regret, as events proved. But it could not surrender white supremacy, "especially," notes Carl Degler, "when it was imposed by a North whose hands in this respect were far from clean." To be sure, slavery supplied an instrument of racial adjustment, and independence constituted a long-shot effort to ensure freedom of action on racial as well as other issues; but state rights and honor remained, state rights to provide a political ideology that permitted local control of racial relations, and honor to require that southerners shape their own institutions without outside pressure. Thus today's historian, like Henry James on his southern tour early in the twentieth century, must come to the realization that "the negro had always been, and could absolutely not fail to be, intensely 'on the nerves' of the South, and that as, in the other time [before the war], the observer from without had always, as a tribute to this truth, to tread the scene on tiptoe, so even yet, in the presence of the immitigable fact, a like discretion is imposed on him."[13]

In the antebellum era and throughout most of the war, the desire to preserve slavery exemplified this constant concern. And slavery turned out to have a far-reaching effect on the strategy of the Civil War, for it made unlikely a Confederate resort to its most promising means of resistance, "general insurrection." Clausewitz and Jomini made a strong case that a resort to guerrilla warfare constituted an inefficient means of defense because the results of such a total effort were "not commensurate with the energies" expended. More relevant, such a strategy incurred high nonmilitary costs. Clausewitz noted one of these costs when he pointed out that guerrilla warfare could be considered "a state of legalized anarchy that is as much a threat to the social order at home as it is to the enemy." When that social order included race relations, it would have been dangerous for the Confederacy to have resorted to it, as some Confederate Unionists had realized in 1861.[14]

Further, by 1863 the black population had proved itself willing to enlist in the Union army and had surprised skeptics by its military effectiveness when adequately trained. In any guerrilla resistance the black population in the Confederacy would constitute a resource for an enormously powerful indigenous counterinsurgency force. The turmoil introduced into the countryside would have made slavery more precarious, not less, and would have provided slaves with even more opportunity to subvert the Confederate war effort, perhaps by sabotage and espionage, but more likely by escape and enlistment in the Union army. The Union would certainly have used this formidable weapon, and its use would have changed race relations well beyond the point that the actual events did change them, even beyond the possibility of recognition or restoration.

By surrendering without resort to wholesale use of guerrillas, southerners had, as John Shy has pointed out, "saved the basic elements—with the exception of slavery itself—of the Southern social, that is to say racial, order. The social order could not possibly have survived the guerrilla warfare which a continued resistance movement would have required." Thus slavery brought on the conflict, but, with the underlying problem of race relations, it paradoxically ended it as well, by making fainthearted southerners too fearful to employ their one, otherwise invincible, military weapon. Under such circumstances, it is unreasonable to expect that a people not fully committed to the war would run the risk of creating another Santo Domingo, or at least breaking down remaining social controls. Doubtless, the reasoning of many southerners did not reach that far. The wholesale desertion that took away 40 percent of the Confederate armies east of the Mississippi in the fall and early winter of 1864–65 showed that, before a full-scale resort to guerrilla warfare loomed as the alternative, a critical number of Confederates had given to the cause all that their commitment warranted.[15]

Clausewitz excoriated such behavior. Although he did not use the word "honor," he demanded that a people fight to preserve it. "No matter how small and weak a state may be in comparison with its enemy," he wrote, "it must not forego these last efforts, or one would conclude that its soul is dead." "There will always be time enough to die," he continued. "Like a drowning man who will clutch instinctively at a straw, it is a natural law of the moral world that a nation that finds itself on the brink of an abyss will try to save itself by any means." Clausewitz felt that a failure to fight to the last shows that the nation "did not deserve to win, and, possibly for that very reason was unable to." But Clausewitz did not take into sufficient account moral and religious factors, such as those that made some Confederates more than willing to surrender slavery. For, when the institution faced severe pressure, a multitude of Confederates were willing to see it go, having "discovered" that they were not fighting for slavery at all, or even for state rights, but for white supremacy, independence, and honor.[16]

But Clausewitz's caustic criticism has relevance only if one assumes that the Confederacy was a nation—that it was sufficiently separated from the Union and the glory of their common history to make it a distinct nationality. Analyzing conflict "between *states of very unequal strength*," Clausewitz noted that "inability to carry on the struggle can, in practice, be replaced by two other grounds for making peace: the first is the improbability of victory; the second is its unacceptable cost." Powerful Union armed forces and sophisticated and innovative strategy supplied the first ground; the insufficiency of a nationalism based on slavery, state rights, and honor meant that the cost of continuing the struggle ran too high. Perhaps no white southerners could contemplate such a war. Slavery, the cause of secession and four years of military conflict, would thus have limited the extent and persistence of the Confederacy's resistance even had it wished to carry on beyond the defeat of the principal armies; but desertion and surrender showed that few Confederates had any such desire.[17]

So the Confederacy succumbed to internal rather than external causes. An insufficient nationalism failed to survive the strains imposed by the lengthy hostilities. Necessary measures alienated planters, who, by planting cotton and husbanding their slaves, already had limited the national effort. Privation affected many yeomen, soldiers, and their families as the costs and shortages of the contest reduced their already meager standards of living. These hardships and the perception of inequitable and unwise actions placed an added strain on a nationalism already taxed by the duration and bloodshed of the conflict. Slavery, in a sense the keystone of secession, became a liability as the Union's fight against slavery and the South's own religious beliefs induced more guilt among more southerners. After three years of essentially successful defense against powerful invading forces, these prolonged strains proved more than Confederate nationalism could bear and, frequently encouraged by a sense that defeat must be the Lord's work, Confederates, by thousands of individual decisions, abandoned the struggle for and allegiance to the Confederate States of America.

The transformation southerners made in identifying the causes of the struggle well illustrates the South's essentially ephemeral allegiance to slavery and devotion to independence, and the rapid development of a powerful central government indicated the slender cord that bound some state-righters to the concept of state rights until they appealed to state rights once again after the war was over. Only the determination to hold fast to honor, and the concomitant desire to dictate the terms of racial adjustment, proved constant.

And yet, in a very real sense, the answer to the question posed by the title of this book is that in some respects the South did not lose the Civil War. Southerners eventually resolved the dissonance between the world as it was and the world as they had wanted it to be by securing enough of their war aims—state rights, white supremacy, and honor—to permit them to claim their share of the victory.

JUST AS the Civil War ended, the landlocked South American republic of Paraguay launched a war that presents interesting parallels with, and at least one sharp contrast to, the Confederacy. The war against the Triple Alliance of Brazil, Uruguay, and Argentina found Paraguay badly outmatched even without important Uruguayan involvement. Brazil's population base alone numbered ten million compared to Paraguay's estimated five hundred thousand; the officially stated strength of the Brazilian national guard nearly equaled the total unenumerated population of Paraguay.

Early in 1865 the armored ships of the Imperial Brazilian Navy smashed the Paraguayan fleet, subsequently imposing a total blockade of the Paraguay River, the country's natural and only useful lifeline to the outside. Paraguayans foolishly swam out into the river to attack Brazilian ships or stole along in canoes camouflaged with water hyacinths. Three thousand Paraguayans held muddy trenches along the river against fifteen thousand invaders and, with a handful of soldiers, maintained a redoubt at Humaita for months against the allied fleet. Interestingly, Paraguay conscripted its few slaves while Brazil offered theirs freedom in exchange for military service.

Contemporaries marveled, as have historians since, at the Paraguayans' tenacity in fighting for five years a steadily losing war against their opponents' larger armies and superior resources. Paraguayans' fanatic resistance depended on the unyielding determination of their autocratic and vainglorious president and their intense, almost tribal, identity. Indian ethnicity and cultural unity lay at the heart of their suicidal fortitude and passionate patriotism, as did a bitter legacy of Brazilian and Argentine encroachments and intimidation.

The military effort raised for this struggle for national survival contrasted markedly with that of the Confederacy. Paraguay fielded an army of sixty thousand men on a population base of about five hundred thousand, for a time the largest standing army on the continent. After four years, every male in Paraguay from the ages of eleven to sixty was at the front on the river approaches, and women and children volunteered much, if not most, of the logistical support. Paraguay's 15 to 20 percent of the population under arms compares impressively with the 10 percent typically maintained by industrialized societies in twentieth-century wars and contrasts tellingly with the 3 to 4 percent sustained under the Confederacy. Although Paraguay's government finally resorted to conscription, most soldiers willingly volunteered.

When heavy casualties, disease, and starvation depleted manpower reserves, children from the ages of ten to fourteen volunteered even as the draft age was lowered to twelve. By the end of the war in 1870–71 militia rolls included even the blind and handicapped, and one military district reported nineteen men between the ages of sixty and sixty-nine, eight between fifty and fifty-nine, two between twenty and thirty-nine, and seven between twelve and nineteen. These were all that remained available; the others had already gone to war, and women provided the agricultural force to feed the army.

The Paraguayans proved fierce fighters, even though many of them had to rely on pikes and knives instead of muskets. One unit armed itself entirely with captured machetes. In spite of heavy casualties, disease, and shortages so severe that even colonels lacked horses, desertion became a problem only after three years of struggle.

Casualty counts well illustrate Paraguayan tenacity. Commencing with 500,000 population, Paraguay was reduced to a total of 221,000 a half-decade later. Of these, 106,250 were women, 86,000 were children, and 28,750 were men. In other words, 56 percent of the population failed to survive the disaster.

Obviously, the Paraguayans displayed an exceptional devotion to their country. Perhaps they would have ended the war sooner, by negotiation if not surrender, had their president not stubbornly refused to consider any concession, even after allied occupation of the capital found him taking refuge in the interior wilderness with the remnants of the palace guard. But Paraguayan tenacity, based on a fundamental commitment to their country and hatred of the invaders, does exhibit how a people can fight when possessed of total conviction. Lacking this determination, the Confederacy yielded after a far less costly resistance against an enemy enjoying resources meager in comparison to the advantage held by the Triple Alliance over Paraguay.

Paraguayans look back upon their wasteful war as a heroic national defense against foreign invaders. They tend to slight the mistakes of their president in precipitating the conflict and his incompetent but not unprepared prosecution of it. Here they avoid risking the dissonance which the idea of a needless contest might contain. Unlike southerners, Paraguayans apparently have no need to find victory in defeat or to conjure up a rationale for salvaging their honor. Paraguayans' genuine and enduring nationalism, to say nothing of their futilely heroic resistance, requires no further justification than resentment of past arrogance and foreign intrusion.

Although the Confederate war effort seems feeble in comparison with that of the Paraguayans, southerners had far less incentive to make such a desperate resistance. But the Confederates fought harder than Americans ever fought, or needed to fight, facing far more formidable opposition than Americans ever confronted, and without allies. And the inadequacy of their motivation to save slavery, their only modest feeling of national distinctiveness, and their fundamentalist Christian faith, explain why they did not do more.

The Politics of Local Defense:
Owsley's State-Rights Thesis

ALTHOUGH the state-rights interpretation of Confederate defeat still has prominence, at least by way of lip service, one notes less and less substantive discussion of it as the years go by. The best-known collection of essays explaining the reasons for the Union victory does, however, contain an essay that carries on the Owsley tradition by advancing the hypothesis that the Confederacy died of democracy. But the historiographical reference to Owsley's work has the tone of an antique catalog listing a curiosity. With the rapidly developing sophistication of historical study, the question of state rights has been transformed into one of nationalism, willpower, southern ideology, democratic resistance to authority, or the natural tendency of a people under stress to clutch at any weapon that might ensure their survival. The result has been to place the Confederacy on the couch and to interpret state rights more as a symptom than as the fatal disease that terminated the Confederate experiment. Equally important in bringing this change of emphasis, today's historians have more skepticism with respect to Owsley's explanation than their counterparts in Owsley's own generation.[1]

To put it bluntly, as one contemporary historian informally characterized Owsley's state rights thesis a few years ago, "nobody believes that anymore." His peers nodded agreement. This conclusion is somewhat exaggerated; Owsley's work is still widely cited. And yet there are doubts, although no one has yet bothered to produce a full and formal critique. David Donald in a sense still reigns as Owsley's potent living interpreter, even though he did not use the term "state rights" in his own assessment of the war's outcome, preferring instead to write that the Confederacy "Died of Democracy." And Donald adds a layer of subtle interpretation that Owsley lacked.[2]

Like Donald, Owsley came from the South, but the generation or more that separates them in age reflects in their emphasis and interpretation. Owsley, born in 1890, did his mature work during the 1920s and 1930s. Although *State Rights in the Confederacy*, his doctoral dissertation, became his first book, published in 1925, he actually had more interest in vindication of the South with respect to the war's causation than he did in investigating what he called "the seamy side" of Confederate history.[3]

His interpretations of the war's causation attracted much attention and won many supporters because, as Thomas J. Pressly has pointed out, historical interpretations of the Civil War typically reflect the milieu in which they took shape. During the 1920s and 1930s, a period of increasing sectional tension, Owsley played an important role as the leader of the historiographical school sometimes known as the "Southern Vindicators"; he was also one of the twelve Nashville Agrarians who wrote the proagrarian manifesto *I'll Take My Stand*. But we are more concerned here with Owsley's conclusions in regard to the war's outcome, which have relevance for us because Owsley became a Beardian. As such, he sought to fasten the blame for "war guilt" upon the North; ironically, Owsley saw the germs of Confederate defeat in a South that rigorously refused to be more like the North.[4]

Owsley authored two books considered revolutionary in their time (the other was *King Cotton Diplomacy*). And he has had respect ever since as an undeniably important historian who dedicated himself to remedying what he perceived as a predominance of southern history written by hostile, indifferent, or factually careless northern historians. But despite all the publicity, Owsley's state-rights thesis has never been universally and uncritically accepted. Charles W. Ramsdell, a careful and perceptive scholar, scathingly reviewed *State Rights in the Confederacy* in the June 1927 issue of the *Mississippi Valley Historical Review*. Ramsdell correctly delineated many of the book's more notable faults, although Ramsdell also propounded the "northern war-guilt" thesis.[5]

Whereas "in earlier years," Ramsdell observed, "the credit [for northern victory] was about equally divided between Providence and the heavier battalions; more recently attention has shifted to the industrial and social differences between the warring sections." Some southern, notably anti-Davis, writers had asserted that the underlying cause of Confederate failure lay in a despotic central government that undermined "public confidence and support." But Owsley had taken a fresh tack, that "state rights jealousy and particularism so weakened the general government that defeat, which otherwise would have been almost impossible, became inevitable."[6]

Ramsdell agreed that "it is not at all difficult to find evidence that state authorities frequently hampered the Confederate government," but he cogently remarked that Owsley "has tried to prove too much and has laid his book open to severe criticism in . . . the handling of evidence." Ramsdell observed that Owsley "has accepted isolated and casual statements as bases for sweeping declarations; he has read into some of his sources statements that are not there even by implication; and he has ignored evidence that tends to disprove or to qualify materially portions of his general thesis. These faults," Ramsdell asserted, "are most frequent in the first two chapters, but they are found throughout the book."[7]

In this appendix, we focus upon Owsley's first chapter, "Local Defense," by far his most important. Mrs. Owsley chose to include this essay, which she regarded as the most representative part of the book, in the memorial volume to her husband that she edited and published in 1969. (She changed its title to "Local Defense and the Downfall of the Confederacy: A Study in State Rights," and we cite that republication rather than Owsley's original book because the footnotes have a better format.) We shall consider some of Owsley's explicit arguments and then look at his sources. Time and again, our comparisons confirm Ramsdell's 1927 observation that "possibly the author became over-enamored of this thesis and, like other lovers, lost something of his critical powers."[8]

As Ramsdell said, Owsley's "rogues' gallery is crowded with governors." Owsley finds little that any of them did to merit anything but condemnation, save for a single instance, when in 1864 the governor of Florida chided the governor of Georgia about resistance to centralized army supply procedures. Specifically, according to Owsley, the state executives, especially those of Georgia and North Carolina, interfered with the war's prosecution in the name of local interests and decentralization. Owsley believes they prevented the Confederacy from achieving victory during the first year, when it could have done so decisively, and then continued their cantankerous obstruction for three more years to the bitter end, thus furthering their direct contributions to defeat. But again, as Ramsdell pointed out, Owsley ignored many ways all of the governors supported and aided the war effort, even, in some cases, going "beyond their constitutional power" in extending aid to the Confederacy.[9]

For example, Richard M. McMurry assessed Joseph E. Brown of Georgia, rightly we believe, as having conducted "a very efficient and on the whole successful wartime administration." Interestingly, Brown "was often forced to take actions that ignored constitutional rights." He performed a most important service to the Confederacy "in raising troops . . . providing help for the thousands of refugees who streamed through Georgia and for the families of Georgia soldiers. . . . Food was provided for both groups and a settlement was established for refugees in Terrell County . . . the governor seized hoards of salt and distributed that valuable commodity to the public. . . . Brown attempted to curb the cultivation of cotton and to have the state's agricultural efforts devoted to the growing of food crops . . . [he waged a] campaign against illegal distilleries. Grain, he argued, was needed for food and copper for military purposes. He sought to promote the manufacture of cloth . . . and to manufacture implements of war." But since he did all of this without direction and coordination provided by the central government, Owsley, almost inevitably, ignored it.[10]

Owsley believed that a "veritable tug of war between the central and local governments" existed. He thought that "if the individual states had immediately placed the arms in their possession in the hands of the Confederate armies . . . the Confederate government would have been able to put a much larger army in the field in 1861." In this conjecture, Owsley ignored problems of organizing, training, feeding, and moving the host that he implied might have done the job in one fell swoop. But even Owsley immediately admitted that "the states did transfer the arms and munitions captured with the United States arsenals," though "in actual practice the several governors each disposed of a large part of these arms according to the interests of their respective states or according to his own individual judgment." But this statement admits that the states organized and gave arms to new troops. Owsley ridicules Governor Thomas Moore of Louisiana for refusing in July 1861 to supply arms for five or six regiments in Confederate service because "it would take all the guns in the arsenal," and, as Moore said, "we may expect an invasion ourselves in the fall." He missed by half a year: the Federals did invade Louisiana, and New Orleans, inadequately defended, fell the following spring.[11]

The situation in North Carolina became an especial bone of contention for Owsley. Governor Zebulon Vance stands as Owsley's favorite villain, the man who in the end "had on hand in warehouses 92,000 uniforms, thousands of blankets, shoes, and tents. But at the same time Lee's men in Virginia were barefooted, almost without blankets, tents, and clothing. Vance had enough uniforms to give every man in Lee's army two apiece."[12]

Ramsdell immediately took exception to this statement, claiming that "it really does not require much knowledge of conditions in North Carolina and of Vance himself to see the injustice of this view." More recently Marc Kruman has asserted that Owsley, as well as such other historians as Albert Burton Moore (who had already applied Owsley's theme of disaffection to conscription) or Georgia Lee Tatum (who more deeply probed the effects of disloyalty) "dwell upon the symptoms of dissent in the Confederacy but overlook the underlying causes." Owsley, and the generation of historians who accepted his argument almost whole, did not see the forest for the trees, placing entirely too much credence in the harm supposedly wreaked by the manifestation of these understandable phenomena, and, as champions of the South, they could not conclude that the southern cause or the Confederate leadership was wrong. Understandably, they found the solution in scapegoats, and the vociferous Vance and Brown fit their psychological need perfectly.[13]

If Vance served as Owsley's chief villain, Governor Joseph Brown of Georgia never lagged far behind, Owsley actually mentioning him much more often. Here, too, Ramsdell found faults, asserting that "there seems to be no ground for the assertion (p. 15) that Brown, not content with holding on to the state's arms, was determined 'to get as much more as possible out of the Confederate government.'" Owsley noted that Brown carried out a "selfish policy" and "did not refrain from engaging in frequent, unnecessary, and far-fetched quarrels with the sorely-beset Richmond government." Nowhere does Owsley credit Brown with the very tangible and meaningful services that he performed in behalf of the war effort, not only within Georgia but for the benefit of the entire Confederacy. (See Chapter 10.)[14]

Owsley sometimes seemed to impose his conclusions on the data. For example, he said that Governor Brown "was successfully attempting to bring under his control the entire management of the coast defense of Georgia," which was not an unreasonable desire, especially in the fall of 1861 when the states were raising troops and Confederate forces and command still lacked much of the organization they would have later. The letter Owsley cites to prove his contention supports Brown's aim but greatly exaggerates his success. Brigadier General A. R. Lawton, the commander of the Department of Georgia, reported to the secretary of war only that "Governor Brown has suddenly shown a disposition to exercise a good deal of authority over, and claim credit for, the coast defense, and his desire now is to make such appointments as will secure the control to him in case of attack." Despite the claim of Owsley's text, however, the Confederate Department of Georgia remained firmly under War Department control, even though its commander came from Governor Brown's state.[15]

Owsley's next footnote cites support for his statement that "by the application of high pressure" Brown had induced Lawton to seize the cargo of a blockade-runner and to place the rifles thereon into the hands of local defense troops. The footnote adds that "Brown had shown Lawton a message from Richmond that convinced the latter of an imminent invasion. From the well-known tactics of Brown," Owsley commented, "one can readily understand what that persistent individual was up to." But the passage in the *Official Records* that Owsley cited contains another letter from Lawton to Secretary of War Benjamin, attempting to justify and explain why Lawton, on his own initiative, had seized the rifles. It indicates that "for several days after the arrival of the *Bermuda* at Savannah it was impossible to ascertain here whether the arms and munitions by the steamer were public or private property. Sorely pressed for the want of arms, and authorized as I was by the War Department . . . I am not aware that I transcended my authority . . . was there no emergency to justify my act?" Not only had the governor shown Lawton a private dispatch from Richmond warning of an imminent invasion, but the same information also reached Lawton from Howell Cobb and from Secretary Benjamin himself. "High pressure" seems to have been applied by Yankee threats, not by Governor Brown. Furthermore, Owsley's next clause implies that Lawton kept the entire cargo. But in the source cited, Lawton reported that "most of these arms will probably be placed in the hands of troops actually mustered into the service of the Confederate States" and that he would "be happy to direct the shipment of the remainder to such places as may be directed."[16]

Owsley at last concludes a tedious argument concerning the use (or misuse) of arms during the war's first year by claiming that "the initial advantages of better trained soldiery and better generals were lost and the popular enthusiasm for war was dissipated: State rights had reaped its first harvest." This stricture, however, rests not only on the easy and unwarranted supposition that the Confederacy had better soldiers and generals but also on some unstated assumption about the use of such forces when stationary northern armies spent their time coping with the same problems of organization and training as those the South faced. Owsley ascribed the failure to have larger armies on the frontier initially to lack of arms for the troops and subsequently to inadequate manpower, both attributable to the governors' hoarding resources for local defense.[17]

But local defense amounted to little more than coast defense, and governors like other authorities made the mistake of expecting the Union to use its command of the sea to mount invasions of the South. Jefferson Davis and his secretaries of war made the same error, initially allocating far too many men to guard the coasts. Thus the governors' concern for their sea and gulf frontiers harmonized with the initial Confederate strategy and, later, their continuing concern and creation of state forces enabled the Confederacy to leave much of the responsibility for seaboard defense to the states and so concentrate more Confederate troops against the main Union invading armies. Moreover, many of the men enrolled in local defense forces were also engaged in essential occupations on the home front.

In striving to show the tyranny of local over national defense, Owsley's enthusiasm sometimes exceeded what his sources warranted. For example, when Confederate Brigadier General Lawton learned that he might have to conform to the orders of his senior, Major General W. H. T. Walker of the

Georgia state forces, Owsley described Lawton as "so dejected over the prospect that he predicted disaster and asked to be relieved of his place." Though this placed Lawton in danger of being outranked, a situation that had happened elsewhere and spurred the creation of higher ranks in the Confederate army, it was by an "old friend," a West Point graduate and experienced regular officer who would become a Confederate major general in 1863. Lawton does not appear to have been "dejected," but he did feel pique at being superseded when he had organized his department to suit himself, and he understandably felt uncomfortable because the disgruntled Walker had just left the Confederate service. Hardly dejected or predicting disaster, Lawton did fear "embarrassment" and asked to be relieved of his command at the prospect of his department passing under state control when Walker and Governor Brown had both displayed hostility to the War Department. Soon R. E. Lee, a full general, would command in South Carolina and Georgia and outrank all state commanders.[18]

PART II of Owsley's essay on local defense covers the war's next three years. Its point of departure is the rebuilding of the various state military organizations after they had been broken up by the implementation of the conscript law of April 1862. "Nine-tenths of the men in many of the organizations," Owsley asserted, "were subject to general service, which, added to the notorious inefficiency and cowardice of such organizations [a statement for which Owsley cited no source], made it absolutely necessary that the Confederate government should obtain control of them." Beginning a series of descriptions of the process in each state, Owsley blasted the first fusillade at Alabama's Governor John Gill Shorter.[19]

Proceeding through a series of steps in his supposed attempt to grasp local power, "Governor Shorter came out with the bold request that the war department allow him to enlist for state defense all the conscripts in the counties of Barbour, Pike, Henry, Dale, Coffee, and Covington." But the War Department readily acceded to his request to muster these men "into service for coast defense" and assured the governor that the department wished to give Shorter "all that you ask" and that the troops could remain in state service to protect "the coast in case of any invasion" unless "the demand for service elsewhere becomes more imperious," an eventuality the War Department doubted would occur.[20]

This augmenting of state forces resulted from an effort by Governor Shorter and the governors of Georgia and Florida to strengthen the defense of the coast by organizing a new department and leaving a company of state sharpshooters obligated for Confederate service along the coast. Shorter had secured the allocation of conscripts from the counties along the Gulf because he convinced the War Department that if Colonel James H. Clanton, a popular local commander, could strengthen his command, he could protect the country and its "salt manufacturers on the coast which are of urgent and great importance." The importance of salt in diets and for curing meat always made this a pressing consideration as the Confederacy sought to protect its logistic base from Union forces.[21]

Governor Shorter's "bold request" also exemplifies effective state collaboration with the overall war effort. This more positive description also would fit what Owsley characterized as Shorter's effort, when "emboldened by success," to acquire for the state forces "all *the rest* of the conscripts in Alabama who showed any reluctance in going into the Confederate service." But Shorter was not as imperious as Owsley made him appear. Facing a serious draft-resistance problem, he merely sought to attract to the state forces that "class of men over the State liable to conscription who are hiding out and dodging enrollment officers." These he thought his popular Colonel Clanton could recruit and at the same time reduce resistance to the conscription act. Although the governor did not believe Clanton could raise more men than he needed, if he did recruit a larger force, Shorter explained that it would enable the War Department "to re-enforce Mobile." Again Owsley's example seems to illustrate a helpful rather than a hindering attitude on the part of Governor Shorter.[22]

In pursuing his thesis that state-inspired local defense efforts handicapped the Confederate war effort, Owsley depicted Georgia as not far behind North Carolina in this category. He attacked the usually prickly Governor Brown for asking the Georgia legislature, soon after the passage of the second conscription act, to re-create a state force. "Spoiling, as usual, for a quarrel with President Davis," Owsley wrote, Brown believed "that Georgia had a right to every able-bodied man not in actual Confederate service . . . [and] he enforced his arguments by a garbled quotation from Davis himself." Owsley cited a long letter by Brown to Davis in which Brown informed the president that he had formed a mere two regiments (eighteen hundred men) of state troops to protect against invasion and to perform police duty. Brown's words contained no twisting of Davis's meaning. The governor quoted an earlier letter from the president: "The State has not surrendered the power to call them [militia] forth to execute State laws." Rather, "Congress may call them forth to repel invasion; so may the State, for it has expressly reserved this right." These words do not support Owsley's contention that Brown was claiming for Georgia a "right" to every able-bodied man not in actual Confederate service, although one could interpret the letter and appended enclosures to mean that the legislature did make the claim. Clearly, from his tone, Brown was not "spoiling . . . for a quarrel." Rather, he wanted to ensure that the ambiguities created by "concurrent jurisdiction" of Confederate and state governments over these men would *not* create a conflict. So Brown simply informed Davis that the *legislature* had not waived the right to the entire militia, but that he was going to raise the two regiments "out of any of the militia of this State who are not in the active service of the Confederacy or out of any other able-bodied men who may volunteer." Continuing, Brown wrote, "Sincerely desiring harmony and concord between the State and the Confederate authorities in all matters pertaining to the common defense, I have instructed the militia officers of this State, in mustering volunteers into her service, 'to muster in no one between the ages of 18 and 45 who has been actually enrolled into Confederate service.'"[23]

Brown then asked that Davis, in turn, order the enrolling officers to respect the validity of the formation of the militia units—certainly not to refrain from recruiting altogether; that would indeed have been a claim to all men not "in actual Confederate service." Brown did not garble his quotation of Davis. He may have wanted to score debating points, a trait he shared with his contentious president, but he desired primarily to avoid the confusions created by overlapping jurisdictions by abiding by Davis's interpretation of the Constitution and laws. This, Owsley asserted, indicated a desire for a quarrel. Even when Brown agreed with Davis, Owsley placed him in the wrong. "Certainly Davis had no intention of surrendering conscripts to Brown when he wrote this," noted Owsley correctly, but then, Brown was not asking him to surrender conscripts—only to avoid future conscription of those actually mustered into the militia. Again, Brown, though always argumentative, did not seem to be hindering the war effort. Rather, he wished to employ state resources to create a militia that would have some military value, especially in defense of the coast. He asked only that the Confederacy not conscript the men he enlisted in his militia.[24]

After completing a survey of the process in each of the other states, whereby "the local defense organizations [had] grown up and multiplied until, like the barnacles on the hulk of a foundering ship, they threatened to drag the Confederacy down to destruction," Owsley returned to Governor Brown. And again, Owsley construed as obstruction the difficult governor's desire for clarification. Secretary of War Seddon had proposed that organizations be raised for local defense made up of men above and below the military age, and he subsequently had gone further and pronounced an alternative method of obtaining them: the War Department might simply call upon each governor for an approximate levy. Owsley misinterpreted Brown and Brown's resistance.[25]

The controversy had to do with Brown's concern that the South could not legally force men outside the draft age to serve: they would have to be induced

to do so. Brown objected to Confederate agents operating in Georgia and trying to do the job apart from any process performed by state administration; he
wanted the matter left in his hands and said that he sincerely believed he could
do it more efficiently. Brown does not appear here as belligerent, although he
may have shown some impatience, and he certainly—at least in the passages
cited by Owsley—did not "instantly" wash "his hands of the whole affair," as
Owsley contended. Brown did request permission to take some of the men
between the ages of forty and forty-five (who, Brown admitted, were by this
time liable to call by the draft) "till the President shall have ordered them to
be enrolled as conscripts, when they are to be dropped from these organizations. Many of them would be willing to volunteer, for the time, for home
defense and I think it good policy to permit them to do so." This request does
not seem unreasonable.[26]

The discussion of South Carolina's raising of local defense forces along the
lines of Seddon's suggestion contains similiar misinterpretation. Already that
state was "possessed of a large force in which there were seven conscripts out
of every eight men," wrote Owsley. But Owsley's source indicates that "fully
seven-eights of those *liable* to conscription" belonged to such organizations;
being liable to conscription, the words used by the commandant of conscripts
in South Carolina, differed from being a conscript, the word used by Owsley.[27]

Next Owsley criticized Brown's request to the secretary of war that, after
the Battle of Chickamauga, the six-months troops be allowed "to go home until
another big battle was to be fought, in order that they might attend their
crops." Owsley said that in this matter "Brown's wrath knew no bounds." But
the source that Owsley cited contains a rational and reasoned argument, a
letter, neither nasty nor rude, from Brown to Davis, November 13, 1863.
Truly, the Confederate government had broken faith with these troops: although Seddon had called them out on a temporary basis, he decided to keep
them in continuous service. Brown wrote,

> We must retain a producing class at home to furnish supplies to the Army, or it
> becomes a mere question of time when we must submit to the enemy on account of
> our inability longer to support our armies.
>   The Home Guards are composed of this reserved producing class, and their ser-
> vices in the agricultural fields are absolutely indispensable for the continuance of
> our troops in the military field. They are willing to do military service for short
> periods in sudden emergencies, but they cannot leave their homes for regular ser-
> vice without ruin to themselves and their country. Much of their crop of the present
> year has been and is now being wasted in the field. . . . Their wheat is not yet
> sowed, and cannot be unless they have furloughs.[28]

Brown concluded with the specific passage that Owsley cited and misinterpreted: "I again most respectively and earnestly claim for them the right to return home and attend to their home interests till another exigency calls for their services. They are now organized, and if they were at the end of each emergency permitted to return home, they would at all times be ready to make prompt response to each call." This does not sound like the demand of a sour, unreasoning man who, "we may safely assume," Owsley told us, "never ceased night or day in his waking hours—or perhaps in his dreams—to throw obstacles in the path of the Confederacy." Rather, it seems that Brown was taking a temperate position with respect to the constant tug of war between the manpower needs of the army and the economy.[29]

One last element in the local defense argument relates to the Conscription Act of February 17, 1864, which included a provision that would nationalize by draft all state forces, again increasing the age span of liability, by calling all men seventeen years old or between forty-five and fifty into Confederate units for use in state defense. Many Confederates thought that the central government was attempting by this law to deprive the states of sufficient producers at home and to circumvent the states from maintaining any "troops of war." These two concerns had been "of minor importance in all the states except Georgia and North Carolina," Owsley asserted, but now they became more pressing. In Georgia it precipitated "the bitterest controversy of the whole war."[30]

Even if Owsley was correct in claiming "that the greater part of the hostility to conscription, except in Georgia and North Carolina, developed after the passage of the law of February, 1864, and . . . that the law proposed to divest the states of their . . . *sine qua non* of . . . sovereignty," it hardly follows, as Owsley implied, that this constituted one last major contribution to Confederate defeat. Perhaps, in this case, especially considering the universality of disapproval that came from all the states, the central government had resorted to an unwise measure—one that, however practical it looked on the statute books, went against the grain of the people. But "never once throughout the book," as Ramsdell pointed out, "does the author suggest that any policy or act of the Confederate government or of any high Confederate official could be mistaken."[31]

Owsley's "bitterest controversy of the whole war" occurred after Confederates had failed miserably to capitalize upon their victory at Chickamauga, had suffered defeat in the struggle for Chattanooga, and had allowed an invasion route to be opened into Georgia with Chattanooga as a base of operations—a route along which the Federals did indeed begin thrusting a few months later, when William T. Sherman's forces pushed forward into the very heart of

Brown's state. Brown was not satisfied with the efficacy of Confederate resistance and response to the unfolding situation, and it might be persuasively argued that he was correct in his dissatisfaction. So, as Owsley said, "By a proclamation declaring that Georgia was abandoned to her own defense," Brown "drafted into state forces all the Confederate details . . . [and] exempts, unless he had also exempted them." He also drafted men in "the Confederate local-defense companies, and all persons subject to military service but not yet actually under Confederate control." It seems a matter of tortuous logic to see Owsley's position: "Thus he [Brown] took the Confederate details and exempts and left his own unmolested. Those whom the Confederate government had desired to leave at home, he took; those the Confederate government had desired to see in military service Governor Brown left alone. It was typical of the man. But he must needs add insult to injury."[32]

Actually Brown mustered an impressive force, a division-sized organization, and he committed it to combat, subordinate to the command of the Confederate field general, first Joseph E. Johnston and later John Bell Hood. Now, Owsley stated, with condemnation and a touch of incredulity at Brown's attitude, that "even while Atlanta was falling into the hands of the enemy . . . the Governor praised the troops for their service and gallantry, and told them that it was their due, as the emergency was over, that opportunity be given them to put their houses in order and take a breathing spell." He gave them "a thirty-day furlough, during the most critical moments of the campaign around Atlanta." But this statement is misleading; the "critical moments" had ended a week earlier. Atlanta fell on the first two days of September, "fairly won," as Sherman put it, whereas Brown ordered the furlough on the tenth of September. And Governor Brown's proclamation, cited by Owsley, gives a convincing rationale for furloughing these men during what seemed a lull in the campaign.[33]

"You entered the service for the defense of Atlanta," Brown told the troops, and "that city has for the time fallen into the hands of the enemy. . . . The fall of Atlanta leaves the State exposed to further invasion. The enemy will fortify that place [there Brown proved wrong], accumulate supplies, and prepare for a winter campaign against Macon and other interior points." Brown correctly asserted that the crops badly needed attention, and he observed that each man had pressing duties to provide for the future needs of his dependents. But he additionally ordered "that all persons over the age of fifty years be detailed until further orders to perform necessary patrol duty at home, and to arrest and send forward, when the division returns to the field, all who are subject who do not report." Brown admonished that "it is very important that the division reassemble in its full strength at the time appointed, [and] it is not expected that any will be absent at roll-call. All who are thus absent," the governor warned, "will be considered deserters."[34]

Thus Brown's forces seemed to vindicate the concept of state troops. Low in military effectiveness because many were militia and most younger or older than the prime military age, these men managed to give the Confederate army valuable aid and proved formidable in defending the elaborate entrenchments that both sides had learned to dig by 1864. Yet Georgia could field this military force without the burden on the economy that full-time soldiering inevitably would have entailed. Brown's zeal in conscripting even Confederate soldiers may have been excessive, but the energy of the state government did augment Confederate military strength beyond what it would have been without the manpower resources enlisted by Governor Brown and his legislature.

In none of this does Brown sound like a man who wrote "with his pen fairly reeking with gall," as Owsley said. Saying that Brown "regarded [Davis] as a regular Nero," Owsley noted that, when asked by Secretary Seddon to give his militia to regular service, Brown chose to "refuse to 'gratify the President's ambition . . . and surrender the last vestige of the sovereignty of the state.'" Although upset when he wrote his long reply to Seddon, Brown did not engage in irrational vituperation. Governor Brown thought that Seddon had been unfair to Georgia and Georgians; perhaps he was right. Brown actually wrote, "While I refuse to gratify the President's ambition *in this particular* [the requisition for ten thousand militia, not the President's ambition per se] and to surrender the last vestige of the sovereignty of the State . . . I beg to assure you that I shall not hesitate to order them to the front, and they will not shun the thickest of the fight, when the enemy is to be met upon the soil of their beloved State. Nor will I withhold them from the temporary command of the Confederate general who controls the army during great emergencies when he needs their aid." Brown also observed that "Georgia now has upon the soil of Virginia nearly fifty regiments of as brave troops as ever met the enemy . . . [and] she has many others equally gallant aiding in the defense of other States. Indeed, the blood of her sons has crimsoned almost every battle-field east of the Mississippi from the first Manassas to the fall of Atlanta."[35]

One might well argue that Brown actually aided the overall war effort, not only by taking appropriate steps for state defense and the continued functioning of the economy but also by making compulsory militia service more efficient. "It is reported," Brown said in his order granting the furlough, "that many persons in the cities of the State have avoided service by uniting with what are usually called local companies." And he ordered that when the militiamen who fought in the field before Atlanta's fall returned to the field, they should "bring with them, under arrest if necessary, all persons subject . . .

together with all persons who remained at home attending to their ordinary business under Confederate exemptions or details" who no longer had any exemptions or details in effect.[36]

And so it seems difficult to share Owsley's conclusion that "altogether, local defense contributed very materially to the defeat of the Confederacy." The conclusion, so plausible at first glance, comes from too many instances of imposing a thesis upon the data, a fairly easy fault to commit in view of the disputatious tone of some of the correspondence. The most notable instance of the last remains the famous point about Governor Vance's ninety-two thousand hoarded uniforms, "enough uniforms to give every man in Lee's army [at war's end] two apiece."[37]

This impressive statistic in support of his thesis proved hard to trace because *State Rights in the Confederacy* cites no source for this oft-repeated statement, which appears in a summary chapter entitled "Conclusion." Owsley had completed his dissertation without this summation; when he readied his book for publication he took parts from various chapters of the dissertation to create the conclusion, and this was one of them. The source got lost in the shuffle. In the dissertation, still available at the University of Chicago, the passage appears on page 96, near the end of Owsley's chapter, "Relation of the States to Their Troops in the Confederate Service." Here Owsley cited two sources. But a check reveals that they are essentially verbatim repetitions of a speech delivered by Vance. Owsley says that Vance made his famous boast "at the end of the war," which seems to mean sometime in 1865, or 1866 at the latest. But Vance actually delivered the speech on August 18, 1875, to the Southern Historical Society, and on February 23, 1885, to the Association of the Maryland Line. So, at best the authority for the hoard's existence and its size lies in a single, though repeated, boast by the governor a decade and more after the war's end. And even then Owsley did not relate precisely what Vance said: "At the surrender . . . the State had on hand, ready-made and in cloth, 92,000 suits of uniforms." Even if Vance did have that much, and perhaps he did not, how many were still mere bolts of cloth?[38]

If the state of North Carolina had such a vast stock of uniforms and cloth, what purpose did it have? If it could have clothed Lee's army twice, it would have provided a new uniform each year for the North Carolina state forces beyond the remainder of the decade. If in fact the state had so much, perhaps it is less a criticism of the action of the state and more of an indictment of Confederate finance and the Confederate quartermaster general that the Confederacy did not have such a lavish abundance also.

But using Owsley's sources and applying to them the contrary hypothesis, one could easily conclude just the opposite from Owsley about the effect of the local-defense issue upon Confederate defeat. We do not find that the records reflect any criticism of local defense coming from regular officers. Every state in the Confederacy had cause for nervousness, those on the coast as well as those on the inland frontier. All needed, and the Confederacy wanted them to have, what the Germans called *Landsturm*, last-ditch forces for local defense. It seems probable that, in his anxiety to prove a doubtful thesis, Owsley overlooked the implications of some of his sources and misread others. This part of the work, like many dissertations before and since, bears the earmarks of failure to double-check adequately. Sometimes it displays hasty research in which the author makes loaded words carry part of the heavy burden of proof that the sources alone, at this reading, do not always seem able to support.

But the main criticism of Owsley's pioneering and important work does not lie in these evidences of overzealousness for his interpretation. Rather, as is evident after decades of additional research and writing, state rights clearly provided a shield for opposition, was a symptom more than a cause, did less harm than Owsley supposed, and permitted the energies and resources of the states to contribute significantly to the Confederate war effort.

Appendix Two

Attack and Die: Confederate
Casualties and War Effort

G RADY MCWHINEY and Perry D. Jamieson have presented a major interpretation of the cause, course, and outcome of the Civil War. They base their interpretation on patterns of immigration which brought Celts from Cornwall, Wales, Ireland, and Scotland to the South, where they became the dominant group, others in the region becoming "culturally Celticized." English immigration, on the other hand, dominated the North, creating a "cultural dichotomy" which constituted, they believe, "the major cause of the Civil War."[1]

This difference also "explains why the war was fought the way it was. Because the Civil War was basically a continuation of the centuries-old conflict between Celts and Englishmen, it is understandable that southerners would fight as their Celtic ancestors had and that Yankees would follow the ways of their English forebears." Celtic warfare had one salient feature, its reliance on the frontal charge, and southerners continued to rely on it because "the reckless charge was too deeply ingrained in Celtic warfare to be abandoned."[2]

McWhiney and Jamieson also trace the origin of a Confederate belief in offensive charges to the experience of the Mexican War, which gave the United States Army a conviction of the supremacy of the tactical offensive. They believe that the soldiers who participated in the war ignored the war's many turning movements and concentrated instead on the frontal attacks that succeeded. Thus Mexican War veterans generalized the winning frontal attacks, even ignoring the assistance provided by simultaneous turning or enveloping movements. The West Point teaching of Professor Dennis Hart Mahan, as understood and misunderstood, reinforced these lessons.[3]

But when the regular army divided for the Civil War, most southerners took this offensive tradition with them while the northerners, if they had imbibed it, practiced it very little as compared with their southern opponents. The explanation for this difference in applying the United States Army's offensive tradition must lie in the Celtic culture of the Confederates and the English background of the Union leaders. Union generals usually avoided the tactical offensive in the first two years of the war whereas, McWhiney and Jamieson insist, the Confederates attacked. The tradition of the Celtic charge explains the divergent behaviors of military leaders brought up in the same school, army, and war. Thus the Confederates assumed the offensive in two-thirds of the first twelve major campaigns or battles of the war. They suffered appalling casualties in constant attacks and counterattacks, and "by attacking instead of defending, the Confederates murdered themselves," suffering defeat in the war because they piled up unsustainable casualties in vain frontal attacks. Thus "Southerners lost the Civil War because they were too Celtic and their opponents were too English."[4]

In support of their thesis that "reckless charges accounted for most Confederate casualties" and that the Confederates suffered defeat because they "destroyed themselves by making bold and repeated attacks," McWhiney and Jamieson calculate losses in the "first twelve major campaigns or battles in which total casualties exceeded 6,000 men." They found that the Confederates attacked in eight of these twelve and lost 152,841 men, 24.6 percent of their forces, compared with 113,160, or 13.9 percent of the Union forces.[5]

In reaching these conclusions, McWhiney and Jamieson used the statistics given in Table 1.[6]

This table mixes some prisoners, usually classified among the missing, with the killed and wounded. To treat killed and wounded separately from missing so as to deal more consistently with the data, we reproduce in Table 2 data from the eleven campaigns and battles only, deleting the prisoners surrendered at Vicksburg. But we add the casualties of the assault on Vicksburg, a relatively minor action, to the eighteen additional combats that occurred during 1861–63, which appear in Thomas L. Livermore's *Numbers and Losses in the Civil War in America, 1861–65*, from which McWhiney and Jamieson also drew their data. Treating all operations up through 1863 includes most of those for which Colonel Livermore gives Confederate as well as Union losses and all of the principal operations in the period for which uniform casualty data exist and upon which McWhiney and Jamieson rest much of their thesis of excessive losses.

Table 2 thus repeats all campaigns, battles, and combats during this period, including killed and wounded only. The table refers to the actions explained in the previous paragraph and for which we have Colonel Livermore's authoritative and consistently derived data.[7]

Table 2 shows that in all actions the absolute numbers of killed and wounded were about the same, 144,000, for both sides. But, having fewer men, the Confederates suffered a higher percentage of losses. The smaller battles and campaigns, together with deleting the Vicksburg prisoners, altered the casu-

TABLE 1

The First Twelve Major Campaigns or Battles of the War in Which
Total Casualties Exceeded 6,000 Men

Battle or campaign	Tactical offensive	Number of men engaged		Losses and percent lost			
		US	CS	US		CS	
Shiloh	US & CS	62,682	40,335	10,162	(16.2)	9,735	(24.1)
Fair Oaks	CS	41,797	41,816	4,384	(10.5)	5,729	(13.7)
Seven Days	CS	91,169	95,481	9,796	(10.7)	19,739	(20.7)
Second Manassas	US & CS	75,696	48,527	10,096	(13.3)	9,108	(18.8)
Sharpsburg	US	75,316	51,844	11,657	(15.5)	11,724	(22.6)
Perryville	CS	36,940	16,000	3,696	(10.0)	3,145	(19.7)
Fredericksburg	US	100,007	72,497	10,884	(10.9)	4,656	(6.4)
Murfreesboro	CS	41,400	34,732	9,220	(22.3)	9,239	(26.6)
Chancellorsville	CS	97,382	57,352	11,116	(11.4)	10,746	(18.7)
Vicksburg	US	45,556	22,301	3,052	(6.7)	29,396*	(100.0)
Gettysburg	CS	83,289	75,054	17,684	(21.2)	22,638	(30.2)
Chickamauga	CS	58,222	66,326	11,413	(19.6)	16,986	(25.6)
Totals		809,456	622,265	113,160		152,841	

Total engaged in these twelve campaigns

  US = 809,456

  CS = 622,265

    187,191 more US troops engaged

Total losses in these twelve campaigns

  US = 113,160 (or 13.9 percent of those engaged)

  CS = 152,841 (or 24.6 percent of those engaged)

  39,681 more CS troops lost

*Captured.

Source: Grady McWhiney and Perry D. Jamieson, *Attack and Die: Civil War Military Tactics and the Southern Heritage* (University: University of Alabama Press, 1982), p. 8. © 1982 by The University of Alabama Press.

alty proportions significantly as well as shifted the balance in the incidence of attack; the Confederates attacked in thirteen, the Union in seventeen.

Since killed and wounded are not the only casualties, Table 3 shows the missing in the foregoing campaigns, battles, and combats. It then adds in the major capitulations of Vicksburg, Port Hudson, and Harpers Ferry. Previous tables had omitted these actions because their surrender was not sufficiently associated with any combat important enough to warrant Colonel Livermore's including it.

Table 3 shows that the Confederates suffered absolutely as well as proportionately higher losses of missing. Although small compared to the killed and

TABLE 2
TABLE 1 in *Attack and Die* Modified and Extended

	Number of men engaged		Number and percent killed and wounded			
	US	CS	US		CS	
a. Eleven campaigns or battles (Vicksburg deleted from the original twelve) in which the Confederates attacked in eight and the Union attacked in three.	769,903	599,964	110,108	(14.3)	123,445	(20.6)
b. Nineteen additional combats (assault on Vicksburg included) found in Livermore's *Numbers and Losses* for the years 1861–63, inclusive. The Confederates attacked in five, and the Union attacked in thirteen.	467,859	345,555	34,601	(7.49)	21,384	(6.2)
c. Total of the thirty foregoing campaigns, battles, or combats in 1861–63. The Confederates attacked in thirteen, and the Union attacked in seventeen.	1,237,762	945,519	144,709	(11.7)	144,829	(15.3)

wounded, the category of missing seems to display greater Confederate weakness than the category of losses directly caused by enemy bullets.

Table 4 consolidates previous tables, combining killed and wounded with missing to give total casualties.

Table 4 shows results which in their impact do not differ markedly from those of McWhiney and Jamieson, reproduced in Table 1. The numbers are larger on both sides, but the percentages maintain much of their original relationship. The Union percentage of loss rises from 13.9 percent to 16.3 percent, and the Confederate ratio drops only from 24.6 to 23 percent. Table 2, which

Appendix Two

TABLE 3

Table 1 in *Attack and Die* with Different Modifications and Extensions

	Number of men engaged		Number and percent missing (includes prisoners)			
	US	CS	US		CS	
a. Eleven campaigns or battles (Vicksburg deleted from the original twelve). The Confederates attacked in eight, and the Union attacked in three.	769,903	599,964	38,066	(4.9)	16,643	(2.8)
b. Nineteen additional combats (assault on Vicksburg included) found in Livermore's *Numbers and Losses* for the years 1861–63, inclusive. The Confederates attacked in five, and the Union attacked in thirteen.	467,859	345,555	10,264	(2.2)	28,582	(8.3)
c. Total of thirty campaigns, battles, or combats in 1861–63. The Confederates attacked in thirteen, and the Union attacked in seventeen.	1,237,762	945,519	48,330	(3.9)	45,225	(4.8)
Add Vicksburg prisoners		29,396			29,396	
Add Port Hudson prisoners		6,340			6,340	
Add prisoners from Harpers Ferry	11,000		11,000			
Totals	1,248,762	981,255	59,330	(4.8)	80,961	(8.3)

includes only killed and wounded, may, however, offer a better measure of the tactical effects of frontal attacks than does Table 4, which includes prisoners.

Table 5 seeks to remove all numbers related to strategic rather than tactical factors. Thus it deletes the losses at Vicksburg, Port Hudson, and Fort Donelson, all of which are connected to strategic blunders. For consistency we have also deleted the casualties resulting from the assaults on these places. Although a tactical rather than a strategic mistake caused the capitulation of

TABLE 4
Tables 2 and 3 consolidated: Thirty Battles, Campaigns, and Combats
from 1861 through 1863

Number of men engaged		Number and percent of casualties (killed, wounded, and missing)			
US	CS	US		CS	
1,248,762	981,255	204,039	(16.3)	225,790	(23)

Harpers Ferry, it seemed consistent to remove it also to allow the resulting data, used in a later table, to reflect tactical variables more accurately.

Table 5 simply shows the derivation of the numbers needed in Table 6, in which we present the casualties that resulted from tactical action only.

These calculations have used all of Livermore's data for 1861, 1862, and 1863, the years for which he has adequate Confederate as well as Union data. We added the numbers surrendered at Harpers Ferry, Vicksburg, and Port

TABLE 5
Actions Resulting from Confederate Strategic Blunders in Trapping Themselves in Vicksburg, Port Hudson, and Fort Donelson and the Union's Egregiously Faulty Defense at Harpers Ferry

	Number of men engaged		Killed and wounded		Missing	
	US	CS	US	CS	US	CS
Assault on Vicksburg	45,556	22,301	3,052	825*	147	0
Vicksburg prisoners		29,340				29,340
First assault on Port Hudson	13,000	4,192	1,838	235	157	0
Second assault on Port Hudson	6,000	3,487	1,604	47	188	0
Port Hudson prisoners		6,340				6,340
Fort Donelson	27,000	21,000	2,608	2,000	224	14,623
Harpers Ferry prisoners	11,000				11,000	
Totals	102,556	86,660	9,102	3,107	11,716	50,303
Total US casualties deleted = 20,818						
Total CS casualties deleted = 53,410						

*The figure is missing in Livermore; 825 is comparable to the defenders' losses in defending Port Hudson against two assaults.

TABLE 6
Comparison of Tactical Casualties Only

	Number of men engaged		Number and percent of casualties (killed, wounded, and missing)			
	US	CS	US		CS	
Table 4	1,237,762	981,255	204,039	(15.6)	225,790	(23)
Subtract results of Table 5	102,556	86,660	20,818		53,410	
	1,146,206	894,595	183,221	(16)	172,380	(19.3)

Hudson (Tables 3 and 4) before, in Table 5, subtracting these, the assault on Vicksburg, two assaults on Port Hudson, and the action and capitulation at Fort Donelson (Table 5). The data are now purged of many of the losses resulting almost exclusively from strategic rather than tactical ineptitude.

This change reduces the number of battles, campaigns, and combats to twenty-six, in which the Confederates attacked in twelve and the Union in fourteen.[8] Taking all of Livermore's 1861–63 engagements, including missing, but excluding capitulations resulting from major strategic, rather than tactical, blunders creates this comparison with our Table 1, identical with Table 1 in McWhiney and Jamieson, *Attack and Die*, shown in Table 7.

To summarize the point of these seven tables, we note that if one uses all thirty of the battles in Livermore for the 1861–63 period, the Confederates attacked in only thirteen and the casualties were as follows: Confederates— 225,790 or 23 percent of their forces; Union—204,039 or 16.3 percent. If one compares in these thirty battles killed and wounded only, the Confederates

TABLE 7
A Comparison of McWhiney and Jamieson's Casualty Results with the Tactical
Casualties of Table 6

	Numbers engaged		Losses (killed, wounded, and missing)			
	US	CS	US		CS	Percent
Table 1	809,456	622,265	113,160	(13.9)	152,841	(24.6)
Table 6	1,146,206	894,595	183,221	(16)	172,380	(19.3)

lost 144,829 or 15.3 percent, and the Union lost 144,709 or 11.7 percent. In some respects the numbers of killed and wounded only offer a better measure of the tactical effects of frontal attacks.

The source of greater Confederate casualties becomes clearer when one notes the origin of the Confederate missing and prisoners. These amount to 80,961 (8.3 percent) for the Confederates and 59,330 (4.8 percent) for the Union. But of these, 50,303 Confederate and 11,716 Union missing and prisoners derive from Confederate strategic blunders of trapping themselves in Vicksburg, Port Hudson, and Fort Donelson and the Union's faulty defense of Harpers Ferry. Thus the Confederacy lost well over half of its missing troops when on the defensive, in prisoners rather than killed and wounded, and because of strategic rather than tactical blunders. Of the remaining missing and prisoners the Confederates lost 30,658 (3.1 percent) and the Union 47,614 (3.8 percent).

Isolating casualties resulting from tactical rather than clearly strategic action (excepting the Union defense at Harpers Ferry), the Confederates lost 172,380, or 19.3 percent and the Union 183,221, or 16 percent. Thus a thorough analysis of the numbers does not substantiate the thesis that a Confederate mistake in assuming the tactical offensive caused them to murder themselves in bold and repeated attacks. In fact, the difference of only 3.3 in the percentage of casualties does not seem large enough to explain Confederate defeat through self-destruction.

These more complete data do not fit McWhiney and Jamieson's thesis nearly as well as do their own preliminary data presented in Table 1. In fact, the data may very well render unnecessary their thesis of differing tactical doctrines in the Union and Confederate armies. Actually, the foundation of their thesis contains a critical flaw. Their point about the Celtic way of war depends a great deal on illustrations drawn from ancient and medieval warfare. In these eras the Celts had nothing distinctive in their combat methods. The Romans and the Celts each fought the other the same way that the Scots often fought the English, on foot with spears and swords. Fighting in this way, rather than mounted or with missiles, tended to characterize combat in rugged or forested country. In addition, poorer people and militias tended to rely less on the more expensive mounted weapon systems.

The ancient Greeks fought in this manner also and always sought an elevated position down from which to rush their opponent. Men who fight hand to hand seem to believe in momentum, the Roman soldier hurling his pilum and dashing forward just before meeting the enemy. The now pacific but very well-prepared Swiss long had great fame for the rapidity, even impetuosity, of their

charge with spears. Thus the Celtic preference for the charge did not differentiate them from many others who fought the same way, on foot and hand to
hand.

Thus McWhiney and Jamieson seem to have confused the Celtic way of war
with the shock-action methods characteristic of heavy infantry. The sixteenth-
century Scottish battles also have these features and, at Culloden in 1746, the
Scotch employed shock action when they met disciplined British regulars
drilled to use the musket. But tactically, the Scottish militia had little choice in
fighting regular infantry trained in the rapid-fire methods typical of eighteenth-century armies. Although their attack failed, they had more chance of
success with shock action than with trying to match volleys with regulars. Of
course, Prince Charles, ignoring the advice of an experienced soldier, made a
military error to fight where he did.

That the battles which McWhiney and Jamieson cite consisted of frontal
combat does not distinguish them from most other battles of ancient, medieval, and early modern times. Armies then usually lacked the means, through
maneuver, to compel an enemy to fight under disadvantageous terms and did
not have adequate tactical methods to attack an enemy's flank in battle. Thus,
like the Scotch and others, the Duke of Marlborough, the greatest English
general of the eighteenth century, had to win his famous victories over the
French in essentially frontal battles in which he took the offensive.

In their analysis of Celtic warfare against the English, McWhiney and Jamieson overlook strategy. This leads them to ignore, for example, the Welsh
practice of avoiding battle with the English armies and relying primarily on
guerrilla warfare. If the Welsh had depended more on major battles, the English might well have completed their conquest of Wales in less than the two
centuries it actually required.

The McWhiney-Jamieson interpretation rests upon an ethnic rather than a
weapons system approach to tactics. Yet this interpretation is essential to
their thesis that the Confederates had faith in frontal attacks and Union soldiers did not. It matters not whether one accepts their thesis that the Mexican
War taught the effectiveness of the tactical offensive, as they believe, or the
efficacy of the constantly practiced turning movements as Herman Hattaway
and Archer Jones contend in *How the North Won*.

But the evidence seems readily to support the existence of officers in the
United States Army before the Civil War who had considerable faith in the
likelihood of the success of a frontal assault; equally many had much less conviction about this or even believed the attacker faced insuperable odds, especially if the defender entrenched. At least partially independent of this dichotomy of thought there existed another body of opinion impressed by the

turning movement, so well exemplified in Scott's Mexican War campaigns. Nor does there seem to be much correlation between the two schools. Lee and Mc-Clellan, for example, both valued the turning movement; but McClellan began the war lacking much belief in the frontal attack while Lee initially had substantial faith that it could succeed. Of course this division between officers with more and less confidence in the likelihood of the success of a frontal attack doubtless excluded a large number who never turned their minds to the question at all. The same certainly held true also of those who believed in turning movements and others who considered such a separation of an army dangerous.

But prewar ideas about the efficacy of frontal attacks constituted only one of many motives for carrying them out. If, as seems doubtful, the prewar army had a predominant faith in frontal attacks, then the northerners would have had to ignore it because they were English and southerners embrace it because they were Celts. On the other hand, even the soldiers who had disavowed frontal attacks and had learned to turn the enemy as an alternative would, if southerners, have disregarded it because they were Celts. The existence of two prewar points of view about efficacy of the tactical offensive would actually better accommodate the Celtic-English thesis because it would permit each ethnic group to choose the doctrine most congenial to its heritage.

Yet this distinction between the Celtic and English way of war cannot satisfactorily rely on the examples they cite because they do not adequately distinguish the early warfare of the Celts from that of their contemporaries. Nor do the complete data for thirty battles support their thesis of a difference in offensive-mindedness between the two armies; the Confederates attacked in thirteen and the Union in seventeen. Thus, they do not seem to have needed their Celtic warfare thesis.

So we are left with the tactical ideas and conditions of the Civil War. Given a free choice, few commanders would prefer to attack an enemy in front rather than in the flank or rear. But, since no military leader would willingly defend with his flank or rear, attackers rarely had the opportunity to assail the vulnerable part of hostile forces. It would, therefore, be a false antithesis to presume a choice between a frontal assault and some other kind. Presumably, therefore, the difference between belief in and doubts about the efficacy of the frontal attack would show itself not in their prevalence in battle but in the willingness of commanders to engage in offensive battles.

Whereas the opponents of turning movements could avoid their use, the skeptics of frontal attacks could not eschew them in an offensive battle if only because the enemy would rarely dispose himself so as to make a flank or rear attack possible. Further, even a tactical turning movement would often require a frontal attack to engage the attention and forces of the hostile commander in front in order to facilitate the move of the detachment passing the enemy flank. And, even in a defensive battle, the defender could well have to resort to a frontal counterattack.

McWhiney and Jamieson point out the prevalence of counterattacks and their effect in raising casualties. But counterattacks have an integral part in the defense in battles. In strategy Clausewitz enjoined that "within the limits of his strength a defender must always seek to change over to the attack as soon as he has gained the benefit of the defense." Here he noted that, when confronted with a defender going over to the offensive, the attacker improvises a defense, one naturally of "a less effective kind" because he had not prepared his defense. Likewise Clausewitz urged counterattacks in battle where *"the defender is better placed to spring surprises by the strength and direction of his own attacks."* And he argued that even "where a counterattack is not enough to win victory, it may suffice to provide protection" against having the defeated army's retreat interrupted.[9]

Although battles may have had their main tactical significance in their attrition, they also involved the self-esteem and reputation of those involved. But beyond these natural human motives for gaining victory, defeat had, Clausewitz contended, "a greater psychological effect on the loser than the winner. This in turn gives rise to additional loss of material strength, which is echoed in loss of morale; the two become mutually interactive as each enhances and intensifies the other." In addition to psychological and material losses, defeats can have a significant impact on civilian morale, even resulting in "a complete crushing of self-confidence." Certainly the Confederate success in winning half of the twenty-six combats used for tactical analysis had much to do with sustaining their will to win and with offsetting the depressing effect of the battles lost and the capitulations at Fort Donelson, Vicksburg, and Port Hudson. And since counterattacks play a part in winning defensive battles, the Confederates had little choice but to employ them. Rarely, one would think, would a general fighting a defensive battle risk defeat merely to avoid a frontal counterattack; the cost of defeat would certainly outweigh the losses in such an assault.[10]

Combat conditions in the Civil War did enhance the power of the defense compared with the era of Napoleon. The increased range and accuracy of the rifle rendered unnecessary two or even three lines of defenders firing; one line could have as much power as two with smoothbores, repelling an attack by beginning fire at longer range and with greater accuracy than could smoothbores. Further, in the absence of a numerous hostile cavalry trained to charge with the sabre, defenders did not need to remain erect to protect themselves against a sabre attack with a wall of bayonets as well as with volleys on command. This meant that defending soldiers would emulate skirmishers by taking cover in ditches and sunken roads and behind fences, walls, standing or fallen trees, stumps, and embankments. Given even a few minutes, soldiers on the defensive learned to improvise cover by digging or, for example, making a low breastwork of fence rails. The need for only one line of men firing facilitated this type of seeking cover from which to deliver fire; defenders thus enjoyed an additional advantage over their predecessors in Napoleon's time by having this cover from their assailant's fire.

At the same time the attackers lost some of the tactical resources they had enjoyed fifty years earlier. In addition to the absence of heavy cavalry to charge suddenly against a weak point, troops on the offensive usually found it impractical to employ columns to rush the enemy in order to use their bayonets; the excellent target presented by a column together with the ability of the longer-range rifle to converge its fire over a wider segment of the front rendered this mode of attack almost useless. And the artillery, always more effective on the defense than offense, had lost its old offensive ability to advance and bring defenders under fire with their very effective cannister shot because the rifle outranged the cannister, exposing the gunners to too much danger. Further, defenders under cover had a diminished vulnerability to artillery.

Increasingly defenders entrenched, not merely to protect themselves from fire during the assault but because attackers often took cover themselves and fired at the defenders. Frequently before an attack, as well as when it paused or had failed, the troops on the offensive took cover within range of the defending line and began firing. If the defense were to enjoy any advantage over the attack under these circumstances, the defenders must erect field fortifications in order to give them cover and firing positions better than those of their assailants. This proved easy to do because the defenders knew in advance where they would make their stand.

So the rifle and the more powerful defensive dispositions which it helped make possible and necessary strengthened the defenders. Further, since infantry no longer needed protection against cavalry, these same factors gave much utility to quite simple entrenchments which only covered the riflemen from fire because they needed no physical barrier against cavalry. Thus defenders could erect useful entrenchments much more rapidly than in earlier wars. In addition to other resources of Napoleon's attackers which they had lost, Civil War attackers no longer had another, the fire of skirmishers against infantry arrayed in line and standing erect. Only concentration of superior numbers or the opportunity to turn or envelop a hostile line remained available to the attackers. With so many changes in combat circumstances, it is not surprising that Civil War soldiers failed immediately to comprehend their effect on the offensive as well as only gradually to make full use of the new resources available to the defenders.

With these changes adding to the defense's primacy, soldiers should certainly have displayed more reluctance to engage in frontal battles. But, since strategy had undergone no comparable modification, the need for offensive battles had not diminished. Lincoln's urging of an attack on Lee's entrenched position soon after the Battle of Gettysburg, justified by the strategic opportunities, and Meade's reluctance to undertake what he regarded as a hopeless battle clearly illustrate the tension between strategy and tactics. This tension had always existed, but the enhanced power of the tactical defense and weakening of the offensive only slowly altered the strategic assumptions which had governed the warfare of the French Revolution and Napoleon.

Battles remained as essentially frontal as had been those of Napoleon, Lee's plan for the arrival of Jackson's turning contingent in the Seven Days' Battles being as rare as the arrival of a force on the enemy's flank or rear, as occurred in Napoleon's battles at Castiglione and Bautzen. The length of the combatants' lines also remained similar to those in Napoleon's time when compared to the number engaged, thus augmenting the strength of the defense because of enhanced firepower. No other change compensated for this increase in the strength of the defense. With armies of comparable leadership—belonging to essentially the same culture, trained in the same military academy, and having fundamentally the same doctrine—the Union and Confederate forces were remarkably evenly matched.

This similarity helps account for the failure of either army often to have the important results with the tactical turning movement which Scott had enjoyed in Mexico. Both sides did, however, use the strategic turning movement as much or more than had Napoleon, but with more success in forcing the enemy back than in obtaining decisive strategic results. Thus McClellan and Rosecrans, like Lee and Bragg, drove the enemy back by maneuver rather than battle, but only Grant obtained decisive results—at Vicksburg and Appomattox. In strategy, as in tactics, decisive victories usually eluded the evenly matched contestants.

Nevertheless, the data leave us with the problem of explaining why the Confederates suffered a higher percentage of casualties when, in fact, they fought more often on the defensive. Here the numbers engaged bear a critical relationship to the casualties incurred. In all twenty-six combats the Confederates had 885,598 men compared to the Union's 1,150,540, meaning that Union soldiers outnumbered Confederate by about 1.28 to 1. Thus, since the Union soldiers faced fewer enemies and did not have as many bullets directed at them, they could expect to lose fewer men. The range of the rifle, as compared with the smoothbore, enabled a larger number of soldiers to participate in the engagements, and the combats with the rifle came to approach F. W. Lanchester's model in which every soldier could fire on every other. Of course, this was far from being completely true, and defensive cover and entrenchments, as well as the training and experience of the soldiers, made conditions depart even more from Lanchester's model. But the range of the rifle greatly enhanced the advantages of numerical superiority, and the Union enjoyed this superiority both as an average for all battles and in twenty-four of the twenty-six combats that enter into our tactical calculations.

To illustrate the importance of Lanchester's idea about every soldier's ability to fire at every other, suppose two equally armed forces met under conditions in which all soldiers on each side could fire at all others on the opposing side. If one contestant had twice the force, it could, in the first unit of time, shoot twice as many soldiers in the smaller force as the men in the smaller force could shoot in the larger. Thus in the first unit of time the smaller force would suffer double the number of casualties of the larger. But as the combat continued into the second unit of time, the larger force would then have more than a two-to-one superiority and so could shoot more than twice as many men of the smaller force than it lost from the smaller enemy's fire. This led F. W. Lanchester to conclude that under such conditions the combat effectiveness of armies was not directly proportional to their numbers, but, rather, it compared as the square of the strengths of the two armies. A force of 1,000 men could, in a fight to the finish under these conditions, hit every man in an opposing force of 500 and still have only 134 of its own men hit. The larger unit would suffer 13.4 percent casualties while the smaller would sustain a 100 percent rate of killed or wounded.

Lanchester called this his square law, and it helps explain high casualties even when a force is acting on the defensive. In three major battles—Worth, Gravelotte, and Sedan—at the opening of the Franco-Prussian War, for example, the Prussians, outnumbering the French 1.7 to 1, attacked. Although the Prussians were not only on the offensive but very aggressively so, losing 8,000 men in an attack lasting less than an hour, they suffered only 8.5 percent casualties while the smaller French forces lost 14 percent of their men. This occurred in spite of the equipment of the French regulars, who carried a breech-loading rifle superior to that of the Prussians.

Joseph E. Johnston's experience defending against Sherman's prudent advance in May 1864 also illustrates the attrition resulting in part from such long-range weapons. Although neither army attacked, they had much contact through their pickets and reconnaissances as Sherman turned back the careful Johnston. In this circumspect warfare Sherman, whose men entrenched at every opportunity, lost 10,528 killed and wounded, 9.6 percent of his 110,123 men; but Johnston lost 9,187, 13.9 percent of his 66,089. Thus even the most judicious defense, which made the maximum use of entrenchments, entailed substantial casualties for the numerically inferior force. Ironically, Lee, in defending against Grant's aggressive simultaneous advance, suffered little or no higher percentage of casualties in his army than did Grant in his. Grant's attacks on Lee's breastworks counterbalanced the factor that kept Sherman's casualties proportionately smaller than Johnston's.

So, if everything else were equal, and the same share of each army fired at the other, a force of 1,150,540—30 percent stronger than a force of 885,598— would be 69 percent stronger in combat power because of squaring the numbers on each side. The long range of the rifle made Lanchester's ideas relevant, and the Civil War became the first major war in which both sides were ultimately fully equipped with rifles. This 69 percent greater combat power must go far to account for the Confederates suffering only 11,000, or 6 percent, fewer casualties than did the Union in these battles (see Table 7). The Union's numerical advantage, suddenly multiplied by the substitution of the rifle for the smoothbore, readily explains why the Confederates suffered a higher percentage loss in spite of being on the defensive more often.

So the data not only no longer support the thesis that the Confederates murdered themselves by making reckless charges, but, in view of the Union's numerical superiority and the tactical benefit given by having greater numbers of men armed with rifles, it no longer becomes necessary to try to account for the proportionately higher Confederate casualties by attributing them to rash assaults. In fact, the Confederates attacked less often than the Union in the battles we considered for these calculations of tactical losses; moreover, they attacked in only one of the four omitted campaigns and battles.

Lanchester's square law, used for combat operations research today, also enables us to calculate the relative preponderance of the defensive over the offensive and the comparative combat effectiveness of the two forces. On the offensive the Confederates had, using Lanchester's method, 92 percent of the combat effectiveness of the Union defenders; Union troops on the offensive against Confederates had, however, only 42 percent of the combat effectiveness of the defending Confederates. These figures argue strongly both for the primacy of the defense and for the tactical ascendancy of the Confederate soldier and his leaders. The most likely explanation for the relatively low combat effectiveness of Union troops is their shorter terms of service and the policy of many northern states to form new units rather than, as did the Confederates, send recruits to their veteran regiments. Nevertheless, this presumed Confederate combat superiority argues strongly against a special Confederate tactical ineptitude displayed in an unfounded faith in frontal attacks.[11]

Inexperience in managing large bodies of troops or any prewar practice in large-scale maneuvers as well as untrained regimental and higher commanders may offer a reason for the war to exhibit so few instances of successful tactical turning movements. That McClellan, an opponent of frontal attacks, should fight a frontal battle at Antietam suggests this as a likely interpretation for much of such behavior on both sides. Union and Confederate commanders often either lacked the understanding and skill to avoid bloody frontal battles like Antietam, Fredericksburg, and Chickamauga or found their opponents too adept to leave their flanks vulnerable. And blunders played a part as Grant and Lee, who both relied on the turning movement, displayed when each carried out a hopeless frontal attack—Grant at Cold Harbor and Lee on the third day of Gettysburg.

Participation in the Mexican War must have taught many of its participants the wrong lesson, one which the subsequent introduction of the rifle rendered even more erroneous. But the initially amateur character of the armies must have played a major part, and they were evenly matched as much in this regard as they were in the quality of their high commands and their high level of skill at the end of the war. So the initial lack of experience in any combat of most of the subordinate leaders also must have contributed to the prevalence of frontal attacks. A direct assault occurs most readily to the uninitiated, and an attack that circumvents the front of an opposing force requires more skill by the commander and mastery of drill by the men. Even contempt for the enemy may have motivated some early frontal assaults. Clearly, many factors must have contributed to the number of ill-advised frontal attacks, Grant's responsiveness in 1864 to public opinion constituting just one more.

If tactical ineptitude and mistakes even by capable, veteran leaders provide a major reason for the frequency of frontal battles, then combat effectiveness must say something about the relative level of competence of each contestant. For example, Union troops, in their doomed attack at Fredericksburg in December 1862, had combat effectiveness of less than 30 percent of that of the defending Confederates. The average effectiveness for all Confederate offensive battles was 92 percent. This creates a presumption that the representative Confederate attack had a more rational basis than a faith in the primacy of the offensive or a tactical sophistication unchanged by the advent of firearms and modern drill and methods. But a tactical analysis sufficiently thorough to test new hypotheses goes beyond the scope of this work.

And strategic reasons, rather than tactical optimism, dictated many offen-

sive battles. For example, the cautious Joseph E. Johnston as well as the aggressive Lee attacked McClellan's army in the spring of 1862 because both of
them believed that the Union army threatened a siege that would inevitably
take Richmond. McClellan's skillful use of his two-sided base had brought him
to the gates of Richmond, thus putting the Confederates in a position which
they judged too threatening. As a result of the Seven Days' Battles, Lee resolved to avoid further battles, using instead strategic turning movements
to force the enemy back. Immediately employing his own two-sided base,
he turned the Union army back in the Second Manassas and Antietam campaigns. Retreating, and so losing territory and damaging civilian morale, the
defensive-minded McClellan as well as the combative Pope felt compelled to
take the offensive against Lee's army.

Similar motives dictated an assault when a Union exploitation of a faulty
position led to the entrapment of the Confederate force in Fort Donelson. But
the frontal attack at Shiloh, where the Confederates gained tactical surprise,
illustrates the principal consideration behind most Confederate offensive
moves. The Union advances in Kentucky, Missouri, and Tennessee had given
them control of a territory approximately the size of France. The Confederates
had lost areas that could supply men to the army as well as valuable agricultural and industrial resources. They had suffered political damage as well in
the elevation of Union and loss of Confederate morale. So they counterattacked in an effort to recover lost territory. At Chancellorsville, when Lee,
instead of retreating, took the offensive to turn Hooker's turning movement,
he acted to protect the area between the Rappahannock River and Richmond,
an important source of supplies for his army. Like the offensive engagement at
Shiloh, that at Chickamauga aimed to recover a position in Tennessee lost to
earlier Union successes.

But a few battles had no particular strategic context. At Murfreesboro in
December 1862 Rosecrans advanced on Bragg, planning to attack him in a
decisive onslaught; but Bragg anticipated him, making his assault first. Rosecrans learned a lesson from this bloody conflict and resorted to turning movements thereafter; but Bragg did not, and he later made an essentially frontal
attack at Chickamauga. In his advance at Fredericksburg, also in December
1862, Burnside sought out the enemy to attack him, and, unlike Bragg, Lee
clearly displayed pleasure in having him do so.

But, of the twelve major campaigns or battles which McWhiney and Jamieson cite, in nine the offensive resulted from a response to turning movements,
and in two—Murfreesboro and Fredericksburg—from a straightforward
fighting advance. The twelfth, Gettysburg, had its origin in Lee's turning
movement, but he, rather than the Union commander, attacked. Wishing
to spend the summer in Maryland or Pennsylvania, feeding his forces

at Union expense and stymieing an enemy movement in Virginia, Lee realized that he could not remain concentrated in the presence of Meade's army because he could not supply his men and horses under such circumstances. He thus attempted to defeat the careful Meade before he had concentrated the Union army and to drive him back to allow the Confederates the opportunity to disperse and forage. His attack on the third day, when Pickett charged, constituted, of course, an egregious tactical blunder comparable to Grant's at Cold Harbor.

Yet two-thirds of the Confederate offensive battles listed by McWhiney and Jamieson resulted primarily from strategic considerations, counterattacks to recover territory lost to Union offensive action. Excessive optimism about the prospects of success in battle may have had a part, but the strategic imperative to recover lost logistic resources and restore morale and political strength depleted by retreat played the dominant role.

Nevertheless, Confederate casualties remain. The Confederates, in suffering tactically related losses of 172,380 men as compared with 183,221 for the Union (Table 6) sustained 94 percent as many combat casualties as the Union and lost 19.3 percent of their forces compared to 16 percent for the Union. These heavy losses occurred in spite of attacking no more than the Union and notwithstanding the Confederates' apparently superior tactical skill. But greater Union numbers of rifle-armed men did much to offset the advantage that should have resulted from better Confederate combat effectiveness. In the absence of direct assault on entrenchments, greater numbers even offset the advantage in attrition which normally would have redounded to the benefit of the defender.

Even when in 1864 Lee resisted Grant's advance and his assaults on entrenched Confederate positions, Lee's smaller army suffered proportionately as many casualties as the Union force. Counterattacks, necessary to avoid defeat in battle, also contributed to raising the casualties of the defender.

Some belief in the greater efficacy of the tactical offensive may well have animated more Confederate than Union leaders and may be reflected in casualty figures. But in view of the impact of the rifle combined with larger numbers, it is not a necessary hypothesis to explain the Confederates' absolutely fewer casualties and such a modest disparity in percentage of combat casualties, 19.3 compared to 16 percent.

And when combined with mistakes that lost many prisoners at Fort Donelson, Vicksburg, and Port Hudson, these factors raised Confederate casualties until they actually exceeded, in absolute numbers, those of the Union in the battles, campaigns, and combats in the previous tables. Table 8 recapitulates these numbers.

The number of missing actually constituted a greater immediate drain on

TABLE 8
Total Casualties for Campaigns and Battles in Previous Tables

	US	CS
	Killed and wounded	Killed and wounded
Thirty battles, campaigns, and combats, killed and wounded only	144,709	144,829
Number of missing, including Fort Donelson, Vicksburg, Port Hudson, and Harpers Ferry	59,330	80,961
Total	204,039	225,790

manpower than did the deaths resulting from battle. In all thirty campaigns, battles, and combats, the Confederates suffered 24,525 battle deaths and the Union 24,463. If we use the Union army's overall ratio of 13.3 percent for wounded who died, and the French army's World War I percentage of 32.3 percent of the dead to stand for the wounded discharged because of their injuries, we can estimate the number of men lost to each side as a result of killed and wounded in battle (Table 9).[12]

Of course, these numbers overstate the losses because many missing, who were not prisoners, returned to their units, and the armies exchanged many prisoners. But the gross number of Confederate missing, 80,961, exceeds the 48,447 directly attributable to the enemy's fire. In fact, the 50,303 prisoners lost because of the strategic error of bottling men up in forts at Fort Donelson, Vicksburg, and Port Hudson exceeds this computation of the deaths directly attributable to enemy fire.

Although neither a more thorough treatment of the data nor some of the

TABLE 9
Numbers Killed and Wounded in Battle

	US	CS
1. Deaths in battle	24,463	24,525
2. Wounded	120,246	120,304
3. Line 2 × .133	15,993	16,000
4. Line 1 × .323	7,902	7,922
5. Sum of lines 1, 3, and 4	48,358	48,447
Number missing	59,330	80,961
Total lost to service	107,688	129,408

ethnic military assumptions supports the McWhiney and Jamieson thesis, their more fundamental question remains. Could the high casualty rate have so crippled the Confederacy as to lead to its defeat? Such losses did not prevent the French from winning in World War I. If the Confederacy had about 100,000 combat deaths, perhaps as many as 120,000, they would amount to no more than 2.2 percent of the Confederacy's 5,500,000 whites. Such a loss compares with France's loss in World War I of 3.3 percent of its population. At the close of that war France, with a population of 40,000,000 and armed forces in excess of 4,000,000, took the offensive and, together with powerful allies, marched to victory.[13]

Of course, the higher proportion of nonbattle deaths in the Confederacy mitigates this comparison with France. Epidemics such as measles and far more primitive medicine assured higher nonbattle deaths. On the other hand, the Confederacy had a much younger population than France's, providing a higher proportion of men of military age. But since the Confederacy's percentage of battle deaths is significantly lower than that of the French, the cases are essentially parallel. The strongly nationalistic French, with a highly developed antipathy for the Germans and the assistance of a fresh ally, the United States, provided leadership and weapons for the forces opposing Germany and carried the war to an offensive conclusion; the Confederacy proved unable to sustain a continued defensive as long as the four and one-fourth years of World War I.

In World War II Germany fought longer and suffered even more heavily than France in the previous war, losing through armed forces fatalities about 5 percent of its population. In addition, enemies inflicted substantial civilian casualties in air raids. Nevertheless, Germany fought for five and a half years, continuing an increasingly hopeless resistance after its principal European ally, Italy, left the war. Linguistic and historical distinctness from the enemies with whom it had recently fought another long war and ideological differences, especially with the Russian regime, undoubtedly supported a firm national resistance under the leadership of Germany's powerful autocratic government. Compared to the Confederacy, Germany lost more than double the percentage of combat deaths. But the overrunning of Germany, a comparatively small country, by millions of hostile soldiers cut short the resistance, one that Hitler would doubtless have prolonged had he had the advantage of a land area comparable in size to the South's. Nevertheless, against enemies demanding unconditional surrender, the divergence in combat deaths between Germany and the South may serve as an indicator of the disparity in the intensity of nationalism between the two and the different consequences southerners and Germans saw in defeat, as well as of the far greater authority which the Nazi regime exercised over its people.

If the Confederates had half of the Union's nonbattle deaths of 224,097, another 112,000 would have been added to their wartime losses even though many of these would also have occurred in civilian life from accidents and natural causes. Together these estimates of combat and noncombat deaths approximately equal the quarter of a million estimated by Charles P. Roland. This would have amounted to about a fourth of the probable Confederate combat manpower pool. If, following the French ratio in World War I, about 40,000 received discharge owing to wounds, and unexchanged prisoners alive at the end of the war amounted to about 63,000,[14] the Confederacy suffered casualties as follows:

Battle and nonbattle deaths	250,000
Discharged for wounds	40,000
Prisoners	63,000
Total losses to the armed forces	353,000

Thus by the end of the war, the Confederacy had lost a third of its more than one million available men which Colonel Livermore believes the Confederacy actually brought into service. Thus there remained to the South at the end of the war a potential armed force of about 650,000 to 700,000, a number considerably more than its total strength at any one time. The government had fully or partially exempted many of these men for essential civilian occupations.

Confederate forces in the field fluctuated during the war as Table 10 exhibits.[15]

The numbers display considerable consistency over time. For example, in spite of the losses at Gettysburg and Chickamauga and the capitulations at Vicksburg and Port Hudson, the Confederate forces had suffered a net decrease of fewer than 9,000 when commanders submitted returns at the end of 1863.

TABLE 10
Nominal Strength of the Confederate Army
at Various Times

Date	Numbers on Rolls
December 31, 1861	326,768
June 30, 1862	328,049
December 31, 1862	449,439
June 30, 1863	473,058
December 31, 1863	464,646
June 30, 1864	413,311
December 31, 1864	400,787
Last reports	358,692

The odds against the Confederates remained constant through 1863, the Confederates, averaging 408,392, having 55 percent of the Union's 704,974. But by June 30, 1864, the Union forces amounted to 1,001,782, and the Confederates still had only 413,311. For both reporting dates in 1864 Confederate strength had dropped to about 42 percent of the Union's. Nevertheless, this number sufficed to hold Richmond and, if Sherman had not used a raiding strategy, to keep him in north Georgia. It therefore apparently still provided an adequate force to carry out a basically successful defense against a conventional strategy. Further, the Confederate rosters in December 1864 carried only 400,000 of the 650,000–700,000 remaining in the manpower pool. In spite of pressing civilian and war production needs, the Confederacy could, hypothetically, have found some additional men.

Clearly the casualties of the war placed a very severe strain on the Confederacy's available white males of military age and, consequently, on its economy and morale. It was maintaining enrolled in its active forces 4.5 percent of its total population, over 7 percent of its white population, as compared with the approximately 9 percent of its native population which France had with the colors in 1918. Whether it could bear that strain would depend on its nationalism, expectations of success, and the value the Confederates placed on victory.

The number of men present with their units sheds light on this problem. The disparity between the numbers on the rolls and those present in the field changed during the war. At the end of 1861, Confederate forces had 21 percent of the men on their rosters absent. But by June 1862 the number absent had risen to over 30 percent and fluctuated around 30 percent for the next twelve months. This figure compares with the initial Union absence rate of 10.5 percent, which rose to 20 percent by June 1862 and remained about 25 percent for the next twelve months. This difference is readily explicable considering the greater degree of compulsion used by the Confederacy and by its need to draw more heavily on its far smaller manpower pool, forcing it to call up men with less commitment to the war.

But by the end of the fall of 1863 the percentage of Confederate absentees had risen almost to 40 percent; the Union absence rate rose, too, but remained well under 30 percent. Evidently the dimmed prospects for victory after Gettsyburg, Vicksburg, and Chattanooga had raised the desertion rate. But the percentage absent remained constant during the spring and summer while the Union rate rose slightly, to just over 30 percent. Thus on June 30, 1864, the Confederate armies had about 413,000 men on their rolls but only about 257,000 counted present with their units. Declining morale since the summer of 1863 had helped to increase a tremendous gap between nominal and actual strength.

In the fall of 1864 the proportion of absentees increased dramatically, rising from less than 40 percent at the end of June to 53 percent in the return of December 31, 1864. The fall of Atlanta and the reelection of Lincoln had obviously depressed morale. This rise in absenteeism continued, attaining nearly 60 percent in the last returns. But these, showing only 117,144 present, certainly lack reliability because the Union received the surrender of 174,223.[16]

Clearly Confederate numbers fluctuated more by the number present than by the total force available. Although men taken prisoner account for some of the increase in absences, the prospects for victory seem to have exercised the principal impact. The close correlation of increases in the rate of absence with military and political events strongly suggests that these, and the conscription of the less committed, constituted the primary causes of increases in absences, or that they exacerbated the problem "that Southerners, like all Celts, lacked tenacity."[17]

So, though the Confederacy could keep the nominal strength of its army at 400,000 men almost to the end, it could not supply the want of confidence in victory and belief that it had worth enough to warrant additional sacrifices. Certainly the heavy casualties depressed morale as well as required the Confederacy to dig deeper into the more reluctant levels of the manpower barrel. But as the experience of France and Germany shows, such casualties do not preclude a vigorous and successful war effort. And the Confederacy's casualties did not prevent it from fielding an adequate force. At the end of the war the Union had a nominal strength still little more than double the Confederacy's, but the Union had at least four times as many men with their units.

The original McWhiney and Jamieson thesis began with the assumption of a particular Celtic way of war characterized by an impetuous charge. But this provided a faulty basis for elaborating a peculiarly Celtic way of war because most of the examples upon which they based their thesis involved men armed with swords and spears or were drawn from the times when all armies conducted essentially frontal battles. An inadequate basis for a hypothesis does not necessarily indicate its falsity, but a more thorough examination of the data did not substantiate their preliminary investigation, which had shown more numerous Confederate attacks and vastly greater casualties. Instead, the Confederates attacked slightly less often than the Union armies and suffered only a little higher percentage of casualties. Since strategic reasons accounted for a large number of the Confederate offensive battles, and other factors, including inexperience and the blunders of even competent and seasoned leaders, could readily account for the prevalence of offensive frontal battles on both sides, no ethnic explanation seemed needed for the conduct of the war by either side. High Confederate combat effectiveness further argued against the tactical ineptitude implied by the original Celtic warfare hypothesis. Further, superior Union numbers in the first major war with both sides armed with rifles readily help us understand the comparatively heavy Confederate casualties.

Since the 80,961 missing in the thirty larger battles and campaigns in the first three years of the war substantially exceeded the estimate of 48,447 for those lost to service by death or battle disability, combat itself proved a less significant source of casualties than prisoners and other missing. In fact, the 53,410 men lost during this period through strategic mistakes may exceed the estimated number permanently lost to bullets in these thirty campaigns and battles in 1861, 1862, and 1863. Thus it is at least as difficult to find support for the thesis of defeat because of battle casualties as it is to substantiate a Celtic way of war or a Confederate propensity for frontal attacks.

But from this examination emerged a more fundamental hypothesis. Did Confederate manpower losses from every cause, including the 66,000 prisoners remaining alive in Union hands at the end of the war, cause Confederate defeat? Such a hypothesis need not depend on any special tactical or strategic explanation; the mere fact of heavy loss of life in an intensively fought four-year war provided an ample basis for asking this question. And the inquiry shows very serious casualties. Nevertheless, the Confederacy maintained the strength of its armies virtually unimpaired right through the campaigns of 1864. But this strength represented nominal numbers only, the proportion of men with the armies having declined during the war and, along with morale, had fallen precipitously at the end.

The Confederacy suffered heavy losses but less as a percentage of its white population than France in World War I or Germany in World War II. Enough men remained available to keep the armies at full strength and to continue effectively to exploit the power of the defense and the great size of the country to make a continued formidable resistance. But casualties, like defeats, helped depress morale, and the Confederacy's desire for the fruits of victory, its nationalism, and its willingness to suffer disruption of slavery and race relations did not equal the challenge of continuing the struggle.

Notes

INTRODUCTION

1. Henry Steele Commager, "How 'The Lost Cause' Was Lost," *New York Times Magazine*, August 4, 1963, p. 10.

2. John Russell Bartlett, *The Literature of the Rebellion: A Catalogue of Books and Pamphlets Relating to the Civil War in the United States . . .* (Boston, 1866).

3. David Donald, ed., *Why the North Won the Civil War* (Baton Rouge, 1960).

CHAPTER ONE

1. Donald, ed., *Why the North Won the Civil War*. For brief surveys of the historiography of Confederate defeat, see Donald's short preface to *Why the North Won* and the essay by Mary Elizabeth Massey, "The Confederate States of America: The Homefront," in Arthur S. Link and Rembert W. Patrick, eds., *Writing Southern History: Essays in Historiography in Honor of Fletcher M. Green* (Baton Rouge, 1965); James G. Randall and David Donald, *The Civil War and Reconstruction*, 2d ed., rev. (Lexington, Mass., 1969), 514–22; David Donald, *Liberty and Union* (Lexington, Mass., 1978), 162–66. The lack of a two-party political system was also part of David Potter's argument in his essay "Jefferson Davis and the Political Factors in Confederate Defeat," in Donald, ed., *Why the North Won the Civil War*, 113–14.

2. Charles W. Ramsdell, *Behind the Lines in the Southern Confederacy* (1944; rpr. New York, 1969), 113; E. Merton Coulter, *The Confederate States of America, 1861–1865* (Baton Rouge, 1950), 566; and Charles Grier Sellers, Jr., "The Travail of Slavery," in Sellers, ed., *The Southerner as American* (Chapel Hill, 1960), 44, 71.

3. Frank L. Owsley, *State Rights in the Confederacy* (Chicago, 1925), 1.

4. *Richmond Enquirer*, January 9, 1865, quoted in Hamilton J. Eckenrode, *Jefferson Davis: President of the South* (New York, 1930), 45; Jefferson Davis,

The Rise and Fall of the Confederate Government, 2 vols. (New York, 1881), 1:518.

5. Bell Irvin Wiley, *The Road to Appomattox* (1956; rpr. New York, 1968), 101; Donald, ed., *Why the North Won the Civil War,* 90.

6. Ludwell H. Johnson, "Jefferson Davis and Abraham Lincoln as War Presidents: Nothing Succeeds Like Success," *Civil War History* 27 (March 1981):49–63; Donald, ed., *Why the North Won the Civil War,* 79, 80, 85.

7. Donald, ed., *Why the North Won the Civil War,* 90.

8. Ibid., 31, 15.

9. Raimondo Luraghi, *The Rise and Fall of the Plantation South* (New York, 1978), 123; Emory M. Thomas, *The Confederacy as a Revolutionary Experience* (Englewood Cliffs, N.J., 1971), 134. See also Emory M. Thomas, *The Confederate Nation, 1861–1865* (New York, 1979), 212 and passim.

10. Luraghi, *Plantation South,* 127; Maurice Kaye Melton, "Major Military Industries of the Confederate Government" (Ph.D. dissertation, Emory University, 1978), 86.

11. Stanley Lebergott, "Why the South Lost: Commercial Purpose in the Confederacy, 1861–1865," *Journal of American History* 70 (June 1983):58–74; the quotation is from 74.

12. Ibid., 66–72.

13. William N. Still, Jr., *Confederate Shipbuilding* (Athens, Ga., 1969), 80.

14. Charles B. Dew, *Ironmaker to the Confederacy: Joseph R. Anderson and the Tredegar Iron Works* (New Haven, 1966), 267.

15. Thomas, *Confederate Nation,* 201.

16. Still, *Confederate Shipbulding,* 77. The best study of Confederate railroads is Robert C. Black III, *The Railroads of the Confederacy* (Chapel Hill, 1952).

17. Grady McWhiney and Perry D. Jamieson, *Attack and Die: Civil War Military Tactics and the Southern Heritage* (University, Ala., 1982), 124.

18. U.S. Surgeon-General's Office, *The Medical and Surgical History of the War of the Rebellion,* 6 vols. (Washington, D.C., 1875–83), ser. 2, vol. 2, pp. 685–86.

19. McWhiney and Jamieson, *Attack and Die,* 59–60, 112–25; Archer Jones, *Confederate Strategy from Shiloh to Vicksburg* (Baton Rouge, 1961), 9–12; Grady McWhiney, *Southerners and Other Americans* (New York, 1973), 103–27.

20. John G. Moore, "Mobility and Strategy in the Civil War," *Military Affairs* 24 (Summer 1960):68–77.

21. T. Harry Williams, "The Military Leadership of North and South," in Donald, ed., *Why the North Won the Civil War,* 29–31, 35, 37.

22. Ibid., 42–47.

23. Ibid., 38.

24. Ibid., 41, 46.

25. Williams's interpretation of Jomini relates to that in his *Lincoln and His Generals* (New York, 1952), which itself has much in common with the attack on Union generals carried on during the war by radical and other civilian critics of Union generals. The thesis about the extent and nature of Jomini's influence provides an explanation of why most generals differed with Lincoln and harmonizes with the wartime conviction held by many civilians that a West Point education made its graduates unable to conduct offensive warfare. That the West Point curriculum included Jomini provided, for Williams, the explanation for its debilitating effect on its graduates. Since then there have been thorough expositions of a more traditional view of Jomini as well as of his minor place in the West Point curriculum. See Archer Jones, "Jomini and the Strategy of the American Civil War: A Reinterpretation," *Military Affairs* 34 (December 1970):127–31; Thomas L. Connelly and Archer Jones, *Politics of Command: Factions and Ideas in Confederate Strategy* (Baton Rouge, 1973), 24–30 and passim; and James L. Morrison, "Educating Civil War Generals: West Point, 1833–1861," *Military Affairs* 38 (October 1974):108–11. Nevertheless, this interpretation lives on, appearing, for example, in Michael C. C. Adams, *Our Masters the Rebels: A Speculation on Union Military Failure in the East, 1861–1865* (Cambridge, Mass., 1978), 92, 172–73. For more bibliography and an exposition of the source of confusion about Jomini's views, see John R. Elting, "Jomini: Disciple of Napoleon?" *Military Affairs* 28 (Spring 1964):17–26, and Herman Hattaway and Archer Jones, *How the North Won: A Military History of the Civil War* (Urbana, Ill., 1983), 21–24.

In *Lincoln Reconsidered: Essays on the Civil War Era* (New York, 1956), David Donald presented an exposition of Jomini similar to that of Williams. For example, he apparently followed Sir Basil Liddell Hart in criticizing Lee for following Jomini's offensive prescription, thus forecasting an interpretation of Lee later advocated by T. L. Connelly and presented in Connelly and Jones, *Politics of Command.*

26. Joseph L. Harsh, "Battlesword and Rapier: Clausewitz, Jomini, and the American Civil War," *Military Affairs* 38 (December 1974):133–38, and T. Harry Williams, "The Return of Jomini: Some Thoughts on Recent Civil War Writing," *Military Affairs* 39 (December 1975):204–6.

27. Among the disciples of Jomini studied by soldiers in the nineteenth century are P. L. MacDougall, *The Theory of War*, 2d ed. (London, 1858); and Edward Bruce Hamley, *The Operations of War Explained and Illustrated*, 4th ed. (London, 1878). Both MacDougall and Hamley followed Jomini in explain-

ing military operations. John Bigelow, Jr., *The Principles of Strategy Illustrated Mainly from American Campaigns* (New York, 1891), has more originality. John I. Alger, *The Quest for Victory: The History of the Principles of War* (Westport, Conn., 1982), explains Jomini's role in the development of the concept of the principles of war; see esp. pp. 17–46, 176–78, 185–86, 202–9, 210–12. In U.S. Army, *FM 100-5, Operations* (Washington, D.C., 1982), see esp. pp. 7-4, 8-2, 8-4, 8-10, 8-11, 9-7, 10-1, 10-2, 13-2. In this manual the army expounds its basic operational doctrine for the conduct of campaigns and battles. For Grant's Vicksburg campaign as an example of a turning movement see pp. 8-1 through 8-3. *FM 100-5* relies on the offensive principle of concentration against weakness, implicit in Clausewitz and Jomini, but originating with Jacques de Guibert and other eighteenth-century French writers who influenced Napoleon. These operational ideas suffered some eclipse in the United States in the twentieth century. Instead, views of Grant like those espoused by Williams had powerful influence in the U.S. Army in the period between World Wars I and II and influenced the U.S. strategic perspective in World War II. See Russell F. Weigley, "Shaping the American Army of World War II: Mobility versus Power," *Parameters, Journal of the U.S. Army War College* 11 (September 1981), 13–21.

28. Ramsdell, *Behind the Lines in the Southern Confederacy,* esp. 85, 113.

29. Clement Eaton, *A History of the Southern Confederacy* (1954; rpr. New York, 1965), chap. 13; Charles P. Roland, *The Confederacy* (Chicago, 1960), 193–94.

30. Edward Channing, *A History of the United States,* vol. 6, *The War for Southern Independence, 1849–1865* (New York, 1925), 612–15; Charles H. Wesley, *The Collapse of the Confederacy* (1937; rpr. New York, 1968), 167–68, 171; Coulter, *Confederate States of America,* 566–67.

31. Sellers, "Travail of Slavery," 44, 61, 67–71.

32. Wiley, *Road to Appomattox,* 101, 103–5; Carl N. Degler, *Place over Time: The Continuity of Southern Distinctiveness* (Baton Rouge, 1977), 107; Kenneth M. Stampp, "The Southern Road to Appomattox," in Stampp, ed., *The Imperiled Union: Essays on the Background of the Civil War* (New York, 1980), 251–52, 255.

33. Potter, "Jefferson Davis and the Political Factors in Confederate Defeat," in Donald, ed., *Why the North Won the Civil War,* 103; Eaton, *History of the Southern Confederacy,* 251. For Confederate propaganda in Europe, see Charles P. Cullop, *Confederate Propaganda in Europe, 1861–1865* (Coral Gables, Fla., 1969), 135 and passim. The unsystematic, haphazard nature of Confederate propaganda on the home front is discussed in James W. Silver, "Propaganda in the Confederacy," *Journal of Southern History* 11 (November 1945):487–503.

34. John Hall Stewart, *A Documentary Survey of the French Revolution* (New York, 1951), 472–73.

35. Jefferson Davis to Hugh Davis, January 8, 1865, Jefferson Davis, *Jefferson Davis: Private Letters, 1823–1889*, ed. Hudson Strode (New York, 1966), 140.

36. *Daily Conservative*, October 8, 1864. The letter was widely printed in newspapers throughout the Confederacy.

37. Jon L. Wakelyn, *Biographical Dictionary of the Confederacy* (Westport, Conn., 1977), 333–34; Thomas B. Alexander and Richard E. Beringer, *The Anatomy of the Confederate Congress: A Study of the Influence of Member Characteristics on Legislative Voting Behavior, 1861–1865* (Nashville, 1972), 14, 69, 170, 238, 403; "Proceedings of the . . . Confederate Congress" [title varies], *Southern Historical Society Papers* 45 (May 1925):159; W. S. Oldham to Jefferson Davis, February 11, 1865, U.S. War Department, *The War of the Rebellion: A Compilation of the Official Records of the Union and Confederate Armies,* 70 vols. in 128 parts (Washington, D.C., 1880–1901), ser. 4, vol. 3, pp. 1078–79, hereafter cited as *OR;* U.S. Congress, Senate, *Journal of the Congress of the Confederate States of America, 1861–1865*, 7 vols. (Washington, D.C., 1904–5), 4:491, 742; 7:408–9, 497; Williamson S. Oldham, "Memoirs of W. S. Oldham, Confederate Senator, 1861–1865" (typescript, 31, 33, 137, 138, Barker Texas History Center, University of Texas, Austin). Oldham's typescript memoirs are apparently a draft of a series of articles he later published under the title "Last Days of the Confederacy," *De Bow's Review*, 2d ser., 7–8 (October 1869–September 1870).

38. Oldham, "Memoirs," 137–41.

39. Ibid., 143–45, 148–61, 163, 191, 301.

40. Ibid., 138 and passim.

CHAPTER TWO

1. H. de Jomini, *The Art of War*, trans. G. H. Mendell and W. P. Craighill (Philadelphia, 1862), 44, 49, hereafter cited as Jomini.

2. Jomini, 44.

3. Jomini, 43.

4. Carl von Clausewitz, *On War*, ed. and trans. Michael Howard and Peter Paret (Princeton, 1976), 145, hereafter cited as Clausewitz; Jomini, 55.

5. Clausewitz, 145; Jomini, 56.

6. William S. McFeely, *Grant: A Biography* (New York, 1981), 78; John Russell Young, *Around the World with General Grant*, 2 vols. (New York, 1879), 2:352; John H. Brinton, *The Personal Memoirs of John H. Brinton, Major and Surgeon, U.S.V., 1861–1865* (New York, 1914), 239.

7. Jomini, 43; Clausewitz, 607. In the same place Clausewitz wrote that "subordinating the political point of view to the military would be absurd."

8. Davis to W. P. Harris, December 13, 1861, Jefferson Davis, *Jefferson Davis, Constitutionalist: His Letters, Papers and Speeches*, ed. Dunbar Rowland, 10 vols. (Jackson, Miss., 1923), 5:179.

9. Jomini, 53, 57, 335.

10. Jomini, 56.

11. Clausewitz, 145–47.

12. Most Civil War officers in high command justified Jomini's faith when he wrote: "Correct theories, founded upon right principles, sustained by the actual events of wars, and added to accurate military history, will form a true school of instruction for generals. If these means do not produce great men, they will at least produce generals of sufficient skill to take rank next after the natural masters of the art of war" (Jomini, 325).

13. Clausewitz, 358, 600; Jomini, pp. 72–74, 96, 121–22, 166, 184, 186, 189, 202–3, 353, 359, 360; Frank E. Vandiver, *Their Tattered Flags* (New York, 1970), 88–89, 94; Frank E. Vandiver, "Jefferson Davis and Confederate Strategy," in Bernard Mayo, ed., *The American Tragedy: The Civil War in Retrospect* (Hampden-Sydney, Va., 1959), 19–32.

14. Clausewitz, 223; see also 290–93, 315–18, 361, 418–19, 433, 508–9, 615.

15. Jomini, 179, 188, 341, 343; see also 200–201, 204, 207.

16. Clausewitz, 161, 214, 391, 460, 625.

17. Clausewitz, 390, 406–7, 409–14, 492, 496, 505, 535–37; Jomini, 68, 96, 153–57, 181, 201, 211–15, 223, 244.

18. Clausewitz, 80, 81, 809; see also 75; Jomini, 16–35, 50.

19. Clausewitz, 90–97, 501; see also 513, 517, 597, 601, 626; Jomini, 72, 88–89, 107.

20. Clausewitz, 472, 597; Jomini, 23; see also Clausewitz, 472–75, 480, 562–63, 611–12, 627, 633; Jomini, 90, 98–99, 151.

21. Clausewitz, 632–34.

22. Clausewitz, 627; George W. Randolph to Molly Randolph, October 10, 1861, Edgehill-Randolph Papers, Alderman Library, University of Virginia, Charlottesville.

CHAPTER THREE

1. Part of this chapter in another form has appeared in William N. Still, Jr., "A Naval Sieve: The Union Blockade in the Civil War," *Naval War College Review* 36 (May–June 1983):34–45.

2. U.S. Congress, Senate, Executive Document No. 1, Annual Report of the Secretary of the Navy, December 2, 1861, 37th Cong., 2d sess., 1861, 3 (serial 1119).

3. Coulter, *Confederate States of America*, 294; Bern Anderson, *By Sea and by River: The Naval History of the Civil War* (New York, 1962), 232; Roland, *The Confederacy*, 137.

4. James R. Soley, *The Blockade and the Cruisers* (New York, 1883), 44–45.

5. Frank L. Owsley, *King Cotton Diplomacy: Foreign Relations of the Confederate States of America* (1931, 2d ed. Chicago, 1959), 229–67.

6. Marcus W. Price, "Ships That Tested the Blockade of the Carolina Ports, 1861–1865," *American Neptune* 8 (July 1948):196–241; Price, "Ships That Tested the Blockade of the Gulf Ports, 1861–1865," *American Neptune* 11 (October 1951):262–97; Price, "Ships That Tested the Blockade of the Georgia and East Florida Ports, 1861–1865," *American Neptune* 15 (April 1955):97–132; Richard Everett Wood, "Port Town at War: Wilmington, North Carolina, 1860–1865" (Ph.D. dissertation, Florida State University, 1976), 183–84. The most complete study of the Union blockade is Stephen Robert Wise, "Lifeline of the Confederacy: Blockade Running during the Civil War" (Ph.D. dissertation, University of South Carolina, 1983).

7. Frank E. Vandiver, ed., *Confederate Blockade Running through Bermuda, 1861–1865* (Austin, Tex., 1947), xli; Vandiver, *Their Tattered Flags*, 233–34.

8. Richard I. Lester, *Confederate Finance and Purchasing in Great Britain* (Charlottesville, Va., 1975), 49, 165, 168, 177, 197, 199; Richard D. Goff, *Confederate Supply* (Durham, N.C., 1969), 139; Anderson, *By Sea and by River*, 288.

9. William N. Still, Jr., *Iron Afloat: The Story of the Confederate Armorclads* (Nashville, 1971).

10. See his address to Congress, January 12, 1863, Davis, *Jefferson Davis, Constitutionalist*, 5:405; Davis to Tucker, January 15, 1865, *OR*, ser. 1, vol. 47, pt. 2, p. 1014.

11. Seddon to Davis, November 26, 1863, *OR*, ser. 1, vol. 2, p. 1015; Luraghi, *Plantation South*, 136; Goff, *Confederate Supply*, 145, 247; *Richmond Daily Dispatch*, March 27, 1865.

12. Luraghi, *Plantation South*, 129; Thomas, *Confederacy as a Revolutionary Experience;* Thomas, *Confederate Nation;* Vandiver, *Their Tattered Flags;* Frank E. Vandiver, *Ploughshares into Swords: Josiah Gorgas and Confederate Ordnance* (Austin, Tex., 1952); Goff, *Confederate Supply;* Still, *Confederate Shipbuilding*.

13. Wood, "Port Town," 178; *OR*, ser. 4, vol. 3, pp. 78–80.

14. "Official Regulations to carry into effect the act 'to impose regulations upon the foreign commerce of the Confederate States to provide for the public defense,'" signed and approved by Secretary of War James A. Seddon and Secretary of the Treasury C. G. Memminger, March 5, 1864, *OR*, ser. 4, vol. 3, pp. 187–89; ibid., 80–82; U.S., Congress, Senate, *Journal of the Congress of the Confederate States*, 6:702.

15. Davis to House of Representatives, December 20, 1864, *OR*, ser. 4, vol. 3, p. 949; Davis to House of Representatives, June 10, 1864, James D. Richardson, ed., *A Compilation of the Messages and Papers of the Confederacy, Including Diplomatic Correspondence*, 2 vols. (Nashville, 1905), 1:467; Davis to House of Representatives, December 20, 1864, *OR*, ser. 4, vol. 3, p. 951.

16. Seddon to Davis, December 10, 1864, *OR*, ser. 4, vol. 3, p. 928; Davis to House of Representatives, December 20, 1864, ibid., 952. See also Wilfred Buck Yearns, *The Confederate Congress* (Athens, Ga., 1960), 137–39; Alexander and Beringer, *Anatomy of the Confederate Congress*, 205–6; Louise B. Hill, *State Socialism in the Confederate States of America* (Charlottesville, Va., 1936).

17. Robert Browning, "The Blockade of Wilmington, North Carolina, 1861–1865" (M.A. thesis, East Carolina University, 1980), 136–77.

18. Goff, *Confederate Supply*, 141.

19. Robert Erwin Johnson, "Investment by Sea: The Civil War Blockade," *American Neptune* 32 (January 1972):53–54; Browning, "Blockade of Wilmington," 58–59.

20. Lee to Ludlow Case, September 4, 1863, U.S. Navy, *Official Records of the Union and Confederate Navies in the War of the Rebellion*, 30 vols. (Washington, D.C., 1894–1927), ser. 1, vol. 9, p. 191, hereafter cited as *OR, Navies*.

21. Hill, *State Socialism*, 12.

CHAPTER FOUR

1. See Hill, *State Socialism*, and Luraghi, *Plantation South*, 84, 150.

2. Frank E. Vandiver, *Jefferson Davis and the Confederate State* (Oxford, 1964), 2; Vandiver, *Their Tattered Flags*, 130; Vandiver, "Jefferson Davis—Leader without Legend," *Journal of Southern History* 43 (February 1977):17; Jefferson Davis to Hugh Davis, January 8, 1865, Davis, *Jefferson Davis: Private Letters*, 140. For a parallel text of the United States and Confederate constitutions that indicates clearly the great inherent power in the latter, see Charles Robert Lee, Jr., *The Confederate Constitutions* (Chapel Hill, 1963), appendix.

3. Thomas, *Confederate Nation*, 147, 224.

4. Paul D. Escott, *After Secession: Jefferson Davis and the Failure of Confederate Nationalism* (Baton Rouge, 1978), xi, 74.

5. Stampp, "Southern Road to Appomattox," 257, 255–60; the quote is from 257.

6. Worth to Joseph Utley, May 28, 1861, Jonathan Worth, *The Correspondence of Jonathan Worth*, ed. J. G. de Roulhac Hamilton, 2 vols. (Raleigh, 1909), 1:150.

7. *Nashville Republican Banner*, April 17, 1861.

8. Pardon petition of Robert L. Caruthers, Amnesty Papers, Tennessee, Records of the Adjutant General's Office, Record Group 94, National Archives, Washington, D.C.; Graham to Robert C. Winthrop, February 1, 1867, Robert Charles Winthrop Papers, Massachusetts Historical Society, Boston.

9. Ralph A. Wooster, *The Secession Conventions of the South* (Princeton, 1962).

10. Steven A. Channing, "Slavery and Confederate Nationalism," in Walter J. Fraser, Jr., and Winfred B. Moore, eds., *From the Old South to the New: Essays on the Transitional South* (Westport, Conn., 1981), 221–24.

11. Lillian A. Pereyra, *James Lusk Alcorn: Persistent Whig* (Baton Rouge, 1966), 401; Percy Lee Rainwater, *Mississippi: Storm Center of Secession, 1856–1861* (1938; rpr. New York, 1969), 219; Marc W. Kruman, *Parties and Politics in North Carolina, 1836–1865* (Baton Rouge, 1983), 207–8.

12. Elizabeth Blair Lee to Samuel Phillips Lee, January 22, 1861, Virginia Jeans Laas, "'On the Qui Vive for the Long Letter': Washington Letters from a Navy Wife, 1861," *Civil War History* 29 (March 1983):41.

13. Steven A. Channing, *Crisis of Fear: Secession in South Carolina* (New York, 1970), 145–47; John E. Johns, *Florida during the Civil War* (Gainesville, 1963), 1, quoting from Ellen Call Long, *Florida Breezes, or, Florida New and Old* (1883; rpr. Gainesville, 1962), 306–8.

14. Mary Boykin Chesnut, *Mary Chesnut's Civil War*, ed. C. Vann Woodward (New Haven, 1981), 241, entry for November 20, 1861; George H. Reese, ed., *Proceedings of the Virginia State Convention of 1861*, 4 vols. (Richmond, 1965), 3:169.

15. Worth to J. J. Jackson, December 17, 1860, Worth, *Correspondence*, 1:127; *Raleigh Daily Conservative*, January 2, 1865; see also Richard L. Zuber, *Jonathan Worth: A Biography of a Southern Unionist* (Chapel Hill, 1965), 119, and James L. Roark, *Masters without Slaves: Southern Planters in the Civil War and Reconstruction* (New York, 1977), 2–7.

16. Lincoln to Joshua F. Speed, August 24, 1855, Abraham Lincoln, *The Collected Works of Abraham Lincoln*, ed. Roy P. Basler, 8 vols. (New Brunswick, N.J., 1953), 2:320.

17. William J, Northen, ed., *Men of Mark in Georgia . . .* , 6 vols. (Atlanta, 1907–12), 3:558; Johns, *Florida during the Civil War*, 21. Johns gives no source for the quotation.

18. J. P. Eller to Vance, January 28, 1861, Zebulon Baird Vance, *The Papers of Zebulon Baird Vance*, ed. Frontis W. Johnston, vol. 1, 1843–1862 (Raleigh, 1963), 93; Benjamin Harvey Hill, Jr., *Senator Benjamin H. Hill of Georgia: His Life, Speeches, and Writings* (Atlanta, 1893), 39–40; Herschel V. Johnson, "From the Autobiography of Herschel V. Johnson, 1856–1867," *American Historical Review* 30 (January 1925):327.

19. *Nashville Republican Banner*, August 3, 1861.

20. Walter L. Buenger, "Secession Revisited: The Texas Experience," *Civil War History* 30 (December 1984):293–305; Phillip Shaw Paludan, *Victims: A True Story of the Civil War* (Knoxville, 1981), 64; Jeremiah Clemens to "My Dear Daughter," September 5, 1862, *Civil War Times–Illustrated* Collection, U.S. Army Military History Institute, Carlisle Barracks, Pa.

21. Message to the second session of the Provisional Congress, April 29, 1861, Richardson, ed., *Messages and Papers*, 1:82. The phrase caught on, and Confederates probably repeated it more often than anything else Davis said or wrote during the war. Governor Vance of North Carolina repeated it back to him, December 30, 1863, Davis, *Jefferson Davis, Constitutionalist*, 6:141. It appears twice in the messages of Georgia's Governor Brown to the state legislature, November 6, 1862, and November 5, 1863, Allen D. Candler, ed., *The Confederate Records of the State of Georgia*, 6 vols. (Atlanta, 1909–11), 2:284, 482. It is even found in a geography textbook designed for use in Confederate elementary schools: Mrs. M. B. Moore, *Primary Geography Arranged as a Reading Book for Common Schools* (1864), in Malcolm C. McMillan, ed., *The Alabama Confederate Reader* (University, Ala., 1963), 359–60.

22. See, for example, Brown to Davis, May 8, 1862, *OR*, ser. 4, vol. 1, pp. 1116, 1120; U.S., Congress, Senate, *Journal of the Congress of the Confederate States*, 1:845; Henry Cleveland, *Alexander H. Stephens in Public and Private: With Letters and Speeches, before, during, and since the War* (Philadelphia, 1866), 718, 721, 725; Speech at Augusta, Georgia, October 5, 1864, Davis, *Jefferson Davis, Constitutionalist*, 6:357. J. D. B. De Bow claimed that "we are not revolutionists—we are resisting revolution" (De Bow, "Our Danger and Our Duty," *De Bow's Review*, 1st ser., 33 [1862]:44).

23. Wooster, *Secession Conventions of the South*, 195, 198–99; Vandiver, *Their Tattered Flags*, 19; Robert L. Kerby, "Why the Confederacy Lost," *Review of Politics* 35 (July 1973):342–43.

24. David M. Potter, "The Historian's Use of Nationalism and Vice Versa," in Potter, *The South and the Sectional Conflict* (Baton Rouge, 1968); Chan-

ning, "Slavery and Confederate Nationalism," 219–26; Georgia Lee Tatum, *Disloyalty in the Confederacy* (1934; rpr. New York, 1970); Paludan, *Victims*.

25. Alexander and Beringer, *Anatomy of the Confederate Congress*, 339–40.

26. Buenger, "Secession Revisited," p. 305.

27. McWhiney, *Southerners and Other Americans*, 3–4; Edward Pessen, "How Different from Each Other Were the Antebellum North and South?" *American Historical Review* 85 (December 1980):1122, 1147, 1149.

28. Potter, "The Historian's Use of Nationalism," 76.

29. On this point see Rollin G. Osterweis, *Romanticism and Nationalism in the Old South* (New Haven, 1949), although Osterweis takes southern nationalism more seriously than we are inclined to do. Quote is from 137.

30. Herman Hattaway, "Via Confederate Post," *Civil War Times Illustrated* 15 (April 1976):22–29.

31. Potter, "The Historian's Use of Nationalism," 65–69; Frank L. Owsley, "The Fundamental Cause of the Civil War: Egocentric Sectionalism," *Journal of Southern History* 7 (February 1941):8–9.

32. James M. McPherson, "Antebellum Southern Exceptionalism: A New Look at an Old Question," *Civil War History* 29 (September 1983):242–44.

33. Potter, "The Historian's Use of Nationalism," 68–69, 78–80.

34. Buenger, "Secession Revisited," passim; *Nashville Republican Banner*, April 11, 1861; Charles Reagan Wilson, "Robert Lewis Dabney: Religion and the Southern Holocaust," *Virginia Magazine of History and Biography* 89 (January 1981):81. The alleged remarks were attributed to James L. Petigru. Unfortunately, the source has been lost.

35. Avery O. Craven, *The Growth of Southern Nationalism, 1848–1861* (Baton Rouge, 1953), ix, 171, 205, and chaps. 13 and 14.

36. John McCardell, *The Idea of a Southern Nation: Southern Nationalists and Southern Nationalism, 1830–1860* (New York, 1979), 2–3, 9, 337–38.

37. David M. Potter, *The Impending Crisis, 1848–1861*, completed and edited by Don E. Fehrenbacher (New York, 1976), 462–63, 469, 473–74, 478, 484. See also Carl N. Degler, *Place over Time: The Continuity of Southern Distinctiveness* (Baton Rouge, 1977), 106–7, who contends that slavery had made the South distinctive, though not so distinctive as to create a special worldview.

CHAPTER FIVE

1. Davis to F. W. Pickens, January 13, 1861, Davis, *Jefferson Davis, Constitutionalist*, 5:37. See also Davis, *Rise and Fall*, 1:227, 230–31; Davis to

Franklin Pierce, January 20, 1861, Davis, *Jefferson Davis: Private Letters*, 122; Davis to Varina Davis, February 20, 1861, ibid., 123.

2. Thomas, *Confederate Nation*, 21; Paul C. Nagel, *One Nation Indivisible: The Union in American Thought, 1776–1861* (New York, 1971).

3. Samuel S. Hill, Jr., *The South and the North in American Religion* (Athens, Ga., 1980), xi.

4. Ibid., 47, 51; Thomas, *Confederate Nation*, 21.

5. Sydney E. Ahlstrom, *A Religious History of the American People* (New Haven, 1972), 654–65, 667; James E. Wood, Jr., "Religious Fundamentalism and the New Right," *Religion Journal of Kansas* 20 (October 1982):2, reprinted from *Journal of Church and State* 22 (Autumn 1980):409–21; Hill, *The South and the North in American Religion*, 69.

6. William W. Sweet, *The Story of Religion in America*, 2d ed. (New York, 1950), 312; Hill, *The South and the North in American Religion*, 87; Ahlstrom, *Religious History of the American People*, 673.

7. After the war, some of the Radical Republicans carped against what they asserted had been the pope's recognition of the Confederate government—the only recognition by a "foreign sovereign." In fact, it consisted simply of the pope's having addressed Jefferson Davis in an 1863 letter as "Your Excellency" (Ahlstrom, *Religious History of the American People*, 670).

8. Benjamin J. Bleid, *Catholics and the Civil War* (Milwaukee, 1945), 40, 50, 53, 61, 62, 69.

9. W. Harrison Daniel, "Protestantism and Patriotism in the Confederacy," *Mississippi Quarterly* 24 (Spring 1971):119–23.

10. Ahlstrom, *Religious History of the American People*, 670–71.

11. Ibid.

12. Bleid, *Catholics and the Civil War*, 55.

13. Quoted in Coulter, *Confederate States of America*, 518.

14. Francis Butler Simkins, *A History of the South*, 3d ed. (New York, 1967), 223; Thomas C. DeLeon, *Belles, Beaux and Brains of the 60's* (New York, 1909), 56; Thomas Reade Rootes Cobb, "Correspondence of Thomas Reade Rootes Cobb, 1860–1862," ed. A. L. Hull, *Publications of the Southern History Association* 11 (1907):166; *Nashville Republican Banner*, August 7, 1861; Leon Litwack, *Been in the Storm So Long: The Aftermath of Slavery* (New York, 1979), 5, quoted from George P. Rawick, ed., *The American Slave: A Composite Autobiography*, 19 vols. (Westport, Conn., 1972–79), 14:192.

15. Special message of Governor Joseph E. Brown to the Senate and House of Representatives, November 7, 1860, Candler, ed., *Confederate Records of the State of Georgia*, 1:55.

16. Betty L. Mitchell, *Edmund Ruffin: A Biography* (Bloomington, Ind., 1981), 165, 185, 241.

17. Davis, *Rise and Fall*, 1:227, 304.

18. Martha Wolfenstein, *Disaster: A Psychological Essay* (London, 1957), 147.

19. Chesnut, *Mary Chesnut's Civil War*, 29, 246, entries for March 18 and November 28, 1861.

20. John W. Blassingame, *The Slave Community: Plantation Life in the Antebellum South*, rev. ed. (New York, 1979), 268–70; McMillan, ed., *Alabama Confederate Reader*, 360.

21. Hill, *The South and the North in American Religion*, 3–5, 10, italics added.

22. James F. Maclear, "The Republic and the Millennium," in Elwyn A. Smith, ed., *The Religion of the Republic* (Philadelphia, 1971), 184; Hill, *The South and the North in American Religion*, 29–30.

23. Clement Eaton, *A History of the Old South: The Emergence of a Reluctant Nation*, 3d ed. (New York, 1975), 382; James H. Moorhead, *American Apocalypse: Yankee Protestants and the Civil War, 1860–1869* (New Haven, 1978), 45; see also Samuel S. Hill, Jr., ed., *Religion in the Southern States: A Historical Study* (Macon, 1983), and Donald G. Mathews, *Religion in the Old South* (Chicago, 1977).

24. Moorhead, *American Apocalypse*, 55; Daniel, "Protestantism and Patriotism in the Confederacy," 117; John Brown Gordon, *Reminiscences of the Civil War* (New York, 1903), 417.

25. Thomas, *Confederate Nation*, 21.

26. Ibid., 22–23. See also Degler, *Place over Time*, 22–23, who contends that even today religion "helps to set the South apart from the nation not only because it is conservative, but because it is taken seriously by southerners."

27. Hill, *The South and the North in American Religion*, 37–38.

28. Revelation 16:16; Moorhead, *American Apocalypse*, ix–xiii, and passim.

29. Moorhead, *American Apocalypse*, 3–7, 9, 21n; Charles Reagan Wilson, *Baptized in Blood: The Religion of the Lost Cause, 1865–1920* (Athens, Ga., 1980), 64. Moorhead has addressed the subject of Civil War–era millennialism in other contexts as well as in his book on northern mainline Protestants. But he appears to be more knowledgeable about the part of the topic he treated in his book than he does on its southern manifestations. He says in "Millennialism," in Samuel S. Hill, Jr., ed., *Encyclopedia of Religion in the South* (Macon, 1984), 478, that "the majority of antebellum Southern clergymen appear to have been postmillennialists . . . [but that] Southern postmillen-

nialism, however, differed from its Northern counterpart in one important particular. Whereas the latter was frequently allied with a free-labor capitalism, the former increasingly made a virtue of slavery." And he deals with the entire topic, across a broader time spectrum, in his article "Between Progress and Apocalypse: A Reassessment of Millennialism in American Religious Thought, 1800–1880," *Journal of American History* 71 (December 1984):524–42. But even there, he tells us much more about postmillennialism than he does about premillennialism, which suggests that he may still be a bit hazy about the latter. He is convincing in his assertion that "by the early twentieth century an explicit postmillennialism had largely vanished from American Protestantism" (pp. 541–42). But he hints, at the conclusion of his latest article, that perhaps the [southern] Protestant conservatives had by and large embraced premillennialism. Perhaps, as we believe, that is what they had been all along—when they were millennialists at all, and most of the time they were not. Charles Reagan Wilson, in private conversation with Hattaway, has agreed, suggesting that nineteenth-century southern Protestant thinkers generally always had held any doctrine of millennialism at arm's length, regarding it as "too New Englandish."

30. Daniel, "Protestantism and Patriotism in the Confederacy," 117; Ahlstrom, *Religious History of the American People*, 672.

31. W. Harrison Daniel, "Bible Publication and Procurement in the Confederacy," *Journal of Southern History* 24 (May 1958):198–99, nn. 38, 43; Thomas, *Confederate Nation*, 246; James I. Robertson, Jr., "Chaplain William E. Wiatt: Soldier of the Cloth," in James I. Robertson, Jr., and Richard M. McMurry, eds., *Rank and File: Civil War Essays in Honor of Bell Irvin Wiley* (San Rafael, Calif., 1976), 118.

32. Ahlstrom, *Religious History of the American People*, 672.

33. Thomas, *Confederate Nation*, 245; Proclamation of May 28 and Proclamation of October 31, 1861, in Richardson, ed., *Messages and Papers*, 1:103, 135.

34. Daniel, "Protestantism and Patriotism in the Confederacy," 117–18; Chesnut's diary is also quoted by Daniel.

35. William Cowper, "Light Shining Out of Darkness," *Olney Hymns* (London, 1779), quoted in Brian Spiller, *Cowper Verse and Letters* (Cambridge, Mass., 1968), 154.

36. Jefferson Davis, Proclamation to the Soldiers of the Confederate States, undated, but probably August 1, 1863, *OR*, ser. 4, vol. 2, p. 687.

37. Thomas, *Confederate Nation*, 246; Daniel, "Protestantism and Patriotism in the Confederacy," 118. Religious thinking also inspired anti-Confederate activities among Quakers, Unitarians, and other sects, though their

numbers were small. See Samuel Horst, *Mennonites in the Confederacy: A Study in Civil War Pacifism* (Scottsdale, Pa., 1967).

38. Daniel, "Protestantism and Patriotism in the Confederacy," 131–33.

39. John Bones to Robert Hughes, March 29, 1861, Hughes Family Papers, Southern Historical Collection, quoted in Roark, *Masters without Slaves*, 9; *Nashville Republican Banner*, April 16, 17, 1861; *North Carolina Standard*, July 17, 1863.

40. De Bow, "Our Danger and Our Duty," 45; *Montgomery Weekly Advertiser*, December 5, 12, 1860.

41. Daniel, "Protestantism and Patriotism in the Confederacy," 125, 129.

42. Robertson and McMurry, eds., *Rank and File*, 131–32.

43. James B. Sheeran, *Confederate Chaplain: A War Journal* (Milwaukee, 1960), v–vi, 5–6, 8–9, 20, 25, 29, 31–32.

44. Daniel, "Bible Publication and Procurement," 199 n. 43; Jay Monaghan, *Civil War on the Western Border, 1854–1865* (New York, 1955), 195.

45. Bleid, *Catholics and the Civil War*, 64.

46. John Keegan, *The Face of Battle* (New York, 1976), 114, 237–38, 326.

47. James W. Silver, *Confederate Morale and Church Propaganda* (New York, 1957), 101.

48. Ahlstrom, *Religious History of the American People*, 677.

49. Ibid.

PART THREE

1. Rev. C. C. Jones to Lt. Charles C. Jones, Jr., March 24, 1862, Robert Manson Myers, ed., *The Children of Pride: A True Story of Georgia and the Civil War* (New Haven, 1972), 866.

CHAPTER SIX

1. Jomini, 40.

2. Clausewitz, 516, 179; Jomini, 102; see also Clausewitz, 135–36, 163, 196–97, 364, 367–69, 466, 476, 541.

3. Jomini, 102–32, 274–75.

4. Clausewitz, 547.

5. Louis M. Starr, *Reporting the Civil War: The Bohemian Brigade in Action, 1861–65* (New York, 1962), 34.

6. Clausewitz, 391.

7. Clausewitz, 261.

8. Clausewitz, 261, 71.

9. Clausewitz, 263.

10. Clausewitz, 260–65, 613.

11. Clausewitz, 422; see also Jomini, 70, 80.

12. Clausewitz, 375, 328, 338, 340; Jomini, 138, 146, 246.

13. *OR Navies*, ser. 1, vol. 25, p. 474; Louis C. Hunter, *Steamboats on the Western Rivers: An Economic and Technological History* (Cambridge, Mass., 1949), 555.

14. Quoted in John D. Milligan, *Gunboats down the Mississippi* (Annapolis, Md., 1965), 19; *OR Navies*, ser. 1, vol. 22, p. 356.

15. Jomini, 217–18.

16. William T. Sherman, *Memoirs of Gen. W. T. Sherman. . .* , 2 vols. 4th ed. (New York, 1891), 1:248.

17. McFeely, *Grant*, xii.

18. Clausewitz, 299; Jomini, 341, 343.

19. Clausewitz, 364.

20. Halleck to McClellan, March 4, 1862, *OR*, ser. 1, vol. 7, p. 683; U.S. Army, *F-M 100-5, Operations*, 7–8.

21. Davis to the Senate and House of Representatives of the Confederate States, February 25, 1862, Richardson, ed., *Messages and Papers*, 1:189.

22. Speech of Henry S. Foote, February 20, 1862, "Proceedings," *Southern Historical Society Papers* 44 (June 1923):28; Joseph E. Brown, "A Proclamation to the Mechanics of Georgia," February 20, 1862; Candler, ed., *Confederate Records of the State of Georgia*, 2:199–200.

23. Jefferson Davis, A Proclamation to the People of the Confederate States, February 20, 1862, Richardson, ed., *Messages and Papers*, 1:218; Joseph E. Brown, A Proclamation, February 18, 1862, Candler, ed., *Confederate Records of the State of Georgia*, 1:197; Resolution of May 9, 1862, Virginia, *Acts of the General Assembly of the State of Virginia, at the Extra Session, 1862 . . .* (Richmond, 1862), 28.

CHAPTER SEVEN

1. Thomas Bragg Diary, 1861–62 (No. 3304), microfilm, entries for February 7, 10, and 26, 1862, frames 457–59, 471, microfilm copy of original in Southern Historical Collection, Library of the University of North Carolina at Chapel Hill.

2. Clausewitz, 365; see also Clausewitz, 341–47, 446; Jomini, 76, 144–45, 172–74, 177.

3. Clausewitz, 198, 199; see also 363, 445, 557–61.

4. Jomini, 328, 74; Clausewitz, 204; see also Jomini, 70, 73, 90, 96, 115, 117, 139, 176, 178, 186–87, 329, 333, 342; Clausewitz, 204, 542, 549, 552, 596–97, 612, 617, 619, 621–23. The Confederates could also easily have been following the point of the United States Army's 1982 operations manual that "concentration increases the chances of success." This work also enjoins that "an underlying purpose of all defensive operations is to create the opportunity to change to the offensive." Although the Confederates had not planned a counterattack in their bungled defense in Tennessee and Kentucky, they followed its spirit when they did counterattack. And by intending to attack Grant before Buell joined him, they followed the manual's injunction to "concentrate attacking forces against enemy weaknesses" (U.S. Army, *FM 100-5, Operations*, 7-9, 9-9, 10-3). Of course, such actions equally reflected the ideas of Jomini and Clausewitz.

5. Ulysses S. Grant, *Personal Memoirs of U.S. Grant*, 2 vols. (New York, 1885–86), 1:222, 368–69, 354–55.

6. Clausewitz, 472–73.

7. Grant, *Memoirs*, 1:381; Grant to E. B. Washburne, June 1, 1862, Ulysses S. Grant, *The Papers of Ulysses S. Grant*, John Y. Simon, ed., 12 vols. to date (Carbondale, Ill., 1967–), 5:136; Sherman, *Memoirs*, 1:282.

8. Scott to McClellan, May 3, 1861, *OR*, ser. 1, vol. 51, pt. 1, p. 369.

9. Rowena Reed, *Combined Operations in the Civil War* (Annapolis, Md., 1978), 39.

10. Anderson, *By Sea and by River*, 51.

11. Reed, *Combined Operations*, 44–51; Samuel Francis Du Pont, *Samuel Francis Du Pont: A Selection from His Civil War Letters*, ed. John Daniel Hayes, 3 vols. (Ithaca, N.Y., 1969), 1:lxxi–lxxiii.

12. John G. Barrett, *The Civil War in North Carolina* (Chapel Hill, 1963), 66; Reed, *Combined Operations*, 39–40.

13. William N. Still, Jr., "Admiral Goldsborough's Feisty Career," *Civil War Times–Illustrated* 17 (February 1979):20.

14. Grant, *Memoirs*, 2:539.

15. Clausewitz, 611, 617–19, 633–34.

16. Bell Irvin Wiley, *The Life of Billy Yank: The Common Soldier of the Union* (New York, 1952), 164.

17. Clausewitz, 204–5, 209, 211, 612; see also Jomini, 311.

18. McClellan to Lincoln, January 31, 1862, Lincoln, *Collected Works*, 5:120–25; Clausewitz, 546.

19. Clausewitz, 546.

20. Clausewitz, 233; Jomini, 328; see also Clausewitz, 625; Jomini, 178–79, 189, 342–43.

21. Clausewitz, 552, 525, 502–4; see also Clausewitz, 166, 181–82; Jomini, 107–8, 152–53.

22. Clausewitz, 234.

23. Very likely Clausewitz would have shared Lincoln's apprehension about a "sack" of Washington. He would have thought that the Union should adequately fortify the capital and that it should "have sufficient powers of resistance to protect it against capture or plunder by any raiding party that happens to come along." But he would, like Jomini, certainly have disparaged the substantial division of forces involved because of the large number of men Lincoln retained between Richmond and Washington (Clausewitz, 475; see also Clausewitz, 402, 619–23; Jomini, 106, 217).

24. Mallory to Conrad, May 10, 1861, *OR Navies*, ser. 2, vol. 2, pp. 67–69.

25. Goldsborough to Welles, April 19, 1862, ibid., ser. 1, vol. 7, pp. 246–47.

26. Clausewitz, 192.

27. Clausewitz, 464.

28. Clausewitz, 501.

29. Clausewitz, 283.

30. U.S. Army, *FM 100-5, Operations*, 10-4, 8-4, 8-6.

31. Clausewitz, 600, 535, 360–71, 546–47; see also Clausewitz, 233, 390, 392, 437, 530.

32. Reed, *Combined Operations*, 187.

33. Clausewitz, 234, 263, 558; Lincoln to de Gasparin, August 4, 1862, Lincoln, *Collected Works*, 5:355.

34. Clausewitz, 615.

35. Chesnut, *Mary Chesnut's Civil War*, 400–401, entry for June 29, 1862; Proclamation to the People of the Confederate States, February 20, 1862, Richardson, ed., *Messages and Papers*, 1:217–18.

CHAPTER EIGHT

1. Stampp, "Southern Road to Appomattox," 258–59; Lee, *Confederate Constitutions*, 114–16. The *Montgomery Weekly Advertiser*, January 16, 1861, claimed that "separate State action is necessary before that effectual co-operation can be had, which alone can produce reconstruction—and if the Northern people are not hopelessly blinded by the fanaticism that pervades their communities, they will recognize in the peaceable secession of South Carolina and

other States the only hope of subsequent reconstruction." On January 19, 1861, pro-Union delegate T. W. Alexander moved, in the Georgia secession convention, "that the people of Georgia would be willing that the Federal Union, now broken and dissolved, should be reconstructed whenever the same can be done on a basis that would secure, permanently and unequivocally, the measure of the rights and equality of the people of the slave-holding States." These resolutions were referred to committee and never reported back. See Candler, ed., *Confederate Records of the State of Georgia*, 1:262.

2. U.S., Congress, Senate, *Journal of the Congress of the Confederate States*, 1:75–77, 895; *OR*, ser. 4, vol. 1, pp. 111–12.

3. U.S., Congress, Senate, *Journal of the Congress of the Confederate States*, 2:277–78.

4. Vandiver, *Their Tattered Flags*, 156–58.

5. Davis to Lee, Bragg, and Kirby Smith, September 7, 1862, Davis, *Jefferson Davis, Constitutionalist*, 5:338–39; Larry E. Nelson, *Bullets, Ballots, and Rhetoric: Confederate Policy for the United States Presidential Contest of 1864* (University, Ala., 1980), 18–19.

6. Lee to Davis, September 3, 4, 5, 1862, *OR*, ser. 1, vol. 19, pt. 2, pp. 590–94.

7. Clausewitz, 516, 135–36, 341–44, 547; Jomini, 66–67, 77–84, 119–20; Heinrich Dietrich von Bülow, *The Spirit of the Modern System of War* (London, 1806), 1–75, hereafter cited as Bülow.

8. Jomini, 77–84.

9. R. Ernest Dupuy and Trevor N. Dupuy, *The Compact History of the Civil War* (New York, 1960), 142.

10. Clausewitz, 466; Jomini 204; see also Clausewitz, 465, 542; Jomini, 207.

11. Clausewitz, 466.

12. Clausewitz, 548–49.

13. Lee to Davis, September 3, 4, 1862, *OR*, ser. 1, vol. 19, pt. 2, pp. 590–91.

14. Lee to Davis, September 12, 1862, and September 5, 1862, *OR*, ser. 1, vol. 19, pt. 2, pp. 604–5, 593. See Clausewitz, 71, 415, 416, 492–94, 546; Jomini, 78, 82, 162, 237, 239–41.

15. Lee to Davis, September 3, 1862, *OR*, ser. 1, vol. 19, pt. 2, p. 591.

16. Clausewitz, 411–12.

17. James M. McPherson, *Ordeal by Fire: The Civil War and Reconstruction* (New York, 1982), 283.

18. Lee to the People of Maryland, September 8, 1862, *OR*, ser. 1, vol. 19, pt. 2, pp. 601–2; Lee to Davis, September 7, 8, 1862, ibid., 596–97, 600.

19. See Clausewitz, 174, 286, 288, 291.

20. Bell Irvin Wiley, *The Life of Johnny Reb: The Common Soldier of the Confederacy* (Indianapolis, 1943), 341.

21. Jomini, 313–14; Clausewitz, 562; see also Jomini, 202, 288–89, 304–15, Clauswitz, 453, 460–61, 465, 562–64, 568, 614.

22. Jomini, 29, 144, 27; see also Jomini, 29–34, 41, 72, 95, 167, 233, 337.

23. Clausewitz, 480; see also 161, 346–47, 350, 373, 414, 424–26, 452, 463, 465, 473, 479–81, 483.

24. Jomini had noted how formidable guerrillas and raiders were: "Irregular troops supported by disciplined troops may be of greatest value in destroying convoys, intercepting communications &c." Clausewitz felt "no need to elaborate" on the problems of communication in a hostile country in a national war. He placed great emphasis on the desirability that lines of communications form a right angle with the front, rendering them relatively secure. But with guerrillas in the rear to help the raiders, "action against the enemy's lines of communication is possible even if they join his front at a right angle; our raiders did not constantly have to fall back on their own forces, but can find plenty of shelter simply by vanishing into the countryside" (Jomini, 72, 142; Clauswitz, 340; see also Jomini, 122, 144, 246; Clausewitz, 328, 338, 375).

25. Jomini, 42n; Clausewitz, 463, 550, 556, 562–63; see also Clausewitz, 299, 461–63.

26. Jomini, 262–63; see also Clausewitz, 464–65, 555–56.

27. Bragg to Cooper, August 1, 1862, *OR*, ser. 1, vol. 16, pt. 2, p. 741; Bragg to Kirby Smith, August 15, 1862, ibid., 759; Kirby Smith to Davis, August 11, 1862, ibid., 753; Kirby Smith to the East Tennesseeans in the U.S. Army, August 13, 1862, ibid., 756; Kirby Smith to Bragg, August 20, 1862, ibid., 766–67; Kirby Smith to Davis, August 21, 1862, ibid., 768–69.

28. Jno. W. Crockett and others to Jefferson Davis, August 18, 1862, ibid., 771–72; Kirby Smith to Cooper, August 24, 1862, ibid., 777–78; Kirby Smith to Davis, August 26, 1862, ibid., 780.

29. Proclamation by Braxton Bragg, September 14, 1862, ibid., 822; Sam. Jones to Henry C. Wayne, September 16, 1862, ibid., 835.

30. J. P. McCown to Kirby Smith, September 16, 1862, ibid., 836; Kirby Smith to Bragg, September 18, 1862, ibid., 845–46; Bragg to the adjutant general, C.S. Army, September 25, 1862, ibid., 876; Bragg to Leonidas Polk, October 1, 1862, ibid., 895.

31. Jomini, 200–201, 346, 67, 333.

32. Clausewitz, 261, 195; see also Clausewitz, 360, 391, 530–31, 535, 546, 560, 625.

33. Clausewitz, 263, 267, 261; see also 261–72, 349, 509; Jomini, 183.

34. Clausewitz, 617–32, 509. Clausewitz believed that most campaigns fell "between the two poles" of seeking a decision and a strict limitation on objectives (Clausewitz, 501).

35. Address of Hon. T. A. R. Nelson to the People of East Tennessee, newspaper clipping reprinted in *OR*, ser. 1, vol. 16, pt. 2, pp. 909–11.

36. Jefferson Davis to T. H. Holmes, October 21, 1862, Davis, *Jefferson Davis, Constitutionalist,* 5:356.

37. Proclamation by Braxton Bragg, September 14, 1862, *OR*, ser. 1, vol. 16, pt. 2, p. 822.

38. Clausewitz, 549–50, 372; see also Clausewitz, 363–66; Jomini, 121–22. Clausewitz believed the pursuit of such territorial goals might lead to "major or minor engagements," but such battles "will neither be sought, nor will they be treated as objectives in themselves, but rather as necessary evils. They cannot rise before a certain level of magnitude and importance" (Clausewitz, 549–50).

39. Clausewitz, 488–98, 501–19, 600; Jomini, 74, 96, 184; see also Clausewitz, 364, 405, 451, 460–68. Unlike Jomini, Clausewitz believed that the strategic turning movement had a "far greater affinity" for the defense than the offense. Thus he listed it among his "methods of the defense" (Clausewitz, 460).

40. Clausewitz, 503, 506.

41. Clausewitz, 507, 505.

42. Clausewitz, 512.

43. Clausewitz, 511, 562; see also 512, 513, 564.

CHAPTER NINE

1. McPherson, *Ordeal by Fire,* 172.

2. *OR Navies,* ser. 1, vol. 27, pp. 418, 619–28, 682–83.

3. Hunter, *Steamboats on the Western Rivers,* 555.

4. William N. Still, Jr., "Porter . . . Is the Best Man," *Civil War Times–Illustrated* 16 (May 1977):4–9, 44–47.

5. Ibid., 47.

6. Milligan, *Gunboats down the Mississippi,* 178.

7. *OR Navies,* ser. 1, vol. 26, pp. 679–80.

8. Louis Phillippe Albert d'Orleans, Comte de Paris, *History of the Civil War in America,* 4 vols. (Philadelphia, 1875–88), 3:215–16.

9. William N. Still, Jr., "The New Ironclads," in William C. Davis, ed., *The Image of War, 1861–1865,* vol. 2, *The Guns of '62* (Garden City, 1982), 59.

10. Anderson, *By Sea and by River,* 175, 177.

11. J. A. Dahlgren to W. T. Sherman, April 20, 1865, Sherman, *Memoirs,* 2:319; W. T. Sherman to Grant, December 24, 1864, ibid., 225.

12. Lee to Welles, *OR Navies*, ser. 1, vol. 9, pp. 370–71.

13. Browning, "Blockade of Wilmington," 19–20.

14. James M. Merrill, *The Rebel Shore: The Story of Union Sea Power in the Civil War* (Boston, 1957), 220–21.

15. Reed, *Combined Operations*, 377; Jay Luvaas, "The Fall of Fort Fisher," *Civil War Times–Illustrated* 3 (August 1964):5–9, 31–35; Anderson, *By Sea and by River*, 284.

16. Davis to Brooks, March 15, 1862, *OR*, ser. 4, vol. 1, p. 998.

CHAPTER TEN

1. Owsley, *State Rights in the Confederacy*, 1, 19, 26, 38.

2. Merrill, *Rebel Shore*, vi, 13–14; see also 25, 52–53.

3. Kruman, *Parties and Politics*, 243; Marc W. Kruman, "Dissent in the Confederacy: The North Carolina Experience," *Civil War History* 27 (December 1981):297, 298–99.

4. Kruman, *Parties and Politics*, 245, 247; Kruman, "Dissent," 299–300, 301.

5. Kruman, *Parties and Politics*, 259, 260, italics added; Kruman, "Dissent," 306–8.

6. Kruman, *Parties and Politics*, 266; Kruman, "Dissent," 311; Randall and Donald, *Civil War and Reconstruction*, 457–58; Donald, *Lincoln Reconsidered*, chap. 4.

7. David M. Potter, "Jefferson Davis and the Political Factors in Confederate Defeat," in Donald, ed., *Why the North Won the Civil War*, 111–12.

8. Lewis O. Saum, "Schlesinger and 'The State Rights Fetish': A Note," *Civil War History* 24 (December 1978):357–59.

9. Kruman, "Dissent," 311–12; Kruman, *Parties and Politics*, 266; Hugh T. Lefler and Albert R. Newsome, *North Carolina: The History of a Southern State*, rev. ed. (Chapel Hill, 1963), 437–38; Horace W. Raper, "William W. Holden and the Peace Movement in North Carolina," *North Carolina Historical Review* 31 (October 1954):495–96; Eaton, *History of the Southern Confederacy*, 258.

10. Kruman, "Dissent," 312; Kruman, *Parties and Politics*, 267; John S. Preston to J. C. Breckinridge, February 1865, Tabulations A and B, *OR*, ser. 4, vol. 3, p. 1101.

11. David D. Scarboro, "North Carolina and the Confederacy: The Weakness of States' Rights during the Civil War," *North Carolina Historical Review* 56 (April 1979):134.

12. Eaton, *History of the Southern Confederacy*, 256; Newsome and Lefler, *North Carolina*, 438–39; Vance, *Papers*, 1:xli–xiv; Thos. Miller to Vance, November 10, 1862, ibid., 324; Martha Coletrane to Vance, November 18, 1862, ibid., 374.

13. Scarboro, "North Carolina and the Confederacy."

14. James Alex Baggett, "Origins of Upper South Scalawag Leadership," *Civil War History* 29 (March 1983):69.

15. John B. Jones, *A Rebel War Clerk's Diary at the Confederate States Capital*, 2 vols. (Philadelphia, 1866), 1:197, entry for November 27, 1862; Z. B. Vance to Jefferson Davis, May 13, 1863, Davis, *Jefferson Davis, Constitutionalist*, 5:486–87.

16. Escott, *After Secession*, 54–55.

17. Ibid., 55ff.

18. "Proceedings," *Southern Historical Society Papers* 47 (December 1930):208–10, 220–21; U.S. Congress, Senate, *Journal of the Congress of the Confederate States*, 1:781–82.

19. Richard D. Brown, *Modernization: The Transformation of American Life, 1600–1865* (New York, 1976), 173–75, 181.

20. Hill, *State Socialism;* Coulter, *Confederate States of America*, 202–7, 210–11.

21. Eaton, *History of the Southern Confederacy*, 241–42; Roland, *The Confederacy*, 66–69.

22. Vandiver, *Their Tattered Flags*, 240–42, 245.

23. Frank E. Vandiver, "The Civil War as an Institutionalizing Force," in William F. Holmes and Harold M. Hollingsworth, eds., *Essays on the American Civil War*, Walter Prescott Webb Memorial Lectures (Austin, Tex., 1968), 85–86; see also Vandiver, *Ploughshares into Swords;* Josiah Gorgas, *The Civil War Diary of General Josiah Gorgas*, ed. Frank E. Vandiver (University, Ala., 1947).

24. Thomas, *Confederate Nation*, 206–14, quotes on 212–13.

25. Luraghi, *Plantation South*, 113. Needless to say, we do not agree with all of Luraghi's conclusions. We doubt, for example, that "the cultural history of the Old South has . . . its deepest roots . . . in Italy" (15).

26. Ibid., 118.

27. Ibid., 123–24. A general law of the maximum, however, was introduced in the Confederate Senate in November 1864, bounced between committees, and killed. See U.S., Congress, Senate, *Journal of the Congress of the Confederate States*, 4:262, 269, 283.

28. Luraghi, *Plantation South*, 124.

29. Ibid., 125, 127.

30. Ibid., 129–30.

31. Ibid., 131–32.

32. Thomas H. Watts to James A. Seddon, January 19, 1864, *OR*, ser. 4, vol. 3, p. 37; Watts to Seddon, April 12, 1864, Yancey Papers, Executive Correspondence, Maps and Manuscripts Division, Alabama Department of Archives and History, Montgomery; Escott, *After Secession*, 66. For example, see Joseph E. Brown to James A. Seddon, November 9, 1863, *OR*, ser. 4, vol. 2, pp. 943–44; General Assembly of North Carolina, December 12, 1863, ibid., 1066; and John Milton to James A. Seddon, January 26, 1864, ibid., 3, 46. See also Lebergott, "Why the South Lost," 70–72.

33. Escott, *After Secession*, 68; Jefferson Davis, To the Senate and House of Representatives of the Confederate States, December 7, 1863, Richardson, ed., *Messages and Papers*, 1:364–67; Curtis Arthur Amlund, *Federalism in the Southern Confederacy* (Washington, D.C., 1966), 38–39.

34. Escott, *After Secession*, 73, 76, 75.

35. Ibid., 88; John Brawner Robbins, "Confederate Nationalism: Politics and Government in the Confederate South, 1861–1865" (Ph.D. dissertation, Rice University, 1964), 108–9; James G. Randall, *Constitutional Problems under Lincoln*, rev. ed. (Urbana, Ill., 1964), 11–12, 259.

36. Escott, *After Secession*, 90, citing Amlund, *Federalism*, 105, q.v.

37. Alexander and Beringer, *Anatomy of the Confederate Congress;* Escott, *After Secession*, 90 n. 77, 92; Saum, "Schlesinger and 'The State Rights Fetish,'" 358–59.

38. Escott, *After Secession*, 137 n. 2, 135–37.

39. Robbins, "Confederate Nationalism," 29, 30; see also Lee, *Confederate Constitutions*, for a detailed analysis of both provisional and permanent constitutions.

40. Robbins, "Confederate Nationalism," 64, 65.

41. Ibid., 68.

42. Ibid., 70, 81–82; Owsley, *State Rights in the Confederacy*, 184–91.

43. Robbins, "Confederate Nationalism," 85, 86. Contemporary Confederate politicians were quick to note this geographic relationship, which many of them thoroughly resented. For example, Josiah Turner, Jr., a North Carolina congressman, declared that he "would rather plough and feed hogs than legislate . . . with Missouri and Kentucky to help me" (quoted in Yearns, *Confederate Congress*, 225).

44. Owsley, *State Rights in the Confederacy*, 176–202; William M. Robinson, *Justice in Grey: A History of the Judicial System of the Confederate States of America* (Cambridge, Mass., 1941); Robbins, "Confederate Nationalism," 93 n. 68, 87, 94; Alexander and Beringer, *Anatomy of the Confederate Congress*, 167, 172. Brown's remarks are found in "Proceedings," *South-*

ern Historical Society Papers 50 (December 1953):133. Militia drafts were held during the colonial period, and conscription was discussed in Congress during the War of 1812.

45. Robbins, "Confederate Nationalism," 97, 98, 99, quoting James M. Matthews, *Statutes at Large, 1 Cong. 1 Sess.*, chap. 31; U.S., Congress, Senate, *Journal of the Congress of the Confederate States*, 5:220–21; 2:153–54.

46. Robbins, "Confederate Nationalism," 104, 106.

47. Ibid., 106, 107; Jefferson Davis to the governor and Executive Council of South Carolina, September 3, 1862, Davis, *Jefferson Davis, Constitutionalist*, 5:334–37.

48. Robbins, "Confederate Nationalism," 108, 116.

49. Ibid., 121; Emory Upton, *The Military Policy of the United States* (Washington, 1912), 468–69.

50. Escott, *After Secession*, 137–38.

51. Paul D. Escott, "Poverty and Governmental Aid for the Poor in Confederate North Carolina," *North Carolina Historical Review* 61 (October 1984):462–80.

52. Escott, *After Secession*, 138–49, 151, 152–53, quote on 149, 151; Thomas, *Confederate Nation*, 202–5; Coulter, *Confederate States of America*, 422–23.

53. Frank L. Owsley, "Local Defense and the Overthrow of the Confederacy: A Study in State Rights," 64; Frank L. Owsley, "Defeatism in the Confederacy," 97–98; both in Frank L. Owsley, *The South, Old and New Frontiers: Selected Essays of Frank Lawrence Owsley*, ed. Harriet C. Owsley (Athens, Ga., 1969).

54. Owsley, "Defeatism," 99.

55. John Adams to T. Jordon, May 8, 1862, *OR*, ser. 1, vol. 52, pt. 2, p. 312; O. M. Mitchell to E. M. Stanton, May 19, 1862, ibid., vol. 10, pt. 2, p. 204.

56. Clausewitz, 77; Report of Brigadier General Grenville M. Dodge, May 5, 1863, *OR*, ser. 1, vol. 23, pt. 1, p. 248.

57. Owsley, "Defeatism," 99; Ella Lonn, *Salt as a Factor in the Confederacy* (University, Ala., 1965), 112.

58. Thomas, *Confederate Nation*, 202–5; Coulter, *Confederate States of America*, 422–23; Escott, "Poverty and Governmental Aid for the Poor in Confederate North Carolina."

59. Owsley, "Defeatism," 101, 104; statement of Col. Jefferson Faulkner and A. R. Hill, undated but ca. May 8, 1864, *OR*, ser. 4, vol. 3, p. 398.

60. Owsley, "Defeatism," 97, 99; Robert S. Hudson to Davis, October 5, 1863, *OR*, ser. 4, vol. 2, pp. 856–58; James M. Arrington to J. M. Withers, January 30, 1865, ibid., vol. 3, pp. 1042–43; M. A. Baldwin to Jones M. Withers, January 30, 1865, ibid., 1043–44.

61. Lebergott, "Why the South Lost," 72, quoting Joseph E. Johnston, *Narrative of Military Operations Directed, during the Late War between the States* (1874; rpr. Bloomington, Ind., 1959), 424–25.

62. Ramsdell, *Behind the Lines in the Southern Confederacy*, 61–67.

63. Lebergott, "Why the South Lost," 62–66; Paul D. Escott, "Serving Two Masters: The Political Acumen of Georgia's Joseph E. Brown," published under the title "Georgia," in W. Buck Yearns, ed., *The Confederate Governors* (Athens, Ga., 1985), 75–76. We draw heavily on this article but do not present Escott's intriguing and convincing main thesis only because it is not sufficiently germane to our principal purpose.

64. Escott, "Georgia," 73, 75, 77.

65. Ibid., 70, 77.

66. Ibid., 76–77. Quote is from Brown to George T. Anderson, May 2, 1864, *OR*, ser. 4, vol. 3, pp. 373–74.

67. Peter Wallenstein, "Rich Man's War, Rich Man's Fight: Civil War and the Transformation of Public Finance in Georgia," *Journal of Southern History* 50 (February 1984):24, 34, 32.

68. Ibid., 30, 35, 17; Escott, "Georgia," 76.

69. Escott, "Georgia," 78.

70. Escott, *After Secession*, 152–53.

71. Ibid., 160; Paul Escott, "'The Cry of the Sufferers': The Problem of Welfare in the Confederacy," *Civil War History* 23 (September 1977):228, 238.

CHAPTER ELEVEN

1. R. E. Lee to Thomas J. Jackson, November 14, 1862, *OR*, ser. 1, vol. 19, pt. 2, p. 720.

2. Lincoln to McClellan, October 13, 1862, Lincoln, *Collected Works*, 5:461; Jomini, 70, 80.

3. Lee to Gustavus W. Smith, November 6, 1862, *OR*, ser. 1, vol. 19, pt. 2, p. 697; Lee to Davis, November 6, 1862, ibid., 698; Lee to Jackson, November 18, 1862, ibid., vol. 21, 1018–19; Lee to Davis, November 19, 1862, ibid., 1020–21; Lee to Cooper, November 21, 1862, ibid., 1026.

4. Lee to Jackson, November 23, 1862, *OR*, ser. 1, vol. 21, 1027; Lee to Davis, November 25, 1862, ibid., 1028–29; Davis to Lee, December 8, 1862, Davis, *Jefferson Davis, Constitutionalist*, 5:385.

5. R. E. Lee to Jefferson Davis, December 6, 1862, *OR*, ser. 1, vol. 21, pp. 1049–50; Lee to Cooper, December 13, 1862, ibid., 1061.

6. Clausewitz, 97.

7. Kirby Smith to Joseph E. Johnston, December 26, 1862, *OR*, ser. 1, vol. 20, pt. 2, p. 462.

8. Clausewitz, 271.

9. James A. Seddon to Kirby Smith, January 4, 1863, *OR*, ser. 1, vol. 20, pt. 2, p. 484; J. E. Johnston to Cooper, January 6, 1863, ibid., 487; Johnston to R. S. Ewell, January 6, 1863, ibid.; Johnston to Jefferson Davis, January 7, 1863, ibid., 487–88; P. G. T. Beauregard to Braxton Bragg, January 8, 1863, ibid., 490.

10. Edwin C. Bearss, *Decision in Mississippi: Mississippi's Important Role in the War between the States* (Jackson, 1962), 110–11; see Jomini, 221, 224.

11. Herman Hattaway, "Confederate Mythmaking: Top Command and the Chickasaw Bayou Campaign," *Journal of Mississippi History* 32 (November 1970):311–26.

12. Oliver P. Morton to E. M. Stanton, January 3, 1863, *OR*, ser. 1, vol. 20, pt. 2, p. 297; Lincoln to Oliver P. Morton, February 1, 1863, *OR*, ser. 3, vol. 3, p. 23; J. M. Hofer, "Development of the Peace Movement in Illinois during the Civil War," *Journal of the Illinois State Historical Society* 24 (April 1931):119. Clausewitz noted the adverse effects "on the people and the government" produced by "a sudden collapse of the most anxious expectations," such as those entertained for the December campaigns (Clausewitz, 255).

13. Hubert H. Wubben, *Civil War Iowa and the Copperhead Movement* (Ames, 1980), 93–95; Samuel J. Kirkwood to Edwin M. Stanton, March 10, 1863, *OR*, ser. 3, vol. 3, p. 62; Kirkwood to Stanton, March 11, 1863, ibid., 62; Kirkwood to Stanton, March 13, 1863, with enclosures, ibid., 66–72; Orville Hickman Browning, *The Diary of Orville Hickman Browning*, vol. 1, *1850–1864*, Theodore Calvin Pease and James G. Randall, eds., in *Collections of the Illinois State Historical Library* (Springfield, 1925), 20, 600, entry for December 18, 1862.

14. James A. Seddon to Jefferson Davis, January 3, 1863, *OR*, ser. 4, vol. 2, pp. 280, 285, 293.

15. Davis to the Senate and House of Representatives of the Confederate States, January 12, 1863, Richardson, ed., *Messages and Papers*, 1:277; Jones, *Rebel War Clerk's Diary*, 1:224, 228, entries for December 25, 1862, and January 1, 1863; William T. Sherman to David Tod, March 12, 1863, *OR*, ser. 3, vol. 3, p. 65.

16. Jomini, 216; see also Clausewitz, 460.

17. Clausewitz, 339, 343, 510, 346, 347; see also Clausewitz, 340, 365.

18. Jomini, 31.

19. Sherman to Rawlins, July 8, 1862, *OR*, ser. 1, vol. 17, pt. 2, p. 84; Sherman to John Sherman, December 24, 1861, William T. Sherman, *The Sherman Letters: Correspondence between General and Senator Sherman, 1837 to 1891*, ed. Rachel Sherman Thorndike (1894; rpr. New York, 1969), 136; Sherman to

David Tod, March 12, 1863, *OR*, ser. 3, vol. 3, pp. 3, 65–66. Clausewitz would have believed that forested, "obstructed terrain," of which the South had an abundance, helped guerrillas in a "truly national" resistance, and guerrillas aided and were encouraged by "skillful raiders" who learned to "move daringly in small detachments and attack boldly, assaulting the enemy's weaker garrisons, convoys, and minor units on the march" (Clausewitz, 350, 465, 460; see also Clausewitz, 188, 347, 480–83, 562–64; Jomini, 42, 216, 218, 221).

20. Davis to Polk, March 28, 1848, Jefferson Davis, *The Papers of Jefferson Davis*, ed. Haskell M. Monroe, Jr., et al., 4 vols. to date (Baton Rouge, 1971–), 3:290.

21. Jomini, 224.

22. Clausewitz, 381, 379, 384, 477, 472; see also Clausewitz, 381–83, 469–78, and Chapter 8, above.

23. Clausewitz, 479. Clausewitz believed that a large theater of war, with "its natural obstacles and its sheer expanse of surface," provided "immobile forces," which aided the defense (Clausewitz, 499).

24. Jomini, 169.

25. Clausewitz, 577, 595–96, 92; see also 526.

26. Oldham, "Memoirs," 298.

27. Clausewitz believed that as "any considerable weakening of the forces will generally lead to a loss of territory," so any "considerable loss of territory" will lead to a weakening of the armed forces; but only "in the long run" would the armed forces feel the effect of the diminution of the country's extent (Clausewitz, 484–85).

28. Clausewitz, 382–83, 566, 598, 611, 613; see Jomini, 72.

29. Wiley, *Life of Billy Yank*, 27.

30. Jomini, 147.

31. Clausewitz, 391.

32. U.S. Army, *FM 100-5, Operations*, 8-2.

33. Robert Garlick Hill Kean, *Inside the Confederate Government: The Diary of Robert Garlick Hill Kean*, ed. Edward Younger (New York, 1957), 74, entry for June 17, 1864. Kean wrote that Campbell hesitated and declined to discuss Napoleon with Seddon because "it would do no good."

34. Clausewitz, 554.

35. Halleck to Grant, August 1, 1863, *OR*, ser. 1, vol. 24, pt. 1, p. 63; Jomini, 137.

36. Jomini, 176, 137, 70.

37. Jomini, 156, 42; Clausewitz, 412; Theodore Lyman, *Meade's Headquarters, 1863–1865; Letters of Colonel Theodore Lyman from the Wilderness to Appomattox*, ed. George R. Agassiz (Boston, 1922), 102. Clausewitz did allow

for the success of the strategic turning movement when, as in this case, the enemy made *"major, obvious, and exceptional mistakes"* (Clausewitz, 364).

38. Rosecrans to Halleck, June 2, 1863, *OR*, ser. 1, vol. 24, pt. 3, p. 376.

39. Rosecrans to Stanton, July 7, 1863, *OR*, ser. 1, vol. 23, pt. 2, p. 518; Clausewitz, 529.

40. Jomini, 74; Clausewitz, 370; Jefferson Davis to Robert E. Lee, May 31, 1863, Davis, *Jefferson Davis, Constitutionalist,* 5:502.

41. Lee to Davis, June 7, 1863, Davis, *Jefferson Davis, Constitutionalist,* 5:507; see, e.g., Lee to Davis, June 23, 1863, ibid., 531.

42. Lincoln to Hooker, May 14, June 5, 1863, Lincoln, *Collected Works,* 6:217–18, 249–50.

43. George G. Meade to Margaretta Meade, February 6, 1863, George G. Meade, *The Life and Letters of George Gordon Meade, Major General United States Army,* ed. George Gordon Meade, 2 vols. (New York, 1913), 1:354.

44. Abraham Lincoln to Henry W. Halleck, July 6, 1863, Lincoln, *Collected Works,* 6:318; Lincoln to Meade, July 14, 1863, ibid., 328. Although the letter to Meade was never sent, Meade understood Lincoln's disappointment from Halleck's dispatches and, sent or not, it reveals Lincoln's thoughts well. See also Clausewitz, 370.

45. Lee to Davis, July 31, 1863, *OR*, ser. 1, vol. 27, pt. 2, p. 305.

46. Lawrence N. Powell and Michael S. Wayne, "Self-Interest and the Decline of Confederate Nationalism," in Harry P. Owens and James J. Cooke, eds., *The Old South in the Crucible of War* (Jackson, Miss., 1983), 32–33.

47. Kean, *Inside the Confederate Government,* 79–81.

48. Consolidated abstract from returns of the Confederate army on or about June 30, 1863, *OR*, ser. 4, vol. 2, p. 615; consolidated abstract from returns of the Confederate army on or about December 31, 1863, ibid., 1073; Robert D. Graham to William A. Graham, August 20, 1863, William Alexander Graham, *The Papers of William Alexander Graham,* ed. J. G. de Roulhac Hamilton and Max R. Williams, 6 vols. (Raleigh, N.C., 1957–76), 5:521.

49. Lee to Davis, July 8, 1863, Davis, *Jefferson Davis, Constitutionalist,* 5:538; Davis to Robert Ward Johnson, July 14, 1863, ibid., 548.

CHAPTER TWELVE

1. Proclamation, October 31, 1861, Richardson, ed. *Messages and Papers,* 1:135; Resolution of November 19, 1862, *Acts of the General Assembly of the State of Georgia, Passed in Milledgeville, at an Annual Session in November and December 1862: Also Extra Session of 1863* (Milledgeville, 1863), 101.

2. *North Carolina Christian Advocate* and *Fayetteville Presbyterian*, both quoted in the *Raleigh Register*, August 12, 1863; Resolution of November 17, 1863, in *Acts of the General Assembly of the State of Georgia, Passed in Milledgeville, at an Annual Session in November and December, 1863; Also, Extra Session of 1864* (Milledgeville, 1864), 101.

3. Silver, *Confederate Morale and Church Propaganda*, 25.

4. *Daily Lynchburg Virginian*, September 8, 1862.

5. *Lynchburg Virginian*, September 28, 1864.

6. Silver, *Confederate Morale and Church Propaganda*, 31–32, 36.

7. Reply to Members of the Presbyterian General Assembly, June 2, 1863, Lincoln, *Collected Works*, 6:244; Meditation on the Divine Will, September 2, 1862?, ibid., 5:403–4.

8. Proclamation Appointing a National Fast Day, March 30, 1863, ibid., 6:155–56; Proclamation of Thanksgiving, July 15, 1863, ibid., 332; Abraham Lincoln to Eliza P. Gurney, September 4, 1864, ibid., 7:535.

9. Cushing Strout, *The New Heavens and New Earth: Political Religion in America* (New York, 1974), 196–98.

10. *Spirit of the Times*, date unknown, copied in the *Milledgeville Confederate Union*, June 31, 1864, and the *Richmond Dispatch*, June 11, 1864.

11. Bertram Wyatt-Brown, *Southern Honor: Ethics and Behavior in the Old South* (New York, 1982), 107.

12. Joseph E. Brown, Inaugural Address, November 8, 1861, Candler, ed., *Confederate Records of the State of Georgia*, 2:128–29.

13. A Proclamation, September 4, 1862, Richardson, ed., *Messages and Papers*, 1:268; *Lynchburg Daily Virginian*, March 26, 27, 1863; *Memphis Daily Appeal*, July 13, 21, 1863.

14. *Milledgeville Confederate Union*, August 18, 1863; A Proclamation, July 25, 1863, Richardson, ed., *Messages and Papers*, 1:328.

15. Joseph E. Brown to the Senate and House of Representatives, November 5, 1863, Candler, ed., *Confederate Records of the State of Georgia*, 2:535; Alabama, *Acts of the Called Session, 1863, and of the Third Regular Annual Session of the General Assembly of Alabama . . .* (Montgomery, 1864), 215; Mississippi, *Laws of the State of Mississippi, Passed at a Called and Regular Session of the Mississippi Legislature . . . Dec. 1862 and Nov. 1863* (Selma, Ala., 1864), 232, 228–29; Florida, *The Acts and Resolutions Adopted by the General Assembly of Florida, at Its 12th Session . . .* (Tallahassee, 1863), 53.

16. *Daily Lynchburg Virginian*, September 18, 1862.

17. Mary Jones to Col. Charles C. Jones, Jr., July 14, 1863, Myers, ed., *Children of Pride*, 1076; ibid., 1233, entry for December 22, 1864; Reverend

John Jones to Mary Jones, September 23, 1864, ibid., 1203; *Raleigh Daily Progress*, July 15, 1863, quoted in *North Carolina Standard*, July 17, 1863; C. D. Smith to James Ramsay, November 17, 1863, James G. Ramsay Papers (No. 1568), Southern Historical Collection, Library of the University of North Carolina at Chapel Hill.

18. *Daily Lynchburg Virginian*, April 4, 1863.

19. *Milledgeville Confederate Union*, August 25, 1863, quoting the *Athens Watchman*, date unknown. The *Savannah News* also noted the article in the *Watchman* and condemned it.

20. *Raleigh Daily Conservative*, April 16, 1864; *Lynchburg Virginian*, March 20, 1865.

21. Ramsdell, *Behind the Lines in the Southern Confederacy*.

22. *Raleigh Daily Conservative*, December 20, 1864.

23. Abraham K. Korman, *The Psychology of Motivation* (Englewood Cliffs, N.J., 1974), 169.

24. Leon Festinger, "Cognitive Dissonance," *Scientific American* 207 (October 1962):93, 94. This article is a popularized explanation of the theory presented at length in Festinger's *A Theory of Cognitive Dissonance* (Evanston, 1957).

25. *Lynchburg Daily Virginian*, March 27, 1863.

26. William Alexander Graham to Zebulon B. Vance, February 12, 1865, Graham, *Papers*, 6:232; *Lynchburg Republican*, date unknown, quoted in the *North Carolina Standard*, November 4, 1864.

27. *Raleigh Daily Conservative*, September 23, October 15, December 20, 1864; see also ibid., May 4, 1864.

28. Festinger, *Theory of Cognitive Dissonance*, 25–34, 137, 195, 244–47, 265; Festinger, "Cognitive Dissonance," 95; and Jack W. Brehm and Arthur R. Cohen, *Explorations in Cognitive Dissonance* (New York, 1962), 300. Other helpful sources for the study of cognitive dissonance include Leon Festinger, *Conflict, Decision, and Dissonance* (Stanford, 1964); Philip G. Zimbardo, *The Cognitive Control of Motivation: The Consequences of Choice and Dissonance* (Glenview, Ill., 1969); and Robert B. Zajonc, "Thinking: Cognitive Organization and Processes," in David L. Sills, ed., *International Encyclopedia of the Social Sciences*, 17 vols. ([New York], 1968), 15:615–22, esp. 618–21. Two works that employ dissonance theory to understand problems of guilt, slavery, and war goals are Robert M. Cover, *Justice Accused: Anti-Slavery and the Judicial Process* (New Haven, 1975), which deals with the dissonance created when antislavery judges made proslavery decisions, and Escott, *After Secession*, chap. 8, which uses dissonance theory to understand the decision process by which Confederates changed their war goal from preservation of slavery to

achievement of independence for its own sake. For a discussion of the useful-
ness of the concept of cognitive dissonance for historians, see Richard E.
Beringer, *Historical Analysis: Contemporary Approaches to Clio's Craft*
(New York, 1978), chap. 9.

29. James Phillips to William A. Graham, April 3, 1865, Graham, *Papers*,
6:290–91.

30. Message to the [Georgia] Senate and House of Representatives,
November 6, 1862, Candler, ed., *Confederate Records of the State of Georgia*,
2:305–7; Joseph E. Brown to George T. Anderson, May 2, 1864, ibid., 3:512;
message to the [Georgia] Senate and House of Representatives, November 6,
1862, ibid., 2:285, 301; message to the [Georgia] Senate and House of Representatives, February 18, 1865, ibid., 2:844.

31. "Proceedings," *Southern Historical Society Papers* 45 (May 1925):26,
213; ibid., 47 (December 1930):205; Zebulon Vance to Jefferson Davis, December 30, 1863, Davis, *Jefferson Davis, Constitutionalist*, 6:141; Paludan,
Victims, 69; see also Joseph E. Brown, Message to the [Georgia] Senate and
House of Representatives, November 6, 1862, Candler, ed., *Confederate Records of the State of Georgia*, 2:284.

32. Alexander H. Stephens to Herschel V. Johnson, April 8, 1864, *OR*, ser.
4, vol. 3, pp. 279–80; *Raleigh Daily Conservative*, April 25, 1864, reprinting
Stephens's speech of March 16, 1864.

33. Message to the General Assembly of Georgia, November 3, 1864, Candler, ed., *Confederate Records of the State of Georgia*, 2:738–39; Governor
Brown to the [Georgia] Senate and House of Representatives, February 18,
1865, ibid., 854.

34. "Proceedings, *Southern Historical Society Papers* 51 (March 1959):28;
Richard C. Puryear to William A. Graham, May 10, 1864, Graham, *Papers*,
6:102; James T. Leach to William A. Graham, January 6, 1864, ibid., 3.

35. *Raleigh Daily Conservative*, April 5, 1865.

36. William W. Boyce to Jefferson Davis, September 29, 1864, published in
the *Raleigh Daily Conservative*, October 8, 1864.

37. David Donald, "Died of Democracy," in *Why the North Won the Civil
War;* "Proceedings," *Southern Historical Society Papers* 51 (March 1959):125.

38. Jefferson Davis to Robert W. Johnson, July 14, 1863, Davis, *Jefferson
Davis, Constitutionalist*, 5:550; *Raleigh Daily Conservative*, January 2, April
5, 1865.

39. Alexander and Beringer, *Anatomy of the Confederate Congress*, 44–45;
David M. Carter to William A. Graham, March 16, 1864, Graham, *Papers*,
6:45.

40. Johnson, "From the Autobiography of Herschel V. Johnson, 1856–
1867," 334; Herschel V. Johnson to Gentlemen, September 25, 1864, in *Raleigh*

Daily Conservative, October 11, 1864; Augustus S. Merrimom to William A. Graham, February 22, 1864, Graham, *Papers,* 6:28.

41. David M. Carter to William A. Graham, March 16, 1864, Graham, *Papers,* 6:46.

CHAPTER THIRTEEN

1. Jomini, 75; Clausewitz believed that "the use of interior lines is associated with defense" (Clausewitz, 542).

2. Clausewitz, 294.

3. Clausewitz, 492.

4. Message to the Senate and House of Representatives of the Confederate States, December 7, 1863, Richardson, ed., *Messages and Papers,* 1:345–48, 369.

5. Clausewitz, 573; Gorgas, *Civil War Diary,* 72, entry for December 7, 1863.

6. Clausewitz, 614, 511.

7. Clausewitz, 511, 283, 358, 359.

8. Proclamation of Amnesty and Reconstruction, December 8, 1863, Lincoln, *Collected Works,* 7:53–56; Lincoln to Ogden Hoffman, December 15, 1863, ibid., 67–68.

9. *Richmond Whig,* December 14, 1863; ibid., December 17, 1863; Jones, *Rebel War Clerk's Diary,* 2:115, entry for December 14, 1863; Kean, *Inside the Confederate Government,* 127, entry for December 14, 1863; *Richmond Whig,* December 14, 1863, "Proceedings," *Southern Historical Society Papers* 50 (December 1953):67, 68.

10. Clausewitz, 347; Jomini, 33. Clausewitz had some ideas for dealing with guerrilla warfare but said that these suggestions were "less an objective analysis than a groping for truth. The reason is that this sort of warfare is not as yet very common" (Clausewitz, 483).

11. William T. Sherman, "The Grand Strategy of the Last Year of the War," in Robert U. Johnson and Clarence C. Buel, eds., *Battles and Leaders of the Civil War,* 4 vols. (New York, 1884–88), 4:247; Clausewitz, 612; Jomini, 123, 127; see also Jomini, 126, 129, 330. Clausewitz had taken the same view as Jomini, also warning against a concentric attack if the enemy would have "a chance to equalize his strength by using his interior lines." But he, too, had made a significant exception, regarding interior lines as most suitable for the defense, "the stronger form with the passive purpose," and exterior lines, or what he called a convergent attack, as best for the offensive, "the weaker form

with the active purpose," He summarized: "Both in strategy and tactics a convergent attack always holds out promise of *increased* results, for if it succeeds the enemy is not just beaten; he is virtually cut off. The convergent attack, then, is always the more promising; but since forces are divided and the theatre is enlarged, it also carried a greater risk. As with attack and defense, the weaker form promises the greater success. All depends, therefore, on whether the attacker feels strong enough to go after such a prize" (Clausewitz, 619; see also Clausewitz, 63, 135, 367–68, 620–21, 630).

12. Clausewitz, 363.

13. Bülow, 2–3, 202, 254, 81, 184, 82.

14. Bülow, 257, 107–8.

15. Bülow, 184, 256; see also 286.

16. Clausewitz, 259. Clausewitz often seems to be reacting against Bülow's ideas, especially in his constant stress on the importance of battles. His work is full of allusions to Bülow, mostly uncomplimentary. See Clausewitz, 95, 132, 135, 136, 140, 144, 149, 168, 178, 184, 193, 196, 197, 199, 214, 215, 218, 227, 228, 260, 268, 272, 299, 342, 461, 476, 516.

17. Clausewitz, 562; U. S. Grant to W. T. Sherman, April 4, 1864, U.S. Congress, Senate, *Supplemental Report of the Joint Committee on the Conduct of the War*, 39th Cong., 1st sess., 2 vols. (Washington, D.C., 1866), 1:27–28, hereafter referred to as *Supplemental Report*.

18. Jomini, 59–60.

19. Grant, *Memoirs*, 2:143.

20. Edward Wightman to "Tom," June 22, 1864, in Edward Wightman, "The Roughest Kind of Campaigning: Letters of Sergeant Edward Wightman, Third New York Volunteers, May–July 1864," ed. Edward G. Longacre, *Civil War History* 28 (December 1982):342; Clausewitz, 234.

21. Jomini, 129.

22. Clausewitz, 349, 544.

23. Jomini, 327.

24. Jomini would have believed that he was denied "decisive results" because *"the attacks were made in front,"* a judgment with which Clausewitz and Bülow would have agreed. In fact, Clausewitz could not envision a frontal battle "in today's tactics, where outflanking the enemy is the aim of every engagement" (Jomini, 333; Clausewitz, 214; see also Clausewitz, 178, 233, 367; Bülow, 101, 103, 117–19, 164; Jomini, 200).

25. Jomini, 145.

26. Grant, *Memoirs*, 2:331–32.

27. Bülow, 82; see also Clausewitz, 367.

28. Nelson, *Bullets, Ballots, and Rhetoric*, xi, 17, 81–84, 117, 132–34, 157; quotes on xi, 83, 132.

29. Thomas Lawrence Connelly, *Autumn of Glory: The Army of Tennessee, 1862–1865* (Baton Rouge, 1971), 430.

30. Clausewitz, 190, 192.

31. Bülow, 77, 83–84.

32. Jomini, 240; Clausewitz, 461; see also Bülow, 17–175; Jomini, 77–84, 119–20; Clausewitz, 299, 461–63.

33. Bülow, 102, 286.

34. Clausewitz, 475; see also 383, 472–74.

35. Some of the psychological mechanisms by which military defeat in the Atlanta campaign undermined the morale of the Confederate military are summarized in William J. McNeill, "Confederate Morale: A Psycho-Historical Assessment of the Impact of the Federal Invasion of Georgia and the Carolinas," a paper presented at the annual meeting of the Southern Historical Association, November 1984; the quote is from page 7.

36. Clausewitz, 503.

37. Clausewitz, 511, 512; see also 501–19.

38. Sherman to Grant, October 9, 1864, *Supplemental Report*, 1:221–22; Sherman to Halleck, October 19, 1864, ibid., 235–36.

39. Clausewitz, 612.

40. Grant to Sheridan, February 20, 1865, *OR*, ser. 1, vol. 46, pt. 2, p. 606.

41. Jomini, 220, 221; Clausewitz, 263–69. Clausewitz would have seen in this campaign reason for his warning that "a line of retreat that deviates considerably from a straight line always involves considerable risk" (Clausewitz, 546).

42. H. de Jomini, *Précis de l'art de la guerre ou nouveau tableau analytique des principales combinaisons de la stratégie, de la grande tactique, et de la politique militaire*, ed. F. Lecomte, 2 vols. (Paris, 1894), 2:403.

43. Consolidated abstract from returns of the Confederate army on or about June 30, 1864, *OR*, ser. 4, vol. 3, p. 520; consolidated abstract from returns of the Confederate army on or about December 31, 1864, ibid., 989.

44. T. J. Stokes to Missouri Stokes, June 5, 1864, Mary A. H. Gay, *Life in Dixie during the War, 1861–1862–1863–1864–1865* (1892; rpr. Atlanta, 1979), 93; *Richmond Daily Dispatch*, January 17, 1865; Alexander Reeves to William A. Graham, January 18, 1865, Graham, *Papers*, 6:218; Thomas C. Fuller to William A. Graham, March 24, 1865, ibid., 287; *Lynchburg Virginian*, January 23, 1865.

CHAPTER FOURTEEN

1. Clausewitz, 92.
2. Clausewitz, 94.

3. Grant's strategy of raids followed Clausewitz's prescription for operations to make the war more costly to the foe: "The immediate object here is neither to conquer the enemy's country nor to destroy its army, but simply *to cause general damage.*" Of course, Grant's objective, including destruction of railroads and factories, was more specific and sophisticated than wreaking general damage, but it wholly harmonized with Clausewitz's objective (Clausewitz, 93).

4. John Shy, *A People Numerous and Armed: Reflections on the Military Struggle for American Independence* (New York, 1976), 244.

5. Jomini, 29–30, 95; Clausewitz, 479, 483.

6. Jomini, 31.

7. Jomini, 31, italics added; see Jomini, 15, 24, 29–30, 32–35, 41, 42, 72, 144, 167, 263, 313–14; Clausewitz, 161, 186, 220, 346–47, 350, 373, 396, 399, 414, 424–26, 452, 463, 465, 473, 563.

8. Jomini, 29, 34.

9. Jomini, 33–34, 29.

10. Jomini, 34.

11. Ibid.

12. McFeely, *Grant*, 209, 228; Lloyd Lewis, *Sherman: Fighting Prophet* (New York, 1932), 535; Basil H. Liddell Hart, *Sherman: Soldier, Realist, American* (1929; rpt. New York, 1958), 385, 391, 394, 397; Sherman, *Memoirs*, 2:351; Sherman to Grant, April 18, 25, 28, 1865, ibid., 355, 362, 366.

13. Liddell Hart, *Sherman*, 146.

14. Kerby, "Why the Confederacy Lost," 326, 328, 332–34; De Bow, "Our Danger and Our Duty," 47–48.

15. Clausewitz understood the potential of guerrilla warfare and would have said that a national resistance, that powerful "strategic means of defense," would have intensified the effect of the South's large spaces and the Union's comparatively small armies. The "thunder clouds" of guerrilla warfare would "build up all around the invader the farther he advances." Small units of the Confederate field armies would "harass the more considerable units" of the enemy and "arouse uneasiness and fear, and deepen the psychological effect of the insurrection as a whole. Its effect is like that of the process of evaporation: it depends on how much surface is exposed. The greater the surface and the area of contact between it and the enemy forces, the thinner the latter have to be spread, the greater the effect of a general uprising. Like smoldering embers, it consumes the basic foundations of the enemy's forces." The Union had already found this out; as early as 1863 it had devoted one-third of its armies to the task of protecting communications and garrisoning conquered territory. It would not have surprised Jomini had the Union needed to use one-half of its men for this purpose (Clausewitz, 482, 479–81; Jomini, 34).

16. War Department, Adjutant General's Office, General Orders No. 100, April 24, 1863, *OR*, ser. 3, vol. 3, pp. 150, 153, 155.

17. Herman Hattaway, *General Stephen D. Lee* (Jackson, Miss., 1976), 100; Randolph endorsement on G. J. Rains to D. H. Hill, May 14, 1862, *OR*, ser. 1, vol. 11, pt. 3, p. 510.

18. Johnston, *Narrative of Military Operations*, 411, 398–99.

19. Paludan, *Victims*.

20. E. P. Alexander, *Military Memoirs of a Confederate: A Critical Narrative* (New York, 1912), 604–5; *New York Times*, June 15, 1902.

21. Stampp, "Southern Road to Appomattox," 268–69; Degler, *Place over Time*, 107–9; Sherman to John Sherman, April 8, 1865, Sherman, *Sherman Letters*, 248; McFeely, *Grant*, 240.

22. Stampp, "Southern Road to Appomattox," 266–69.

23. Nelson, *Bullets, Ballots, and Rhetoric*, chap. 3.

24. Gorgas, *Civil War Diary*, 150, entry for November 17, 1864.

25. Resolution approved December 13, 1864, Alabama, *Acts of the Called Session, 1864, and of the Fourth Regular Annual Session of the General Assembly of Alabama, Held in the City of Montgomery, Commencing on the 27th Day of September and the 2nd Monday in November 1864* (Montgomery, 1864), 185; Herschel V. Johnson to Gentlemen, September 25, 1864, *Raleigh Daily Conservative*, October 11, 1864.

26. Resolution approved December 7, 1864, Florida, *Acts and Resolutions Adopted at its 13th Session*, 45; Speech at Columbia, South Carolina, quoted in Nelson, *Bullets, Ballots, and Rhetoric*, 132.

27. Lincoln, Memorandum, August 23, 1864, Lincoln, *Collected Works*, 7:514; Lincoln to William T. Sherman, September 19, 1864, ibid., 8:11. At the beginning of the war, Clausewitz more than likely would have conceived that Confederates expected to yield little or no territory because they anticipated "a state of balance in which the side with the positive aim (the side with the stronger grounds for action) was the one that had the weaker forces. The balance would then result from the combined effects of aim and strength." Even if they gave up some territory they could count on the superiority of the defense providing "the natural formula for outlasting the enemy, for wearing him down." If the use of all of the resources of the defense, including space and forested terrain with poor roads, gave "an advantage in war, the advantage need only be enough to *balance* any superiority the opponent may possess; in the end his political object will not seem worth the effort it costs" (Clausewitz, 82, 94).

28. Sherman to Thomas, October 20, 1864, *OR*, ser. 1, vol. 39, pt. 3, p. 378; Sherman, *Memoirs*, 2:137–40; quote is from Sherman to Lincoln, September 17, 1864, ibid., 139.

29. Clausewitz, 92, 94, 97; Sherman to Grant, November 6, 1864, *OR*, ser. 1, vol. 39, pt. 3, p. 660.

30. Clausewitz, 77, 90.

31. Clausewitz, 92, 88.

32. Nelson, *Bullets, Ballots, and Rhetoric*, 119, 157.

33. Gorgas, *Civil War Diary*, 50–51, entry for July 17, 1863; Resolution of March 4, 1865, Mississippi, *Laws of the State of Mississippi, Passed at a Called Session of the Mississippi Legislature, Held in Columbus, February and March, 1865* (Meridian, Miss., 1865), 59–60; *Lynchburg Virginian*, March 14, 1865.

34. Moorhead, *American Apocalypse*, 99, 110–11, 126.

35. Gorgas, *Civil War Diary*, 113, 164, entries for June 6, 1864, and January 6, 1865.

36. J. O. L. Goggin to unknown, n.d., *Richmond Whig*, March 29, 1865; *Lynchburg Virginian*, March 6, 1865; Circular letter of Julian Hartridge, *Milledgeville Confederate Union*, January 31, 1865; R. M. T. Hunter, speech at the African Church, February 9, 1865, *Lynchburg Virginian*, February 13, 1865.

37. *Lynchburg Virginian*, February 7, 1865; speech of Jefferson Davis in Richmond, January 5, 1863, Davis, *Jefferson Davis, Constitutionalist*, 5:393; Gorgas, *Civil War Diary*, 167, 174, entries for January 30 and March 6, 1865.

38. *Lynchburg Virginian*, September 22, 1864; *Milledgeville Confederate Union*, January 24, 1865; *Memphis Daily Appeal* (published in Atlanta), June 9, 1864; see, e.g., Mary E. Robarts to Susan M. Cumming, November 28, 1864; Mary Jones to Susan M. Cumming, December 9, 1864; Susan M. Cumming to Mary Jones, December 10, 1864; and Laura E. Buttolph to Mary Jones, December 10, 1864, Myers, ed., *Children of Pride*, 1215–19.

39. *Richmond Daily Dispatch*, March 8, 9, 10, 1865; Silver, *Confederate Morale and Church Propaganda*, 53, 66–68; *Tuscaloosa Observer*, May 8, 1865.

40. *Lynchburg Virginian*, September 22, 1864; *Milledgeville Confederate Union*, January 24, 1865; Silver, *Confederate Morale and Church Propaganda*, 41, 68–69; *Richmond Daily Dispatch*, January 30, 1865; Bell I. Wiley, "The Movement to Humanize the Institution of Slavery during the Confederacy," *Emory University Quarterly* 5 (December 1949):207–20, esp. 208, 215, 217.

41. Clausewitz, 77.

42. Clausewitz, 81.

43. Henry Yates Thompson, *An Englishman in the American Civil War: The Diaries of Henry Yates Thompson*, ed. Sir Christopher Chancellor (New York, 1971), 90, 92.

44. Clausewitz, 88, 92, 81.

45. Stampp, "Southern Road to Appomattox," 11, 251–52, 255. This essay is a revision of an earlier piece published under the same title in the Cotton Memorial Papers, No. 4 (El Paso, 1969).

46. Ibid., 255, 259. This suggestion is most certainly true for North Carolinians.

47. Ibid., 266–67.

48. Thomas Jefferson, *Notes on the State of Virginia*, ed. William Peden (Chapel Hill, 1955), 163; Chesnut, *Mary Chesnut's Civil War*, 29, 255, diary entries for March 18 and December 6, 1861; Osterweis, *Romanticism and Nationalism in the Old South*, 15.

49. W. J. Cash, *The Mind of the South* (New York, 1941), 60; Sellers, "Travail of Slavery," 41, 44; Wiley, *Road to Appomattox*, 102–5. Robert Penn Warren, *The Legacy of the Civil War* (1961; rpr. Cambridge, Mass., 1983), 8; Degler, *Place over Time*, 108.

50. James Oakes, *The Ruling Race: A History of American Slaveholders* (New York, 1982), chap. 4, passim, but esp. 98, 100, 103–5, 108, 114–15, 120, 122.

51. Roark, *Masters without Slaves*, 97; Eugene D. Genovese, *The World the Slaveholders Made: Two Essays in Interpretation* (New York, 1969), 146; James Brewer Stewart, "'A Great Talking and Eating Machine': Patriarchy, Mobilization and the Dynamics of Nullification in South Carolina," *Civil War History* 27 (September 1981):209, 208.

52. Romans 3:10, 23.

53. Gay, *Life in Dixie during the War*, 195.

54. Diary of Edward Fontaine, entry for May 11, 1865, in John K. Bettersworth, ed., *Mississippi in the Confederacy*, vol. 1, *As They Saw It* (Jackson, Miss., 1961), 358; Gay, *Life in Dixie during the War*, 195.

55. Moorhead, *American Apocalypse*, 21, 27, 111–12. Dagon was the national idol-god to which the Philistines made sacrifice. It was a very strong, and indeed a revealing statement, for this Union clergyman to make; it not only asserted that the South prayed to a fake god; but that the Jewish-Christian God (Jehovah) would, as He had done before, smite down that false god and destroy the people who had followed him. See Judges 16:23 and 1 Samuel 5:3–9.

56. Lincoln, *Collected Works*, 8:333.

57. Quoted in W. R. Brock, *An American Crisis: Congress and Reconstruction, 1865–1867* (London, 1963), 75.

58. Lincoln, *Collected Works*, 7:20, November 19, 1863, newspaper text; Garfield to J. Harrison Rhodes, May 1, 1862, James A. Garfield, *The Wild Life of the Army: Civil War Letters of James A. Garfield*, ed. Frederick D. Williams (East Lansing, Mich., 1964), 90.

59. *Raleigh Daily Conservative*, April 16, June 10, 1864.

60. *Raleigh Register*, August 12, 1863, discussing an article in the *Biblical Recorder*.

61. Chesnut, *Mary Chesnut's Civil War*, 798, entry for May 1865; "A Proclamation," March 12, 1864, Richardson, ed., *Messages and Papers*, 1:413; "A Proclamation," October 26, 1864, ibid., 564; "A Proclamation," January 25, 1865, ibid., 567.

62. Herschel V. Johnson to A. E. Cochrane, October 25, 1862, quoted in Wiley, *Road to Appomattox*, 104; John Jones to Mary Jones, December 7, 1863, Myers, ed., *Children of Pride*, 1122.

63. Roark, *Masters without Slaves*, 89; Dolly Burge Diary, November 8, 1864, Burge-Gray Papers, Emory University, quoted in ibid., 97; Elisha Franklin Paxton, ed., *The Civil War Letters of General Frank "Bull" Paxton, C.S.A., A Lieutenant of Lee and Jackson*, ed. John Gallatin Paxton (Hillsboro, Tex., 1978), 59–60; W. H. Morgan to Jefferson Davis, January 30, 1888, Jefferson Davis, *Calendar of the Jefferson Davis Postwar Manuscripts in the Louisiana Historical Collection, Confederate Memorial Hall* (1943; rpr. New York, 1970), 276; "A Proclamation," February 20, 1862, Richardson, ed., *Messages and Papers*, 1:218; "Studies in the South," *Atlantic* 50 (December 1882):754.

CHAPTER FIFTEEN

1. "Proceedings," *Southern Historical Society Papers* 47 (December 1930):7–8, September 29, 1862; Joint Resolution on the Subject of Retaliation, May 1, 1863, Confederate States of America, *Public Laws of the Confederate States of America, Passed at the Third Session of the First Congress*, 1863, ed. James M. Matthews (Richmond, 1863), 167–68.

2. P. R. Cleburne and others to Commanding General, the Corps, Division, Brigade, and Regimental Commanders of the Army of Tennessee, January 2, 1864, *OR*, ser. 1, vol. 52, pt. 2, pp. 587–92.

3. Kean, *Inside the Confederate Government*, 67, diary entry for May 29, 1863.

4. Davis to W. H. T. Walker, January 13, 1864, *OR*, ser. 1, vol. 52, pt. 2, p. 596; James A. Seddon to Joseph E. Johnston, January 24, 1864, ibid., 606–7. Davis remembered this as "the first time any officer of the Army proposed the enrolment [sic] of negroes as soldiers" (Davis to Campbell Brown, June 14, 1886, in Johnson and Buel, eds., *Battles and Leaders*, vol. 2, facing p. 98, Extra-Illustrated Edition, RB 298000, Huntington Library, San Marino, California.

5. Message to Congress, November 7, 1864, Richardson, ed., *Messages and Papers*, 1:495.

6. When requested to give permission for raising a regiment of black troops, Secretary of War James A. Seddon abruptly replied that "it is not probable that any such policy will be prescribed by Congress" (Seddon to Major E. B. Briggs, November 24, 1864, *OR*, ser. 4, vol. 3, p. 846); Benjamin to Fred A. Porcher, December 21, 1864, ibid., 959–60; Davis to John Forsyth, February 21, 1865, ibid., 1110; Davis to Campbell Brown, June 14, 1886, Johnson and Buel, eds., *Battles and Leaders*, vol. 2, facing p. 98, Extra-Illustrated Edition, RB 298000, Huntington Libary, San Marino, California; Davis, *Rise and Fall*, 1:518.

7. *Jackson Mississippian*, August 1863, quoted in Bettersworth, ed., *Mississippi in the Confederacy*, 245–46; Akin to Nathan Land, October 31, 1864, Warren Akin, *Letters of Warren Akin: Confederate Congressman*, ed. Bell Irvin Wiley (Athens, Ga., 1959), 32–33.

8. Vest to Gov. Thomas Canute Reynolds, February 17, 1865, Eldridge Papers, EG Box 61, Huntington Library, San Marino, California; Gorgas, *Civil War Diary*, 142–44, entries for September 25, 29, and October 2, 1864; Samuel Clayton to Jefferson Davis, January 10, 1865, *OR*, ser. 4, vol. 3, p. 1011; anonymous to Howell Cobb, January 13, 1865, Robert Toombs, *The Correspondence of Robert Toombs, Alexander H. Stephens, and Howell Cobb*, ed. Ulrich B. Phillips, American Historical Association *Annual Report for the Year 1911*, vol. 2 (Washington, 1913), 656, 657.

9. Lee to Andrew Hunter, January 11, 1865, *OR*, ser. 4, vol. 3, pp. 1012–13.

10. *Charleston Mercury*, February 3, 1865; U.S. Congress, House, *Report of the Joint Committee on Reconstruction*, House Report No. 30, pt. 2, 39th Cong., 1st sess., 1866, p. 136.

11. J. H. Stringfellow to Jefferson Davis, February 8, 1865, *OR*, ser. 4, vol. 3, pp. 1069–70.

12. Kean, *Inside the Confederate Government*, 177, diary entry for November 20, 1864.

13. Alexander and Beringer, *Anatomy of the Confederate Congress*, 261; Warren Akin to Nathan Land, October 31, 1864, Akin, *Letters*, 33.

14. Pardon petition of Edmund S. Dargan, August 13, 1865, Amnesty Papers, Alabama, Record Group 94, National Archives; "Proceedings," *Southern Historical Society Papers* 52 (July 1959):241–42, January 27, 1865.

15. *Milledgeville Confederate Union*, August 18, 1863, quoting the *Mobile Advertiser* of unknown date; *Raleigh Daily Conservative*, April 16, 1864; *Lynchburg Virginian*, January 25, 1865; Oldham, "Memoirs", 302; William A. Graham to David L. Swain, January 28, 1865, Graham, *Papers*, 6:225; Graham

to Zebulon B. Vance, February 12, 1865, ibid., 232; J. A. Orr, "Reminiscences of J. A. Orr," typescript, 4, 7, Mississippi Department of Archives and History, Jackson. The text of the spring 1864 proposal is not found in the *Journal of the Confederate Congress.*

16. "An Act to increase the military force of the Confederate States, Approved March 13, 1865," Confederate States of America, *Laws and Joint Resolutions of the Last Session of the Confederate Congress . . .* , ed. Charles W. Ramsdell (Durham, N.C., 1941), 118–19; Paragraph 4, General Orders No. 14, Adjt. and Insp. General's Office, March 23, 1865, *OR*, ser. 4, vol. 3, pp. 1161–62; Robert F. Durden, *The Gray and the Black: The Confederate Debate on Emancipation* (Baton Rouge, 1972); Chesnut, *Mary Chesnut's Civil War*, 255, 407, entries for December 6, 1861, and July 3, 1862.

17. *Milledgeville Confederate Union*, November 1, 1864, quoting the *Lynchburg Republican* of unknown date; *Raleigh Daily Conservative*, October 21, 1864; Address of Governor Vance, February 22, 1864, ibid., April 16, 1864; *North Carolina Standard*, February 21, 1865.

18. Robert Hardy Smith, *An Address to the Citizens of Alabama on the Constitution and Laws of the Confederate States of America* (Mobile, 1861), 16.

19. Frank Moore, ed., *The Rebellion Record: A Diary of American Events, with Documents, Narratives, Illustrative Incidents, Poetry, etc.*, 11 vols. and supplement (New York, 1861–68), 1: pt. 3, pp. 45–46. The scriptural reference is to Matthew 21:42; *Congressional Globe*, 36th Cong. 1st sess., quoted in Allan Nevins, *The Emergence of Lincoln*, vol. 2, *Prologue to Civil War, 1859–1861* (New York, 1950), 126; R. M. T. Hunter to James R. Micou, Thomas Croxton, and others signing the call, December 10, 1860, Robert M. T. Hunter, *Correspondence of Robert M. T. Hunter, 1826–1876*, ed. Charles Henry Ambler, American Historical Association *Annual Report for the Year 1916*, vol. 2 (Washington, D.C., 1918), 340, 347.

20. *Nashville Union and American*, January 25, 1861; "Address to the People of Davidson County," ibid., January 29, 1861; *Congressional Globe*, 36th Cong., 2d sess., pt. 1, p. 59, December 11, 1860; Reuben Davis, *Recollections of Mississippi and Mississippians* (Boston, 1890), 399–400.

21. See Davis's resolution of February 2, 1860, 36th Cong., 1st sess., Senate Miscellaneous Document No. 11 (Serial 1038), and its revision, March 1, 1860, 36th Cong., 1st sess., Senate Miscellaneous Document No. 24 (Serial 1038) (the major difference is the deletion of the threat); *Congressional Globe*, 36th Cong., 2d sess., pt. 1, p. 487, January 21, 1861; Message to Congress, April 29, 1861, Richardson, ed., *Messages and Papers*, 1:67–68.

22. [J. L. M. Curry], *Address of Congress to the People of the Confederate*

States (Richmond, 1864), 1. The address is also found in the *Southern Historical Society Papers* 1 (January 1876):23–39; *Charleston Mercury*, February 5, 1865, 1. We do not wish to become involved in an argument over the actual causes of the Civil War. For now, we simply assume that, whatever else contemporaries (and historians) may say, slavery was the basic cause of the war: not state rights, not economics, not class conflict, not irresponsible agitation, but slavery. In any event, what concerns us here are not actual causes, but causes as Confederates perceived them. The difference is important.

23. Durden, *The Gray and the Black;* C. C. Jones to Charles C. Jones, Jr., March 24, 1862, Myers, ed., *Children of Pride,* 867; Speech of Herschel V. Johnson, December 4, 1862, *Milledgeville Confederate Union,* December 16, 1862; Johnson to several gentlemen, September 25, 1864, ibid., October 18, 1864; Address of Congress to the People of the Confederate States, *Richmond Whig,* March 20, 1865 (the text of this joint resolution does not appear in the *Journal of the Congress*); *Lynchburg Virginian,* March 24, 1865; ibid., October 8 and November 3, 1864, from the *Richmond Enquirer,* October 6, 1864, and the *Mobile Register,* date not given; *Milledgeville Confederate Union,* August 18, 1863, from the *Mobile Advertiser,* date not given; *Milledgeville Confederate Union,* August 16, 1864, from the *Richmond Examiner,* date not given. See also Escott, *After Secession,* chap. 8.

24. *Milledgeville Confederate Union,* January 17, 1865; *Atlanta Southern Confederacy* from ibid.; *Raleigh Daily Conservative,* January 2, 3, 1865.

25. *Raleigh Daily Conservative,* October 15, 1864; Joseph E. Brown to the Senate and House of Representatives, February 18, 1865, Candler, ed., *Confederate Records of the State of Georgia,* 2:853–54; *Milledgeville Confederate Union,* May 10, 1864.

26. Wyatt-Brown, *Southern Honor,* passim.

27. Jones, *Rebel War Clerk's Diary,* 2:402–3, entries for January 29, 30, 1865; *Raleigh Daily Conservative,* July 14, 1864; "Proceedings of the Confederate Congress," *Southern Historical Society Papers* 52 (July 1959): 12–14, 20, December 16–17, 1864; *Mary Chesnut's Civil War,* 644, 809, entries for September 21, 1864, and May 10, 1865; *Richmond Daily Dispatch,* January 19, 1865.

28. Lamkin to wife, January 3, 1865, Eldridge Papers, EG Box 34, Huntington Library, San Marino, California; *Milledgeville Confederate Union,* January 17, 1865, from the *Atlanta Southern Confederacy,* date unknown; Mrs. Akin to Akin, January 8, 1865, Akin, *Letters,* 117.

29. Mrs. Akin to Warren Akin, January 8, 1865, Akin, *Letters,* 117; *Lynchburg Virginian,* October 8, 1864.

30. *Jackson News,* March 1865, quoted in Bettersworth, ed., *Mississippi in*

the Confederacy, 246; John W. Brown, typescript diaries (No. 1924), microfilm copy of original, 290, entry for April 6, 1865, Southern Historical Collection, Library of the University of North Carolina at Chapel Hill; *Lynchburg Republican*, date unknown, quoted in the *North Carolina Standard*, November 4, 1864.

31. Quoted in the *Raleigh Daily Conservative*, December 30, 1864.

32. *Raleigh Daily Conservative*, October 13, 1864, January 2, 1865; Vance message reprinted in the *Raleigh Daily Conservative*, November 23, 1864; *North Carolina Standard*, February 3, 1865; Graham to David L. Swain, January 28, 1865, Graham, *Papers*, 6:226–27; Smith to Senate of Virginia, March 6, 1865, Brock Papers, BR Box 239, Huntington Library, San Marino, California.

33. Escott, *After Secession*, chap. 8.

34. "Proceedings of the Confederate Congress," *Southern Historical Society Papers* 51 (March 1959):294–95, November 10, 1864.

35. Thomas S. Gholson, *Speech of Hon. Thos. S. Gholson, of Virginia, on the Policy of Employing Negro Troops, and the Duty of All Classes to Aid in the Prosecution of the War* (Richmond, 1865), 5–6; Cobb to James A. Seddon, January 8, 1865, *OR*, ser. 4, vol. 3, p. 1009; John M. Daniel, *The Richmond Examiner during the War; or, The Writings of John M. Daniel, with a Memoir of His Life, by His Brother*, ed. Frederick S. Daniel (New York, 1868), 213, 214; *Charleston Mercury*, November 12, 1864, p. 1.

36. *Raleigh Daily Conservative*, February 27, 1865; Governor Joseph E. Brown to the Senate and House of Representatives, February 15, 1865, Candler, ed., *Confederate Records of the State of Georgia*, 2:833–34.

37. Howell Cobb to James A. Seddon, January 8, 1865, *OR*, ser. 4, vol. 3, p. 1009.

38. Clement Eaton, *Jefferson Davis* (New York, 1977), 172–73; Roland, *The Confederacy*, 185–86; Durden, *The Gray and the Black*, 147–51. The standard study of Confederate diplomacy is Owsley, *King Cotton Diplomacy*.

39. *Milledgeville Confederate Union*, February 14, 1865.

40. Henry Adams, *The Education of Henry Adams* (1918; rpt. New York, 1931), 246; Chesnut, *Mary Chesnut's Civil War*, 412, 439, 702, entries for July 10, 1862, an unspecified date in 1863, and January 16, 1865.

41. *Raleigh Daily Progress*, July 15, 1863, quoted in *North Carolina Standard*, July 17, 1863; *Raleigh Daily Conservative*, April 27, 1864, September 23, 1864.

42. *Raleigh Daily Conservative*, July 8, 1864; Chesnut, *Mary Chesnut's Civil War*, 805, entry for May 7, 1865.

43. "Resolution declaring the ground on which the Confederate States

stand in this War and the terms on which peace ought to be offered to the enemy," March 19, 1864, in Georgia, *Acts of the General Assembly, March 1864*, 158.

44. *Lynchburg Virginian*, December 26, 1864; *North Carolina Standard*, February 17, 1865.

45. *The American Annual Cyclopaedia and Register of Important Events of the Year 1864* . . . (New York, 1867), 218; *Charleston Mercury*, January 15, 1865.

46. Ernest Gordon Rupp, *The Righteousness of God: Luther Studies* (London, 1953), 109, from *Luthers Werke*, 44.504, 4.602.7 (1509–12).

47. Sellers, "Travail of Slavery," 44; see also Wiley, *Road to Appomattox*, 102–5.

48. W. E. Burghardt Du Bois, *The Souls of the Black Folk: Essays and Sketches* (1903; rpt. New York, 1953), 186. For discussion of this reaction see Wolfenstein, *Disaster*, passim, but esp. 200.

49. Wolfenstein, *Disaster*, 155; Stampp, "Southern Road to Appomattox," 267; Henry S. Foote, *War of the Rebellion; or, Scylla and Charybdis* . . . (New York, 1866), 421–22; anonymous letter of October 30, 1865, quoted in Ralph A. Graves, "Marching through Georgia Sixty Years After," *National Geographic* 50 (September 1926):309–10; Kenneth M. Stampp, *The Peculiar Institution: Slavery in the Antebellum South* (New York, 1956), 425. See, e.g., Chesnut, *Mary Chesnut's Civil War*, 809, entry for May 10, 1865.

50. Commentary by Dan T. Carter, session titled "A Culture in Crisis: The Response of the White South to Defeat," Southern Historical Association, November 1980; *Milledgeville Confederate Union*, January 17, 1865; Wilson, *Baptized in Blood*, 102; "Studies in the South," 754.

51. Gay, *Life in Dixie during the War*, 232; Thomas L. Connelly and Barbara Bellows, *God and General Longstreet: The Lost Cause and the Southern Mind* (Baton Rouge, 1982), 12–16; Rives to S. L. M. Barlow, August 10, 1866, Barlow Papers, BW Box 62, Huntington Library, San Marino, California; see also Willie Lee Rose, *Slavery and Freedom*, ed. William W. Freehling (New York, 1982), 76–77.

52. Mrs. W. H. Stiles to children, August 20, 1865, MacKay and Stiles Family Papers, Southern Historical Collection, University of North Carolina Library, Chapel Hill, quoted in Roark, *Masters without Slaves*, 161; Testimony of Colonel Orlando Brown, U.S. Congress, House, *Report of the Joint Committee on Reconstruction*, pt. 2, p. 126; William Heyward to James Gregorie, June 4, 1868, Gregorie and Elliott Family Papers, Southern Historical Collection, University of North Carolina Library, Chapel Hill, quoted in Roark, *Masters without Slaves*, 161; William B. Hesseltine, *Confederate Leaders in*

the New South (Baton Rouge, 1950), 12; George C. Rable, "Bourbonism, Reconstruction, and the Persistence of Southern Distinctiveness," *Civil War History* 29 (June 1983):138–39; Degler, *Place over Time*, 106; Clement Eaton, *The Waning of the Old South Civilization, 1860–1880s* (1968; rpr. New York, 1969), 114.

53. Foote, *War of the Rebellion*, 415–16; W. R. Drinkard to James Lyons, January 20, 1869 (of course, the slaves were no longer slaves, but fixed habits of speech die hard); L. Q. Washington to James Lyons, December 13, 1868; James Robb to James Lyons, May 4, 1869, all in Brock Papers, BR Box 37, Huntington Library, San Marino, California.

54. Daniel A. Novak, *The Wheel of Servitude: Black Forced Labor after Slavery* (Lexington, Ky., 1978), 41; Pete Daniel, *The Shadow of Slavery: Peonage in the South, 1901–1969* (Urbana, Ill., 1972), ix, 11, 139; Henry W. Grady, address to the New England Club, New York, December 21, 1886, Henry W. Grady, *Life of Henry W. Grady, Including His Writings and Speeches*, ed. Joel Chandler Harris (New York, 1890), 90, 87–88.

CHAPTER SIXTEEN

1. William J. Cooper, Jr., *The South and the Politics of Slavery, 1828–1856* (Baton Rouge, 1978), 69, 73, 371, 373, quotes on 371, 373.

2. Jefferson Davis to Hugh Davis, January 8, 1865, Davis, *Jefferson Davis: Private Letters*, 139–40.

3. Durden, *The Gray and the Black*, 3; Channing, *Crisis of Fear*, 237, 289–92, quote on 292; Eaton, *The Waning of the Old South Civilization*, 113; Stampp, "Southern Road to Appomattox," 260–64, 268, quote on 268; Roark, *Slaves without Masters*, 105.

4. Chesnut, *Mary Chesnut's Civil War*, 334, diary entry for May 6, 1862.

5. Davis, *Recollections of Mississippi and Mississippians*, 298; Sidney Andrews, *The South since the War . . .* (Boston, 1866), 92–93; Douglas Southall Freeman, *R. E. Lee: A Biography*, 4 vols. (New York, 1934–35), 4:159; Jones, *Rebel War Clerk's Diary*, 2:424, entry for February 17, 1865, italics added.

6. Waldo W. Braden, "Repining over an Irrevocable Past: The Ceremonial Orator in a Defeated Society, 1865–1900," in Braden, ed., *Oratory in the New South* (Baton Rouge, 1979), 17, 20–21; Howard Dorgan, "Rhetoric of the United Confederate Veterans: A Lost Cause Mythology in the Making," ibid., 148–55, quotes on 155.

7. *Charleston Mercury*, November 19, 1866, 2; R. Barnwell Rhett, "The Confederate Constitution," *De Bow's Review*, 2d ser., 7 (November 1869):930 (this article is a reprint of an 1867 letter); Williamson S. Oldham, "True Cause and Issues of the Civil War," ibid. (August 1869):674–75.

8. Robert M. T. Hunter, "Origin of the Late War," *Southern Historical Society Papers* 1 (January 1876):1, 13.

9. Henry S. Foote, *Casket of Reminiscences* (Washington, D.C., 1874), 148ff; Davis, *Recollections of Mississippi and Mississippians*, 297–98.

10. Albert T. Bledsoe, *The War between the States, or, Was Secession a Constitutional Right Previous to the War of 1861–65?* (Lynchburg, Va., 1915) (this book is a condensation of *Is Davis a Traitor?*, which Bledsoe wrote immediately after the war and published in 1866); J. L. M. Curry, *The Southern States of the American Union, Considered in Their Relations to the Constitution of the United States and to the Resulting Union* (Richmond, 1895), 210. Curry expressed much the same view in his *Civil History of the Government of the Confederate States, with Some Personal Reminiscences* (Richmond, 1901), 26–29.

11. Alexander H. Stephens, *A Constitutional View of the Late War between the States: Its Causes, Character, Conduct and Results, Presented in a Series of Colloquies at Liberty Hall*, 2 vols. (Philadelphia, 1868–70), 1:10; Stephens to Henry Huntley Haight, January 14, 1870, Haight Papers, Huntington Library, San Marino, California.

12. Davis, *Rise and Fall*, 2:762–63; Festinger, *Theory of Cognitive Dissonance*, 247; Degler, *Place over Time*, 105, quoting William Faulkner, *Intruder in the Dust* (New York, 1948), 194–95.

13. Robert A. Lively, *Fiction Fights the Civil War: An Unfinished Chapter in the Literary History of the American People* (Chapel Hill, 1957), 95–101.

14. Stampp, "Southern Road to Appomattox," 268–69; Degler, *Place over Time*, 109.

15. James D. Bullock to Jefferson Davis, October 16, 1886, Davis, *Calendar of the Jefferson Davis Postwar Manuscripts*, 254.

16. Wyatt-Brown, *Southern Honor*, xviii; Rable, "Bourbonism, Reconstruction, and the Persistence of Southern Distinctiveness," 138, 146, 151, 153; Shy, *People Numerous and Armed*, 244–45.

17. James Phillips to William A. Graham, April 3, 1865, Graham, *Papers*, 6:290–91.

18. Chesnut, *Mary Chesnut's Civil War*, 809, entry for May 10, 1865; I. W. Avery, quoted in Connelly and Bellows, *God and General Longstreet*, 24; Ramsdell, *Behind the Lines in the Southern Confederacy*, 121–22.

19. A. W. Venable to Davis, August 8, 1874, Davis, *Jefferson Davis, Constitutionalist*, 7:393; Stephen D. Lee, "Gen. Lee's Address," *Confederate Veteran* 12 (July 1904):326.

20. "The Old Confederate Veteran: Speech of Gen. E. Porter Alexander, on Alumni Day, at West Point," *New York Times*, June 15, 1902, p. 24.

21. *Public Opinion*, November 5, 1887, p. 1, reprinted from the *Macon* (Georgia) *Telegraph*.

22. Davis to Frank Stringfellow, June 4, 1878, Davis, *Jefferson Davis: Private Letters*, 483.

23. William M. Browne to Howell Cobb, March 28, 1866, Toombs, *Correspondence of Toombs, Stephens, and Cobb*, 2:678; Dan T. Carter, "Honor and Southern Intransigence in Reconstruction, 1865–67," paper presented at the annual meeting of the Southern Historical Association, 1982.

24. Hesseltine, *Confederate Leaders in the New South*, 147; Tourgée quoted in Otto H. Olsen, *Carpetbagger's Crusade: The Life of Albion Winegar Tourgée* (Baltimore, 1965).

25. Stephens, *Constitutional View*, 1:31; John Vines Wright to Benjamin Perry, November 23, 1887, Eldridge Papers, EG Box 66, Huntington Library, San Marino, California.

26. Wilson, *Baptized in Blood*, 164–65; Edward A. Pollard, *The Lost Cause Regained* (New York, 1868), 135, quoted in Jack P. Maddex, Jr., "Pollard's *The Lost Cause Regained:* A Mask for Southern Accommodation," *Journal of Southern History* 40 (November 1974):606; Jefferson Davis to Lucius B. Northrop, date unknown, referenced in Northrop to Davis, July 1882, Davis, *Jefferson Davis, Constitutionalist*, 9:180; Davis to Stringfellow, June 4, 1878, Davis, *Jefferson Davis: Private Letters*, 483; W. W. Mann to Davis, August 31, 1879, Davis, *Calendar of the Jefferson Davis Postwar Manuscripts*, 148; J. H. Vandegrift to Davis, July 13, 1887, ibid., 267.

27. Walter Neale, *The Sovereignty of the States: An Oration . . .* (New York, 1910), 2. Neale's stirring words were part of an attack on the income tax amendment, the protective tariff, and the pension laws; Bullock to Davis, July 24, 1884, in Davis, *Calendar of the Jefferson Davis Postwar Manuscripts*, 215; Maddex, "Pollard's *The Lost Cause Regained*," 612.

28. Jerry L. Russell, ed., *Civil War Round Table Digest* 9 (December 1978):17–18 (this comment should not be construed as a value judgment of Russell's remarks or as a negative attitude toward the important cause of historic preservation to which Russell devotes much of his time and energy; Civil War historians ought to be especially appreciative of his work); *Argus Suburbia-Reporter*, October 10, 1979.

29. Shy, *People Numerous and Armed*, 245.

PART FIVE

1. Antoine de Saint-Exupéry, *Flight to Arras*, in *Airman's Odyssey* (New York, 1942), 403, 414.

2. Rable, "Bourbonism, Reconstruction, and the Persistence of Southern Distinctiveness," 152.

CHAPTER SEVENTEEN

1. P. G. T. Beauregard, "The First Battle of Bull Run," in Johnson and Buel, eds., *Battles and Leaders*, 1:222–26, quotes on 222.

2. Clement Eaton, *Jefferson Davis* (New York, 1977), 175, 232 (see also chap. 23); Oldham, "Memoirs," 138.

3. Owsley, "Defeatism," 98.

4. Springboards to further understanding are Robert N. Bellah, *The Broken Covenant: American Civil Religion in Time of Trial* (New York, 1975); Leland D. Baldwin, *The American Quest for the City of God* (Macon, Ga., 1981); and Carlton J. H. Hayes, *Nationalism: A Religion* (New York, 1960).

5. The occasion was the 1975 Symposium on Military History at the United States Air Force Academy.

6. Edmund Wilson, "The Union as Religious Mysticism," *New Yorker* 29 (March 14, 1953):116, 119–26, 129–36, quote on 131; but see also Sidney E. Mead, *The Lively Experiment: The Shaping of Christianity in America* (New York, 1963), esp. chap. 5; David Elton Trueblood, *Abraham Lincoln: Theologian of American Anguish* (New York, 1973), chap. 6 and esp. 121; and Glen E. Thurow, *Abraham Lincoln and American Political Religion* (Albany, 1976); Martin Marty to Herman Hattaway, July 2, 1984, in possession of Herman Hattaway; Kenneth S. Kantzer, Editorial, *Christianity Today* 18 (July 13, 1984):14.

7. See primarily H. Shelton Smith, *In His Image, But . . . : Racism in Southern Religion, 1780–1910* (Durham, 1972), esp. chaps. 4 and 5; for additional insight into the Southern Baptists see Rufus B. Spain, *At Ease in Zion: Social History of Southern Baptists, 1865–1900* (Nashville, 1961), and John Lee Eighmy, *Churches in Cultural Captivity: A History of the Social Attitudes of Southern Baptists* (Knoxville, 1972); for religion and the lost cause see Wilson, *Baptized in Blood.*

8. Owsley, "Local Defense," 64.

9. Jomini, 29.

10. Lebergott, "Why the South Lost," 59–66, 69–74.

11. Escott, "Georgia," 80; see also Escott, *After Secession*, 90, 92, 244–48, 252–55, 272–73.

12. Sherman to Grant, November 6, 1864, *OR*, ser. 1, vol. 39, pt. 3, pp. 658–61.

13. Ulrich B. Phillips, "The Central Theme of Southern History," *American Historical Review* 34 (October 1928):31; Degler, *Place over Time*, 110; Henry James, *The American Scene* (1907; rpr. New York, 1946), 376.

14. Clausewitz, 479; see also Jomini, 33–34.

15. Shy, *People Numerous and Armed*, 244.

16. Clausewitz, 483.

17. Clausewitz, 91.

APPENDIX ONE

1. Donald, ed., *Why the North Won the Civil War*, xi.

2. Ibid., 90.

3. Owsley, *State Rights in the Confederacy*, vii.

4. Thomas J. Pressly, *Americans Interpret Their Civil War* (1954; 2d ed., 1962), New York, 280–83.

5. Harriet Chappell Owsley, "Introduction," Owsley, *The South*, xvi.

6. Charles W. Ramsdell, review of *State Rights in the Confederacy*, by Frank Lawrence Owsley, *Mississippi Valley Historical Review* 14 (June 1927):107.

7. Ibid., 107–8.

8. Ibid., 108.

9. Ibid., 110, 109.

10. Richard M. McMurry, "Joseph E. Brown of Georgia," *Civil War Times Illustrated* 10 (November 1971):37.

11. Owsley, "Local Defense," in Owsley, *The South*, 65, 66.

12. Owsley, *State Rights in the Confederacy*, 276–77.

13. Ramsdell, review of Owsley, 109; Kruman, "Dissent," 293–94; see also Albert B. Moore, *Conscription and Conflict in the Confederacy* (New York, 1924); Tatum, *Disloyalty in the Confederacy*.

14. Ramsdell, review of Owsley, 108; Owsley, "Local Defense," 68.

15. Owsley, "Local Defense," 70; Lawton to Benjamin, November 1, 1861, *OR*, ser. 1, vol. 4, p. 307.

16. Owsley, "Local Defense," 70–71; Lawton to Benjamin, October 5, 1861, *OR*, ser. 4, vol. 1, p. 668; Benjamin to Lawton, September 25, 1861, ibid., ser. 1, vol. 6, p. 283; Lawton to Samuel Cooper, September 25, 1861, ibid., ser. 4, vol. 1, pp. 617–18.

17. Owsley, "Local Defense," 71.

18. Ibid., 71, 73; Lawton to Benjamin, November 1, 1861, *OR*, ser. 1, vol. 4, pp. 306–7. Owsley's source, ibid., refers only to correspondence between Brown and Benjamin in September 1861, not March 1862, as his context implies. The only index reference to W. H. T. Walker leads to the November 1, 1861, Lawton letter cited, and this must have been the reference Owsley had in mind.

19. Owsley, "Local Defense," 75.

20. Ibid., John A. Campbell to Shorter, January 23, 1863, *OR*, ser. 1, vol. 52, pt. 2, pp. 414–15.

21. Shorter to Seddon, January 14, 1863, *OR*, ser. 1, vol. 15, pp. 946–48; see Ella Lonn, *Salt as a Factor in the Confederacy* (University, Ala., 1965), esp. chaps. 1, 11, and 12, and p. 172.

22. Owsley, "Local Defense," 75–76, italics added; Shorter to Seddon, March 5, 1863, *OR*, ser. 4, vol. 2, pp. 419–20.

23. Owsley, "Local Defense," 76; Brown to Davis, December 29, 1862, *OR*, ser. 4, vol. 2, pp. 263–64.

24. See Davis's original statement in his letter of May 29, 1862, *OR*, ser. 4, vol. 1, pp. 1135–36; Owsley, "Local Defense," 76.

25. Owsley, "Local Defense," 78; see also 80, nn. 119, 120, and 121.

26. Owsley, "Local Defense," 80; Brown to Seddon, *OR*, ser. 4, vol. 2, p. 592.

27. Owsley, "Local Defense, 79; C. D. Melton to John S. Preston, September 12, 1863, *OR*, ser. 4, vol. 2, p. 813, italics added.

28. Owsley, "Local Defense," 81; Brown to Seddon, *OR*, ser., 4, vol. 2, pp. 952–53.

29. Brown to Seddon, *OR*, ser. 4, vol. 2, pp. 952–53; Owsley, "Local Defense," 82.

30. The text of this law is found in *OR*, ser. 4, vol. 3, pp. 178–81; Owsley, "Local Defense," 82, 87.

31. Owsley, "Local Defense," 83; Ramsdell, review of Owsley, 110.

32. See, for example, Connelly, *Autumn of Glory*, chaps. 9–15; Owsley, "Local Defense," 87–88.

33. Owsley, "Local Defense," 89.

34. See *OR*, ser. 1, vol. 52, pt. 2, pp. 735–36.

35. Owsley, "Local Defense," 89; Brown to Seddon, *OR*, ser. 1, vol. 52, pt. 2, pp. 736–40, italics added.

36. To the Militia Composing the First Division, September 10, 1864, *OR*, ser. 1, vol. 52, pt. 2, pp. 735–36.

37. Owsley, "Local Defense," 91; Owsley, *State Rights in the Confederacy*, 266–67.

38. Thesis No. T11718, Department of Photoduplication, University of Chicago Library; Walter Clark, ed., *Histories of the Several Regiments and Battalions from North Carolina in the Great War 1861–65*, 5 vols. (Raleigh, 1901), 1:34–35; "Address Delivered by Governor Z. B. Vance, of North Carolina, Before the Southern Historical Society, at White Sulphur Springs, West Virginia, August 18th, 1875," *Southern Historical Society Papers* 14 (1886):513; Owsley, *State Rights in the Confederacy*, 276.

APPENDIX TWO

1. McWhiney and Jamieson, *Attack and Die*, 178.
2. Ibid., 178, 191.
3. Ibid., 27, 28, 33–40, 144–57, 159, 160, 168, 169.
4. Ibid., 24, 180.
5. Ibid., 8, 9, 11.
6. Ibid., 8.
7. Thomas L. Livermore, *Numbers and Losses in the Civil War in America, 1861–65* (Boston, 1900), 77–108. Succeeding tables, unless otherwise noted, rely on these pages.
8. We use McWhiney's and Jamieson's classification although Chancellorsville, for example, might tenably be viewed as a Union offensive battle.
9. Clausewitz, 600, 524–25, 361, 391.
10. Clausewitz, 253, 255.
11. Hattaway and Jones, *How the North Won*, 728. This investigation of combat effectiveness and Lanchester's method of calculation is explained more thoroughly on pp. 721–28.
12. We used extrapolations to divide Confederate casualties where not divided between killed and wounded, including the 825 casualties assumed in defending Vicksburg against Grant's assault. For the French ratio, see C. R. M. F. Cruttwell, *A History of the Great War, 1914–1918* (Oxford, 1934), 631. In the absence of such data for the Civil War, we have used the French data because of their ready availability. Because of the superiority of French medicine and the firmer hold the French army had over its men, we can assume that this figure is too small for the Civil War. Armies often collected casualty data very informally, and various armies used different definitions. Greater precision would doubtless alter this table significantly but not the overall conclusions of this appendix.
13. We base this estimate of 120,000 on expanding the 94,000 Confederate battle deaths cited as a minimum by Livermore in the same proportions as the

Historical Statistics increased to 140,000 the original War Department figure of 110,000 for Union battle deaths. The figure of 120,000 is consistent with the ratio of Union and Confederate deaths in Livermore's combats for 1861–63 and the fact that the Confederates stood on the defensive more and had better entrenchments in 1864 and 1865. Charles P. Roland, however, estimates only 100,000 battle deaths. See Livermore, *Numbers and Losses*, 5; U.S. Bureau of the Census, *Historical Statistics of the United States, Colonial Times to 1957* (Washington, 1960), 735; Roland, *The Confederacy*, 194.

14. Roland, *The Confederacy*, 194–95; Livermore, *Numbers and Losses*, 5–7, 10–40, 61.

15. *OR*, ser. 4, vol. 1, pp. 822, 1176, vol. 2, pp. 278, 615, 1073, vol. 3, pp. 520, 989, 1182. The figure for June 30, 1864, is adjusted by adding an estimate of 28,000 on the rolls of Early's unreported corps. This is based on the assumption that he had about 15,000 present for duty. In lieu of the incomplete trans-Mississippi returns, we have used 73,843, the average of the December 31, 1863, and the December 31, 1864, returns. Subsequent data rely on these references.

16. For Confederate numbers, *OR*, ser. 4, vol. 1, pp. 822, 1176, vol. 2, pp. 278, 615, 1073, vol. 3, pp. 520, 989, 1182; for Union numbers, ibid., ser. 3, vol. 1, p. 775, vol. 2, pp. 185, 957, vol. 3, pp. 460, 1198, vol. 4, pp. 465, 1031, 1283; for number surrendered, Livermore, *Numbers and Losses*, 7. Units evidently carried prisoners on their rolls. See Livermore, *Numbers and Losses*, 7 and 46. For Livermore's comparisons of strength, see 42–47. Throughout the war the percentage of those present for duty remained constant at roughly 80 percent of the aggregate present, the number we use to compute the number absent.

17. McWhiney and Jamieson, *Attack and Die*, 189.

Bibliography

Adams, Henry, *The Education of Henry Adams*. 1918. Reprint. New York, 1931.

Adams, Michael C. C. *Our Masters the Rebels: A Speculation on Union Military Failure in the East, 1861–1865*. Cambridge, Mass., 1978.

Ahlstrom, Sydney E. *A Religious History of the American People*. New Haven, 1972.

Akin, Warren. *Letters of Warren Akin: Confederate Congressman*. Edited by Bell I. Wiley. Athens, Ga., 1960.

Alabama. *Acts of the Called Session, 1863, and of the Third Regular Annual Session of the General Assembly of Alabama Held in The City of Montgomery, Commencing on the 27th Day of September and the 2nd Monday in November 1864*. Montgomery, 1864.

_____. *Acts of the Called Session, 1864, and of the Fourth Regular Annual Session of the General Assembly of Alabama . . . 1864*. Montgomery, 1864.

Alexander, E. P. *Military Memoirs of a Confederate: A Critical Narrative*. New York, 1912.

Alexander, Thomas B., and Beringer, Richard E. *The Anatomy of the Confederate Congress: A Study of the Influence of Member Characteristics on Legislative Voting Behavior, 1861–1865*. Nashville, 1972.

Alger, John I. *The Quest for Victory: The History of the Principles of War*. Westport, Conn., 1982.

The American Annual Cyclopaedia and Register of Important Events of the Year 1864. . . . Vol. 4. New York, 1867.

The American Slave: A Composite Autobiography Edited by George P. Rawick. 19 vols. Westport, Conn., 1972–79.

Amlund, Curtis Arthur. *Federalism in the Southern Confederacy*. Washington, D.C., 1966.

Anderson, Bern. *By Sea and by River: The Naval History of the Civil War*. New York, 1962.

Andrews, Sidney. *The South since the War. . . .* Boston, 1866.

Argus Suburbia-Reporter (Bellaire/West University Place, Texas).

Atlanta Southern Confederacy.

Baggett, James Alex. "Origins of Upper South Scalawag Leadership." *Civil War History* 29 (March 1983): 53–73.

Baldwin, Leland D. *The American Quest for the City of God.* Macon, Ga., 1981.

Barlow, Samuel Latham Mitchill. Papers. Henry E. Huntington Library, San Marino, Calif.

Barrett, John G. *The Civil War in North Carolina.* Chapel Hill, 1963.

Bartlett, John Russell. *The Literature of the Rebellion: A Catalogue of Books and Pamphlets Relating to the Civil War in the United States. . . .* Boston, 1866.

Bearss, Edwin C. *Decision in Mississippi: Mississippi's Important Role in the War between the States.* Jackson, Miss., 1962.

Bellah, Robert N. *The Broken Convenant: American Civil Religion in Time of Trial.* New York, 1975.

Beringer, Richard E. *Historical Analysis: Contemporary Approaches to Clio's Craft.* New York, 1978.

Bettersworth, John K., ed. *Mississippi in the Confederacy.* Vol. 1, *As They Saw It.* Jackson, Miss., 1961.

Bigelow, John, Jr. *The Principles of Strategy Illustrated Mainly from American Campaigns.* New York, 1891.

Black, Robert C., III. *The Railroads of the Confederacy.* Chapel Hill, 1952.

Blassingame, John W. *The Slave Community: Plantation Life in the Antebellum South.* Rev. ed. New York, 1979.

Bledsoe, Albert T. *The War between the States; or Was Secession a Constitutional Right Previous to the War of 1861–65?* Lynchburg, Va., 1915.

Bleid, Benjamin J. *Catholics and the Civil War.* Milwaukee, 1945.

Braden, Waldo W. "Repining over an Irrevocable Past: The Ceremonial Orator in a Defeated Society, 1865–1900." In Waldo W. Braden, ed., *Oratory in the New South.* Baton Rouge, 1979.

Bragg, Thomas. Diary, 1861–1862, No. 3304. Microfilm copy of original in Southern Historical Collection, University of North Carolina Library, Chapel Hill.

Brehm, Jack W., and Cohen, Arthur R. *Explorations in Cognitive Dissonance.* New York, 1962.

Brinton, John H. *The Personal Memoirs of John H. Brinton, Major and Surgeon, U.S.V., 1861–1865.* New York, 1914.

Brock, Robert Alonzo. Papers. Henry E. Huntington Library, San Marino, Calif.

Brock, W. R. *An American Crisis: Congress and Reconstruction, 1865–1867.* London, 1963.

Brown, John W. Typescript Diary, No. 1924. Microfilm copy of original, Southern Historical Collection, University of North Carolina Library, Chapel Hill.

Brown, Richard D. *Modernization: The Transformation of American Life, 1600–1865*. New York, 1976.

Browning, Orville Hickman. *The Diary of Orville Hickman Browning*. Vol. 1, *1850–1864*. Edited by Theodore Calvin Pease and James G. Randall. *Collections of the Illinois State Historical Library*. Springfield, 1925.

Browning, Robert. "The Blockade of Wilmington, North Carolina, 1861–1865." M.A. thesis, East Carolina University, 1980.

Buenger, Walter L. "Secession Revisited: The Texas Experience." *Civil War History* 30 (December 1984):293–305.

Bülow, Heinrich Dietrich von. *The Spirit of the Modern System of War*. London, 1806.

Candler, Allen D., ed. *The Confederate Records of the State of Georgia*. 5 vols. Atlanta, 1909–11.

Carter, Dan T. Commentary at session on "A Culture in Crisis: The Response of the White South to Defeat." Southern Historical Association, November 1980, Atlanta, Ga.

————. "Honor and Southern Intransigence in Reconstruction, 1865–67." Paper presented at the annual meeting of the Southern Historical Association, 1982, Memphis, Tenn.

Cash, W. J. *The Mind of the South*. New York, 1941.

Channing, Edward. *A History of the United States*. Vol. 6, *The War for Southern Independence, 1849–1865*. New York, 1925.

Channing, Steven A. *Crisis of Fear: Secession in South Carolina*. New York, 1970.

————. "Slavery and Confederate Nationalism." In Walter J. Fraser, Jr., and Winfred B. Moore, eds., *From the Old South to the New: Essays on the Transitional South*. Westport, Conn., 1981.

Charleston Mercury.

Chesnut, Mary Boykin. *Mary Chesnut's Civil War*. Edited by C. Vann Woodward. New Haven, 1981.

Civil War Times–Illustrated Collection. U.S. Army Military History Institute, Carlisle Barracks, Pa.

Clark, Walter, ed. *Histories of the Several Regiments and Battalions from North Carolina in the Great War, 1861–65*. 5 vols. Raleigh, N.C., 1901.

von Clausewitz, Carl. *On War*. Edited and translated by Michael Howard and Peter Paret. Princeton, 1976.

Cleveland, Henry. *Alexander H. Stephens in Public and Private: With Letters and Speeches, before, during and since the War*. Philadelphia, 1866.

Cobb, Thomas Reade Rootes. "Correspondence of Thomas Reade Rootes

Cobb, 1860–1862." Edited by A. L. Hull. *Publications of the Southern History Association* 11 (1907).

Commager, Henry Steele. "How 'The Lost Cause' Was Lost." *New York Times Magazine*, August 4, 1963, pp. 10–11, 66–67.

Confederate States of America. *Laws and Joint Resolutions of the Last Session of the Confederate Congress. . . .* Edited by Charles W. Ramsdell. Durham, N.C., 1941.

––––––. *Public Laws of the Confederate States of America, Passed at the Third Session of the First Congress, 1863.* Edited by James M. Matthews. Richmond, 1863.

––––––. *The Statutes at Large of the Confederate States of America, Commencing with the First Session of the First Congress: 1862. . . .* Edited by James M. Matthews. Richmond, 1862.

––––––. *The Statutes at Large of the Provisional Government of the Confederate States of America. . . .* Edited by James M. Matthews. Richmond, 1864.

Connelly, Thomas Lawrence. *Autumn of Glory: The Army of Tennessee, 1862–1865.* Baton Rouge, 1971.

Connelly, Thomas L., and Bellows, Barbara. *God and General Longstreet: The Lost Cause and the Southern Mind.* Baton Rouge, 1982.

Connelly, Thomas L., and Jones, Archer. *Politics of Command: Factions and Ideas in Confederate Strategy.* Baton Rouge, 1973.

Cooper, William J., Jr. *The South and the Politics of Slavery, 1828–1856.* Baton Rouge, 1978.

Coulter, E. Merton. *The Confederate States of America, 1861–1865.* Baton Rouge, 1950.

Cover, Robert M. *Justice Accused: Anti-Slavery and the Judicial Process.* New Haven, 1975.

Cowper, William. "Light Shining Out of Darkness." *Olney Hymns.* London, 1779. Quoted in Brian Spiller, *Cowper: Verse and Letters.* Cambridge, Mass., 1968.

Craven, Avery O. *The Growth of Southern Nationalism, 1848–1861.* Baton Rouge, 1953.

Cruttwell, C. R. M. F. *A History of the Great War, 1914–1918.* Oxford, 1934.

[Curry, J. L. M.] *Address of Congress to the People of the Confederate States.* Richmond, 1864.

––––––. *Civil History of the Government of the Confederate States, with Some Personal Reminiscences.* Richmond, 1901.

––––––. *The Southern States of the American Union, Considered in Their Relations to the Constitution of the United States and to the Resulting Union.* Richmond, 1895.

Daniel, John M. *The Richmond Examiner during the War; The Writings of John M. Daniel, with a Memoir of His Life, by His Brother.* Edited by Frederick S. Daniel. New York, 1868.

Daniel, Pete. *The Shadow of Slavery: Peonage in the South, 1901–1969.* Urbana, Ill., 1972.

Daniel, W. Harrison. "Bible Publication and Procurement in the Confederacy." *Journal of Southern History* 24 (May 1958):191–201.

―――. "Protestantism and Patriotism in the Confederacy." *Mississippi Quarterly* 24 (Spring 1971):117–34.

Davis, Jefferson. *Calendar of the Jefferson Davis Postwar Manuscripts in the Louisiana Historical Association Collection, Confederate Memorial Hall.* New Orleans, 1943. Reprint. New York, 1970.

―――. *Jefferson Davis, Constitutionalist: His Letters, Papers and Speeches.* Edited by Dunbar Rowland. 10 vols. Jackson, Miss., 1923.

―――. *Jefferson Davis: Private Letters, 1823–1889.* Edited by Hudson Strode. New York, 1966.

―――. *The Papers of Jefferson Davis.* Edited by Haskell M. Monroe, Jr., et al. 5 vols. to date. Baton Rouge, 1971–.

―――. *The Rise and Fall of the Confederate Government.* 2 vols. New York, 1881.

Davis, Reuben. *Recollections of Mississippi and Mississippians.* Boston, 1890.

De Bow, J. D. B. "Our Danger and Our Duty." *De Bow's Review,* 1st ser. 33 (1862):43–51.

Degler, Carl N. *Place over Time: The Continuity of Southern Distinctiveness.* Baton Rouge, 1977.

DeLeon, Thomas C. *Belles, Beaux and Brains of the 60's.* New York, 1909.

Dew, Charles B. *Ironmaker to the Confederacy: Joseph R. Anderson and the Tredegar Iron Works.* New Haven, 1966.

Donald, David. *Liberty and Union.* Lexington, Mass., 1978.

―――. *Lincoln Reconsidered: Essays on the Civil War Era.* New York, 1956.

―――, ed. *Why the North Won the Civil War.* Baton Rouge, 1960.

Dorgan, Howard. "Rhetoric of the United Confederate Veterans: A Lost Cause Mythology in the Making." In Waldo W. Braden, ed., *Oratory in the New South.* Baton Rouge, 1979.

Du Bois, W. E. Burghardt. *The Souls of the Black Folk: Essays and Sketches.* 1903. Reprint. New York, 1953.

Du Pont, Samuel Francis. *Samuel Francis Du Pont: A Selection from His Civil War Letters.* Edited by John Daniel Hayes, 3 vols. Ithaca, N.Y., 1969.

Dupuy, R. Ernest, and Dupuy, Trevor N. *The Compact History of the Civil War.* New York, 1960.

Durden, Robert F. *The Gray and the Black: The Confederate Debate on Emancipation*. Baton Rouge, 1972.

Eaton, Clement. *A History of the Old South: The Emergence of a Reluctant Nation*. 3d ed. New York, 1975.

_____. *A History of the Southern Confederacy*. 1954. Reprint. New York, 1965.

_____. *Jefferson Davis*. New York, 1977.

_____. *The Waning of the Old South Civilization, 1860–1880's*. 1968. Reprint. New York, 1969.

Eckenrode, Hamilton J. *Jefferson Davis: President of the South*. New York, 1930.

Edgehill-Randolph Papers. Alderman Library, University of Virginia, Charlottesville.

Eighmy, John Lee. *Churches in Cultural Captivity: A History of the Social Attitudes of Southern Baptists*. Knoxville, 1972.

Eldridge, James William. Papers. Henry E. Huntington Library, San Marino, Calif.

Elting, John R. "Jomini: Disciple of Napoleon?" *Military Affairs* 28 (Spring 1964):17–26.

Escott, Paul D. *After Secession: Jefferson Davis and the Failure of Confederate Nationalism*. Baton Rouge, 1978.

_____. "'The Cry of the Sufferers': The Problem of Welfare in the Confederacy." *Civil War History* 23 (September 1977):228–40.

_____. "Georgia." In W. Buck Yearns, ed., *The Confederate Governors*. Athens, Ga., 1985.

_____. "Poverty and Governmental Aid for the Poor in Confederate North Carolina." *North Carolina Historical Review*, 61 (October 1984):462–80.

Faulkner, William. *Intruder in the Dust*. New York, 1948.

Festinger, Leon. "Cognitive Dissonance." *Scientific American* 207 (October 1962):93–102.

_____. *Conflict, Decision, and Dissonance*. Stanford, 1964.

_____. *A Theory of Cognitive Dissonance*. Evanston, 1957.

Florida. *The Acts and Resolutions Adopted by the General Assembly of Florida, at Its 12th Session*. Tallahassee, 1863.

_____. *The Acts and Resolutions Adopted by the General Assembly of Florida, at Its 13th Session*. Tallahassee, 1865.

Foote, Henry S. *Casket of Reminiscenses*. Washington, D.C., 1874.

_____. *War of the Rebellion; or, Scylla and Charybdis*. . . . New York, 1866.

Freeman, Douglas Southall. *R. E. Lee: A Biography*. 4 vols. New York, 1934–35.

Garfield, James A. *The Wild Life of the Army: Civil War Letters of James A. Garfield.* Edited by Frederick D. Williams. East Lansing, Mich., 1964.

Gay, Mary A. H. *Life in Dixie during the War, 1861–1862–1863–1864–1865.* 1892. Reprint. Atlanta, 1979.

Genovese, Eugene D. *The World the Slaveholders Made: Two Essays in Interpretation.* New York, 1969.

Georgia. *Acts of the General Assembly of the State of Georgia, Passed in Milledgeville, at an Annual Session in November and December 1862: Also Extra Session of 1863.* Milledgeville, 1863.

_____. *Acts of the General Assembly of the State of Georgia, Passed in Milledgeville, at an Annual Session in November and December, 1863; Also, Extra Session of 1864.* Milledgeville, 1864.

_____. *Acts of the General Assembly of the State of Georgia, Passed in Milledgeville, at the Called Session. In March 1864.* Milledgeville, 1864.

Gholson, Thomas S. *Speech of Hon. Thos. S. Gholson, of Virginia, on the Policy of Employing Negro Troops, and the Duty of All Classes to Aid in the Prosecution of the War.* Richmond, 1865.

Goff, Richard D. *Confederate Supply.* Durham, N.C., 1969.

Gordon, John Brown. *Reminiscences of the Civil War.* New York, 1903.

Gorgas, Josiah. *The Civil War Diary of General Josiah Gorgas.* Edited by Frank E. Vandiver. University, Ala., 1947.

Grady, Henry W. *Life of Henry W. Grady, Including His Writings and Speeches.* Edited by Joel Chandler Harris. New York, 1890.

Graham, William Alexander. *The Papers of William Alexander Graham.* Edited by J. G. de Roulhac Hamilton and Max R. Williams. 6 vols. Raleigh, N.C., 1957–76.

Grant, Ulysses S. *The Papers of Ulysses S. Grant.* Edited by John Y. Simon. 12 vols. to date. Carbondale, Ill., 1967–.

_____. *Personal Memoirs of U.S. Grant.* 2 vols. New York, 1885–86.

Graves, Ralph A. "Marching through Georgia Sixty Years After." *National Geographic* 50 (September 1926):259–311.

Haight, Henry Huntley. Papers. Henry E. Huntington Library. San Marino, Calif.

Hamley, Edward Bruce. *The Operations of War Explained and Illustrated.* 4th ed. London, 1878.

Harsh, Joseph L. "Battlesword and Rapier: Clausewitz, Jomini, and the American Civil War." *Military Affairs* 38 (December 1974):133–38.

Hattaway, Herman. "Confederate Mythmaking: Top Command and the Chickasaw Bayou Campaign." *Journal of Mississippi History* 32 (November 1970):311–26.

————. *General Stephen D. Lee.* Jackson, Miss., 1976.

————. "Via Confederate Post." *Civil War Times–Illustrated* 15 (April 1976):22–29.

Hattaway, Herman, and Jones, Archer. *How the North Won: A Military History of the Civil War.* Urbana, Ill., 1983.

Hayes, Carlton J. H. *Nationalism: A Religion.* New York, 1960.

Hesseltine, William B. *Confederate Leaders in the New South.* Baton Rouge, 1950.

Hill, Benjamin Harvey, Jr. *Senator Benjamin H. Hill of Georgia: His Life, Speeches, and Writings.* Atlanta, 1893.

Hill, Louise B. *State Socialism in the Confederate States of America.* Charlottesville, Va., 1936.

Hill, Samuel S., Jr. *Religion in the Southern States: A Historical Study.* Macon, Ga., 1983.

————. *The South and the North in American Religion.* Athens, Ga., 1980.

————, ed. *Encyclopedia of Religion in the South.* Macon, Ga., 1984.

Hofer, J. M. "Development of the Peace Movement in Illinois during the Civil War." *Journal of the Illinois State Historical Society* 24 (April 1931):110–28.

Horst, Samuel. *Mennonites in the Confederacy: A Study in Civil War Pacifism.* Scottsdale, Pa., 1967.

Hughes, Robert M. Papers. Property of R. M. Hughes III, of Norfolk, Va.

Hunter, Louis C. *Steamboats on the Western Rivers: An Economic and Technological History.* Cambridge, Mass., 1949.

Hunter, Robert M. T. *Correspondence of Robert M. T. Hunter, 1826–1876.* Edited by Charles Henry Ambler. American Historical Association *Annual Report for the Year 1916,* vol. 2. Washington, D.C., 1918.

————. "Origin of the Late War." *Southern Historical Society Papers* 1 (January 1876):1–13.

James, Henry. *The American Scene.* 1907. Reprint. New York, 1946.

Jefferson, Thomas. *Notes on the State of Virginia.* Edited by William Peden. Chapel Hill, 1955.

Johns, John E. *Florida during the Civil War.* Gainesville, 1963.

Johnson, Herschel V. "From the Autobiography of Herschel V. Johnson, 1856–1867." *American Historical Review* 30 (January 1925):311–36.

Johnson, Ludwell H. "Jefferson Davis and Abraham Lincoln as War Presidents: Nothing Succeeds Like Success." *Civil War History* 27 (March 1981):49–63.

Johnson, Robert Erwin. "Investment by Sea: The Civil War Blockade." *American Neptune* 32 (January 1972):45–57.

Johnson, Robert U., and Buel, Clarence C., eds. *Battles and Leaders of the*

Civil War. 4 vols. New York, 1884–88 (Extra-illustrated Edition, Huntington Library, San Marino, Calif.).

Johnston, Joseph E. *Narrative of Military Operations Directed, during the Late War between the States.* 1874. Reprint. Bloomington, Ind., 1959.

Jomini, H. de. *The Art of War.* Translated by G. H. Mendell and W. P. Craighill. Philadelphia, 1862.

―――. *Précis de l'art de la guerre ou nouveau tableau analytique des principales combinaisons de la stratégie, de la grande tactique, et de la politique militaire.* Edited by F. Lecomte. 2 vols. Paris, 1894.

Jones, Archer. *Confederate Strategy from Shiloh to Vicksburg.* Baton Rouge, 1961.

―――. "Jomini and the Strategy of the American Civil War: A Reinterpretation." *Military Affairs* 34 (December 1970):127–31.

Jones, John B. *A Rebel War Clerk's Diary at the Confederate States Capital.* 2 vols. Philadelphia, 1866.

Kantzer, Kenneth S. Editorial. *Christianity Today,* July 13, 1984, pp. 14–15.

Kean, Robert Garlick Hill. *Inside the Confederate Government: The Diary of Robert Garlick Hill Kean.* Edited by Edward Younger. New York, 1957.

Keegan, John. *The Face of Battle.* New York, 1976.

Kerby, Robert L. "Why the Confederacy Lost." *Review of Politics* 35 (July 1973):326–45.

Korman, Abraham K. *The Psychology of Motivation.* Englewood Cliffs, N.J., 1974.

Kruman, Marc W. "Dissent in the Confederacy: The North Carolina Experience." *Civil War History* 27 (December 1981):293–313.

―――. *Parties and Politics in North Carolina, 1836–1865.* Baton Rouge, 1983.

Laas, Virginia Jeans. "'On the Qui Vive for the Long Letter:' Washington Letters from a Navy Wife, 1861." *Civil War History* 29 (March 1983): 28–52.

Lebergott, Stanley "Why the South Lost: Commercial Purpose in the Confederacy, 1861–1865." *Journal of American History* 70 (June 1983):58–74.

Lee, Charles Robert, Jr. *The Confederate Constitutions.* Chapel Hill, 1963.

Lee, Stephen D. "General Lee's Address." *Confederate Veteran* 12 (July 1904):325–27.

Lefler, Hugh T., and Newsome, Albert R. *North Carolina: The History of a Southern State.* Rev. ed. Chapel Hill, 1963.

Lester, Richard I. *Confederate Finance and Purchasing in Great Britain.* Charlottesville, Va., 1975.

Lewis, Lloyd. *Sherman: Fighting Prophet.* New York, 1932.

Liddell Hart, Basil H. *Sherman: Soldier, Realist, American.* 1929. Reprint. New York, 1958.

Lincoln, Abraham. *The Collected Works of Abraham Lincoln.* Edited by Roy P. Basler. 8 vols. New Brunswick, N.J., 1953.

Litwack, Leon. *Been in the Storm So Long: The Aftermath of Slavery.* New York, 1979.

Lively, Robert A. *Fiction Fights the Civil War: An Unfinished Chapter in the Literary History of the American People.* Chapel Hill, 1957.

Livermore, Thomas L. *Numbers and Losses in the Civil War in America, 1861–65.* Boston, 1900.

Long, Ellen Call. *Florida Breezes, or Florida New and Old.* 1883. Reprint. Gainesville, 1962.

Lonn, Ella. *Desertion during the Civil War.* 1929. Reprint. Gloucester, Mass., 1966.

――――. *Salt as a Factor in the Confederacy.* 1933. Reprint. University, Ala. 1965.

Luraghi, Raimondo. *The Rise and Fall of the Plantation South.* New York, 1978.

Luvaas, Jay. "The Fall of Fort Fisher." *Civil War Times–Illustrated* 3 (August 1964):5–9, 31–35.

Lyman, Theodore. *Meade's Headquarters, 1863–1865: Letters of Colonel Theodore Lyman from the Wilderness to Appomattox.* Edited by George R. Agassiz. Boston, 1922.

Lynchburg Republican.

Lynchburg Virginian.

MacDougall, P. L. *The Theory of War.* 2d ed. London, 1858.

Maclear, James F. "The Republic and the Millennium." In Elwyn A. Smith, ed., *The Religion of the Republic.* Philadelphia, 1971.

Macon (Georgia) *Telegraph.*

Maddex, Jack P., Jr. "Pollard's *The Lost Cause Regained:* A Mask for Southern Accommodation." *Journal of Southern History* 40 (November 1974): 595–612.

Massey, Mary Elizabeth. "The Confederate States of America: The Homefront." In Arthur S. Link and Rembert W. Patrick, eds., *Writing Southern History: Essays in Historiography in Honor of Fletcher M. Green.* Baton Rouge, 1965.

Mathews, Donald G. *Religion in the Old South.* Chicago, 1977.

McCardell, John. *The Idea of a Southern Nation: Southern Nationalists and Southern Nationalism, 1830–1860.* New York, 1979.

McFeely, William S. *Grant: A Biography.* New York, 1981.

McMillan, Malcolm C., ed. *The Alabama Confederate Reader*. University, Ala., 1963.

McMurry, Richard M. "Joseph E. Brown of Georgia." *Civil War Times–Illustrated* 10 (November 1971):29–39.

McNeill, William J. "Confederate Morale: A Psycho-Historical Assessment of the Impact of the Federal Invasion of Georgia and the Carolinas." Paper presented at the annual meeting of the Southern Historical Association, November 1984, Louisville, Ky.

McPherson, James M. "Antebellum Southern Exceptionalism: A New Look at an Old Question." *Civil War History* 29 (September 1983):230–44.

———. *Ordeal by Fire: The Civil War and Reconstruction*. New York, 1982.

McWhiney, Grady. *Southerners and Other Americans*. New York, 1973.

McWhiney, Grady, and Jamieson, Perry D. *Attack and Die: Civil War Military Tactics and the Southern Heritage*. University, Ala., 1982.

Mead, Sidney E. *The Lively Experiment: The Shaping of Christianity in America*. New York, 1963.

Meade, George G. *The Life and Letters of George Gordon Meade, Major-General United States Army*. 2 vols. Edited by George Gordon Meade. New York, 1913.

Melton, Maurice Kaye. "Major Military Industries of the Confederate Government." Ph.D. dissertation, Emory University, 1978.

Memphis Daily Appeal.

Merrill, James M. *The Rebel Shore: The Story of Union Sea Power in the Civil War*. Boston, 1957.

Milledgeville Confederate Union.

Milligan, John D. *Gunboats down the Mississippi*. Annapolis, Md., 1965.

Mississippi. *Laws of the State of Mississippi, Passed at a Called and Regular Session of the Mississippi Legislature . . . Dec. 1862 and Nov. 1863*. Selma, Ala., 1864.

———. *Laws of the State of Mississippi, Passed at a Called Session of the Mississippi Legislature, Held in Columbus, February and March 1865*. Meridian, Miss., 1865.

Mitchell, Betty L. *Edmund Ruffin: A Biography*. Bloomington, Ind., 1981.

Monaghan, Jay. *Civil War on the Western Border, 1854–1865*. Boston, 1955.

Montgomery Weekly Advertiser.

Moore, Albert B. *Conscription and Conflict in the Confederacy*. New York, 1924.

Moore, Frank, ed. *The Rebellion Record: A Diary of American Events, with Documents, Narratives, Illustrative Incidents, Poetry, etc.* 11 vols. and supplement. New York, 1861–68.

Moore, John G. "Mobility and Strategy in the Civil War." *Military Affairs* 24 (Summer 1960):68–77.

Moorhead, James H. *American Apocalypse, Yankee Protestants and the Civil War, 1860–1869*. New Haven, 1978.

_____. "Between Progress and Apocalypse: A Reassessment of Millennialism in American Religious Thought, 1800–1880." *Journal of American History* 71 (December 1984):524–42.

_____. "Millennialism." In *Encyclopedia of Religion in the South*, edited by Samuel S. Hill. Macon, Ga., 1984.

Morrison, James L. "Educating Civil War Generals: West Point, 1833–1861." *Military Affairs* 38 (October 1974):108–11.

Myers, Robert Manson, ed. *The Children of Pride: A True Story of Georgia and the Civil War*. New Haven, 1972.

Nagel, Paul C. *One Nation Indivisible: The Union in American Thought, 1776–1861*. New York, 1971.

Nashville Republican Banner.

Nashville Union and American.

Neale, Walter. *The Sovereignty of the States: An Oration. . . .* New York, 1910.

Nelson, Larry E. *Bullets, Ballots, and Rhetoric: Confederate Policy for the United States Presidential Contest of 1864*. University, Ala., 1980.

Nevins, Allan. *The Emergence of Lincoln*. Vol. 2, *Prologue to Civil War, 1859–1861*. New York, 1950.

New York Times.

North Carolina Standard.

Northen, William J., ed. *Men of Mark in Georgia* . . . 6 vols. Atlanta, 1907–12.

Novak, Daniel A. *The Wheel of Servitude: Black Forced Labor after Slavery*. Lexington, Ky., 1978.

Oakes, James. *The Ruling Race: A History of American Slaveholders*. New York, 1982.

Oldham, Williamson S. "Last Days of the Confederacy." *De Bow's Review*, 2d ser., 7–8 (October 1869–September 1870).

_____. "Memoirs of W. S. Oldham, Confederate Senator, 1861–1865." Typescript, Barker Texas History Center, University of Texas, Austin.

_____. "True Cause and Issues of the Civil War." *De Bow's Review.*, 2d ser., 7 (August 1869):674–88.

Olsen, Otto H. *Carpetbagger's Crusade: The Life of Albion Winegar Tourgée*. Baltimore, 1965.

Orleans, Louis Phillippe Albert d', Comte de Paris. *History of the Civil War in America*. 4 vols. Philadelphia, 1875–88.

Orr, J. A. "Reminiscenses of J. A. Orr." Typescript. Mississippi Department of Archives and History, Jackson.

Osterweis, Rollin G. *Romanticism and Nationalism in the Old South*. New Haven, 1949.

Owsley, Frank L. "Defeatism in the Confederacy." *North Carolina Historical Review* 3 (July 1926):446–56.

_____. "The Fundamental Cause of the Civil War: Egocentric Sectionalism." *Journal of Southern History* 7 (February 1941):3–18.

_____. *King Cotton Diplomacy: Foreign Relations of the Confederate States of America*. 1931. 2d ed., rev. Chicago, 1959.

_____. "Local Defense and the Overthrow of the Confederacy: A Study in State Rights." *Mississippi Valley Historical Review* 11 (March 1925):492–525.

_____. *The South, Old and New Frontiers: Selected Essays of Frank Lawrence Owsley*. Edited by Harriet C. Owsley. Athens, Ga., 1969.

_____. *State Rights in the Confederacy*. Chicago, 1925. (Also as Ph.D. dissertation, number T11718, University of Chicago Library.)

Paludan, Phillip Shaw. *Victims: A True Story of the Civil War*. Knoxville, 1981.

Pardon Petitions. Amnesty Papers. Records of the Adjutant General's Office. Record Group 94, National Archives, Washington, D.C.

Paxton, Elisha Franklin. *The Civil War Letters of General Frank "Bull" Paxton, C.S.A., A Lieutenant of Lee and Jackson*. Edited by John Gallatin Paxton. Hillsboro, Tex., 1978.

Pereyra, Lillian A. *James Lusk Alcorn: Persistent Whig*. Baton Rouge, 1966.

Pessen, Edward. "How Different from Each Other Were the Antebellum North and South?" *American Historical Review* 85 (December 1980):1119–49.

Phillips, Ulrich B. "The Central Theme of Southern History." *American Historical Review* 34 (October 1928):30–43.

Pollard, Edward A. *The Lost Cause Regained*. New York, 1868.

Potter, David M. *The Impending Crisis, 1848–1861*. Completed and edited by Don E. Fehrenbacher. New York, 1976.

_____. *The South and the Sectional Conflict*. Baton Rouge, 1968.

Powell, Lawrence N., and Wayne, Michael S. "Self-Interest and the Decline of Confederate Nationalism." In Harry P. Owens and James J. Cooke, eds., *The Old South in the Crucible of War*. Jackson, Miss., 1983.

Pressly, Thomas J. *Americans Interpret Their Civil War*, 1954. 2d ed. New York, 1962.

Price, Marcus W. "Ships That Tested the Blockade of the Carolina Ports, 1861–1865." *American Neptune* 8 (July 1948):196–241.

———. "Ships That Tested the Blockade of the Georgia and East Florida Ports, 1861–1865." *American Neptune* 15 (April 1955):97–132.

———. "Ships That Tested the Blockade of the Gulf Ports, 1861–1865." *American Neptune* 11 (October 1951):262–90.

"Proceedings of the . . . Confederate Congress" (title varies). *Southern Historical Society Papers* 44–54 (June 1923–July 1959).

Rable, George C. "Bourbonism, Reconstruction, and the Persistence of Southern Distinctiveness." *Civil War History* 29 (June 1983):135–53.

Rainwater, Percy Lee. *Mississippi: Storm Center of Secession, 1856–1861.* 1938. Reprint. New York, 1969.

Raleigh Daily Conservative; Daily Conservative (title varies).

Raleigh Daily Progress.

Raleigh Register.

Ramsay, James. Papers, No. 1568. Southern Historical Collection. University of North Carolina Library, Chapel Hill.

Ramsdell, Charles W. *Behind the Lines in the Southern Confederacy.* 1944. Reprint. New York, 1969.

———. Review of *State Rights in the Confederacy*, by Frank Lawrence Owsley. *Mississippi Valley Historical Review* 14 (June 1927):107–11.

Randall, James G. *Constitutional Problems under Lincoln.* Rev. ed. Urbana, Ill., 1964.

Randall, James G., and Donald, David. *The Civil War and Reconstruction.* 2d ed., rev. Lexington, Mass., 1969.

Raper, Horace W. "William W. Holden and the Peace Movement in North Carolina." *North Carolina Historical Review* 31 (October 1954):493–516.

Rawick, George P., ed. *The American Slave: A Composite Autobiography.* 19 vols. Westport, Conn., 1972–79.

Reed, Rowena. *Combined Operations in the Civil War.* Annapolis, Md., 1978.

Reese, George H., ed. *Proceedings of the Virginia State Convention of 1861.* 4 vols. Richmond, 1965.

Rhett, R. Barnwell. "The Confederate Constitution." *De Bow's Review*, 2d ser. 7 (November 1869):930.

Richardson, James D., ed. *A Compilation of the Messages and Papers of the Confederacy, Including Diplomatic Correspondence, 1861–1865.* 2 vols. Nashville, Tenn., 1905.

Richmond Dispatch; Richmond Daily Dispatch (title varies).

Richmond Enquirer.

Richmond Examiner.

Richmond Whig.

Roark, James L. *Masters without Slaves: Southern Planters in the Civil War and Reconstruction.* New York, 1977.

Robbins, John Brawner. "Confederate Nationalism: Politics and Government in the Confederate South, 1861–1865." Ph.D. dissertation, Rice University, 1964.

Robertson, James I., Jr. "Chaplain William E. Wiatt: Soldier of the Cloth." In James I. Robertson, Jr., and Richard M. McMurry, eds., *Rank and File: Civil War Essays in Honor of Bell Irvin Wiley*. San Rafael, Calif., 1976.

Robinson, William N. *Justice in Grey: A History of the Judicial System of the Confederate States of America*. Cambridge, Mass., 1941.

Roland, Charles P. *The Confederacy*. Chicago, 1960.

Rose, Willie Lee. *Slavery and Freedom*. Edited by William W. Freehling. New York, 1982.

Rupp, Ernest Gordon. *The Righteousness of God: Luther Studies*. London, 1953.

Russell, Jerry L., ed. *Civil War Round Table Digest* 9 (December 1978).

Saint-Exupéry, Antoine de. *Flight to Arras*. In *Airman's Odyssey*. New York, 1942.

Saum, Lewis O. "Schlesinger and 'The State Rights Fetish': A Note." *Civil War History* 24 (December 1978):351–59.

Savannah News.

Scarboro, David D. "North Carolina and the Confederacy: The Weakness of States' Rights during the Civil War." *North Carolina Historical Review* 56 (April 1979):133–49.

Sellers, Charles Grier, Jr. "The Travail of Slavery." In Charles Grier Sellers, Jr., ed., *The Southerner as American*. Chapel Hill, 1960.

Sheeran, James B. *Confederate Chaplain: A War Journal*. Milwaukee, 1960.

Sherman, William T. *Memoirs of Gen. W. T. Sherman. . . .* 2 vols. 4th ed. New York, 1891.

———. *The Sherman Letters: Correspondence between General and Senator Sherman, 1837 to 1891*. Edited by Rachel Sherman Thorndike. 1894. Reprint. New York, 1969.

Shy, John. *A People Numerous and Armed: Reflections on the Military Struggle for American Independence*. New York, 1976.

Silver, James W. *Confederate Morale and Church Propaganda*. New York, 1957.

———. "Propaganda in the Confederacy." *Journal of Southern History* 11 (November 1945):487–503.

Simkins, Francis Butler. *A History of the South*. 3d ed. New York, 1967.

Smith, H. Shelton. *In His Image, But . . . : Racism in Southern Religion, 1780–1910*. Durham, 1972.

Smith, Robert Hardy. *An Address to the Citizens of Alabama on the Constitution and Laws of the Confederate States of America*. Mobile, 1861.

Soley, James R. *The Blockade and the Cruisers*. New York, 1883.

Southern Historical Society Papers. 52 vols. Richmond, 1876–59.

Spain, Rufus B. *At Ease in Zion: Social History of Southern Baptists, 1865–1900*. Nashville, 1961.

Stampp, Kenneth M. *The Peculiar Institution: Slavery in the Antebellum South*. New York, 1956.

_____. "The Southern Road to Appomattox." In Kenneth M. Stampp, ed., *The Imperiled Union: Essays on the Background of the Civil War*. New York, 1980.

Starr, Louis M. *Reporting the Civil War: The Bohemian Brigade in Action, 1861–65*. New York, 1962.

Stephens, Alexander H. *A Constitutional View of the Late War between the States: Its Causes, Character, Conduct and Results, Presented in a Series of Colloquies at Liberty Hall*. 2 vols. Philadelphia, 1868–70.

Stewart, James Brewer. "'A Great Talking and Eating Machine': Patriarchy, Mobilization and the Dynamics of Nullification in South Carolina." *Civil War History* 27 (September 1981):197–220.

Stewart, John Hall. *A Documentary Survey of the French Revolution*. New York, 1951.

Still, William N., Jr. "Admiral Goldsborough's Feisty Career." *Civil War Times–Illustrated* 17 (February 1979):12–20.

_____. *Confederate Shipbuilding*. Athens, Ga., 1969.

_____. *Iron Afloat: The Story of the Confederate Armorclads*. Nashville, 1971.

_____. "A Naval Sieve: The Union Blockade in the Civil War." *Naval War College Review* 36 (May–June 1983):34–45.

_____. "The New Ironclads." In William C. Davis, ed., *The Image of War, 1861–1865*. Vol. 2, *The Guns of '62*. Garden City, 1982.

_____. "Porter . . . Is the Best Man." *Civil War Times–Illustrated* 16 (May 1977):4–9, 44–47.

Strout, Cushing. *The New Heavens and New Earth: Political Religion in America*. New York, 1974.

"Studies in the South." *Atlantic* 50 (December 1882):750–63.

Sweet, William W. *The Story of Religion in America*. 2d ed. New York, 1950.

Tatum, George Lee. *Disloyalty in the Confederacy*. 1934. Reprint. New York, 1970.

Thomas, Emory M. *The Confederacy as a Revolutionary Experience*. Englewood Cliffs, N.J., 1971.

_____. *The Confederate Nation, 1861–1865*. New York, 1979.

Thompson, Henry Yates. *An Englishman in the American Civil War: The*

Diaries of Henry Yates Thompson, 1863. Edited by Sir Christopher Chancellor. New York, 1971.

Thurow, Glen E. *Abraham Lincoln and American Political Religion*. Albany, 1976.

Toombs, Robert. *The Correspondence of Robert Toombs, Alexander H. Stephens, and Howell Cobb*. Edited by Ulrich B. Phillips. American Historical Association *Annual Report for the Year 1911*, vol. 2. Washington, D.C., 1913.

Trueblood, David Elton. *Abraham Lincoln: Theologian of American Anguish*. New York, 1973.

Tuscaloosa Observer.

U.S. Adjutant General's Office. Pardon Petitions. Amnesty Papers. Record Group 94, National Archives, Washington, D.C.

U.S. Army. *F-M 100-5, Operations* (Washington, D.C.: 1982).

U.S. Bureau of the Census. *Historical Statistics of the United States, Colonial Times to 1957*. Washington, D.C., 1960.

U.S. Congress. *Congressional Globe, Containing the Debates and Proceedings*. 36th Cong., 1st and 2d sess.

U.S. Congress. House. *Report of the Joint Committee on Reconstruction*. House Report No. 30, pt. 2, 39th Cong., 1st sess., 1866. Washington, D.C., 1866.

U.S. Congress. Senate. Executive Document No. 1. Annual Report of the Secretary of the Navy, December 2, 1861. 37th Cong., 2d sess., 1861.

———. *Journal of the Congress of the Confederate States of America, 1861–1865*. 7 vols. Senate Document No. 234. 58th Cong., 2d sess. Washington, D.C., 1904–5.

———. Miscellaneous Document No. 11. Resolutions of Mr. Davis, February 2, 1860. 36th Cong., 1st sess., 1860.

———. Miscellaneous Document No. 24. Resolutions of Mr. Davis, March 1, 1860. 36th Cong., 1st sess., 1860.

———. *Supplemental Report of the Joint Committee on the Conduct of the War*. 39th Cong., 1st sess. 2 vols. Washington, D.C., 1866.

U.S. Naval War Records Office. *Official Records of the Union and Confederate Navies in the War of the Rebellion*. 30 vols. Washington, D.C., 1894–1927.

U.S. Surgeon-General's Office. *The Medical and Surgical History of the War of the Rebellion*. 6 vols. Washington, 1875–83.

U.S. War Department. *The War of the Rebellion: A Compilation of the Official Records of the Union and Confederate Armies*. 70 vols. in 128 parts. Washington, D.C., 1880–1901.

Upton, Emory. *The Military Policy of the United States*. Washington, D.C., 1912.

Vance, Zebulon Baird. *The Papers of Zebulon Baird Vance.* Edited by Frontis W. Johnston, Vol. 1, *1843–1862.* Raleigh, 1963.

Vandiver, Frank E. "The Civil War as an Institutionalizing Force." In William F. Holmes and Harold M. Hollingsworth, eds., *Essays on the American Civil War.* Walter Prescott Webb Memorial Lectures. Austin, Tex., 1968.

_____. *Jefferson Davis and the Confederate State.* Oxford, 1964.

_____. "Jefferson Davis and Confederate Strategy." In Bernard Mayo, ed., *The American Tragedy: The Civil War in Retrospect.* Hampden-Sydney, Va., 1959.

_____. "Jefferson Davis—Leader without Legend." *Journal of Southern History* 43 (February 1977):3–18.

_____. *Ploughshares into Swords: Josiah Gorgas and Confederate Ordnance.* Austin, Tex., 1952.

_____. *Their Tattered Flags.* New York, 1970.

_____, ed. *Confederate Blockade Running through Bermuda, 1861–1865.* Austin, Tex., 1947.

Virginia. *Acts of the General Assembly of the State of Virginia, at the Extra Session, 1862. . . .* Richmond, 1862.

_____. *Acts of the General Assembly of the State of Virginia, Passed at the Session of 1863–4. . . .* Richmond, 1864.

Wakelyn, Jon L. *Biographical Dictionary of the Confederacy.* Westport, Conn., 1977.

Wallenstein, Peter. "Rich Man's War, Rich Man's Fight: Civil War and the Transformation of Public Finance in Georgia." *Journal of Southern History* 50 (February 1984):15–42.

Warren, Robert Penn. *The Legacy of the Civil War.* 1961. Reprint. Cambridge, Mass., 1983.

Weigley, Russell F. "Shaping the American Army of World War II: Mobility versus Power." *Parameters, Journal of the U.S. Army War College"* (September 1981):13–21.

Wesley, Charles H. *The Collapse of the Confederacy.* 1937. Reprint. New York, 1968.

Wightman, Edward. "The Roughest Kind of Campaigning: Letters of Sergeant Edward Wightman, Third New York Volunteers, May–July, 1864," edited by Edward G. Longacre. *Civil War History* 28 (December 1982):324–50.

Wiley, Bell Irvin. *The Life of Billy Yank: The Common Soldier of the Union.* Indianapolis, 1952.

_____. *The Life of Johnny Reb: The Common Soldier of the Confederacy.* Indianapolis, 1943.

———. "The Movement to Humanize the Institution of Slavery during the Confederacy." *Emory University Quarterly* 5 (December 1949):207–20.

———. *The Road to Appomattox*. 1956. Reprint. New York, 1968.

Williams, T. Harry. *Lincoln and His Generals*. New York, 1952.

———. "The Return of Jomini: Some Thoughts on Recent Civil War Writing." *Military Affairs* 39 (December 1975):204–6.

Wilson, Charles Reagan. *Baptized in Blood: The Religion of the Lost Cause, 1865–1920*. Athens, Ga., 1980.

———. "Robert Lewis Dabney: Religion and the Southern Holocaust." *Virginia Magazine of History and Biography* 89 (January 1981):79–89.

Wilson, Edmund. "The Union as Religious Mysticism." *New Yorker* 29 (March 14, 1953):116, 119–26, 129–36.

Winthrop, Robert Charles. Papers. Massachusetts Historical Society, Boston.

Wise, Stephen Robert. "Lifeline of the Confederacy: Blockade Running during the Civil War." Ph.D. dissertation, University of South Carolina, 1983.

Wolfenstein, Martha. *Disaster: A Psychological Essay*. London, 1957.

Wood, James E., Jr. "Religious Fundamentalism and the New Right." *Religion Journal of Kansas* 20 (October 1982), reprinted from *Journal of Church and State* 22 (Autumn 1980):409–21.

Wood, Richard Everett. "Port Town at War: Wilmington, North Carolina, 1860–1865." Ph.D. dissertation, Florida State University, 1976.

Wooster, Ralph A. *The Secession Conventions of the South*. Princeton, 1962.

Worth, Jonathan. *The Correspondence of Jonathan Worth*. Edited by J. G. de Roulhac Hamilton. 2 vols. Raleigh, N.C., 1909.

Wubben, Hubert H. *Civil War Iowa and the Cooperhead Movement*. Ames, 1980.

Wyatt-Brown, Bertram. *Southern Honor: Ethics and Behavior in the Old South*. New York, 1982.

Yearns, Wilfred Buck. *The Confederate Congress*. Athens, Ga., 1960.

———, ed. *The Confederate Governors*. Athens, Ga., 1985.

Young, John Russell. *Around the World with General Grant*. 2 vols. New York, 1879.

Zajonc, Robert B. "Thinking: Cognitive Organization and Processes." In David L. Sills, ed., *International Encyclopedia of the Social Sciences*. 17 vols. New York, 1968. 15:615–22.

Zimbardo, Philip G. *The Cognitive Control of Motivation: The Consequences of Choice and Dissonance*. Glenview, Ill., 1969.

Zuber, Richard L. *Jonathan Worth: A Biography of a Southern Unionist*. Chapel Hill, 1965.

Index

Abolition: and secession decision, 72; religious justification for, 96

Abolitionists, 414

Ahlstron, Sydney E. (religious historian): opinions and assessments of, 83–84, 86, 93, 95, 101–2

Akin, Warren (C.S.A. congressman), 372, 374; wife of, 382–83

Aircraft, 247

Alabama, 11, 51, 449–50; Davis tours, 29; views of populace, 85, 98, 374; governor protests impressment, 218–19; peace movement in, 230; relief efforts in, 231; legislature of, 275, 348

Alabama (C.S.A. war vessel), 57

Alabama River, 310, 314

Alcorn, James L. (Mississippi Unionist), 69

Alexander, E. Porter (C.S.A. general): proposes guerrilla action, 346; as veteran, 411

Alexander, T. W. (delegate to Georgia secession convention), 501 (n. 1)

Alexander, Thomas B. (political historian): opinions and assessments of, 6–7, 220, 223

Alger, John I. (Jominian scholar), 485–86 (n. 27)

Allatoona Pass, Georgia: Confederates turned at, 322

American Protestantism. *See* Protestants, Religion

American Revolution, 329; bicentennial of, 428; as example of national resistance, 431

Amlund, Curtis A. (political historian): opinions and assessments of, 219–20; *Federalism in the Southern Confederacy*, 219

Amnesty, 307–9

Amnesty proclamation, 348

Amphibious operation, 196–97

Anaconda plan: strategy propounded by Scott, 53, 134. *See also* Blockade, naval

Anderson, Bern (naval historian), 55–57; quoted, 194

Anderson, Robert (U.S.A. general), 54

Andrews, Sidney (essayist): and cognitive dissonance, 403–4

Anglican Church. *See* Episcopal Church

Anglicanism: Davis converts to, 95

Anglo-Saxon heritage, 458–81

Annihilation, military: as unlikely possibility, 338

Antebellum South. *See* The South

Anxiety, 198–99, 201–2

A. O. Tyler (U.S.A. gunboat), 119

Appalachia: opposition to C.S.A. in, 74

Appomattox Court House, 332, 398, 404

Aquia, Virginia: and Battle of First Manassas, 111

Argentina, 440

Arkansas: rivers in, and C.S.A. communication lines, 117; and Price's Raid, 326

Arkansas (C.S.A. war vessel), 58, 189

Armageddon: Civil War seen as, 93–94. *See also* Religion

Armored vessels: ordered constructed, 58

Army of Northern Virginia, 185, 195, 198

Army of Tennessee, 324, 337–38, 369; destroyed in Nashville campaign, 331

Army of Virginia, 163, 167

Army of the James, 317

Army of the Potomac, 138, 140, 141, 148, 163, 167, 185, 238, 252, 253, 259–61, 264–65, 303

Artillery: as defensive weapon, 14, 15

Ashby, Turner (C.S.A. officer), 170

Association of the Maryland Line, 456

Atlanta, 454–55; and civil-military decisions, 25; fall of, 28–29; industry in, 217; bread riots in, 229; and Gov. Brown's exemptions, 233

Atlantic Coast, 200–201

Atlantic Ocean, 195

Atlantic Squadron, 135

223; and secession, 72–73, 291, 361, 492 (n. 21); and Confederate governors, 73, 208–11, 450–51, 455; depicted on Confederate postal stamps, 77; realistic in initial outlook, 82, 87–89; and religion, 95–96, 126, 154, 269, 274–75, 353, 366; and free navigation of Mississippi River, 157–58; and suspension of habeas corpus, 206, 223; and C.S.A. Constitution, 219, 222, 290, 378; and conscription, 225; messages to C.S.A. Congress, 245, 305; opposition to his policies, 288–89; leadership assessed, 323, 424–26; birthday as holiday, 347; and political leverage, 347–48; efforts for diplomatic recognition, 387–88; ideology of, 402; memoirs, 407; postwar views, 408; anti-Davis writers, 444
Davis, Nicholas (chaplain of Hood's Texas Brigade), 99
Davis, Reuben C.S.A. analyst), 287, 377, 404, 406
DeBow, James D. B. (editor of *DeBow's Review*), 98, 343, 395
Deception: at Murfreesboro, 241
Defeat, military: assessed, 236; significance in approach of, 276–77; early Confederate response to, 299; misperceptions of, 300; relative insignificance of, 303; unconscious desire for, 361; perceived as inevitable, 363, 366–67; acceptance of, 382, 384, 389–91, 393, 395–96; causes of, 430; impact of, on will, 434; psychological impact of, at Atlanta, 517 (n. 35)
Defeatism: prevails in the South, 335, 365
Defense: significance and desirability of, 47, 116, 139, 340, 431, 424, 518 (n. 15); power of, demonstrated, 114, 241, 302–3, 322
DeForest, John W. (U.S.A. officer): on war's causes, 403
Degler, Carl N. (historian), 436–37; on guilt and Confederate defeat, 23; on guerrilla action, 346; on emancipation, 358; on slavery and southern identity, 493 (n. 37)
Deism, 362
Democratic party: and Election of 1862, 179, 207; and Election of 1864, 206
Democrats, Secession: and 1863 election lost to Union whigs, 292

Demoralization. *See* Morale
Department of East Tennessee, Army of, 173
Department of Georgia, 447
Department of Mississippi and East Louisiana, 321
Depression, 335. *See also* Morale
Deprivation: as strategic ploy, 314
Desertion, 266, 327, 334, 384, 397; and relief efforts, 233; as a factor in defeat, 435, 439
Determination, 245, 249, 307, 329. *See also* Will and public morale
Discouragement of populace: and Lee's strategy, 253, 334
Disillusion, 391
Dissonance, cognitive. *See* Cognitive dissonance
Diversion, military, 236, 241, 306, 328, 334
Division of Territory, 251. *See also* Territory
Donald, David (historian): opinions and assessments of, 4–8, 32, 290, 356, 485 (n. 25); editor of *Why the North Won the Civil War*, 443
Dorgan, Howard (analyst of postwar oratory), 405
Douglas, Stephen A., 71
The Draft. *See* Conscription
Draft riots: in New York, 224, 323
Dragoons, 247
Drewry's Bluff, Virginia, Battle of, 148, 317, 318
DuBois, William E. B., 393
DuPont, Samuel F. (U.S. admiral), 193, 195; and Port Royal Expedition, 136; strengthens blockade, 137
Durden, Robert F. (historian): on emancipation, 375, 379, 402
Durham Station, North Carolina, 339, 398

Eads, James B. (engineer), 119
Early, Jubal A. (C.S.A. general), 336; and use of the base and turning movements, 162; attempts to raid Washington, D.C., 320; significance of loss in battle with Sheridan, 435
East Gulf Blockading Squadron, 136
Eaton, Clement (historian): on morale, 21; on propaganda, 26; on state rights, 209–11; on the blockade, 214–15; on